A Reading Course in Homeric Greek

BOOK 1

Third Edition, Revised

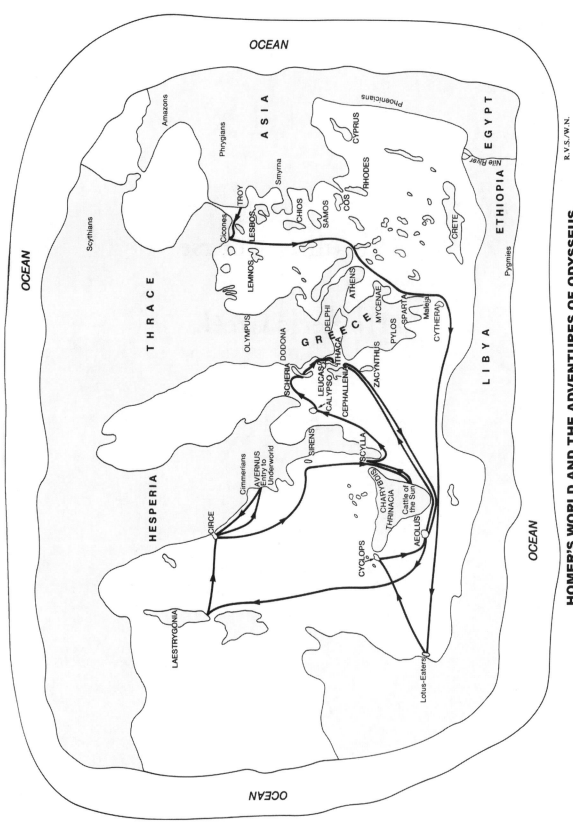

HOMER'S WORLD AND THE ADVENTURES OF ODYSSEUS

A Reading Course in Homeric Greek

BOOK 1

Third Edition, Revised

Raymond V. Schoder, S.J., M.A., Ph.D.
Vincent C. Horrigan, S.J., M.A.

Revised, with additional material by
Leslie Collins Edwards

focus Publishing
R. Pullins Company
Newburyport, MA 01950

Table of Contents

A Reading Course in Homeric Greek

On Using This Book

Structure of the Course

The entire book is scientifically built up on the basis of a complete statistical tabulation of just what forms, rules, and words *actually occur in the text* which will be read in this course. As a result, emphasis is distributed according to the degree of frequency with which each particular item will be met during the two years' work. Grammar and vocabulary are thus streamlined, that the efforts of the class may be directed efficiently to matters which are actively important for reading the Homeric text.

Only those principal parts of verbs, and only those special forms of -μι verbs are assigned which actually occur at least three times in the readings from Homer in this course. Thus the *memory burden is greatly reduced,* with no unneeded items included, yet is fully adequate for reading the selections from Homer provided.

These items cover, at the same time, the essentials of Homeric and Greek grammar, thus providing a solid foundation for further reading in Homer or in other Greek authors. Nevertheless, the student who cannot go on in Greek beyond the present course will find satisfaction in having repeatedly seen and used within the course itself every principle that he has learned. The book, then, forms a unit in itself, offering material of intrinsic worth and interest; it is not merely a preparation for something else.

Reading Real Greek

In the first sixty lessons, the Readings are all actual quotations from various authors over the whole range of Greek literature. The quotations have, where necessary, been simplified or adapted to fit a limited vocabulary and syntax and the Homeric dialect, but they remain faithful to the original thought. These selections thus provide a certain contact with writers other than Homer, and with general Greek thinking. Already by Lesson 11 you will be reading real Greek!

The Homer readings are held off until the student has the key forms, rules, and words well in hand. Reading Homer thus becomes easy—most of the language is already familiar, while any new forms or words are explained as they come up, when needed.

The heavy work of the course, held to its statistically verified minimum of forms, rules, and words needed to read the Homer selections provided, is concentrated in the first quarter of the program (first sixty lessons); the remaining three quarters are then fun—"downhill," "cashing in" on the wealth of forms and vocabulary accumulated in the first sixty lessons. Meanwhile the short Readings from other Greek authors are an early reward for the grammar and vocabulary being progressively learned.

The text of Homer himself is over ninety-nine percent unaltered. Where an especially rare or troublesome form has been reduced to simpler terms, the change is always strictly in accord with Homeric usage. Care has been taken to include in the selections read those passages on which Vergil draws in the *Aeneid,* Bk. 1, 2, 4, 6.

Lesson Design

It should be noted that the exercises entitled TRANSLATE and PUT INTO GREEK all drill on the matter just learned, and that the English sentences headed WRITE IN GREEK always draw exclusively on review grammar, not on the forms or syntax first seen in that day's lesson.

Everything learned is constantly reused and thus kept active as the course progresses.

In general, with classes of fifty minutes, the Lessons are designed to be taken one a day, with a class free every eight or ten days for thorough and detailed vocabulary review. However, Lessons 16, 21, 29, 35, 45, and 83 are intended to take two class periods apiece, while Lessons 59 and 60, general review of the first sixty lessons, will each supply matter for three days' class, if desired. Many of the easier lessons, especially from Lesson 61 on, can be covered two to a class. Where class periods are longer than fifty minutes, more than one lesson can be taken, as the teacher judges feasible.

— R.V. Schoder
V.C. Horrigan

REVISED EDITION

Why this revised edition

Approaching the learning of Ancient Greek through Homeric Greek makes particular sense for the student of today, who often has only a year or two to spend on the study of Greek. Homeric Greek is somewhat simpler syntactically than Attic Greek, so that reading with some proficiency and even pleasure is attainable within that abbreviated time-span. Moreover, of all the ancient texts still read today, certainly none is more widely read or enjoyed than Homer's *Odyssey*; students are often drawn to the study of the Greek language by their experience with Homer in translation. Yet the extant Homeric Greek textbooks were not written for today's student; they assumed familiarity with grammatical terminology and syntactical concepts that are no longer covered in the educational curriculum.

What has been changed

Schoder and Horrigan's *Reading Course in Homeric Greek* had several virtues which kept me returning to it year after year for my own Greek classes. First, it is organized around the verb system, proceeding in the order of the six principal parts from the present system through the aorist passive system. This logical arrangement seems to convey to the student the "big picture" of the Greek grammatical system more effectively than any other I have tried. Second, the book is, compared to other Greek texts available now, quite concise; it is possible to cover the material in it in the allotted meeting times, without skipping over readings and longer explanations. Finally, and most importantly, it is a gratifying course, because it relatively quickly prepares the student to read something they will certainly enjoy—the Lotus Eaters and Cyclops episodes from Book 9 of the *Odyssey*.

There were some weaknesses in the text that I have tried to address in this revised edition. Based on my experience using Schoder and Horrigan's text, I have added fuller explanations of syntactical concepts where the original edition's versions seemed too thin for today's students. Paradigms have been labeled clearly; participle and adjective paradigms have been declined in full.

I have also included, early in the text, explicit explanations of grammatical terminology. But I have striven to keep the book from becoming a very long book, since I find that shorter texts work better in today's teaching schedules and with today's students. Other changes and additions include:

- Self-correcting review exercises for the non-review lessons from Lesson 10-54. These exercises offer extra drilling of and basic practice with new morphology and syntax, on the model of Wheelock's excellent self-correcting exercises at the back of his Latin textbook.

- New and updated essays. Essays on topics related to the Homeric poems, including oral composition, social and political organization, folktales, and the Geometric style, have been added. Some of the essays from the original edition have been updated and expanded. In addition, the essays are presented in a more logical order. Essays focused on Homer are placed in earlier chapters of the third unit (on the *Odyssey*), followed in roughly historical sequence by the essays on other authors, genres and topics.

- Expanded and updated Notes and Commentary on the *Odyssey*. Notes have been augmented with more detail and cross-references to grammatical explanations elsewhere in the book. The Commentary has been re-written and updated.

- The text of the *Odyssey* now follows the highly regarded text of P. von der Muehll (Basel 1962). I have adopted the readings currently most widely accepted by scholars, and have included notes where necessary to explain unfamiliar forms.

- Sentences and Passages from the Septuagint have been added to the Readings. One strength of Schoder and Horrigan's book was its ample inclusion of New Testament and early Christian Greek authors in the Readings. I have added to these some passages from the Septuagint, the Greek translation of the Hebrew Torah. One of the new essays also briefly introduces the Jewish and Christian literature written in Koine.

- New information has been added to the Greek-English Vocabulary at the end of the book. Students will now find in parentheses the lesson in which a word was first introduced. In addition, here and in the MEMORIZE sections of the Lessons I have written out the full genitive of third declension nouns, instead of just the genitive endings. Many of the entries have been reorganized for greater clarity. Other information about peculiarities of usage has been added where appropriate.

- Two new indices have been added. The grammatical index and a general index at the back of the book should, if used in conjunction with the Table of Contents and the Vocabularies, help students locate information within the book.

—L. Collins Edwards, 2004

Abbreviations

acc.	accusative	**m.-p.**	middle-passive
act.	active	**n.**	neuter
adj.	adjective	**neg.**	negative
adv.	adverb	**no.**	number
aor.	aorist	**nom.**	nominative
comp.	comparative	**obj.**	object
conj.	conjunction	**opt.**	optative
conjg.	conjugation	**pass.**	passive
cp.	compare	**pers.**	person
dat.	dative	**pf.**	perfect
decl.	declension	**pl.**	plural
def.	definite	**plpf.**	pluperfect
f.	feminine	**prep.**	preposition
fut.	future	**pres.**	present
gen.	genitive	**pron.**	pronoun
gend.	gender	**ptc.**	participle
impf.	imperfect	**rel.**	relative
impt.	imperative	**sg.**	singular
ind.	indicative	**sub.**	subject
indecl.	indeclinable	**subj.**	subjunctive
indef.	indefinite	**supl.**	superlative
inf.	infinitive	**syst.**	system
interr.	interrogative	**trans.**	transitive
intr.	intransitive	**vb.**	verb
irreg.	irregular	**voc.**	vocative
m.	masculine	**w.**	with
mid.	middle	**+**	followed by, with

Lesson 1

The Forms and Sounds of the Greek Alphabet

1. THE GREEK ALPHABET

LETTER		NAME	PRONUNCIATION	GREEK EXAMPLE
A	α	alpha	dra**ma**	δρα-μα
B	β	beta	**b**iography	βι-ος
Γ	γ	gamma	**gang**lion	γαγ-γλι-ον
Δ	δ	delta	**d**emocracy	δη-μος
E	ε	epsilon	**e**pidemic	ε-πι
Z	ζ	zeta	a**dz**e	τρα-πε-ζα
H	η	eta	th**ey**	αθ-λη-της
Θ	θ	theta	**th**eology	θε-ος
I	ι	iota	ph**y**sique	φυ-σι-κος
K	κ	kappa	**c**osmic	κοσ-μος
Λ	λ	lambda	**l**ogic	λο-γος
M	μ	mu	**m**eter	με-τρον
N	ν	nu	**n**ectar	νεκ-ταρ
Ξ	ξ	xi	clima**x**	κλι-μαξ
O	ο	omicron	**o**steopath	οσ-τε-ον
Π	π	pi	**p**lanet	πλα-νη-της
P	ρ	rho	c**r**isis	κρι-σις
Σ	σ, ς	sigma	**s**ophist	σο-φισ-της
T	τ	tau	**t**echnical	τεχ-νι-κος
Y	υ	upsilon	r**u**le, p**u**t	ψυ-χη, υπ-νος
Φ	φ	phi	gra**ph**ite	γρα-φω
X	χ	chi	**ch**aos	χα-ος
Ψ	ψ	psi	a**ps**e	α-ψις
Ω	ω	omega	**o**de	ω-δη

2. NOTES

a.   There are five vowels in Greek, and these five vowels represent five short vowel sounds and five corresponding long vowel sounds. Two of the Greek vowels are always long (η, ω), two are always short (ε, ο), while the rest (α, ι, υ) can be either long or short. Long vowel sounds were held longer than short.

Long vowels:	Short vowels:
α	α
η	ε
ι	ι
ω	ο
υ	υ

b. If the α is long, it sounds like the first **a** in 'drama'; if short, like the second **a**.

c. If the ι is long, it sounds like the **i** in 'physique'; if short, like the **y**.

d. If the υ is long, it sounds like the **u** in 'rule'; if short, like the **u** in 'put'. Or it may be sounded more like an English vowel **y**—if long, like the **y** in 'philosophy', if short like the **i**.

e. γ is always hard, as in 'go', never soft as in 'gem.' Before κ, γ, χ, ξ it has the sound of English *ng* (as in 'ganglion').

f. ς is used at the end of words; otherwise σ (e.g. λυσις).

g. Distinguish carefully the sounds of α and ο. The α should be sounded like the English word *Ah!*, the ο like *awe*.

h. θ and φ were not originally pronounced as English *th* and *ph*, but were closer to our *t* and *p* — they were "aspirated," i.e., 'stop' consonants (like *t* and *p*) followed by a puff of air.

3. PRONOUNCE AND COPY CAREFULLY IN GREEK

1. φι-λο-σο-φι-η
2. δι-α-λο-γος
3. μι-κρο-φω-νος
4. φωσ-φο-ρος
5. α-να-λυ-σις
6. πνευ-μο-νι-η
7. δρα-μα-τι-κος
8. σκε-λε-τον
9. θε-α-τρον
10. βαπ-τισ- μα
11. μα-θη-μα-τι-κος
12. πο-λι-τι-κος
13. α-ρω-μα
14. αμ-φι-βι-ος
15. στρα-τη-γι-κος
16. α-γω-νι-η
17. αρ-χι-τεκ-των
18. ορ-χησ-τρα
19. με-λαγ-χω-λι-η
20. πο-λυ-γω-νον
21. γυμ-να-σι-ον

Lesson 2

The Greek Dipthongs And Their Sounds
How To Divide Greek Words Into Syllables

4. DIPHTHONGS

The Greek vowels are: α, ε, η, ι, ο, ω, υ. When two of these vowels combine to produce one continuous sound, the combination is called a diphthong. (δι- double, φθόγγος sound)

DIPHTHONG	SOUND	EXAMPLE
αι	ai in *aisle*	βι-αι
αυ	ow in *cow*	αυ-τος
ει	ei in *eight*	ει-πον
ευ	ε + υ	Ζευς
ηυ	η + υ	ηυ-ρον
οι	oi in *oil*	οι-κος
ου	oo in *soon*	ου-δεν
υι	we in *weak*	υι-ος

5. IOTA SUBSCRIPT

When the vowel ι follows η, ω, and long α it is usually written and printed beneath them instead of after them:

> ηι is written ῃ
> ωι is written ῳ
> αι is written ᾳ

This iota is called **iota subscript**. In our modern standard pronunciation of Ancient Greek, the iota subscript is not pronounced.

The practice of subscribing the iota is not earlier than the twelfth century A.D. In the eighth century B.C. (the century in which "Homer" is usually placed) and in the Classical period, iota after η, ω, and long α would have been pronounced as well as written on the line (**iota adscript** e.g., βίηι rather than βίῃ). By the first century B.C., when the iota after η, ω, and long α was no longer pronounced, it began to be sometimes omitted in writing as well.

With capital letters, the iota after η, ω, and long α is written on the line, e.g., ΒΙΗΙ for βίῃ.

6. SYLLABLES

a. A word has as many syllables as it has vowels or diphthongs.

b. A single consonant between two vowels or diphthongs is pronounced with the following vowel or diphthong. But a final letter of a preposition in compound words stays with the preposition, never going with the following word.

c. Two consonants are usually split, except τρ and γρ. For practical purposes, however, it is sufficient to follow the English method of syllable division. Thus: α-λη-θει-η, φι-λε-ο-με-νη, παρ-ο-δος, αι-ει, θα-λασ-σα, πε-τρη, υ-γρος, ερ-γον.

7. EXERCISE

Write out, dividing properly into syllables:

1. τανταλιζω
2. αιων
3. αστρονομιη
4. φαλαγγος
5. λαβυρινθος
6. συλλαβη
7. μετα-φορη
8. γεωμετριη
9. μεθοδος*
10. αριθμητικος
11. επι-ταφιον
12. μηχανικος
13. μητροπολις
14. συμμετριη
15. κατα-στροφη
16. δια-γραμμα
17. ελαστικος
18. θησαυρος
19. μονοτονος
20. τροπαιον
21. μονοπωλιη

*μεθ- is from the preposition μετα-

Lesson 3

How to Stress Greek Words

8. STRESS AND PITCH

a. In English, and most modern languages, stress is placed on one syllable of a word (e.g., *noth*-ing, ma-*tu*-ri-ty). In Ancient Greek, instead of increased stress, one syllable of most words was given a slightly different musical **pitch**. The accent marks you see over printed Greek indicate the sort of variation in pitch required for each word; the next lesson will give you a brief introduction to pitch marks. However, it is standard practice for English speakers today simply to stress the accented syllable of an ancient Greek word.

b. As was suggested in Section 2 above, the Greeks did observe the **quantity** of syllables, always prolonging in pronunciation those syllables that are 'long' and running over more rapidly those that are 'short'. To the modern ear this resembles a sort of emphasis on the prolonged syllable, and it is the basis for metrical pronunciation of Greek poetry. Here is the basic rule for determining the quantity of a syllable:

A syllable is **long by nature** if it contains a long vowel or diphthong (Section 2). It is **long by position** if its vowel is followed by two consonants or by a double consonant. There are three double consonants: ζ (= dz), ξ (= ks), and ψ (= ps).

9. NOTE

Where a short syllable would take one beat of a musical metronome, a long syllable would extend over two beats. To attempt to preserve the quantity of Greek syllables may be impractical or merely beyond the limits of your patience at this point in the course. However, you may find it more pleasant to attempt once you have studied Homeric meter and are reading the Homer selections later in this book, where the distinctive rhythmic pattern is based on the sequence and interrelationship of long and short syllables.

10. DRILL

Pronounce any syllable with a pitch mark with a slight stress.

1. βάπτισμα
2. διάλογος
3. λωτός
4. Κύκλωψ
5. ἄρωμα
6. πολύγωνον
7. πολιτικός
8. οἶνος
9. ῥυθμός
10. γυμνάσιον
11. θέατρον
12. γεωμετρίη
13. θησαυρός
14. φάλαγξ
15. μετα-φορή

Lesson 4

Names of the Greek Letters
The Meaning of Breathings and Pitch Marks

11. ALPHABET NAMES

ἄλφα	ζῆτα	λάμβδα	πῖ	φῖ
βῆτα	ἦτα	μῦ	ῥῶ	χῖ
γάμμα	θῆτα	νῦ	σίγμα	ψῖ
δέλτα	ἰῶτα	ξῖ	ταῦ	ὦ μέγα
ἒ ψιλόν	κάππα	ὂ μικρόν	ὖ ψιλόν	

12. BREATHINGS

Every Greek word beginning with a vowel or diphthong must have a **breathing mark**. The rough breathing (ʽ) shows that *h* is to be sounded with the initial vowel or dipthong. The smooth breathing (ʼ) means that *h* is not to be pronounced. The breathing is written directly above the initial vowel, but if a diphthong begins the word it is written above the second vowel of the diphthong (αἰών).

Initial ρ always has the sound of *rh*; consequently, it is always written with a rough breathing (ῥ).

13. PITCH MARKS

Ancient Greek was a musical language. Besides the effect of long and short syllables on the sound pattern of words and sentences, there was also, as we have noted, a musical variation in tone or pitch of voice—a rising and falling of tune level. It is impractical, and unnecessary, for us today to try to recapture this subtle quality of spoken Greek.

The marking of pitch by special signs was introduced only very late, around 200 B.C. apparently by the great scholar and librarian Aristophanes of Byzantium, as an aid to Romans and other foreigners learning Greek. Only much later yet, around the second century A.D., did it become common to write these **pitch marks** on all manuscripts. The symbols used are:

ʹ	Acute accent	indicating a rising tone.
ˋ	Grave accent	indicating a falling tone.
˜	Circumflex accent	a combination of Acute and Grave, a rising and then falling of pitch in the same syllable.

These symbols had nothing to do with stress; they did not mean that the syllable over which they were written was given more emphasis of voice than other syllables in the word. Their very design clearly represented rising, falling, or rising then falling of the voice: its level of pitch or tone, not of strength or stress. This is further evident from the name of these marks: προσῳδία (musical accompaniment) and the Latin equivalent: *accentus* ('singing along with')—from which our word 'accent' is descended. Only long after the Classical period of Greek literature, around the first century A.D., did the syllable bearing the pitch-mark also come to be stressed more than the others: what we mean by 'accent' today. Medieval and modern Greek stresses syllables bearing the pitch-mark, and, as we have noted, it is standard for modern readers of Ancient Greek to do so as well. Yet, as we shall see in our reading of Homer, the written pitchmarks or 'accents' have no effect on the metrical pattern of poetry and are universally ignored in connection with the poetic rhythm even by those who treat them in prose as indicating stress.

You and your teacher may prefer to postpone learning the complicated rules governing the kind and position of the pitch-marks until later in the year. (The rules are given, for reference, in Appendix C at the back of the book.) But the pitch-marks will be written on all Greek words in this course, as is common practice. Besides, in a very few cases, the pitch-mark differentiates between words which are otherwise identical in spelling, e.g., ἄλλα ('other things'), ἀλλά ('but'); εἶμι ('I will go'), εἰμί ('I am'); τίς ('who?'), τις ('someone'). And since the circumflex may stand only over a long vowel (or diphthong), it helps us recognize that the vowel is long when this is not otherwise clear.

14. EXERCISE

Write out in Greek the names of all the letters of the alphabet, including pitch marks. Memorize them, in sequence.

Write in full the Greek alphabet (letters, not names!) ten times, spacing in fives. Thus: αβγδε, ζηθικ, etc. Memorize the sequence.

Lesson 5

Greek Punctuation. Review of Lessons 1-4

15. PUNCTUATION MARKS

Greek has four marks of punctuation:

a.   ,   comma, as in English.

b.   .   period, as in English.

c.   ·   a point above the line, equivalent to both the colon and semicolon in English.

d.   ;   question mark, which is the same in form as the English semicolon.

16. DRILL

Copy in Greek, dividing into syllables and encircling the syllable to be stressed according to Section 8.

1.	ἱπποπόταμος	10.	ὅμοῖος
2.	ῥινοκέρως	11.	ἁρμονίη
3.	ψυχή	12.	ὀφθαλμός
4.	ἀρχή	13.	ὑπερβολή
5.	ἄνθρωπος	14.	χρόνος
6.	ῥυθμός	15.	φωνή
7.	ῥευματισμός	16.	ἱστορίη
8.	ξεῖνος	17.	εὐδήσω
9.	σύμ-πτωμα	18.	ὑψηλός

17. EXERCISE

Copy these English sentences, punctuating them with the proper Greek punctuation marks:

1. How are you George
2. He came   however   it was too late
3. Who did this   Did you   Or did Jim
4. Review the following   pronunciation   syllabification   stress   breathings and punctuation

Lesson 6

A Preview of the Greek Declensions

18. THE CASES AND THEIR USE AND MEANING

Greek, like Latin, is an **inflected** language—its words have different endings added to their basic stem as a way of indicating their grammatical function and relationship to other words in a clause. The inflection of nouns (words for names of persons, places. things, etc.), and adjectives (words describing nouns), is called **declension** and nouns and adjectives are said to be **declined** as they change their endings. The inflection of verbs (words for actions, or states of being) is **conjugation**, and verbs are said to be **conjugated** as they change their endings. Participles, which are verbal adjectives, are declined like nouns and adjectives. Adverbs (words which describe verbs, adjectives, other adverbs, etc.) are not declined or conjugated.

The different endings which are attached to the stem of nouns and adjectives as they are declined are called **case endings** and the noun or adjective is said to be in a particular **case** according to the ending it shows. Thus, for example, the noun meaning "force" is spelled βίη in one case, but βίης in another. βίη is in the **dative case**, and means "by force" whereas βίης is in the **genitive case** and means "of force."

Pronouns provide the closest parallel in English to the Greek case system. For example, "they" must be the subject of a clause, while "them" must function as some sort of object, either of a verb or of a preposition; "their" shows possession. In general, however, word order and prepositions rather than inflection show the syntactical role of a noun or adjective in English:

> *Murray gave Tucker a big carrot.*

In this sentence, the **subject** (Murray), **direct object** (carrot), and **indirect object** (Tucker) of the verb are identifiable only thanks to word order. Even the **adjective** (big) modifying "carrot" is identifiable as such because of its placement. The sentence could also be written *Murray gave a big carrot to Tucker,* where the preposition "to" helps to identify the indirect object. But in Greek, the order of words in a sentence such as this one would not indicate their syntactical roles, which would instead be marked by their endings.

Omitting the **vocative** (for direct address; treated Lesson 57), there are in Greek four cases (that is, classes of endings):

a. **Nominative**: indicating the *subject* of a verb (e.g., 'the *water* flows', 'the *water* is heated by the fire').

b. **Genitive**: indicating *source, possession, separation,* with basic meanings 'of', 'from', but many other special relations and functions: 'water *of the Nile*' (Gen. of source)
  'a temple *of stone*'   (Gen. of material)
  'a temple *of Apollo*'   (Gen. of possession)

'a jar *of wine*'	(Gen. of contents)
'six *of the men*'	(Partitive Gen.)
'We ceased *from work*.'	(Gen. of separation)
'They came *from Troy*.'	(Gen. of place from which)
'during the time *of winter*'	(Gen. of time during which)
'nowhere in all *of the land*'	(Gen. of place within which)
'my love *of my mother*'	(Objective Gen.)
'*my mother's* love for me'	(Subjective Gen.)
'He is younger *than his brother*.'	(Gen. of comparison)
'a march *of seven days*'	(Gen. of extent)
'He is worthy *of a large gift*.'	(Gen. of price)

c. **Dative**: indicating *reference, place, means,* with basic meanings 'to', 'for'; 'in', 'on'; 'by', 'with' and other special relations and functions:

'He gave the shield *to me*.'	(Dat. of indirect object)
'They built this house *for me*.'	(Dat. of reference)
'He grieved *in his heart*.'	(Dat. of place where)
'They came *on the fifth day*.'	(Dat. of time when)
'He was struck *by a rock*.'	(Dat. of means)
'They came *with a loud shout*.'	(Dat. of manner/accompaniment)
'dangerous *because of its speed*.'	(Dat. of cause)
'Let us fight *along with him*.'	(Dat. of association)
'This was done *by us*.'	(Dat. of agent)
'There is no cover *to the box*.'	(Dat. of possession)
'She was younger *by six years*.'	(Dat. of degree of difference)
'The story was *for me* very sad.'	(Ethical Dat.)
'Aeolus gave gifts to him *in friendship*.'	(Dat. of interest/benefit)

d. **Accusative**: used as the *direct object of verbs,* indicating the *object* or *receiver* of an action. Also indicates that in *regard to which* something is true, and expresses the concept of *motion toward, extent of space,* or *time*:

'He killed *the lion*.'	(Acc. of direct object)
'They fought a *hard fight*.'	(Cognate acc.) (the noun has a meaning closely related to that of the verb)
'He was swift *of foot* (= *in regard to feet*).'	(Acc. of respect)
'They came *the quickest way*.'	(Adverbial acc.)
'They came *to the cave*.'	(Acc. of place to which)
'We marched *ten days/ten miles*.'	(Acc. of extent of time or space)
'The messenger spoke *to the king*.'	(Acc. with. verbs. of speaking)
'They considered *him* to be *a fool*.'	(Acc. in indirect statement)
'They asked *him* (for) *food*.'	(Double acc.)

Note: Some of the meanings given above for genitive, dative, and accusative are conveyed by the case ending itself; but some are conveyed by a preposition, which in turn "takes" a particular case. Sometimes one preposition will have different meanings, depending on the case of the noun that follows it. Examples are seen in Section 19 below and in later lessons.

19. MEMORIZE

ἀπό   [prep. + gen.] away from, from

γὰρ   [conj.; never first word] for

ἐκ   [ἐξ before vowels] [prep. + gen.] out of

καί   [conj.] and; even, also

σύν   [prep. + dat.] with

ἐν   [prep. + dat.] in, on, among

ἐπί   [prep. + gen.] upon
        [prep. +dat.] on, at, beside
        [prep. + acc.] to, towards; after [in search or attack]

ὑπό   [prep. + gen.] from under; under the influence of, = by [personal or impersonal agent]
        [prep. + dat.] under [at rest]
        [prep. + acc.] under [motion to]

20. DRILL

Which construction of the dative is exemplified by the italicized words in the following?

1. He was wounded *by a spear.*
2. They built *him* a house.
3. He died *last month.*
4. I fought *with great bravery.*
5. They offered *me* a reward.
6. The gods dwell *in heaven.*
7. Apollo gave *him* strength.
8. Will Odysseus give some wine *to Polyphemus?*
9. Accomplish *for me* this wish.
10. Grant *me* this prayer.
11. May he atone *with tears.*
12. You are hateful *to me.*
13. Stand *on the highest peak.*
14. Do *me* this favor.
15. There is no depth *to him.*
16. I helped *with words and hands.*
17. They took him away *with a cry.*
18. He lived *in Ithaca.*
19. I will not fight *with you.*
20. He angered me *by his pride.*

21. EXERCISE

Write original sentences illustrating six different uses of the genitive and accusative. Underline and identify by name each construction.

22. PREPOSITION USE

For the sake of clarity, or to express relationships not indicated by the cases alone, prepositions are used. In the following sentences, indicate what preposition with which case you would use to express the italicized words in Greek. Refer to Section 19.

1.   They came *towards the city.*
2.   Release them *from under the yoke.*
3.   She came *out of the palace.*
4.   Drive the cattle *upon the ship.*
5.   My father is *in the city.*
6.   He was killed *by Odysseus.*
7.   He sank *under the sea.*
8.   Odysseus swam *from the ship.*
9.   He lay *on the raft.*
10.   The king came *with many followers.*
11.   He slept *under the trees.*
12.   The ship was lifted *by the waves.*

Lesson 7

The First Declension in -η

23. ENDINGS

In Section 18 we saw that the change in endings of nouns and adjectives is called **declension**. But there are three different patterns according to which Greek noun- and adjective-endings change, and each of these patterns is called a declension. Each noun follows only one of these patterns, and is said to "belong to" either the **first, second** or **third declension**. Adjectives, as we shall see a little later, generally belong to more than one declension.

Within a declension, there are sub-classes. There are two are classes of nouns, adjectives and participles in the first declension: Those ending in -η, and those ending in -α.

Nouns, adjectives, participles in -η add these endings:

	Sg.	Pl.
N.	-η	-αι
G.	-ης	-αων
D.	-ῃ	-ῃσι
A.	-ην	-ας

Thus βίη *force* is declined:

	Sg.	Pl.
N.	βίη	βίαι
G.	βίης	βιάων
D.	βίῃ	βίῃσι, βίῃς
A.	βίην	βίας

24. GENDER

All first declension nouns ending in -η and -α are **feminine** in **gender**. It is important to understand that gender as used here is a purely grammatical category which does not coincide with sex, even though, in general, words that refer to living things will be of the same grammatical gender as the sex of the living thing. Yet, nouns that refer to inanimate things without sex still possess grammatical gender in Greek. For example, our first declension paradigm noun, βίη, is grammatically feminine, even though the referent of "force" has no gender.

25. MEMORIZE

ἀληθείη, -ης   [f.] truth

ἀρετή, -ῆς   [f.] manliness, virtue

βίη, -ης   [f.] force

δίκη, -ης   [f.] justice; custom

εἰρήνη, -ης   [f.] peace

καλή, -ῆς   [f. adj.] beautiful, noble

πέτρη, -ης   [f.] rock

ψυχή, -ῆς   [f.] soul; life

26. TRANSLATE

1. καλάων ἀρετάων
2. ἐν ἀληθείη
3. ὑπὸ πέτρῃσι
4. ἀπὸ ψυχῆς καλῆς
5. ἐξ εἰρήνης
6. ἐπὶ πέτρας
7. εἰρήνη ψυχῇ
8. ἀρεταὶ ἐν καλῇσι ψυχῇσι
9. ἐπὶ γὰρ πετράων
10. δίκη καὶ εἰρήνη

27. PUT INTO GREEK

1. in peace
2. for the noble soul
3. upon the beautiful rocks
4. with justice
5. the truths (as object)
6. in the soul
7. by force
8. of souls
9. by virtues
10. of truth

28. WORD STUDY

There are over 500,000 English words that have been taken over by our language from Greek! Most of these are technical terms in the sciences, but very many are common words of daily life which an educated person is expected to know and be able to use correctly. In this book, the most useful common words derived from the Greek vocabulary of each lesson will be listed in a special section of the lesson called Word Study. Use these word studies to a double advantage: to help you remember the meaning of the Greek words themselves, and to build up your personal English vocabulary for reading and expression. Careful attention to this part of the lesson day by day will bring the substantial reward of a steadily expanding knowledge of important English words; and you will know why they mean what they do, since you will have traced them back to their origin. See if you recognize the following from the vocabulary above:

IRENIC, IRENE — SALTPETER — PSYCHIC, PSYCHOLOGY (from ψυχή soul, + λόγος account, study, word).

Lesson 8

The First Declension in -α

29. ENDINGS

Some nouns, adjectives and participles in the first declension have α in the nominative and accusative singular, instead of η. Feminine nouns, adjectives, and participles in -α add these endings:

	Sg.	Pl..
N.	-α	-αι
G.	-ης	-αων
D.	-η	-ησ(ι)
A.	-αν	-ας

Thus γαῖα *earth* is declined:

	Sg.	Pl.
N.	γαῖα	γαῖαι
G.	γαίης	γαιάων
D.	γαίη	γαίησι, γαίης
A.	γαῖαν	γαίας

30. OMISSION OF VERB

Sometimes no verb is expressed in a Greek sentence. In such cases, *is* or *are* must be understood.

E.g. πέτραι καλαί. *The rocks (are) beautiful.*
δίκη ἀρετή. *Justice (is) a virtue.*

(Notice the period! It indicates a complete sentence.)

31. MEMORIZE

ἀλλά	[conj.] but
γαῖα, -ης	[f.] earth, land
δόξα, -ης	[f.] opinion; glory
ἡδεῖα, -ης	[f. adj.; m. and n. to be introduced later] sweet, pleasant
θάλασσα, -ης	[f.] sea
μέν.....δέ	[correlative particles marking contrast] indeed ... but; on the one hand....on the other; δέ [without μέν] but, however; and
οὐ	[οὐκ before smooth breathing, οὐχ before rough breathing] not, no

οὔτε   and not, nor [following a negative clause]

οὔτε.....οὔτε   neither .... nor

32. TRANSLATE

1. ὑπὸ θάλασσαν
2. ἡδεῖα ἀλλὰ οὐ καλή
3. ἐπὶ γαίῃ
4. ψυχαὶ καλαί
5. ἀληθείη ἀρετὴ ψυχῆς.
6. γαίῃ μέν, οὐ δὲ θαλάσσῃ
7. εἰρήνη ἡδεῖα ψυχῇ.
8. δόξα μέν, οὐ δὲ εἰρήνη.
9. εἰρήνη σὺν δίκῃ
10. ὑπὸ γαίης

33. PUT INTO GREEK

1. on land and on sea
2. noble glory
3. Glory is sweet.
4. not beautiful and not pleasant
5. from the sea to the land
6. Truth and justice are virtues of the soul.
7. force indeed, but not justice
8. by noble souls
9. of truth
10. Justice is the rock of peace.

34. WORD STUDY

DOXOLOGY (a hymn in praise of God, as the Gloria in the Mass); — GEOGRAPHY (γράφω I draw; a drawing or description of the earth); — UTOPIA (τόπος place; 'no-place', an imaginary idealized land or world, from St. Thomas More's famous book *Utopia*).

Lesson 9

Review of The First Declension

35. NOTE

All feminine nouns of the first declension, and the feminine of all adjectives and participles, are declined as βίη or γαῖα. If their nominative singular ends in -η, they follow the declension of βίη. If in -α, they follow γαῖα.

N.	βίη	βίαι	γαῖα	γαῖαι
G.	βίης	βιάων	γαίης	γαιάων
D.	βίη	βίησ(ι)	γαίη	γαίησι(ι)
A.	βίην	βίας	γαῖαν	γαίας

36. MEMORIZE

ἀγαθή, -ῆς	[f. adj.]	good, brave
αἰεί	[adv.]	ever, always, forever
ἀνάγκη, -ης	[f.]	necessity, need
ἀρχή, -ῆς	[f.]	beginning
δή	[adv.]	clearly, indeed
νῦν	[adv.]	now, at the present time
οὕτως	[adv.]	thus, in this way, so
φωνή, -ῆς	[f.]	voice, sound

37. TRANSLATE

1. ἐξ ἀγαθῆς ἀρχῆς
2. φωνῇ καλῇ
3. ἀρεταὶ δὴ ἀνάγκη ψυχάων.
4. γαῖα ἀγαθή.
5. ἀρεταὶ δὴ ἀνάγκη
6. ἐξ ἀληθείης ἀρχὴ δόξης.
7. ἐν ἀρχῇ
8. νῦν δὲ ἀνάγκη εἰρήνης.
9. δίκη αἰεὶ ἀγαθή.
10. οὕτως ἀγαθῇσι ψυχῇσι αἰεὶ εἰρήνη.

38. PUT INTO GREEK

1. Peace with justice is always a necessity.
2. by necessity
3. Sweet is the voice of the sea.
4. The beginnings of virtue are not always sweet.
5. Necessity is sweet.
6. Virtue is the beginning of glory.
7. upon the rocks in the sea
8. Souls are not always noble.
9. with a pleasant voice
10. Justice is the soul of peace.

39. WORD STUDY

AGATHA — ARCHAIC (from the beginning, ancient), ARCHAEOLOGY (science of ancient civilizations), ARCHETYPE (first pattern or model); — PHONETIC (representing the sound, as a 'phonetic alphabet'), PHONETICS (science of determining the sounds of languages), PHONOGRAPH (γράφω I write), EARPHONE, DICTAPHONE (Latin *dicta*, sayings), SAXOPHONE (invented by Sax), XYLOPHONE (ξῦλον wood), SYMPHONY (συν-, a harmony of sounds with one another).

Lesson 10

The Present and Imperfect Indicative and The Present Infinitive of εἰμί I AM

40. TERMINOLOGY

In the classification of verb forms, **indicative** identifies the **mood**, which indicates the type of statement that the verb is making. **Indicative** means that mood which expresses or indicates situations of fact, in distinction to hypothesis, wish, command, which are expressed by other verbal moods.

The **infinitive** is the most general expression of the verb's action, unrestricted by factors of who or how many. In other words, the infinitive has no person or number, and so it is not conjugated. It is identified in English by the pre-form 'to'—for example, 'to see' is the infinitive of that verb, while 'he sees, they saw,' etc. are indicative forms.

The **present tense** (time-frame) indicates an action going on, continuous, or progressing. The **imperfect** specifies that the action was continuous in the past. Thus 'She laughs/is laughing' is in present tense, 'She was laughing' is imperfect. Note that, in Greek, the same verb form is used for 'She laughs' as for 'She is laughing.' (More on this in Lesson 16.)

The verb εἰμί is **conjugated** for you in Section 41. That is, it is shown in the **first person**, **second person** and **third person**, both **singular** and **plural**. If a verb is in the first person, its subject is *I* or *we*; if second person, *you* or *you all*; if third person, *he, she, it* or *they*. If the subject is a single person or thing, then the verb is said to be singular; the verb is plural if the subject is more than one person or thing.

41. FORMS

The verb *to be*, as in English, Latin, and other languages, is quite irregular. But it is a very high frequency word (you will meet it hundreds of times in the present course). Hence you must simply memorize it until you master it. Note: before a vowel, ἐστίν and εἰσίν are used.

Verb **paradigms** will be presented throughout this text in the form you see here.

PRES. IND.

	Sg.		*Pl.*	
1st pers.	εἰμί	I am	εἰμέν	we are
2nd pers.	ἐσσί (εἰς)	you are	ἐστέ	you (pl.) are
3rd pers.	ἐστί(ν)	he/she/it is	εἰσί(ν)	they are

IMPF. IND.

	Sg.		*Pl.*	
1st pers.	ἦα	I was	ἦμεν	we were
2nd pers.	ἦσθα	you were	ἦτε	you all were
3rd pers.	ἦεν (ἦν, ἔην)	he/she/it was	ἦσαν (ἔσαν)	they were

PRES. INF.

εἶναι (ἔμμεν, ἔμμεναι)   to be

Notes:

1. The third person singular or plural may also be translated *there is, there are, there was, there were*, in impersonal statements.

2. The subject of a verb in Greek is not always expressed. For example, εἰμί by itself means "I am," even without the pronoun ἐγώ ("I"). In such a case, the subject is said to be "in the verb" or "not expressed."

42. MEMORIZE

αἶψα   [adv.] quickly, suddenly

εἰ   [conj.] if

εἰς   [prep. + acc.] into, to

κατά   [prep. + gen.] down from; [prep. + acc.] down (along); throughout; according to

ποτέ   [enclitic adv.] ever, (at) some time, once

πρός   [prep. + gen.] from; [prep. + dat] on, at; [prep. + acc.] to, towards

φίλη, -ης   [f. adj.] dear (to), friendly (to) [+ dat.]

43. TRANSLATE

1. ἦσαν πέτραι ἐν θαλάσσῃ.
2. κατὰ ἀληθείην
3. οὔ ποτε ἦεν πρὸς πέτρῃ.
4. αἶψα εἰς καλὴν γαῖαν
5. ἦν ἀνάγκη ἀληθείης.
6. δίκη ἐστιν ἀνάγκη ἀγαθῆς εἰρήνης.
7. ἐπὶ γὰρ γαίῃ νῦν εἰμεν.
8. εἰρήνη μὲν ἔην, οὐ δὲ δίκη.
9. πρὸς θάλασσαν
10. ἀληθείη ἐστὶν αἰεὶ καλή.

44. PUT INTO GREEK

1. Manliness is dear to good souls.
2. We were under the rocks.
3. There was a voice from the sea.
4. throughout the land
5. according to justice, not force
6. You (sg.) were on the land.
7. Truth was in the beginning.
8. down from the rocks
9. There is always glory in manliness.
10. Truth is a virtue.

45. WORD STUDY

CATACLYSM (κλυσμός deluge; hence, any overwhelming change 'flooding down' upon men's lives), CATACOMB (κύμβη a hollow place; therefore, a cave dug down under the earth, as those in Rome), CATAPULT (πάλτης hurler), CATALOG (λέγω—hence, an index of items going 'down the list' in order), CATASTROPHE (στροφή a turning; therefore, a sudden 'downward shift' in human affairs).

Lesson 11

The Second Declension—Masculine.
Adjectives: Agreement With Nouns, Substantives

46. FORMS

The second declension has two divisions: those whose nominative ends in -ος are masculine; those in -ον are always neuter. Three exceptions (words in -ος which are feminine, not masculine) will be noted in the vocabularies when they first occur.

All masculine nouns, adjectives, and participles in -ος have the following endings:

	Sg.	*Pl.*
N.	-ος	-οι
G.	-ου, -οιο	-ων
D.	-ῳ	-οισι, -οις
A.	-ον	-ους

Thus θεός *god* is declined:

	Sg.	*Pl.*
N.	θεός	θεοί
G.	θεοῦ, θεοῖο	θεῶν
D.	θεῷ	θεοῖσι, θεοῖς
A.	θεόν	θεούς

Notes:

1. Except for ἡδεῖα, the feminine forms of the adjectives introduced so far have their masculine and neuter forms in the second declension:

	masculine nominative	neuter nominative
ἀγαθή :	ἀγαθός	ἀγαθόν
καλή :	καλός	καλόν
φίλη :	φίλος	φίλον

2. Adjectives and participles (which are adjectival forms of verbs) **agree** with the noun or pronoun that they go with in thought. They take the same type of ending as the noun or pronoun they modify (nominative, genitive, dative, or accusative case, singular or plural number, and masculine, feminine, or neuter gender). Thus, 'beautiful gods' in the nominative plural would be καλοὶ θεοί. Because θεός is a masculine noun, the masculine form of the adjective is used to modify it. Likewise, 'of a pleasant peace' would be ἡδείης εἰρήνης, feminine singular and genitive.

3. Sometimes the adjective is used alone, with the noun it modifies unexpressed or "understood." This **substantive use of the adjective** is also possible in English, as in the sentence, "The rich get richer, and the poor get poorer." (= "The rich people get richer, and the poor people get poorer.") Here are some examples in Greek of substantives:

καλός	*(the) noble man*
ἀγαθαί	*(the) good women*
ἀγαθόν	*(the) good (thing)*

4. Henceforth, adjectives will be listed only in the nominative form, with masculine, feminine and neuter endings indicated (for example, καλός, -ή, -όν); nouns, on the other hand, will be listed in the nominative with their genitive ending indicated (for example, λόγος, -ου [m.] word).

47. MEMORIZE

ἀγαθός, -ή, -όν	good, brave
ἄνθρωπος, -ου	[m.] man, human being
θεός, -οῦ	[m., f.] god, goddess
ἰητρός, -οῦ	[m.] physician
καλός, -ή, -όν	beautiful, noble
λόγος, -ου	[m.] word; account
μοῦνος, -η, -ον	alone, only
νήπιος, -η, -ον	simple; foolish
σοφός, -ή, -όν	wise
ὑψηλός, -ή, -όν	high
φίλος, -η, -ον	dear (to), friendly (to) [+ dat.]
φίλος, -ου	[m. adj. as noun] friend

48. TRANSLATE

1. λόγος σοφοῦ σοφός ἐστιν.
2. ὑψηλῇσι πέτρῃσι
3. ἀνθρώπων ψυχάς
4. νηπίου λόγοι οὔ ποτε σοφοί.
5. φίλῳ μούνῳ
6. δίκῃ μούνῃ
7. λόγοισι ἰητρῶν
8. φίλος ἀνθρώποισι σοφοῖσι
9. ἰητροὶ ἔσαν ἀγαθοί.
10. θεὸς σοφός ἐστιν.

49. PUT INTO GREEK

1. of the wise physicians
2. He was not a friend of truth.
3. of the foolish man
4. by the force of truth
5. Physicians are noble.
6. down from the high rocks
7. Truth is a wise man's glory.
8. Justice and peace are noble.
9. Gods are friendly to men.
10. by the words of wise men

50. READINGS

Note: In these READINGS sections from now on, actual quotations are given from ancient Greek authors, and from the New Testament (originally written in Greek), adapted where necessary to the special Homeric forms. You are therefore already reading authentic Greek literature selections!

1. μοῦνος σοφός ἐστιν ἐλεύθερος.   (Stoic motto)
2. λύπης ἰητρός ἐστιν ἀνθρώποισι λόγος.   (Menander)
3. ἐν ἀρχῇ ἦν λόγος, καὶ λόγος ἦν σὺν θεῷ, καὶ λόγος ἦν θεός.   (St. John)
4. δόξα ἐν ὑψηλοῖσι θεῷ, καὶ ἐπὶ γαίης εἰρήνη ἐν ἀνθρώποις εὐδοκίης.   (St. Luke)
5. νήπιός εἰμι· σκάφην σκάφην λέγω.   (Fragment of a Greek comedy)
6. κατὰ ἀληθείην, μοῦνος ἀγαθός ἐστι τιμητός.   (Aristotle)

ἐλεύθερος, -η, -ον	free
εὐδοκίη, -ης	[f.] good will
λέγω	I call, I say (that something is something)
λύπη, -ης	[f.] grief
σκάφη, -ης	[f.] tub
τιμητός, -ή, -όν	deserving of honor

> *Note:* In all Readings, including the Homer passages from Lesson 61 on, words not assigned for memory are explained below the text. All memory words can be found in the Vocabulary at the end of the book.

51. WORD STUDY

PHILANTHROPIST (one who is friendly to other men and helps them), ANTHROPOLOGY (science of man in his physical history); — THEISM, THEOLOGY (study of God), THEOCENTRIC, THEOPHILUS;— PSYCHIATRIST (healer of souls or minds); — GEOLOGY (γαῖα or γῆ, study of the earth's formation), the suffix -(O)LOGY ending a word means 'scientific study of' that thing; DECALOG (δέκα 10; the Ten Commandments); LOGIC, LOGICAL (correct thinking, thought and word being but two sides of the same process),

LOGARITHM (ἀριθμός number [Cp. ARITHMETIC]; list of numbers) —
MONOLOGUE (a speech by only one person), MONARCH, MONARCHY
(ἄρχω I rule; government by one supreme head), MONK (μόναχος, from ἔχω I
hold; hence, 'one holding alone', living away from other men), MONOPLANE (with
Latin *planus*, therefore, one-surfaced, one-winged), MONOGRAM (γράμμα letter;
two or more letters intertwined into one), MONOGRAPH (γράφω I write; a
complete or scholarly essay on one subject), MONOMANIAC (μανίη madness; a
person made crazy by concentrating on one idea), MONOSYLLABLE,
MONOTHEISM (belief in one God), MONOTONE, MONOTONOUS (τονή
pitch; in one unvaried tone or pitch); — PHILOSOPHY, PHILOSOPHER (lover of
wisdom), PHILOLOGY (love of learning; science of languages), FRANCOPHILE,
etc. (lover of France, etc.); — SOPHIST (wise man; now = a pretender at wisdom),
SOPHISM (falsely wise argument); — TIMOTHY ('honored by God').

Lesson 12

The Second Declension—Neuter

52. FORMS

All neuter nouns, adjectives, and participles of second declension add these endings. Notice that the accusative is always the same as the nominative:

	Sg.	Pl.
N.	-ον	-α
G.	-ου, -οιο	-ων
D.	-ῳ	-οισ(ι)
A.	-ον	-α

Thus ἔργον *work* is declined:

	Sg.	Pl.
N.	ἔργον	ἔργα
G.	ἔργου, ἔργοιο	ἔργων
D.	ἔργῳ	ἔργοισι, ἔργοις
A.	ἔργον	ἔργα

53. NOTE

A neuter plural subject generally takes a singular verb.
E.g., δένδρεά ἐστιν ὑψηλά.   *The trees are high.*

54. MEMORIZE

βίος, -ου	[m.] life
δένδρεον, -ου	[n.] tree
δίκαιος, -η, -ον	just, honorable
εἵνεκα	[prep. + gen.] on account of, for the sake of
θάνατος, -ου	[m.] death
κακός, -ή, -όν	cowardly, bad, evil
ὁμοῖος, -η, -ον	like to, similar to [+ dat.]
π(τ)όλεμος, -ου	[m.] war
χρυσός, -οῦ	[m.] gold

55. TRANSLATE

1. ἐν βίῳ δικαίῳ
2. δένδρεα ὑψηλά
3. εἴνεκα πτολέμοιο
4. ὁμοῖόν ἐστι χρυσῷ.
5. δένδρεόν ἐστι καλόν.
6. ἐν δικαίῃ εἰρήνῃ
7. θάνατος οὐκ αἰεὶ κακός.
8. εἴνεκα ἀνθρώπων δικαίων
9. εἴνεκα ἀρετάων
10. δένδρεα ἦεν καλά.

56. PUT INTO GREEK

1. under the high tree
2. Life is a war.
3. by a cowardly death
4. The trees were good.
5. wars for the sake of peace
6. down from the tree
7. death in war
8. We were always just.
9. by means of gold
10. from under the trees

57. READINGS

1. ὁμοῖόν ἐστιν ὁμοίῳ φίλον.   (Greek Proverb)
2. οὐ γὰρ χρυσός, οὔτε ἐπὶ γαίης οὔτε ὑπὸ γαίης, ἀρετῇ ἐστιν ἶσος.   (Plato)
3. εἰρήνη οὔκ ἐστιν εἴνεκα πολέμοιο, ἀλλὰ πόλεμός ἐστιν εἴνεκα εἰρήνης. (Aristotle)
4. οὐκ ἔστιν κακὸν ἀνθρώπῳ ἀγαθῷ, οὔτε ἐν βίῳ οὔτε ἐν θανάτῳ.   (Plato)
5. δίκη καὶ δίκαιόν ἐστι καλόν.   (Plato)

   ἶσος, -η, -ον   equal to

58. WRITE IN GREEK

1. Only the good man's life is truly life. [For "truly" use κατὰ ἀληθείην.]
2. Truth is the soul's life.
3. There is a lofty tree beside the sea.

59. WORD STUDY

BIO-CHEMISTRY (chemistry of living things), BIOLOGY, BIOGRAPHY, BIOGRAPHER (γράφω I write); — RHODODENDRON (a flowery shrub somewhat like the rose, ῥόδος); — "Thanatopsis" (Bryant's poem, the title meaning "a vision of Death"); — CACOPHONY (clashing uproar of unpleasant sounds); — HOMEOTHERAPY (θεραπεία curing; hence, medical curing by treating with small doses of a germ like that to be conquered); — POLEMIC (controversial, disputing) — CHRYSANTHEMUM (ἄνθεμον flower; 'goldflower')

Lesson **13**

Review of the First and Second Declension; Types of Nouns, Adjectives, and Participles

60. ADJECTIVES AND PARTICIPLES

There are two types of adjectives and participles:

a. Masculine and neuter are declined according to the second declension; feminine is declined according to the first declension in -η. See Section 61.

b. Masculine and neuter are declined according to the third declension; feminine is declined according to the first declension in -α. (Third declension forms will be seen in Lessons 27 and 29).

61. DECLENSION

Therefore adjectives and participles that have -ος in the masculine will have -η in the feminine and -ον in the neuter. Here is the complete declension of καλός, -ή, -όν *beautiful, noble.*

	MASCULINE	FEMININE	NEUTER
	Sg.		
N.	καλός	καλή	καλόν
G.	καλοῦ	καλῆς	καλοῦ
D.	καλῷ	καλῇ	καλῷ
A.	καλόν	καλήν	καλόν
	Pl.		
N.	καλοί	καλαί	καλά
G.	καλῶν	καλάων	καλῶν
D.	καλοῖσι, καλοῖς	καλῆσι, καλῆς	καλοῖσι, καλοῖς
A.	καλούς	καλάς	καλά

Note: Adjectives have gender, number and case, just as nouns do. Some, like καλός, -ή, -όν, resemble nouns of the first and second declension, while others in their masculine and neuter forms resemble nouns of a declension we have yet to meet.

62. MEMORIZE

δῶρον, -ου	[n.] gift
ἔργον, -ου	[n.] work, deed
ἐσθλός, -ή, -όν	noble, excellent

θυμός, -οῦ	[m.] heart, spirit
ξεῖνος, -ου	[m.] guest, stranger
ὀλίγος, -η, -ον	small, few
σχέτλιος, -η, -ον	cruel, pitiless; reckless
τέ	[postpositive conj.] and
τέ…τέ	both…and
τέ…καί	both…and

63. TRANSLATE

1. δῶρά ἐστιν ὀλίγα.
2. φίλος ξείνοις ἦεν.
3. ἐν ἐσθλῷ θυμῷ
4. ἔργοις σχετλίοις
5. σύν τε καλοῖσι καὶ κακοῖσι
6. ξεῖνοί εἰσι φίλοι θεοῖσι.
7. ἐπὶ ὀλίγη πέτρη
8. ἀρεταὶ ἐσθλάων ψυχάων
9. ἀρχή ἐστιν ἀγαθή.
10. δῶρα ἦεν καλά τε φίλα τε.

64. PUT INTO GREEK

1. gifts for the noble stranger
2. death on the pitiless sea
3. gifts small indeed but dear
4. by just works
5. of the excellent physician
6. towards the high rocks
7. The men are cruel.
8. The bad are always foolish.
9. Gold was the beginning of the evil deeds.
10. The deeds were not noble.

65. READINGS

1. πρὸς γὰρ θεοῦ εἰσι ξεῖνοί τε πτωχοί τε.   (Homer)
2. θεοί τέ εἰσι, καί εἰσι δίκαιοι.   (Plato)
3. οὐ μέν σχέτλια ἔργα ἐστὶ φίλα θεοῖσι, ἀλλὰ δίκη καὶ ἀγαθὰ ἔργα. (Homer)
4. ἄνθρωπος ἐκ πείρης ἐστὶν ἀγαθὸς καὶ σοφός.   (Plato)
5. ἀγαθῶν ἀνθρώπων ἐσθλὸς μέν ἐστι λόγος, ἐσθλὰ δὲ ἔργα.   (Theognis)
6. ὀλίγον δῶρον, ἀλλὰ ἀπὸ θυμοῦ.   (Greek Anthology)

| πτωχός, -οῦ | [m.] beggar |
| πείρη, -ης | [f.] experience |

66. WRITE IN GREEK

1. Death for the sake of justice and virtue is always noble.
2. Gold is an evil for foolish men, but a good for the just in heart.
3. A coward's life is, indeed, like to death.

67. WORD STUDY

THEODORE, DOROTHY ('gift of God'), ISIDORE (Isis, Egyptian goddess); — ERG (measure of work done, a unit of energy in physics), ENERGY (inner force for work); — OLIGARCH, OLIGARCHY (ἄρχω I rule; government by the few); — EMPIRIC, EMPIRICAL (based on experience or experiment; drawn from observation, not theory, 'empirical psychology').

Lesson 14

The Declension and Meaning of Intensive and Demonstrative Pronouns/Adjectives

68. MEANINGS

Pronouns are used instead of specific nouns, to designate persons and things more generically. (e.g., *he, they* instead of *Hector, Trojans*) There are several types, two of which are introduced here. Each of these pronouns can be used as adjectives as well (e.g., *those Trojans*).

a. The **intensive** pronoun/adjective (*self, same, very; himself, herself, itself*) αὐτός, αὐτή, αὐτό gives force or emphasis to the noun it modifies or represents. For example, ψυχὴ αὐτή, *the soul itself* (intensive adjective) or αὐτοί, *they themselves* (intensive pronoun).

b. **Demonstrative** pronouns/adjectives "point out" nouns. The demonstrative (ἐ)κεῖνος, (ἐ)κείνη, (ἐ)κεῖνο *that, that one* (plural *those*) describes something that is relatively distant in space or time: ἐκείνου δενδρέου *of that tree* (cf. the somewhat archaic *yonder tree*). The demonstrative equivalent to English *this, these* will be presented in the next lesson.

69. FORMS

These pronouns/adjectives are declined according to the first and second declensions, except that -ον of the neuter is shortened to -ο. Thus:

	M.	*F.*	*N.*
Sg.			
N.	αὐτός	αὐτή	αὐτό
G.	αὐτοῦ, αὐτοῖο	αὐτῆς	αὐτοῦ, αὐτοῖο
D.	αὐτῷ	αὐτῇ	αὐτῷ
A.	αὐτόν	αὐτήν	αὐτό
Pl.			
N.	αὐτοί	αὐταί	αὐτά
G.	αὐτῶν	αὐτάων, αὐτῶν	αὐτῶν
D.	αὐτοῖσ(ι)	αὐτῇσ(ι)	αὐτοῖσ(ι)
A.	αὐτούς	αὐτάς	αὐτά
Sg.			
N.	(ἐ)κεῖνος	(ἐ)κείνη	(ἐ)κεῖνο
G.	(ἐ)κείνου	(ἐ)κείνης	(ἐ)κείνου

	M.	*F.*	*N.*
D.	(ἐ)κείνῳ	(ἐ)κείνῃ	(ἐ)κείνῳ
A.	(ἐ)κεῖνον	(ἐ)κείνην	(ἐ)κεῖνο
	Pl.		
N.	(ἐ)κεῖνοι	(ἐ)κεῖναι	(ἐ)κεῖνα
G.	(ἐ)κείνων	(ἐ)κεινάων, (ἐ)κεῖνων	(ἐ)κείνων
D.	(ἐ)κείνοισ(ι)	(ἐ)κείνῃσ(ι)	(ἐ)κείνοισ(ι)
A.	(ἐ)κείνους	(ἐ)κείνας	(ἐ)κεῖνα

70. NOTE

a. When standing alone, αὐτός, -ή, -ό and (ἐ)κεῖνος, -η, -ο are pronouns; when modifying a noun they have adjectival force. Cp. Latin *ipse* and *ille*.

b. Occasionally αὐτός, when not in the nominative or beginning a clause, lacks the intensive sense and is merely an unemphatic *him, her, it*. E.g., δῶρα ἀπὸ αὐτοῦ *gifts from him*.

71. MEMORIZE

ἐγγύς	[adv.; prep. + gen.] near
ἕτερος, -η, -ον	(the) other
ἡμέτερος, -η, -ον	our
καρπός, -οῦ	[m.] fruit
ὀφθαλμός, οῦ	[m.] eye
πολλός, -ή, -όν	much; many
πόνος, -ου	[m.] toil, trouble
ποταμός, οῦ	[m.] river

72. TRANSLATE

1. ἐγγὺς θαλάσσης
2. πολλάων ἀρετάων
3. αὐτοί εἰσι σοφοί.
4. ὑπὸ αὐτὰς πέτρας
5. ἐκ κείνης ἀρχῆς
6. ἀρεταὶ αὐταί εἰσιν ἐν ψυχῇ.
7. ἐν βίῳ ἡμετέρῳ
8. εἵνεκα αὐτοῖο πολέμοιο
9. ἐξ ἐκείνων πόνων δόξα.
10. καρπὸς πολλὸς ἐπὶ κείνοισι δενδρέοισι.

73. PUT INTO GREEK

1. in our noble hearts
2. among those rocks
3. for the wise man himself
4. of the same men
5. under those high trees

6. That peace was not just.
7. near that small river
8. The other tree is high.
9. Those are the words of a wise man.
10. There were many rivers in the same land.

74. READINGS

1. φίλος γάρ ἐστιν ἕτερος αὐτός.   (Aristotle)
2. πολλὰ οὔκ ἐστιν αὐτὰ αἰεί. (Plato)

75. WRITE IN GREEK

1. Manliness of soul is an excellent gift.
2. The words of a noble friend are life to the soul.
3. Even a small gift from a good man is dear, if from the heart.

76. WORD STUDY

HETERODOX (holding a different opinion than the commonly accepted one, especially in religion), HETEROGENEOUS (γένος kind, race; of different kinds or elements); — OPHTHALMIA (inflammation of the eyes); — HIPPOPOTAMUS (ἵππος horse; 'riverhorse'); — AUTOBIOGRAPHY (a life written by the person himself), AUTOMOBILE (Latin mobile; 'self-moving). AUTOGRAPH (one's own signature), AUTOCRACY, AUTOCRAT (κράτος power; 'self-governing'), AUTONOMY, AUTONOMOUS (νόμος law; 'self-ruling', independent), AUTOSUGGESTION (convincing oneself of undergoing some experience, as suffering from a supposed headache until it becomes real), AUTOGYRO ('selfrotator', since the revolving wing rotor is not power-driven as in the helicopter), AUTHENTIC (ἔντης author; 'by the author himself', genuine, original), AUTHENTICITY, AUTHENTICATE (make authoritative).

Lesson **15**

The Declension and Meaning of ὁ, ἡ, τό
and the Demonstrative ὅδε, ἥδε, τόδε

77. FORMS

	M.	*F.*	*N.*
Sg.			
N.	ὁ	ἡ	τό
G.	τοῦ, τοῖο	τῆς	τοῦ, τοῖο
D.	τῷ	τῇ	τῷ
A.	τόν	τήν	τό
Pl.			
N.	οἱ (τοί)	αἱ (ταί)	τά
G.	τῶν	τάων	τῶν
D.	τοῖσι, τοῖς	τῇσι, τῇς	τοῖσι, τοῖς
A.	τούς	τάς	τά
Sg.			
N.	ὅδε	ἥδε	τόδε
G.	τοῦδε, τοῖοδε	τῆσδε	τοῦδε, τοῖοδε
D.	τῷδε	τῇδε	τῷδε
A.	τόνδε	τήνδε	τόδε
Pl.			
N.	οἵδε (τοίδε)	αἵδε (ταίδε)	τάδε
G.	τῶνδε	τάωνδε (τῶνδε)	τῶνδε
D.	τοῖσ(ι)δε	τῇσ(ι)δε	τοῖσ(ι)δε
A.	τούσδε	τάσδε	τάδε

Note: The dative masculine/neuter plural is sometimes τοῖσδεσ(σ)ι instead of τοῖσ(ι)δε.

78. USES

a.   ὁ, ἡ, τό is the most common pronoun in Greek. It has three meanings: When it modifies a noun, it has the force of a weak demonstrative adjective: *that*, occasionally equivalent to *the*. When it has a definite antecedent, it has the force of a relative: *who, which, what*. This use and meaning will be explained in a later lesson. Finally, when it merely stands in place of a noun already mentioned, it has the force of a personal pronoun: *he, she, it, that.*

b.   In the nominative plural, τοί and ταί are never used as pronouns. They are frequently used as demonstratives, and for relative force.

c.   ὅδε, ἥδε, τόδε, a strengthened form of ὁ, ἡ, τό, is always demonstrative (adjective or pronoun), *this (one)*. It refers to what is near in place, time, or thought.

d.   Examples:

(1).   as demonstrative adjective:

τοῖο δενδρέοιο καρποί εἰσι καλοί, ἀλλὰ τοῦδε εἰσὶ κακοί.

The fruits of that tree are fine, but this one's are bad.

(2).   as personal pronoun:

ὅδε ἐστὶ φίλος ἡμέτερος. τοῦ λόγοι εἰσὶ σοφοί.

This man is our friend. His (= of him) words are wise.

79.   MEMORIZE

βροτός, -ή, -όν	mortal, human
ἑός, -ή, -όν	own; his, her
θησαυρός, οῦ	[m.] treasure
θνητός, -ή, -όν	mortal
κρατερός, -ή, -όν	strong
νόος, -ου	[m.] mind
νοῦσος, -ου	[f.] disease
πονηρός, -ή, -όν	worthless, base, wicked
χαλεπός, -ή, -όν	difficult

80.   TRANSLATE

1.   τοῖσι θάνατος οὐ χαλεπός.

2.   κεῖνοι πονηροί εἰσι· τῶν ἔργα ἐστὶ κακά.

3.   τοῖο νόος ἦεν κρατερός.

4.   τῶνδε πόνων καρπὸς δόξα.

5.   δενδρέοισι ὅδε ποταμός ἐστιν ἀγαθός.

6.   ἐγγὺς τῆς πέτρης ἦν θησαυρός.

7.   αἵδε οὔκ εἰσι πονηραί, ἀλλὰ τάων χαλεπός ἐστι βίος.

8.   ἑοῖσι φίλοις ἀγαθός ἐστι θησαυρός.

9.   τῆς ὀφθαλμοὶ ἦσαν καλοί.

10.   ἥδε ἐστὶν ἀρχὴ τοῦ λόγου.

81. WRITE IN GREEK

1.   The fruit of our tall tree is abundant. ["abundant" = "much"]

2.   That account is not opinion, but the truth.

3.   The man is Truth's friend and is clearly our friend also.

82. WORD STUDY

AMBROSE (ἀμ-βρόσιος for ἀμ-βρότιος im-mortal); — THESAURUS (a dictionary of words arranged by synonyms, etc.), TREASURE, TREASURY (by change in pronunciation from 'thesury').

Lesson 16

A Map of the Greek Verb

Note: This lesson is not as hard as it looks! Its purpose is to provide you with an overall view of the divisions of the Greek verb, so that when you learn these various divisions one by one in coming lessons you will understand how they fit into the whole grammatical picture. It tells us what the verb divisions *are*, and what they *mean*, before you deal with their actual forms or verb endings. As you will see by turning to Appendix A at the end of the book, these endings are quite simple, and many of them are alike. Before long, as you work through later lessons, this will all become clear and familiar. This 'map' will help you on your way. Don't expect to remember it all now, but use it for frequent reference to keep your bearings. Besides, there is only one conjugation in Greek—not four, as in Latin; and it is not nearly as complicated as the verb-system in many other languages, such as Russian.

This lesson should be spread over two days. On the first day, study Sections 83, 84, 86; on the second, Sections 85, 87, 88 and review the whole.

83. DIVISIONS OF THE VERB

a.   This lesson includes a "map" of the Greek verb. Every verb form you will meet can be located in one of the squares on this chart.

b.   Notice that there are eight possible **systems**. A system is the collection of all the verb forms which are derived from the same **stem**. Scarcely any Greek verb has all eight systems or stems. Most verbs have six, and these are indicated, as in Latin, by the **principal parts** of that verb, as given in the vocabulary.

c.   There are three **voices**:

(1).   **Active** voice: the subject acts upon something else.

E.g., *They washed the clothes.*

(2).   **Middle** voice: the subject acts on himself or for himself.

E.g., *They washed themselves.*
They washed their clothes. (= They washed clothes for themselves.)

(3).   **Passive** voice: the subject is acted upon by someone else.

E.g., *The clothes were washed by them.*

d.   There are four **moods** (i.e., types or qualities of meaning), besides the infinitive and participles, namely: **Indicative** (for statements of fact), **Subjunctive** (implying subordination, dependence, intention), **Optative** (for wishes and hypothetical quality), **Imperative** (for commands). Rules for their use will be seen in later lessons.

e.   There are six **tenses**. In all the moods, each tense expresses a different **aspect**. By aspect is meant whether the verbal action is viewed as a) in progress, b) completed, or c) simple, that is, occurring without completion or incompletion specified. Sometimes, as in the indicative mood, tense gives information about time-value (i.e., whether the verbal action is in present, past, or future time). The tenses in the indicative mood have the following significance of time and aspect: **Present** (indicating an action in the present time and of progressive aspect), **Imperfect** (past time, progressive aspect), **Future** (future time and either in progress or simple), **Aorist** (past time, with simple aspect), **Perfect** (present time, completed), **Pluperfect** (past time, already completed earlier). For some grammatical relationships, the tenses are divided into two classes:

PRIMARY TENSES	SECONDARY TENSES
Present	Imperfect
Future	Aorist
Perfect	Pluperfect

f.   Verbs that are conjugated so as to reflect person and number are called **finite**. The indicative, subjunctive, optative and imperative are referred to as finite moods because verbs in these moods show person and number.

84. MEANING OF THE TENSES

a.   In the indicative, all six tenses are used, with the differences in meaning indicated above in #83e. In the indicative mood the meanings of the tenses for the English verb 'write' are as follows:

	PAST TIME	*PRESENT TIME*	*FUTURE TIME*
COMPLETED ASPECT	pluperfect *I had written*	perfect *I have written*	future perfect *I shall have written*
PROGRESSIVE ASPECT	imperfect *I was writing*	present *I am writing*	future *I shall be writing*
SIMPLE ASPECT	aorist *I wrote*	present *I write*	future *I shall write*

Notes:

1. To express simple past action (e.g., *He spoke*), Homer sometimes uses the imperfect, rather than the aorist— implying but not stressing the continuing nature of the action.

2. The future perfect tense is not introduced in this book, because of its rarity in Homer (as in Ancient Greek generally).

b.   In the subjunctive, optative, and imperative there are only three tenses. Only three are needed. Why? Because in the subjunctive, optative and imperative the different tenses do not denote a difference of **time** but only of kind of action, or **aspect**. The present has the idea of the continuance of action (irrespective of when the action occurred); the aorist has the idea of a simple occurrence of an action (no matter when it happened); and the perfect (which is rarely used in these moods) has the idea of completion with finality.

For example:

1. Honor thy father and mother.   The *present* imperative is used.
2. Meet me at nine o'clock.   The *aorist* imperative is used.
3. Die, then, and go to your ancestors.   The *perfect* imperative is used.

c.   In the infinitive, also, the tenses represent **aspect** or kind of action, not time, except in accusative and infinitive construction. On the relationship of tenses in indirect statement, see the note under Section 114b3).

d.   In the participle, the tenses indicate **time** of action—but in relation to that of the main verb. Thus:

1. Hearing this (present participle), I marveled. (contemporaneous action)
2. I came, being about to ask (future participle) what had happened. (subsequent to main action)
3. Having said this (aorist participle), I walked away. (antecedent to main action)
4. After dying (perfect participle), he was forever honored. (completed before main action)

e.   Henceforth, in the MEMORIZE vocabularies, the tense-systems of verbs will be indicated by listing the verb's **Principal Parts**— the first singular active indicative form of the Present, Future, Aorist, Perfect, Perfect Middle/Passive and Aorist Passive. For most verbs, only those principal parts are assigned for memory which actually occur in the Homer readings in this book.

85. MEMORIZE

αἰσχρός, -ή, -όν	shameful
γίγνώσκω, γνώσομαι, γνῶν, ἔγνωκα, ἔγνωσμαι, γνώσθην	I know
λίθος, -ου	[m.] stone
λύω, λύσω, λύσα, λέλυκα, λέλυμαι, λύθην	I loose, I release
ὄλβος, -ου	[m.] happiness, prosperity
ὁράω, ὄψομαι, ἴδον, ἑώρακα, ἑώραμαι, ὄφθην	I see, I look at
ῥηίδιος, -η, -ον	easy
χρόνος, -ου	[m.] time

86. QUIZ IN MAP ANALYSIS

1.   Which systems of the Greek verb are confined to the active voice?
2.   Which to the passive voice?
3.   What moods does the future system lack? The perfect middle system?
4.   What is similar about the way the imperfect and the pluperfect fit into the general line-up of the verb?

5.   Name all possible infinitives, stating both tense and voice.

6.   Which tenses and voices have no imperative listed?

7.   Which aorist has no middle forms?

8.   What principal part supplies the stem for the passive of all aorists—first, second and third?

9.   The fourth principal part of a verb cannot be used in which third(s) of the map: top, middle or bottom? Why?

10.   In what mood alone can an imperfect occur?

87.   PLOTTING SITUATIONS ON THE MAP

State in full (by tense, mood, voice) the precise block of the map in which the underlined portions of the following sentences belong. (The number in parentheses after the sentence indicates how many forms are to be explained, lest the compound English forms mislead you).

1.   They *were walking* along the shore. (1)

2.   He intends *to burn* the new tie that she *gave* him. (2)

3.   I *have* never *been* so *praised* before. (1)

4.   While *defending* himself, he *was wounded* and *died*. (3)

5.   I *am coming*, mother! (1)

6.   *Give* me that translation! (1)

7.   Socrates repeatedly said, "*Do always* only what is right." (1)

8.   It *will be* glorious *to be respected* by all, he *said* daily. (3)

9.   We *had left* already before he *came*. (2)

10.   They *made themselves* a fortune, but *will be hated* by those who *have been defrauded*. (3)

88.   WORD STUDY

GNOSTICS (ancient heretical sect claiming inner 'knowledge' of religious truths); — MONOLITH (a structure carved from a single block of stone), LITHOGRAPH (printing from stone or metal plate carrying design in soapy ink); — ANALYZE (ἀνά up; to 'break up' or dissolve into parts for better understanding), CATALYST (κατά —; a chemical agent which helps 'break down' or change chemicals without being changed itself), ELECTROLYSIS (to loose or break up chemical compounds by an electric current; — ELECTRIC is from the word for amber, easily electrified by friction), LYSOL (a dissolving disinfectant); — CHRONOLOGICAL (in 'order of time', as a chronological chart of American presidents), CHRONIC (continuing a long time, lingering, as 'chronic rheumatism'), CHRONICLE (a register of events in the order of time occurrence, a history), SYNCHRONIZE (put into same time or beat with something else, as to 'synchronize watches or gears'); — AUTOPSY ('seeing for oneself,' especially in coroner's examination of body to determine cause of death).

MAP OF THE GREEK VERB

SYSTEMS
(principal parts)

1.	2.	3. 1st Aor.	2nd Aor.	3rd Aor.	4. Pf.	5. m.-p. Pf.	6. Aor. Pass.
Pres.	Fut.						
ACTIVE VOICE:							
pres. ind. impf. ind.	ind.	ind.	ind.	ind.	pf. ind. plpf. ind.	—	—
subj.	—	subj.	subj.	subj.	subj.	—	—
opt.	[opt.]	opt.	opt.	opt.	opt.	—	—
impt.	—	impt.	impt.	impt.	impt.	—	—
inf.	inf.	inf.	inf.	inf.	inf.	—	—
ptc.	ptc.	ptc.	ptc.	ptc.	ptc.	—	—
MIDDLE VOICE:							
pres. ind. impf. ind.	ind.	ind.	—	—	—	pf. ind. plpf. ind.	—
subj.	—	subj.	subj.	—	—	[subj.]	—
opt.	[opt.]	opt.	opt.	—	—	[opt.]	—
impt.	—	impt.	impt.	—	—	impt.	—
inf.	inf.	inf.	inf.	—	—	inf.	—
ptc.	ptc.	ptc.	ptc.	—	—	ptc.	—
PASSIVE VOICE:							
pres. ind. impf. ind.	[ind.]	—	—	—	—	pf. ind. plpf. ind.	ind.
subj.	—	—	—	—	—	[subj.]	subj.
opt.	[opt.]	—	—	—	—	[opt.]	opt.
impt.	—	—	—	—	—	[impt.]	impt.
inf.	[inf.]	—	—	—	—	inf.	inf.
ptc.	[ptc.]	—	—	—	—	ptc.	ptc.

Notes:

1. Forms in brackets are not presented in this book, either because they are not Homeric, or are exceedingly rare.

2. There is no spot on this chart for the Future Perfect, which is formed on the stem of the perfect middle, though it is generally passive in sense.

Lesson 17

The Present and Imperfect Indicative Active.
Constructions in Statements of Fact, and of Past Contrary to Fact

89. STEM AND ENDINGS

The stem of the present system is obtained from the first principal part (the present indicative active), by dropping the ending. Thus λύω = I loose, present stem λυ-. The endings are these:

PRES. IND. ENDINGS

	Sg.	*Pl.*
1st pers.	-ω	-ομεν
2nd pers.	-εις	-ετε
3rd pers.	-ει	-ουσι(ν)

PRES. IND.

	Sg.		*Pl.*	
1st pers.	λύω	I loose	λύομεν	we loose
2nd pers.	λύεις	you loose	λύετε	you loose
3rd pers.	λύει	he/ she/ it looses	λύουσι(ν)	they loose

IMPF. IND. ENDINGS

	Sg.	*Pl.*
1st pers.	-ον	-ομεν
2nd pers.	-ες	-ετε
3rd pers.	-ε	-ον

IMPF. IND.

	Sg.		*Pl.*	
1st pers.	λύον	I was loosing	λύομεν	we were loosing
2nd pers.	λύες	you were loosing	λύετε	you were loosing
3rd pers	λύε	he/ she/ it was loosing	λύον	they were loosing

90. νῦ MOVABLE

Words ending in -σι, and the third person singular ending in -ε, may add an extra letter ν, called "νῦ-movable", before a vowel or at the end of the sentence, occasionally before a consonant. A few other words also take νῦ-movable, as you will see when you meet them. (Cp. English: a pear, an apple.)

91. USES OF THE INDICATIVE

a. The indicative (all tenses) without a particle is the mood of **fact**, as in English. The negative is οὐ.

    Examples:

    οὐ λέγω τόδε. *I do not say this.*
    βροτοὶ θνήσκουσιν. *Mortals die.*

b. Contrary to Fact Conditions: With the particles ἄν or κε(ν) [untranslatable, merely giving a less factual turn to the thought], the indicative is used in **contrary to fact** conditional sentences in present or past time. The imperfect or aorist tense is used in both clauses; ἄν or κε(ν) in conclusion only. The negative is μή in the if-clause, but οὐ in the conclusion.

    Examples:

    εἰ μὴ αἰεὶ εὗδεν, πολλά κε μάνθανεν.
    If he were not always sleeping, he would be learning many things.

    εἰ δῶρα φέρε, φιλέομεν ἄν αὐτόν.
    If he were bearing gifts, we would love (=be loving) him.

    Note: The if-clause (called a **protasis**) in a contrary-to-fact condition contains a supposition which the speaker believes to be false. The conclusion (called an **apodosis**) is based on this unreal supposition. Thus, in the examples above, he *is*, in fact always sleeping (and therefore is not learning much), and he is *not* bearing gifts (so we do not love him).

92. MEMORIZE

ἄγω, ἄξω, ἄγαγον	I lead
εὕδω, εὑδήσω, εὕδησα	I sleep
θνήσκω, θανέομαι, θάνον	I die
λέγω	I say, I tell; I call
μανθάνω, μαθήσομαι, μάθον	I learn
μή	not; μηδέ and not, nor, not even
φέρω, οἴσω, ἔνεικα	I bear, I bring
φιλέω, φιλήσω, φίλησα	I love
ὡς	[adv. and conj.] as, that, how

93. TRANSLATE

1. τόδε λέγεις αὐτός;
2. ἑὸν φίλον οὐ γιγνώσκει.
3. κεῖνοι φέρον λίθον.
4. εἰ μὴ λέγες, οὐκ ἄν γίγνωσκον.

5. οὔ κε μανθάνετε ἀληθείην, εἰ μὴ θνῆσκεν.
6. ἀρετὴ φέρει ὄλβον.
7. αἰεὶ εὕδετε;
8. καὶ ἀγαθοὶ θνήσκουσιν.
9. νοῦσοι φέρον θάνατον.
10. ἡμέτερα ἔργα οὔκ ἐστιν αἰσχρά.

94. PUT INTO GREEK

1. Did you (sg.) know that?
2. Gold does not always bring happiness.
3. Mortals do not know much.
4. If he were not dying, he would not be sleeping.
5. If it were bad, we would not love it.
6. Men love gold and treasures.
7. A strong mind knows the truth.
8. He kept saying, "I know, I know."
9. Time brings both good and bad.
10. We see many stones in that river.

95. READINGS

1. ἀπὸ ἐχθρῶν δὴ πολλὰ μανθάνουσι σοφοί.   (Aristophanes)
2. αἰεὶ τὸν ὁμοῖον ἄγει θεὸς πρὸς τὸν ὁμοῖον.   (Homer)
3. οὐχ εὕδει θεοῦ ὀφθαλμός, ἐγγὺς δέ ἐστιν ἀνθρώπων πόνοις.   (Stobaeus)
4. πόνος γάρ, ὡς λέγουσι, δόξης ἀρχή ἐστιν.   (Euripides)
5. κακὸν φέρουσι καρπὸν κακοὶ φίλοι.   (Menander)

ἐχθρός, -ή, -όν   hateful
νέος, -η, -ον   young, new

96. WORD STUDY

MATHEMATICS (μάθ-ον); — PERIPHERY (περί around, about; the line which 'carries around' the area of a body, its circumference or surface); — NEO- a prefix meaning "new, revived", as in NEO-PLATONIC, NEO-SCHOLASTICISM, NEO-CLASSICAL, NEO-LITHIC (an archeological period, the New Stone Age), NEON (the 'new' element, when discovered in 1898);— CHRISTOPHER ('Christ-bearer').

Lesson 18

The Present Subjunctive Active; The Subjunctive of εἰμί.
Hortatory and Purpose Constructions

97. ENDINGS

	PRES. SUBJ. ENDINGS		PRES. SUBJ.		SUBJ. OF εἰμί	
	Sg.	*Pl.*	*Sg.*	*Pl.*	*Sg.*	*Pl.*
1st pers.	-ω	-ωμεν	λύω	λύωμεν	ὦ	ὦμεν
2nd. pers.	-ῃς	-ητε	λύῃς	λύητε	ᾖς	ἦτε
3rd pers.	-ῃ	-ωσι(ν)	λύῃ	λύωσι(ν)	ᾖ	ὦσι

Notes:

1. These endings are similar to the present indicative, the vowels merely becoming long, and iota being subscribed when it occurs.

2. No translation of the subjunctive is given with the paradigm because the translation of a subjunctive varies according to the type of construction in which it appears. For some examples, see Section 98 below.

98. USES OF THE SUBJUNCTIVE

a. **Hortatory:** Requested or proposed actions referring to the speaker himself, alone or among others, are put into the subjunctive. Negative μή.

   Examples:

   μὴ λέγωμεν αἰσχρά.   *Let us not say shameful things.*
   δῶρον φέρω.   *Let me carry the gift.*

b. **Purpose:** purpose clauses are introduced by ἵνα, ὡς, ὅπως, or ὄφρα = *that, in order that, to.* After a primary main verb they take the subjunctive, sometimes also after a secondary main verb. Negative ἵνα μή. ὡς μή, ὅπως μή, ὄφρα μή, occasionally μή alone.

   Examples:

   οὐ λέγει, ἵνα μὴ γιγνώσκωμεν.
   He does not tell, (in order) that we may not know.

   δῶρα θεοῖσι φέρομεν, ὄφρα ἀνθρώπους φιλέωσιν.
   We bring gifts to the gods, (in order) that they may love men.

99. MEMORIZE

ἐννέπω, ἐνίψω, ἔνισπον	I say, I tell
ἐπεί	[conj.] when; since
ἔχω, ἕξω or σχήσω, σχόν or σχέθον	I have, I hold

ἵνα [adv.] where; [conj.] that, in order that, to

κεύθω, κεύσω, κύθον   I hide

ὅπως [conj.] that, in order that, to

ὅτι [conj.] that; because

ὄφρα [conj.] that, in order that, to

παρ-έχω, παρ-έξω or παρα-σχήσω, παρά-σχον   I supply

[*Note:* A compound verb is a verb (ἔχω) prefixed with a preposition (παρά); in some of the forms of compound verbs, as here in the case of παρ-έχω, the spelling of the prefix may be altered because of the vowel or consonant which follows it.]

ῥέζω, ῥέξω, ῥέξα   I do

100. TRANSLATE

1. ἀληθείην αἰεὶ ἐννέπωμεν.
2. εὕδομεν ἵνα μὴ θνήσκωμεν.
3. δίκην φιλέει ὄφρα ὄλβον ἔχῃ.
4. χαλεπὰ δὴ φέρωμεν.
5. λέγω ὡς μανθάνητε.
6. τάδε δὴ ῥέζον, ἵνα δόξαν νῦν ἔχωσιν.
7. ἐννέπω [subjunctive] ὅπως γιγνώσκῃς.
8. θνήσκει ἵνα βίον ἔχητε αὐτοί.
9. ἀληθείην μὴ κεύθωμεν.
10. πόνους φέρουσιν ὄφρα χρυσὸν ἔχωσιν.

101. PUT INTO GREEK

1. Let us lead a noble life!
2. I hide the treasure [in order] that he may not see it.
3. He supplies fruit in order that we may be strong.
4. Let us bear this difficult disease.
5. They die in order that you (sg.) may not die.
6. Let us always have justice.
7. If we know the truth, let us not hide it.
8. Let us love our friends from the heart.
9. We learn in order that our mind may be strong.
10. Let us not do evil things nor wicked deeds.

102. READINGS

1. μὴ φιλέωμεν ἐν λόγῳ μηδὲ ἐν γλώσσῃ, ἀλλὰ ἐν ἔργῳ καὶ ἀληθείῃ. οὕτως δὴ γιγνώσκομεν ὅτι ἐξ ἀληθείης εἰμέν.   (St. John)
2. τάδε ῥέζω ἵνα δόξαν ἐν ἀνθρώποισιν ἔχῃ.   (Homer; Zeus, speaking of Odysseus)

3. ῥέζωμεν δὴ οὕτως, ἐπεὶ θεὸς οὕτως ἄγει. (Plato)

4. λέγει, καὶ οὐ κεύθει νόῳ, ἵνα καὶ αὐτὴ γιγνώσκω [subjunctive]. (Homer)

5. τλητὸν γὰρ θεοὶ θυμὸν πάρ-εχον ἀνθρώποισιν. (Homer)

γλῶσσα, -ης   [f.] tongue, language
τλητός, -ή, -όν   enduring

103. WRITE IN GREEK

1. I would not have done it if I had known it was evil.

2. Many diseases bring death to mortals.

3. Even if it had been difficult, he would have said it.

104. WORD STUDY

GLOSSARY (a dictionary of obscure or foreign words in some authors, explaining their meaning), GLOSS (a marginal note in old manuscripts), hence also to GLOSS (over) some statement by a plausible explanation covering its defects; POLYGLOT (πολύ many; in many tongues or languages, as a 'polyglot bible').

Lesson 19

The Present Optative Active: Wishes and Purpose Construction After Secondary Main Verbs

105. ENDINGS

	PRES. OPT. ENDINGS		PRES. OPT.	
	Sg.	*Pl.*	*Sg.*	*Pl.*
1st pers.	-οιμι	-οιμεν	λύοιμι	λύοιμεν
2nd. pers.	-οις	-οιτε	λύοις	λύοιτε
3rd. pers.	-οι	-οιεν	λύοι	λύοιεν

Note: As with the subjunctive, and for the same reasons (Section 97, note 2), no translation of the optative is given with the paradigms.

106. USES OF THE OPTATIVE

a.   **Wishes:** Both possible and impossible wishes are expressed by the optative alone (hence its name, from Latin *opto*, I wish or hope). Sometimes εἰ, εἴθε, or εἰ γὰρ (= "would that", "if only") introduce the wish, especially if it is an impossible one. Negative μή. Note that a wish often = a polite imperative.

Examples:

μανθάνοιμι.   *May I learn! I hope I learn.*
μὴ τόδε κελεύοις.   *Please don't command this.*

b.   **Purpose:** after a secondary main verb, ἵνα, ὡς, ὅπως, or ὄφρα generally take the optative (occasionally the subjunctive; cp. 98b) to express purpose. Negative ἵνα μή, etc. Thus,

πολλοὺς φέρε πόνους ἵνα καλὰ μανθάνοι.
He bore many labors (in order) that he might learn noble things.

Note: As indicated here and in Section 98b, the mood of the verb in a purpose clause depends on the tense of the main verb of the sentence. This relation between the tenses and moods of the verbs in complex sentences is called **sequence of moods**. A primary tense (Section 83e) of the main verb requires a subjunctive in the purpose clause; this is termed **primary sequence**. A secondary tense requires an optative; this is called **secondary sequence**. Sequence of moods will apply in other constructions besides purpose constructions.

107. MEMORIZE

ἀδικέω, ἀδικήσω, ἀδίκησα	I (do) wrong, I injure
διώκω, διώξω, δίωξα	I pursue
ἐσθίω, ἔδομαι, φάγον	I eat
ἱκάνω	[pres. system only] I come
κελεύω, κελεύσω, κέλευσα	I command [+ acc., dat., inf.]
ποιέω, ποιήσω, ποίησα	I make, I produce, I do
φοιτάω, φοιτήσω, φοίτησα	I roam (back and forth)

108. TRANSLATE

1.   μή ποτε ἀδικέοιμι.
2.   κεῦθον χρυσὸν ἵνα μὴ τὸν ὁράοις.
3.   ὄλβον αἰεὶ ἔχοιμεν.
4.   ἔσθιεν ὅπως μὴ θνήσκοι.
5.   εἰ γὰρ βίον ἔχοιμι ῥηίδιον.
6.   ἵκανεν ὄφρα ποταμὸν ὁράοι.
7.   καρποὺς φέρομεν ἵνα ἐσθίοιτε.
8.   λόγους ἐσθλῶν μανθάνοιμεν.
9.   πολλὰ χαλεπὰ ῥέζε ἵνα ὄλβον ἔχοι.
10.   ὀφθαλμοὺς ἡμετέρους ἔχομεν ὄφρα ὁράωμεν.

109. PUT INTO GREEK

1.   He brought fruit (in order) that we might eat.
2.   May we always do noble things!
3.   He roamed back and forth in order to see the river.
4.   If only she loved those things!
5.   The foolish fellows slept, in order that they might not learn.
6.   Please don't say that.
7.   Did you (pl.) hide the fruit in order that we might not eat it?
8.   May you (sg.) never do wrong!
9.   They bore the other labors also, in order that they might not die.
10.   May I learn the same truths!

110. READINGS

1.   ἄγνωστον δὲ φίλῳ καλὸν μή ποτε ἔχοιμι.   (Callimachus)
2.   ἀλλὰ ἄνθρωπος σιγῇ δῶρα θεῶν ἔχοι.   (Homer)
3.   νοῦσοι δὲ εἰς ἀνθρώπους ἱκάνουσιν αὐτόμαται καὶ πολλὰ κακὰ
     θνητοῖσι φέρουσιν. σιγῇ δὲ φοιτάουσι, ἐπεὶ οὐκ ἔχουσι
     φωνήν.   (Hesiod)

4. ἀγαθὸς μὲν ἄνθρωπος ἐξ ἀγαθοῦ θησαυροῦ ἑῆς κραδίης προ-φέρει ἀγαθόν, πονηρὸς δὲ ἐκ πονηροῦ πονηρόν.   (St. Matthew)

5. αἶψα γὰρ ἐν κακοῖσι βροτοὶ γηράσκουσιν.   (Homer)

ἄγνωστος, -η, -ον	unknown
αὐτόματος, -η, -ον	spontaneous
γηράσκω	I grow old
κραδίη, -ης	heart
προ-φέρω	I bring forth
σιγή, -ῆς	silence

111. WRITE IN GREEK

1. Foolish people sleep [in order] that they may not learn difficult things. [Do not translate "people"]

2. If he commands this, let us do it as for a friend.

3. Men who have a noble mind pursue truth and justice, that they may never do wrong.

112. WORD STUDY

ESOPHAGUS (οἴσω from φέρω, and φάγον, 'the food bearer', the tube through which food passes from mouth to stomach); — POET (ποιη-τής a maker), POEM (ποίη-μα a thing made), POETIC; — AGNOSTIC ('unknowing', one who denies certain knowledge is possible, a full skeptic), AGNOSTICISM: — AUTOMATIC (self-moving, self-operating), AUTOMATON (a mechanical device imitating human actions; a person whose actions seem to be mechanical and involuntary, a 'living machine'); — CARDIAC (from καρδία. variant spelling for κραδίη -of the heart, as 'cardiac glands').

Lesson 20

The Present Active Imperative, Infinitive and Participle. Commands. Accusative With Infinitive in Indirect Statement.

113. FORMS

PRES. IMPT. ENDINGS			PRES. IMPT.			
	Sg.	*Pl.*	*Sg.*		*Pl.*	
2nd. pers.	-ε	-ετε	λύε	loose/ be loosing	λύετε	loose/ be loosing

PRES. INF. ENDINGS	PRES. INF.	
-ειν or	λύειν or	
-(ε)μεν or	λύ(ε)μεν or	to be loosing/ to loose
-(ε)μεναι	λύ(ε)μεναι	

PRES. PTC. ENDINGS	PRES. PTC.
m. f. n.	m. f. n.
-ων, -ουσα, -ον	λύων, λύουσα, λῦον

114. USES

1. The **imperative** expresses a command. Negative μή.

   Example: μὴ τὸ ἐσθίετε.   *Do not eat that!*

2. Some of the constructions in which the **infinitive** is used are the following:

   a. **Complementary infinitive:** after verbs of wishing, planning, etc., as in English.

      Example: ἐθέλει μανθάνειν.   *He wishes to learn.*

   b. as a **noun**. When used as nouns, infinitives are always neuter in gender.

      Example: ἀδικέειν αἰσχρόν ἐστιν.
      To do evil is shameful. (= *evil-doing* is shameful).

   c. **Indirect Statement:** When statements are quoted indirectly, they are introduced by verbs of saying, thinking, believing, perceiving, and knowing (e.g., "She says that the guest is sleeping."). After some Greek verbs, such as λέγω and νομίζω, the verb in the quoted statement is put into the infinitive mood, and the subject of that verb is put into the accusative case. Direct and indirect objects retain their 'original' cases. The negative of the infinitive is οὐ.

      Examples:

      λέγει ξεῖνον οὐχ εὕδειν.   *She is saying that the guest is not sleeping.*
      (The subject of the infinitive is the accusative ξεῖνον.)

νομίζομεν ἐκεῖνον εἶναι σοφόν.   *We consider that man to be wise.*
(= We think that that man is wise. The subject of the infinitive εἶναι is
ἐκεῖνον, with the predicate adjective σοφόν modifying it.

ἰητρὸς λέγε τούσδε νοῦσον φεύγειν.
The doctor was saying that these people were escaping the disease.
The subject of the infinitive φεύγειν is τούσδε; its direct object is
νοῦσον.

Note: The action denoted by the *present* infinitive is contemporaneous with the
action of the main verb, i.e., the guest is not sleeping when she speaks; that
man is wise as we speak, and the people were escaping the disease at the
same time as the doctor was saying that they were escaping. As new tenses
are introduced, so will new tense relations in indirect statement be
presented. We shall see that the tense of the infinitive in indirect statement
represents the tense of the finite verb in the direct statement.

3.   Declension, uses and translations of the participle will be introduced in Lessons
29 and 30. Participles will not appear in exercises until then.

115. MEMORIZE

ἐθέλω, ἐθελήσω, ἐθέλησα	I wish
ζώω, ζώσω, ζῶσα	I live
ἠδέ	[conj.] and
νοέω, νοήσω, νόησα	I think, I perceive
νομίζω, νομιῶ, νόμισα	I consider, I think, I believe
παρά	[prep. + gen.] from [prep. + dat.]at, beside [prep. + ace.]to, along
φεύγω, φεύξομαι, φύγον	I flee, I escape

116. TRANSLATE

1. ἐθέλω πολλὰ μανθάνειν.
2. λέγω ἀρχὴν εἶναι ἀγαθήν.
3. μή ποτε ἀδικέετε.
4. κεῖνοι λέγον δένδρεον θνήσκειν.
5. αἰσχρὰ μὴ νόεε θυμῷ.
6. τὴν λέγει νῦν ἱκανέμεν.
7. νήπιος ἐθέλει καρπὸν ἐὸν καὶ ἔχειν καὶ ἐσθίειν.
8. δένδρεα ἠδὲ πέτρας παρὰ ποταμὸν ὁράετε.
9. ὡς δίκαιος ἐθέλω αἰεὶ ζωέμεναι.
10. νομίζει ἐκείνους πονηροὺς κεύθειν θησαυρόν.

117. PUT INTO GREEK

1.   We always wished to eat.

2.   Let us never wish to injure a friend.

3.   He said that the women were bringing gold and treasure.

4.   He is saying that it is easy to do wrong, but hard to hide the base deeds.

5.   To live in peace and justice is good.

6.   May our mind perceive the truth!

7.   They say you (sg.) are just.

8.   Speak, in order that many people may know.

9.   To wrong a friend is wicked and foolish.

10.   Let us learn from noble men never to do wrong.

118. READINGS

1.   Σωκράτης λέγει πολλοὺς ἀνθρώπους ζώειν ἵνα ἐσθίωσιν· αὐτὸς δὲ ἔσθιε ἵνα ζώοι.   (Xenophon)

2.   χαλεπὸν ποιέειν, κελεύειν δὲ ῥηίδιον.   (Philemon)

3.   ἀγαθὸν οὔκ ἐστιν μὴ ἀδικέειν, ἀλλὰ μηδὲ ἐθέλειν ἀδικέειν.   (Democritus)

Σωκράτης   Socrates

119. WRITE IN GREEK

1.   They kept roaming back and forth in order to see the trees and rocks along the river.

2.   May we love and do the same things!

3.   He always did just deeds, that he might live forever in the minds of mortals.

120. WORD STUDY

ZOOLOGY (science of animals as living things), ZOO (abbreviation for zoological park, a place for displaying various animals); — PARADOX (a contradictory statement, or one seeming to be contradictory), PARADIGM (δεῖγμα a showing; hence, a chart showing the forms of a word beside one another), PARAGRAPH (γράφω I write; originally a mark in the margin 'written beside' the word beginning a new division of the thought; hence, a division of thought in composition), PARALYSIS (a loosening of the muscles beside the bones, resulting in inability to move the limbs).

Lesson 21

Review of the Present System Active
The 'Alpha Privative'

121. ENDINGS

PRESENT SYSTEM ACTIVE

-ω	-ομεν
-εις	-ετε
-ει	-ουσι(ν)
-ον	-ομεν
-ες	-ετε
-ε(ν)	-ον
-ω	-ωμεν
-ῃς	-ητε
-ῃ	-ωσι(ν)
-οιμι	-οιμεν
-οις	-οιτε
-οι	-οιεν
-ε	-ετε
-ειν	
-(ε)μεν	
-(ε)μεναι	
-ων, -ουσα, -ον	

122. SYNTAX

1. *Indicative:* Imperfect or Aorist Indicative in both clauses, ἄν or κέ(ν) in conclusion, to express contrary-to-fact condition in the past. (Negative μή in if-clause, οὐ in conclusion).

2. *Subjunctive:* Exhortation. (Neg., μή)
   Purpose: ἵνα, ὡς, ὅπως, ὄφρα (Negative μή)

3. *Optative:* Wishes. (Neg. μή)
   Purpose: ἵνα, ὡς, ὅπως, ὄφρα (Negative μή)

4. *Imperative:* Commands. (Neg. μή)

5. *Infinitive:* After verb of wishing, etc., (Neg. μή)
   As a noun. (Neg. μή)
   In Indirect Statement (Neg. οὐ)

Note: the general distinction between οὐ and μή is that οὐ negates statements of concrete fact; μή, the others (possibility, condition, general, etc.).

123. THE ALPHA PRIVATIVE

In the ancient Indo-European mother language from which Greek, Latin, and English are descended, the vocalic-n sound (ṇ) prefixed to words, often negatived their meaning. This sound became ἀ(ν)- in Greek, *in* in Latin, *un-* in English (e.g., ἀδικέω, *in-vincibilis*, un-kind). Notice this negative or privative force of α- or αν- in many Greek words which you will meet. (Can you find the two instances in which it has already occurred?). Not all initial alphas, of course, have this negative force.

124. MEMORIZE

ἀθάνατος, -η, -ον	immortal, eternal
ἁμαρτάνω, ἁμαρτήσομαι, ἅμαρτον	I fail of, I miss, I err [often + gen.]
διδάσκω, διδάξω, δίδαξα	I teach
δίς	[adv.] twice, a second time
δοκέω, δοκήσω, δόκησα	I seem, I appear
ὄμβρος, -ου	[m.] rain, storm
οὐδέ	and not, nor, not even
παντοῖος, -η, -ον	of all sorts
πάρ-ειμι	I am present
πίπτω, πέσομαι, πέσον	I fall
που	[indefinite adv.] perhaps, I suppose, of course, no doubt
ποῦ	[interr. adv., always with circumflex] where?
σπεύδω, σπεύσω, σπεῦσα	I hasten
τρέφω, θρέψω, θρέψα	I nourish, I feed, I rear
φρονέω, φρονήσω, φρόνησα	I consider, I have understanding

125. TRANSLATE

1. παντοῖα ἀγαθὰ βροτοὶ ἐθέλουσιν ἐχέμεν.
2. ἔργον δίκης εἰρήνη ἐστίν.
3. σχέτλιος μὴ καὶ δοκέοιμι ἔμμεν.
4. σπεῦδε πρὸς θάλασσαν.
5. πολλοὶ παρ-ῆσαν, ὅπως μανθάνοιεν.
6. ἰητρὸς τάδε κελεύει ποιέειν, ἵνα βίον ἔχῃς κρατερόν.
7. λέγε τήνδε πέτρην πίπτειν εἰς ποταμόν.
8. οὐκ ἂν θνῆσκεν, εἰ μὴ ἁμάρτανε καὶ πίπτε.
9. ἑτέρους διδάσκωμεν παντοίους φιλέειν.
10. μὴ σπεύδετε, ὄφρα μὴ πίπτητε.
11. σοφοὶ νομίζουσιν ἀρετὴν δόξαν φέρειν.

126. PUT INTO GREEK

1. If you (sg.) wish to have happiness, do noble things.

2. If he were fleeing the rain, he would be hastening.

3. Truth nourishes our mind.

4. I say men's souls are immortal.

5. Let us eat in order that we may live.

6. If they were considering all sorts of things, they would not err.

7. Time teaches mortals both good and bad.

8. Don't flee toil, lest you seem to be a coward.

9. May we live forever!

10. Only the foolish do not love beautiful things.

127. READINGS

1. καί που δοκέεις ἀγαθὸς ἔμμεναι ἠδὲ κρατερός, ὅτι παρὰ ὀλίγοις καὶ οὐκ ἀγαθοῖσιν ὁμιλέεις.   (Homer)

2. σοφῷ γὰρ αἰσχρόν ἐστιν ἁμαρτάνειν.   (Aeschylus)

3. οὐ γὰρ χρόνος διδάσκει φρονέειν, αλλὰ ἀγαθὴ τροφή τε καὶ ψυχή.
   (Democritus)

4. ὄλβος ἀνθρώπου ἐστὶ βίος κατὰ νόον καὶ ἀρετήν· τάδε γὰρ μάλιστά ἐστιν ἄνθρωπος.   (Aristotle)

5. δὶς ἐπὶ αὐτῷ λίθῳ πίπτειν αἰσχρόν ἐστιν.   (Greek proverb)

6. εἰρήνη γεωργὸν καὶ ἐν πέτρῃσι τρέφει καλῶς, πόλεμος δὲ καὶ ἐν πεδίῳ κακῶς.   (Menander)

7. σπεῦδε βραδέως.   (Augustus' favorite maxim, quoted by Suetonius.)

βραδέως	[adv.] slowly
γεωργός, -οῦ	[m.] farmer
κακῶς	[adv. of κακός] badly
καλῶς	[adv. of καλός] beautifully, well
μάλιστα	[adv.] especially
ὁμιλέω	I associate with
πεδίον, -ου	[n.] plain
τροφή, -ῆς	[f.] rearing

128. WRITE IN GREEK

1. Let us learn all sorts of things, in order that we may live with men according to justice and truth. [Do not translate "of things"]

2. We know the soul is immortal, both by our own mind and by the words of the wise.

3. Let us not wish to seem noble and brave, but to be, [in order] that our friends may be many.

129. WORD STUDY

ATHANASIUS ('the immortal one'); — DIDACTIC (aimed at teaching something, as 'didactic poetry'); — DISSYLABLE (a word of two syllables); —GEORGE, GEORGIA, Vergil's *Georgics* (poems on the art of farming).

Lesson 22

The Present and Imperfect Middle and Passive Indicative. Deponent Verbs

130. NOTE

In all systems except the aorist, the form (but not the meaning) of the middle and the passive are exactly alike. For the meaning of middle and passive voice verbs, see the paradigms below and review Section 83c.

131. ENDINGS

PRES. IND. M.-P. ENDINGS

	Sg.	*Pl.*
1st pers.	-ομαι	-ομεθα
2nd pers.	-εαι	-εσθε
3rd pers.	-εται	-ονται

PRESENT IND. M.-P.

	Sg.	
1st pers.	λύομαι	I loose for myself/ am loosed
2nd pers.	λύεαι	you loose for yourself/ are loosed
3rd pers.	λύεται	he looses for himself/ is loosed

	Pl.	
1st pers.	λυόμεθα	we loose for ourselves/ are loosed
2nd pers.	λύεσθε	you loose for yourselves/ are loosed
3rd pers.	λύονται	they loose for themselves/ are loosed

IMPF. IND. M.-P. ENDINGS

	Sg.	*Pl.*
1st pers.	-ομην	-ομεθα
2nd. pers.	-εο	-εσθε
3rd. pers.	-ετο	-ονто

IMPF. IND. M.-P.

	Sg.	
1st pers.	λυόμην	I was loosing for myself/ was being loosed
2nd. pers.	λύεο	you were loosing for yourself/ were being loosed
3rd. pers.	λύετο	he was loosing for himself/ was being loosed

Pl.

1st pers.	λυόμεθα	we were loosing for ourselves/ were being loosed
2nd pers.	λύεσθε	you were loosing for yourselves/ were being loosed
3rd pers.	λύοντο	they were loosing for themselves/ were being loosed

Note: Sometimes -ομεσθα is used for -ομεθα

132. DEPONENT VERBS

Some Greek verbs have no active forms, but their middle or passive forms have active meaning. These are called **deponent verbs** because they "lay aside" some of their forms. They are easily recognized in the vocabularies by the fact that the first form given has middle endings, while the meaning remains active. There is an example in the vocabulary of this lesson. The middle of deponent and of active verbs often has **intransitive** force. That is, the action does not 'go over' onto another object. E.g., τρέπομαι *I turn (myself)*, in distinction to the transitive τρέπω *I turn (something else)*.

133. MEMORIZE

ἀέξω, ἀεξήσω, ἀέξησα	I enlarge, I increase [trans.]; [in mid.]: I increase (myself), I grow [intr.]
αἰτέω, αἰτήσω, αἴτησα	I ask, I request
ἥδομαι, ἥσομαι, ἡσάμην	I am pleased with [+ dat.]
λαμβάνω, λήψομαι, λάβον	I take, get
μάχομαι (μαχέομαι), μαχήσομαι, μαχεσ(σ)άμην	I fight (against)
μετά	[prep. + dat.] among, with; [prep. + acc.] into the midst, after
οὖν	therefore, then [not of time!]
πλησίος, -η, -ον	near; neighbor(ing)
τρέπω, τρέψω, τρέψα	I turn [trans.]; [in mid.]: I turn (myself) [intr.]

134. TRANSLATE

1. πόνοις μούνοις πολλὰ μανθάνεται.
2. βροτοὶ ὄλβον διώκονται αἰεί.
3. καρποὶ φέροντο πρὸς πλησίους ἡμετέρους.
4. ἰητρὸς οὐκ αἰτέεται χρυσόν, ἀλλὰ ὄλβον ἑτέροις.
5. ἔργοισι ἀγαθοῖσι ἀέξεται ἀρετή.
6. ὑπὸ φίλων γιγνωσκόμεθα.
7. ἐγγὺς πετράων τρέπετο ποταμός.
8. νόος ἀληθείῃ ἥδεται.

9. πλησίοισι ἀγαθοῖσι μαχέεσθε;

10. πολλὰ καὶ ὑπὸ σοφῶν οὐ νοέεται.

135. PUT INTO GREEK

1. The treasure was hidden among the trees.

2. I was pleased with the gifts.

3. The wise, then, teach themselves all sorts of things.

4. You (sg.) are said to be brave.

5. The stones were being taken by force and borne to the sea.

6. The evil man was being pursued by many.

7. We are pleased with this gift.

8. After a rain, the rivers increase.

9. Let us nourish our souls with truth and justice.

10. Are you pleased with her voice?

136. READINGS

1. θέος ὁράει ἀνθρώπους, καὶ πλησίος πάρ-εστιν, ὅς δικαίοις ἥδεται καὶ οὐκ ἀδίκοις.   (Menander)

2. Αἴγυπτος λέγεται ἔμμεν δῶρον Νείλου ποταμοῦ.   (Herodotus)

3. αἰτέετε καὶ οὐ λαμβάνετε ὅτι κακῶς αἰτέεσθε.   (St. James)

4. ἀνάγκη γὰρ οὐδὲ θεοὶ μάχονται.   (Simonides)

5. ἀέξεται ἀρετὴ μετὰ σοφοῖσιν ἀνθρώπων μετά τε δικαίοις, ὡς δένδρεον ὑπὸ ὄμβρου· χρειὼ δὲ παντοίη ἐστὶ φίλων ἀνθρώπων.   (Pindar)

6. οὐ γὰρ αἶψα θεῶν ἀθανάτων τρέπεται νόος.   (Homer)

ἄδικος, -ον	unjust
Αἴγυπτος, -ου	[f.] Egypt
κακῶς	[adv. of κακός] badly, wrongly
ὅς	[rel. pronoun] who
Νεῖλος, -ου	[m.] Nile
χρειὼ	[indecl. f.] need

137. WRITE IN GREEK

1. Let us, then, hasten to learn all sorts of noble deeds and to flee from cruel (deeds).

2. Take (pl.) the gold and hide it in the earth, that it may not be the beginning of war among friends. [Omit "it" both times.]

3. If you (sg.) wished to increase the life of the soul, you would do only what is just and excellent.

138. WORD STUDY

HEDONIST (one who does only what is pleasant, an extreme pleasure-lover); — METAPHYSICS ('the treatise after the Physics' in Aristotle's writings; hence, the science of ultimate principles underlying all things, the philosophy of Being)— METAMORPHOSIS (μορφή form; a change into one form or state after another, a transformation)— METAPHOR (φορή, a carrying, from φέρω : hence, a comparison where one idea 'carries after it' its implications directly to another object without use of like, as, etc.; e.g., "He is a lion on parade, but a rabbit in battle."); — SYLLABLE (part of a word 'taken together' as a unit of sound) — SYLLABUS (a brief outline or schedule of studies, etc. 'taken together' in a concise view of the whole).

Lesson 23

The Present Subjunctive and Optative, Middle and Passive

139.

	PRES. SUBJ. M.-P. ENDINGS		PRES. SUBJ. M.-P.	
	Sg.	*Pl.*	*Sg.*	*Pl.*
1st pers.	-ωμαι	-ωμεθα	λύωμαι	λυώμεθα
2nd pers.	-ηαι	-ησθε	λύηαι	λύησθε
3rd pers.	-ηται	-ωνται	λύηται	λύωνται

140.

	PRES. OPT. M.-P. ENDINGS		PRES. OPT. M.-P.	
	Sg.	*Pl.*	*Sg.*	*Pl.*
1st pers.	-οιμην	-οιμεθα	λυοίμην	λυοίμεθα
2nd pers.	-οιο	-οισθε	λύοιο	λύοισθε
3rd pers.	-οιτο	-οιατο	λύοιτο	λυοίατο

Note:

In the optative middle (pres. and aor.) and also in the Perfect middle indicative (see Sections 269 and 338) the 3 pl. ending is -ατο not the expected -ντο —which is the 3 pl. optative middle-passive ending in later, Classical Greek.

141. MEMORIZE

ἀν-έχομαι, ἀν-έξομαι or ἀνα-σχήσομαι, ἀνά-σχον or -σχεθον	I hold up under, I endure
γίγνομαι, γενήσομαι, γενόμην, γέγαα	I am born, I become, I am, I happen
ἑταῖρος, -ου	[m.] companion, comrade
ἠέλιος, -ου	[m.] sun
μισέω, μισήσω, μίσησα	I hate
ὀρθός, -ή, -όν	straight, true
πίνω, πίομαι, πίον	I drink
ὦ	O! [in direct address]

142. TRANSLATE

1. μὴ μισέωμεν ἑταίρους, ἵνα μὴ καὶ μισεώμεθα.
2. χαλεπὰ ἀν-έχοιο, ὄφρα ποτὲ ἔχῃαι καλά.
3. μάχετο, ὅπως μὴ λαμβάνοιτο.
4. ἐσθλὰ αἰεὶ διώκωμεν.
5. γίγνοιτο εἰρήνη ὀρθή τε καὶ δικαίη.
6. πίπτει εἰς γαῖαν ὄμβρος, ἵνα δένδρεα ἀέξηται.
7. ἡδοίμεθα αἰεὶ κείνοις.
8. πονηροὶ κεύθονται, ἵνα μὴ ὁράωνται.
9. πολλὰ ἀν-εχόμην, ἵνα γιγνοίμην σοφός.
10. μή ποτε τρέποισθε ἀπὸ ἀληθείης νηπίων λόγοις.
11. ἀέξεται ὄλβος, ἐπεὶ δίκαιοι ἦσαν.

143. PUT INTO GREEK

1. Let us nourish our minds with good things.
2. We eat and drink [in order] to become strong.
3. May he endure sickness as a brave man.
4. They fled, lest they be seen.
5. Didn't you (sg.) bring this that it might be eaten?
6. Hide (pl.) the treasure in the rocks, that it may not be taken.
7. "May I always fight for the sake of truth and justice," he said.
8. He wished to die that he might not be said to be a coward.
9. May our hearts be pleased with good things, as our eyes are with the beautiful.
10. Let us fight and die as brave men.

144. READINGS

1. γαῖα κελαινὴ πίνει ὄμβρον, πίνει δὲ δένδρεα γαῖαν· ποταμοὺς πίνει
θάλασσα, ἥλιος δὲ θάλασσαν· ἀν-έχοισθε οὖν, ὦ ἑταῖροι, εἰ καὶ
αὐτὸς ἐθέλω πίνειν.
(Anacreontic)
2. μὴ σπεῦδε πλουτέειν, μὴ αἶψα πτωχὸς γίγνηαι.   (Menander)
3. τόδε οὔκ ἐστι χαλεπόν — θάνατον φεύγειν. ἀλλὰ φεύγειν πονηροὺς
καὶ πονηρά, τόδε δή ἐστι χαλεπόν.   (Plato)

κελαινός. -ή, -όν	black
πλουτέω	I am rich
πτωχός, -οῦ	[m.] beggar

145. WRITE IN GREEK

1. Many men are pleased with truth and beautiful things; but many think life is to eat and to drink.

2. The sun is said by the foolish to drink from the rivers and the sea.

3. He fought in the war, that we might live and die in peace.

146. WORD STUDY

NITROGEN (a 'nitrate-born' element), GENESIS (the first book of the Bible, telling of the 'birth' or making of the world);, — HELIOTROPE (ἥλιος, later spelling for ἠέλιος, and τροπή from τρέπω : hence 'sun-turner', a purple flower which turns to face the sun), HELIUM (an element first discovered in the sun); — MISANTHROPE (a hater of mankind); —ORTHODOX (holding the true opinion, un-heretical), ORTHOGRAPHY (γράφω I write; correct spelling or writing); — PLUTOCRAT, PLUTOCRACY (κράτος power; government by the wealthy), PLUTO (god of the underworld of the dead in ancient mythology, as being 'rich' in possessions).

Lesson 24

The Present Imperative, Infinitive, Participle Middle and Passive
The Use of Infinitive For Imperative

147. FORMS

PRES. IMPT. M.-P. ENDINGS

	Sg.	Pl.
2nd pers.	-εο or -ευ	-εσθε

PRES. IMPT. M.-P.

	Sg.		Pl.	
2nd pers.	λύεο or λύευ	loose for yourself be loosing for yourself be loosed	λύεσθε	loose for yourselves be loosing for yourselves be loosed

PRES. INF. M.-P. ENDINGS	PRES. INF. M.-P.	
-εσθαι	λύεσθαι	to loose for oneself to be loosed

PRES. PTC. M.-P. ENDINGS	PRES. PTC. M.-P.
m. f. n.	m. f. n.
-μενος, -η, -ον	λυόμενος, λυομένη, λυόμενον

Note: The present participle middle-passive declines like καλός, -ή, -όν

148. INFINITIVE AS IMPERATIVE

Not infrequently the infinitive is used in an independent clause with the force of an imperative, e.g., πονηρὰ φεύγειν. *Flee from base things!*

149. MEMORIZE

ἄπ-ειμι	I am away
αὐτάρ	but, yet
δυνατός, -ή, -όν	able, possible [+ εἰμί and infinitive] able (to do something)
μέλλω, μελλήσω, μέλλησα	I am about, I am going, I intend, I am destined (to do something) [+ infinitive]

ὄφρα	(in order) that, to [+ subjunctive or optative in purpose construction]; while, until [+ indicative if purely factual, + purpose construction if anticipatory]

πέλω, —, πέλον
  or deponent form:
  πέλομαι, —, πλόμην
	I come to be, I am

πέμπω, πέμψω, πέμψα	I send
σός, -ή, -όν	your [sg.]
τοί	surely, you see [postpositive]

150. TRANSLATE

1. μὴ λαμβάνεο τάδε ἡμέτερα.
2. λέγει πολλοὺς πέμπεσθαι.
3. λύεσθαί που ἐθέλει, ἵνα φοιτάῃ.
4. μέλλες σὸν ξεῖνον πέμπειν;
5. μὴ φεύγετε, ἀλλὰ ἀν-έχεσθε.
6. εἵνεκα βίοιο μάχοντο.
7. ἀγαθὸς πέλευ ὄφρα ἑταῖρος σὸς ἄπ-εστιν.
8. τοῖσδε οὖν ἥδεσθαι, ἐπεὶ αὐτὸς φέρες.
9. μὴ τρέπευ, ὄφρα μὴ πίπτῃς.
10. καρποὶ μέλλον ἀπὸ δενδρέων λαμβάνεσθαι, αὐτὰρ ὄμβρος ἵκανε, καὶ εἰς γαῖαν πίπτον.
11. δυνατοί εἰσιν πολλοὺς πόνους ἀν-έχεσθαι.

151. PUT INTO GREEK

1. While they are away, hide yourself!
2. To be hated is an evil thing.
3. They were being taken by force.
4. Are you (pl.) now able to fight?
5. He seems to endure both good and bad with a noble spirit.
6. Good and noble things were done by your (sg.) companions.
7. Surely you (sg.) wish to be taught!
8. He said your companions are being pursued in war.
9. Endure (pl.) troubles, until you become strong in heart.
10. If only we were not destined to be sent to that land!

152. READINGS

1. φίλων, οἵ τε πάρ-εισι καὶ οἳ ἄπ-εισι, μιμνήσκεο.   (Thales)
2. μή ποτέ τοι κακὸν ἄνθρωπον φίλον ποιέεσθαι ἑταῖρον, ἀλλὰ αἰεὶ φεύγειν ὥς τε κακὸν ὅρμον.   (Theognis)

3. μὴ ζῶε ὡς μέλλων ζώειν αἰεί. θάνατος πάρ-εστι· ὄφρα ζώεις, ὄφρα δυνατός ἐσσι, ἀγαθὸς γίγνεο.   (Marcus Aurelius)

4. αὐτὰρ ἐπεὶ τόνδε πόνον πέμπον θεοὶ ἀθάνατοι, ἀν-έχεο, μηδὲ ὀδύρεο σὸν κατὰ θυμόν.   (Homer)

μέλλων	nom. m. ptc, modifying subject: translate: "(one) destined" [+ infinitive]
μιμνήσκω	I am mindful of [+ gen.]
ὀδύρομαι	I grieve
οἵ	[relative pronoun] who
ὅρμος, -ου	[m.] harbor

153. WRITE IN GREEK

1. Those people wish to learn many things, that they may become wise.

2. This wise man endured many and difficult toils, that he might come to be strong and just.

3. "Let us fight as brave men," he said, "in order that we may be loved by many."

154. WORD STUDY

POMP (πομπή a sending; a grand procession or pageant; hence, ostentatious display, a show of magnificence.)

Lesson **25**

Review of the Whole Present System

155. ENDINGS

IND.

    PRES.

        ACT.   M.-P.

-ω	-ομεν	-ομαι	-ομεθα
-εις	-ετε	-εαι	-εσθε
-ει	-ουσι(ν)	-εται	-ονται

    IMPF.

        ACT.   M.-P.

-ον	-ομεν	-ομην	-ομεθα
-ες	-ετε	-εο	-εσθε
-ε	-ον	-ετο	-οντο

SUBJ.

    PRES.

        ACT.   M.-P.

-ω	-ωμεν	-ωμαι	-ωμεθα
-ῃς	-ητε	-ηαι	-ησθε
-ῃ	-ωσι(ν)	-ηται	-ωνται

OPT.

    PRES.

        ACT.   M.-P.

-οιμι	-οιμεν	-οιμην	-οιμεθα
-οις	-οιτε	-οιο	-οισθε
-οι	-οιεν	-οιτο	-οιατο

IMPT.

    PRES.

        ACT.   M.-P.

-ε	-ετε	-εο, -ευ	-εσθε

INF.

    PRES.

        ACT.   M.-P.

-ειν, -(ε)μεν, -(ε)μεναι   -εσθαι

PTC.

    PRES.

        ACT.   M.-P.

-ων, -ουσα, -ον   -ομενος, -ομενη, -ομενον

156. COMMENTS ON THE PRESENT SYSTEM

a. Notice that the subjunctive endings are simply lengthened forms of the present indicative. These same endings are used for the subjunctive of all tenses.

b. Note that every ending begins with a vowel. This vowel is called a **thematic** vowel. In the present system, it is always ο or ε, or a lengthened form of them.

c. You will find that the optative of all systems always has an iota diphthong (οι, αι, εαι, ει, υι) to match the one here. Use this fact as a clue in recognizing an optative ending.

157. MEMORIZE

ἀμείβομαι, ἀμείψομαι, ἀμειψάμην	I (ex)change; I reply
γε	[enclitic particle] at least, in fact
δείδω, δείσομαι, δεῖσα, δείδια	I fear [+ infinitive or μή and purpose construction]
εἴρομαι, εἰρήσομαι, ἐρόμην	I ask
ἱερός, -ή, -όν	holy, sacred
νηός, -οῦ	[m.] temple
πεύθομαι, πεύσομαι, πυθόμην	I learn (by inquiry), I inquire (from), I hear of [+ acc. of thing heard, + gen. of person heard]
πρῶτος, -η, -ον	first
σώζω, σώσω, σῶσα	I save

158. TRANSLATE

1. πολλὰ πεύθεαι σοῖς ὀφθαλμοῖς.
2. νήπιοι δείδουσι μὴ εἰς γαῖαν πίπτῃ ἠέλιος.
3. αἶψα ποιέωμεν, ἐπεὶ χρόνος σπεύδει.
4. νομίζεις τόνδε νηὸν ἱερόν εἶναι;
5. μή γε νήπια εἴρευ.
6. ἑταίρους κέλευε ἱκανέμεν, ὄφρα μαχεοίατο.
7. ἐσθλός τε πέλει καὶ δοκέει σοφὸς ἔμμεν.
8. μή ποτε δείδοιτε παντοίους ἐχέμεναι φίλους.
9. μάχοντο ἵνα ἑταίρους σώζοιεν.
10. διδάσκω ἠδὲ ἀμείβομαι, ὄφρα μανθάνητε.

159. PUT INTO GREEK

1. An evil man fights with his own soul.
2. Do you (sg.) see her?
3. Take (pl.) those stones and bring them to the river.
4. Neither the earth nor the sea is (use πέλομαι) always the same.
5. The trees grew straight and high.

6. We learn by inquiry (use πεύθομαι) in order not to become foolish.

7. While drinking, don't (sg.) fall into the river!

8. If you (sg.) wish to have glory, bear up under hard things.

9. May peace come, the fruit of justice and truth!

10. Please don't fight (pl.), but become friends.

160. READINGS

1. πολλὰ δὴ κακὰ ἀν-έχεο σὸν κατὰ θυμόν.   (Homer)

2. δένδρεον ἀγαθὸν καρποὺς καλοὺς ποιέει, πονηρὸν δὲ πονηροὺς ποιέει καρπούς.   (St. Matthew)

3. ψυχῇ ἄνθρωπος δυνατός ἐστι φεύγειν μὲν κακόν, διώκειν δὲ καὶ λαμβάνειν ἀγαθόν.   (Plato)

4. μὴ δείδεο· πρῶτός εἰμι καὶ ἔσχατος. νεκρὸς ἦα, καὶ νῦν ζώω εἰς αἰεί. (Apocalypse)

5. οὐ γιγνώσκετε ὅτι νηὸς θεοῦ ἐστε; νηὸς δὲ θεοῦ ἐστιν ἱερός. (St. Paul)

6. σοφὸς ἐν ἑῇ ψυχῇ περι-φέρει ἑὰ ἀγαθά.   (Menander)

ἔσχατος, -η, -ον	last
νεκρός, -οῦ	[m.]dead body; dead
περι-φέρω	I carry around

161. WRITE IN GREEK

1. Let us learn those these truths by inquiry.

2. Evil men fear death, but to the holy it seems good and the beginning of eternal life.

3. A few things you (sg.) know; learn also these, that you may be able to speak (λεγ-) among the wise.

162. WORD STUDY

AMEBA (the simplest form of animal life, consisting of a single cell frequently changing shape); — HIERARCHY (ἀρχή rule; the clergy as a group, 'the rulers of holy things', i.e., the Church; sometimes applied to any other group of persons or things similarly organized according to degree and rank, as "in the hierarchy of the sciences, Theology has the highest place"), HIEROGLYPH (γλυφή a carving; picture-writing, as that invented by the priests of ancient Egypt and carved on sacred monuments; hence, humorously, illegible or unintelligible writing); — PROTON (the 'first constituent' of an atom, carrying the positive charge and larger than its complementary part, the electron), PROTEIN (a basic food-element in meat, etc., a 'first essential' of a healthy diet), PROTOPLASM (πλᾶσμα molded form; the basic molded or organized substance from which living cells are formed), PROTOTYPE (the original form or model of something, the standard pattern to which other things of the same kind should conform).

Lesson 26

The Future System
Relative Pronoun and Relative Clauses

163. FORMATION OF THE FUTURE

The future system is formed by adding the endings of the present system to the **future stem**. This future stem is found by dropping the -ω or -ομαι of the **second principal part** of the verb.

For instance, to form the future passive infinitive of λύω, take the future stem λυσ- from the second principal part (λύσω) and add -εσθαι. λύσεσθαι: *to be about to be loosed.* Similarly for the other forms: λύσεις, λύσει, λύσ-ουσι, etc. See full list of forms in Appendix A. For example, here is the future active indicative of λύω:

	Sg.		*Pl.*	
1st pers.	λύσω	I shall loose	λύσομεν	we shall loose
2nd pers.	λύσεις	you will loose	λύσετε	you will loose
3rd pers.	λύσει	he will loose	λύσουσι(ν)	they will loose

Remember that the subjunctive, optative and imperative are not used in the future system!

> *Note:* Regarding Indirect Statement involving the future tense. As noted in Section 114, a present infinitive in indirect statement indicates that the action of the infinitive is contemporaneous with that of the main (introducing) verb. Likewise, if an infinitive in indirect statement is in the future tense, then the action of the infinitive is future in respect to that of the main verb.

λέγει ξεῖνον οὐχ εὑδήσειν.   *She is saying that the guest will not be sleeping.*

ἰητρὸς λέγε τούσδε νοῦσον φεύξεσθαι.   *The physician was saying that these people would escape (be escaping) the disease.*

164. RELATIVE PRONOUN AND RELATIVE CLAUSES

1. The **relative pronoun** ("who, which, what, that") is declined according to the first and second declension, and in particular resembles the demonstrative pronoun/adjective ὁ, ἡ, τό.

	M.	*F.*	*N.*
	Sg.		
N.	ὅς	ἥ	ὅ
G.	οὗ	ἧς	οὗ
D.	ᾧ	ᾗ	ᾧ
A.	ὅν	ἥν	ὅ

	M.	F.	N.
Pl.			
N.	οἵ	αἵ	ἅ
G.	ὧν	ὧν	ὧν
D.	οἷσ(ι)	ᾗσ(ι)	οἷσ(ι)
A.	οὕς	ἅς	ἅ

2. In the English sentence, *"The man who sent the gift is noble"* the noun 'man' is modified (described) by a dependent clause ('who sent the gift') known as a **relative clause**. The relative clause is linked to its **antecedent** (man) in the main clause by a **relative pronoun** ('who') which stands for the noun 'man.'

Within its own relative clause, the relative pronoun has a grammatical role. In this example, the relative pronoun 'who' is the subject of its clause. In Greek the nominative case is used for subjects, so the relative pronoun in this case would have to be nominative (ὅς):

ἄνθρωπος ὃς δῶρον πέμπε ἐσθλός ἐστιν.

But compare the roles of the relative pronouns in the following English sentences:

I saw the treasures that you were hiding. (direct object)

The trees on which much fruit grows are tall. (object of preposition)

The companion whose brother is dying will request food. (possesive)

In Greek, each of these relative pronouns would have to be put into the proper **case** to signal its grammatical role (cp. Section 18). The Greek equivalents would be:

ὅραον θησαυροὺς οὓς κεύθες. (accusative)

δένδρεα ὑψηλά ἐστιν ἐπὶ οἷσι πολλὸς καρπὸς ἀέξεται. (dative after ἐπὶ)

ὁ ἑταῖρος οὗ κασιγνητὸς θνήσκει αἰτήσεται σῖτον. (genitive)

Notice that each of the pronouns has the same **gender** and **number** as its antecedent in the main clause. In our first sentence, ὅς is masculine and singular because its antecedent ἄνθρωπος is masculine and singular. In the second sentence, οὓς is masculine and plural as is its antecedent θησαυρούς. In the third sentence, οἷσι is neuter and plural as is δένδρεα. And in the last sentence, οὗ is masculine and singular as is ἑταῖρος.

To summarize: the gender and number of a relative pronoun will be the same as its antecedent in the main clause, but its case will be determined by its grammatical role within its own relative clause.

3. Besides the relative pronoun introduced and declined in this Lesson, the demonstrative pronoun/adjective ὁ, ἡ, τό is also used by Homer as a relative pronoun. E.g., ἄνθρωποί τοί εἰσιν ἀγαθοί, πολλῶν φίλοι εἰσίν. *Men who are good are friends of many.*

165. MEMORIZE

ἀπ-ολλύω, ἀπ-ολέσω, ἀπ-όλεσ(σ)α, ἀπ-όλωλα, 2 aor. mid.: ἀπ-ολόμην	I kill, I destroy; I lose; [in pf. and mid.] I perish, I am lost
ἐμός, -ή, -όν	my, mine
ἔρχομαι, ἐλεύσομαι, ἔλ(υ)θον, ἐλήλουθα	I come, I go
ζωή, -ῆς	[f.] life
κασιγνητός, -οῦ	[m.] brother
οὐρανός, -οῦ	[m.] heaven, sky
παρ-έρχομαι	I go past, I pass
πῶς	[interr. adv.] how?
πως	[enclitic adv.] somehow, in any way
σῖτος, -ου	[m.] bread, food

166. TRANSLATE

1. ἐκεῖνα πεύσομαι ἃ οὐ γιγνώσκω.
2. οἵ ποιέουσι καλὰ ἔργα γενήσονται καλοί.
3. πολλοὶ βροτοὶ οἷσι θεὸς πέμπει νοῦσον θανέονται.
4. πόνους ἕξεις, αὐτὰρ καὶ δόξαν.
5. θάνατον οὔ πως φευξόμεθα βροτοί.
6. λέγει κασιγνητοὺς ἑοὺς ἐλεύσεσθαι.
7. μέλλει ὄψεσθαι οὐρανὸν ἐξ οὗ ὄμβρος πεσέεται.
8. "πῶς ζωὴν ἐμὴν σώσω;" εἴρετο.
9. πολλά τοι οὔ ποτε γνώσεσθε.
10. ἔρχευ, καὶ σοῖσι ὀφθαλμοῖσι ὄψεαι θάλασσαν.
11. οἵδε νόμιζον ἱερὸν νηὸν οὔ ποτε ἀπ-ολέσεσθαι.
12. τὸν σῖτον ὃν μέλλεις ἔδεσθαι μισέω.

167. PUT INTO GREEK

1. Command! (sg.) We shall do what you say.
2. Mortal men will never flee (i.e., escape) death.
3. He is about to take the gold, but he will be taken himself.
4. True justice will never be turned away from evil deeds.
5. My brother, whom you were pursuing, will take this treasure and hide (it).
6. Rain is falling; the rivers, then, will suddenly increase.
7. I don't know, but I shall inquire and find out. (use a form of πεύθομαι)
8. There are many things that we mortals shall never learn.

9.   He will bring bread that we will eat.

10.   Evil men, who are never wise, will always fear justice.

11.   She is about to wrong a man whom I love.

168. READINGS

1.   ὃν θεοὶ φιλέουσι, θνῄσκει νέος.   (Menander)

2.   οἵ ποτε ἦτε τῆλε ἀπὸ θεοῖο, νῦν ἐγγύς ἐστε, ἐν Χριστῷ. αὐτὸς γάρ ἐστιν ἡμετέρη εἰρήνη.

3.   οὐρανὸς καὶ γαῖα παρ-ελεύσονται, λόγοι δὲ ἐμοὶ οὔ ποτε παρ-ελεύσονται.   (St. Matthew)

4.   ὃ μὲν καλόν ἐστιν, φίλον ἐστίν. ὃ δὲ οὐ καλόν, οὐ φίλον ἐστίν.   (Theognis)

5.   ἀθανάτη ἐστὶν ἡμετέρη ψυχὴ καὶ οὔ ποτε ἀπ-ολέσεται.   (Plato)

6.   τόδε γε θαυμάσιον ἔχω ἀγαθόν, ᾧ σῴζομαι· οὐ γὰρ αἰσχύνομαι μανθάνειν, ἀλλὰ πεύθομαι καὶ εἴρομαι, καὶ φιλέω τὸν ὃς ἀμείβεται.   (Socrates, in Plato)

αἰσχύνομαι	I am ashamed
θαυμάσιος, -η, -ον	marvelous
τῆλε	[adv.] far, far away
Χριστός, -οῦ	[m.] Christ, the Anointed One

169. WRITE IN GREEK

1.   We shall pass the river, which turns near those rocks and goes into the sea

2.   Life is difficult but supplies men many good things by which we are always pleased.

3.   Strong rain, which falls to earth from the sky, will forever destroy many works of men.

170. WORD STUDY

URANUS (a planet named after the Greek god of the heavens, grandfather of Zeus), URANIUM an element named after Uranus); — PARASITE (one who eats at a rich man's table, getting a place 'beside the food' by means of flattery; hence, an animal or person living off another's resources and doing no work of its own); — HOMILY (an explanation of some text from Scripture, etc. for 'gathering' or 'association' of people).

Lesson 27

The Third Declension—Masculine and Feminine.
Rules of Gender

171. GENDER

The third declension contains masculine, feminine, and neuter forms. The gender can easily be told from the word's stem (found by dropping the -ος of the genitive ending.) The general rules are these:

> stems ending in ατ-, αρ-, α-, ε- (ἀτάραε) are neuter,
> stems ending in δ-, ι-, θ-, ιτ-, τητ- (διθιττητ) are feminine,
> all others are masculine.

There are a few exceptions to the above rules. In any case, the gender of nouns is indicated in the Memorize sections and Vocabularies.

172. ENDINGS of third declension masculine and feminine nouns, adjectives, participles:

	Sg.	*Pl.*
N.	—	-ες
G.	-ος	-ων
D.	-ι	-σι, -εσσι
A.	-α, (-ν)	-ας

173. NOTE

a. Many nouns have alternative endings other than the above, especially in the dative and accusative. When these occur in the readings, they will be identified.

b. Stems in ι- or υ- take -ν in the accusative singular (e.g., πόλι-ν, ἰχθύ-ν). Adjectives in -υς take accusative singular masculine in -υν.

c. In the dative plural, a τ, δ, θ, or ν ending the stem drop out before the ending, while a κ, γ, or χ blend with the σ of the ending into a ξ. Thus, ἄνακτ-σι becomes ἄνακ-σι, then ἄναξι. When both ν and τ drop, the vowel lengthens in compensation: γέροντ-σι becomes γέρουσι.

174. EXAMPLES OF THIRD DECLENSION NOUNS

Sg.

N.	ἄναξ [m.] lord	παῖς [m., f.] child	πατήρ [m.] father
G.	ἄνακτος	παιδός	πατέρος, πατρός
D.	ἄνακτι	παιδί	πατέρι, πατρί
A.	ἄνακτα	παῖδα	πατέρα

Pl.

N.	ἄνακτες	παῖδες	πατέρες
G.	ἀνάκτων	παίδων	πατέρων, πατρῶν
D.	ἀνάκτεσσι, ἄναξι	παίδεσσι, παισί	πατράσι
A.	ἄνακτας	παῖδας	πατέρας

Sg.

N.	πόλις [f.] city	γέρων [m.] old man
G.	πόλιος, πόληος	γέροντος
D.	πόλει, πόληι	γέροντι
A.	πόλιν	γέροντα

Pl.

N.	πόλιες, πόληες	γέροντες
G.	πολίων	γερόντων
D.	πολίεσσι	γερόντεσσι, γέρουσι
A.	πόλιας, πόλεις, πόληας	γέροντας

Notes:

1.   For clarity's sake, the full genitive (not just the ending) of each third declension noun listed in the Memorize sections will be given.

2.   Present and Future participles in -ων have their stem in -οντ- e.g., λύων, λύοντος, λύοντι, λύοντα, etc. Participle stems will be seen in Lesson 29.

175. MEMORIZE

ἄναξ, ἄνακτος	[m] king, lord
ἀνήρ, ἀνέρος or ἀνδρός	[m.] dat. pl. ἄνδρεσσι or ἀνδράσι man, male
γέρων, γέροντος	[m.] old man
ἕκαστος, -η, -ον	each
ἤ or, than; ἤ ... ἤ	either ... or, whether ... or
μέτρον, -ου	[n.] measure
παῖς, παιδός	[m., f.] child, boy, girl
πατήρ, πατέρος or πατρός	[m.] father
περ	[enclitic particle] surely, by far [adds force]; [+ participle] though
πόλις, πόλιος or πόληος	[f.] city
φύσις, φύσιος	[f.] nature

φαίνω, φανέω, φῆνα	I show, I reveal; in mid: φαίνομαι, φανέομαι.
	aor. pass. w. act. force: φάνην I show myself, I appear

176. TRANSLATE

1. τὸν λέγουσιν ἔμμεναι ἄνδρα κρατερόν.
2. παιδὶ θάλασσαν φαίνωμεν.
3. παντοίους ἄνδρας τρέφει πόλις ἑκάστη.
4. ἄνακτες δίκην φιλέουσιν ἠδὲ δικαίους.
5. ὑπὸ ἀνδρῶν σοφῶν αἰεὶ φιλήσεται ἀληθείη.
6. ἕκαστος κατὰ ἑὴν φύσιν ζώει.
7. ἀνδρῶν ἔργων μέτρον ἀρετή.
8. παισὶ ἀγαθοῖσι πολλὰ δῶρα πατέρες παρ-έχουσι.
9. ἀνέρι ἑκάστῳ περ ζωή ἐστιν ἡδεῖα.
10. ἀνάκτεσσι πόνους αἰεὶ παρα-σχήσει ἢ εἰρήνη ἢ πόλεμος.

177. PUT INTO GREEK

1. Let us tell the king what our companions saw.
2. Each thing grows toward the measure of its own nature.
3. Only an evil man will take bread away from children.
4. The city will be saved by strong men.
5. He appears (use φαίνομαι) to be just, but he is pitiless.
6. They are coming to show the boys the gold.
7. To each man death will sometime come.
8. May we reveal our nature by our deeds!
9. Please show yourselves men, not children!
10. Do you (sg.) see the rain that is falling among the trees?

178. READINGS

1. δὶς παῖδές εἰσι γέροντες. (Menander)
2. ἀνδρὸς χαρακτὴρ ἐκ λόγου γιγνώσκεται. (Menander)
3. θνήσκειν μὴ λέγε ἄνδρας ἀγαθούς. (Callimachus)
4. ἄνθρωπος φύσιι πολιτικόν ἐστι ζωόν. (Aristotle)
5. χρόνος δίκαιον ἄνδρα φαίνει μοῦνος. (Sophocles)
6. πολλοὶ μὲν ἄνθρωποι, ὀλίγοι δὲ ἄνδρες. (Herodotus, of the Persian army. ἀνήρ often has the meaning of *man* in distinction to *woman*, as in Latin *vir* is more specific than *homo*).
7. ἕκαστος ἑὸν μισθὸν λήψεται, κατὰ ἑὸν πόνον· θεοῖο γάρ εἰμεν συν-εργοί.
   (St. Paul)

γέρων, γέροντος	[m.] old man

ζωός, -ή, -όν	living
μισθός, -οῦ	[m.] wages
πολιτικόν, -ή, -όν	living in a community, social
συν-εργός, -όν	working together; a cooperator
χαρακτήρ, χαρακτῆρος	[m.] stamp, character

179. WRITE IN GREEK

1. A strong storm that comes from the sky will destroy both fruits and trees.

2. I shall go, then, to your brother and request the gold, of which I shall have need in order to live.

3. He will indeed be pleased with the gifts, which will appear to be yours, not ours.

180. WORD STUDY

ANDREW ("manly," "strong"); — METRE or METER (the 'measure' of poetic rhythm, a verse structure), hence HEXAMETER, PENTAMETER, etc. (six, five, etc. feet or 'measures' to a line, in poetry), — METER (a measuring instrument, as in SPEEDOMETER, VOLTMETER, THERMOMETER [θέρμος heat], etc.), GEOMETRY (γῆ, variant form of γαῖα, the science of mathematical laws growing out of the measurement of space; so called because the Greeks who invented geometry at first drew their figures in the earth or dust); — PEDAGOGUE (ἀγωγός a leader: cp. ἄγαγον. Originally a slave who led children to school; thence, a school-master, teacher), PEDAGOGY, PEDAGOGIC (the science of education); —PHYSICS (the science of natural laws of weight, gravity, light, electricity, etc.), PHYSICIST (a professional expert in physics), PHYSICAL, PHYSICIAN (one who cares for man's natural powers and body, a doctor), PHYSIC (a medicine helping nature readjust itself); — PHENOMENON ('that which appears or reveals itself'; hence, a visible appearance or effect; also, an unusual event, a marvel), PHENOMENAL (in appearance only; more commonly: extraordinary, marvelous), CELLOPHANE (plastic wrapper through whose cells the contents appear), EPIPHANY (feast of the 'Revealing' of Christ to the world); — POLITICAL, POLITICS (pertaining to community administration and public policy); — CHARACTER, CHARACTERISTIC (distinctive quality stamped on an individual).

Lesson 28

The Third Declension—Neuter

181. FORMS

Neuter nouns, adjectives, and participles of the third declension have endings identical with masculine and feminine except in the nominative and accusative. Thus. ἔπος, ἔπεος (*word*) is declined:

	Sg.	Pl.	Sg.	Pl.
N.	—	-α	ἔπος	ἔπεα
G.	-ος	-ων	ἔπεος	ἐπέων
D.	-ι	-σι, -εσσι	ἔπει	ἔπεσι or ἐπέεσσι
A.	—	-α	ἔπος	ἔπεα

Note:

Third declension nouns whose nominative ends in -ος are always neuter.
Be careful to distinguish them from masculine nouns of the second declension.
The genitive ending (-ος rather than -ου) supplies the clue.

182. MEMORIZE

διά	[prep. + gen.] through
	[prep. + acc.] through; among, on account of
ἔπος, ἔπεος	[n.] word
κῆρ, κῆρος	[n.] heart
μῆκος, μήκεος	[n.] length
πρᾶγμα, πράγματος	[n.] deed; [in pl.]: trouble, deeds
πῦρ, πυρός	[n.] fire
σῶμα, σώματος	[n.] body, corpse
τῇ	where [rel. adv.]; there
τῇδε	[adv.] here
φάος, φάεος	[n.] light
χρῆμα, χρήματος	[n.] possession, property; [in pl.] wealth

183. TRANSLATE

1. μὴ φιλέωμεν χρήματα ἀνδρός, ἀλλὰ ἄνδρα αὐτόν.
2. νήπιοι παῖδες διὰ πυρὸς ἐθέλουσι φοιτάειν.
3. νόον ἀνδράσι φαίνομεν ἐπέεσσιν.

4. κῆρι ἀνέρος πονηροῦ κεύθεται σχέτλια ἔργα.

5. σπεύσω κασιγνητὸν ἐμὸν καὶ παῖδας ἐκ πυρὸς σώζειν.

6. οὔ τοι μῆκος βίοιο, ἀλλὰ ἀρετὴ φέρει δόξαν.

7. ἐκ πραγμάτων γνώσεται ἀνήρ ἀληθείην.

8. σώμασι θνητῶν νοῦσοι φέρουσι θάνατον, οὐ δὲ ψυχῆσιν.

9. φάει ἠελίοιο δυνατοὶ πέλονται ὀφθαλμοὶ ὁράειν.

10. τῇ χρήματα, τῇ ἐστι καὶ πράγματα.

184. PUT INTO GREEK

1. The soul supplies life to the body.

2. "Wealth is the man," says the fool.

3. We hastened down the river in order to flee the king.

4. May virtue ever increase in your soul and heart!

5. By the light of the fire, many trees were seen.

6. He said this temple, which is the property of a god, is therefore holy.

7. Shameful deeds reveal a base mind and heart.

8. That light was similar to a fire that is falling in the sky.

9. They wanted to take the stranger's property for themselves.

10. We learn many things from the words of our friends.

185. READINGS

1. κακῆς ἀπὸ ἀρχῆς γίγνεται τέλος κακόν.   (Euripides)

2. καὶ ἦν Ἰωσὴφ καλὸς τῷ εἴδει καὶ ὡραῖος τῇ ὄψει σφόδρα.
   (Genesis XXXIX 6, from the Septuagint, the Greek translation of the
   Hebrew Bible)

3. τῇ γὰρ ἐστι σὸς θησαυρός, τῇ ἐστι καὶ σὸν κῆρ.   (St. Matthew)

4. εἰς αὐτὸ πῦρ ἐκ καπνοῦ.   (Lucian)

5. ἄγει δὲ πρὸς φάος ἀληθείην χρόνος.   (Greek proverb)

6. χρήματα γὰρ ψυχὴ πέλεται δειλοῖσι βροτοῖσιν.   (Hesiod)

7. ἕκαστος διὰ ἑὰ πράγματα ἐσθλός ἐστιν ἢ κακός.   (Apollodorus)

8. μέτρον βίου ἐστὶ κάλλος, οὐ χρόνου μῆκος.   (Plutarch)

9. κεῖνο ἐν ψυχῇ εἰσι λόγοι ὅ περ κάλλος ἐν σώματι.   (Aristides)

δειλός, -ή, -όν	wretched, worthless
εἶδος, εἴδεος	[n.] figure, appearance, "looks"
Ἰωσὴφ	[indecl.] Joseph, a son of Jacob, sold by his jealous brothers into slavery in Egypt
καπνός, -οῦ	[m.] smoke
κάλλος, -εος	[n.] beauty, nobleness
ὄψις, ὄψεος	[f.] face
σφόδρα	[adv.] exceedingly
τέλος, -εος	[n.] end
ὡραῖος, -η, -ον	beautiful

186. WRITE IN GREEK

1.   The boys hastened to the tall tree among the rocks near the sea, since the treasure was said to be hidden there.

2.   I shall do what the king commands, for he is noble.

3.   By his very nature, man wishes to learn the truth, in order that his mind may live and grow; for truth is the mind's food.

187. WORD STUDY

DIAMETER (the 'measure through' the center of a circle or sphere), DIAGONAL (γωνίη angle; a line cutting at an oblique angle through a figure), DIAGRAM (an outline or sketch which 'writes' the essential lines 'through' the fuller plan; i.e., puts the skeletal structure, around which the whole is built, in clearer view), DIALOGUE (a 'word or discourse among' two or more speakers), DIALECT (λέγω 'a way of speaking among' certain people, a special modified form of a language used among certain classes, groups, or localities), DIAPHRAGM (φράγμα barrier, fence; the midriff, a muscle which lies between the thorax and abdomen as a 'barrier through' the body under the lungs; it controls breathing; hence, a similar dividing partition in a mechanical device); — PRAGMATISM (the doctrine that concrete results are the only test of truth); — PYRE (a pile of inflammable materials arranged for burning a dead body), PYRAMID (so called, it is thought, because pointed like a bonfire), PYROTECHNICS (τεχνή art; art of making and using fireworks), PYREX (trade name for fire-hardened glass utensils); — PHOSPHOROUS (φῶς by contraction of φάος + φέρω— 'light-bearer', a soft yellow element that glows under certain conditions), PHOTOGRAPH ('drawing or picture made by light'). PHOTOELECTRIC (pertaining to combined action of light and electricity); — CALLISTHENICS (σθένος strength; light exercises to promote gracefulness and health); — TELEOLOGY (the philosophical doctrine that all activity is purposive, directed at some goal or 'end'); — EPIC (a long narrative poem celebrating in exalted 'words' the adventures of some national hero).

Lesson 29

How To Predict the Stems of Adjectives and Participles. The Participle of εἰμί

188. THE PROBLEM

While the genitive form of a noun is given in vocabularies and dictionaries in order to indicate the noun's declension, adjectives and participles are conventionally listed in the vocabularies only in the nominative forms. But the genitive and other cases, just as with nouns, are all built on the stem, not directly on the nominative form. It is essential, then, to know how to tell from the nominative itself (i.e., the dictionary entry) what the stem (and hence the other cases) will be. The clue lies in being able to identify the particular declension type of adjective or participle to which the word in question belongs.

189. ADJECTIVE DECLENSION TYPES (review Sections 60-61)

Type A. *First and second declension:* masculine and neuter belong to the second declension, feminine to first in -η. Hence, if an adjective or participle ends in -ος, -η, -ον, you at once know its stem (the nominative form minus the -ος, -η, or -ον), and know that its genitive ends in -ου, -ης, -ου, with the other cases following regularly.

Notes:

(1). All middle participles are of this type. Here is the Present Middle-Passive Participle of our paradigm verb λύω:

	M.	*F.*	*N.*
Sg.			
N.	λυόμενος	λυομένη	λυόμενον
G.	λυομένου	λυομένης	λυομένου
D.	λυομένῳ	λυομένῃ	λυομένῳ
A.	λυόμενον	λυομένην	λυόμενον
Pl.			
N.	λυόμενοι	λυόμεναι	λυόμενα
G.	λυομένων	λυομένων	λυομένων
D.	λυομένοισ(ι)	λυομένῃσ(ι)	λυομένοισ(ι)
A.	λυομένους	λυομένας	λυόμενα

(2). A few adjectives (mostly compounds) have no separate feminine forms, but use masculine endings when modifying either masculine or feminine words. Hence their nominative is listed as -ος, -ον.

For a paradigm of the Type A adjective, see the complete declension of καλός, -ή, -όν in Section 61.

Type B. *First and third declension:* masculine and neuter belong to third declension, feminine to first in -α (not in -η as with type A!). There are these divisions:

Adjectives, two kinds (*Note:* the differences in the accusative masculine singular, and the nominative and accusative neuter singular between these two adjectives):

	M.	F.	N.	M.	F.	N.
Sg.						
N.	ἡδύς	ἡδεῖα	ἡδύ	πτερόεις	πτερόεσσα	πτερόεν
G.	ἡδέος	ἡδείης	ἡδέος	πτερόεντος	πτεροέσσης	πτερόεντος
D.	ἡδέι	ἡδείῃ	ἡδέι	πτερόεντι	πτεροέσσῃ	πτερόεντι
A.	ἡδύν	ἡδεῖαν	ἡδύ	πτερόεντα	πτερόεσσαν	πτερόεν
Pl.						
N.	ἡδέες	ἡδεῖαι	ἡδέα	πτερόεντες	πτερόεσσαι	πτερόεντα
G.	ἡδέων	ἡδείων	ἡδέων	πτεροέντων	πτεροέσσων	πτεροέντων
D.	ἡδέεσσι	ἡδείῃσι	ἡδέεσσι	πτερόεσσι	πτεροέσσῃς	πτερόεσσι
A.	ἡδέας	ἡδείας	ἡδέα	πτερόεντας	πτεροέσσας	πτερόεντα

Note: Masculine and neuter πτερόεσσι are contracted from πτεροέντεσσι.

Participles, four kinds:

1.	PRES. ACT.			FUT. ACT.		
	M.	F.	N.	M.	F.	N.
Sg.						
N.	λύων	λύουσα	λῦον	λύσων	λύσουσα	λῦσον
G.	λύοντος	λυούσης	λύοντος	λύσοντος	λυσούσης	λύσοντος
D.	λύοντι	λυούσῃ	λύοντι	λύσοντι	λυσούσῃ	λύσοντι
A.	λύοντα	λύουσαν	λῦον	λύσοντα	λύσουσαν	λῦσον
Pl.						
N.	λύοντες	λύουσαι	λύοντα	λύσοντες	λύσουσαι	λύσοντα
G.	λυόντων	λυουσάων	λυόντων	λυσόντων	λυσουσάων	λυσόντων
D.	λυόντεσσι (λύουσι)	λυούσῃσ(ι)	λυόντεσσι (λύουσι)	λυσόντεσσι (λύσουσι)	λυσούσῃσ(ι)	λυσόντεσσι (λύσουσι)
A.	λύοντας	λυούσας	λύοντα	λύσοντας	λυσούσας	λύσοντα

Note: Types 2-4 belong to tense systems which are yet to be introduced. They are given here for future reference.

2. *FIRST AOR. ACT.*

	M.	F.	N.	M.	F.	N.
	Sg.			*Pl.*		
N.	λύσας	λύσασα	λῦσαν	λύσαντες	λύσασαι	λύσαντα
G.	λύσαντος	λυσάσης	λύσαντος	λυσάντων	λυσασάων	λυσάντων
D.	λύσαντι	λυσάσῃ	λύσαντι	λυσάντεσσι (λύσασι)	λυσάσῃσ(ι)	λυσάντεσσι (λύσασι)
A.	λύσαντα	λύσασαν	λῦσαν	λύσαντας	λυσάσας	λύσαντα

3. *PERF. ACT.*

	M.	F.	N.	M.	F.	N.
	Sg.			*Pl.*		
N.	λελυκώς	λελυκυῖα	λελυκός	λελυκότες	λελυκυῖαι	λελυκότα
G.	λελυκότος	λελυκυίης	λελυκότος	λελυκότων	λελυκιάων	λελυκότων
D.	λελυκότι	λελυκυίῃ	λελυκότι	λελυκότεσσι (λελυκόσι)	λελυκυίῃσ(ι)	λελυκότεσσι (λελυκόσι)
A.	λελυκότα	λελυκυῖαν	λελυκός	λελυκότας	λελυκυίας	λελυκότα

4. *AOR. PASS.*

	M.	F.	N.	M.	F.	N.
	Sg.			*Pl.*		
N.	λυθείς	λυθεῖσα	λυθέν	λυθέντες	λυθεῖσαι	λυθέντα
G.	λυθέντος	λυθείσης	λυθέντος	λυθέντων	λυθεισάων	λυθέντων
D.	λυθέντι	λυθείσῃ	λυθέντι	λυθέντεσσι (λυθεῖσι)	λυθείσῃσ(ι)	λυθέντεσσι (λυθεῖσι)
A.	λυθέντα	λυθεῖσαν	λυθέν	λυθέντας	λυθείσας	λυθέντα

Type C. *Third declension only:* all forms belong to third declension; there are no special feminine endings. In some cases, the word has *two* terminations (one for masculine and feminine, and the other for neuter), in others, only *one* (serving for all genders). Three kinds:

	M./F.	N.	M./F.	N.
	Sg.		*Sg.*	
N.	ἀληθής	αληθές	πρόφρων	πρόφρον
G.	ἀληθέος	ἀληθέος	πρόφρονος	πρόφρονος
D.	ἀληθέι	ἀληθέι	πρόφρονι	πρόφρονι
A.	ἀληθέα	ἀληθές	πρόφρονα	πρόφρον

	M./F.	*N.*	*M./F.*	*N.*
	Pl.		*Pl.*	
N.	ἀληθέες	ἀληθέα	πρόφρονες	πρόφρονα
G.	ἀληθέων	ἀληθέων	προφρόνων	προφρόνων
D.	ἀληθέσσι	ἀληθέσσι	προφρόνεσσι	προφρόνεσσι
A.	ἀληθέας	ἀληθέα	πρόφρονας	πρόφρονα

	Sg.
N.	μάκαρ
G.	μάκαρος
D.	μάκαρι
A.	μάκαρα
	Pl.
N.	μάκαρες
G.	μακάρων
D.	μακάρεσσι
A.	μάκαρας

Note:

1. μάκαρ and other adjectives of one termination occur only occasionally as neuter, and then solely in the oblique cases (i.e., genitive and dative).

2. In words of one termination (like μάκαρ), the genitive will be given in the vocabularies, as with third declension nouns, for convenience in determining the stem, since these words have to be treated individually, as they do not fall into a pattern.

3. There are no participles in Type C, but only adjectives.

190. PRESENT PARTICIPLE OF εἰμί

ἐών, ἐοῦσα, ἐόν is declined like λύων, λύουσα, λῦον (genitive: ἐόντος, ἐούσης, ἐόντος).

191. MEMORIZE

αἱρέω, αἱρήσω, ἕλον	I seize; [in mid.] I pick for myself, I choose
ἀληθής, ές	true
ἡδονή, -ῆς	[f.] pleasure
ἡδύς, ἡδεῖα, ἡδύ	sweet, pleasant
κρίνω, κρινέω, κρῖνα	I pick out; I separate; I judge
μάκαρ, -αρος	happy, blessed
πρόφρων, -ον	willing, eager, ready

πτερόεις, -εσσα, -εν   winged

χρηστός, -ή, -όν   worthy, good

192. TRANSLATE

1. σοφοῖσι μανθάνειν ἀληθέα παρ-έχει ἡδονήν.

2. τόδε που πρόφρονι θυμῷ ποιήσω.

3. μάκαρ ἄνθρωπος ὃς δυνατός ἐστιν χρήματα ἐᾷ σώζειν ἀπὸ πυρός τε καὶ ὄμβρου.

4. ἀνδρὸς χρηστοῦ ψυχὴ μετὰ μακάρεσσι ζώσει αἰεί.

5. ἔπεα πτερόεντα τὰ κῆρι ἔχεις, λέγε.

6. χρηστὰ κρίνεται ὑπὸ χρηστῶν.

7. ἐκεῖνος ἄναξ ἀπὸ οὗ ἐμὸς κασίγνητος φεύγει καὶ ἑὴν παῖδα ἀδίκεεν.

8. οὐκ ἐπέεσσι ἡδέεσσι φανέεται ἀληθείη.

9. ἀνέρα μάκαρα φαίνουσιν ὃς αἴρεε τὰ χρήματα.

10. μὴ ἡδὺ αἰεί αἱρέεσθε, ἀλλὰ ὅ ἐστι χρηστόν.

193. PUT INTO GREEK

1. That tree bears sweet fruit.

2. He said the voice of a true friend is always pleasant and good.

3. They chose to die, that they might have glory among the living.

4. Who loves pleasure, loves a winged thing that quickly perishes.

5. I know your companion will come eagerly.

6. Each of my companions is a brave and worthy man.

7. These are gifts for the king, who is a friend of my brother's.

8. They did not seem to be the words of evil men who were about to seize our gold.

9. I hope to choose true pleasures.

10. Justice is winged, and pursues mortals doing evil.

194. READINGS

1. σῶμα μέν Πλάτωνος ἥδε γαῖα κατ-έχει, ψυχὴ δὲ θεοειδὴς ἐν μακάρεσσίν ἐστιν.   (Speusippus)

2. ἀληθὲς γὰρ οὔ ποτε ἐλέγχεται.   (Plato)

3. χρηστὸς ἀνὴρ ἕκαστα κρίνει ὀρθῶς, καὶ ἐν ἑκάστοις ἀληθείη τῷ φαίνεται. ἕτεροι δὲ πολλοὶ διὰ ἡδονὴν ἁμαρτάνουσι· ἡδὺ γάρ, οὐκ ἐὸν αἰεὶ ἀγαθόν, ὡς ἀγαθὸν αἱρέονται. λύπην δὲ ὡς κακὸν φεύγουσιν. μοῦνος οὖν χρηστὸς ὃ ἀληθές ἐστιν ἐν ἑκάστοις ὁράει.   (Aristotle)

4. οὐχ ὅρκοι εἰσὶν πίστις ἀνδρὸς ἀλλὰ ὅρκων ἀνήρ.   (Aeschylus)

5. καὶ ἐξέρχετο ἀνὴρ δυνατὸς ἐκ τῆς παρατάξεος τῶν ἀλλοφύλων,
    Γολιὰθ ὄνομα αὐτῷ, ἐκ Γέθ· ὕψος αὐτοῦ τεσσάρων πήχεων καὶ
    σπιθαμῆς.   (i Kings XVII 4, from the Septuagint, the Greek translation of the
    Hebrew Bible)

ἀλλόφυλλοι, -ων	[m.] foreigners [here = Philistines]
Γέθ	[indecl.] Gath, a major Philistine city [here = gen., obj. of prep.]
Γολιὰθ	[m. indecl.] Goliath, a Philistine giant who would be killed by David's slingshot
δυνατός, -ή, -όν	strong
ἐλέγχω	I put to shame; I refute
ἐξ-έρχομαι	I come out (of)
θεοειδὴς, -ές	[m.] godlike
κατ-έχω	I hold down, contain
λύπη, -ης	[f.] pain
ὄνομα, ονόματος	[n.] name
ὀρθῶς	[adv.] rightly, correctly
ὅρκος, -ου	[m.] oath, pledge
παράταξις, παρατάξεος	[f.] battle line
πῆχυς, πήχεος	[m.] fore-arm; cubit (18 inches)
πίστις, πίστιος	[f.] faith; guarantee
Πλάτων, -ωνος	Plato, the famous philosopher
σπιθαμή, -ῆς	[f.] the space one can span with thumb and pinkie: a span [about 8 inches]
τέσσαρες, -ων	[m., f.] four
ὕψος, ὕψεος	[n.] height

195. WRITE IN GREEK

1. Of those trees, many will fall on account of storms, and many will be destroyed
    by fire, but others will grow where they were.

2. We fear lest they are about to fight with our good neighbors.

196. WORD STUDY

HERETIC ('one who picks and chooses' among religious or other serious doctrines,
thus separating himself from those who hold the entire and common belief),
HERESY; HERESIARCH (one who begins a heresy); — HEDONISM (the
philosophical system which makes pleasure the only good and the test of all things);
— CRISIS (κρί-σις a separation or judgment; hence, the turning point at which
events are decided one way or the other), CRITIC (one who separates good from bad,
true from false; a judge), CRITICAL (at the crisis or turning point; decisive),
CRITERION (a standard or test by which to judge things for correctness).

Lesson 30

Review of the Third Declension
Uses of the Participle

197. FORMS

Masculine and feminine nouns are declined as ἄναξ, neuters as ἔπος. Third declension adjectives and participles follow the same models.

	Sg.	*Pl.*		*Sg.*	*Pl.*
N.	ἄναξ	ἄνακτες		ἔπος	ἔπεα
G.	ἄνακτος	ἀνάκτων		ἔπεος	ἐπέων
D.	ἄνακτι	ἄναξι, ἀνάκτεσσι		ἔπει	ἔπεσι or ἐπέεσσι
A.	ἄνακτα	ἄνακτας		ἔπος	ἔπεα

198. NOTES

1. Stems in ι- and υ- end in -ν in accusative singular.

2. Masculine adjectives with nominatives in -υς have accusative singular in -υν.

3. A κ, γ, or χ blends with σ to become ξ.

4. In neuters, the accusative is always like the nominative.

5. Gender of nouns: stems in ατ-, αρ-, α-, ε- are neuter; stems in δ-, ι-, θ-, ιτ-, τητ- are feminine; the rest are masculine.

199. USES OF THE PARTICIPLE

Participles are both verbs and adjectives, and as such possess both verbal and adjectival characteristics and functions.

1. As verbs, participles:

   a. have tense and voice

   b. are built from the principal parts of verbs

   c. have subjects and may have objects

2. As adjectives, participles:

   a. have gender, case and number

   b. agree in gender, case and number with the noun or pronoun they modify (which may also be thought of as the participle's subject)

Participles in Greek are used

1. Where a **relative clause** might be used:

The man speaking winged words is not my brother. (The man who is speaking winged words is not my brother.)

ἀνὴρ ἔπεα πτερόεντα λέγων ἐμὸς κασιγνητὸς οὔκ ἐστιν.

In this type of **participial clause** (the participle, its subject, and any objects), the participle is modifying the noun it modifies (its subject) in the same way that a relative clause would. Note that λέγων agrees in case, gender and number with its nominative, masculine and singular subject ἀνὴρ. Of course, a participial clause need not be nominative:

We sent gifts to the man speaking winged words. (We sent gifts to the man who was speaking winged words.)

δῶρα πέμπομεν ἀνδρὶ ἔπεα πτερόεντα λέγοντι .

Here the participle λέγοντι is dative, in agreement with its subject ἀνδρί, which is a dative indirect object of the verb πέμπομεν. In both sample sentences, ἔπεα πτερόεντα is accusative because it is the direct object of the participle in its clause.

2. To express some type of **circumstance** attendant upon the action of the main verb. The negative with all circumstantial participles is οὐ, with the exception of those that express a condition, where μή is used.

a. Cause:

Because she loved my brother, she saved him. (Loving my brother, she saved him.)

φιλέουσα ἐμὸν κασιγνητὸν σῶζεν.

b. Time (with the tense of the participle denoting a point of time relative to that of the main verb of the sentence):

They died while saving the city.

θνῆσκον πόλιν σώζοντες.

They will die while saving the city.

θανέονται πόλιν σώζοντες.

c. Purpose or Intention (usually with the future participle):

He comes in order to (intending to) ransom his brother.

ἔρχεται λυσόμενος ἐὸν κασιγνητόν.

d. Concession (often with περ):

Although we are able to conceal the truth, we reveal (it). (Being able to conceal the truth, we [nevertheless] reveal it.)

δυνατοί περ ἐόντες ἀληθείην κεύθειν, φαίνομεν.

e. Condition

Not seeming wise, I would not be loved. (If I did not seem wise, I would not be loved.)

μὴ φαινόμενος σοφός, οὐκ ἂν φιλεόμην.

3. After certain verbs, e.g., ὁράω, πεύθομαι, γιγνώσκω and ἀκούω, to express **indirect statement**. The subject of the participle in the subordinate clause, if different from the subject of the introductory verb, is put in the accusative case, just as the subject of the infinitive is put into the accusative case after λέγω and νομίζω. The tense of the participle represents a point of time relative to the tense of the introductory verb; it may also be thought of as representing the corresponding tense of the verb in the "original" statement.

> *I see that she is hiding the gold.* (I see "χρυσὸν κεύθει.")
>
> χρυσὸν κεύθουσαν ὁράω.
>
> *I saw that she was hiding the gold.* (I saw "χρυσὸν κεύθει.")
>
> χρυσὸν κεύθουσαν ὄραον.
>
> *I saw that she was (being) about to hide the gold.* (I saw "χρυσὸν κεύσει.")
>
> χρυσὸν κεύσουσαν ὄραον.

Note: ὁράω, πεύθομαι and ἀκούω in indirect statement denote *intellectual* perception, and are essentially equivalent to an English verb such as "realize" or "know." When ἀκούω denotes sense perception, it takes a genitive object:

> *I hear the king speaking winged words.*
>
> ἄνακτος ἔπεα πτερόεντα λέγοντος ἀκούω.

Likewise can πεύθομαι take a genitive when it means "hear (tell) of":

> *I hear of his being away.*
>
> πεύθομαι ἀπέοντος.

When ὁράω denotes actual "seeing" as opposed to "realizing", however, it still takes an accusative object, so that, for example, the first sample sentence above could be translated, "I see her hiding the gold."

200. MEMORIZE

ἀκούω, ἀκούσομαι, ἄκουσα	I hear
ἅπας, ἅπασα, ἅπαν	[m./ n. gen. ἅπαντος] all, the whole
εἷς, μία, ἕν [m./n. gen. ἑνός]	one
ἥμισυς, (-εια), -υ	half
μηδείς, μηδεμία, μηδέν	[for gen., see under εἷς] no one, none
οὐδείς, οὐδεμία, οὐδέν	[for gen., see under εἷς] no one, none
πᾶς, πᾶσα, πᾶν	[m./ n. gen. παντός] all, every, the whole
πειράω, πειρήσω, πείρησα	I make trial of [+ gen.]; I attempt, I try [+ gen., or + inf.]
πατρίς, πατρίδος	[f.] fatherland, country; [as f. adj.]: of one's fathers, ancestral

201. TRANSLATE

1. πάντες ἐθέλουσιν ζώειν τε καὶ μάκαρες ἔμμεν.

2. οὐδείς ἐστιν ὃς ἐὴν πατρίδα οὐ φιλέει.

3. ἑνὸς τοῦδε δενδρέοιο ἅπαντες οἵδε καρποί εἰσιν.

4. εἰ μὴ δυνατός ἐσσι πᾶν λαμβάνεσθαι, ἥμισύ γε αἱρέεο.

5. ἀνδρὸς ἀρετῆς πειράει πτόλεμος.

6. ὁράεις τήνδε πέτρην πίπτουσαν εἰς ποταμόν;

7. πᾶσι βροτοῖσι νοῦσοι πέλονται χαλεπαὶ φέρειν.

8. μηδενὶ ἑτέρῳ κεῖνο ἐμὸν δῶρον φαίνοιτε.

9. πασάων ψυχάων ἀθανάτη ἐστὶ ζωή, σῶμα δὲ θνήσκει.

10. ἀκούομεν ἐκείνους πονηροὺς ἐν πάσησι πολίεσσι ἐόντας.

11. εἰς πατρίδα ἔρχετο ἄνακτος πειρήσουσα.

12. τόδε ποίεε πίνων.

13. μισέω τούσδε ἐμὸν φίλον ἀδικέοντας.

14. μὴ παρ-έχοντες δῶρα, οὐκ ἂν νῦν φεῦγον.

202. PUT INTO GREEK

1. To all men, the sun seems to be like a fire in the sky.

2. Half of every deed is the beginning.

3. To no one seeing it from the river does this rock seem high.

4. Do you (sg.) not see that it is noble to save our fatherland now?

5. Let us make trial of all the food that she says is there.

6. These are gifts for the king, who is (use participle) a friend of my brother's.

7. To die for the sake of your country is not indeed pleasant, but it is noble.

8. The king is coming to see his brother's children.

9. Of all men, only the just and good have true happiness.

10. The sun was said to be Nature's eye, seeing everything.

11. The mind of a man falling to death quickly considers many things.

12. That is the only sea of the whole earth which he does not know.

13. Although all men are mortal, nevertheless many attempt to live forever.

14. While roaming back and forth I saw many things.

203. READINGS

1. εἷς ἀνὴρ οὐδεὶς ἀνήρ.   (Greek maxim)

2. φίλους ἔχων νόεε θησαυροὺς ἔχειν.   (Greek proverb)

3. ἀρχὴ δέ τοι ἥμισυ παντός.   (Greek proverb)

4. ἄνθρωπος θάνατον φεύγων διώκει.   (Democritus)

5. ἀδύνατόν ἐστι πολλὰ πειραόμενον ἄνθρωπον πάντα καλῶς ποιέειν. (Xenophon)

6. οὐκ ἐπὶ σίτῳ μούνῳ ζώει ἄνθρωπος, ἀλλὰ ἐπὶ παντὶ λόγῳ ἐξ-ερχομένῳ διὰ στόματος θεοῦ.   (St. Matthew)

7. ἔργον ἐστὶν οὐδὲν ὄνειδος, ἀεργίη δὲ ὄνειδος.   (Hesiod)

8. ἅπαντα καλοῖς ἄνδρεσσι ἀγαθά.   (Greek proverb)

9. οὐδεὶς θεὸς δύσ-νοος ἀνθρώποις.   (Plato)

10. ἅπασα γαῖα ἀνδρὶ σοφῷ πατρίς.   (Thales)

11. σκηνή ἐστι πᾶς βίος.   (Palladas) Can you translate this into Shakespeare's famous words for the same idea?

12. γηράσκω δὲ αἰεὶ πολλὰ διδασκόμενος.   (Solon)

ἀεργίη, -ης	[f.] idleness	
ἀδύνατος, -ον	unable (ἀδύνατόν ἐστι + acc. and infinitive "it is impossible")	
γηράσκω	I grow old	
δύσ-νοος, -ον	unfriendly to, ill-minded towards	
εξ-έρχομαι	I come out	
καλῶς	[adv.] well	
ὄνειδος	[n.] reproach, disgrace	
σκηνή, -ῆς	[f.] tent; stage	
στόμα, -ατος	[n.] mouth	

204. WRITE IN GREEK

1. To a wise man judging the works of mortal men, not all deeds appear worthy, and many seem foolish.

2. Now is the time to teach all men that war, even though just, is the beginning of many evils, both to the fatherland and to the whole earth. [Use the participle of εἰμί after "though"].

3. Since pleasures are winged, they are not true happiness, which only virtue and a noble life are able to supply.

4. The light of a fire near the sea is pleasant to one seeing (it) from these high rocks where we now are.

205. WORD STUDY

ACE (a single-spot card; a unit); — HEMISPHERE (σφαῖρα ball, sphere; the 'half-sphere', half of the earth's surface, divided either at the equator or through the poles); — PATRIOT (one devoted to his fatherland), PATRIOTIC, PATRIOTISM; — PAN- (a prefix meaning 'including all', e.g., PAN-AMERICAN, PAN-SLAVIC, PANCHROMATIC [χρῶμα color]), PANORAMA ('a seeing of all,' a complete view in all directions; a series of pictures or scenes following one another to give a view of the whole sweep of some large topic, e.g., of American frontier life), PANTHEISM (the doctrine that 'all is God,' i.e., everything is but an aspect of divinity), PANTHEON (a great Roman temple 'all divine' [θεῖον], designed by Emperor Hadrian), PANTS (colloquial abbreviation from PANTALOONS, (a type of trousers worn by renaissance Venetians, who were nicknamed Pantaloons from their connection with St. Pantaleon ['all-lion', mighty]), PANTOMIME (μῖμος imitator; the conveying of ideas or a story 'all by imitation', i.e., by imitative gestures and actions; a play without dialog, only expressive action), DIAPASON ('through all' stops of an organ at once; hence, the complete range of a thing's powers all exerted at one time); — PIRATE (one who 'makes attempts on' ships); — STOMACH (the 'mouth' of the digestive organs), CHRYSOSTOM ('golden-mouthed,' honorary title of St. John, archbishop of Constantinople in 5th century, most famous as a preacher); — SCENE (originally, painted stage-effects, SCENERY; hence, a division of a play by change of setting; also, a striking view), SCENIC, SCENARIO.

REVIEW EXERCISES

206. READINGS

1. μηδὲν ἄγαν   (Greek maxim; imperative implied. One of the most basic and often quoted principles of the Greek philosophy of life.)

2. ἀνδρὶ σοφῷ ξεῖνον οὐδέν.   (Antisthenes)

3. ᾧ μὴ εἷς καὶ αὐτός ἐστιν αἰεὶ βίου σκοπός, κεῖνος εἷς καὶ αὐτὸς διὰ οὔλοιο βίοιο ἔμμεναι οὔκ ἐστι δυνατός.   (Antoninus)

4. Σωκράτης ἔφη θεοὺς πάντα γιγνώσκειν.   (Xenophon)

5. οὐ διὰ πολλὸν ἄνθρωποι ζώομεν χρόνον, ἀλλὰ ὀλίγον· ψυχὴ δὲ ἀθανάτη καὶ ἀγήρως ζώει διὰ χρόνου παντός.   (Phocylides)

6. γιγνώσκομεν ὅτι ἀνθρώποισι φιλεόντεσσι θεὸν πάντα συν-εργέει εἰς ἀγαθόν.   (St. Paul)

7. ἀληθείη δὴ πάντων μὲν ἀγαθῶν θεοῖς εστι πρῶτον, πάντων δὲ ἀνθρώποις.   (Plato)

8. ἆ Σόλων, Σόλων, Ἕλληνες αἰεὶ παῖδές ἐστε, γέρων δὲ Ἕλλην οὔκ ἐστιν· νέοι γάρ ἐστε ψυχῇσι πάντες.   (An Egyptian priest to Solon the philosopher on a visit to Egypt; quoted by Plato)

9. ἀλλὰ Ζεὺς πάντων ὁράει τέλος.   (Solon)

10. ἡμέτερον γὰρ πολίτευμα ἐν οὐρανοῖς ἐστιν.   (St. Paul)

11. βροτοῖς ἅπασιν συν-είδησις θεός.   (Menander, referring to the commands of reason which man must obey in his mortal life)

12. φιλοσοφίη βίου κυβερνήτης.   (Motto of Phi Beta Kappa fraternity)

13. ἅπαντα σιγάων θεὸς τελέει.   (Menander)

14. ἐκ γαίης μὲν πάντα γίγνεται, καὶ εἰς γαῖαν πάντα τελέεται.   (Xenophanes)

15. χρόνος κρυπτὰ πάντα πρὸς φάος φέρει.   (Menander)

16. ἄνθρωποι δὲ νήπια νοέομεν, γιγνώσκοντες οὐδέν· θεοὶ δὲ κατὰ σφέτερον νόον πάντα τελέουσι.   (Theognis)

17. χρυσός ἐστι αἷμα καὶ ψυχὴ βροτοῖς.   (Antiphanes)

18. πάντες δὲ θεῶν χατέουσι ἄνθρωποι.   (Homer)

19. ὑπὸ παντὶ λίθῳ σκόρπιος εὕδει.   (Greek proverb)

---

20. γηράσκει πάντα ὑπὸ χρόνου.   (Aristotle)

21. οὐδὲ μάκαρ οὐδεὶς πέλεται βροτός, ἀλλὰ πονηροὶ πάντες θνητῶν τοὺς ἠέλιος ὁράει.   (Solon)

22. ἀπ-ολλύουσιν ἤθεα χρηστὰ ὁμιλίαι κακαί.   (Menander)

23. οὔ τοι χρήματα ἴδια ἔχουσι βροτοί.   (Euripides; take ἴδια here as predicate adj., not modifier)

24. πᾶν ἦθος διὰ ἔθος.   (Plato)

25. φίλους ἐχέμεναι οὐ μοῦνον ἀνάγκη ἐστὶν ἀλλὰ καὶ καλόν· ἄνδρας γὰρ φιλοφίλους πάντες αἰνέομεν.   (Aristotle)

ἅ	[exclamation] ah!
ἄγαν	[adv.] to excess, beyond reasonable bounds
ἀγήρως, -ων	ageless, undecaying
αἷμα, -ατος	[n.] blood
αἰνέω	I praise
γέρων, -οντος	[m.] old man
γηράσκω	I grow old
ἔθος, -εος	[n.] habit
Ἕλλην, -ηνος	[m.] a Greek (cp. HELLENISM: Greek culture; HELLENIST: a lover of Greek literature and culture; HELLENISTIC age: C. 333-19 B.C., when Greek culture and language were most widespread)
ἦθος, -εος	[n.] character, moral trait (cp. ETHICS: the philosophy of character and morality; ETHICAL)
ἴδιος, -η, -ον	private, personal, one's own (cp. IDIOM: an expression confined to or peculiar to a particular language and not literally translatable into another; IDIOT: an imbecile, a private, common, ignorant person; IDIOSYNCRASY [σύν-κρασις a mingling together], hence, a personal distinctive peculiarity or mannerism)
κρυπτός, -ή, -όν	hidden, secret
κυβερνήτης, -ου	[m.: a variation of the first declension] pilot, steersman
νέος, -η, -ον	young, new
ξεῖνος, -η, -ον	strange, foreign
ὁμιλίη, -ης	[f.] association, company
οὖλος, -η, -ον	whole, entire
ὅτι	[conj.] that [introducing a subordinate clause in indirect statement, just as in English; its use is confined to certain verbs, including λέγω]
πολίτευμα, -ατος	true country, place of citizenship
σιγάω	I keep silent
σκοπός, -οῦ	[m.] goal, aim
σκόρπιος, -ου	[m.] scorpion
συν-είδησις, -ιος	conscience, perception of right and wrong
συν-εργέω	I work together, I cooperate
σφέτερος, -η, -ον	their
τελέω	I accomplish, I bring to its completion or end
τέλος, -εος	[n.] end; object, aim
φιλο-σοφίη, -ης	[f.] philosophy, i.e., 'love of wisdom'
φιλό-φιλος, -η, -ον	friend-loving, affectionate
χατέω	I have need of, I have a natural yearning after [+ gen.]

207. PUT INTO GREEK

1. Every man pursues happiness according to his own nature.

2. Life is like war— it shows a man to be either brave or a coward.

3.   "Let us fight," he said, "with all spirit, that our children may have true peace."

4.   If he had not taught it, how would we have learned to love all other men?

5.   Choose (pl.) what you wish, for I brought everything that it might be eaten.

6.   Yet at that very time, I suppose, we were near the rock where the treasure was!

7.   They will supply your brother food of all sorts, as a gift from the king.

8.   May I never be turned away from the truth a second time by the voice of fools!

9.   Though requesting only what is just, they fail of that for the sake of which the king sent them.

10.   Only strong men are able thus to endure what they at heart hate.

11.   We did not see that they were seizing the possessions.

12.   Because they pursue pleasure (use participle), they love sweet things.

208. IDENTIFY, by stating completely the precise *form* of the word (e.g., 3 decl. m. dat. pl.; pres. mid. ind. 2 sg.); then give the exact meaning of the word in that form. (Where there are two words, translate both but identify only the second):

1.   ἄπ-εσσι

2.   δείσονται

3.   ἡδονάων

4.   εἴροιτο

5.   ἐπεὶ ἀπ-ῆα

6.   κεῖνο πτερόεν

7.   παρ-εόντι

8.   τρεφομένης

9.   ὄφρα ὦ

10.   ἡδέων καρπῶν

11.   λύσασι

12.   ἐούσης

13.   ἄγωμεν

14.   ζωήν

15.   ἵνα ἦτε

16.   μὴ ἀδικέοις

17.   λυόμην

18.   πάρ-εις;

19.   λύουσαι

20.   θανάτοιο

21.   ὅπως ὦσι

22.   λύοντος

23.   ξεῖνοι

24.   κεν πίπτετε

25.   κελεύσεις

26.   παρ-ῆμεν

27.   ἥδοιο

28.   ἀρχῇ

29.   ἵνα ᾖς

30.   μὴ θνήσκοι

31.   λύε

32.   ὅπως λαμβάνητε

33.   λυόντεσσι

34.   μελλέμεν

35.   ἄπ-ειμεν

36.   ἵνα αἱρέωμαι

37.   οὔτε ἦσαν

38.   μὴ κρινοίμεθα

39.   ὦμεν

40.   ὄφρα πίνῃς

41.   λαμβάνετε (!)

42.   ἀληθές

43.   μηδὲ σωζοίατο

44.   ὡς φεύγοιμι

45.   λύσοντες

46.   ἀπ-ῆσθα;

47.   ὀφθαλμοῖσι

48.   λύετο

49.   πτερόεις

50.   πυρὸς ὑψηλοῖο

51.	φρόνεες	66.	παρ-έην
52.	σπεῦδε (!)	67.	ἵνα ἔρχηται
53.	ἱερῷ νηῷ	68.	σχέτλια πράγματα
54.	ὄφρα φοιτάῃ	69.	εἰμί
55.	πρόφρον	70.	πτερόεσσα
56.	αἱρήσομαι	71.	ἱκάνοιεν
57.	ἵνα γίγνωνται	72.	λύευ
58.	μήκει	73.	πλησία
59.	μαχεόμην	74.	ἐόν
60.	πελόμεσθα	75.	ἐόν
61.	ἥδεσθε	76.	ποῦ ἔσαν;
62.	ὄφρα κελεύησθε	77.	ἡδύς
63.	αἱρέεο (!)	78.	αὐτό
64.	διώκετο	79.	ἵνα ᾖ
65.	λύμεν	80.	ἀληθής

209. TRANSLATE

1. οὐκ οὖν γιγνώσκεις λόγους ψυχῆς ἐόντας ἰητρόν;
2. ποταμὸν νῦν αἶψα ἱκάνοιτέ τε καὶ τῇ κεύθοισθε μετὰ δενδρέοις.
3. ποιεόντεσσι χαλεπά, τάδε γε ῥηίδια εἶναι δοκήσει τά ποτε οὐκ ἔθελον πειράειν.
4. ἑταῖροι ἐμοί παρ-ερχόμενοι, εὗδεν ἐπὶ θαλάσσῃ.
5. εἴθε δίκην, οὐ βίην, νοέοιμεν πάντες ἀληθές μὲν πέλεσθαι πατρίδος μέτρον, ἀληθέα δὲ δόξαν.
6. πολλὰς τοῦ σώματος νούσους πρόφρων φέρουσα, ὀρθή φαίνεαι θεοῖο φίλη. [τοῦ here is the article, "the"]
7. ἔργοιο ἑκάστοιο ἥμισυ μέν αἱρέευ ἥμισυ δὲ ῥέξω αὐτός.
8. κῆρι ἐσθλῷ ἀεξήσεται ὑπὸ πόνων ἀρετή.
9. μή ποτε ἔπος αἰσχρὸν ἐννεπέμεν, ἵνα μὴ φαίνηαι αἰσχρὸς καὶ αὐτός.
10. λέγει ἀνθρώπους λόγοισι ἀμειβομένους ἀληθέσι φίλους διδάσκειν, ἠδὲ σὺν τοῖς ἀληθείην πεύθεσθαι.

END OF FIRST UNIT

Lesson 31

The Interrogative And Indefinite Pronouns/Adjectives

210. MEANING

When it is a pronoun, the **interrogative** τίς, τί means "who?, what?" It can also modify other nouns as an adjective, just as demonstratives do; in this case it means "which?, what?"

> τίς ἔρχεται; *Who is coming?* (Pronoun)
>
> τίς ἀνὴρ ἔρχεται; *Which/What man is coming?* (Adjective)
>
> τῷ τόδε δῶρον χρηστὸν φαίνεται εἶναι; *To whom does this gift seem to be useful?* (Pronoun)
>
> τῷ νηπίῳ τόδε δῶρον χρηστὸν φαίνεται εἶναι; *To what fool does this gift seem to be useful?* (Adjective)

When it is a pronoun, the **indefinite** τις, τι means "someone/anyone, something/anything." But as an adjective, it means "some, any, certain."

> ἔρχεταί τις. *Someone is coming.* (Pronoun)
>
> ἀνήρ τις ἔρχεται. *A certain man is coming.* (Adjective)
>
> ὁράει τινα ἔρχοντα. *He sees someone coming.* (Pronoun)
>
> ὁράει ἀνέρα τινὰ ἔρχοντα. *He sees some man coming.* (Adjective)

211. MORPHOLOGY

The forms of the indefinite and interrogative pronouns are spelled alike. They must be distinguished by their pitch mark. The interrogative always has a pitch mark and has it always on the first syllable. The indefinite is an **enclitic** and very seldom has a pitch mark, and then on the last or second-last syllable. (See the Appendix C for more on enclitics.) There is no distinct form for the feminine gender, which shares one form with the masculine.

212. FORMS

τίς, τί *who? which? what?*			τις, τι *some(one), some(thing), certain, any(one), any(thing)*	

	M./F.	N.	M./F.	N.
	Sg.		Sg.	
N.	τίς	τί	τις	τι
G.	τεῦ	τεῦ	τευ	τευ
D.	τῷ, τέῳ	τῷ, τέῳ	τῳ, τεῳ	τῳ, τεῳ
A.	τίνα	τί	τινα	τι
	Pl.		Pl.	
N.	τίνες	τίνα	τινες	τινα
G.	τέων	τέων	τεων	τεων
D.	τέοισι	τέοισι	τεοισι	τεοισι
A.	τίνας	τίνα	τινας	τινα

213. NOTES

a. The neuter τί is often used as an adverb meaning "why?"

b. The neuter τι is often used as an adverb meaning "somehow," "in some respect."

c. The indefinite pronoun, when used as an adjective, generally follows the word it modifies, and gives it a vague, undefined sense; e.g., ἄνθρωπός τις *some man or other, a certain man* (whose name I do not know or will not mention).

214. THE INDEFINITE RELATIVE PRONOUN/ADJECTIVE AND INDIRECT INTERROGATIVE PRONOUN/ADJECTIVE

1.   The indefinite relative pronoun is ὅς τις, ἥ τις, ὅ τι (ὅττι): *whoever, whatever.* It is generally written as two words in the nominative and accusative, both parts being declined (e.g., ὅν τινα, ἅς τινας). Sometimes in the nominative and accusative, and always in the genitive and dative, the masculine and neuter forms are written as one word, only the last part being declined, the first part shortening to -ὁ (e.g., ὅτευ, ὁτέοισι, ὅτις).

	M.	F.	N.
	Sg.		
N.	ὅς τις (ὅτις)	ἥ τις	ὅ τι (ὅττι)
G.	ὅτευ (ὅττευ)	ὅτευ (ὅττευ)	ὅτευ (ὅττευ)
D.	ὅτῳ (ὅτεῳ)	ὅτῳ (ὅτεῳ)	ὅτῳ (ὅτεῳ)
A.	ὅν τινα (ὅτινα)	ἥν τινα	ὅ τι (ὅττι)
	Pl.		
N.	οἵ τινες	αἵ τινες	ἅ τινα (ἅσσα)
G.	ὅτων (ὁτέων)	ὅτων (ὁτέων)	ὅτων (ὁτέων)
D.	ὁτέοισ(ι)	ὁτέοισ(ι)	ὁτέοισ(ι)
A.	οὕς τινας (ὅτινας)	ἅς τινας	ἅ τινα (ἅσσα)

ὅς τις ἔρχεται, δῶρον αἱρήσει. *Whoever is coming will choose a gift.*

ὅ τι αἱρέεο, αἱρέεο αἶψα. *Whatever you choose, choose immediately.*

2.   The same forms are also used as **indirect interrogative pronouns**. As such they introduce an **indirect question**, which is a question quoted within a complex sentence (cf. **indirect statement**).

They ask who is coming. (They ask, "Who is coming?")

αἰτέουσιν ὅς τις ἔρχεται. (αἰτέουσιν, "τίς ἔρχεται;")

When the main verb introducing an indirect question is in a secondary (i.e., past) tense, the verb in the subordinate clause may be put into the optative mood (same tense as the "original" question). Or the indicative may be retained:

They asked who was coming. (They asked, "Who is coming?")

αἴτεον ὅς τις ἔρχοιτο. (αἴτεον, "τίς ἔρχεται;")

αἴτεον ὅς τις ἔρχεται.

Alternatively, the direct interrogative pronoun may be retained:

αἰτέουσιν τίς ἔρχεται. (*They ask who is coming.*)

Other ways to introduce an indirect question will be seen later.

215. MEMORIZE

ἄνεμος, -ου	[m.] wind
ἄρα, ῥα	[postpositive] therefore, then [not of time!]
ἔρδω, ἔρξω, ἔρξα	I do
ἔτι	[adv.] yet, still;
οὐκ ἔτι	no longer
νέκταρ, νέκταρος	[n.] nectar [the special drink of the gods]
πείθω, πείσω, πεῖσα or πέπιθον, 2 aor. mid. πιθόμην	I persuade, I win over; [in mid.] I am persuaded by, I am obedient to, I obey [+ dat.]

216. TRANSLATE

1. τίς δυνατός ἐστι πάντα ἐρδέμεν;
2. ὁράω τινὰ παρὰ ποταμὸν φοιτάοντα.
3. τέοισι πόλεμος ἡδὺς φαίνεται εἶναι;
4. πρᾶγμά τι καλὸν ἄρα ἔρδωμεν, ἵνα δόξαν ἔχωμεν.
5. τίνα ῥα πείσετε ἔργον οὕτως χαλεπὸν ἔρδειν;
6. οἵ τινες τόδε λέγουσιν ἁμαρτάνουσιν.
7. τί σπεύδεις; χρόνος ἔτι ἔστι πολλός.
8. ὅς τις θεοῖς πείθεται, ὅδε σοφὸς πέλεται ἠδὲ ἱερός.
9. πάντες που φίλοι εἰμὲν τεοισι, καί τινας ἔχομεν φίλους.
10. ὅτευ δὴ ὁ χρυσός ἐστιν, σός γέ οὐκ ἔστιν.
11. αἰτήσω ἄσσα ἐθέλεις σώζειν.
12. ὁ παῖς αἴτεεν οἵ τινες ἑταῖροι παρ-ερχοίατο.
13. βροτὸς ἕκαστος φύσιν τινὰ ἔχει.
14. φανέει πού τις τὸν νηὸν ἱερόν.

217. PUT INTO GREEK

1. All men are in some respect good and noble.
2. The rain was being borne along by some wind or other.
3. Never do (pl.) anything that is shameful!
4. Some of my companions are no longer able to endure the toil.
5. Whom (pl.) did he say to be present?
6. With whom (pl.) are you (pl.) fighting, and for the sake of what?
7. No one who attempts to persuade all men is wise.
8. Why do mortals not drink nectar?
9. A certain king once hid his treasure under those rocks.
10. Have you (sg.) any friends who are also mine? Which?
11. We ask what words he is able to hear.
12. We asked what words they said.

218. READINGS

1. τίς ἄρα ὅδε ἐστίν, ᾧ καὶ ἄνεμος καὶ θάλασσα πείθονται; (St. Mark)

2. οὐ πᾶς ἔρδων τι διὰ ἡδονὴν αἰσχρός ἐστιν, ἀλλὰ κεῖνος ὃς διὰ ἡδονὴν αἰσχρόν τι ἔρδει. (Aristotle)

3. ὅ τι καλόν, φίλον αἰεί. (Euripides. Keats said, "A thing of beauty is a joy for-ever.")

4. ἔστι τις οὕτως νήπιος, ὃς νοέει θεοὺς οὐκ εἶναι; (Socrates, quoted by Plato)

5. οὐχ ἥδομαι τροφῇ φθορῆς οὐδὲ ἡδονῇσι τοῦδε βίου· σῖτον θεοῦ ἐθέλω, ὅ ἐστι σῶμα Χριστοῖο, καὶ πίνειν ἐθέλω αἷμα αὐτοῦ, ὅ ἐστιν ἀγάπη ἀθανάτη. (St. Ignatius of Antioch)

6. Πύρρων ἔφη μηδὲν δια-φέρειν ζώειν ἢ θνήσκειν. εἴρετο ἄρα τις· "τί οὖν οὐ θνήσκεις;" ὁ δὲ ἔφη, "ὅτι οὐδὲν δια-φέρει." (Diogenes Laertius)

ἀγάπη, -ης	[f.] love
αἷμα, -ατος	[n.] blood
δια-φέρειν, δια-φέρει	[impersonal] it makes a difference
ἔφη	(he) said
ὅτι	[conj.] because
Πύρρων	Pyrrho of Elis, philosopher, friend of Alexander the Great and founder of the Skeptics
τροφή, -ῆς	[f.] nourishment, food
φθορή, -ῆς	[f.] decay [meaning here this passing world]

219. WRITE IN GREEK

1. That beautiful and lofty tree which we all knew and loved is no longer there beside the sea.

2. Of all my friends, none is so wise and good and pleasant as my brother.

3. Only those, then, who always do what is noble and true are happy.

220. WORD STUDY

ANEMONE ('wind-flower', a beautiful spring flower of the woods); — NECTAR (now any delicious drink), NECTARINE (a variety of peach 'fit for the gods'); — ATROPHY (a wasting of part of the body from 'lack of nourishment').

Lesson 32

The Forms of the First Personal Pronoun

221. FORMS of ἐγώ ("I") and ἡμεῖς ("we")

	Sg.	*Pl.*
N.	ἐγώ(ν)	ἡμεῖς (ἄμμες)
G.	μευ (ἐμεῖο)	ἡμέων
D.	ἐμοί, μοι	ἡμῖν (ἄμμιν)
A.	ἐμέ, με	ἡμέας (ἄμμε)

Note:

1.   The English **personal pronoun** shows case, as does Greek; the "objective case" of the nominative *I* and *we* is *me* and *us*.

2.   The unaccented forms above are enclitic (see Appendix C) and are less emphatic.

3.   A Greek verb form contains the subject (e.g., φαίνω *I reveal*) so the nominative personal pronoun appears only where emphasis on the subject is intended. For example:

> φαίνω θησαυρόν.
> *I reveal the treasure.*

> ἐγώ φαίνω θησαυρόν.
> <u>*I*</u> *reveal the treasure.*

4.   The genitive of the first- or second-person personal pronouns may be used to show possession. Thus the sentence

> φιλέω κασιγνητόν μευ.
> *I love my brother.*

means the same thing as

> φιλέω ἐμὸν κασιγνητόν.

which uses the **possessive adjective** rather than the genitive of the personal pronoun. (See Sections 79, 149, and 165 on the possessive adjectives.)

222. MEMORIZE

ἄλλος, -η, -ο	other, another, else
βούλομαι, βουλήσομαι, βουλόμην	I desire, I prefer
γλυκύς, -εῖα, -ύ	sweet, delightful
ἔνθεν	[adv.] from there; then [of time]

μίσγω, μίξω, μίξα	I mix (something, in acc.) with (something, in dat.), I mingle with
Μοῦσα, -ης	[f.] Muse [a goddess of poetry and art]
ὕδωρ, ὕδατος	[n.] water
φρήν, φρενός	[f.] mind, spirit

223. TRANSLATE

1. τί μοι βούλεαι γίγνεσθαι;
2. "οἵδε εἰσί μευ παῖδες," λέγεν ἐκεῖνος.
3. κελεύει με ἰκανέμεν, ὄφρα ἐμοὶ χρυσὸν παρ-έχῃ.
4. θεοὶ μὲν νέκταρ πίνουσιν, ἡμεῖς δὲ ὕδωρ— ἢ ἄλλο τι.
5. ἡμέων ἁπάντων κεῖνος αἰεὶ πρῶτος κρίνεται.
6. εἰς ποταμὸν ἔρχεσθε, καὶ ἔνθεν φέρετέ μοι ὕδατος μέτρον.
7. μίσγοισθε ἡμῖν ὡς φίλοισι φίλοι.
8. ἐγὼ δὴ Μουσάων γλυκείῃ ἥδομαι φωνῇ.
9. ἡμέας οὖν πέμψει πρὸς ἄνακτα.
10. ἄμμες ἄρα βουλόμεθα τόδε, οὐδέ τι ἄλλο.
11. ὅδε φίλος ἐστί μοι, ὅς τις ἐμοὶ πείθεται.
12. πάντες αἰτέουσιν ἅ τινα ἐγὼ βούλομαι μανθάνειν.

224. PUT INTO GREEK

1. He seems to me a brave and strong fellow.
2. They would have brought us food, had they known our need.
3. Which of us will learn all this first? I?
4. The Muses teach us many beautiful things.
5. He is my true friend; who else, indeed, is so good to me?
6. Mix (sg.) everything with water, then bring it to me (use πρός).
7. We, at least, prefer to die like brave men, not flee as cowards.
8. He saw us pursuing his brother among the trees.
9. I know that man —he once fought near me in the war.
10. Truth is dear to me, and food for my mind.

225. READINGS

1. οὔ ποτε ὕδωρ καὶ πῦρ μίξονται, οὐδέ ποτε ἡμεῖς φίλοι γενησόμεθα. (Theognis)
2. μή μοι γίγνοιτο τὰ βούλομαι, ἀλλὰ τά μοι συμ-φέρει.   (Menander)
3. ἀντὶ πόνων πωλέουσιν ἡμῖν πάντα ἀγαθὰ θεοί.   (Epicharmus)
4. καὶ ἐγὼ νέκταρ χυτόν, Μουσάων δῶρον, ἄνδρεσσι φίλοις πέμπω, γλυκὺν καρπὸν φρενός.   (Pindar)

5. μή με ἔπεσι μὲν φίλεε, νόον δὲ ἔχων καὶ φρένας ἄλλας, εἴ γέ με φιλέεις καὶ ἀληθέα ἔχεις νόον.   (Theognis)

6. ζώω οὐκ ἔτι ἐγώ, ζώει δὲ ἐν ἐμοὶ Χριστός.   (St. Paul)

7. εἷς σῖτος, ἕν σῶμα εἰμὲν ἄμμες πολλοί. πάντες γὰρ ἐξ ἑνὸς σίτοιο ἐσθίομεν.   (St. Paul)

ἀντί	[prep. + gen.] for, in place of, over against
πωλέω	I sell, I exchange
συμ-φέρω	I am of benefit to, I am good for
χυτός, -ή, -όν	out-poured

226. WRITE IN GREEK

1. Certain of the gods drink only nectar; nor do they desire anything else, so delightful does it seem.

2. What, then, shall lead me away from justice? Shall war? or death? or toil? or pleasure? Nothing!

3. Of which Muse is your delightful voice the gift?

227. WORD STUDY

ALLERGIC (ἔργον, 'other-working', in a condition of heightened susceptibility to a certain infection, a second exposure to which 'reacts otherwise' than the first, which was harmless, the second being violent), ALLEGORY (ἀγορεύω I speak; an elaborate literary simile 'speaking' of one truth by telling of some 'other' similar to it, which is an illustrative parallel; e.g., Bunyan's *Pilgrim's Progress*, Spenser's *Faerie Queene*); — GLUCOSE (a sweet sugar-compound), GLYCERINE, NITROGLYCERINE; — MUSIC ('the Muses' art'), MUSICAL, MUSICIAN; MUSEUM (a temple of the Muses, i.e., of the arts); — HYDROGEN (a 'water-born, water-producing' element), HYDRANT (a water valve), HYDRAULIC (αὐλός pipe; moving by the force of water-pressure in pipes, e.g., hydraulic brakes), HYDROPLANE (an airplane which can operate from the water); — FRENETIC, or FRANTIC (suffering from excessive mental agitation), FRENZY (violent fury, mental delirium; literally, 'inflammation of the brain'); — ANTI- (a prefix to many words, meaning 'opposed to, against'; e.g., ANTI-AIRCRAFT, ANTI-CHRIST, ANTI-CLIMAX, ANTI-SOCIAL), ANTIDOTE (δότη f. adj., 'given'; a medicine given to counteract a poison or other harmful substance), ANTISEPTIC (σηπτικός making rotten, corrupting; an acid, etc., acting against or preventing the corruptive effect of germ-laden matter), ANTITOXIN (τοξικός poison; a substance formed in the living tissues of an animal to neutralize the poisonous effect of the germs whose activity produced the antitoxin itself); — MONOPOLY ('only selling', the exclusive control of a product or service so that there is no price-competition).

Lesson 33

The Forms of the Second Personal Pronoun

228. FORMS of σύ ("you") and ὑμεῖς ("you all")

	Sg.	Pl.
N.	σύ	ὑμεῖς
G.	σεῦ (σεῖο)	ὑμέων
D.	σοί (τοι)	ὑμῖν
A.	σέ	ὑμέας

229. MEMORIZE

δέχομαι, δέξομαι, δεξάμην	I receive, I accept
εὑρίσκω, εὑρήσω, εὗρον	I find, I discover
εὐρύς, -εῖα, -ύ	wide, broad
λαός, -οῦ	[m.] people [a nation]; followers
ὁδός, -οῦ	[f.] way, road; journey
οἶνος, -ου	[m.] wine
πόθεν	[interr. adv.] from what source? whence?

230. TRANSLATE

1. οὔ τοι πείσομαι, ἐπεὶ κακόν ἐστιν ὃ κελεύεις.
2. σεῖο ἐστὶ τόδε δῶρον, ἢ ἄλλου τευ;
3. ἔρχοισθε· δεξόμεθα γὰρ ὑμέας ὡς φίλους.
4. ἡμεῖς μὲν κεῖνον βουλόμεθα πρῶτον εἶναι· ὑμεῖς δὲ τίνα;
5. πάντα σοὶ ἀγαθὰ παρ-έχει θεός.
6. καλόν τι ἔρδειν, καί σευ δόξα μετὰ πᾶσιν ἀεξήσεται.
7. νῦν δέ τις ὑμέων ὕδατι τὸν οἶνον μίσγοι, ἵνα πίνωμεν.
8. σὺ δὲ τίνας σοι αἱρέεαι ἑταίρους;
9. φαίνεταί που ὑμῖν ῥηίδιον ἔμμεναι εὑρίσκειν ὁδὸν οὕτως εὐρεῖαν.
10. πόθεν σὲ ἱκανέμεν λέξω;

231. PUT INTO GREEK

1. How shall we find you (pl.)?
2. We are your (sg.) friends; do whatever you wish here.
3. I shall show you (pl.) the road leading towards the sea.

4.   Bring (sg.) me that rock, and I will call you strong!

5.   Why does he seem to you (sg.) so wise?

6.   Which of you drank that wine?

7.   You (pl.) are my companions; let us fight that we may save our fatherland.

8.   I know the king is pleased with you(sg.) as with a true friend.

9.   Who sends you (pl.) to me? From where?

10.   You (pl.) bring the food, but you (sg.) the water.

232. READINGS

1.   ἀγαπήσεις πλησίον σευ ὡς σὲ αὐτόν.   (St. Matthew. An instance of the 'future of command', as in "thou shalt…," "you shall…")

2.   πόθεν πόλεμοι καὶ πόθεν μάχαι ἐν ὑμῖν; οὐκ ἔνθεν, ἐκ ἡδονάων ὑμέων πολεμεουσάων ἐν ὑμῖν; ἐπι-θυμέετε καὶ οὐκ ἔχετε, μάχεσθε οὖν καὶ πολεμέετε.   (St. James)

3.   καὶ σύ τέκνον.   (The dying Caesar to Brutus, according to Suetonius)

4.   πάντων ἰητρὸς κακῶν χρόνος ἐστίν· κεῖνος καὶ σὲ νῦν ἰάσεται. (Menander)

ἀγαπάω	I love
ἐπι-θυμέω	I set my heart upon something, I covet
ἰάομαι, ἰάσομαι	I cure, I heal
μάχη, -ης	[f.] battle, conflict
πολεμέω	I wage war
τέκνον, -ου	[n.] child, son

233. WRITE IN GREEK

1.   I, at least, shall not obey, because it does not seem to me just or noble. ["or" here, after a negative, = "nor"].

2.   From what source will we receive food and wine and water for the king and his people?

234. WORD STUDY

LAITY ('the people', as distinguished from the clergy, or from members of a profession), LAYMAN, LAY (of the laity; non-professional); — ELECTRODE (a 'road for electrons or electricity', one of the poles of a battery or dynamo), ANODE (ἀνά up; the positive electrode, providing the entry or 'way up' for the current into something), CATHODE (καθ', from κατά, the negative pole, the exit or 'way down' for the current).

Lesson 34

The Forms of the Third Personal Pronoun. The Future of εἰμί

235. NOTE

a. The nominative case of the third personal pronoun (*he, she, it* and *they*) is generally unexpressed, being contained in the verb ending. When it is expressed for the purpose of emphasis or contrast, ὁ, ἡ, τό or (ἐ)κεῖνος, -η, -ο are used. (See Lessons 14, 15.)

b. Generally, whenever one of the third personal pronoun forms listed in section 236 has a pitch mark (as the forms in parentheses below), it is reflexive in sense. Thus, λέγει ἑὸν παῖδα ὁμοῖον οἷ ἔμμεν. *He says his son is like him(self).* Sometimes αὐτός, -ή, -ό is added, in the same case as the pronoun.

236. FORMS

	Sg.	*Pl.*
N.	—	—
G.	ἑο (ἕο)	σφεων (σφέων)
D.	οἱ (οἷ)	σφι(ν), σφισι (σφίσι)
A.	ἑ, μιν (ἕ)	σφεας (σφέας)

237. FUTURE OF εἰμί

IND.

	Sg.	*Pl.*
1st pers.	ἔσ(σ)ομαι	ἐσ(σ)όμεθα
2nd pers.	ἔσ(σ)εαι	ἔσ(σ)εσθε
3rd pers.	ἔσ(σ)εται / ἔσται	ἔσ(σ)ονται

PTC.	*INF.*
m. f.. n.	
ἐσόμενος, -η, -ον	ἔσεσθαι

238. MEMORIZE

γόνυ, γούνατος	[n.] knee
εἰσ-έρχομαι, εἰσ-ελεύσομαι, εἴσ-ελθον	I enter
ἐντολή, -ῆς	[f.] command, order
ζητέω, ζητήσω, ζήτησα	I seek, I search after
πύλη, -ης	[f.] gate, entrance
υἱός, -οῦ or υἱέος	[m.] son

108

239. TRANSLATE

1. εἷς σφεων θνῆσκεν, ἕτεροι δὲ ἔτι φεύγουσιν.

2. οὐδεὶς ἐστι θνητῶν, οὐδὲ ἦν ποτε οὐδὲ ἔσεται, ὅς πάντα γιγνώσκει.

3. κέλευέ σφεας πρός ἑ ἀγέμεναι κασιγνητόν σφεων.

4. εὑρήσεις μιν καί ἑο υἱοὺς ὑπὸ δενδρέοισι ἐσθίοντας.

5. πάντας βούλονται σφίσι πείθεσθαι.

6. αἴτεέ σφεας εἰσ-έρχεσθαι, οἱ δὲ οὔκ ἔθελον.

7. ζητέωμέν μιν, ὄφρα ἑ σώζωμεν.

8. ἄνακτος πείθεσθε ἐντολῇσι, καὶ ὑμέας φιλήσει καὶ εἰς εἰρήνην ἄξει.

9. τίνες σφέων υἱοί σευ εἰσίν;

10. πονηροῖο υἱέες πονηροὺς ζητήσουσιν ἑταίρους, καί σφιν ἤσονται.

240. PUT INTO GREEK

1. They said he seemed to them to be a man of noble mind.

2. I shall be to him a true friend, as he also will be to me.

3. They fell at (εἰς) his knees and requested gifts.

4. Hasten! (sg.) and you will be able to save her and her sons.

5. Who of us does not love himself?

6. Death will be for them the gate of glory, for they did noble deeds.

7. We tried to hide the children, so that no one might find them.

8. The river was not wide, yet its length was great (πολλόν).

9. She has a noble mind, but they seize everything for themselves.

10. I shall eagerly receive them as companions.

241. READINGS

1. οὐδὲ ἔτι μιν παῖδες πρὸς γούνασι παππάζουσιν   (Homer, of a dead warrior)

2. εἰσ-έρχεσθε διὰ στεινῆς πύλης· στεινὴ δὲ πύλη καὶ ὁδὸς ἣ ἄγει εἰς βίον, καὶ ὀλίγοι εἰσὶν οἵ μιν εὑρίσκουσιν.   (St. Matthew)

3. ἡμεῖς γὰρ νηὸς θεοῦ ζώοντός εἰμεν, ὡς λέγει θεός· "ἐν-οικήσω ἐν σφιν, καὶ ἔσομαί σφεων θεός, καὶ αὐτοὶ ἔσονταί μευ λαός." (St. Paul)

4. εἰ φιλέετε ἐμέ, ἐντολὰς ἐμὰς φυλάσσετε. ὅς τις ἔχει ἐντολὰς ἐμὰς καὶ φυλάσσει, κεῖνός ἐστιν ὃς φιλέει με, καὶ ἐγὼ φιλήσω μιν καὶ φανέω οἱ ἐμὲ αὐτόν.   (St. John)

5. κακοῖς ὁμιλέων αὐτὸς ἐκ-βήσεαι κακός, σοφοῖσι δὲ σοφός.   (Menander)

ἐκ-βαίνω, ἐκ-βήσομαι	I come out, I turn out
ἐν-οικέω, ἐν-οικήσω	I dwell in
ὁμιλέω	I associate (with) [+ dat.]
παππάζω	I call someone "papa," "father"

στεινός, -ή, -όν	narrow
φυλάσσω	I observe, I keep (literally, I stand guard over)

242. WRITE IN GREEK

1. Which of you is able to discover the road leading through the trees to the river?

2. If he had known you (sg.) were present, he would no doubt have spoken to you personally. ["personally" = "himself"]

3. She was searching after her son among all our companions' children.

243. WORD STUDY

POLYGON ('many-angled,' from γωνίη 'joint' or 'angle', a word derived from γόνυ. Hence also PENTAGON, HEXAGON, OCTAGON, etc., the prefix being the Greek number for 5, 6, 8, etc.); — PYLON (in architecture, a massive doorway to a temple or other building flanked by a pyramidal tower; in aviation, a tower serving as turning-point in the racecourse); — PAPACY, POPE (office and name of the 'Holy Father'); — STENOGRAPHER ('narrow-writer', i.e., one who uses shorthand).

Lesson 35

The First Aorist System Indicative and Subjunctive Active.
Present General and Future More Vivid Conditions

244. TYPES OF AORIST

From the map of the verb (Lesson 16) you have noticed that there are three different aorist systems in the active voice. Almost every verb has only one of these systems. Look at the third principal part. If it ends in -α, it is **first (1st) aorist**. If it ends in -ον, it is **second (2nd) aorist**. If it ends in a long vowel plus ν (e.g., βῆν, γνῶν, δῦν), it is **third (3rd) aorist**.

245. NOTE

1. The characteristic vowel of the first aorist indicative is α. To form the first aorist indicative active, remove the -α ending from the third Principal Part (Sections 83-84) to find the **aorist tense stem**. Add the first aorist indicative endings (below) to this stem.

2. The subjunctive endings of all tense-systems, including the aorist, are alike (cp. Section 156a). To form the first aorist subjunctive active, use the aorist stem as described above, and add the subjunctive endings.

3. For the meaning of the aorist tense in the indicative, refer to Section 84a. For the subjunctive, see Section 84b and Section 247, below.

246. ENDINGS

1st AOR. IND.

	Sg.	*Pl.*	*Sg.*		*Pl.*	
1st pers.	-α	-αμεν	λῦσα	I loosed	λύσαμεν	we loosed
2nd pers.	-ας	-ατε	λῦσας	you loosed	λύσατε	you loosed
3rd pers.	-ε(ν)	-αν	λῦσε(ν)	he loosed	λῦσαν	they loosed

1st AOR. SUBJ.

	Sg.	*Pl.*	*Sg.*	*Pl.*
1st pers.	-ω	-ωμεν	λύσω	λύσωμεν
2nd pers.	-ῃς	-ητε	λύσῃς	λύσητε
3rd pers.	-ῃ	-ωσι(ν)	λύσῃ	λύσωσι(ν)

247. FURTHER USES OF THE SUBJUNCTIVE

a. Future More Vivid Condition

When a probable future supposition forms the basis for a conclusion (**apodosis**, cp. Section 91) in the future indicative or an imperative, the verb of the supposition (the **protasis**, cp. Section 91) is put into the subjunctive. This subjunctive may be introduced by ἄν or κε(ν). The supposition itself may be introduced by εἰ or ἤν (*if*); ὅτε, ἐπεί, or ἐπήν (*when*); or forms of the indefinite relative ὅς τις (*whoever*). Thus:

(1). θάνατον δὲ ἐγὼ δέξομαι, ὅτε ἄν δὴ Ζεὺς ἐθέλῃ πέμπειν ἠδὲ ἀθάνατοι θεοὶ ἄλλοι. *But I shall accept death* [conclusion]*whenever Zeus and the other deathless gods wish to send it.* [supposition: the gods will probably wish to send death]

(2). εἴ κεν πέμψῃ σε, ἔρχευ πρόφρων. *If he sends you* [supposition: it is likely he will send you], *go willingly!* [conclusion]

(3). οἵ τινες ἐκ τοῦδε καρποῦ ἐσθίωσιν, αἶψα θανέονται. *Whoever eat(s) of this fruit* [supposition: people will likely eat the fruit] *will quickly die.* [conclusion]

b. Present General Condition

When the protasis implies repeated occurrence in the present, the subjunctive is used to express the supposition; the verb in the conclusion (apodosis) is in the present indicative. The subjunctive sometimes has ἄν or κε(ν). The protasis may be introduced by εἰ or ἤν (*if*); ὅτε, ἐπεί, or ἐπήν (*when*); or forms of the relative or indefinite relative ὅς / ὅς τις (*who, whoever*). Thus:

ὅτε ἄν βούληται, ἐπὶ θάλασσαν ἔρχεται. *Whenever he wishes* [supposition: he often or repeatedly wishes], *he goes to the sea.* [conclusion]

c. Hence, these two constructions differ in their main verb, the apodosis or conclusion; but both put the verb of the protasis in the subjunctive. The subjunctive is the mood of supposition, likelihood, and exhortation, not of plain fact.

d. Whether the subjunctive in the protasis is present or aorist depends, according to the regular rule (Section 84b), on the aspect, or kind of action implied. Present subjunctive is used if the verb's action is thought of as continuing; aorist subjunctive is used if the action is thought of as simply occurring, without attention to whether or not it is continuous or completed.

e. The negative of both conditions is μή in the protasis, but οὐ in the apodosis, just as in the contrary-to-fact conditions introduced earlier (cp. Section 91b).

248. MEMORIZE

Ἀπόλλων, Ἀπόλλωνος	[m.] Apollo [the god]
δύω or δύο	[indecl.] two
ἐπήν	contraction of ἐπεὶ ἄν
ἤν	contraction of εἰ ἄν
μάλα	[adv.] very, quite, greatly

ὅτε   [adv.] when, whenever

τεύχω, τεύξω, τεῦξα,   I build; I make ready. [In pf. pass. often = I am]
   pf. mid.: τέτυγμαι

249. TRANSLATE

1. κέλευσέ σφεας πρὸς ἓ ἱκανέμεν.

2. εἴ κεν ἐκ τοῖο δενδρέοιο πίπτῃ, θανέεται.

3. νηὸν παρὰ θαλάσσῃ τεῦξαν θεῷ.

4. ὅτε παῖδες καρπούς τινας ὁράωσι, βούλονταί σφεας ἐσθίειν.

5. ζητήσαμέν σε, οὐ δὲ δυνατοὶ ἦμεν εὑρίσκειν.

6. ἢν με αἰτήσῃς ἥμισυ μὲν ῥέζειν, ῥέζω, οὐ δὲ πᾶν.

7. οὐκ ἂν φρονήσατέ μιν οὕτως εἶναι κακόν, εἰ μὴ τόδε ἔρξεν.

8. δύω πέμποις ἑταίρους, ἵνα μηδὲν δείσωμεν.

9. ἐπὴν τὸν λίθον τρέψητε, θησαυρόν που εὑρήσετε.

10. τόνδε οἶνον ὕδατι μίξωμεν· μάλα γὰρ γλυκὺς πέλεται.

11. ὅς τις πέμπηται εἰς ἐμὴν πατρίδα, κεῖνος φιλήσεται ὑπὸ πάντων.

12. ἅ τινα τεύξῃ, τεύχει πρόφρων.

250. PUT INTO GREEK

(*Note:* from this lesson on, translate mere past statements by the aorist, using the imperfect to express action continued or repeated in the past. This will aid clarity and uniformity. When later you meet again in the text of Homer imperfects with non-continuous force, you will recognize the fact from context or from the word's meaning.)

1. Whoever does that is evil.

2. When he teaches us anything, we learn!

3. If they send the strangers to the king, he will kill them.

4. We always hasten to the gate if we see anyone entering.

5. When the gods loose rain from heaven, the rivers increase.

6. If she had sought her son here, she would have saved him quickly.

7. When we know all these things, we shall be very happy.

8. Whatever evil they request, say (sg.) that you will not do (it).

9. If you (sg.) send me into the war, I shall fear greatly.

10. Whenever you (sg.) are with me, I am happy.

251. READINGS

1. ὃς ἔχῃ υἱὸν θεοῦ ἔχει ζωήν· ὃς μὴ ἔχῃ υἱὸν θεοῦ ζωὴν οὐκ ἔχει.
   (St. John)

2. τοὺς δύω Ἀπόλλων ποίησε, Ἀσκληπιὸν ἠδὲ Πλάτωνα, τὸν μὲν ἵνα
   ψυχήν, τὸν δὲ ἵνα σῶμα σῴζοι.   (Anonymous inscription)

3. μάλα γὰρ ἐχθρός μοι κεῖνος ὃς ἕτερον μὲν κεύθῃ ἐν φρεσί, ἄλλο δὲ
    λέγῃ. (Achilles, in Homer)

4. οἶνον τοι πολλὸν πίνειν κακόν· ἢν δέ τις πίνῃ ἑ σοφῶς, οὐ κακὸς
    ἀλλὰ ἀγαθός. (Theognis)

5. ὃς γάρ κεν ἐθέλῃ σώζειν ψυχὴν ἕο αὐτοῦ, ἀπ-ολέσει μιν· ὃς δὲ ἀπ-
    ολέσῃ ψυχὴν εἵνεκα ἐμεῖο, εὑρήσει μιν. (St. Matthew)

6. ὅτε ἄν τι μέλλῃς σὸν πλησίον κακ-ηγορέειν, πρῶτον σεῦ αὐτοῦ ἐπι-
    σκέπτεο κακά. (Menander)

Ἀσκληπιός, -οῦ	Asclepius [a minor god, inventor of medical arts]
ἐπι-σκέπτομαι	I pass in review, I examine
ἐχθρός, -ή, -όν	hateful to
κατ-ηγορέω	I criticize, I say evil against
Πλάτων, -ωνος	Plato [the philosopher]
σοφῶς	[adv.] wisely, sensibly

252. WRITE IN GREEK

1. I shall bring them half of all the fruit from our trees; for I love them as very
    friendly [use φίλος, -η, -ον] neighbors.

2. None of them was able to find the treasure, yet two were very near it twice.

3. Send (sg.) her these two gifts from (use παρά) me, and request her to receive
    my brother kindly. [Put "receive" last]

253. WORD STUDY

HENDIADYS (ἓν διὰ δύω, a literary figure of speech in which one idea is expressed
through two related words, e.g., 'with might and main', = 'with all one's strength', or
Vergil's 'they drank from cups and gold', i.e., from golden cups); — PENTATEUCH
(τεῦχος book [originally, a case built to hold written pages, thence coming to mean
the book itself], 'the five books' ascribed to Moses and forming a unit at the beginning
of the Bible, e.g., Genesis, Exodus, etc.).

Lesson 36

The First Aorist Optative, Imperative, Infinitive, and Participle Active

254. ENDINGS

1st AOR. OPT.

	Sg.	Pl.	Sg.	Pl.
1st pers.	-αιμι	-αιμεν	λύσαιμι	λύσαιμεν
2nd pers.	-ειας	-αιτε	λύσειας	λύσαιτε
3rd pers.	-ειε(ν)	-ειαν	λύσειε(ν)	λύσειαν

1st AOR. IMPT.

	Sg.	Pl.	Sg.	Pl.		
2nd. pers.	-ον	-ατε	λῦσον	λύσατε	loose!	loose!

1st AOR. INF.

-αι	λῦσαι	to loose

1st AOR. PTC.

m. f. n. nom.	m. f. n. nom.
-ας, -ασα, -αν	λύσας, λύσασα, λῦσαν

255. NOTE

1. In the optative the iota diphthong is characteristic (see Section 156c).

2. Review the force of the aorist tense in these moods (Section 84). The aorist participle generally represents a point of time prior to that of the main verb, just as other tenses of the participle represent points of time relative to the tense of the main verb. Review Section 199.

    θνῆσκον πόλιν σώσαντες.
    They died after saving the city.

    ὁράω θησαυρὸν διώξασαν.
    I see that she pursued the treasure.

3. For the declension of the first aorist participle, see Lesson 29.

256. MEMORIZE

βουλεύω, βουλεύσω, βούλευσα	I plan, I consider whether to or how to [+ inf., or ὅπως and purpose construction]
βουλή, -ῆς	[f.] plan, advice, will
γαμέω, γαμέω, γάμησα or γῆμα	I marry
θέμις, θέμιστος	[f.] a right, custom; θέμις ἐστί it is right, lawful [+ acc. and inf.]

| λανθάνω, λήσω, λάθον | I elude, I escape someone's notice, I deceive; [in mid.] I am forgetful of |
| πω | [adv., + negative] never yet, in no way, not at all |

257. TRANSLATE

1. μηδέν πω αἰτήσειας ἀπὸ ἐμεῖο πονηρόν.

2. πῶς τις γαμήσας μάκαρ ἔσται, ἢν μὴ πολλὰ ἀν-έχηται πρόφρων;

3. τῆσι οὐδεμία φαίνεται ὁδός, ζητησάσῃσι περ διὰ χρόνου πολλοῦ.

4. θέμις ἐστὶ κακόν τι ἄνδρα ποιήσαντα καὶ κακὰ δέχεσθαι;

5. ἀδικῆσαι μὲν αἰσχρόν, μάλα δὲ αἰσχρὸν ἀδικέειν.

6. εἰ οἶνος γλυκὺς πέλετο, οὐκ ἄν τὸν μίξα σὺν ὕδατι.

7. σχέτλια ἔργα μή ποτε ῥέξον.

8. τοὺς βούλετο λανθανέμεν, ἵνα μή ἑ ἀπολέσειαν.

9. σπεῦσα ἱκανέμεν, ὄφρα ὑμέας σώσαιμι.

10. γαμήσασι πολλά που ἔσσεται καὶ χαλεπὰ καὶ ἡδέα.

11. ἰητροῖο ἄνδρα ἐκ νούσων λύσαντος ἀέξεται δόξα.

258. PUT INTO GREEK

1. Whenever you (pl.) plan to do something fine, do it!

2. Having mingled its water with the sea, the river perishes.

3. He said they persuaded him to send them the gold.

4. We feared (aor.) that you (sg.) would destroy us.

5. It was being built thus, so that no one might loose the wine into the ground.

6. It was the advice of the man who sent us. (use ptc., not rel. pron.)

7. Whatever you (sg.) build, make it strong and beautiful.

8. They were being led by force, so that the king might judge them.

9. May you (pl.) never in any way do evil!

10. To separate good from bad is a virtue of our mind.

259. READINGS

1. οἵ γε αὐτῷ κακὰ τεύχει ἀνὴρ ἄλλῳ κακὰ τεύχων, κακὴ δὲ βουλὴ βουλεύσαντι μάλιστα κακή. (Hesiod)

2. πᾶς λόγος, εἴ κεν ἀπ-ῇ ἔργα, νήπιος φαίνεται. (Demosthenes)

3. οὐδείς πω ξεῖνον ἀπατήσας ἀθανάτους λανθάνει. (Theognis)

4. οὐκ ἔστι θνητοῖσιν πρὸς θεοὺς πολεμῆσαι· οὐδενὶ τόδε θέμις ἐστίν. (Theognis)

5. "οὐκ ἔστι γαμήσας ὅς τις οὐ χειμάζεται," λέγουσιν πάντες, καὶ γαμέουσιν γιγνώσκοντες. (Greek Anthology)

6. Σωκράτης ἔφη πολλοὺς ἀνθρώπους ζώειν ἵνα ἐσθίωσιν· αὐτὸς δὲ ἔσθιε ἵνα ζώοι.

ἀπατάω, ἀπατήσω, ἀπάτησα	I deceive
ἔφη	[3rd. pers. sg. impf. of φημί] (he) said
μάλιστα	[adv.] especially
οὐκ ἔστι	[+ inf.] it is not possible (to do something);
οὐκ ἔστι…. ὅς τις	there is no one who; nobody
πολεμέω, πολεμήσω, πολέμησα	I wage war
Σωκράτης	Socrates, the philosopher
χειμάζομαι	I am storm-tossed

260. WRITE IN GREEK

1. In the beginning, God made the heavens and the earth and the light of the sun, and separated the waters into seas. And He said, "Let us make man similar to Ourselves, and king of all things which are seen."

2. To whom (pl.) did you (sg.) show the gold that my brother sent you?

261. WORD STUDY

BIGAMY (with Latin *bis*, = 'twice-married', the practice of marrying again while still married to another living person), BIGAMIST (one guilty of bigamy), MONOGAMY ('single-marriage'), POLYGAMY (simultaneous 'marriage with many' persons); — LETHARGY (ἔργον, 'causing to forget work', a state of powerless inactivity, stupor, apathy), LETHARGIC (like one affected by lethargy; drowsy, hard to rouse to activity); — GENEALOGY (the account of one's race, lineage, offspring, a 'family tree' listing descendants and relatives within several generations), HOMOGENEOUS (similarity throughout the whole, as 'a homogeneous group'); — CINEMA ('moving pictures').

Lesson 37

The First Aorist Indicative and Subjunctive Middle

262. ENDINGS

1st AOR. MIDDLE IND.

	Sg.	Pl.	Sg.	Pl.
1st pers.	-αμην	-αμεθα	λυσάμην	λυσάμεθα
2nd pers.	-αο	-ασθε	λύσαο	λύσασθε
3rd pers.	-ατο	-αντο	λύσατο	λύσαντο

1st. AOR. MIDDLE SUBJ.

	Sg.	Pl.	Sg.	Pl.
1st pers.	-ωμαι	-ωμεθα	λύσωμαι	λυσώμεθα
2nd pers.	-ηαι	-ησθε	λύσηαι	λύσησθε
3rd pers.	-ηται	-ωνται	λύσηται	λύσωνται

Note:

Remember that in the aorist system, middle endings do not also have passive force; there are special aorist passive endings (Lessons 51-52). Thus, the indicative forms above would mean: *I loosed for myself, You loosed for yourself, He loosed for himself,* etc.

263. MEMORIZE

βασιλείη, -ης	[f.] kingdom
ἐάω, ἐάσω, ἔασα	I leave (alone); permit, allow (to do or be something) [+ inf.]
πάσχω, πείσομαι, πάθον	I suffer, I experience
πονέομαι, πονήσομαι, πονησάμην	I labor, I toil at, I am busy about
χάρις, χάριτος, acc. sg. χάριν	[f.] grace; beauty, charm

264. TRANSLATE

1. ὀλίγα αἰτησάμην· μοῦνον σῖτον, ἵνα ζώοιμι.
2. κασιγνητόν σευ πεμψώμεθα· μάλα γὰρ σοφός ἐστιν.
3. πολλοὺς νοήσαντες ἐρχομένους, τρεψάμεθα καὶ φεύγομεν.
4. ἢν πράγματα πονήσασθε χρηστά, κρατερὴ ἂν ἦεν βασιλείη.
5. Ἀπόλλων σχετλίοισί σφεων πράγμασι οὔ πω ἤσατο.
6. χρήματα πολλὰ οὐκ ἕξεις, εἰ μή κε πονήσηαι.
7. ὅτι μαχέοντο ὡς ἄνδρες ἀγαθοί, πατρίδα σώσαντο.

8. ὅτε αἰσχρόν τι ῥέξωνται βροτοί, πείσονταί τινες.

9. παντοίας βουλεύσασθε βουλάς, τὰς ἐγὼν οὐκ ἐάσω ἄνακτα
    λανθάνειν.

10. ἐπὴν τρέψηται πρῶτος, τρέπονται καὶ ἕτεροι πάντες.

11. ἥδε ἐστὶ φωνὴ φίλου παῖδας ἱκανέμεν κελεύοντος.

12. παισὶ μανθάνουσι σπεύδει χρόνος.

265. PUT INTO GREEK

1. When he kept asking, "Who are you (pl.)?" what did you reply?

2. We prepared ourselves much food, that we might all eat.

3. All of them fought with much glory.

4. Whatever custom requests of us, let us do it willingly.

5. I was pleased with the charm of your (sg.) voice.

6. I shall lead my brother to you (pl.), that you may receive him as a companion.

7. Who taught you (sg.) that? Or did you teach yourself?

8. Let us build ourselves a temple to the Muses by the sea.

9. If you (sg.) accept my advice, you will save the whole kingdom.

10. He reared his two sons into men of many virtues.

266. READINGS

1. καλέσας πρὸς ἓ αὐτὸν παῖδας, ἔφη Ἰησοῦς, "ἐάετε παῖδας πρός με
    ἔρχεσθαι, καὶ μὴ κωλύσατέ σφεας. τοίων γάρ ἐστι βασιλείη θεοῦ. καὶ
    λέγω ὑμῖν, ὃς ἂν μὴ δέξηται βασιλείην θεοῦ ὡς παῖς, οὔ ποτε εἴς μιν
    εἰσ-ελεύσεται."   (St. Luke)

2. χάριτι θεοῦ εἰμι ὃ εἰμι. καὶ χάρις θεοῦ εἰς ἐμὲ οὐ κενεὴ ἦεν. πολλὰ
    πονησάμην· οὐκ ἐγὼ δέ, ἀλλὰ χάρις θεοῖο σὺν ἐμοί.   (St. Paul. εἰς ἐμέ
    = "given me" or "toward me")

3. οὐκ ἔστιν οὐδεὶς ὅς τις οὐχ οἷ αὐτῷ φίλος.   (Menander)

4. τήνδε ἐντολὴν ἔχομεν ἀπὸ θεοῦ, ἵνα ὅς τις φιλέει θεόν, φιλέῃ καὶ ἑὸν
    κασιγνητόν.   (St. John)

5. ἄνθρωπος μὴ φιλέων ἑὸν κασιγνητὸν τὸν ὁράει, θεὸν τὸν οὐχ ὁράει
    πῶς φιλήσει;   (Phocylides)

Ἰησοῦς, -οῦ	Jesus
καλέω, καλέω, κάλεσα	I call
κενεός, -ή, -όν	empty; fruitless
κωλύω, κωλύσω, κώλυσα	I forbid, I prevent
τοῖος, -η, -ον	of such a kind, such

267. WRITE IN GREEK

1. Having planned what they wished to do (aor.), they hastened to the river and
    hid themselves (impf.) among the trees.

2. Leave (pl., aor.) all your possessions, and flee (pres.)! May the cruel king not destroy us too!

3. We built the gate so high and strong, that no one might even try to enter and seize our gold.

268. WORD STUDY

PSYCHOPATHIC ('suffering in the soul' from mental disease; in an overwrought and upset state of mind), TELEPATHY ('suffering or experiencing at a distance', the supposed psychic phenomenon of direct communication of thought to another mind far away without any external expression through words, etc.; usually termed 'mental telepathy'), PATHOS (the quality of an event or artistic representation which causes one to experience a 'suffering', i.e., a feeling or an emotion, of pity, compassion, or sadness), PATHETIC (arousing pathos; sad, pitiable), APATHETIC (unfeeling, emotionless, unmoved by stirring events), APATHY (the state of being insensible, indifferent, experiencing no emotion); — CLETUS ("called," "chosen out"), PARACLETE one 'called alongside' as a helper or official protector, a special name or title of the Holy Spirit as Divine Intercessor or comforter of the soul), ECCLESIA (the people's legislative assembly in ancient Greek cities, composed of citizens 'called out' to vote on some law; a church, the assembly of the faithful 'called out or chosen' by God into His special religious society), ECCLESIASTIC (a churchman, a member of the clergy or hierarchy), ECCLESIASTICAL (pertaining to the Church, as 'ecclesiastical ceremonies').

Lesson 38

The First Aorist Optative, Imperative, Infinitive, Participle Middle. The Impersonal Verb χρή.

269. ENDINGS

1st AOR. MIDDLE OPT.

	Sg.	Pl.	Sg.	Pl.
1st pers.	-αιμην	-αιμεθα	λυσαίμην	λυσαίμεθα
2nd pers.	-αιο	-αισθε	λύσαιο	λύσαισθε
3rd pers.	-αιτο	-αιατο	λύσαιτο	λυσαίατο

1st AOR. MIDDLE IMPT.

	Sg.	Pl.	Sg.		Pl.	
2nd pers.	-αι	-ασθε	λῦσαι	loose for yourself!	λύσασθε	loose for yourselves!

1st AOR. MIDDLE INF.

-ασθαι   λύσασθαι   to loose for oneself

1st AOR. MIDDLE PTC.

m. f. n. nom	m. f. n. nom.
-αμενος, -η, -ον	λυσάμενος, -η, -ον

270. THE IMPERSONAL VERB χρή

The "verb" χρή, translated *it is necessary*, is actually an indeclinable noun, with an understood ἐστί. χρή is thus a 3rd person singular verb, but it has no definite subject. Instead, an infinitive stands as its subject; the infinitive, if it has a subject, has an accusative subject. Because χρή has no definite subject, it is called an "impersonal" verb.

χρὴ ὑμέας τὸν θησαυρὸν ζητῆσαι.

It is necessary for you all to search for the treasure. (Literally: For you all to search for the treasure is necessary.)

271. MEMORIZE

ἀείρω, —, ἄειρα	I lift up, I take up, I raise
ἦμαρ, ἤματος	[n.] day
μῆλον, -ου	[n.] sheep; flock
πιστεύω, πιστεύσω, πίστευσα	I believe (in), I have faith in [+ dat.]
χαίρω, χαιρήσω, χάρην	I rejoice (in); χάρην aor. pass. with act. force
χρή	it is necessary [+ inf. w. acc. sub.: see Section 270]

272. TRANSLATE

1. εἴ γε βουλεύσησθε, εἰς ἀγαθὸν πατρίδος βουλεύσασθε.

2. χρήματα ἐὰ ἀείραιτο καὶ ἔρχοιτο· μισέομεν γάρ ἑ πάντες.

3. ἄνθρωπον χρὴ κατὰ ἑὴν φύσιν ζώειν

4. λέγει σφέας δώροισι ὑμέων μάλα ἥσασθαι.

5. βουλόμεθά σε ἱκανέμεν, ὄφρα σε πρὸς ἄνακτα πεμψαίμεθα.

6. εἰ μῆλά σευ εὑρίσκειν ἐθέλεις, ζήτησαι αὐτός.

7. τόδε ῥέξαν, ἵνα ἀρετῆς σευ πειρησαίατο.

8. πολλὰ χρὴ ἄνθρωπον ἑοῖσιν ὀφθαλμοῖσι πεύθεσθαι.

9. ἔργοισιν ἐπέεσί τε ὀρθοῖσιν πονεώμεθα εἵνεκα δίκης.

10. κείνους τρεψαμένους καὶ φεύγοντας διώκει.

11. μῆλα σὰ ἀπὸ ἐμῶν κρίναιο, ὡς γιγνώσκωμεν τεῦ ἐστιν ἕκαστον.

12. διὰ ἤματος παντὸς πονησάμενοι, νῦν εὕδομεν.

273. PUT INTO GREEK

1. Receive (pl.) them as friends for my sake.

2. I know he toiled; but I toiled, too.

3. Loose (sg.) your flocks, in order that they may eat under the trees.

4. We wished to hide the gold, so that not even after searching might they find it.

5. We considered how you might release yourselves and flee.

6. We were fighting, that we might save our property from the evil king.

7. Answer (pl.) quickly, that I may rejoice in the truth.

8. Having turned near the river, they were now passing the high rocks beside the sea.

9. Believe (pl.) me! I did this only that you might be pleased.

10. He said the strangers, after building themselves something or other under the trees, are fleeing.

11. It is necessary for you (sg.) to do this deed.

12. Those children ought to learn useful (χρηστός, -ή, -όν) things.

274. READINGS

1. εἴ τις ἐθέλει ὀπίσω μευ ἔρχεσθαι, χρή μιν ἀρνήσασθαι ἑ αὐτὸν καὶ ἀείρειν ἑὸν σταυρὸν παντὶ ἤματι, καὶ ἔπεσθαί μοι. (St. Luke)

2. κατανοήσας δὲ Μωυσῆς τὸν πόνον τῶν υἱῶν Ἰσραὴλ ὁράει ἄνθρωπον Αἰγύπτιον τύπτοντά τινα Ἑβραῖον τῶν ἑαυτοῦ ἀδελφῶν τῶν υἱῶν Ἰσραήλ· περιβλεψάμενος δὲ ὧδε καὶ ὧδε οὐχ ὁράει οὐδένα, καὶ πατάξας τὸν Αἰγύπτιον κρύψεν αὐτὸν ἐν τῇ ἄμμῳ. (Exodus II 11, from the Septuagint, the Greek translation of the Hebrew Bible)

3. Χριστὸν οὐχ ὁράοντες φιλέετε καὶ τῷ πιστεύετε· μάλα οὖν χαιρήσετε δεξάμενοι τέλος πίστιος ὑμέων, σωτηρίην ψυχάων.   (St. Peter)

4. ὄλβον αἱρεόμεθα αἰεὶ διὰ αὐτὸ καὶ οὔ ποτε διὰ ἄλλο τι. δόξαν δὲ καὶ ἡδονὴν καὶ νόον καὶ πᾶσαν ἀρετὴν αἱρεόμεθα μὲν καὶ διὰ αὐτὰ καὶ εἵνεκα ὄλβου, νοέοντες οὕτως ὄλβον ἕξειν. ὄλβον δὲ εἵνεκα κείνων οὐχ αἱρεόμεθα οὐδὲ διὰ ἄλλο τι, διὰ δὲ αὐτό. ἔστι γὰρ ἀγαθὸν ἐν οἷ αὐτῷ.   (Aristotle)

5. δίκαιον οὖν ἐστι μὴ λιποτακτέειν ἡμέας ἀπὸ βουλῆς θεοῦ.   (St. Clement of Rome, the fourth Pope)

6. χρὴ ἡμέας παῖδα ἔτι ἐόντα διδασκέμεν καλὰ ἔργα.   (Phocylides)

7. ζητέειν χρὴ θεόν, ἐπεί γε οὐ τῆλε ἀπὸ ἑνὸς ἑκάστου ἡμέων ἐστίν. ἐν τῷ γὰρ ζώομεν καὶ κινεόμεθα καὶ εἰμέν· "τοῦ γὰρ καὶ γένος εἰμέν," ὡς καί τινες ὑμέων ποιητάων λέγουσιν.   (St. Paul, at the end quoting Aratus.)

ἀδελφός, -οῦ	[m.] brother, kinsman
Αἰγύπτιος, -η, -ον	Egyptian
ἄμμος, -ου	[f.] sand
ἀρνέομαι, ἀρνήσομαι, ἀρνησάμην	I renounce, I deny
γένος, -εος	[n.] race, offspring
δίκαιόν ἐστι	it is right [+ acc. and inf.]
ἑαυτοῦ, -ῆς, -οῦ	of himself (herself, itself)
Ἑβραῖος, -ου	[m.] a Hebrew
ἕπομαι	I come along with, I follow
ἔστι	there is [ἔστι at the beginning of a sentence accented in this way has this meaning]
Ἰσραήλ	[indecl.] Israel [here= gen. "of Israel"]
κατα-νοέω, κατα-νοήσω, κατα-νόησα	I observe
κινέομαι	I move about
κρύπτω, κρύψω, κρύψα	I hide, I cover
λιποτακτέω	I abandon my post, I am a deserter
Μωυσῆς, -οῦ	[m.] Moses, an Israelite leader
νόος	here = wisdom
ὀπίσω	[adv., prep. + gen.] after
πατάσσω, πατάξω, πάταξα	I slay by striking
περι-βλέπομαι, περι-βλέψομαι, περι-βλεψάμην	I look around
πίστις, πίστιος	[f.] faith
ποιηταί, -άων	[m.] poets
σταυρός, -οῦ	[m.] cross
σωτηρίη, -ης	[f.] salvation, safety
τέλος, -εος	[n.] goal, consummation, fulfillment
τῆλε	[adv.] afar off, at a distance
τύπτω	I beat
ὧδε καὶ ὧδε	"this way and that"

275. WRITE IN GREEK

1. If you (sg.) fight for your country's sake, you will have much glory; for it is a noble thing in the eyes of all men.

2. They received your (pl.) gifts rejoicing, and wish you to know they are greatly pleased.

3. The wise king replied that to command is easy and pleasant, but to obey is sometimes very difficult.

4. It is difficult to be always good; yet we ought to make the attempt, for that is the way to happiness.

276. WORD STUDY

EPHEMERAL (ἔφ᾽ from ἐπί + ἡμέρη an alternative form for ἦμαρ, hence, 'on a day', i.e., for a short time only, transient, quickly passing, short-lived, as in the sentence 'His enthusiasms are usually ephemeral.')

Lesson 39

Review of The First Aorist System

277. ENDINGS

See Appendix A for complete list of endings.

278. MEMORIZE

ἄκρος, -η, -ον	top(most), outermost, extreme; [as n. noun:] edge, tip
ἄλληλοι, -ων	[pl. only] one another, each other
ἅμα	[adv., or prep. + dat.] at the same time, together, with
ἔπειτα	then, thereupon
κόσμος, -ου	[m.] world
μακρός, -ή, -όν	long, large [in space or time]

279. IDENTIFY AND TRANSLATE

Stating the exact form in tense, voice, mood, etc.
(e.g., aor. mid. ptc. n. nom.-acc. sg.):

1. πέμψαντι
2. λύσειαν
3. ἀδικῆσαι
4. τρέψατο
5. ἢν ποιήσῃς
6. θρέψατε
7. πονησαμένους
8. ῥέξαιμι
9. μὴ μαχέσασθε
10. ἔρξαι
11. σώσαμεν
12. ἵνα ἀμείψαιο
13. νόησε
14. δέξαιτο
15. ἀπ-ολέσαντες
16. ἀείραιμι
17. εἰ φρονήσατε
18. αἰτήσαο
19. ἤσασθαι
20. δίδαξον
21. τρεψάσης
22. πιστεύσας
23. ἢν πειρήσηαι
24. πείσειας

280. SIGHT READING

The Road to Inner Peace

φιλέωμεν οὖν ἀλλήλους, ὅπως ἱκάνωμεν πάντες εἰς βασιλείην θεοῦ.
κασιγνητοί μευ, ποιήσωμεν βουλὴν θεοῖο καλέσαντος ἡμέας, ἵνα
ζώσωμεν· καὶ διώξωμεν ἀρετήν, κακίην δὲ φεύγωμεν ἠδὲ ἀσεβείην, μὴ
ἡμέας κατα-λαμβάνῃ κακά. ἢν γὰρ ἀγαθὰ ποιέωμεν πρόφρονες,

125

διώξεται ἡμέας εἰρήνη. ἡμεῖς ἄρα ἐν καθαρῷ κῆρι δουλεύσωμεν θεῷ, καὶ ἐσόμεθα δίκαιοι. ποιέοντες γὰρ βουλὴν Χριστοῦ, εὑρήσομεν ἀνάπαυσιν.

(From the earliest preserved Christian homily, c. 130 A.D., by an unknown author; formerly attributed to St. Clement of Rome.)

ἀνάπαυσις, -ιος	[f.] rest, peaceful repose
ἀσεβείη, -ης	[f.] evil-doing
δουλεύω, δουλεύσω, δούλευσα	I am a slave to, I serve
καθαρός, -ή, -όν	pure, clean
κακίη, -ης	[f.] wickedness
καλέω, καλέω, κάλεσα	I call, I choose out
κατα-λαμβάνω	I seize upon, I befall

281. READINGS

1. πολλοὶ ἰητροὶ εἰσ-ερχόμενοί με ἀπ-όλεσαν. (Droll epitaph on a Greek tomb)

2. μοῦνος ἦεν ἢ πρῶτος θνητῶν ὃς φῆνε ἑῷ τε βίῳ καὶ ἐπέεσσι, ὡς ἅμα ἀγαθὸς καὶ μάκαρ γίγνεται ἀνήρ. (Aristotle's tribute to Plato, inscribed on an altar erected in his honor)

3. μακρὴ δὲ καὶ ὀρθή ἐστιν ὁδὸς εἰς ἀρετήν, καὶ ἐν ἀρχῇ χαλεπή. ἐπὴν δέ τις εἰς ἄκρον ἱκάνῃ, ῥηιδίη δὴ ἔπειτα πέλει ὁδός. (Hesiod)

4. αἰτέω ὅπως πάντες ἓν ὦσιν, ὡς σὺ ἐν ἐμοὶ καὶ ἐγὼ ἐν σοί—ὅπως καὶ οἵδε ἐν ἡμῖν ἓν ὦσιν, ἐγὼ ἔν σφιν καὶ σὺ ἐν ἐμοί, ὄφρα γιγνώσκῃ κόσμος ὅτι φίλησάς σφεας ὡς ἐμὲ φίλησας. ἐθέλω δέ σφεας εἶναι μετά μοι, ἵνα ὁράωσι δόξαν ἐμήν. (Christ's prayer to His Father at the Last Supper; from St. John)

5. σῖτος θεοῦ καταβαίνων ἐξ οὐρανοῖο ζωὴν παρ-έχει ἀνθρώποισιν. αὐτός εἰμι σῖτος ζωῆς. (St. John)

6. ἀλλὰ καὶ ὑμέας χρή, ὦ ἄνδρες, εὐ-έλπιδας εἶναι πρὸς θάνατον, καὶ ἕν τι τόδε νοέειν ἀληθές· ὅτι οὐκ ἔστιν ἀνδρὶ ἀγαθῷ οὐδὲν κακὸν οὔτε ζώοντι οὔτε θνήσκοντι, οὐδὲ θεοὶ ἀμελέουσι τοῦδε πραγμάτων. (Socrates' final address to the jury; from Plato)

ἀμελέω	I am neglectful of, I am unconcerned about [+ gen.]
εὔ-ελπις, -ιδος	of good hope
κατα-βαίνω	I come down

282. WRITE IN GREEK

1. Don't flee (pl.), but keep hiding under the rock while he is passing, lest he perceive and destroy you. [Determine carefully which of these verbs are aorist, and which middle!]

2. There are many treasures in the world, but it is not lawful to take whatever we desire from one another.

283. WORD STUDY

AKRON ('city on the heights'), ACROBAT (βάτης a walker, 'one who walks on his outermost limbs', i.e., on tiptoe), ACROBATIC; ACROSTIC (στῖχος line, a cleverly devised poem or prose piece in which the 'outermost line' of initial or final letters themselves spell something when read down the line in order); — PARALLEL (lines uniformly running 'beside one another'; a close likeness between things, as a 'literary parallel' between pieces of writing similar to each other), PARALLELISM, PARALLELOGRAM; — COSMOS (the world or universe as a whole; any orderly system organized out of confusion and chaos), COSMIC (universal; coming from distant worlds, as 'cosmic-rays') — MACRON (a long mark over a vowel to show it is long in pronunciation; — CATHERINE ('pure').

Lesson 40

The Second Aorist System Active.
Should-Would and Potential Constructions

284. ENDINGS

So far, the aorists we have seen in sentences and readings have had third principal parts ending in -α or -αμην, including our paradigm verb λύω. In other words, we have been using only **first aorists**. However, all along in our vocabulary lists we have seen verbs whose third principal parts end in -ον or -ομην; such verbs are said to have **second aorists**. (For example, πάσχω, introduced in Lesson 37, has as its third principal part πάθον. The deponent verb γίγνομαι, with its third principal part γενόμην, was introduced in Lesson 23. Both of these verbs have second aorists.) The distinction between first and second aorists is strictly "morphological," i.e., there is no difference in meaning between the two types of aorist.

The second aorist system endings are exactly the same as for the present system (including the imperfect, for indicative forms); the infinitive ending -ειν sometimes becomes -εειν. See Appendix A for list of endings separately. Thus ἴδον (I saw), second aorist and third principal part of ὁράω, is conjugated in the active:

2nd AOR. ACT.

	IND.	*SUBJ.*	*OPT.*	*IMPT.*
	Sg.			
1st pers.	ἴδον	ἴδω	ἴδοιμι	
2nd pers.	ἴδες	ἴδης	ἴδοις	ἴδε (or ἰδέ)*
3rd pers.	ἴδε	ἴδη	ἴδοι	
	Pl.			
1st pers.	ἴδομεν	ἴδωμεν	ἴδοιμεν	
2nd pers.	ἴδετε	ἴδητε	ἴδοιτε	ἴδετε
3rd pers.	ἴδον	ἴδωσι	ἴδοιεν	

INF.   *PTC. (m.f. n. nom.)*

ἰδεῖν, ἰδέειν, ἰδέμεν(αι) or ἴδμεν(αι)   ἰδών, ἰδοῦσα, ἰδόν

*The second pers. sg. 2nd aor. act impt. of five verbs is accented on the final syllable. These are: λαβέ, εὑρέ, εἰπέ, ἐλθέ and, in Attic Greek, ἰδέ. However, ἰδέ appears in Homer as ἴδε.

285. FURTHER USES OF THE OPTATIVE

a.   **Should-would (Future Less Vivid) condition**

When a less likely future supposition is to be expressed, it is put into the optative, sometimes with ἄν or κε(ν) added; negative μή. This supposition, or protasis, is generally accompanied by a conclusion (apodosis) stating what would result if the supposition were to come true. Such a theoretical conclusion, being itself only a rather vague future possibility, is also put into the optative (negative οὐ); if ἄν or κε(ν) is added, it makes the conclusion more definite, = "in that case, then, under those circumstances" (not necessarily to be translated explicitly). For example:

εἴ κεν ἔλθοι, χαίροιμεν.
If he should come, we would rejoice.

εἰ πέσοι ὁ λίθος, πάντες ἂν θάνοιτε.
If that rock happened to fall, you would all [in that case] die.

In English, a Future Less Vivid Condition may be expressed in four ways; using the first example above, these are: (1) If he should come, we would rejoice. (2) If he happens/happened to come, we would rejoice. (3) If he came, we would rejoice (4) If he were to come, we would rejoice.

It is possible, of course, that the conclusion should not be a vague but a definite reaction— an ordinary imperative or hortatory subjunctive, e.g., "If he should come, receive him gladly" (or "…let us receive him gladly"). Such a sentence is a mixed construction, not a true should-would condition.

b.   **Potential optative**

When an opinion as to what might, could, or would happen is expressed, without explicitly stating the conditions or circumstances which would bring it about, the verb is again put into the optative, usually with κε(ν) or ἄν (negative οὐ). Such a statement is really equivalent to the conclusion (apodosis) of a should-would sentence in which the supposition or protasis on which the conclusion depends is not expressed. Hence, it follows the same rule: For instance:

τίνα κεν εἶναί μιν λέγοις;
Who would you say he is? [if you were to be asked]

οὐδὲ κρατερὸς τόδε ἂν ποιήσειεν.
Not even a strong man could do that. [if he should try]

c.   *Note:* Remember that "would have" in English refers to past contrary to fact, and is therefore expressed in Greek by the imperfect or aorist indicative with κε(ν) or ἄν (see Section 91b). Sometimes, however, Homer uses the optative with κε(ν) in this sense, as the context makes clear in each case.

286. MEMORIZE

αὐλή, -ῆς	[f.] courtyard, farmyard, fold
ἔλπω or ἔλπομαι	[present system only] I expect, I hope, I suppose [+ inf.]
εὔχομαι, εὔξομαι, εὐξάμην	I claim to be, I boast, I exult; I pray (to) [+ inf.]
ποιμήν, ποιμένος	[m.] shepherd

287. TRANSLATE

1. ἔλθετε καὶ ἴδετε τί εὗρον.
2. εἰ κακόν τι πάθοις, ἀνέχεο ὡς ἀνήρ.
3. εὐξάμεθα θεοῖς πᾶσιν, ὄφρα σώσειαν ἡμέας ἀπὸ θανάτου.
4. ἑταίρους ἔλπεται ἀγαγεῖν εἰς πατρίδα ἄλλην.
5. πολλὰ περ μαθόντας καὶ ἄλλα πολλὰ χρὴ ὑμέας μαθεῖν.
6. εἰ χρυσὸν τῇδε κύθοιτε, οὐδείς ποτέ μιν εὕροι.
7. ἀλλὰ τί κε ῥέξαιμι, ἐπεὶ οὐκ ἔλθον ἑταῖροι;
8. πάντα ἑὰ μῆλα εἰς αὐλὴν ἀγαγών, ποιμὴν νῦν εὕδει.
9. τί ἔνθεν λάβοιεν;
10. σῶσον ἡμέας, ἵνα μὴ θάνωμεν.
11. πεμπομένοισι λέγε ἃ χρὴ ποιέειν.
12. οὐχ ἕνα μοῦνον ἀλλὰ πάντας χρὴ εἵνεκα πατρίδος πράγματα ἀν-έχεσθαι.

288. PUT INTO GREEK

1. How did you (sg.) miss my words?
2. Having eluded the shepherd, they seized two sheep and fled.
3. May you (pl.) learn much while you are still boys.
4. If they should come now, what would you (sg.) do?
5. Command (pl.) them not to take anything.
6. What else could I eat, since we had only bread?
7. We expect to find all the sheep sleeping in the fold.
8. Bring (sg.) me your sons, that I may see them.
9. From what place did you (sg.) take the wine?
10. (On) seeing us they (f.) greatly rejoiced.

289. READINGS

1. λάβετε, φάγετε· τόδε ἐστὶ σῶμά μευ.   (St. Matthew)
2. ἄνθρωπος ἐών ἄμαρτον· μὴ θαύμαζε.   (Menander)
3. εἰ κακὰ ποίησας, κακὰ καὶ παθεῖν σε χρή.   (Sophocles)
4. εἰ δὲ θεὸν ἀνήρ τις ἔλπεται λαθέμεν ἔρδων τι, ἁμαρτάνει.   (Pindar)
5. εἰ μὴ γαμέοι ἄνθρωπος, οὐκ ἂν ἔχοι κακά.   (Menander)

6. τί δὲ ἔχεις ὃ οὐ λάβες παρὰ θεοῦ; εἰ δὲ καὶ λάβες, τί εὔχεαι ὡς μὴ λαβών;   (St. Paul)

7. οὐκ ἔστιν εὑρεῖν βίον ἄλυπον οὐδένος.   (Menander)

8. ἐγώ εἰμι ποιμὴν καλός. ποιμὴν καλὸς θνήσκει εἵνεκα μήλων. ἐγὼ γιγνώσκω μῆλα ἐμὰ καὶ γιγνώσκουσιν ἐμέ, καὶ ἕπονταί μοι. ἄλλα δὲ μῆλα ἔχω τὰ οὐκ ἔστιν ἐκ τῆσδε αὐλῆς. τὰ χρὴ ἐμὲ ἀγαγεῖν, καὶ φωνῆς ἐμῆς ἀκούσουσι καὶ γενήσονται μία ποίμνη, εἷς ποιμήν.
(St. John)

ἀκούω, ἀκούσω	I hear the sound of, I hear [+ gen.]
ἄλυπος, -ον	free from sorrow
ἕπομαι	I follow [+ dat.]
οὐκ ἔστιν	[+ inf.] it is not possible (to do something)
θαυμάζω	I wonder, I am surprised
ποίμνη, -ης	[f.] flock

290. WRITE IN GREEK

1. He replied that his brother persuaded all his companions not to allow the king to receive them.

2. If men did not do cruel deeds to one another, there would be peace always; for peace is the fruit of justice.

291. WORD STUDY

ACOUSTIC (suitable for, or pertaining to, hearing, as 'good acoustic qualities' of a hall, making it easy to hear), ACOUSTICS (the science of sound and the laws of hearing).

Lesson **41**

The Second Aorist System Middle

292. ENDINGS

Identical with those of the present system (including the imperfect, for indicative forms). See Appendix A. Thus ἴδον (I saw) is conjugated in the middle:

2nd AOR. MIDDLE

	IND.	*SUBJ.*	*OPT.*	*IMPT.*
Sg.				
1st pers.	ἰδόμην	ἴδωμαι	ἰδοίμην	
2nd pers.	ἴδεο	ἴδηαι	ἴδοιο	ἴδεο, ἴδευ
3rd pers.	ἴδετο	ἴδηται	ἴδοιτο	
Pl.				
1st pers.	ἰδόμεθα	ἰδώμεθα	ἰδοίμεθα	
2nd pers.	ἴδεσθε	ἴδησθε	ἴδοισθε	ἴδεσθε
3rd pers.	ἴδοντο	ἴδωνται	ἰδοίατο	

AOR. INF.	*PTC. (m. f. n. nom.)*
ἰδέσθαι	ἰδόμενος, -η, -ον

293. MEMORIZE

ἀπάνευθε	[adv., and prep. + gen.] away (from), apart (from), afar
εἶπον	[2 aor. system only] I said, I told
περί	[adv.] round about; especially [prep. + gen.] about; excelling [prep. + dat. or acc.] about; for
πόρον	[2 aor. system only] I gave, I offered
τελέω, τελέω, τέλεσα	I fulfill, I accomplish, I complete

294. TRANSLATE

1. σοφοὶ γενοίμεθα· χρὴ γάρ.
2. οὐ βούλοντο περὶ ἑτέροις κακὰ ἐνισπεῖν.
3. εἴ γε πρόφρων ζητέοις, πολλά που πύθοιο.
4. λάθον ἡμέας ἀπάνευθε παρ-ερχόμενοι.
5. οὐκ ἐάσω σε ὃ ἐμοὶ πόρε λαβέσθαι.
6. ἐν ἀρχῇ εἶπε θεός, "γένοιτο φάος," καὶ γένετο.
7. πολλοὺς ἀνα-σχομένη πόνους βίον τέλεσε καλόν.

8. πῶς δὴ ἑλοίμην ἄν, ἐπεὶ ἕν μοῦνόν μοι πόρες;

9. εἰ μὴ λάβοιτο ἄλλων χρήματα, οὔ κε πονηρὸς πέλοι ἀνήρ.

10. εὔχετο σοφὸς ἔμμεναι, ὄφρα πολλοί οἱ πιστεύοιεν.

11. ἐρομένοισι χρὴ ἀληθείην εἰπεῖν.

12. μαχεόμενοι πολλοὶ θάνον.

13. μαχομένους εἵνεκα βίοιο οὐκ ἴδετε;

295. PUT INTO GREEK

1. To desire and to accomplish are not the same (thing).

2. Let us endure even this for our country's sake.

3. What would happen if he should come?

4. If a storm should suddenly come, the topmost trees would all fall.

5. Having made your (pl.) choice of anything, do not quickly choose something else.

6. To endure fools is never easy.

7. If you (sg.) asked, I would tell you all I know about them.

8. Of these two (pieces of) fruit, choose (sg.) one and give me the other.

9. He would not obey, not even if I should command it.

10. Whenever you (sg.) desire to learn something, inquire.

296. READINGS

1. καί σοι πάντα γένοιτο, ἅ τινα φρεσὶ σῇσι βούλεαι.   (Homer)

2. ἡδύ ἐστι καὶ πυθέσθαι.   (Hesiod)

3. μάλα γὰρ φίλησε θεὸς κόσμον, καὶ πόρε ἑὸν υἱὸν μοῦνον, ἵνα πᾶς πιστεύων οἱ μὴ ἀπ-όληται.   (St. John)

4. θανέειν γὰρ καλὸν ἐν προμάχοισι πεσόντα ἄνδρα ἀγαθὸν περὶ ἑῇ πατρίδι μαχόμενον.   (Tyrtaeus)

5. τόδε τοι λέγοιμι ἄν σοι, μηδένα πώ ποτε λαβόντα, ἔτι νέον ἐόντα, τήνδε δόξαν περὶ θεῶν, ὡς οὔκ εἰσιν, βίον τελέσαι πρὸς γῆρας μείναντα ἐν τῇδε δόξῃ.   (Plato)

6. ἀπάνευθε φίλων οὐδεὶς ἕλοιτό κε ζώειν, ἔχων περ ἄλλα ἀγαθὰ πάντα. (Aristotle)

7. ἐξ ἀρχῆς βίου αἰεί μισέειν μὲν τὰ ἃ χρὴ μισέειν καὶ φιλέειν τὰ ἃ χρὴ φιλέειν, — τόδε ἐστὶν ὀρθὴ παιδείη.   (Plato)

γῆρας, -αος	[n.] old age
μένω, μενέω, μεῖνα	I remain
νέος, -η, -ον	young
παιδείη, -ης	[f.] education
πρόμαχος, -ου	[m.] front-line fighter

297. WRITE IN GREEK

1. The shepherd hid all his sheep away from the road, so that no one going past might discover them.

2. Having eaten half of the food and drunk all the wine, the two strangers fled, fearing someone might discover and seize them. (For "fearing" use the aor. ptc. + μή.]

298. WORD STUDY

PERIMETER ('the measure around', the line bounding a two-dimensional figure), PERIOD (the 'way around', a space of time marked by the recurrence or 'coming around again' of some event, e.g., the ringing of a bell to mark beginning and end of a class period; in literature, a sentence in which the flow of thought is complete and clear only when the last word is reached and the 'journey around' from main subject to main verb is completed), PERIODIC (recurrent, as 'periodic explosions'), PERIODICAL (magazine coming out at recurrent intervals), PERIPHRASTIC (by 'round about expression', as a 'periphrastic conjugation', where a verb form is constructed by use of a helping verb, instead of inflection of the verb itself, e.g., Latin *erat docens* ["was teaching"] for *docebat*), PERISCOPE (σκοπέω I look; an instrument for 'looking around corners' by means of mirrors or prisms properly arranged).

Lesson 42

The Third Aorist Indicative And Subjunctive Active

299. ENDINGS

Many of the verb endings seen so far comprise two parts: the **person marker** (e.g., -ς for the 2nd person singular active, -μεν for the 1st person plural active, -σθε for the 2nd person plural middle/passive); and the **thematic vowel** (ο before μ or ν, ε before other consonants), which comes between the verb stem and the person marker. The third aorist has no thematic vowel between the root/stem and the endings. It is therefore sometimes called a 'root aorist'. The root always ends in a long vowel. Examples are βῆν (from βαίνω), στῆν (from ἵστημι), γνῶν (from γιγνώσκω), and δῦν (from δύω). There are very few others.

3rd AOR. IND. ENDINGS

	Sg.	Pl.
1st pers.	-ν	-μεν
2nd pers.	-ς	-τε
3rd pers.	—	-σαν

Thus βῆν (*I went*), γνῶν (*I knew*), δῦν (*I entered, I sank into, I set*)

	Sg.	Pl.	Sg.	Pl.	Sg.	Pl.
1st pers.	βῆν	βῆμεν	γνῶν	γνῶμεν	δῦν	δῦμεν
2nd pers.	βῆς	βῆτε	γνῶς	γνῶτε	δῦς	δῦτε
3rd pers.	βῆ	βῆσαν	γνῶ	γνῶσαν	δῦ	δῦσαν / δῦν

3rd AOR. SUBJ. ENDINGS

	Sg.	Pl.
1st pers.	-ω	-ωμεν
2nd pers.	-ῃς	-ητε
3rd pers.	-ῃ	-ωσι

	Sg.	Pl.	Sg.	Pl.	Sg.	Pl.
1st pers.	βήω	βήωμεν	γνώω	γνώωμεν	δύω	δύωμεν
2nd pers.	βήῃς	βήητε	γνώῃς	γνώητε	δύῃς	δύητε
3rd pers.	βήῃ	βήωσι	γνώῃ	γνώωσι	δύῃ	δύωσι

300. MEMORIZE

βαίνω, βήσομαι, βῆν, βέβηκα	I go
δύω, δύσω, δῦν	I enter
ῥέω	[pres. syst.] I flow
στῆν	[3 aor. syst. of ἵστημι I stand] I stood (intr.)
τλάω, τλήσομαι, τλῆν	I endure (something) patiently, I have the heart, I dare (to do something) [+ inf.]

301. TRANSLATE

1. στῆ ἀπάνευθε, ὄφρα μή ἑ ἴδοιεν.
2. τὴν γνῶμεν ὅτε ἔτι παῖς ἦεν.
3. ἢν τλήῃς τήνδε νοῦσον, δόξαν ἕξεις οὐκ ὀλίγην.
4. δείδω μὴ βήῃ παῖς εἰς ποταμὸν καὶ ἀπ-όληται.
5. διδάσκοις ἡμέας περὶ κακῆς τῆσδε νούσου, ἵνα μὴ θάνωμεν.
6. στῆσαν ἐγγὺς πέτρης, ἐξ ἧς ὕδωρ ῥέε γλυκύ.
7. οὐδεὶς τλῆ οἱ ἐνισπεῖν περὶ θανάτου ἑοῖο υἱοῖο.
8. φανέω ὑμῖν χρυσὸν ἅπαντα, ὅτε κε βήωσι.
9. λέγε τίς ἐσσι, ἵνα γνώῃ ἄναξ.
10. τί οὐκ εἰς-έλθετε, ἀλλὰ παρὰ πύλῃσι στῆτε;
11. οἵ τινες γνώωσι πολλὰ καλὰ γίγνονται καλοί.
12. ὅτε ἡέλιος δύῃ εἰς θάλασσαν, ὁ ποιμὴν μῆλα ἄγει εἰς αὐλήν.

302. PUT INTO GREEK

1. He knew many (people) from (ἐκ) that land.
2. Let us endure patiently whatever life might bring us.
3. If you (sg.) stand upon that rock, you will be able to see the sea.
4. When they saw the shepherd coming, the sheep went into the fold.
5. The physicians did not know the disease that he had.
6. Because you (sg.) dared fight with many, I knew you were a brave man.
7. Two of them went down the road, two towards the river.
8. If we had known that, we would not have come.
9. When you (pl.) stood afar, you seemed very small.
10. Which of you had the heart to seize the child from the fire?

303. READINGS

1. πολλῶν ἀνθρώπων ἴδεν ἄστεα καὶ νόον γνῶ.   (Homer, of Odysseus' benefits from his travels)

2. νῦν υἱοὶ θεοῦ εἰμεν, καὶ οὔ πω φανερόν ἐστι τί ἐσόμεθα. γιγνώσκομεν ὅτι ὅμοιοι θεῷ ἐσόμεθα, ὅτι ὀψόμεθά μιν ὡς ἐστιν.   (St. John; the second ὅτι has a different meaning from the first!)

3. φῦ μὲν οὐδεὶς βροτῶν ὅς τις οὐ πονέεται.   (Euripides)

4. εἰ ἀνάγκη γένοιτο ἢ ἀδικέειν ἢ ἀδικέεσθαι, ἑλοίμην ἂν μᾶλλον
   ἀδικέεσθαι ἢ ἀδικέειν.   (Plato)

5. ὁ δὲ μάκαρ ἐστίν, ὅν τινα Μοῦσαι φιλέονται· τοῦ ἀπὸ στόματος
   γλυκεῖα ῥέει φωνή.   (Hesiod)

6. ἕτερος ἐξ ἑτέρου σοφὸς καὶ πάλαι καὶ νῦν, οὐδὲ γὰρ ῥηίδιον
   ἀρρήτων ἐπέων πύλας εὑρεῖν.   (Bacchylides)

7. ἃ δὲ ἂν μάθῃ παῖς, τά που σώσονται πρὸς γῆρας.   (Euripides)

8. μὴ ζῶε ὡς μέλλων ζώειν αἰεί. θάνατος πάρ-εστι· ὄφρα ζώεις, ὄφρα
   δυνατός ἔσσι, ἀγαθὸς γίγνεο.   (Marcus Aurelius)

9. καὶ ἀνάστη Γολιὰθ καὶ βῆ εἰς συνάντησιν Δαυείδ. καὶ ἐκτείνεν
   Δαυεὶδ τὴν χεῖρα αὐτοῦ εἰς τὸ κάδιον καὶ λάβεν ἐκεῖθεν λίθον ἕνα,
   καὶ σφενδόνησεν καὶ πάταξεν Γολιὰθ ἐπὶ τὸ μέτωπον αὐτοῦ, καὶ δῦ
   ὁ λίθος διὰ τῆς περικεφαλαίης εἰς τὸ μέτωπον αὐτοῦ, καὶ πέσεν ἐπὶ
   πρόσωπον αὐτοῦ ἐπὶ τὴν γαῖαν.   (i Kings XVII 48-49, from the
   Septuagint, the Greek translation of the Hebrew Bible)

ἀνάστη	aor. 3 of ἀν-ίστημι, I stand up [intr.]
ἄρρητος, -ον	unspoken
ἄστυ, -εος	[n.] city
γῆρας, -αος	[n.] old age
Γολιάθ	[m. indecl.] Goliath, a Philistine giant
Δαυείδ	[m. indecl.] David, a future king of Israel and Judah, here still a youth
ἐκεῖθεν	[adv.] from that place, thence
ἐκ-τείνω	I stretch out
ἕτερος…ἕτερος	[idiom] one…another
κάδιον, -ου	[n.] vessel
μᾶλλον	[adv.] rather
μέτωπον, -ου	[n.] forehead
πάλαι	[adv.] in the past, long ago
πατάσσω, πατάξω, πάταξα	I strike
περικεφαλαία, -ης	[f.] helmet
πρόσωπον, -ου	[n.] face
στόμα, -ατος	[n.] mouth, lips
σφενδονάω, σφενδονήσω, σφενδόνησα	I sling
συνάντησις, -ιος	[f.] a meeting ες συνάντησιν Δαυείδ = "to meet David"
φανερός, -ή, -όν	evident, known
φῦν	[3 aor. of φύω] I was born, I was
χείρ, χειρός	[f.] hand

304. WRITE IN GREEK

1. (On) hearing of the death of your (sg.) two sons, we desired to come, but the
   length of the journey did not allow it. ["On hearing" = aor. ptc.]

2. If she had married the king's son, she would now be very happy.

3. I feared to enter, lest I should fall into the fire and perish.

305. WORD STUDY

RHEOSTAT (an instrument for 'regulating the flow' of an electrical current), RHEUMATISM (a 'flowing' or shifting inflammation of the nerve-structure of the muscles and joints), CATARRH (an excessive secretion of mucous membrane 'flowing down' from the sinus, as in head colds); — PALEOGRAPHY (the science of working out ancient systems of writing or old manuscripts and inscriptions), PALEOZOIC (name of the lowest geological layer, containing fossils of the 'life long ago').

Lesson 43

The Third Aorist Optative, Imperative,
Infinitive, Participle Active

306. ENDINGS

3rd AOR. OPT. ENDINGS

	Sg.	*Pl.*
1st pers.	-ιην	-ιμεν
2nd pers.	-ιης	-ιτε
3rd pers.	-ιη	-ιεν

	Sg.	*Pl.*	*Sg.*	*Pl.*
1st pers.	βαίην	βαῖμεν	γνοίην	γνοῖμεν
2nd pers.	βαίης	βαῖτε	γνοίης	γνοῖτε
3rd sing.	βαίη	βαῖεν	γνοίη	γνοῖεν

	Sg.	*Pl.*
1st pers.	δύην/δυίην	δῦμεν/δυῖμεν
2nd pers.	δύης/δυίης	δῦτε/δυῖτε
3rd pers.	δύη/δυίη	δῦεν/δυῖεν

3rd. AOR. IMPT. ENDINGS

	Sg.	*Pl.*
2nd pers.	-θι	-τε

	Sg.	*Pl.*	*Sg.*	*Pl.*	*Sg.*	*Pl.*
2nd pers.	βῆθι	βῆτε	γνῶθι	γνῶτε	δῦθι	δῦτε

3rd. AOR. INF. ENDINGS

-ναι   βῆναι   γνῶναι   δῦναι

3rd. AOR. PTC. ENDINGS (m. f. n. nom.)

-ς, -σα, -ν   βάς, βᾶσα, βάν   γνούς, γνοῦσα, γνόν   δύς, δῦσα, δύν

> *Notes:*
>
> 1. In the optative and participle the root-vowel is absorbed into the endings.
>
> 2. The genitives of the masculine and neuter singular participles are: βάντος, γνόντος, and δύντος. The feminine participles decline like γαῖα.

307. MEMORIZE

ἄλγος, ἄλγεος	[n.] pain, distress, woe
λείπω, λείψω, λίπον	I leave
ὀΐω or ὀΐομαι, ὀΐσομαι, ὀϊσάμην	I think, I suppose, I imagine
ποθέω, ποθήσω, πόθεσα	I long (to do something), I yearn (to do something) [+ inf.], I miss (a person or thing)

308. TRANSLATE

1. γνῶθί σφεας οὐκ ἔτι βάντας.
2. ἄλγος τι εἵνεκα φίλης τλῆναι ἡδύ ἐστι φιλέοντι.
3. οὐδείς μιν ἴδε εἰς ποταμὸν δύντα, τῇ ἀπ-όλετο.
4. εἰ τῇδε σταίης, φύγοις κεν ὄμβρον τε ἄνεμόν τε.
5. πολλά περ γνόντα, ἔτι ἂν διδάσκοιμί σε ἄλλα πολλά.
6. εἰς ἄκρην πέτρην βῆναι μὲν ποθέω, οὐ δὲ τλάω.
7. στῆτε τῇ ἐστε, ὄφρα κεν παρ-έλθῃ ἄναξ.
8. δῶρα παντοῖα πόρε ἡμῖν ξεῖνος, ἵνα γνοῖμέν ἑ μάλα ἡμῖν φίλον ἐόντα.
9. ἑταίρους ἐμοὺς κρατερὰ τλάντας σύν μοι ἄλγεα οὔ ποτε λείψω.
10. ὀΐομαί μιν εἰς πόλεμον βῆναι, οὐ δὲ γιγνώσκω.
11. πεμπομένοισι λέγε ἃ χρὴ τλῆναι.

309. PUT INTO GREEK

1. If a difficult disease should bring us pain, we ought to endure (it) like men.
2. Stand (sg.) apart from the others, that I may see you alone.
3. "Please go (sg.) to the temple and offer Apollo our gifts," he said.
4. Who would have the heart to destroy so beautiful a tree?
5. (After) standing near the road throughout the whole day, the sheep are now going to the fold.
6. I expect to find that great treasure for the sake of which many fought (impf.) and died.
7. Know (pl.) this! that I shall never leave my sons.
8. Having endured the toils of war, he now yearns after peace.
9. If I knew all things, I would not be (πελ-) mortal, but a god.
10. Even if you (pl.) were to go to another land, you would still love this country most of (περί) all.

310. READINGS

1. πάντες ἄνθρωποι γνῶναι ποθέουσι φύσιι.   (Aristotle)
2. ἃ μὴ γίγνώσκω, τὰ οὐδὲ ὀΐομαι γνῶναι.   (Plato)
3. γνῶθι σὲ αὐτόν.   (Thales; later inscribed on the Delphic temple)

4. δὶς εἰς αὐτὸν ποταμὸν οὐκ ἂν βαίης.   (Heraclitus)

5. αἰσχρόν ἐστι πλουτέειν καὶ ἄλλο μηδὲν γνῶναι.   (Euripides)

6. οὐ δυνατός εἰμι πάντα σοι παρα-σχεῖν, ὦ κῆρ, τὰ βούλεαι· τλῆθι, καλῶν οὔ τι σὺ μοῦνος ποθέεις.   (Theognis)

7. τί οὖν ἐστι ζώειν; οὐ ψυχῆς φήσομεν ἔργον εἶναι;   (Plato)

8. διὰ πολλάων θλίψεων χρὴ ἡμέας εἰς-ελθεῖν εἰς βασιλείην θεοῦ.
   (Acts of the Apostles)

9. χρὴ γὰρ φιλέειν κεῖνον ὃν θεὸς φιλέει.   (Greek Anthology)

θλῦψις, -εος or -εως	[f.] affliction, hardship
πλουτέω	I am wealthy, rich
φημί, φήσω, φῆσα	I say, I claim [+ acc. and inf. in indirect statement]

311. WRITE IN GREEK

1. Why did you (sg.) stand upon that very rock from which your brother fell and perished? [Express "fell and" by the aor. ptc. alone ='falling']

2. (After) passing the river we found a wide and straight road, and went quickly down it to the sea.

3. Say (sg.) what is in your mind, that we may all know what you believe about these things.

312. WORD STUDY

NEURALGIA (νεῦρον nerve; a sharp 'pain in the nerve' tissues, often accompanied by partial paralysis), ANALGESIC (ἀν- privative; a medicine bringing 'painlessness', as an anaesthetic); — ECLIPSE (a 'leaving out' or fading out of a bright object when a dark body comes between it and the observer; figuratively, to cast someone into the shadow by superior excellence, e.g., 'he eclipses all other singers'), ELLIPTICAL (ἐλ- for ἐκ- before λ: 'leaving something out', as an 'elliptical construction' omitting the verb or other words in a sentence).

Lesson 44

Review of All Aorists—Active and Middle

313. REVIEW

Endings from complete list in Appendix A.

314. MEMORIZE

βάλλω, βαλέω, βάλον	I throw, I strike
εὖ	[adv.] well
μένω, μενέω, μεῖνα	I remain, I stay; I await
σάρξ, σαρκός	[f.] flesh

315. SIGHT READING

Life of Our Life

ἐγώ εἰμι ἄμπελος, ὑμεῖς ὄζοι. ὅς τις μένῃ ἐν ἐμοὶ καὶ ἐγὼ ἐν οἱ, κεῖνος φέρει καρπὸν πολλόν. ἀπάνευθε δὲ ἐμεῖο, οὐ δυνατοὶ ἔσεσθε ποιέειν οὐδέν, ὡς ὄζος, ἣν μὴ μένῃ ἐν ἀμπέλῳ. μείνατε ἐν ἐμοί, καὶ ἐγὼ ἐν ὑμῖν· ἣν μείνητε ἐν ἐμοὶ καὶ λόγοι μευ ἐν ὑμῖν μείνωσιν, ὅττι κεν ἐθέλητε, αἰτήσασθε, καὶ γενήσεται ὑμῖν.

(Jesus at the Last Supper; from St. John)

ἄμπελος, -ου	[f.]	vine
ὄζος, -ου	[m.]	branch

316. PUT INTO GREEK

1. We received other gifts too from our friends. (pl.)
2. Stay! (pl.), don't leave us, lest we perish.
3. The strong wind threw many trees to the ground.
4. If I offered you (sg.) gold or happiness, what would you choose?
5. If you do not remain here with him, he will flee to his own country.
6. Whatever you (sg.) do, do it well
7. They hid all their possessions, that you might not take anything.
8. We sent two companions to bring them food, water, and wine.
9. Though they threw (ptc.) the rock with much force, they missed (ἁμαρτ-) the tree.
10. Because *you* (sg.) commanded it, I eagerly obeyed.

317. READINGS

1. τόδε "γνῶθι σὲ αὐτόν" ἐστι γνῶναι σὰ πράγματα καὶ τί χρή σε ποιέειν.   (Menander)

2. ἐγώ εἰμι σῖτος ζώων ἐξ οὐρανοῖο κατα-βάς. ἤν τις φάγῃ ἐκ τοῦδε σίτου, ζώσει εἰς αἰεί. καὶ σῖτος, ὂν ἐγὼ δωρήσομαι, σάρξ μεύ ἐστιν εἰς ζωὴν κόσμου.   (St. John)

3. ἀγαπητοί, εἰ οὕτως θεὸς φίλησεν ἡμέας, χρὴ καὶ ἡμέας ἀλλήλους φιλέειν.   (St. John)

4. εἰ γὰρ θεὸς ὑπὲρ ἡμέων ἐστί, τίς ἄντα ἡμέων; ὅς γε ἑοῦ υἱοῦ οὐ φείσατο, ἀλλὰ εἵνεκα ἡμέων πάντων δωρήσατό μιν—πῶς οὐ καὶ σὺν αὐτῷ πάντα ἡμῖν δωρήσεται;   (St. Paul)

5. ἀλλὰ τί κε ῥέξαιμι; θεὸς γὰρ διὰ πάντα τελέει ἑὴν βουλήν.   (Homer)

6. χρὴ θνητὸν ἀνάγκας ἐκ θεῶν φέρειν.   (Euripides)

ἀγαπητός, -ή, -όν	beloved
ἄντα	[prep. + gen.] against
δωρέομαι, δωρήσομαι, δωρησάμην	I give
κατα-βαίνω	I come down
ὑπέρ	[prep. + gen.] on the side of, for; above
φείδομαι, φείσομαι, φεισάμην	[+ gen.] I spare, I keep back

318. WRITE IN GREEK

1. I suppose they went along the river until they found the gold which we left under the fallen tree. ["They went" is in acc. and inf. construction, but not the rest of the sentence.]

2. The king well planned how he might (by) fighting destroy the enemy (ἐχθρούς) and save his people. ["how" is ὅπως— cp. Section 256, under βουλεύω]

3. Not daring (aor.) to remain, he stood apart from the others, and thus escaped our notice.

319. WORD STUDY

DEVIL (by false pronunciation of διά-βολος, 'the one who throws through a person's character', 'slanderer'), DIABOLIC, DIABOLICAL (devilish, satanic), METABOLISM (the complete process of assimilating food, 'throwing it into' another form; digestion in the broad sense; hence, 'metabolism tests', etc.); — EUGENE ('well-born', noble), EUGENICS (the movement devoted to improving the human species by controlling hereditary factors in mating), EULOGY ('well speaking' or praise of a person or thing, 'a good word', commendation), EUCHARIST (χάρις grace, thanks; 'thanks-giving', because Christ "taking bread into His hands gave thanks" before instituting the Sacrament), EUCHARISTIC (pertaining to the Blessed Sacrament), EUCALYPTUS (καλυπτός, -ή, -όν covered; a large type of evergreen tree with 'well-covered' seed pods), EUPHONY ('sounding well', a pleasant combination of sounds or word-order), EUPHONIOUS (melodious, pleasant to the ear), EUTHANASIA ('pleasant death', the theory that persons very old or greatly suffering should be painlessly put to death for their own or society's benefit),

EUSTACE (στάχιος, -ον of ripe grain; 'well-harvesting', prosperous); —
SARCASM ('flesh-tearing' irony or scornful taunt), SARCASTIC (taunting, 'biting'),
SARCOPHAGUS ('flesh-eating', applied to a kind of corrosive limestone used by the
Greeks for coffins, thence to a coffin or funeral monument in general).

Lesson 45

The Perfect And Pluperfect Indicative Active. Reduplication

320. ENDINGS

PF. ACT. IND.

	Sg.	*Pl.*	*Sg.*	*Pl.*
1st pers.	-α	-αμεν	λέλυκα	λελύκαμεν
2nd pers.	-ας	-ατε	λέλυκας	λελύκατε
3rd pers.	-ε(ν)	-ασι(ν)	λέλυκε(ν)	λελύκασι(ν)

PLPF. ACT. IND.

	Sg.	*Pl.*	*Sg.*	*Pl.*
1st pers.	-εα, -η	-εμεν	λελύκεα, λελύκη	λελύκεμεν
2nd pers.	-ης	-ετε	λελύκης	λελύκετε
3rd pers.	-ει	-εσαν	λελύκει	λελύκεσαν

Notes:

1. The α of the 3rd plural ending is usually short, but occasionally long.

2. For the meaning of the perfect and pluperfect in the indicative mood, see Section 84.

3. Sometimes the perfect has present force, and the pluperfect has imperfect force. For an example, see ἔοικα in Section 323.

321. REDUPLICATION

As an aid in remembering and identifying the principal parts of verbs, notice the characteristic of the perfect systems: **reduplication** or doubling of the sound at the beginning of the verb. (Cp. Latin *cano, canere, cecini; cado, cecidi; parco, peperci,* etc.) Reduplication in Greek is of three kinds:

a. Verbs beginning with a single consonant are reduplicated by placing the initial consonant with ε before the stem:

λύω   λέλυκα (perfect active)   λέλυμαι (perfect middle-passive)

(However, initial ῥ- becomes ἐρρ-: for example, ῥέω becomes ἐρρύηκα, and ῥίπτω becomes ἔρριφα.)

b. Verbs beginning with two consonants simply prefix ἐ:

στέλλω   ἔσταλκα (perfect active)   ἔσταλμαι (perfect middle-passive)

A Reading Course in Homeric Greek

c. Verbs beginning with a short vowel or a diphthong lengthen the initial vowel. (If the first vowel of an iota diphthong is lengthened, the ι is subscribed):

ἁμαρτάνω   ἡμάρτηκα (perfect active)   ἡμάρτημαι (perfect middle-passive)
αὐξάνω   ηὔξηκα   ηὔξημαι
αἱρέω   ᾕρηκα   ᾕρημαι

d. Some verbs begin with a combination of a mute (π, β, φ, κ, γ, χ, τ, δ, θ) and a liquid (λ, μ, ν, ρ). The combination of a mute and a liquid, because easy to pronounce, is generally treated as a single consonant; such verbs reduplicate by placing the *initial* consonant with ε before the stem. However, γν is treated as two consonants:

γράφω   γέγραφα (perfect active)   γέγραμμαι (perfect middle-passive)
(γι)γνώσκω   ἔγνωκα   ἔγνωσμαι

e. Initial mutes which contain an "h" sound (called **aspirates** or **rough consonants**) reduplicate without the "h", φ becoming π, χ becoming κ, θ becoming τ:

φιλέω   πεφίληκα (perfect active)   πεφίλημαι (perfect middle-passive)

f. Some reduplications are irregular; these forms should simply be learned from the vocabularies as the actual principal parts of the verbs in question.

322. DRILL

It is generally possible to recognize the perfect stem on the basis of the present stem. For practice, identify and translate the following perfects and pluperfects, using the hints given on characteristics of the various classes of verbs; note that a few of these verbs will be unfamiliar to you:

A. Class 1: from present stems ending in a long vowel or diphthong; perfect stem reduplicates, ends in κ:

1. κεκελεύκασι   4. ἐπταίκαμεν (πταίω stumble)
2. πεπίστευκας   5. κεκρούκει (κρούω beat)
3. δεδύκαμεν (δύω enter) 6. πεπαύκετε (παύω cease)

B. Class 2: from present stems ending in ε; perfect stem reduplicates, ends in ηκ (ε lengthening to η):

1. νενοήκατε   3. πεφρονήκαμεν   5. πεποιήκεα
2. ᾕρήκασι   4. πεφιλήκης   6. γεγαμήκετε

C. Class 3: from present stems ending in a consonant; perfect stem reduplicates, ends in κ, stem vowel may change or drop:

1. κέκρικας   3. τεθνήκει   5. βέβληκα
2. βεβήκεα   4. ἐγνώκασι   6. ἡμαρτήκατε

D. Class 4: irregular; stem-vowel of present may change or drop, reduplication irregular, perfect stem may end in other letter than κ; but not hard to recognize if first three principal parts are known:

1. πέφευγε   3. εἰληλούθει   5. ἑωράκατε
2. λελοίπετε   4. ἀπ-ολώλης   6. γεγάασι

323. MEMORIZE

ἀγάπη, -ης	[f.] love, charity
γυνή, γυναικός	[f.] woman, wife
δόλος, -ου	[m.] cunning, craftiness; trickery; bait for catching fish
ἔοικα	[pf. with pres. force; ἐῴκεα plpf. with impf. force] I seem, I am like to [+ dat.]; [in 3 sg. impers. construction, which may take acc. and inf.] it is fitting

324. TRANSLATE

1. πολλὰ ἑώρακα, οὐδὲν δὲ οὕτως καλόν.
2. πάντες βεβήκετε, ὅτε ἔλθον ἐγώ.
3. φίλος ἀληθὴς ἔοικεν εἶναι.
4. οὔ πω εἰληλούθει γυνὴ κασιγνητοῖο ἐμοῖο.
5. τοῖο ἀγάπην ἀληθέα ἐοῦσαν ἐγνώκαμεν διὰ ἔργων τοῦ ἀγαθῶν.
6. λίθους λελύκεσαν ὄμβροι· πολλοὶ οὖν πίπτον.
7. πολέμῳ ἀπ-όλωλεν ἄναξ, οὔ γε βίῃ ἀλλὰ δόλῳ.
8. γυναῖκας οὐκ ἀδίκησαν· οὐ γὰρ ἐῴκει.
9. ψυχὴν ἀπὸ σώματος λέλυκε θάνατος.
10. τί χαλεπὰ μὲν δείδιας, οὐ δὲ αἰσχρά;

325. PUT INTO GREEK

1. We have come eagerly.
2. None of them had ever seen a sheep.
3. To love money is sometimes the beginning of many evils.
4. Two of my sons have gone to war, the other still remains with me.
5. It is fitting to have faith in others, and not imagine guile in all their deeds.
6. Why have evil men not yet perished from the earth?
7. He has known your (sg.) craftiness from the beginning.
8. Where have you (sg.) ever seen so tall a tree?
9. The children had not yet come when the stone fell.
10. The light was like to the sun falling from the sky.

326. READINGS

1. χρηστὸς ἀνήρ, ὡς ἔοικε, καὶ ἄλλους χρηστοὺς ποιέει.   (Menander)

2. ἐγὼ φάος εἰς κόσμον εἰλήλουθα, ἵνα πᾶς ὃς πιστεύῃ μοι μὴ μείνῃ ἐν ζόφῳ.   (St. John)

3. ὃς δὲ γυναικὶ πέποιθε, πέποιθεν ὅ γε δόλῳ.   (Hesiod)

4. τῷ λέγει Ἰησοῦς, "ὅτι ἑώρακάς με, πεπίστευκας; μάκαρες κεῖνοι οἵ, οὐκ ἰδόντες, πεπιστεύκασιν."   (Christ to His doubting Apostle, Thomas; from St. John)

5. εὕρηκα.   (Archimedes, on discovering the law of displacement of liquids)

6. οὐδὲ τεθνήκασι θανόντες.   (Simonides, epitaph for the heroes of the great battle of Plataea)

7. καὶ εἶπεν ὁ θεὸς πάλιν πρὸς Μωυσῆν, "οὕτως ἐρεῖς τοῖς υἱοῖς Ἰσραήλ Κύριος ὁ θεὸς τῶν πατέρων ὑμῶν, θεὸς Ἀβραὰμ καὶ θεὸς Ἰσαὰκ καὶ θεὸς Ἰακώβ, ἀπέσταλκέν με πρὸς ὑμᾶς.' "   (Exodus III 15, from the Septuagint, the Greek translation of the Hebrew Bible)

8. ἐν τῷδε ἐγνώκαμεν ἀγάπην θεοῦ, ὅτι κεῖνος θάνεν εἵνεκα ἡμέων. καὶ ἡμέας ἄρα χρὴ θανεῖν εἵνεκα ἡμετέρων κασιγνητῶν.   (St. John)

Ἀβραὰμ	[indecl.] Abraham, the first patriarch of the Hebrews [here = gen., "of Abraham"]
ἀπο-στέλλω	pf. ἀπέσταλκα I despatch (on some service)
εἴρω, ερῶ	I announce
εὕρηκα	pf. of εὑρίσκω
ζόφος, -ου	[m.] darkness, gloom
Ἰακώβ	[indecl.] Jacob, son of Isaac and father of the founders of the 12 tribes of Israel [here = gen., "of Jacob"]
Ἰσαὰκ	[indecl.] Isaac, son of Abraham and father of Jacob [here = gen., "of Isaac"]
Ἰσραήλ	[indecl.] Israel [here= gen. "of Israel"]
κύριος, -ου	[m.] lord [Κύριος ὁ θεός = the Lord God]
Μωυσῆς, -οῦ	[m.] acc. Μωυσῆν Moses, an Israelite leader
πάλιν	[adv.] back, again, here= also
πατήρ, πατέρος	[m.] father
πέποιθα	pf. of πείθω [with pres. mid. force] = I trust
πεπίστευχα	pf. of πιστεύω
τέθνηκα	pf. of θνήσκω [with present force]= I am dead
ὑμᾶς	= contraction of ὑμέας
ὑμῶν	= contraction of ὑμέων

327. WRITE IN GREEK

1. You (sg.) left some food there, no doubt, that my companions might find it and eat, if they should happen to come. (For "find it and," use aor. ptc. alone]

2. Don't stand (pl.) in the light, but hide yourselves among the trees until he passes. [Make all vb. forms aor.]

3. The shepherd replied to our questioning that some of the sheep went into the river and perished, others died along the road, and only two still remained in the fold. ["to our questioning" = "to us asking."]

328. WORD STUDY

AGAPE (the early Christian name for the Mass or Communion-assemblies, as 'feast of divine love'); — MISOGYNIST ('woman-hater'); — EUREKA! (an exclamation of joyous discovery, 'I have it!').

Lesson 46

The Perfect Subjunctive, Optative, Imperative, Infinitive, Participle Active

329. ENDINGS

The endings of the perfect subjunctive, optative and imperative active are the same as those of the present system. Thus:

	PF. SUBJ. ACT.		PF. OPT. ACT.	
	Sg.	*Pl.*	*Sg.*	*Pl.*
1st pers.	λελύκω	λελύκωμεν	λελύκοιμι	λελύκοιμεν
2nd pers.	λελύκῃς	λελύκητε	λελύκοις	λελύκοιτε
3rd pers.	λελύκῃ	λελύκωσι	λελύκοι	λελύκοιεν

	PF. IMPT. ACT.	
2nd pers.	λέλυκε	λελύκετε

PF. INF. ACT.

-εναι, or -εμεν(αι)   λελυκέναι or λελυκέμεν(αι)

PF. PTC. ACT. *(m. f. n. nom.)*

-ως, -υια, -ος   λελυκώς, λελυκυῖα, λελυκός

330. NOTES

1. The perfect indicative expresses completed action in the present time. Thus λέλυκα means *I have just loosed.*

2. Remember that the perfect, outside the indicative (or the infinitive or participle in indirect discourse) does not signify past time, but state of the action as one completed with finality. For examples, review Section 84.

3. The genitive singular of the masculine and neuter perfect participle of λύω is λελυκότος. They belong to the third declension, while the feminine is declined like γαῖα. See Lesson 29 for the full declension.

331. MEMORIZE

μέσ(σ)ος, -η, -ον	middle (of), midst (of) [followed by noun in same case]
οἶκος, -ου	[m.] house, home
πάλιν	[adv.] back (again); again
σφέτερος, -η, -ον	their(s)

332. TRANSLATE

1. κασιγνητούς μευ πρὸς οἶκον ἐκ πολεμοῖο εἰληλουθότας χαίρων δεξάμην.

2. μείνατε ἀπάνευθε πυρός, ὄφρα μὴ ἀπολώλητε.

3. φίλον ἐξ ἄλγεος λελυκέμεν ἢ σώματος ἢ ψυχῆς, καλὸν πέλει.

4. βέβηκε· ἢν γὰρ πάλιν σε ἴδω ἐγγὺς οἴκου ἐμοῦ, βαλέω σε εἰς ποταμόν.

333. PUT INTO GREEK

1. He said the woman had come from the middle of the house, carrying food and water.

2. He said death is for the good a gate into life and happiness.

3. Two shepherds seem to be coming, no doubt that they may release (pf.) their sheep from under the tree.

4. The king's brother died fighting so that the king himself might not perish.

334. TRANSLATE AT SIGHT

ἔφη Ἰησοῦς· "ἐγώ εἰμι ἀνάστασις καὶ ζωή· ὅς τις πιστεύῃ εἰς ἐμέ, κἂν θάνῃ, ζώσεται, καὶ πᾶς ζώων ἠδὲ πιστεύων εἰς ἐμὲ οὔ ποτε θανέεται αἰεί. πιστεύεις τόδε;" λέγει οἱ Μάρθα· "ἐγὼ πεπίστευκα ὅτι σὺ εἰς Χριστός, υἱὸς θεοῦ, εἰς τόνδε κόσμον εἰληλουθώς." (St. John)

ἀνάστασις, -ιος	[f.] resurrection
Ἰησοῦς, -οῦ	Jesus
κἂν	crasis (contraction) for καὶ ἐάν even if, although
Μάρθα	Martha [sister of Lazarus, whom Jesus raises from the dead according to John 11.1-44]

335. READINGS

1. τίς ἄνθρωπος ἐξ ὑμέων ἔχων ἑκατὸν μῆλα καὶ ἀπ-ολέσας ἓν ἐξ σφεων οὐ λείπει ἄλλα πάντα καὶ ἔρχεται ἐπὶ τόδε ἓν ἀπ-ολωλός, ὄφρα ἑ εὕρῃ; καὶ εὑρὼν φέρει χαίρων εἰς οἶκον καὶ κελεύει φίλους ἐοὺς ἠδὲ πλησίους ἐλθεῖν, λέγων σφιν· "χαίρετε σύν μοι, ὅτι εὖρον μῆλόν μευ ἀπ-ολωλός." (St. Luke)

2. γιγνώσκω δὲ τόδε, ὅτι εἰ πάντες ἄνθρωποι σφέτερα κακὰ εἰς μέσον συν-ενείκειαν, βουλόμενοι ἀμείβεσθαι πλησίοισι—ὁράοντες κακὰ πλησίων, ἀσπασίως ἂν ἕκαστοι ἀπο-φεροίατο πάλιν τὰ εἰς-ενηνόχεσαν. (Herodotus)

3. φιλέωμεν ἀλλήλους, ἐπεὶ ἀγάπη ἐκ θεοῦ ἐστιν, καὶ πᾶς ὅς τις φιλέῃ, ἐκ θεοῦ γέγαε καὶ γιγνώσκει θεόν. ὃς δὲ μὴ φιλέῃ, οὐκ ἔγνωκε θεόν· ὅτι θεὸς ἀγάπη ἐστίν. (St. John)

ἀπο-φέρω, ἀπο-οίσω, ἀπο-ένεικα, ἀπο-ενήνοχα	I carry off
ἀσπασίως	[adv.] gladly
εἰσ-φέρω, εἰσ-οίσω, εἰσ-ένεικα, εἰσ-ενήνοχα	I bring in, I bring along

ἑκατόν   [indecl.] a hundred
συν-φέρω, συν-οίσω, συν-ένεικα, συν-ενήνοχα   I bring together

336. WRITE IN GREEK

1. Have you (pl.) ever seen so brave a man? He was like to a rock in the midst of
    the sea being struck again and again by wind and rain. Any other would have
    fled, but he dared to remain and fight.

2. I seek to find the truth, which is sometimes sweet, sometimes difficult— but is
    always good for me.

337. WORD STUDY

MESOPOTAMIA ('the country between the rivers', i.e., between the Tigris and
Euphrates— ancient Assyria and Babylonia); — ECONOMY (-νομίη from νέμω I
manage; 'household management', as in 'domestic economy'; a plan by which something is
managed or run; also, a frugal avoidance of waste, as 'he shows great economy of effort'),
ECONOMICS (the science of household management, or of business and finance on the
broad plane), ECONOMICAL (sparing, well-budgeted or managed, cheap); —
PALINDROME (δρόμος a running; a word or saying in which the letters 'run back
again', i.e., spell the same whether read forward or backward— e.g., the words on a sacred
fountain in the courtyard of Hagia Sophia cathedral in Constantinople: νιψον
ανομηματα μη μοναν οψιν 'Wash your sins, not only your face', or Napoleon's reply
when asked if he could invade England: 'Able I was I ere I saw Elba').

Lesson 47

The Perfect And Pluperfect Indicative, Middle and Passive

338. ENDINGS

PF. M.-P. IND.

	Sg.	*Pl.*	*Sg.*	*Pl.*
1st pers.	-μαι	-μεθα	λέλυμαι	λελύμεθα
2nd pers.	-σαι	-σθε	λέλυσαι	λέλυσθε
3rd pers.	-ται	-αται/-νται	λέλυται	λελύαται/λέλυνται

PLPF. M.-P. IND.

	Sg.	*Pl.*	*Sg.*	*Pl.*
1st pers.	-μην	-μεθα	λελύμην	λελύμεθα
2nd pers.	-σο	-σθε	λέλυσο	λέλυσθε
3rd pers.	-το	-ατο/-ντο	λέλυτο	λελύατο/λέλυντο

Note:

A verb's perfect middle-passive stem can be found by removing -μαι from its fifth principal part. For example, the fifth principle part of γιγνώσκω is ἔγνωσμαι. Thus the verb's perfect middle-passive stem is ἔγνωσ-.

339. CONSONANT CHANGES (For reference; no need to memorize)

a. The perfect middle-passive stem of some verbs ends in a consonant. When the endings are added, certain euphonic changes sometimes take place, to make the combination of sounds easier to pronounce and more pleasing.

b. There are three types of consonant stems, as they appear in the fifth principal part:

(1). ending in -μ, which stands for π, β, or φ.

(2). ending in -γ, which stands for κ, γ, or χ.

(3). ending in -σ which stands for τ, δ, or θ.

c. Rules for changes before consonants of other endings:

1. μ + -σ = ψ	1. γ + -σ = ξ	1. σ + -σ = σ
2. μ + -τ = πτ	2. γ + -τ = κτ	2. σ + -τ = στ
3. μ + -σθ = φθ	3. γ + -σθ = χθ	3. σ + -σθ = σθ
4. μ + -ντ = φατ	4. γ + -ντ = χατ	4. σ + -ντ = θατ

d. **Drill:** What, then, are the perfect middle-passive forms built on λέλειμμαι (from λείπω), τέτυγμαι (from τεύχω), πέπυσμαι (from πεύθομαι) ?

340. MEMORIZE

κεῖμαι	[pf. mid. system] I have been placed, I lie (down)
κρύπτω, κρύψω, κρύψα	I conceal
τότε	[adv.] then

341. TRANSLATE

1. οἶκον παρὰ θαλάσσῃ τετύγμεθα.
2. παῖς ἐπὶ γαίῃ κεῖτο παρ-ερχομένους ἐθέλων λαθέμεν.
3. εὖ δὴ κρύπτεται θησαυρός· οὔ ποτε γὰρ ἑώραται ὑπὸ οὐδενός.
4. μῆλα λέλυτο ποιμήν, ὄφρα παρὰ ποταμὸν φοιτάοιεν.
5. τοῖο πυθόμεθα ἔργα, οὐδεὶς δὲ τότε βούλετό μιν ἐλέειν.
6. τί τέτυχθε πυλὴν οὕτως ὑψηλήν;
7. κεῖσό που ὑπὸ δενδρέῳ, ὄφρα πονέοντο ἕτεροι.
8. ἀπὸ ἀρχῆς ἐγνώσμεθα ὑπὸ ἄνακτος.
9. οὔ πω τέτυκτο οἶκος, ὅτε ὄμβρος ἑ ἀπ-όλεσσεν.
10. "τί τῇδε κεῖσθε," εἶπεν, "οὐδὲ σὺν ἡμῖν ἔρχεσθε;"

342. PUT INTO GREEK

1. Two of my companions have released themselves and are now fleeing.
2. "You (pl.) have been seen!" he said. "Hide quickly!"
3. The woman lay beside the river, looking into the flowing water.
4. The house had been well built, yet it was not beautiful.
5. If it did not seem right to have this, we would not have requested it.
6. Why do you (sg.) lie so near the fire?
7. They had been seen, but no one pursued them.
8. Where have you (sg.) built yourself your house?
9. The man who struck my brother with the rock has never been known.
10. After the storm, many large trees lay on the ground.

343. READINGS

1. ὁ θεὸς τῶν Ἑβραίων προσκέκληται ἡμᾶς. πορευσώμεθα οὖν ὁδὸν τριῶν ἡμερῶν εἰς τὴν ἔρημον, ἵνα θύσωμεν τῷ θεῷ ἡμῶν.
   (The words the Lord instructs Moses to say to the Pharaoh, Exodus III 18, from the Septuagint, the Greek translation of the Hebrew Bible)

2. Χριστῷ συν-εσταύρωμαι.   (St. Paul, referring to the Christian 'death' to things merely of this world)

3. ζωὴ ὑμέων κέκρυπται σὺν Χριστῷ ἐν θεῷ· ὅτε ἂν δὲ Χριστός, ζωὴ ἡμέων, φαίνηται, τότε καὶ ὑμεῖς σὺν οἱ φανέεσθε ἐν δόξῃ.   (St. Paul)

4. πολλὰ πιὼν καὶ πολλὰ φαγὼν καὶ πολλὰ κακὰ εἰπὼν περὶ ἀνθρώπων κεῖμαι Τιμοκρέων Ῥόδιος.   (A mock epitaph by Simonides

for his rival Timocreon, a poet and champion athlete from Rhodes, of somewhat scandalous habits. He was still alive, and wrote a reply to this, to the effect that reports of his demise were somewhat exaggerated— as Simonides would find out if he came around!)

5. εἶπεν Ἰησοῦς Πιλάτῳ· "εἰμὶ δὴ βασιλεύς· ἐγὼ εἰς τόδε γεγένημαι καὶ εἰς τόδε εἰλήλουθα εἰς κόσμον, ἵνα μαρτυρήσω ἀληθείῃ. πᾶς ὃς ᾖ ἐξ ἀληθείης ἀκούει φωνῆς μευ. βασιλείη δὲ ἐμὴ οὔκ ἔστιν ἐκ κόσμου τοῦδε." (St. John)

ἀκούω	[+ gen.] I hear, I listen to
βασιλεύς, -ῆος	[m.] king
γεγένημαι	pf. mid. of γίγνομαι I am born [= γέγαα]
Ἑβραῖος, -ου	[m.] a Hebrew
ἔρημος, -ου	[f.] wilderness, desert
ἡμᾶς	contraction of ἡμέας
ἡμῶν	contraction of ἡμέων
θύω, θύσω, θῦσα	I sacrifice
ὁδὸν τριῶν ἡμερῶν	"a journey of three days" [cognate acc. with πορευσώμεθα— on which see Section 602—and. gen. of extent]
Πιλᾶτος, -ου	Pontius Pilate [1st century A.D. Roman procurator of Judaea, who condemned Jesus to be crucified]
πορεύομαι, πορεύσομαι, πορευσάμην	I travel
προσκέκληται	pf. mid. of προσκαλέομαι I call (to myself)
Ῥόδιος, -η, -ον	of Rhodes
συν-εσταύρωμαι	pf. mid. of συ-σταυρόω I crucify along with
τριῶν ἡμερῶν	see ὁδὸν τριῶν ἡμερῶν above

344. WRITE IN GREEK

1. Be gone (pl.)! For if you come again and try to take anything, I shall seize you and bring you to the king.

2. I had never seen them, but when they had come into the house I quickly knew them to be my brother's sons, and received them rejoicing. ["when they had come" is simply the perfect participle, agreeing in case with the following "them"]

345. WORD STUDY

CRYPTIC ('concealed, secret', as a 'cryptic message'), CRYPT (a concealed chamber or vault, as a basement chapel under a church, or a hidden cemetery vault), GROTTO (from Italian mispronunciation of κρυπτή, a crypt or small cave-like opening in a hillside), GROTESQUE ('like a grotto', i.e., strangely-formed, odd, fantastic); — BASIL ('kingly'), BASILICA (a 'royal' building of special design— oblong, with naves and rows of pillars— used in Greece and Rome as courts of justice, later turned into cathedral churches; a modern cathedral built on the same plan), BASILISK ('little king', a lizard with a crest or crown of scales on the head; a mythological dragon-like beast of the desert said to be able to kill a man by its mere look or fiery breath); — MARTYR ('a witness' to a hated cause), MARTYRDOM ('witness unto death'), MARTYROLOGY (a list or historical account of a series of martyrs).

Lesson 48

The Perfect Imperative, Infinitive, Participle Middle and Passive. Review of All Perfects

346. ENDINGS

PF. IMPT. M.-P.

	Sg.	Pl.	Sg.	Pl.
2nd pers.	-σο	-σθε	λέλυσο	λέλυσθε

PF. INF. M.-P.

-σθαι	λελύσθαι

PF. PTC. M.-P. (m. f. n. nom.)

-μενος, -η, -ον	λελυμένος, λελυμένη, λελυμένον

> *Note:*
>
> a. The same euphonic changes take place as in the indicative.
>
> b. The middle-passive participle declines like καλός, -ή, -ον. See Section 189, under Type A.
>
> c. See Appendix A for complete list of perfect system endings, active and middle-passive, for review.

347. MEMORIZE

ἀμφί	[adv.; prep. + dat. or acc.] on both sides, around, concerning
κτείνω, κτενέω, κτεῖνα or κτάνον	I kill
μήτηρ, μητέρος or μητρός	[f.] mother
πατήρ, πατέρος or πατρός	[m.] father

348. TRANSLATE

1. οὐ γνῶ ἄναξ ἑωραμένους ἡμέας ἠδὲ διωκομένους.
2. ἀμφὶ οἴκῳ κεῖσθε, ὄφρα μή τις λάθῃ ὑμέας εἰσ-ερχόμενος.
3. εὑρεῖν σφεας πειράομεν, οἱ δὲ βεβήκεσαν.
4. πάντες ἐμοὶ υἱέες ἐν τῷδε αὐτῷ οἴκῳ γεγάασιν.
5. δίκη τε καὶ ἀγάπη καὶ εἰρήνη μετὰ πᾶσιν εἰληλούθοιεν ἀνθρώποισιν.
6. καρποὶ πολλοὶ ἐκ δενδρέων λελυμένοι εἰς γαῖαν πίπτον.
7. μάλα που δείσατε, μή πως βεβήκοιμεν.

8. οὐδὲν οὕτως γλυκύ ποτε ἐγνώκαμεν ὡς μητέρων ἡμέων ἀγάπην.

9. ἄνδρα τινὰ κτείνας, εἰς ἑτέρην βέβηκε πατρίδα.

10. μάλα δὴ πατρὶ ἐμῷ ἐῴκει σευ κασιγνητός.

349. PUT INTO GREEK

1. Lying afar under a tree, we saw him concealing the gold.

2. He said the road had been built from the river to the sea.

3. She has never seen her father, who is still away fighting in the war.

4. Lie (sg.) near the temple until they pass; then flee!

5. My mother had gone home, but my brother and I remained with our friends.

6. Since they have come as companions, we ought to receive them.

7. It is easy to seek happiness, but difficult to find it and to hold it.

8. We suffered, in order that you (pl.) might not perish (utterly).

9. Having released the king, they led him into their own country.

10. We shall not kill you (pl.), because you have come as true friends of my father.

350. READINGS

1. χρὴ τλῆναι ἄνδρα χαλεποῖσιν ἐν ἄλγεσι κείμενον, πρός τε θεῶν ἀθανάτων αἰτέειν ἔκ-λυσιν.   (Theognis)

2. θεὸν οὐδείς πώ ποτε ἑώρακεν. ἢν δὲ φιλέωμεν ἀλλήλους, θεὸς ἐν ἡμῖν μένει, καὶ ἀγάπη θεοῦ ἐν ἡμῖν τετελεσμένη ἐστίν. θεὸς ἀγάπη ἐστίν, καὶ ὅς τις μένῃ ἐν ἀγάπῃ, ἐν θεῷ μένει, καὶ θεὸς μένει ἐν οἷ.   (St. John)

3. φάος εἰλήλουθεν εἰς κόσμον, ἀλλὰ φίλησαν ἄνθρωποι μᾶλλον ζόφον, ἢ φάος· ἔργα γάρ σφεων ἦν πονηρά. πᾶς γὰρ πονηρὰ ἔρδων μισέει φάος καὶ οὐκ ἔρχεται πρὸς φάος, ἵνα μὴ κρίνηται ἑὰ ἔργα· ὃς δὲ ἀληθείην ποιέῃ, ἔρχεται πρὸς φάος, ἵνα φαίνηται ἑὰ ἔργα, ὅτι ἐν θεῷ πεποίηνται.   (St. John, developing the idea of Christ as Light of the world)

ἔκ-λυσις, -ιος	[f.] release, relief
ζόφος, -ου	[m.] darkness
μᾶλλον	[adv.] rather, more
πεποίηνται	Attic Greek for πεποίηαται 3rd pers. pl. pf. m.-p. of ποιέω
τετέλεσμαι	pf. m.-p. of τελέω

351. WRITE IN GREEK

1. He who lives in the truth is like to a man who has built (mid.) his house upon a rock. For even if the waters loosed (pf.) from heaven and the storms and winds should strike it, it will not fall; for it has been well built, upon a rock.

2. I had never known you (sg.) or whence you had come.

352. WORD STUDY

AMPHIBIOUS ('living on both sides', i.e., on land or water; used loosely, as 'an amphibious attack'), AMPHIBIAN (e.g., an airplane, operating from both land and water), AMPHITHEATER (an elliptical structure with a 'theater [seeing-place] all around' i.e., at both ends of the oval); — METROPOLIS (πόλις city; 'mother-city', capital of a district or a large city surrounded by suburbs), METROPOLITAN (pertaining to a large city; an archbishop with special dignity and authority over neighboring dioceses); — PATRIARCH (ἄρχω I rule; the 'ruling father' of a tribe or large social family-group [πατριά]; head of a family; hence, a venerable man of authority; a Bishop of the highest rank, ruling great churches like Jerusalem, Constantinople, etc.), PATRISTIC (of the 'Fathers of the Church', the great teachers of the first five centuries).

Lesson 49

The Comparison of Adjectives

353. RULES

Greek adjectives have three **degrees**: positive (e.g., "fine"); comparative (e.g., "finer" or "rather fine"); and superlative (e.g., "finest" or "very fine"). This Section and Section 354 will explain how to form the comparative and superlative degrees. Section 355 will cover their declension.

a. To most second/first declension adjectives, remove the ending -ος from the masculine singular nominative to find the stem; add to this stem:

-ότερος, -οτέρη, -ότερον (comparative) and

-ότατος, -οτάτη, -ότατον (superlative)

if the last syllable of stem is **long** (including syllables long 'by position', i.e., ending in two consonants). Thus:

POSITIVE: δίκαιος, -η, -ον ("just")
COMPARATIVE: δικαι-ότερος, δικαι-οτέρη, δικαι-ότερον ("more just")
SUPERLATIVE: δικαι-ότατος, δικαι-οτάτη, δικαι-ότατον ("most just")

if the last syllable of the stem is **short** add to it:

-ώτερος, -ωτέρη, -ώτερον (comparative) and

-ώτατος, -ωτάτη, -ώτατον (superlative) if the last syllable of the stem is *short*

POSITIVE: χαλεπός, -ή, -όν ("difficult")
COMPARATIVE: χαλεπ-ώτερος, χαλεπ-ωτέρη, χαλεπ-ώτερον ("more difficult")
SUPERLATIVE: χαλεπ-ώτατος, χαλεπ-ωτάτη, χαλεπ-ώτατον ("most difficult")

b. To third declension adjectives in -ης, -ες and to third/ first declension adjectives in -ύς, -εῖα, -ύ, add to the neuter nominative singular (which is identical with the stem) the same suffixes as in (a) above:

POSITIVE: ἀληθής, -ές ("true")
COMPARATIVE: ἀληθέσ-τερος, ἀληθεσ-τέρη, ἀληθέσ-τερον ("truer")
SUPERLATIVE: ἀληθέσ-τατος, ἀληθεσ-τάτη, ἀληθέσ-τατον ("truest")

c. To third declension adjectives in -ων, -ον, add the suffixes -έστερος, -εστέρη, -έστερον (comparative) and -έστατος, -εστάτη, -έστατον (superlative) to the stem, which is found by removing the -ος from the genitive singular:

> POSITIVE: ἄφρων, -ον ("senseless")
> COMPARATIVE: ἀφρον-έστερος, ἀφρον-εστέρη, ἀφρον-έστερον ("more senseless")
> SUPERLATIVE: ἀφρον-έστατος, ἀφρον-εστέρη, ἀφρον-έστατον ("most senseless")

d. To a select group of second/first declension adjectives and third/first declension adjectives, the suffixes -ίων, -ιον (comparative) and -ιστος, -ίστη, -ιστον (superlative) are added to stems that are slightly different from the stem of the positive degree. The comparative and superlative degrees of these adjectives must be learned individually.

> POSITIVE: αἰσχρός, -ή, -όν ("shameful")
> COMPARATIVE: αἰσχ-ίων, αἴσχ-ιον ("more shameful")
> SUPERLATIVE: αἴσχ-ιστος, αἰσχ-ίστη, αἴσχ-ιστον ("most shameful")

> POSITIVE: ἡδύς, ἡδεῖα, ἡδύ ("sweet")
> COMPARATIVE: ἡδ-ίων, ἥδιον ("sweeter")
> SUPERLATIVE: ἥδ-ιστος, ἡδ-ίστη, ἥδ-ιστον ("sweetest")

354. IRREGULAR COMPARISON

As in English, there are Greek adjectives whose comparative and superlative degrees are **irregular**, i.e., based on stems radically altered or entirely different from their positive degree. (Cf. "good", "better" and "best.") The suffixes for such irregular comparatives and superlatives are -ίων, -ιον (or -ων, -ον) (comparative) and -ιστος, -ίστη, -ιστον (superlative), as in (d) above. There is one exception listed below, φίλος, which follows more closely the pattern in (a) above.

The following adjectives introduced in this course have irregular comparison:

> POSITIVE: ἀγαθός, -ή, -όν ("good")
> COMPARATIVE: ἀρείων, ἄρειον or ἀμείνων, ἄμεινον ("better")
> SUPERLATIVE: ἄριστος, -η, -ον ("best")

> POSITIVE: πολλός, -ή, -όν ("many")
> COMPARATIVE: πλείων, πλεῖον ("more")
> SUPERLATIVE: πλεῖστος, -η, -ον ("most")

> POSITIVE: καλός, -ή, -όν ("beautiful")
> COMPARATIVE: καλλίων, κάλλιον ("more beautiful")
> SUPERLATIVE: κάλλιστος, -η, -ον ("most beautiful")

> POSITIVE: μέγας, μεγάλη, μέγα ("big")
> COMPARATIVE: μείζων, μεῖζον ("bigger")
> SUPERLATIVE: μέγιστος, -η, -ον ("biggest")

> POSITIVE: ταχύς, -εῖα, -ύ ("swift")
> COMPARATIVE: θάσσων, θᾶσσον ("swifter")
> SUPERLATIVE: τάχιστος, -η, -ον ("swiftest")

POSITIVE: φίλος, -η, -ον ("dear")

COMPARATIVE: φίλτερος, -η, -ον ("dearer")

SUPERLATIVE: φίλτατος, -η, -ον ("dearest")

355. DECLENSION

Comparatives and superlatives ending in -ος, -η, -ον are declined like καλός, -ή, -όν and comparatives in -ων, -ον like πρόφρων, πρόφρον in Lesson 29.

356. MEMORIZE

ἄφρων, -ον	senseless
δεύτερος, -η, -ον	second
Ζεύς, Διός or Ζηνός	Zeus [father and chief of the gods]
ταχύς, -εῖα, -ύ	swift

357. TRANSLATE

1. ἀληθέστατα δὴ εἶπες.
2. εἰ πλείονες ἦμεν, οὐκ ἂν μαχέσαντο ἀλλὰ φύγον.
3. ἀνθρώπων ἁπάντων πονηρότατοι ἦσαν κεῖνοι.
4. μείζονος δόλου οὐδείς ποτε πέλετο.
5. κάλλιστον ἠδὲ μέγιστον ἔμμεν σφέτερον ὀΐονται οἶκον.
6. πλείονα ἄγει μῆλα ὅδε ποιμὴν ἢ κεῖνος.
7. πασάων γυναικῶν ἀρίστη καὶ καλλίστη καί μοι φιλτάτη μήτηρ πέλετο ἐμή.
8. θάσσων μέν ἐστι κεῖνος ποταμός, πλεῖον δὲ ὕδωρ ἔχει ὅδε.
9. Δία πατέρα ἠδὲ μέγιστον θεῶν εἶναι ὀΐοντό ποτε πολλοί.
10. δευτέρῳ πυρὶ ἀπ-όλετο χρήματα ἡμέτερα πάντα.
11. πατὴρ ἐμός ἴδε ἔργα αἰσχίονα ἢ πάντα ἅ ποτε ἑωράκη ἐγώ.
12. παῖδες αἰεὶ ἐθέλουσι φαγεῖν καρποὺς ἡδίστους.

358. PUT INTO GREEK

1. You (pl.) were hoping, no doubt, to receive more gifts than you did receive.
2. That was the loftiest tree of all that I have ever seen.
3. It is better to be noble than to seem to be noble.
4. He gave most gold to the first and swiftest— myself.
5. The road was longer than you (sg.) would believe.
6. They stood on the very topmost rock, trying to see the sea.
7. He was the bravest man whom I ever knew.
8. It is necessary to build true peace now, if we do not wish to fall into a second and greater war.

9. I love my father as the noblest man whom I have ever known.

10. Endure patiently (sg.)! Others held up under even more, and more difficult, woes.

359. READINGS

1. σοφὸς Σοφοκλῆς, σοφώτερος δὲ Εὐριπίδης, ἀνδρῶν δὲ πάντων
    Σωκράτης σοφώτατος.   (An ancient oracle)

2. οὐ γὰρ δοκέειν ἄριστος, ἀλλὰ εἶναι ἐθέλει.   (Aeschylus)

3. ἐκ μελέτης πλείονες ἢ ἐκ φύσιος ἀγαθοί.   (Critias)

4. αὐτὰρ δεύτεραί πως φροντίδες σοφώτεραι.   (Euripides)

5. νικάειν γὰρ τινά ἑ αὐτὸν πασάων νικάων ἐστὶ πρώτη τε καὶ
    ἀρίστη. (Plato)

6. πάντων κτημάτων ἄριστόν ἐστι φίλος ἀγαθός.   (Xenophon)

7. χαλεπόν ἐστι μὴ φιλῆσαι, χαλεπὸν δὲ καὶ φιλῆσαι, χαλεπώτατον δὲ
    πάντων ἀπο-τυγχάνειν φιλέοντα.   (Anacreontic)

8. ἄριστον μὲν ὕδωρ... (Pindar; Horace disagrees: *"Nulla placere diu nec*
    vivere carmina possunt quae scribuntur aquae potoribus." No poems are able to be
    pleasing nor to survive for long which are written by drinkers of water.)

ἀπο-τυγχάνω	I am unsuccessful
Εὐριπίδης	Euripides [the tragic poet]
κτῆμα, -ατος	[n.] possession
μελέτη, -ης	[f.] careful practice, training
νικάω	I conquer
νίκη, -ης	[f.] victory, conquest
Σοφοκλῆς	Sophocles [the tragic poet]
Σωκράτης	Socrates [the philosopher]
φροντίς, -ίδος	[f.] thought

360. WRITE IN GREEK

1. Have you (sg.) ever known anyone (pl.) so swift to accept pains for the sake
    of others?

2. One temple had been built near the sea to Zeus, a second to Apollo among
    the trees.

3. Our fathers were brave and just, and they left for us a noble country in which we
    now live happily (= happy).

361. WORD STUDY

DEUTERONOMY (νόμος law; 'the second Law', the fifth book of the Old
Testament, containing the second statement or account of the Law of Moses
regulating the life of the Jews); — ARISTOCRACY (κρατέω I rule; 'rule of the
best', i.e., government controlled by a group of nobles or wealthy and prominent
citizens), ARISTOCRAT (a member of the ruling aristocracy; a person of self-
important and refined bearing or attitude); — CALLISTUS, CALLISTA (proper
names); — NICOLAS, NICHOLAS ('victory' + 'the people'), NICODEMUS
(δῆμος people; 'victory' + 'the people').

Lesson 50

The Formation And Comparison of Adverbs

362. FORMATION OF ADVERBS

a. Adverbs are commonly formed from the corresponding adjectives, by adding -ως to the neuter stem. Thus, καλ-ῶς ("beautifully"), ταχέ-ως ("swiftly")

b. Often the neuter accusative, singular or plural, is used as an adverb. E.g., πρῶτον or πρῶτα ("at first"), ἡδύ ("sweetly"), τί ("why?") (cp. Section 213 b, c).

c. We have already learned and used many adverbs not based on adjectives, such as ὅτε ("when") and νῦν ("now"). Such adverbs rarely form comparatives or superlatives.

d. Most prepositions can be used without governing any noun, pronoun, or adjective, thus functioning as adverbs, with the same general meaning as in their prepositional uses. E.g., ἀπό ῥα ἔλθον. ("They therefore went **away**.") ἐγγὺς στῆ. ("He stood **near**.")

363. COMPARISON OF ADVERBS

The neuter accusative *singular* of the comparative adjective is used as the comparative of the adverb; the neuter accusative *plural* of the superlative adjective functions as the superlative form of the adverb. Thus, the comparison of adverbs relies on rule (b) in Section 362 above.

> ἀπό ῥα ἔλθον θᾶσσον. (*They therefore went away more swiftly.*)
>
> ἀπό ῥα ἔλθον τάχιστα. (*They therefore went away most swiftly.*)

364. MEMORIZE

δέκατος, -η, -ον	tenth
μέγας, μεγάλη, μέγα	[m. acc. sg. μέγαν, n. acc. sg. μέγα, rest of m. and n. is 2nd declension, on stem μεγαλ-] great, large, big
νύξ, νυκτός	[f.] night
οἰκέω, οἰκήσω, οἴκησα	I dwell, I inhabit

365. TRANSLATE

1. σοφῶς γε εἶπες, πατὴρ δὲ καὶ σοφώτερον.
2. λίθον μέγαν μακρότατά πως βάλεν.
3. ἔρχευ σύν μοι· ἄλλως γὰρ οὐδὲ βήσομαι αὐτός.
4. οἶκον μὲν ἴδομεν, εἰς δὲ οὐκ ἔλθομεν.
5. εἰ δικαίως μετὰ ἀλλήλοις οἰκέοιεν ἄνθρωποι, εἰρήνην που ἔχοιεν ἄν.

6. ἐπεὶ ἄναξ οὕτως ἐστὶν ἀγαθός, τί οὔ μιν πλεῖον φιλέετε;

7. πάντες μεγάλως χαίρομεν ὅτε σε μάθομεν ἐλεύσεσθαι.

8. τῇδε διὰ νυκτὸς δεκάτης ἀπάσης μείναντες, αἶψα ἅμα ἤματι φαινομένῳ φύγον.

9. καλῶς δὴ ποιήσατε, μητέρα ἐμὴν ἐκ θανατοῖο αἰσχίστου σῴζοντες.

10. ὕδωρ τάχιστα ἐνείκατε, ὄφρα μὴ πάντα πυρὶ ἀπ-ολώλῃ.

366. PUT INTO GREEK

1. We saw a great light falling swiftly through the sky.

2. 1 would have labored more if I had had more time.

3. Whoever comes first will receive the biggest gift.

4. The water fell most swiftly the second night.

5. Lie (sg.) afar, and conceal yourself well.

6. Great winds kept violently (μεγαλ-) striking the house.

7. You (sg.) sleep the most of all boys whom I have ever known!

8. At first we dwelt away from the sea, but now quite near.

9. Whenever rain falls, the rivers flow more swiftly.

10. You have all come most swiftly, and I am greatly pleased.

367. READINGS

1. δοκέει δέ μοι χαλεπώτερον εἶναι εὑρεῖν ἄνδρα καλῶς ἀγαθὰ φέροντα ἢ κακά.   (Xenophon)

2. οὔ τοι ἀπὸ ἀρχῆς πάντα θεοὶ θνητοῖσι φαίνουσι, ἀλλὰ χρόνῳ ζητέοντες εὑρίσκομεν ἄρειον.   (Xenophanes)

3. ἐξ ἔργων δὲ ἄνδρες γίγνονται πλούσιοι, καὶ πονεόμενοι πολλὸν φίλτεροι ἀθανάτοισιν.   (Hesiod)

4. ἀείρεταί τις ὑψηλότερον, ἵνα θᾶσσον πέσῃ.   (Menander)

5. ὡς κακῶς πέλεται πᾶς ἰητρὸς εἴ κε κακῶς μηδεὶς πέλῃ.   (Menander)

6. οὐ ζώειν μέγα τί ἐστίν, ἀλλὰ εὖ ζώειν.   (Plato)

πλούσιος, -η, -ον   rich, wealthy

368. WRITE IN GREEK

1. The man who saved my father when he fell into the sea was the bravest and noblest man whom I have ever known. ["when he fell" = aor. ptc.]

2. I would choose to suffer evil, but not to do evil; for it is nobler.

3. My brother hopes to build a bigger and more beautiful house and dwell in it with his wife and children until he dies.

369. WORD STUDY

DECADE (a period of ten years); — MEGAPHONE (a device for concentrating sound waves to produce a 'great voice'), MEGALOMANIA (μανίη madness; a form of insanity in which a person thinks he is someone great or famous; a tendency to exaggerate one's importance or greatness), MEGALOMANIAC; — ECUMENICAL (pertaining to the whole 'inhabited earth' [οἰκουμένη contracted form of οἰκεομένη], hence worldwide, universal, as an 'ecumenical Council' of Bishops from all countries of the globe), DIOCESE (a region 'inhabited throughout' by members of the Church, a Bishop's territory of government), DIOCESAN (belonging to a diocese).

Lesson 51

The Aorist Indicative and Subjunctive Passive

370. ENDINGS

Aorist passive forms are very similar to those of the 3rd aorist active (see Appendix A). Remember that there is no distinction of first, second, and third aorist in the passive, but only one system. The aorist passive system is built on the stem of the sixth principal part. The aorist passive of our paradigm verb λύω in the indicative 1st person singular λύθην translates as "I was loosed." (Refer to Sections 83c and 84a on the meanings of the tenses and the voices.)

AOR. PASS. IND.

	Sg.	*Pl.*	*Sg.*	*Pl.*
1st pers.	-ην	-ημεν	λύθην	λύθημεν
2nd pers.	-ης	-ητε	λύθης	λύθητε
3rd pers.	-η	-ησαν	λύθη	λύθησαν

AOR. PASS. SUBJ.

	Sg.	*Pl.*	*Sg.*	*Pl.*
1st pers.	-ω	-ωμεν	λυθῶ	λυθῶμεν
2nd pers.	-ῃς	-ητε	λυθῇς	λυθῆτε
3rd pers.	-ῃ	-ωσι(ν)	λυθῇ	λυθῶσι(ν)

371. MEMORIZE

ἄζομαι	[pres. syst. only] I respect, I revere; I hesitate to or shrink from [+ inf.]
μέλος, μέλεος	[n.] member (of the body), limb
χείρ, χε(ι)ρός	[f.] hand

372. TRANSLATE

1. πονέονται ἰητροὶ πολλοί, ἵνα ἐξ ἄλγεος τοῦδε μεγάλου λυθῇς.
2. ὤφθημεν ἠδὲ διωκόμεθα, αὐτάρ σφεας λάθομεν.
3. χρόνος πέλεται βροτοῖσι ἰητρὸς πάντων κακῶν καὶ ἀλγέων.
4. κρύψασθε ταχέως, ὄφρα μὴ γνωσθῆτε παρ-εόντες.
5. πλεῖστά τοι χάρη πατὴρ υἱέα πάλιν ἐκ πολεμοῖο δεξάμενος.
6. δείδω μὴ ὑπὸ πλείονος ὄμβρου λυθῶσιν κεῖνοι λίθοι ἠδὲ πίπτωσιν.
7. εἰ ἐν οἴκῳ μεῖνας, ὡς σε κέλευσα, οὔ κεν ὤφθης.
8. ἄνακτα λαθέμεν πειραόμην, τάχιστα δὲ γνώσθην.

9. τοῖο χεῖρες μὲν ἐξ ὕδατος φάνησαν, ἕτερα δὲ μέλεα κεύθετο πάντα.

10. ἀγαθὸς πέλευ, ἵνα ὅτε ἄν σε ἴδῃ, χάρῃ σευ μήτηρ.

11. ὅς τις μὴ ἄζηται ἀδικέειν, πονηρός ἐστιν.

373. PUT INTO GREEK

1. The water was released and fell into the sea.

2. Say (sg.) what you saw, in order that the whole truth may appear.

3. Seeing him, we rejoiced and seized his hand.

4. My companions were seen, but not I.

5. I was about to eat when you (pl.) appeared afar off on the road.

6. Raise (pl.) the tree, that we may be released and go.

7. Let us hide the food, lest it be seen.

8. We shall remain in the house until you (pl.) appear at the gate.

374. READINGS

1. μὴ κρίνετε, ἵνα μὴ κριθῆτε.   (St. Matthew)

2. ὡς σῶμα ἐστὶν ἕν καὶ μέλεα πολλὰ ἔχει, πάντα δὲ μέλεα σώματος,
    πολλὰ ἐόντα, ἐστὶν ἕν σῶμα, οὕτως καὶ Χριστός. ὑμεῖς γὰρ ἐστε
    σῶμα Χριστοῦ. καὶ γὰρ ἐν ἑνὶ πνεύματι ἡμεῖς πάντες εἰς ἕν σῶμα
    βαπτίσθημεν. καὶ δὴ σῶμα οὐκ ἔστιν ἕν μέλος, ἀλλὰ πολλὰ μέλεα·
    ἢν εἴπῃ πούς· "ὅτι οὐκ εἰμὶ χείρ, οὐκ εἰμὶ ἐκ σώματος," οὐ διὰ τόδε
    οὐκ ἔστιν ἐκ σώματος. νῦν δὲ πολλὰ μὲν μέλεα, ἕν δὲ σῶμα. καὶ εἰ
    πάσχει ἕν μέλος, συμ-πάσχει πάντα μέλεα· εἰ δὲ δόξαν δέχεται ἕν
    μέλος, χαίρει σὺν οἱ πάντα μέλεα.   (St. Paul)

3. ζητέω γὰρ ἀληθείην, τῇ οὐδείς πώ ποτε βλάβη.   (Marcus Aurelius)

βαπτίζω, aor. pass. βαπτίσθην	I baptize
βλάπτω, aor. pass. βλάβην	I harm, I injure
κρίθην	aor. pass. of κρίνω
πνεῦμα, -ατος	[n.] spirit; breath
πούς, ποδός	[m.] foot
συμ-πάσχω	I suffer along with

375. WRITE IN GREEK

1. We ought to respect our father and mother more than anyone else, because they
    love us most and labor long for our sake.

2. If one wishes to be (fut.) king to others, he should first learn to be led by justice
    and truth.

376. WORD STUDY

CHIROPRACTOR (πράκτωρ worker; a doctor who 'works with his hands' to cure ailments by massaging and manipulating the muscles and spinal column), SURGEON (by false pronunciation of χειρουργός 'hand-worker' [cp. ἔργον], a doctor who operates to cure bodily defects or injuries), SURGERY, SURGICAL; — BAPTIZE, BAPTISM, BAPTIST; —PNEUMATIC ('operating by breath or air'), PNEUMONIA (πνεύμων breather, lung; disease of the lungs); — TRIPOD (τρι- three, a 'three-legged' stand), PEW (πόδιον little foot, foot-stool, taken over into French as *peu*, and thence into English as name for church seat); — SYMPATHY ('suffering or feeling along with'), SYMPATHETIC, SYMPATHIZE— ANTIPODES (people on the other side of the world, with their 'feet opposite' ours) — PODIATRIST (a doctor who cures feet).

Lesson 52

The Aorist Optative, Imperative, Infinitive, Participle Passive.
The Optative of εἰμί

377. ENDINGS

AOR. PASS. OPT.

	Sg.	*Pl.*	*Sg.*	*Pl.*
1st pers.	-ειην	-ειμεν	λυθείην	λυθεῖμεν
2nd pers.	-ειης	-ειτε	λυθείης	λυθεῖτε
3rd pers.	-ειη	-ειεν	λυθείη	λυθεῖεν

AOR. PASS. IMPT.

	Sg.	*Pl.*	*Sg.*	*Pl.*
2nd pers.	-ηθι, -ητι	-ητε	λύθητι	λύθητε

> *Note:*
> -ηθι is changed to -ητι when the aorist passive stem ends in a rough
> consonant — φ, θ, or χ— as in the case of λύω [aorist passive stem λυθ-]
> and many other verbs.

AOR. PASS. INF.

-η(με)ναι   λυθῆναι, λυθήμεναι

AOR. PASS. PTC. (m. f. n. nom.)

-εις, -εισα, -εν   λυθείς, λυθεῖσα, λυθέν

> *Note:* For the declension of the aorist passive participle, see Section 189.

378. PRESENT OPTATIVE OF εἰμί

	Sg.	*Pl.*
1st pers.	εἴην	εἶμεν
2nd pers.	εἴης	εἶτε
3rd pers.	εἴη	εἶεν

379. MEMORIZE

ἀνα-βαίνω, ἀνα-βήσομαι, ἀνά-βην	I go up, I ascend
κέρδιον	[comp. adv.] more beneficial, better
λιλαίομαι	[pres. syst. only] I long (to do something) [+ inf.]

380. TRANSLATE

1. εἴ ποτε λίθος κεῖνος λυθείη καὶ πέσοι, κτείνειέ κε πολλούς.
2. μὴ γνωσθέντος οὐδεμία ποτὲ ἀγάπη.
3. εἶπον φάος τι ἀπάνευθε ἐν θαλάσσῃ φανῆναι.
4. κέρδιόν πού κεν εἴη ἡμῖν κακὰ μὴ πάσχειν· νῦν δὲ τλάωμεν ὡς ἄνδρες.
5. χάρητε, ὅτι ἐγγύτερον νῦν εἰμὲν οἴκῳ ἡμετέρῳ καὶ φίλοις.
6. εἰς ἄκρην πέτρην ἀνά-βησαν, ἵνα ὑπὸ πάντων ὀφθεῖεν.
7. λυθήμεναι λιλαίεται μῆλα, οὐ δὲ ἐάσει ποιμήν.
8. εἰπεῖν ἀζόμην, ὄφρα μὴ νήπιος φανείην ἔμμεν.
9. κασιγνητός μευ σοφώτερός σευ ἐστίν, ἀλλὰ οὐ γιγνώσκει πάντα.
10. εἴ κε σὺ τάδε ὀφθείης ἔρδων, καὶ ἕτεροί που καλὰ εἶναι ὀΐοίατο, ἠδὲ ἔρδοιεν αὐτοί.
11. ὄμβρῳ αἶψα λυθέντι πολλὰ ἀπ-ολλύετο.
12. ἡμέας λυθέντας ὅδε ἴδε καὶ δίωξεν.
13. ὀφθεῖσαι σπεύδομεν ἀπό, ἵνα μὴ καὶ γνωσθῶμεν.

381. PUT INTO GREEK

1. It would seem better to remain in the house until he comes.
2. The children, having been seen, fled.
3. It is not lawful to reveal everything (pl.) known about the king.
4. If you (pl.) should be seen, quickly go up into a tree and hide.
5. Her soul longs to be released from the evils of this world and to find (mid.) peace.
6. I brought you (sg.) these gifts, that you might rejoice.
7. They said the stranger's great cunning was known from the beginning.
8. Never appear (sg.) again in this country, or we shall kill you!
9. It is difficult to conceal from others a plan known to many.
10. If he should die, who would then be king?

382. READINGS

1. ἐρωτηθεὶς Ἀριστοτέλης "τί ἐστι φίλος;" ἔφη· "μία ψυχὴ ἐν δύω σώμασιν οἰκέουσα."   (Diogenes Laertius)
2. ἀληθείη παρ-είη σοὶ καὶ ἐμοί, πάντων χρῆμα κάλλιστον.   (Mimnermus)
3. ὡς ἡδύ ἐστι σωθέντα μεμνῆσθαι πόνου.   (Euripides)
4. ἄνθρωπον κτείνας τις ὑπὸ κείνου φίλων διώκετο. τῷ δὲ κατὰ Νεῖλον ποταμὸν βαίνοντι λύκος προσ-έρχεται. φοβηθεὶς οὖν ἀνά-βη ἐπὶ δένδρεον παρὰ ποταμὸν καὶ τῇ κρύπτετο. οὕτως δὲ κείμενος ἑρπετὸν ἴδε προσ-ερχόμενον. εἰς ποταμὸν ἄρα βάλεν ἓ αὐτόν. ἐν τῷ δὲ δεξάμενός μιν φάγε κροκόδειλος.   (Aesop)

5. ἐμοὶ γὰρ ζώειν, Χριστός ἐστι, καὶ θνήσκειν κέρδιον. λιλαίομαι δὲ λυθῆναι καὶ σὺν Χριστῷ εἶναι.   (St. Paul; ζώειν and θνήσκειν here are both nouns and subjects of ἐστι.)

Ἀριστοτέλης	Aristotle [the philosopher]
ἑρπετός, -οῦ	[m.] creeping thing, snake
ἐρωτάω, aor. pass. ἐρωτήθην	I ask
κροκόδειλος, -ου	[m.] crocodile
λύκος, -ου	[m.] wolf
μιμνήσκω, pf. mid. μέμνημαι	I recall the memory of
Νεῖλος, -ου	[m.] Nile
προσ-έρχομαι	I come near (to)
σώθην	aor. pass. of σώζω
φοβέω, aor. pass. φοβήθην	I frighten

383. WRITE IN GREEK

1. If you (sg.) are known to be a friend of the king, you will no doubt receive greater glory from the people.

2. All men ought greatly to revere children, for the happiness of a more beautiful world lies in their hearts and hands.

3. When the sun appears and all my companions are seen, he will quickly flee.

384. WORD STUDY

ARISTOTELIAN (pertaining to the philosophy or followers of Aristotle); — CROCODILE — MNEMONIC (from the root -μνη-; helping remember, as a 'mnemonic rule', e.g., ἀτάραε to tell which third declension nouns are neuter); — PHOBIA (a permanent dominating fear of something, e.g., a phobia of crossing bridges), ACROPHOBIA (excessive 'fear of height'), XENOPHOBIA (a strong 'dislike of strangers'), CLAUSTROPHOBIA (Latin *claustrum*, enclosure; a morbid 'fear of being confined' in small or tight places), HYDROPHOBIA (a disease, rabies, due to the bite of a mad animal, resulting in a 'fear of water', among other symptoms), ANGLOPHOBE, GERMANOPHOBE, etc. (a person with a violent dislike of the British, Germans, etc.).

Lesson 53

Review of The Entire Verb

385. SOME CHARACTERISTICS OF THE VERB

From your knowledge of the entire verb conjugation, and by aid of Appendix A, you can now recognize more clearly certain characteristics of the Greek verb that will help you in remembering the forms. Note in particular that:

a. In the middle, the perfect and pluperfect occur the basic middle endings (primary and secondary) alone, without the joining vowel found in the other systems.

b. In both active and middle, the joining (or "thematic") vowel of the present, future and second aorist endings is o before μ or ν and in the optative, elsewhere ε; the first aorist has α, except in the subjunctive and in four forms of the optative and imperative.

c. Subjunctive endings are alike in all systems, with the thematic vowel lengthened.

d. σ between two vowels drops out. But compare the 2 sg. ind. or impt. of the perfect m.-p., where the σ is retained (λέλυσο, for example), with that of the other middle and m.-p. systems (e.g., λύεο).

e. The optative always has an iota diphthong.

f. The future and second aorist have present system endings.

g. The aorist passive endings closely parallel those of the third aorist active.

h. Special endings occasionally occur: subj. act. 3 sg. -ῃσι for -ῃ , 2 sg. ῃσθα for -ῃς; ind. or opt. mid. 3 pl. -νται, -ντο for -αται, -ατο; mid. subj. 2 sg. -ῃ for -ηαι; mid. 1 pl. -μεσθα for -μεθα.

386. IDENTIFY AND TRANSLATE

Give tense, voice, mood, number; where applicable, give also gender and case.

1. γιγνώσκοιμι
2. ἔρχεσθαι
3. ἢν ἴδωσι
4. ἂν βαίης
5. φάνηθι
6. μαχεομένους
7. μὴ λάβοιτο
8. γνωσθῆναι
9. κρύψαντος
10. μὴ εὖδε
11. πέμψειας
12. δίωκες
13. ποιῆσαι
14. ἐνίσπετε
15. λυθείη
16. δεξαίμεθα
17. κέλευσον
18. λαθέμεν

19. γεγάασι
20. ἔλθοιεν
21. πονήσασθαι
22. τλῆμεν
23. ἵνα αἰτήσαιμεν
24. εἰσ-έρχεσθε
25. βεβηκέμεναι
26. ὄφρα σώσειε
27. λελύσθαι
28. ἵνα εὔχηται
29. μὴ φύγοιτε

30. ἐλευσομένης
31. εἰ ὄϊοιντο
32. ῥέξαν
33. ὄφρα γνώῃς
34. κύθοιο
35. ζητησάσῃ
36. λιπεῖν
37. αἱρέοι
38. τέτυκτο
39. κεν σταίη
40. λυθεισάων

387. MEMORIZE

ἀλέομαι, — , ἀλεάμην or ἀλευάμην	I avoid, I shrink before
θύρη, -ης	[f.] door
κράτος, κρατεος	[n.] strength, power
νηῦς, νηός or νεός, dat. pl. also νηυσί	[f.] ship
οὖλος, -η, -ον	whole, entire

388. READINGS

1. φιλόσοφός τις ἐρωτηθεὶς "τί φιλόσοφοι μὲν ἐπὶ θύρας πλουσίων
   ἔρχονται, πλούσιοι δὲ οὔ ποτε ἐπὶ θύρας φιλοσόφων;" ἔφη· "ὅτι οἱ
   μὲν γιγνώσκουσιν τὰ ὧν δέονται, οἱ δὲ οὐ γιγνώσκουσιν."
   (Diogenes Laertius)

2. ἁλιεύς ποτε ὀλίγον ἰχθὺν λάβεν. ἰχθὺς δέ οἱ ἔφη· "ἰδέ, μάλα ὀλίγος
   εἰμί. νῦν οὖν λῦσόν με, μείζονα δὲ γενόμενον τότε δή με ζήτεε. τὸ
   γάρ σοι ποιέοντι πολλὸν κέρδιον ἔσσεται." ἁλιεύς δὲ ἀμείψατο·
   "ἀλλὰ ἐγὼ δὴ νηπιώτατος ἂν εἴην, εἰ παρ-εὸν ἀγαθὸν μὴ λαβὼν
   ἄδηλον ἐλπίδα διώκοιμι." (Aesop)

3. θεὸς δὴ πάντων μέτρον ἡμῖν εἴη.   (Plato)

ἄδηλος, -ον	uncertain, obscure
ἁλιεύς, -ῆος	[m.] fisherman
δέομαι	I am in need of [+ gen.]
ἐλπίς, ἐλπίδος	[f.] hope
ἐρωτάω, aor. pass, ἐρωτήθην	I ask
ἰχθύς, -ύος	[m.] fish
πλούσιος, -η, -ον	rich, wealthy
φιλόσοφος, -ου	[m.] philosopher

389. WRITE IN GREEK

1. A great fire quickly destroyed the entire ship, but some of the men, fleeing through a small door, threw themselves into the sea and were saved (σωθ-).

2. It would be most base and shameful to avoid pain but not evil deeds.

3. They hid the ships where they would not be seen, because no longer having strength or plan they feared to fight.

390. WORD STUDY

THYROID (a 'door-shaped' gland in the larynx, affecting some of the processes of growth); — the suffix -CRAT (κρατ-) in ARISTOCRAT, PLUTOCRAT, BUREAUCRAT, DEMOCRAT, etc. (= "power or rule of the best, the rich," etc.).

Lesson 54

Use of The Augment. Further Review of The Verb

391. THE AUGMENT

This is a special sign, used by Homer sometimes and by later Greek writers regularly, to point out more sharply the *past* tenses of the *indicative*. Therefore, in reading Homer you will often find the imperfect, aorist, and pluperfect indicative with the augment. The augment ('increase') has two forms, the syllabic and the temporal:

a. **Syllabic.** Stems beginning with a consonant: prefix ἐ, thus adding a syllable. For example:

unaugmented:	*augmented:*
λύον	ἔλυον
λυσάμην	ἐλυσάμην
λελύκετε	ἐλελύκατε

Note:
> initial ρ often doubles after an augment (e.g., ῥέε becomes ἔρρεε).

b. **Temporal.** Stems beginning with a short vowel or diphthong which is not the reduplication: lengthen the initial vowel, thus increasing the *time* required to pronounce the first syllable. When the first vowel of an iota-diphthong is lengthened, iota is subscribed. Here are some forms of the verbs ἄγω, οἰκέω and ἱκάνω:

unaugmented:	*augmented:*	*unaugmented:*	*augmented:*
ἄγοντο	ἤγοντο	οἴκεες	ᾤκεες
ἄγαγον	ἤγαγον	οἴκησα	ᾤκησα
ἄχθην	ἤχθην (aor. pass.)	οἰκήκεμεν	ᾠκήκεμεν (plpf.)

ἵκανε	ἵκανε (spelling is unchanged, but iota is now long)

Note:
> ε is usually lengthened to η; but it becomes ει in a few words, of which you have met or will meet the following: ἔχω, ἐάω, ἕπομαι (I follow), ἕλκω (I drag), ἕρπω or ἑρπύζω (I creep). Note also two 2 aorists: εἶδον (unaugmented ἴδον) and εἷλον (unaugmented ἕλον from αἱρέω).

c. Stems beginning with a long vowel or with a vowel reduplication (recall Section 321) need no augment:

ἡδόμην

ἔγνωσμαι (pf. m.-p.. of γιγνώσκω)

ἔγνωστο (plpf. m.-p. of γιγνώσκω)

392. DRILL

Give the augmented form of the following; then identify by tense, voice, mood, person, and number:

1. λάβεν
2. γνώσθητε
3. οἰκήσαμεν
4. ἔγνωσο
5. ἕλκομεν
6. βεβήκεα
7. φάνησαν
8. αἵρεον
9. ἔχετε
10. λέλυσο

11. ὄφθη
12. ἵκανε
13. ἄγαγες
14. τέτυκτο
15. λάθομεν
16. μαχέσσατο
17. ἔθελον
18. ἑπόμην
19. κέλευσας
20. ἀπ-όλετο

393. TRANSLATE

1. εἰς νῆα ἀν-έβησαν καὶ εἷλον ἄνακτα.
2. ὅτε ἐφάνη ἠέλιος, ὤφθημεν· ἐξ οὖν ἤλθομεν ἠδὲ ἐμαχόμεθα.
3. μάλα δὴ ἤθελόν μιν ἰδέειν, ὁ δὲ ἐβεβήκει.
4. τί ἑταίρους ἐμοὺς ἀπ-ώλεσας;
5. διὰ νυκτὸς ἁπάσης ἔκειντο παρὰ ποταμῷ, ἵνα νέας σευ λάβοιεν παρ-ερχομένας.
6. δύω παῖδες λίθους εἰς ὕδωρ ἔβαλλον.

394. PUT INTO GREEK (using augment wherever allowed)

1. They requested us to come quickly and save them.
2. He kept avoiding (= impf.) us, that we might not ask what evil he had done. (pf. = πεποίηκα; use plpf.)
3. They dwelt in a big house away from the road.
4. We found her roaming back and forth among the children.
5. Why did you (pl.) not allow them to say anything?
6. You (sg.) rejoiced, I suppose, (on) learning he still knows you and your friends.

395. VOCABULARY REVIEW

As the teacher directs.

396. READINGS

1. Σωκράτης εὔχετο πρὸς θεοὺς οὐ χρυσὸν παρ-έχειν οἱ οὐδὲ ἄργυρον, ἀλλὰ μοῦνον εὔχετο ἀγαθὰ παρ-έχειν, ἐπεὶ ἐνόησε θεοὺς ἄριστα γνῶναι ἃ τινά τῳ ἐστιν ἀγαθά. (Xenophon; the τῳ is from τις. See Section 212.)
2. φιλέωμεν θεόν, ἐπεὶ αὐτὸς πρῶτος ἐφίλησεν ἡμέας. (St. John)

3. ἢν καλὸν ἔχῃ τις σῶμα καὶ ψυχὴν κακήν, καλὴν ἔχει νῆα καὶ
   κυβερνητῆρα κακόν.   (Menander)

4. καὶ εἶδεν Γολιὰδ τὸν Δαυεὶδ καὶ ἠτίμασεν αὐτόν, ὅτι αὐτὸς ἦν
   παιδάριον καὶ αὐτὸς πυρράκης μετὰ κάλλεος ὀφθαλμῶν.   (i Kings
   XVII 42, from the Septuagint, the Greek translation of the Hebrew Bible)

5. ἐν ἀρχῇ ἦν Λόγος, καὶ Λόγος ἦν σὺν θεῷ, καὶ ἦν Λόγος θεός. ἐν
   αὐτῷ ζωὴ ἦν, καὶ ζωὴ ἦν φάος ἀνθρώπων—φάος ἀληθές, ὅ
   φωτίζει πάντα ἄνθρωπον. καὶ Λόγος σάρξ ἐγένετο καὶ ᾤκησεν
   μετὰ ἡμῖν (καὶ τοῦ δόξαν εἴδομεν), πλήρης χάριτος καὶ
   ἀληθείης.   (St. John)

ἄργυρος, -ου	[m.] silver
ἀτιμάζω, ἀτιμάσω, ἀτίμασα	I esteem lightly
αὐτός	here = he (i.e., David)
Γολιὰδ	[m. indecl.] Goliath, a Philistine giant whom David will kill [also spelled Γολιάθ]
Δαυείδ	[m. indecl.] David, a future king of Israel and Judah, here still a youth
κάλλος, κάλλεος	[n.] beauty
κυβερνητήρ, -ῆρος	[m.] steersman, pilot
Λόγος, -ου	[m.] the Word, i.e., the Son of God as perfect expression of the Father.
μετά	[prep. + gen.] with
ὅτι	[conj.] because
παιδάριον, -ου	[n.] boy, youth
πλήρης, -ες	full of
πυρράκης, -ες	ruddy
φωτίζω	I enlighten

397. WRITE IN GREEK

1. If you (sg.) threw fire into this ship, you would destroy both it and the others, and perhaps save all your companions from death.

2. Whoever finds a worthy friend finds love and strength and the noblest happiness.

3. I hope they will come quickly, for little time yet remains.

398. WORD STUDY

ARGYROL (trade name for a brown oily silver-protein compound used as an antiseptic); — GOVERN ('to steer the ship of state', to control and guide-the English word coming from Greek by way of the Latin imitation *guberno*), GOVERNOR, GOVERNMENT; GUBERNATORIAL (pertaining to a governor or 'steersman of the state'; cp. Latin *gubernator*, e.g., 'a gubernatorial election').

Lesson 55

**Rules of Vowel-Contraction.
Further Review of The Verb**

399. CONTRACTION OF VOWELS

When a word's stem ends in a vowel, Homer occasionally (later Greek regularly) contracts or fuses this stem-vowel and the vowel of the ending into a single long vowel or diphthong. Such contractions follow these simple rules:

1. α + ε - sound = long α (if iota occurs, it is subscribed). Thus, αε = α (long), αει = ᾳ (long)   (E.g., ὁράεσθαι = ὁρᾶσθαι, ὁράεις = ὁρᾷς).

2. α + ο - sound = ω. Thus, αο, αω, αου = ω   (E.g., ὁράομεν = ὁρῶμεν, ὁράω = ὁρῶ, ὁράουσα = ὁρῶσα).

3. ε + ε or ει = ει. Thus, εε, εει = ει   (E.g., ἐφίλεε = ἐφίλει, φιλέεις = φιλεῖς).

4. ε + ο or ου = ευ or ου . Thus, εο, εου = ευ or ου   (E.g., ἐφίλεον = ἐφίλευν or ἐφίλουν, φιλέουσα = φιλεῦσα or φιλοῦσα).

5. ο + ε or ο = ου. Thus, οε, οο = ου   (E.g., γουνόεσθαι = γουνοῦσθαι, γουνόομαι = γουνοῦμαι [I supplicate]).

400. DRILL

a.   Give the contracted form of the following:

1.	ἐάουσι	6.	δοκέεις
2.	αἱρέετε	7.	γουνοόμην
3.	πειράεις	8.	ὁράεσθαι
4.	βαλέεται	9.	ζητέειν
5.	ἐφοίταον		

b.   What would be the uncontracted form of these words?

1.	ἁλεῖσθε	6.	κτενεῖς
2.	γαμεῦσι	7.	ἀδικεῖ
3.	εἴων	8.	ὁρῶσι
4.	γουνοῦται	9.	φρονεῖτε
5.	φοιτῶντες		

401. TRANSLATE

1.   ᾤκει ξεῖνος ἐν οἴκῳ μεγάλῳ παρὰ θαλάσσῃ.

2.   εἴων μιν ἐλθεῖν, ἐβούλετο γάρ.

3.   πρῶτον μὲν ἥμαρτες· τί δὲ οὐ πάλιν πειρᾷς, ὄφρα ποτὲ ὀρθῶς
     ἀμείψηαι;

4.   ὄλβον ποθεῦντες θεὸν ποθεῦσιν· ὁ γὰρ ἀληθὴς ἀνθρώπων ὄλβος.

5.   τί ποιεῖς; ἔρχευ πρός με, ἵνα ὁρῶ αὐτός.

6.   ἐφοίτα παρὰ ὁδὸν διὰ ἤματος παντός.

402. PUT INTO GREEK (using contracted forms where allowed)

1.   I kept avoiding them, fearing either to fight or flee.

2.   Bring (sg.) us the fruit, in order that we may see it.

3.   Then will peace appear upon the earth, when all men do what is right and just.

4.   He tries to seem wise, but nobody believes him.

5.   We left her roaming back and forth beside the ships, seeking her two sons.

6.   The rain was swiftly flowing down from the higher rocks.

403. VOCABULARY REVIEW

As the teacher directs.

404. READINGS

1.   φαίνεταί μοι κεῖνος ἴσος θεοῖσιν
     ἔμμεναι ἀνὴρ ὃς ἐναντίος τοι
     ἱζάνει καὶ πλησίον ἡδὺ φωνεύσης ὑπ-ακούει.   (Sappho, to a young bride)

2.   οὕτως γὰρ ἄριστα φανεῖ Χριστὸς ἐὸν κράτος, ὅτε ἂν μῆλα λύκων
     περι-γένηται, καὶ ἐν μέσῳ λύκων ἐόντα καὶ πολλὰς λαμβάνοντα
     ὠτειλάς, μὴ μοῦνον μὴ ἀπ-όληται ἀλλὰ καὶ κείνους ἀγάγῃ εἰς
     ἀρείονα βίον.   (St. Chrysostom, commenting on Christ's words to the Apostles,
     "Behold, I send you as sheep among wolves.")

3.   κόσμος παρ-έρχεται· ὅς τις δὲ ποιῇ ἃ θεὸς ἐθέλει μένει εἰς αἰεί.
     (St. John)

4.   ἔφη Ἰησοῦς· "Τόδε ἐστὶν ὃ θεὸς ἐθέλει — πάντα ἄνθρωπον ὃς ὁρᾷ
     υἱὸν θεοῦ καὶ πιστεύῃ αὐτῷ, ἔχειν ζωὴν ἀθανάτην· καὶ ἐγερῶ μιν ἐν
     ἐσχάτῳ ἤματι.   (St. John)

5.   ὁμοίῳ δὴ ὅμοιον αἰεὶ φίλον ἐστίν. ἀνὴρ οὖν ἀγαθός τε καὶ δίκαιος
     ἔσεται θεῷ φίλος. ὅμοιος γάρ.   (Plato)

ἐγείρω, ἐγερέω, ἔγειρα	I rouse from sleep (i.e., from death)
ἐναντίος, -η, -ον	next to
ἔσχατος, -η, -ον	last
ἱζάνω	I sit
ἴσος, -η, -ον	equal to
λύκος, -ου	[m.] wolf
περι-γίγνομαι	I get the better of, I overcome
ὑπ-ακούω	I listen to [+ gen.]
φωνέω	I speak [cp. φωνή]
ὠτειλή, -ῆς	[f.] wound

405. WRITE IN GREEK (using augmented forms)

1. We went up and stood on the very rock where the temple of Apollo had been built, some stones of which still lay upon the ground.

2. If he had not died young, he no doubt would have been a noble and strong king and had much wealth.

406. WORD STUDY

ISOMERES (μέρος part; in chemistry, compounds having the same or equal parts— i.e., basic elements— but different properties and characteristics).

Lesson 56

The Iterative Forms of the Verb.
The Position of Prepositions

407. ITERATIVE VERB-FORMS

Twenty-four times in your reading of Homer in this course you will find him using special verb-forms to emphasize customary or repeated action. These **iterative** forms are simply an expanded form of the imperfect or aorist, made by inserting -(ε)σκ- or -(α)σκ- between the regular stem of the imperfect or aorist indicative, active or middle, and the regular imperfect or second aorist endings (even with first aorist stems). -ασκ- is used mostly with first aorist or α- stems. Iterative forms practically never take the augment. Thus:

ἔχω	imperfect: ἔχον	iterative: ἔχεσκον
καλέω	imperfect: κάλεον	iterative: καλέεσκον
φεύγω	2 aorist: φύγον	iterative: φύγεσκον
ὠθέω	1 aorist: ὦσα	iterative: ὤσασκον

408. POSITION OF PREPOSITIONS

a.   The ordinary position for a preposition is immediately before its noun or pronoun or their modifier, if this precedes. Thus: πρός με, σὺν πολλοῖς ἑταίροις.

b.   Sometimes, for poetic purposes, Homer places a preposition *after* its object (e.g., χειρὸς ἄπο). In such cases, as this example shows, the pitch-mark on the preposition shifts back from the last to the first syllable (κατά becoming κάτα, etc.); this is called **anastrophe**. Sometimes, Homer places a preposition *between* a modifier and its noun or pronoun, e.g., πολλοῖς σὺν ἑταίροις. If you are on the alert for this arrangement and consider the phrase as a whole, it will cause no difficulty.

c.   A preposition may be prefixed directly to a verb, thus forming a compound verb, whose meaning is generally obvious as a combination of the meaning of the verb and preposition alone. E.g., εἰσ-έρχομαι *I go in, I enter,* πάρ-ειμι *I am alongside, I am present.* In such compounds, the preposition really functions as an adverb, since it directly modifies the verb. If the compound governs an object, this is in the same case that the preposition would take if alone, e.g., νηὸς ἐπι-βαίνομεν (= ἐπὶ νηὸς βαίνομεν). Note that prepositional prefixes drop their final vowel if the verb begins with a vowel or has the augment, e.g., πάρ-ειμι (παρά + εἰμί), ἐπ-έβη (ἐπί + ἔβη). For more on this, see the section on **elision** in Lesson 58.

d. When the preposition is used strictly as a detached adverb (recall Section 362), other words may come between it and the word with which it goes in sense, e.g., ἀμφί ῥα πάντες ἔστησαν. (*Everybody, therefore, stood around.*) Such constructions are often the equivalent of a compound verb (ἀμφ-έστησαν), between whose parts certain closely connected words have been slipped in.

409. TRANSLATE

1. πέτρῃ ἔπι ὑψηλῇ κείμενοι νέας ἴδεσκον παρ-ερχομένας.
2. δενδρέων ἄπο ἔπεσον καρποὶ λυθέντες.
3. θύρης δι-ῆλθεν λίθος, καὶ ἔτι μέσσῳ ἐν οἴκῳ κεῖται.
4. ἑταίρων ἑκάστους προσ-ειληλουθότας ὑπό τι δένδρεον κρύπτασκε.
5. φάεα παντοῖα ἀπάνευθε ἐν οὐρανῷ φάνεσκε.
6. μήτηρ παῖδας οὐκ ἔασκε λιλαιομένους περ ὕδωρ εἰσ-βῆναι.
7. οὔ σοι εἰπέσκομεν κακόν μιν ἔμμεν;
8. τί φύγεσκες, οὐ δὲ μείνας ἐμάχεο;

410. PUT INTO GREEK

1. Go down (sg.) into the ship and find me some food.
2. Socrates repeatedly said the same (thing): "Always live justly."
3. All of them perished in the middle of the sea.
4. Why did you (pl.) (repeatedly) not allow us to speak?
5. Stand around (pl.) the house, so that no one may go out.
6. The women, fearing, kept holding each other by the hand(s).
7. We kept taking gold out of the river and bringing it to my father.
8. He always did the most difficult things himself.

411. VOCABULARY REVIEW

As the teacher directs.

412. READINGS

1. αὐτὰρ Ἀχιλλεὺς νηυσὶ παρ-ήμενος ταχείῃς, μήνιεν, οὔτε ποτὲ μετὰ ἑταίρους πωλέσκετο οὔτε ποτὲ εἰς πόλεμον, ἀλλὰ ἀπάνευθε ἔμενε, πόλεμον δὲ ποθέεσκε. (Homer)
2. μή ποτε εἰπὲ ἔπος μέγα· γιγνώσκει γὰρ οὐδεὶς ἀνθρώπων ὅ τι νὺξ καὶ ἦμαρ ἀνδρὶ τελεῖ. (Theognis; μέγα here is idiomatic, = "proud, boastful"; cp. our similar idiom, to "talk big")
3. ὀλίγοισι πόνοις μεγάλα τινὰ πῶς ἄν τις ἕλοι; (Euripides)
4. φιλήσεις θεόν σευ ἐν οὔλῳ κῆρί σευ καὶ ἐν οὔλῃ ψυχῇ σευ καὶ ἐν οὔλῳ νόῳ σευ· ἥδε ἐστὶ μεγάλη καὶ πρώτη ἐντολή. δευτέρη δὲ ὁμοίη ἐστίν· φιλήσεις πλησίον σευ ὡς σὲ αὐτόν. (St. Matthew)
5. Διός τοι νόος μέγας βίοιο ἀνδρῶν οἳ φίλων κυβερνητήρ ἐστιν. (Pindar)

Ἀχιλλεύς, -ῆος	Achilles, central figure of the Iliad, who withdraws his forces from the coalition against Troy after an argument with Agamemnon
κυβερνητήρ, -ῆρος	[m.] pilot
μηνίω	I rage, I am furious
πάρ-ημαι	I sit alongside
πωλέομαι	I go

413. WRITE IN GREEK (use contracted forms)

1. If one has a beautiful body but a wicked soul, his (= to him) is a good ship but a bad pilot. (cp. Sections 18.c and 412.5)

2. Do not allow (pl.) your country to perish; fight! try at least to save it, in peace as also in war.

3. Do you (sg.) see them toiling around the ship? They are trying to complete the work this very night.

414. WORD STUDY

MANIA (fury, insanity; a strong desire or 'craze' for, e.g., 'he has a mania for flying'), MANIAC (a mentally deranged person subject to fits of fury and madness), CLEPTOMANIAC (κλέπτω I steal; a crazed thief, one with a furious and insatiable desire for stealing).

Lesson 57

The Vocative Case of All Declensions. Review of Nouns and Adjectives

415. THE VOCATIVE CASE: MEANING AND RULES FOR FORMATION

a.   The vocative case is the case of direct address. In other words, the person or thing designated by the noun in the vocative case is being spoken to. In the following sentences, the italicized noun(s) would be put into the vocative case in Greek:

> *Hugh*, it is time you started paying attention.

> That is the way the world works, *my dears*.

> O *Summertime*, how I miss you and look forward to your return!

As you would expect, quite often the vocative case occurs with a verb in the imperative mood, and with 2nd person verbs in any mood:

> Stop your squirming, *Tucker*!

> You are capable, *Thomas*, of cleaning the cage yourself.

b.   The vocative is usually spelled the same as the nominative; it is always the same in the plural and in all neuters.

c.   The vocative singular differs from the nominative in the following instances:

   (1).   Second declension masculine -ος takes vocative in ε (e.g., φίλε, ἀγαθέ).

   (2).   Third declension in -ευς and -ις drop the ς (e.g., Ζεῦ, Ὀδυσσεῦ, πόλι *city*).

   (3).   A long vowel in the nominative of the third declension is shortened in the vocative unless it stays long in the genitive and therefore in all other cases (e.g., πάτερ, Ἀγαμέμνον, but κῆρ, Ἀπόλλων).

d.   Irregular vocatives: the vocatives of θεός and γυνή are θεός and γῦναι.

Notes:

1.   The interjection ὦ (English O! in direct address) is not *needed* before the vocative, but it is often used, especially if the vocative is spelled the same as the nominative (e.g., ὦ ἑταῖροι).

2.   Greek seldom expresses by a separate word the "my" before a vocative which is very common in English, but the "my" should often be added when translating a Greek vocative into English, if the context calls for it (e.g., σπεύδετε, φίλοι = "Hurry, my friends!").

416. REVIEW OF NOUNS AND ADJECTIVES

Recall forms, distinctions, and gender-rules of the three declensions by the aid of Lessons 9, 11, 13, 30.

417. VOCABULARY REVIEW

As the teacher directs.

418. TRANSLATE

1. νέα λάβετε, ἑταῖροι, καί σφεας διώκετε.

2. μισεῦμέν σε, κακέ, ὅτι φύγες οὐδὲ εἵνεκα πατρίδος ἐμαχέσαο.

3. δίκαιος ἡμῖν εἴης, ὦ ἄναξ.

4. δόξα σοι εἴη, ἀγαθέ, ἠδὲ ἀγάπη παρὰ ἀνθρώπων ἁπάντων.

5. τί ἔχεις, ὦ παί, σῇ ἐν χειρί;

6. θεὸν οὔ ποτέ τι λήσετε, νήπιοι· κακὰ ἄρα μὴ ῥέζετε.

7. μή με βάλλε, πάτερ, πονηρά περ ἔρξαντα.

8. μὴ ὀίεο, κῆρ, πάντα τοι γενήσεσθαι τὰ ποθέεις.

9. εἰ μὴ κεύθησθε, ξεῖνοι, ὄψονται ὑμέας ἠδὲ αἱρήσουσιν.

10. εἰπέ μοι, Κύκλωψ, τί ἑταίρους ἐμοὺς ἔκτεινας;

419. PUT INTO GREEK

1. Fear not, stranger, no one will do you wrong.

2. We should do to others that which we would desire them to do to us.

3. Always be (πελ-) a man, my son, and a true friend to your friends.

4. Lady, give this to your son as a gift from the king.

5. Let us endure even this patiently, men, that our plan may be more swiftly fulfilled.

6. May I be sent, O king! for I alone know the way.

7. There is no one of mortals who will not have many troubles while he lives.

8. Speak, my friend; for truth, even though not always being pleasant, is a great good.

9. Their voice was carried to the very door of the temple: "Zeus and Apollo, save us!"

10. My brave men, let us remain here and endure until we are commanded to go.

420. READINGS

1. Ζεῦ φίλε, ἄζομαί σε· σὺ γὰρ πάντεσσιν ἀνάσσεις, δόξαν αὐτὸς ἔχων καὶ κράτος μέγα, ἀνθρώπων δὲ εὖ γιγνώσκεις νόον καὶ θυμὸν ἑκάστου, σεῦ δὲ κράτος ἐστὶ μέγιστον, ὦ ἄναξ.   (Theognis)

2. ἕκαστος ἡμέων, ὦ ἄνδρες, οὐχ ἑῷ πατέρι καὶ ἑῇ μητέρι μοῦνον γέγαεν, ἀλλὰ καὶ ἑῇ πατρίδι.   (Demosthenes)

3. ἐγώ εἰμι ὁδὸς καὶ ἀληθείη καὶ ζωή· οὐδεὶς ἔρχεται πρὸς πατέρα εἰ μὴ διὰ ἐμεῖο.   (St. John)

4. οὐδὲν ἐμοὶ ἡδύ ἐστιν εἰ μὴ καὶ ἀληθές.   (Plato)

5. ὅς κε θεοῖς πείθηται, μάλα κλύουσιν αὐτοῦ.   (Homer)

ἀνάσσω   I rule over [+ dat.; cp. ἄναξ]
κλύω   I hear, I give ear to the prayers of [+ gen.]

421. WRITE IN GREEK

1. He kept saying no one was present, but we, knowing it was not true, sought the strangers throughout the house until we found and seized them.

2. Two rivers were (constantly) flowing into the sea, mingling their waters with it and with one another.

3. You showed yourself to be a man of great manliness, because you kept trying until you accomplished this most difficult work.

Lesson 58

Special Case-Endings. Elision

422. SPECIAL CASE-ENDINGS

Homer uses at times a few special endings (remnants of old cases) to give nouns, adjectives, and pronouns a special adverbial force:

a. -δε may be added to the accusative to denote place to which. Thus, οἰκόνδε *homeward*. When it is added to the plural accusative, -δε blends with the preceding α into -ζε. Thus, θυράσ-δε becomes θυράζε *to the doors*.

b. -θεν may be added to a noun or pronoun to denote place from which, source, or separation. E.g., οἴκοθεν *from the house*, Διόθεν *from Zeus*.

c. -φι(ν) may be added to denote various functions of genitive and dative— *by, at, from, with, on* or *in*. Context will make clear which force is meant in a given passage. Thus, βίηφι *by force*, θύρηφιν *at the door*.

   Note:

   To find the form of the word to which -θεν or -φι(ν) should be added, simply drop the final ς or υ of the nominative or genitive. Homer uses these endings only with a certain few words.

423. ELISION

a. Ordinarily, for easier pronunciation, a *short* final vowel (except -υ), and sometimes final -αι or -οι, drop out if the following word begins with a vowel or diphthong. This is called **elision** ("driving out"), and is indicated by an apostrophe (') in the place of the omitted syllable. E.g., ἀπ᾽ ἀρχῆς for ἀπὸ ἀρχῆς.

b. Elision does *not* occur in the dative plural of the third declension, in περί, πρό, ὅτι, τί, and very seldom in monosyllables unless they end in ε. (ὅτ᾽ always = ὅτε, never ὅτι).

c. Forms taking movable ν (Section 90) before a vowel take it instead of eliding; however, ἐστί may do either.

d. Elision also occurs between the parts of compound words, e.g., πάρ-ειμι (πάρειμι), ἐπ-έβη (ἐπέβη). See Section 408c.

e. When elision brings π, τ, or κ directly before a rough breathing at the beginning of the following word, these three consonants change into their corresponding 'rough' or aspirated forms— φ, θ, χ. Thus, κατὰ ὁδόν becomes καθ᾽ ὁδόν, while ἀπό + αἱρέω becomes ἀφ-αιρέω (ἀφαιρέω). Note that the rough breathing is not then written over the second part of the compound word, since its syllable is no longer first.

424. TRANSLATE

1. λίθον τόνδε μέγαν οὐρανόθεν ποτέ πεσεῖν ὀΐσανθ᾽ ἅπαντες.
2. αἶψ᾽ ἀπ᾽ ὀφθαλμῶν ἐφέρετο νηῦς ὑφ᾽ ὕδατος ποταμοῖο ταχὺ ῥέοντος.
3. τί ὑπ᾽ ἐμεῖο κακόν ποτε ἐπάθετε, ἢ ἄλλο τι ὃ οὐ χρὴ φίλον ἔρδειν;
4. πόλεμόνδ᾽ ἐβεβήκεσαν πάντες, οὐδ᾽ εἷς ἔτι παρ-ῆν.
5. ἄνεμος δένδρεα πολλ᾽ εἰς γαῖαν κρατερῆφι βάλε βίηφι.
6. ἐκ σέθεν τόδε δῶρον, ἢ παρά τευ ἄλλου;
7. θύρηφί ῥα στῆτε, ὄφρ᾽ ἂν ἐξ-έλθῃ τις, ἠδ᾽ ὑμῖν τι πόρῃ.
8. βούλομ᾽ ἐγώ γε μενέμεν, οἱ δὲ φυγεῖν λιλαίονται.
9. οἰκόνδε βήωμεν, ἑταῖροι· οὐδὲν γὰρ τῇδε ποιεῖν δυνατοὶ ἐοίκαμεν.
10. ὅτ᾽ ἦλθες ἔτι που εὗδον· οὔ γε φωνήν σευ πυθόμην.

425. PUT INTO GREEK (eliding where proper)

1. According to others, this road is both longer and more difficult.
2. The ships lay upon the water very near one another.
3. The good, though having died (aor. ptc.), will never die, but will always live in the minds of mortals.
4. Night came swiftly down from the sky.
5. He seems to be a brave and noble companion for you.
6. If you (sg.) had stood at the door, as I ordered, they would not easily have fled from the house.
7. If you have faith in me, he said, you will all be very happy.
8. Do you (pl.) see them going away? Or do they still await us?
9. If you (sg.) do not find him, come home quickly.
10. From what place have you come, men? Speak!

426. READINGS

1. ἐννέ᾽ ἔμμεναι Μούσας λέγουσι τινές. ὡς νηπίως· ἴδε, καὶ Σαπφὼ Λεσβόθεν ἐστὶ δεκάτη.   (Plato)
2. ὦ φίλοι, ὅ γε κτείνει με δόλῳ, οὐ δὲ βίηφιν.   (Homer; the giant Polyphemus speaking.)
3. θεόθεν δ᾽ οὐκ ἔστ᾽ ἀλέασθαι.   (Homer; ἔστι + an infinitive often = "it is possible," as here; ἀλέομαι = "evade, hide")
4. Ζεῦ, μεγάλαι ἀρεταὶ θνητοῖς ἔρχοντ᾽ ἐκ σέθεν.   (Pindar)
5. εἷς οἰωνὸς ἄριστος — ἀμύνεσθαι περὶ πατρίδος   (Homer: Hector refuses to withdraw from the battle despite his brother's worry.)
6. οὐκ ἐκ χρημάτων ἀρετὴ γίγνεται, ἀλλ᾽ ἐξ ἀρετῆς χρήματα καὶ ἄλλ᾽ ἀγαθὰ πάντ᾽ ἀνθρώποισιν.   (Plato)

7. ὦ ξεῖν᾽ ἀγγέλλειν Λακεδαιμονίοις ὅτι τῇδε
    κείμεθα, τοῖς κείνων ῥήμασι πειθόμενοι.
    (Simonides' world-famous inscription over the grave of the Spartans
    who died to a man in the heroic stand at Thermopylae.)

ἀγγέλλω	I announce, I report
ἀμύνομαι	I serve as protection, I am a defense
ἐννέα	nine
Λακεδαιμόνιος, -ου	Lacedemonian, Spartan
Λέσβος, -ου	Lesbos [a large and beautiful island in the Aegean sea, near Asia Minor]
οἰωνός, -οῦ	[m.] omen, premonition; a large bird of omen
ῥῆμα, -ατος	[n.] word; command
Σαπφώ	Sappho [the poetess from Lesbos]

427. WRITE IN GREEK

1. If I should become king, O companions, I would give each of you much gold
    and whatever else you might desire.

2. Tell me the truth, son! Why did you strike your brother?

3. Let us pray our sons may be (fut. inf.) very brave and very just; for there is great
    necessity of men living in this way.

428. WORD STUDY

ANGEL ('messenger' of God, announcing His will to men), ANGELIC; ANGELA;
ANGELUS (the thrice-daily prayer to the Blessed Virgin, beginning in Latin with the
words "Angelus Domini…," the former a borrowing from Greek), ARCHANGEL
('ruling-angel', an angel of higher nature and rank), EVANGEL (εὐαγγέλιον the
'good news' of Christ's coming, the Gospel), EVANGELIST (one who writes or
preaches the Gospel, a missionary), EVANGELICAL (pertaining to the Gospels or to
early Christianity); — SAPPHIC (pertaining to Sappho, as 'the Sapphic meter', a
special poetic rhythmic pattern, exemplified by her poem in Section 404).

Lesson 59

General Review of First Unit

429. TOPICS COVERED

In the first thirty lessons, the most important principles studied were the following, which should receive special emphasis in your review, particularly those which you individually feel less confident of having mastered:

1. Pronunciation and stress of Greek words.
2. Syllable-division.
3. The three declensions.
4. Rules of gender.
5. Types and stems of adjectives and participles.
6. The present system of the verb, all tenses, moods, and voices.
7. The future system entire.
8. All forms of εἰμί except the future and optative.
9. ὁ, ἡ, τό and its uses.
10. Relative, intensive, demonstrative pronouns.
11. Significance of the cases.
12. Meaning of the moods and tenses.
13. Syntax rules: statements of fact, contrary-to-fact conditions, exhortations, wishes, purpose constructions, commands, uses of the infinitive, uses of the participle, relative clauses.
14. Vocabulary words.
15. Numerous English derivatives.

430. QUESTIONNAIRE

Use these leading questions to guide your review and to focus it on key points. Be prepared to answer all:

1. What are the rules for syllable division in Greek words?
2. When is a syllable long in Greek? When short?
3. What are the basic meanings of the genitive case? The dative?
4. State the main uses of the accusative.
5. Where do first declension nouns in -α differ in ending from those in -η?
6. Where are second declension neuters different in form from masculines?
7. What is to be noted about neuters in their accusative endings? In the verb of which they are subject?

8. With what declension of the masculine and neuter are feminine adjectives and participles in -α used? Those in -η?

9. What is special about the endings of pronouns which follow the first and second declension?

10. How can you tell grammatically when αὐτός, -ή, -ό, and κεῖνος, -η, -ο are adjectives, not pronouns?

11. What are the different meanings of ὁ, ἡ, τό, and how is it used differently to indicate which meaning is to be taken?

12. Give the meaning and uses of ὅδε, ἥδε, τόδε.

13. How does the middle voice differ in force from the others? When does it have active force?

14. Name the secondary tenses; the primary.

15. When do the tenses indicate time of action? When kind of action?

16. What is the general significance of the aorist stem? The perfect?

17. Which stems of the verb are not used in the middle?

18. In what moods is there no future?

19. State two regular features of subjunctive endings.

20. How does Greek express wishes? Exhortations? Purpose?

21. Explain the relation between the tense of the main (introducing) verb and that of the infinitive in indirect statement.

22. What is the general distinction in use between οὐ and μή?

23. How do you recognize that a verb is deponent?

24. Give two ways of expressing command in Greek.

25. What is a thematic vowel?

26. What is characteristic of all optative endings?

27. What is the rule for gender of third declension nouns?

28. When does the accusative singular of the third declension end in -ν? in -υν?

29. What is the simplest way of predicting the dative plural form of third declension words whose stem ends in a mute?

30. How can you readily tell whether a noun whose nominative singular ends in -ος is of the second or third declension?

31. How do you determine the stem of a third declension adjective or participle?

431. IDENTIFY AND GIVE THE MEANING

1. λίθοισι
2. χαλεπάς
3. ἦεν
4. ἀρχάων
5. πευθοίμην
6. πέλοντο
7. ἐσθλῆς
8. πυρί
9. φάεα
10. ἐστέ
11. πτερόεσσαι
12. ἔργοιο
13. πρόφρονα
14. ἐρχώμεθα
15. φύσιν
16. ἔμμεναι
17. πράγμασι
18. μαχησόμενοι
19. ἢν ἁμαρτάνῃ
20. ἐσθιόντεσσι
21. ἀν-έχοιο
22. ἦσθα
23. πέμπε
24. βίην
25. διώκεσθαι
26. ἠδείη
27. ἐσσί
28. ἀρετάς
29. λαμβάνουσι
30. ἵνα ᾖ
31. μηδένα
32. λέγετε
33. ἐόντας
34. ἐπέεσσι
35. ἀμείβετο
36. ὁράοιμι
37. πέτρης
38. ἦμεν
39. ἀνδράσι
40. πατρίδα

Lesson 60

General Review of Second Unit

432. SUBJECTS FOR REVIEW

In Lessons 31-58, the main items studied were:

1.   The pronouns—indefinite, interrogative, personal.
2.   The three aorist systems.
3.   Perfect, perfect middle, and aorist passive forms.
4.   Further syntax rules: present general, future more vivid, and future less vivid (should-would) conditions, potential constructions, and indirect question.
5.   Future and optative of εἰμί.
6.   Reduplication and augment.
7.   Contraction and elision.
8.   Iterative verb forms.
9.   Vocative, special case endings.
10. Comparison of adjectives.
11. Formation and comparison of adverbs.
12. Use and position of prepositions.
13. Vocabulary words.

433. POINTS TO BE CLEAR ON

1.   How can you tell apart parallel forms of the interrogative and indefinite pronouns?
2.   How does a pitch-mark affect the meaning of a third personal pronoun form?
3.   What determines whether an aorist is of the first, second, or third aorist type?
4.   What is notable about 2nd aorist endings? About first aorist?
5.   In what constructions is ἄν or κε(ν) with the subjunctive used?
6.   How is a vague future (future less vivid) supposition expressed?
7.   What is the difference in thought between a more vivid and a less vivid future supposition?
8.   What type of thought does the potential optative express?
9.   Which consonants are known as 'mutes'? Which are called 'liquids'?
10. Give the rule and an example for each of the three types of reduplication.
11. Give examples illustrating the regular changes undergone by a final consonant of the perfect middle stem when the ending is added.
12. What are the rules for forming the comparative and superlative of adjectives?
13. How are comparative adjectives declined?
14. What is the ordinary way of forming an adverb from an adjective?

15. How are adjectives and prepositions used as adverbs?
16. How do you form the comparative of an adverb? Superlative?
17. In what blocks of the Map of the Verb (Lesson 16) may the augment be used?
18. When is epsilon added for the augment? When is no augment needed?
19. Give examples illustrating the various types of contraction.
20. How are iterative forms constructed? What is their meaning?
21. What are the vocative endings, if different from the nominative?
22. What force do the three special case endings give to a word to which they are added?
23. In what instances may elision occur?

434. DISTINGUISH between the various forms spelled alike for which each of the following might stand (the number in parentheses indicates possibilities). If no pitch-mark is here given, it would be different in the various forms:

1. χρηστά (2)
2. τάχιστα (3)
3. ποιήσω (2)
4. φέρε (2)
5. τῳ (6)
6. πέμπεσθε (6)
7. τελεῖται (4)
8. τι (6)
9. λέγουσι (3)
10. βάλλετε (3)
11. τινα (8)
12. ὦ (2)

435. IDENTIFY AND TRANSLATE

1. τέτυκτο
2. σφίν
3. ποιῆσαι
4. ἐποίει
5. ἀρείονι
6. τευ
7. φανῆναι
8. εἰπέσκες
9. ἐμέ
10. ὁρῶσαι
11. ἀληθεστάτης
12. ἀπ-ολώλει
13. ἔστης
14. θάνατόνδε
15. ὑμεῖς
16. βεβήκαμεν
17. ἔλαθεν
18. ὅτευ
19. ἐλεύσοντ᾽
20. πονηρῶς
21. ἐποθεῦμεν
22. ῥέξον
23. μιν
24. βάλ᾽
25. ἐάσκομεν
26. κακωτέρους
27. γεγάασι
28. τέων
29. ἐᾷς
30. θεόθεν
31. πονεῖται
32. ὅν τινα
33. κεῖσθε
34. παθόντος
35. ἑ
36. ὤφθην
37. βίηφι
38. πειρᾶτε
39. ἐμαχέσαο
40. τέοισι

Honor Work

Optional Supplemental Readings

1. ἡμεῖς δὴ χρῆμα θεῶν εἰμεν.   (Plato)

2. οὐδεὶς ἀνθρώπων οὔτ' ἔσσεται οὔτε γέγαε ὅς τις πᾶσιν ἁδὼν
   ἔρχεται εἰς θάνατον. οὐδὲ γὰρ ὃς θνητοῖσιν καὶ ἀθανάτοισιν
   ἀνάσσει, Ζεύς, θνητοῖς πᾶσιν ἁνδάνει.   (Theognis)
   > ἁνδάνω, ἁδήσω, ἅδον I am pleasing to; ἀνάσσω I am king over,
   > I rule over (+ dat.)

3. λέγει θεός· "ἱεροὶ ἔσεσθε, ὅτι ἱερός εἰμι."   (St. Peter)

4. πάντα χωρεῖ καὶ οὐδὲν μένει.   (Heraclitus)
   > χωρέω I pass on

5. οὐδεὶς ποιῶν πονηρὰ λανθάνει θεόν.   (Menander)

6. νήπιος, ὃς μὲν ἐμὸν νόον φυλάσσει, ἑὰ δὲ πράγματα οὐ νοέει.
   (Theognis)
   > φυλάσσω, φυλάξω, φύλαξα I keep watch over, I observe

7. οὕτως γιγνώσκομεν ὅτι ἐγνώκαμεν θεόν — εἰ τοῦ ἐντολὰς
   φυλάσσωμεν. ὅς τις λέγει ὅτι ἔγνωκέ μιν, καὶ τοῦ ἐντολὰς οὐ
   φυλάσσει, ἐν κείνῳ ἀληθείη οὐκ ἔστιν. ὃς δέ κεν φυλάσσῃ λόγον θεοῦ,
   ἀληθέως ἀγάπη θεοῦ ἔν οἱ τελέεται.   (St. John)
   > φυλάσσω, φυλάξω, φύλαξα I keep watch over, I observe

8. ἐγώ εἰμι ἄλφα καὶ ὦ μέγα, ἀρχὴ καὶ τέλος, λέγει θεός, ὅς εἰμι καὶ ἦα
   καὶ ἔσομαι.   (Apocalypse)
   > τέλος, -εος end

9. θεὸς ἀρχήν τε καὶ τέλος καὶ μέσα ἐόντων ἁπάντων ἔχει.   (Plato)
   > τέλος, -εος end

10. ἅ τινά ἐστιν ἀληθέα, ἅ τινα δίκαια, ἅ τινα ἱερά, ἅ τινα ἀγαθά, τάδε
    φρονέετε· καὶ θεὸς εἰρήνης ἔσεται σὺν ὑμῖν.   (St. Paul)

11. ἐσθλὰ γὰρ ἀπ' ἐσθλῶν μαθήσεαι· ἢν δὲ κακοῖσιν μίσγῃς, ἀπ-ολέσεις
    καὶ τὸν ἔχεις νόον.   (Theognis)

12. Μοῦσαι, νηόν τινα λαβεῖν ὃς οὔ ποτε πεσεῖται ζητεύμεναι, ψυχὴν
    εὗρον Ἀριστοφάνευς.   (Plato)
    > Ἀριστοφάνης -ευς Aristophanes, Athenian comic poet.

13. Ζεῦ πάτερ, ἐσθλὰ μὲν ἡμῖν πόρε καὶ εὐχομένοις καὶ μή, κακὰ δὲ καὶ
    εὐχομένοις μὴ πόροις.   (Socrates, in Plato)

14. δικαίων δὲ ψυχαὶ ἐν χειρὶ θεοῦ, καὶ οὔ ποτε ἅψεταί σφεων ἄλγος.
    ἐδόκησαν ἐν ὀφθαλμοῖς νηπίων θανεῖν, καὶ νοεῖτο θάνατός σφεων
    ὄλεθρος· οἱ δέ εἰσιν ἐν εἰρήνῃ, ὅτι ἐπείρησεν αὐτῶν θεὸς καὶ εὗρέ
    σφεας ἀξίους ἑο αὐτοῦ.   (Book of Wisdom)
    > ἅπτομαι, ἅψομαι I seize hold of; ὄλεθρος, -ου destruction;
    > ἄξιος, -η, -ον worthy of

15. οὐ χρὴ τόδε λανθάνειν ὑμέας, ὅτι ἓν μαρ παρὰ θεῷ ὡς χίλια ἔτεά ἐστιν, καὶ χίλια ἔτεα ὡς ἓν ἦμαρ.   (St. Peter)

   χίλιος, -ου a thousand; ἔτος, -εος year

16. θεὸς φάος ἐστίν, καὶ ζόφος ἔν οἱ οὔκ ἐστιν οὐδέν.   (St. John)

   ζόφος, -ου darkness

17. μέτρον ἄριστον.   (Cleobulus)

18. οὐ γὰρ δὴ ὑπό γε θεῶν ποτε ἀμελεῖται ὃς ἂν πρόφρων ἐθέλῃ δίκαιος γίγνεσθαι καὶ διώκειν ἀρετὴν εἰς ὅσον δυνατὸν ἀνθρώπῳ ὅμοιος πέλεσθαι θεῷ.   (Plato)

   ἀμελέω I neglect, I do not care for; εἰς ὅσον as far as

19. εἴ τε ἐσθίετε εἴ τε πίνετε εἴ τέ τι ποιεῖτε, πάντα εἰς δόξαν θεοῦ ποιεῖτε.   (St. Paul)

20. ἀνθρώπων ἕκαστος δύο πήρας φέρει· μίαν πρόσθεν, δευτέρην δὲ ὄπισθεν· πῆραι δὲ γέμουσι κακῶν. ἀλλ᾽ ἣ μὲν πρόσθεν ἐστίν, ἑτέρων κακὰ ἔχει· ἣ δὲ ὄπισθεν, αὐτοῦ φέροντος ἔχει κακά. διὰ τόδε οὖν ἄνθρωποι σφέων αὐτῶν μὲν κακὰ οὐχ ὁρῶσι, ἑτέρων δὲ μάλα ῥηιδίως γιγνώσκουσιν.   (Aesop)

   πήρη, -ης [f.] knap-sack; πρόσθεν in front; ὄπισθεν in back, behind; γέμω I am full of [+ gen]

21. ἢν φίλος γένηται πονηρός, χρὴ ἄγειν μιν πάλιν εἰς ἀγαθόν· ἄρειον γὰρ καὶ μᾶλλον φίλου ἔργον ἐστὶν βοηθέειν εἰς ἦθος ἢ εἰς χρήματα.   (Aristotle)

   βοηθέω I come to assistance; ἦθος, -εος character, morals; μᾶλλον more

22. γιγνώσκω, καί μοι ἐν φρεσὶ ἄλγεα κεῖται, ὁρῶν πατρίδα ἐμὴν κτεινομένην.   (Solon, referring to political decadence)

23. τάδ᾽ ἔχω, ἃ ἔμαθον καὶ ἐνόησα καὶ καλὰ παρὰ Μουσάων ἔλαβον· ἕτερα δὲ πολλὰ καὶ ἡδέα ἄνεμος ἀφ-είλετο.   (Crates)

24. θνητὰ θνητῶν πάντα, καὶ πάντα παρ-έρχεται ἡμέας· ἢν δὲ μή, ἡμεῖς αὐτὰ παρ-ερχόμεθα.   (Greek Anthology)

25. κελεύω ὑμέας φιλέειν ἀλλήλους, ὡς ἐγὼ ἐφίλησα ὑμέας· οὕτως φιλέετε ἀλλήλους. ἐν τῷδε γνώσονται πάντες ὅτι ἐμοί ἐστε—ἢν φιλέητε ἀλλήλους.   (St. John)

26. χαίρετε ἐν θεῷ αἰεί· πάλιν λέξω, χαίρετε, καὶ εἰρήνη θεοῦ, ἣ ὑπὲρ παντὸς νόου ἐστίν, φυλάξει κῆρ ὑμέων καὶ νόον ἐν Χριστῷ.   (St. Paul)

   ὑπέρ [prep. + gen.] over, above, "beyond the grasp of"; φυλάσσω, -άξω I guard

27. μὴ θαυμάζετε εἰ μισέει ὑμέας κόσμος. γιγνώσκομεν ὅτι βεβήκαμεν ἐκ θανάτοιο εἰς ζωὴν ἐπεὶ φιλέομεν κασιγνητούς. ὃς μὴ φιλέῃ, μένει ἐν θανάτῳ, καὶ πᾶς ὃς μὴ φιλέῃ κασιγνητὸν ἐὸν ἀνθρωποκτόνος ἐστίν.   (St. John)

   θαυμάζω I marvel; ἀνθρωποκτόνος manslayer, murderer

28. μείζονα ἀγάπην ἢ τήνδε οὐδεὶς ἔχει — εἰ θάνοι τις εἵνεκα φίλων ἑῶν. ὑμεῖς φίλοι μεῦ ἐστε, ἢν ποιέητε τὰ ἐγὼ κελεύω ὑμέας.   (St. John)

29. ὀλίγους εὑρήσεις ἄνδρας ἐν χαλεποῖς φίλους ἑταίρους γενομένους,
οἵ τινες ἂν βούλοιντο καὶ ἀγαθῶν καὶ κακῶν μέρος μετά σευ ἔχειν.
(Theognis)

   μέρος, -εος share, portion

30. ἄρειόν ἐστιν σιωπάειν καὶ εἶναι, ἢ λέγοντα μὴ ἔμμεν. καλὸν
διδασκέμεν, ἤν τις λέγων καὶ ποιέῃ.   (St. Ignatius of Antioch)

   σιωπάω I remain silent, I say nothing

31. μεγίστη ὀδύνη πασάων ἐν ἀνθρωποισι ἥδε — πολλὰ φρονέοντα
μηδὲν τελέειν. (Herodotus)

   ὀδύνη, -ης grief, pain, anguish

32. φοιτῶν Χριστὸς παρὰ θάλασσαν ἴδεν δύο κασιγνητούς, Σίμωνα
Πέτρον καὶ Ἀνδρέαν, βάλλοντας δίκτυον εἰς θάλασσαν· ἦσαν γὰρ
ἁλιῆες. καὶ λέγει σφιν· "ἐλθέτε μετ' ἐμέ, καὶ ποιήσω ὑμέας ἁλιῆας
ἀνθρώπων."   (St. Matthew)

   Σίμων, -ωνος Simon; Πέτρος, -ου Peter;
   Ἀνδρέας, acc. -αν Andrew; δίκτυον, -ου net;
   ἁλιεύς, -ῆος fisherman

33. οὐδὲν εἰσ-ενείκαμεν εἰς τόνδε κόσμον, οὐδ' ἐκ-φέρειν τι δυνατοί
εἰμεν.   (St. Paul)

34. εἷς θεὸς ἔν τε θεοῖσι καὶ ἀνθρώποισι μέγιστος, οὐ δέμας θνητοῖσιν
ὅμοιος οὐδὲ νόῳ. οὖλος ὁρᾷ, οὖλος δὲ νοεῖ, οὖλος δέ τ' ἀκούει, καὶ
ἀπάνευθε πόνοιο νοέων φρενὶ πάντα κινεῖ. αἰεὶ δ' ἐν αὐτῷ μένει,
κινεύμενος οὐδέν, οὐδὲ ἔοικέ μιν ἀμείβεσθαι ἄλλοτε
ἄλλῃ.   (Xenophanes)

   δέμας [indecl. n.] shape, build; ἀκούω I hear; κινέω I move;
   ἄλλοτε ἄλλῃ now one way now another; αὐτῷ "in the same state."

35. ἀγάπη Χριστοῦ ὀτρύνει ἡμέας, γιγνώσκοντας ὅτι εἷς εἵνεκα
πάντων θάνε, ἵνα οἳ ζώουσι μηκέτι σφίσι αὐτοῖς ζώωσιν ἀλλὰ
Χριστῷ εἵνεκά σφεων θανόντι καὶ ἐκ νεκρῶν ἐγερθέντι.   (St. Paul)

   ὀτρύνω I urge on; νεκρός, -οῦ corpse, the dead;
   ἐγείρω, aor. pass. ἐγέρθην I raise up, I resurrect

36. οὐδεὶς γὰρ ἡμέων οἳ αὐτῷ ζώει, καὶ οὐδεὶς οἳ αὐτῷ θνήσκει. ἤν τε
γὰρ ζώωμεν, θεῷ ζώομεν, ἤν τε θνήσκωμεν, θεῷ θνήσκομεν. ἤν τε
οὖν ζώωμεν ἤν τε θνήσκωμεν, θεοῦ εἰμεν. εἰς τόδε γὰρ Χριστὸς
ἔθανε καὶ πάλιν ζώει, ἵνα καὶ νεκρῶν καὶ ζωόντων ἄναξ ᾖ.
(St. Paul)

37. πολλοῖς ἀνθρώπων γλώσσῃ θύραι οὐκ ἐπί-κεινται, καὶ πολλὰ
λέγουσι τὰ οὐ χρὴ εἰπεῖν.   (Theognis)

   γλώσση, -ης tongue; ἐπί-κειμαι I am closed [of doors]

38. ἀλλ' εἰσὶ μητρὶ παῖδες ἄγκυραι βίου.   (Sophocles)

   ἄγκυρα, -ης anchor

39. νόμος ἐστὶ πάντων βασιλεύς, θνητῶν τε καὶ ἀθανάτων.   (Pindar)

   νόμος, -ου law; βασιλεύς, -ῆος king

40. γιγνώσκομεν ὅτι ἢν οἶκος ἡμετέρης ζωῆς ἐπὶ γαίῃ λυθῃ, οἶκον
ἀθάνατον ἐκ θεοῦ ἔχομεν ἐν οὐρανοῖς. ὄφρα οὖν ἐν σώματι οἰκέομεν,
ἐκ-δημέομεν ἀπὸ θεοῦ.   (St. Paul)

   ἐκ-δημέω I am in exile

Lesson 61

436. MEMORIZE

Τροίη, -ης   [f.] Troy, Ilion

437. TEXT

The Poem's Theme

Ἄνδρα μοι ἔννεπε, Μοῦσα, πολύτροπον, ὃς μάλα πολλὰ   1
πλάγχθη, ἐπεὶ Τροίης ἱερὸν πτολίεθρον ἔπερσε·

πέρθω, πέρσω, πέρσα	I destroy, I sack
πλάζω, πλάγξω, πλάγξα, —, —, πλάγχθην	I beat; [in pass.] I wander
πολύτροπος, -η, -ον	resourceful
πτολίεθρον, -ου	city, town

438. NOTES

1. ἔννεπε is transitive, = "make known, tell about"

439. COMMENT

1-2. The poem's opening lines give us the theme of the poem (a man), modified by an adjective that conveys the man's essential character and a relative clause that includes general information about his past. This is the story of a man, a man of many twists and turns of mind, versatile, shrewd, up to any demands thrust upon his resourceful-ness by shifting fortune as he is buffeted far and wide on land and sea. Troy, sacred to the gods who had built its lofty walls, has fallen at last to this man's stratagem.

1. ἄνδρα It is the human element that interests Homer, more than mere events. It is this which he puts first, to catch our attention and impress itself upon our minds, under the full weight of the main rhythmic emphasis.

Μοῦσα The poet invokes the Muse, asking her to furnish him with information about things that he has not personally experienced but which she, a goddess, would know all about. Such an invocation is a conventional feature of Greek epic poetry. Later epic poets imitate him. Vergil, for instance: *Musa, mihi causas memora…*, or Milton: "Of man's first disobedience, and the fruit / Of that forbidden tree…sing, Heavenly Muse."

πολύτροπον can mean many things: "turning many ways," "wandering," "ingenious" and "resourceful" are all good translations. The epithet links together several aspects of Odysseus' character; its prominent position makes it clear that crafty intelligence will be the central virtue of this hero.

2. Τροίης...ἔπερσε It was Odysseus who finally stormed impregnable Troy by the wily trick of the Trojan Horse, for he was general of the troops hiding within it. Of course, Odysseus originated the stratagem of the Wooden Horse. You can read the story in both Menelaus' account in Book 4 of the *Odyssey* and Vergil's vivid account in Book 2 of the *Aeneid*.

440. WRITE IN GREEK

1. All men desire to be happy, but not all wish to do the difficult things by which alone true happiness is had.

2. Mother, take the children and hasten home; for I see a great storm coming in from the sea.

3. If you (pl.) had fought more bravely then, you perhaps would have seized Troy in the beginning of the war.

Lesson 62

441. MEMORIZE

ἄστυ, ἄστεος	[n.] town
(ἐ)ρύομαι, (ἐ)ρύσσομαι, (ἐρ)ρυσάμην	I save, I rescue, I protect
νόστος, -ου	[m.] return (home)
πόντος, -ου	[m.] sea, the deep
ὥς, ὧς	[adv.] thus, so [always with pitch-mark]

442. TEXT

Preview of the Story

πολλῶν δ᾽ ἀνθρώπων ἴδεν ἄστεα καὶ νόον ἔγνω,
πολλὰ δ᾽ ὅ γ᾽ ἐν πόντῳ πάθεν ἄλγεα ὃν κατὰ θυμόν,
ἀρνύμενος ἥν τε ψυχὴν καὶ νόστον ἑταίρων.   5
ἀλλ᾽ οὐδ᾽ ὣς ἑτάρους ἐρρύσατο, ἱέμενός περ·

ἄρνυμαι	I seek to gain
ἵεμαι	I desire, I strive

443. NOTES

3. ἔγνω = "came to know, became acquainted with." To review the form, see Lesson 42.

4. ἑός, -ή, -όν is frequently shortened to ὅς, ἥ, ὅν (for ϝός, ϝή, ϝόν), as here and in line 5.

6. οὐδ᾽ ὣς = "not even so." ἕταρος = ἑταῖρος, and is often substituted for it for metrical reasons.

444. COMMENT

3-6. To some, this proem seems to outline in a general way the story the poem is about to tell; others, however, note that it really only covers a part of the poem (roughly Books 5 through 12), and with some inaccuracy.

3. πολλῶν δ᾽ ἀνθρώπων ἴδεν ἄστεα... In fact, the wanderings described by the poem are not so much among the cities of men as among fantastic or at least isolated lands and peoples, far from mainstream human society. The episodes included in this text are examples, but there are others (Circe's island, the Sirens, Scylla and Charybdis, etc.).

πολλῶν…πολλά anaphora, a rhetorical device of repeating a word at the beginning of successive lines or clauses. In this instance, the device serves to emphasize the Odyssean characteristic of many-ness.

5-6. As we shall see, Odysseus will try hard to rescue his companions from the jaws of the Cyclops. It is also Odysseus who has got them into trouble in this case, since his curiosity led him to resist their desire to leave the monster's cave alone. However, in general, Odysseus is not portrayed as driven by a craving for adventure; rather, he seems to be conscientious about his responsibilities as a leader.

445. STRANGE STORY OF A LETTER THAT WAS LOST AND FOUND AGAIN

In the early Greek alphabet, there was an additional sound, equivalent to our w, known as Wau or Digamma ('double-gamma'); it was written ϝ, and came between ε and ζ. By Homer's time, this sound was beginning to be omitted in many words where it formerly occurred, though it was still used with some, at least part of the time. (It was pronounced regularly in one or two local dialects until the second century BCE). Homer seems to have used it often with certain words, especially in traditional phrases and formulas inherited from earlier poets, saying, e.g., ϝέπος, ϝάναξ, αἰϝεί, ϝιδεῖν, ϝοῖνος (cp. Latin *vinum*, English *wine* from the same original root-word). But later Greeks, not using the sound, never wrote it in copying the poems of Homer, and before long forgot that he employed it.

In the 18th century, the great Greek scholar Richard Bentley rediscovered the Homeric use of the digamma by a subtle detective-like study of certain peculiar facts and unexplained 'irregularities' in the rhythm and euphony of Homer's verse. Using as a clue the similarity in sound between many Latin, German, English, and Sanskrit words and their Greek equivalents, except for the absence of a w-sound in the Greek, he proved that these Greek words did have the w-sound too in the beginning and that its influence was still exerted in Homer's verse. Thereby he solved most of the problems of Homeric meter that for centuries had mystified the greatest scholars, even in ancient Greece itself.

The digamma is ordinarily not written in modern texts of Homer, but its influence on the grammar or meter will occasionally be pointed out in the notes.

446. WRITE IN GREEK

1. The ships stood afar off in the middle of the deep, for the king feared to be seen from the city.
2. If they said they desired (inf.) peace, they would not have told the truth.
3. Quickly throw (sg.) water on the fire while it is yet small, for thus you will rescue your possessions and perhaps the city itself.

447. WORD STUDY

NOSTALGIA (painful longing to return home, homesickness).

Lesson 63

448. MEMORIZE

ἀφ-αιρέομαι, ἀφ-αιρήσομαι, ἀφ-ελόμην	I take away
βοῦς, βοός [m., f.] [dat. pl. also βουσί]	ox, cow
θυγάτηρ, θυγατέρος or θυγατρός	[f.] daughter
νόστιμος, -η, -ον	of one's homecoming
ὄλλυμι, ὀλέσω, ὄλεσ(σ)α, ὄλωλα 2 aor. mid. ὀλόμην	I kill, I destroy, I lose; [in pf. and mid.] I perish, I am lost
Ὑπερίων, Ὑπερίονος	[m.] Hyperion [see Notes below]

449. TEXT

The Tragic Undertone

αὐτῶν γὰρ σφετέρῃσιν ἀτασθαλίῃσιν ὄλοντο,
νήπιοι, οἳ κατὰ βοῦς Ὑπερίονος Ἠελίοιο
ἤσθιον· αὐτὰρ ὁ τοῖσιν ἀφείλετο νόστιμον ἦμαρ.
τῶν ἁμόθεν γε, θεά, θύγατερ Διός, εἰπὲ καὶ ἡμῖν.　　10

ἁμόθεν	[adv.] from some point
ἀτασθαλίαι	[pl. f.] recklessness, senseless folly
θεά	[f. of θεός] goddess

450. NOTES

8. κατά here is an adv., with an intensifying sense: "utterly" or "to extinction." βοῦς [= βόας] is acc. pl. of βοῦς. Ὑπερίονος is either a cognomen of Helios the sun god, agreeing with it in the genitive; or else it is a genitive of paternity = "[son] of Hyperion". Hyperion is Helios' father at Hesiod's *Theogony* 374.

10. τῶν is partitive gen. of the demonstrative after εἰπέ , = "tell of these things." καὶ ἡμῖν: "to us, too," either meaning "let us also know what you know;" or perhaps "just as you have told other audiences."

451. COMMENT

7-9. Odysseus' prudence and great clarity of mind are highlighted against the contrasting background of his companions' impulsiveness and folly. If his companions are to perish before reaching home, it will be due to their own moral failing. They cannot blame their leader for lack of concern or wise guidance at crucial moments (cp. lines 5-6). In fact, such a negative assessment of Odysseus' men is not justified by the narrative of the *Odyssey*. Many of the companions die through no fault of their own: for example, eleven of Odysseus' twelve ships are destroyed by the

Laestrygonians, but not because the men are reckless. Indeed, the emphasis placed here upon the men's devouring of the Sun's cattle indeed seems disproportionate to the importance of the story in the narrative. The moral condemnation of them here seems contrary to the spirit in which the episode will be told, for the poem will show the men forced to the brink of starvation by the actions of the gods, and thus well-motivated to do this sacrilegious deed.

ἀτασθαλίῃσιν : in the poem, it will be the suitors, back in Ithaca, who will more notably perish thanks to their ἀτασθαλίῃσιν— not the companions.

10. Homer asks the Muse for help in starting the story of Odysseus from some point, not necessarily the beginning.

452. THE ADVENTURES OF A BREATHING MARK

There is a curious history behind the simple, unpretentious little sign used to indicate the 'breathing' to be employed in pronouncing initial Greek vowels and diphthongs. In the alphabet used at Athens until 403 BCE, the symbol E stood for both ε and η, while H denoted an h-sound. When the Ionian system was adopted, H was used to indicate capital η, thus distinguishing it from ε by its own symbol. But the first half of H was retained to signify a rough breathing, and later the other half was employed to indicate a smooth breathing. Time, and the innate human love of shortcuts, gradually evolved the current symbols,

453. WRITE IN GREEK

1. Though we have suffered (ptc.) much distress both on land and on the deep, we still hope to come to our fatherland and dwell there again in peace.

2. Some strangers destroyed the house and took away all the cows; but not even thus did my wife and two daughters have the heart to leave that land where we had all been born.

3. The mothers greatly rejoiced on the day of their sons' homecoming from the war.

454. WORD STUDY

BUCOLIC (pertaining to herdsmen; pastoral, as 'bucolic poetry', a type of poetry dealing in a pleasantly idealized way with country scenes, and dialogues between men watching their herds); — "HYPERION" (title of a narrative poem by Longfellow connecting the action, laid in Europe, with the myth of the Sun-God).

Lesson 64

455. MEMORIZE

ἀτάρ	but
ἔδω	[pres. system only] I eat
εἶδαρ, εἴδατος	[n.] food
ἐννῆμαρ	[adv.] for nine days
ἐπι-βαίνω, ἐπι-βήσομαι, ἐπί-βην, ἐπι-βέβηκα	[+ gen.] I land upon, I go upon
Λωτοφάγοι, -ων	[m.] Lotus-Eaters [a legendary people]
ὀλοός, -ή, -όν	destructive, deadly

The Adventures of Odysseus

The ten years' war at Troy having ended in total victory for the Greeks, largely by Odysseus' doings, the triumphant princes return with their armies to their various homes in Greece. Odysseus embarks his men on twelve swift ships and sets out for his beloved island kingdom, Ithaca. But the winds carry him northwest, to the southern coast of Thrace, beneath Mt. Ismarus. Finding there a town of the Κίκονες, allies of hated Troy, he destroys it utterly and carries off rich spoils, though sorrowed by the loss of many brave comrades in the battle. A mighty storm threatens to sink the entire fleet as they sail southward for home. Though escaping disaster then, the ships are blown far off their course and are driven for many days across unknown tracts of the sea.

What strange and terrifying experiences befell the heroic band thereafter in their long years of wandering we now learn from the lips of Odysseus himself, as he tells the amazing story to kindly king Alcinous at the termination of his wanderings.

456. TEXT

First Adventure: Landing among the Lotus-Eaters

ἔνθεν δ' ἐννῆμαρ φερόμην ὀλοοῖσ' ἀνέμοισι   11
πόντον ἐπ' ἰχθυόεντα· ἀτὰρ δεκάτῃ ἐπέβημεν
γαίης Λωτοφάγων, οἵ τ' ἄνθινον εἶδαρ ἔδουσιν.

> ἄνθινος, -η, -ον   made of flowers
> ἰχθυόεις, -εσσα, -εν   fish-swarming

457. NOTES

12. δεκάτῃ "on the tenth (day)." Dative of time when.

13. τε often is not to be translated, where it merely indicates the close connection of a relative or subordinate clause with what had gone before.

458. COMMENT

11. ἔνθεν That is, from Cape Maleia, the southernmost tip of Greece, away from which the baneful winds kept forcing Odysseus' fleet, which otherwise would have soon been home. ἐννῆμαρ Nine days is an unusually long voyage at sea.

12. Ancient ships, being fairly small and fragile, generally kept within sight of shore; Odysseus and his men would have feared the open sea toward which the gale has steadily driven them now for over a week.

13. The Lotus-Eaters are named after their staple (and only) food. At this point, Odysseus and his companions have left their familiar Mediterranean world and have entered the realm of fantasy and folktale.

459. THE DUAL IN DECLENSION

There are three **numbers** in the inflection of Greek words: the **singular**, denoting one person or thing; the **plural**, indicating more than one; and the **dual**, signifying two or a pair. The dual is but rarely used, since its meaning is easily carried by the ordinary plural. But if the writer wishes to emphasize that it is two, a pair, of which he is speaking, he will use special endings to call attention to this fact.

Learn, then, the following additional endings of the **nominative** and **accusative dual**:

> 2nd declension: add to stem: -ω
>
> 3rd declension: add to stem: -ε

Thus, τὼδε ἐμὼ χεῖρε *these two hands of mine*
τὼ ῥα ἀπ-ῆλθον χαίροντε. *The pair therefore went away rejoicing.*

460. WRITE IN GREEK

1. Let us go upon the ships now, but not leave this land until our companions bring the delightful food which we received from the Lotus-Eaters.

2. For nine days I lay in a deadly disease, suffering the greatest pains, nor was I able either to eat or to drink.

3. Men might take away my gold and all other things, but never will anyone seize from me my dearest possessions, love of truth and peace of soul.

461. WORD STUDY

LOTUS (a beautiful variety of large creamy water-lily, considered sacred in Egypt and India, and much used in ornamental painting. Different from Homer's lotus, which was probably a prickly shrub with large fruit, similar to the mandrake).

Lesson 65

462. MEMORIZE

ἀφύσσω, ἀφύξω, ἄφυσ(σ)α   I draw; I heap up

δεῖπνον, -ου   [n.] dinner, meal

ἔνθα   [adv.] there, then

θοός, -ή, -όν   swift

463. TEXT

Respite from the Angry Sea

ἔνθα δ᾽ ἐπ᾽ ἠπείρου βῆμεν καὶ ἀφυσσάμεθ᾽ ὕδωρ,

αἶψα δὲ δεῖπνον ἕλοντο θοῆς παρὰ νηυσὶν ἑταῖροι.   15

    ἤπειρος, -ου   [f.] land, mainland

464. COMMENT

14-15. Upon escaping from the prolonged danger and strenuous battle with the sea, Odysseus and his men stand again on dry land. They take a bit of rest, then busy themselves with refilling the water-casks of each ship and preparing a warm meal to eat in weary ease along the shore in the shadow of the towering ships.

465. INDIRECT QUESTIONS (REVIEW; SEE SECTION 214)

a.   Meaning: Direct questions use the actual words of the inquirer, and are independent sentences or clauses (e.g., "Who sent him?"). Indirect questions state the substance of the inquiry, in the same or equivalent words, as a dependent clause which is the object or subject of a verb of asking, knowing, thinking, etc., or in apposition to its object or subject:

    (a) *I asked who sent him.*

    (b) *Who sent him is not yet known.*

b.   Rule: Same as direct question, but after a secondary main verb the dependent verb generally becomes **optative**. This means that when the verb of asking, knowing, etc., on which the question is dependent is in a secondary tense, the verb within the question itself ordinarily shifts from indicative (or subjunctive) to optative; it may stay unchanged, and is always unchanged if the main verb on which it depends is primary. In shifting to the optative, a present, imperfect, or future verb becomes present optative, an aorist becomes the aorist optative, and a perfect becomes the perfect optative. Thus, in example (a) above where the main verb is in a secondary tense, the Greek would be:

    εἰρόμην (ὅς)τίς μιν πέμψειε. (εἰρόμην, "τίς μιν ἔπεμψε;")

  c.   Note: Sometimes the verb of asking, wondering, etc., on which the question depends may not be expressed, but only implied in the context. E.g., *We came [to find out] if you would give us anything.* "Whether" is expressed by εἰ, and "whether…or" by ἦ…ἦε.

466. WRITE IN GREEK

1. I know you (pl.) killed the oxen only in order to have food; but it was not right, for they were not yours but the city's.

2. Raising hands and eyes (dual) towards heaven, he prayed long, asking the gods to protect his daughter and two sons from all evil of body or soul.

3. Swiftly make ready (pl.) a great dinner and draw much wine, for many guests and friends will be present.

Lesson 66

467. REVIEW OF LESSONS 60-65

Go over again thoroughly the text (with notes and comment), vocabulary, and grammar of the preceding five lessons, pointing your review by means of the following questions:

1. What specific things do you learn about Odysseus' character in the introductory ten lines of the poem?

2. What hints of coming events in the story are contained in the first ten lines?

3. What action of Odysseus' companions is foretold here as the turning point in their destiny?

4. What characteristics of the men are already known from the poem's opening lines?

5. From what source does Homer claim to gain his knowledge of the matter contained in this poem?

6. State two events on the homeward journey which precede the landing among the Lotus Eaters.

7. Identify the precise form of the following words:

   a. πολλά (line 1)
   b. Μοῦσα (1)
   c. πλάγχθη (2)
   d. ἄστεα (3)
   e. ἔγνω (3)
   f. ὅ (4)
   g. ἥν (5)
   h. ἐρύσσατο (6)
   i. ἤσθιον (9)
   j. θεά (10)
   k. εἰπέ (10)
   l. φερόμην (11)
   m. ἰχθυόεντα (12)
   n. γαίης (13)
   o. θοῆς (15)

8. Explain the meaning and forms of the dual in declension.

9. Write in Greek:

   a. Protect us, Apollo, and show us the way leading homeward from Troy to our fatherland.

   b. Do not eat (pl.) that food! Though sweet, it is deadly. [Supply the ptc. "being" after "sweet"].

   c. I had never seen oxen and sheep so large and beautiful as here.

   d. If you (pl.) had fought more bravely, they would not have destroyed our town nor carried off all our possessions on swift ships to a land from which we shall never receive them back again.

   e. He died on the very day of his homecoming.

Lesson 67

468. MEMORIZE

δίδωμι, δώσω, δῶκα	I give [see Section 472]
ἵημι, ἥσω, ἧκα or ἕηκα	I send forth, I cast; I place
ἰών, ἰοῦσα, ἰόν	going [pres. act. ptc. of εἶμι I go; gen. ἰόντος, ἰούσης, ἰόντος]
ὀπάζω, ὀπάσσω, ὄπασ(σ)α	I send (someone) as a companion; I present
πατέομαι, —, πασ(σ)άμην	I partake of [+ gen.]
προ-ίημι, προ-ήσω, προ-ῆκα	I send forth, I hurl
τίθημι, θήσω, θῆκα	I put, I place, I cause
χθών, χθονός	[f.] earth

469. TEXT

Reconnaissance

αὐτὰρ ἐπεὶ σίτοιό τ' ἐπασσάμεθ' ἠδὲ ποτῆτος,   16
δὴ τότ' ἐγὼν ἑτάρους προΐην πεύθεσθαι ἰόντας,
οἵ τινες ἀνέρες εἶεν ἐπὶ χθονὶ σῖτον ἔδοντες,
ἄνδρε δύω κρίνας, τρίτατον κήρυχ' ἅμ' ὀπάσσας.

κήρυξ, -υκος	[m.] herald, runner
ποτής, -ῆτος	[f.] drink
τρίτατος, -η, -ον	third

470. NOTES

16. In temporal clauses, the aorist often has the force of a pluperfect.

17. προ-ίην : See Section 473 below for the imperfect of ἵημι.

18. εἶεν : review Section 464.

19. ἄνδρε : review Section 459.

471. COMMENT

17-19. With the crews rested and refreshed and the ships' supply of water renewed, the Greeks are ready again to sail on in search of home. But Odysseus' curiosity about strange countries spurs him before leaving to explore the region on whose coast the storm has driven them. Odysseus, accordingly, dispatches a small group to go into the interior and discover what sort of men dwell in this far-off land. The runner can report anything special, or relay a call for help. Odysseus and the rest wait on the shore.

18. Mortals eat bread, whereas the gods who dwell in the heavens live on nectar and ambrosia.

472. -μι VERBS

There is a group of verbs that have certain irregularities in common and are known as -μι verbs (because the 1 sg. act. ends in -μι not -ω). You met one such verb, ὄλλυμι, in Section 448; a 2 aor. middle form, ὄλοντο, appeared in the passage in Section 449. -μι verbs are irregular only in the present and 2 aor. systems active, where their endings resemble those of εἰμί more than those of the regular -ω verb, and (like εἰμί) lack the thematic vowel between stem and ending. So also in the middle of these systems (where the stem-vowel is always short), the thematic vowel is lacking; but the endings are regular; the subjunctive, however, retains as usual the lengthened thematic vowel, which absorbs an α or ε ending the stem and contracts with ο to ω.

The irregular forms of -μι verbs will occur only rarely in the Homer readings. They will be explained in the notes where they come up, except for a few forms that occur often enough to merit memorizing; these are given individually in this lesson and in three later lessons. There is no need to memorize the other forms that you will not be meeting in the Homer readings.

For your information, however, and as a framework in which to locate the occurring forms, here are some -μι verb patterns for reference:

δίδωμι I give

	Active		Middle	
	Sg.	*Pl.*	*Sg.*	*Pl.*
PRES. IND.				
1st pers.	δίδωμι	δίδομεν	δίδομαι	διδόμε(σ)θα
2nd pers.	διδοῖς(θα)	δίδοτε	δίδοσαι	δίδοσθε
3rd pers.	δίδωσι/διδοῖ	διδοῦσι	δίδοται	δίδονται
IMPF. IND. (often augmented)				
1st pers.	δίδουν	δίδομεν	διδόμην	διδόμε(σ)θα
2nd pers.	δίδους	δίδοτε	δίδοσο	δίδοσθε
3rd pers.	δίδου	δίδοσαν	δίδοτο	δίδοντο
2nd AOR. IND. (often augmented)				
1st pers.	[δῶκα	δόμεν	δόμην	δόμε(σ)θα
2nd pers.	δῶκας	δότε	δοῦ	δόσθε
3rd pers.	δῶκε]*	δόσαν	δότο	δόντο
PRES. SUBJ.				
1st pers.	διδῶ(μι)	διδῶμεν	διδῶμαι	διδώμε(σ)θα
2nd pers.	διδῶσ(θα)	διδῶτε	διδῶαι	διδῶσθε
3rd pers.	διδῷ(σι)	διδῶσι	διδῶται	διδῶνται

PRES. OPT.

1st pers.	διδοίην	διδοῖμεν	διδοίμην	διδοίμε(σ)θα
2nd pers.	διδοίης	διδοῖτε	διδοῖο	διδοῖσθε
3rd pers.	διδοίη	διδοῖεν	διδοῖτο	διδοίατο

2 Aor. Subj. and Opt.: Same as Pres. forms, without initial syllable (δι-): δῶμι, δοίην, etc.

PRES. IMPT.

2nd pers.	δίδου	δίδοτε	δίδοσο	δίδοσθε

2nd AOR. IMPT.

2nd pers.	δός	δότε	δοῦ	δόσθε

PRES. INF.

διδόμεν(αι), διδοῦναι   δίδοσθαι

2nd AOR. INF.

δόμεν(αι), δοῦναι   δόσθαι

PRES. PTC. (nom., m./f./n.)

διδούς, διδοῦσα, διδόν   διδόμενος, -η, -ον

2nd AOR. PTC. (nom., m. f. n.)

δούς, δοῦσα, δόν   δόμενος, -η, -ον

τίθημι I put

	Active		Middle	
	Sg.	*Pl.*	*Sg.*	*Pl.*

PRES. IND.

1st pers.	τίθημι	τίθεμεν	τίθεμαι	τιθέμεθα
2nd pers.	τίθησ(θα)	τίθετε	τίθεσαι	τίθεσθε
3rd pers.	τίθησι/τίθει	τιθεῖσι	τίθεται	τίθενται

IMPF. IND. (often augmented)

1st pers.	τίθην	τίθεμεν	τιθέμην	τιθέμεθα
2nd pers.	τίθεις	τίθετε	τίθεσο	τίθεσθε
3rd pers.	τίθει	τίθεσαν	τίθετο	τίθεντο

2nd AOR. IND. (often augmented)

1st pers.	[θῆκα	θέμεν	θέμην	θέμεθα
2nd pers.	θῆκας	θέτε	θέο	θέσθε
3rd pers.	θῆκε]*	θέσαν	θέτο	θέντο

PRES. SUBJ.

1st pers.	τιθῶ(μι)	τιθῶμεν	τιθῶμαι	τιθώμεθα
2nd pers.	τιθῇσ(θα)	τιθῆτε	τιθῆαι	τιθῆσθε
3rd pers.	τιθῇ(σι)	τιθῶσι	τιθῆται	τιθῶνται

PRES. OPT.

1st pers.	τιθείην	τιθεῖμεν	τιθείμην	τιθείμεθα
2nd pers.	τιθείης	τιθεῖτε	τιθεῖο	τιθεῖσθε
3rd pers.	τιθείη	τιθεῖεν	τιθεῖτο	τιθείατο

2 Aor. Subj. and Opt.: Same as Pres. forms, without initial syllable (τι): θῶ, θείην, etc.

PRES. IMPT.

2nd pers.	τίθει	τίθετε	τίθεσο	τίθεσθε

2nd AOR. IMPT.

2nd pers.	θές	θέτε	θεῦ	θέσθε

PRES. INF.

τιθέμεν(αι)   τιθέσθαι

2nd AOR. INF.

θέμεν(αι), θεῖναι   θέσθαι

PRES. PTC. (nom., m./f./n.)

τιθείς, τιθεῖσα, τιθέν   τιθέμενος, -η, -ον

2nd AOR. PTC. (nom., m./f./n.)

θείς, θεῖσα, θέν   θέμενος, -η, -ον

* These forms are irregular first aorists; they are used in the aorist indicative *singular* instead of second aorist forms.

473. FORMS OF ἵημι AND δίδωμι

Memorize:

ἵημι, ἥσω, ἧκα or ἕηκα   I send forth, I cast; I place

	Sg.	*Pl.*
IMPF.		
1st pers.	ἵειν/ ἵην	ἵεμεν
2nd pers.	ἵεις	ἵετε
3rd pers.	ἵει	ἵεσαν/ ἵεν

δίδωμι, δώσω, δῶκα   I give

2nd AOR. SUBJ.		
1st pers.	δῶ(μι)	δῶμεν
2nd pers.	δῷς(θα)	δῶτε
3rd pers.	δῷ(σι)/δώῃ(σι)	δῶσι

2nd AOR. OPT.

1st pers.	δοίην	δοῖμεν
2nd pers.	δοίης	δοῖτε
3rd pers.	δοίη	δοῖεν

2nd AOR. IMPT.

2nd pers.	δός	δότε

474. WRITE IN GREEK

1. But his companions going out found the Lotus Eaters lying on the earth and partaking of some food which none of us had ever seen.

2. After he had picked out (aor.) two brave men, he sent them forth afar from the ships.

3. They said he would send with us two boys as companions.

475. WORD STUDY

ION (an atom or group of atoms bearing an electric charge and 'going' or moving toward a positive or negative pole), IONIZE (to break up a substance into ions for separating its elements, as by electrolysis).

Lesson 68

476. MEMORIZE

λωτός, -οῦ	[m.] lotus
μήδομαι, μήσομαι, μησάμην	I contrive, I plan
ὄλεθρος, -ου	[m.] destruction

477. TEXT

The Natives' Kindness

οἱ δ᾽ αἶψ᾽ οἰχόμενοι μίγεν ἀνδράσι Λωτοφάγοισιν·   20
οὐδ᾽ ἄρα Λωτοφάγοι μήδονθ᾽ ἑτάροισιν ὄλεθρον
ἡμετέροισ᾽, ἀλλά σφι δόσαν λωτοῖο πάσασθαι.

    οἴχομαι   I proceed

478. NOTES

20. μίγεν : irreg. 3 pl. aor. pass. (for μίχθησαν) of μίσγω. In the passive voice, this verb means "mingle (with)" and takes a dative of association.

22. δόσαν : 3 pl. 2 aor. of δίδωμι. See Section 472.

479. COMMENT

20-22. Contrary to expectation, the inhabitants of this unknown land prove friendly and hospitable. They had not fled inland at sight of the strange ships landing on their coast. Rather, they had drawn near to watch, and when the Greek scouts approach they come forward with lotus fruits as a gift and token of good will. It is to prove more of a peril than a favor.

480. PAST GENERAL CONSTRUCTION

The rules for the **present general construction** were given in Lesson 35. You saw there that when a supposition implies repeated occurrence in the present, the subjunctive (sometimes with ἄν or κεν) is used to express the supposition, while the main verb is in the present indicative.

But if the supposition implies repeated occurrence in **past** time, the optative is used to express the supposition and the main verb is in the imperfect (rarely the aorist) indicative. The supposition may be a conditional, temporal, or relative clause. Such a construction is termed the **past general construction.** Examples:

If (ever) he ordered them to go, they quickly obeyed.
εἴ σφεας βῆναι κελεύοι, αἶψα πείθοντο.

Whenever he ordered them to go, they quickly obeyed.
ὅτε σφεας βῆναι κελεύοι, αἶψα πείθοντο.

Whoever ordered them to go, they quickly obeyed.
ὅς τις σφεας βῆναι κελεύοι, αἶψα πείθοντο.

Observe that the Greek conditional system follows the **sequence of moods** just as do purpose clauses (Section 106b). In conditional sentences, the verb tense of the apodosis is linked to the mood of the verb in the protasis.

481. WRITE IN GREEK

1. Let us not mingle with them, for they might contrive some evil for us or our friends.

2. He once told me who gave him that beautiful lotus, but I no longer know.

3. Whoever plans destruction for others, wrongs himself too, destroying (aor.) the peace of his own soul.

Lesson 69

482. MEMORIZE

αὐτοῦ	[adv.] in the same place, there
μελιηδής, -ές	honey-sweet
νέομαι	[pres. syst. only] I return

483. TEXT

Strange Power of the Lotus

τῶν δ' ὅς τις λωτοῖο φάγοι μελιηδέα καρπόν,
οὐκέτ' ἀπαγγεῖλαι πάλιν ἤθελεν οὐδὲ νέεσθαι,
ἀλλ' αὐτοῦ βούλοντο μετ' ἀνδράσι Λωτοφάγοισι   25
λωτὸν ἐρεπτόμενοι μενέμεν νόστου τε λαθέσθαι.

ἀπ-αγγέλλω, ἀπ-αγγελέω, ἀπ-άγγειλα	I bring back news
ἐρέπτομαι	I feed upon

484. COMMENT

23-26. There are many folktales from around the world about food which, when tasted, prevents a return home from a fabulous land or an underworld. A familiar example is the myth of Persephone, who after swallowing a pomegranate seed is forever bound to the underworld. Here, having sampled the fruit of the lotus, Odysseus' men sink into a mood of listless inactivity. Forgetful of goals, they think only of indulging without stint in this bewitching luxury.

Their mood has been beautifully depicted by Tennyson at the close of his poem, *The Lotos-Eaters:*

> "Dark faces pale against the rosy sun,
> The mild-eyed melancholy Lotos-eaters came
> Branches they bore of that enchanted stem,
> Laden with flower and fruit, whereof they gave
> To each, but whoso did receive of them
> And taste, to him the gushing of the wave
> Far, far away did seem to mourn and rave
> On alien shores; and if his fellow spoke,
> His voice was thin, as voices from the grave;
> And deep-asleep he seem'd, yet all awake,
> And music in his ears his beating heart did make.
> They sat them down upon the yellow sand,
> Between the sun and moon upon the shore;
> And sweet it was to dream of Fatherland,

> Of child, and wife, and slave; but evermore
> Most weary seem'd the sea, weary the oar,
> Weary the wandering fields of barren foam.
> Then someone said, 'We will return no more;'
> And all at once they sang, 'Our island home
> Is far beyond the wave; we will no longer roam.'"

485. FORMS OF τίθημι, to be memorized

τίθημι, θήσω, θῆκα   I put, I cause

Impf. 3 sg.   τίθει
2 aor. Ind. 3 pl.   θέσαν

2 aor. Opt.	1 sg	θείην	1 pl.	θεῖμεν
	2 sg.	θείης	2 pl.	θεῖτε
	3 sg.	θείη	3 pl.	θεῖεν

486. WRITE IN GREEK

1. If they had not eaten this honey-sweet food, they would not have been forgetful of the return home to their fatherland.

2. Whenever anyone partook of the lotus, he never wished to return to his companions or go up again upon the ships.

3. If anyone desired to remain there among those friendly strangers, we all tried to persuade him not to be forgetful of father and mother and home.

Lesson 70

487. MEMORIZE

γλαφυρός, -ή, -όν	hollow
δέω, δήσω, δῆσα	I tie, I fasten
ἐρίηρος, -ον [pl. 3 decl.: ἐρίηρες, etc.]	faithful, loyal
ἐρύω, —, ἔρυσ(σ)α	I drag, I draw
κέλομαι, κελήσομαι, κεκλόμην	I order
κλαίω, κλαύσω, κλαῦσα	I weep, I wail
ὠκύς, -εῖα, -ύ	swift, nimble

488. TEXT

Escape

τοὺς μὲν ἐγὼν ἐπὶ νῆας ἄγον κλαίοντας ἀνάγκῃ,
νηυσὶ δ' ἐνὶ γλαφυρῇσιν ὑπὸ ζυγὰ δῆσα ἐρύσσας·
αὐτὰρ τοὺς ἄλλους κελόμην ἐρίηρας ἑταίρους
σπερχομένους νηῶν ἐπιβαινέμεν ὠκειάων,   30
μή πώς τις λωτοῖο φαγὼν νόστοιο λάθηται.

ζυγά, -ῶν	[n. pl.] rowers' benches
σπέρχομαι	I hurry

489. NOTES

28. ἐν may be written for metrical reasons as ἐνί, εἰν, εἰνί. ὑπὸ ζυγὰ: "under the rowing benches"

490. COMMENT

27-31. When the scouting party does not return, Odysseus and several picked men set out in search. On finding them and discovering their mood, he realizes at once the danger of the situation. Odysseus resolutely resists the temptation to share in the unmanning delights of the lotus, and snatches his companions away from the plant's mysterious and seductive influence.

28. The ζυγά are thwarts or heavy planks joining the side walls of the ship, crossing its width a few feet above the floor and serving as benches on which the oarsmen sit while rowing. The space underneath was used for safe storage, and there Odysseus casts the deserters in chains until they merit release and reinstatement.

491. THE IRREGULAR VERB οἶδα

Memorize:

οἶδα, εἰδήσω   I know

IND. ACT.	PF.		PLPF.		IMPT.	
	(pres. meaning)		(impf. meaning)			
	sg.	*pl.*	*sg.*	*pl.*	*sg.*	*pl.*
1st pers.	οἶδα	ἴδμεν	ἤδεα	ἴδμεν		
2nd pers.	οἶσθα	ἴστε	ἤδης	ἴστε	ἴσθι	ἴστε
3rd pers.	οἶδε	ἴσασι	ἤδη	ἴσαν		

INF. ἴδμεν(αι)

PTC. (m. f. n. nom.)   εἰδώς, εἰδυῖα, εἰδός

492. WRITE IN GREEK

1. May he bind their hands and put them in his swift ship, until they again become faithful and brave companions.

2. Would any father give a stone to his son asking bread? We ought to have faith in those who love us.

3. Whenever I gave him any food or honey-sweet wine, he always cast half into the fire as a gift to some god.

Lesson 71

493. MEMORIZE

ἅλς, ἁλός	[f.] sea
ἕζομαι, —, ἕσα	I sit down; [in aor.] I cause to be seated
ἑξῆς	[adv.] in order, in rows
ἐρετμόν, -οῦ	[n.] oar
καθ-ίζω, —, κάθισα	I seat myself; I cause to be seated
κληΐς, κληῖδος	[f.] oar-lock; bolt
πολιός, (-ή), -όν	grayish, white
τύπτω, τύψω, τύψα	I strike, I beat

494. TEXT

Flight

οἱ δ᾽ αἶψ᾽ εἴσβαινον καὶ ἐπὶ κληῖσι καθῖζον,   32

ἑξῆς δ᾽ ἑζόμενοι πολιὴν ἅλα τύπτον ἐρετμοῖς.

495. COMMENT

32-33. Once again Odysseus and his men escape from a situation threatening disaster, and proceed on their homeward voyage. Not knowing where they are, except far to the south and west of their original course, they can only sail on in what seems the likeliest direction and hope to come across some familiar place or friendly people to guide them in their search. They take their places in the ship and churn the sea into a snowy foam with vigorous rhythmic strokes of the oars.

496. THE HOMERIC SHIP

Ships were a perpetual source of wonder and delight to Homer's mind. His poetic imagination reveled in the beauty and details of their workmanship and the graceful appearance they presented at sea. Vivid descriptions of ships may be found all through both poems. The picture Homer wishes us to see in the present passage, as gathered from these other descriptions, is one of a dozen slender black hulls upon a silver sea, white sails billowing in the evening breeze, the water dancing and gurgling around the sharp prows and twinkling oars, a pattern of gleaming wakes stretching out behind the lofty sterns in the rosy glow of sunset-tinted waters as the graceful shapes plunge swiftly through the waves. It is a picture one does not easily forget.

The Homeric ship, to judge from the evidence of the poems and ancient Greek vase paintings, was generally about 100 feet long, but only 10 to 12 feet wide. Both prow and stern were built up high above the level of the rest, and on each was a raised platform or deck. The rest of the ship was not floored over to form a continuous deck above the water line, but was left open, like our canoe or rowboat, with spaced cross-beams (ζυγά) used for seats. The hull was firmly built, but slender; half-oval in shape, it had a narrow flat bottom allowing it to be dragged up on the beach. Besides a large sail on a central folding mast, there were 20 to 120 oars (most commonly 50); sail and oars were used together. Steering was done by a large paddle held at an angle along the stern. The prow was usually brightly painted, with a large eye to 'guide' the ship and make it seem alive.

497. WRITE IN GREEK

1.   Whenever they sit down in order at the oarlocks, they beat the sea white with their long oars.

2.   If they had put the food under the same rocks as at first, I would have known where it was and made ready the dinner for them.

3.   Everyone who gave them that honey-sweet but deadly food was contriving pain for them and destruction.

498. WORD STUDY

HALOGEN (any of five 'salt-making' chemical elements, fluorine, chlorine, bromine, astatine, and iodine, which form binary salts by union with metals); — POLIOMYELITIS (μυελός marrow; infantile paralysis, attacking the 'gray marrow' of the spinal cord and causing loss of activity in certain muscles); — TYPE (an impression 'beaten' into a hard substance; a mold or pattern; hence a division or class of objects), TYPEWRITER, TYPIST; LINOTYPE (a machine by which a printer sets up type in one mould for each line), TYPOGRAPHY (art of printing), TELETYPE (automatic printing at a distance by wire), TYPICAL ('according to pattern').

Lesson 72

499. REVIEW OF LESSONS 67-71

Restudy these lessons thoroughly, testing your knowledge with this sample examination:

I.   Vocabulary (25%)

   1.   going: n. dat. pl. =

   2.   we shall contrive =

   3.   destruction: dat. sg. =

   4.   they will be tied =

   5.   may he weep (aor.) =

   6.   oarlock: acc. sg. =

   7.   faithful: f. gen. pl. =

   8.   swift: m. dat. pl. =

   9.   honey-sweet: f. acc. sg. =

   10. in order =

II. Text (50%)

   1.   Why did Odysseus have to bind some of his men?

   2.   How many men did he send to investigate the country?

   3.   How were they received?

   4.   Why did Odysseus order his men to leave so quickly?

   5.   In line 18, explain the form and construction of εἶεν.

   6.   In line 19, explain the form of κήρυχ'

   7.   In line 21, explain the form of μήδονθ'.

   8.   In line 30, explain the case of νηῶν.

   9.   In line 31, explain the form and construction of λάθηται .

   10. In line 33, explain the case of ἐρετμοῖς.

III. Grammar (25%)

Translate only the words in italics:

   1.   If we should *put* the oars in your boat, what *would you* (sg.) *give* us?

   2.   Whenever they *ate* the lotus, they no longer knew in what country they once *dwelt*.

   3.   If a ship ever *appeared*, he *sent forth* two companions to meet it.

   4.   Ask him why he *put* the sails under the *hollow rock*.

   5.   Since you (sg.) *knew* it was mine all along, *give* it to me now.

Lesson 73

500. MEMORIZE

ἦμος	[conj.] when
ἠριγένεια, -ης	the early-born (one)
Ἠώς, Ἠόος	[f.] Eos [the personified goddess of the dawn]
μίμνω	[pres. system only] I remain, I await
ῥοδοδάκτυλος, -ον	rosy-fingered

Shortly after leaving the land of the lotus-eaters, the ships are surrounded by an impenetrable mist. In the absence of any stars to indicate direction, the Greeks again do not know where the wind is driving them. Suddenly at dawn they find themselves running up on the beach of a small island near another much larger. They disembark and spend the day in hunting wild goats and in feasting on the delicacy. Seeing smoke and hearing the cries of men and animals on the large island across the strait, they decide to investigate. But as night is near, they first take their sleep along the shore. Odysseus now tells us of the exploration on the next morning and what they found.

Included in the omitted lines (9.105-169) leading up to our passage are sociological and anthropological details about the Cyclopes. Odysseus observes that they have no laws (θέμιστες) and no assemblies (ἀγοραὶ βουληφόροι). Possessing no technology, they neither build ships nor houses; nor do they cultivate the soil, but subsist on the wild foods abundantly available to them. In this sketch, Odysseus introduces the Cyclopes as culturally primitive. Because they lack ships, they have been unable to settle or develop the fertile forested island with its excellent harbor, in which the Greeks have now landed.

501. TEXT

Second Adventure: On the Island of the Cyclops

ἦμος δ᾽ ἠριγένεια φάνη ῥοδοδάκτυλος Ἠώς,
καὶ τότ᾽ ἐγὼν ἀγορὴν θέμενος μετὰ πᾶσιν ἔειπον·   35
"ἄλλοι μὲν νῦν μίμνετ᾽, ἐμοὶ ἐρίηρες ἑταῖροι·
αὐτὰρ ἐγὼ σὺν νηΐ τ᾽ ἐμῇ καὶ ἐμοῖσ᾽ ἑτάροισιν
ἐλθὼν τῶνδ᾽ ἀνδρῶν πειρήσομαι, οἵ τινές εἰσιν,

   ἀγορή, -ῆς [f.] general assembly

222

502. NOTES

35. καὶ τότ᾽ = "at once." θέμενος : 2 aor. ptc. of τίθημι. See Section 472. ἔειπον : since εἶπον formerly began with a digamma, it has a syllabic augment (= ἔϝειπον).

36. ἄλλοι μὲν = "the rest of you" as opposed to the companions on Odysseus' own ship (37)

503. COMMENT

34. The beauty of this famous line, which Homer frequently repeats, is due not only to the vivid metaphor but also to the melodious flow of soft liquid consonants and echoing long vowels. The line represents a highly poetic combination of imaginative charm and skilful word-music. Dawn's "fingers" probably are her spreading crimson/saffron rays along the horizon, reaching out to take over the sky.

36-38. Odysseus' willingness to share in all risks (an essential of great leadership) is one reason why his men have such respect and loyalty for him.

504. DATIVE OF POSSESSION

As was seen in Lesson 6, the personal dative expresses to whom a thing is given, or for whom something is or is done (Dative of reference). When an object is "for" or "belongs to" a person in a special way, the person is said to possess it. Thus a strong Dative of reference, especially when it is a personal pronoun, may be considered a Dative of possession. For example:

ἡμῖν κατ-εκλάσθη ἦτορ. = **Our** heart was crushed.

σφιν νόος ἐστὶ θεουδής. = **Theirs** is a God-fearing mind.

505. WRITE IN GREEK

1. Let us all hope that the dawn of a better day will appear to men suffering (aor.) the many woes and evils of this war.

2. If the others should remain and fight for the sake of our fatherland, would you have the heart to show yourself a coward and hide among the women and children?

3. If we had always made trial of the length and strength of those trees with which we intended to build our ships, the ships no doubt would have been larger, stronger, and swifter than they are now.

506. WORD STUDY

EOLITHIC (the 'dawn of the Stone Age', a very early geological period of the earth's history).

Lesson 74

507. MEMORIZE

ἄγριος, (-η), -ον   wild, savage

ἀνά or ἄμ   [adv.] up; back
           [prep. + gen.] on (to)
           [prep. + dat.] on [at rest]
           [prep. + acc.] on (to), over

508. TEXT

A Fateful Start

ἤ ῥ᾽ οἵ γ᾽ ὑβρισταί τε καὶ ἄγριοι οὐδὲ δίκαιοι,
ἦε φιλόξεινοι, καί σφιν νόος ἐστὶ θεουδής."   40
ὣς εἰπὼν ἀνὰ νηὸς ἔβην, ἐκέλευσα δ᾽ ἑταίρους
αὐτούς τ᾽ ἀμβαίνειν ἀνά τε πρυμνήσια λῦσαι.

     θεουδής, -ές   god-fearing
     πρυμνήσια, -ων   [n. pl.] stern-cables
     ὑβρισταί, άων   [m.] haughty, violent men
     φιλόξεινος, -η, -ον   hospitable

509. NOTES

39-40.   ἤ...ἦε "whether...or" [in indirect question]

41.   ἑταίρους : i.e., the crew of his own flagship.

42.   ἀμβαίνειν : = ἀνα-βαίνειν.   ἀνά...λῦσαι = "loose and draw up"

510. COMMENT

39-42.   Odysseus is driven by his curiosity about the inhabitants of this new land and assumes that encounters with strangers will result in positive experiences—specifically, hospitable entertainment and gift-exchange. However, after his experience as the ξεῖνος of Polyphemus, Odysseus will not evidence so much curiosity or confidence in approaching new experiences.

32.   Greek ships were ordinarily moored in shallow water, their prows facing out to sea for easier departure. The πρυμνήσια were strong rope cables or hawsers binding the stern to some rock, tree, or post on shore. Heavy anchor stones held the prow firmly into the face of the waves.

511. THE CHARACTER OF ODYSSEUS (PART 1)

A look at the opening lines of the *Odyssey* gives an efficient introduction not only to the important themes of the poem but to the basic shape of the hero's character. His name is withheld from us, just as Odysseus will cunningly withhold his name from the Cyclops, Polyphemus. Instead, with his first word Homer refers to him as a man; the emphasis here is not on this hero's immortal glory, but his humanity. We are told that his wanderings were intellectually broadening, but also that he suffered much, all in an effort to survive and to save his companions' lives. That the hero struggled to survive once again underlines his mortality, while his efforts to preserve the lives of others contrasts with heroes of warfare such as Achilles, whose life-destroying wrath is celebrated in the opening lines of the *Iliad*. The proem tells us that Odysseus is a man of many ways (πολύτροπος), who wandered much, saw and learned about many people, and suffered many pains; the reiteration of words with πολ(λ)- points to an essential characteristic of Odysseus, his versatility. It also anticipates the several epithets of Odysseus which convey the versatile nature of his intelligence: besides πολύτροπος, these include πολύφρων (of much intellectual capacity), πολυμήχανος (of many devices), πολύμητις (of much cunning).

When Odysseus withholds his own name from the Cyclops and instead calls himself "Nobody," he is using a form of disguise in order to protect himself and increase his chances of survival, just as he does in other episodes. And as in other episodes featuring a disguised Odysseus, intellectual excellence is being pitted against physical superiority. Odysseus will overcome the more numerous suitors occupying his house in Ithaca in part thanks to his successful disguise as a helpless beggar. The disguised Odysseus is able to penetrate and assess a hostile situation, gathering the information needed to make an assault that makes up for its lack of physical power with its timeliness and opportunism. In Book 4 Helen tells about Odysseus' infiltration into Troy similarly disguised as a beggar. Under the cloak of these unthreatening rags, the wily Odysseus is able to gather information about the layout of Troy in preparation for the Greek attack following their entry inside of the Wooden Horse— another sort of disguise, and a brainchild of Odysseus. Indeed, Menelaus' narrative of the Wooden Horse, also in Book 4, points to another essential aspect of Odysseus' proficiency at disguise. Helen's realistic imitation of the Greek's wives' voices as she circles the Horse fools all the Greeks except Odysseus, and nearly moves them to blow their cover. Only Odysseus is able to resist such an impulse, and thus control the timing of his actions so as to maximize their appropriateness. Moreover, Odysseus' intelligence and self-control saves lives.

The episode we are reading stars a character who is antithetical to Odysseus. Polyphemus is big and strong, but intellectually he is no match for Odysseus, who is able to defeat him with his cunning. Odysseus resists the urge to kill the monster in retaliation for the murder of his companions, knowing that only a live Polyphemus is strong enough to remove the enormous boulder he uses as a door to his cave, allowing the men to escape. Thus, they must manipulate the monster into using his physical force for their benefit. As in many contests in which Odysseus competes, the stronger man must be managed, not just eliminated. As we shall see, this method requires the gathering and/or the controlling of information through disguise and/or observation, and the self-control to wait until the opportune moment.

512. WRITE IN GREEK

1. I remained near the town, that I might learn whether these men were cruel and their (dat.) hearts savage, or honorable and lovers of (ptc.) virtue.

2. We ourselves, indeed, quickly went upon the long ships and sat in order at the oarlocks, but he ordered the others to take the sheep and bring them to the good king. [For "to take…and" use the ptc. only.]

3. It is necessary for all mortals to suffer pain and death; to endure them patiently is difficult but is noble.

513. WORD STUDY

ANACHRONISM (a chronological error which 'throws time back' by projecting something from its own period into an earlier one where it is out of place, e.g., a play showing Abraham Lincoln using a computer), ANAGRAM (a word formed by 'writing over again' the letters of some other word where they are differently arranged, as "own, won, now," or the answer (John 18.38) to Pilate's question to Christ "Quid est veritas?" [*What is truth?*] becoming "Est vir qui adest" [*It is the man who is present*]), ANATOMY, ANATOMICAL (τομή a cutting; 'cutting up' or dissecting a body to learn its structure; the science which studies the structural organization of bodies), ANATHEMA (θέμα, from τίθημι, an official religious curse or denunciation of evil or error, declaring a person or doctrine 'put up' as an object of horror to be avoided and as 'given over' to destruction).

Lesson 75

514. MEMORIZE

ἄγχι	[adv., and prep. + gen.] near, close by
αἴξ, αἰγός	[m., f.] goat
ἀφ-ικνέομαι, ἀφ-ίξομαι, ἀφ-ικόμην	I come to, I arrive [+ acc.]
ὄϊς, ὄϊος	[dat. pl. also ὄεσσι, acc. pl. always ὄϊς] [m., f.] sheep
σπέος, σπέος or σπῆος	[n.] cave
χῶρος, -ου	[m.] place, region

515. TEXT

Arrival

οἱ δ' αἶψ' εἴσβαινον καὶ ἐπὶ κληῖσι καθῖζον,
ἑξῆς δ' ἑζόμενοι πολιὴν ἅλα τύπτον ἐρετμοῖς.
ἀλλ' ὅτε δὴ τὸν χῶρον ἀφικόμεθ' ἐγγὺς ἐόντα,   45
ἔνθα δ' ἐπ' ἐσχατιῇ σπέος εἴδομεν ἄγχι θαλάσσης,
ὑψηλόν, δάφνῃσι κατηρεφές· ἔνθα δὲ πολλὰ
μῆλ', ὄϊές τε καὶ αἶγες, ἰαύεσκον·

δάφνη, -ης	[f.] laurel
ἐσχατιή, -ῆς	[f.] extremity, edge
ἰαύω, ἰαύσω, ἴαυσα	I pass the night
κατ-ηρεφής, -ές	roofed over

516. NOTES

45. τὸν χῶρον : τὸν is here demonstrative = 'that' (i.e., aforementioned) large island across the strait that was mentioned in the summary in Section 500

46. εἴδομεν is the augmented form of ἴδομεν (= ἐϝίδομεν).

48. ὄϊες : for ὄϝιες — which explains why the οι is not a diphthong but two syllables throughout the declension of this word (cp. the Latin for sheep: *ovis*). Whenever the breathing is placed over the first of two vowels, it is a sign that they do not form a diphthong.

517. COMMENT

43-44. It is characteristic of Homer's oral and traditional style, and of epic and ballad technique in general, to repeat certain lines or expressions whenever speaking of the same thing again. This repetition of formulaic phrases and lines was also a welcome aid to the ancient bards who composed orally as they performed. See if you can recognize repeated lines as you read on.

46. The cave, which Odysseus can see from his vantage point, and the flocks sleeping within it, are going to be important in the episode that follows. Moreover, the use of caves for housing instead of built structures is emblematic of a technologically primitive culture.

518. THE CHARACTER OF ODYSSEUS (PART 2)

Wily intelligence, self-control, awareness of mortality, versatility and humanity are the qualities that stand out in the *Odyssey*'s hero. How consistent is this portrait with the Odysseus who appears in the *Iliad* and elsewhere outside of the *Odyssey*?

In a scene in Book 3 of the *Iliad*, Helen suggests that Odysseus' appearance is itself a sort of disguise. To look at Odysseus before he begins to speak, she says, you'd think him a bit simpleminded, for he has an awkward posture and a stare directed at the ground beneath his own feet. But such impressions are dispelled by his powerful and fluent speech, for he is unrivalled as a rhetorician and diplomat. Indeed, Odysseus is Agamemnon's right-hand man in the *Iliad*, serving as his spokesman and ambassador. It is he who is charged with presenting Agamemnon's offer to Achilles to persuade him to rejoin the Greeks in their attack on Troy (Book 9). Thus the *Iliad*'s Odysseus possesses a hidden excellence that seems to gain power beyond that which is intrinsic to it as it emerges from an unlikely cover. Odysseus' oratory ambushes the unsuspecting audience the way a warrior camouflaged by the night might surprise his foe.

And indeed a night ambush is another episode in which Odysseus stars in the *Iliad*. Book 10 tells how Odysseus and Diomedes, on a spying mission, sneak into the Trojan camp at night. They ambush a Trojan scout and trick him, with assurances that he will be released alive, into giving information about Trojan plans and the location of Hector, his gear and horses, as well as the stationing of the various Trojan allies. After he has given them all this information, and even pointed out the camp of the rich King Rhesus and his Thracians, they kill him; they then proceed to kill the sleeping Rhesus and twelve of the Thracians and to steal their splendid horses. This sort of warfare relies on cunning to a much more obvious extent than a battle between spear fighters on a open plain, a type of battle that is more common in the *Iliad*, and in which its physically powerful hero, Achilles, excels. Yet it is easy to see that Odysseus' character suits him well for the ambush, which requires some self-concealment, patience, self-control and good timing in order to surprise the enemy.

The Epic Cycle presents an Odysseus who is inclined towards trickery, but not always for heroic ends. Odysseus is first mentioned in the *Cypria*, according to the evidence we have about that lost epic poem. Because Odysseus had been one of the suitors for the hand of Helen, he had been bound by an oath to fight for her husband should she ever be abducted. Yet, when this very thing happens and recruiters come to Ithaca to collect Odysseus, he feigns insanity—pushing his plow backwards— in order to avoid military service. Palamedes, another wily hero, is able to expose Odysseus' insanity as an act by placing the baby Telemachus in front of the plowshare; Odysseus gives himself away when he opts to save his son. Odysseus later takes revenge on Palamedes by forging a letter from the Trojan King Priam to Palamedes, offering him a generous bribe of gold in return for betraying the Greeks; Odysseus also hides the specified amount of gold in Palamedes' quarters and makes sure that the forged letter is seen by Agamemnon, who has Palamedes stoned by the army.

In the *Little Iliad* Odysseus and Diomedes manage to steal the Trojan guardian statue of the armed Athene called the Palladium. On the way back from this venture, Odysseus tries to get Diomedes killed in order to be able to take all the credit for himself.

519. WRITE IN GREEK

1. In a wide place close by the sea, we came to a very high cave in which we saw many sheep and cows and wild goats.

2. He did not know that some shepherd is always roaming back and forth here among the beautiful white sheep, lest anyone should injure them.

3. Whenever he perceived rosy-fingered Dawn appear over the deep, he took the little sheep that he especially loved and put it at the door of the cave. ["He took…and" = "taking"]

Lesson 76

520. MEMORIZE

ἀπόπροσθεν	[adv.] far away, aloof
ἰδέ	[conj.] and [= ἠδέ]
οἶος, -η, -ον	alone
πελώριος, -η, -ον	gigantic, monstrous

521. TEXT

The Setting

περὶ δ᾽ αὐλὴ
ὑψηλὴ δέδμητο κατωρυχέεσσι λίθοισι
μακρῇσίν τε πίτυσσιν ἰδὲ δρυσὶν ὑψικόμοισιν.   50
ἔνθα δ᾽ ἀνὴρ ἐνίαυε πελώριος, ὅς ῥα τὰ μῆλα
οἶος ποιμαίνεσκεν ἀπόπροθεν· οὐδὲ μετ᾽ ἄλλους
πωλεῖτ᾽, ἀλλ᾽ ἀπάνευθεν ἐὼν ἀθεμίστια ᾔδη.

ἀθεμίστιος, -η, -ον	lawless
δέμω, —, δεῖμα, —, δέδμημαι	I build
δρύς, δρυός	[f.] oak
ἐν-ιαύω	I pass the night in
κατωρυχής, -ες	embedded in the ground
πίτυς, -υος	[f.] pine-tree
ποιμαίνω	I tend, I shepherd
πωλέομαι	I am accustomed to go
ὑψίκομος, -ον	lofty-leafed

522. NOTES

48. περί : round about (the cave's mouth). αὐλή here means "fence" or "wall" (of a farmyard).

53. ἀθεμίστια ᾔδη: i.e., acknowledged no law. For the verb form, see Section 491.

523. COMMENT

48-50. The enormous size of the fence around the fold, built with whole trunks of trees, is the first indication Odysseus has that the natives here are of unusual stature.

51-53. This man turns out to be the giant Polyphemus, a Cyclops ("Circle-eye"). No mention is made of Polyphemus' single eye; aside from the monster's size, the poem's emphasis here is on his asocial character. Note that this information about Polyphemus is not discerned by the hero from his position in the ship, but is gathered later, as the episode unfolds.

524. OPTATIVE OF EXPECTATION

Sometimes a potential optative has the special force of indicating what one desires or expects to happen under the circumstances. This occurs in relative or temporal clauses referring to the future and depending upon some present or projected action of the main verb's subject. This construction follows the regular potential optative rule (optative with κε(ν) or ἄν, cp. Section 285b) but it has to be translated a bit differently in English—by *can*, *will*, or some other less hypothetical expression than *could*, *should*, or *might*. For example:

εὕρωμέν τινα ὅς κεν εἴποι τί ἐστιν.

*Let us find somebody who **can** (or **will**) tell us what it is.*

525. WRITE IN GREEK

1. According to what our companions say, these monstrous shepherds used to remain aloof, and did not wish to be loved or even seen by mortals who go upon the broad sea in hollow ships.

2. He was like to a high tree which the gods put alone on a lofty rock, where it appears to men far away in the middle of the deep.

3. Whenever we feared that something evil was about to happen, we prayed to Apollo, and he always protected us, as (one) well knowing what need we had.

Lesson 77

526. MEMORIZE

ἀρνειός, -οῦ	[m.] (full-grown) ram
θυρεός, -οῦ	[m.] door-stone
ἵστημι, στήσω, στῆσα	I put; I halt [trans.]
ἵσταμαι, στήσομαι, στῆν	I stand, I halt [intr.]
ὄρος, ὄρεος	[n.] mountain

527. TEXT

The Giant Cyclops

καὶ γὰρ θαῦμ᾽ ἐτέτυκτο πελώριον, οὐδὲ ἐῴκει
ἀνδρί γε σιτοφάγῳ, ἀλλὰ ῥίῳ ὑλήεντι   55
ὑψηλῶν ὀρέων, ὅ τε φαίνεται οἶον ἀπ᾽ ἄλλων.
   δὴ τότε τοὺς ἄλλους κελόμην ἐρίηρας ἑταίρους
αὐτοῦ πὰρ νηΐ τε μένειν καὶ νῆα ἔρυσθαι·

θαῦμα, -ατος	[n.] wonder, marvel
ῥίον, -ου	[n.] peak, crag
σιτοφάγος, -η, -ον	bread-eating
ὑλήεις, -εσσα, -εν	tree-covered, wooded

528. NOTES

54. ἐτέτυκτο. Remember that in the pf. pass. system τεύχω often = "I am," etc.

58. πὰρ = παρά. ἔρυσθαι = ἐρύεσθαι .

529. COMMENT

54-56. In describing the vast and terrifying size of the monster who dwelt in this cave, Odysseus is anticipating a bit in his story. At this point, the Greeks have not yet seen the Cyclops; but in narrating things after the event, Odysseus draws on his fuller knowledge and skillfully lets us in on important details necessary to put us in the right mood for grasping the emotional significance of what is to follow. Alfred Noyes has caught the mood of this passage in his imitation of it as the opening of his poem *Forty Singing Seamen*:

> Across the seas of Wonderland to Mogadore we plodded,
> Forty singing seamen in an old black barque,
> And we landed in the twilight where a Polyphemus nodded
> With his battered moon-eye winking red and yellow through the dark
> For his eye was growing mellow

Rich and ripe and red and yellow
As was time, since old Ulysses made him bellow in the dark!
Were they mountains in the gloaming or the giant's ugly shoulders
Just beneath the rolling eyeball, with its bleared and vinous glow,
Red and yellow o'er the purple of the pines among the boulders
And the shaggy horror brooding on the sullen slopes below?
Were they pines among the boulders
Or the hair upon his shoulders?
We were only simple seamen, so of course we didn't know.*

*From *Collected Poems of Alfred Noyes*, Vol. 1 (Copyright, 1906).
Reprinted by permission of the publishers, J. B. Lippincott Co.

57-58. Sensing danger, Odysseus leaves most of his men at the ship, to protect it, keep it in readiness for flight, and at least prevent the whole crew being swallowed up by disaster if things go wrong at the cave.

530. WRITE IN GREEK

1. There the shepherd remained, to protect the rams and goats hiding in a great cave in the middle of the mountain.

2. Whenever a ship appears, we rejoice; for we always fear that it may miss this small place, on account of the storms and great winds.

3. None of us knew whether they gave the gold to some friend or put it under the door-stone of some house where no one might find it.

531. WORD STUDY

ECSTASY (στάσις a standing [cp. ptc. στάς], 'a standing out of oneself' through some overpowering emotion or mental exaltation; rapture, extreme enthusiasm; a religious trance when the soul seems carried out of the body and united to God in prayer), APOSTASY ('a standing away from' some group or cause to which one formerly belonged, especially desertion from one's religion), APOSTATE, APOSTATIZE.

Lesson 78

532. REVIEW OF LESSONS 73-77

In lessons 73-77 you have memorized sixteen new words, have read twenty-five lines of text, and have studied two new points of syntax: the Dative of Possession and the Optative of Expectation. Review thoroughly; then test your review with this sample examination.

I.   Text (30%), 10 minutes:

1.   Translate: μετὰ πᾶσιν ἔειπον.
2.   In 1.38, explain case of ἀνδρῶν .
3.   In 1.42, why is λῦσαι an infinitive?
4.   Translate: οὐδὲ ἐῴκει ἀνδρί.
5.   In 1.40, explain case of σφιν.

II.   Syntax (20%), 10 minutes; translate:

1.   Let us wait here until someone comes who can show us the way.
2.   We asked if these ships were his, and if he built them himself.

III.   Vocabulary (20%), 10 minutes:

1.   Dawn: acc. sg. =
2.   we shall arrive =
3.   ἦμος =
4.   goat: dat. pl. =
5.   wild: masc. dat. pl. =
6.   cave: acc. pl. =
7.   ἄγχι =
8.   ὀρέεσσι =
9.   sheep: acc. pl. =

IV.   Story (30%), 15 minutes:

1.   Write a brief (100 words) but accurate account of the events of these lines.
2.   Was Odysseus a good leader? Cite evidence from the last 25 lines.
3.   Homer's style is unaffected and concrete. In the light of the lines read in the last five lessons, give reasons for accepting or denying this statement.

Lesson 79

533. MEMORIZE

ἀγλαός, -ή, -όν	splendid
ἄμαξα, -ης	[f.] wagon
ἀσκός, -οῦ	[m.] bag
μέλας, μέλαινα, μέλαν	[m. and n. gen. μέλανος] dark, black
ὑψόσε	[adv.] on high, upwards

534. TEXT

A Tactful Approach

αὐτὰρ ἐγὼ κρίνας ἑτάρων δυοκαίδεκ᾽ ἀρίστους
βῆν· ἀτὰρ αἴγεον ἀσκὸν ἔχον μέλανος οἴνοιο,   60
ἡδέος, ὅν μοι δῶκε Μάρων, Εὐάνθεος υἱός,
ἱρεὺς Ἀπόλλωνος, ὃς Ἴσμαρον ἀμφιβεβήκει,
οὕνεκά μιν σὺν παιδὶ περισχόμεθ᾽ ἠδὲ γυναικὶ
ἁζόμενοι· ᾤκει γὰρ ἐν ἄλσεϊ δενδρήεντι
Φοίβου Ἀπόλλωνος. ὁ δέ μοι πόρεν ἀγλαὰ δῶρα·   65

αἴγεος, -η, -ον	of a goat, goatskin
ἄλσος, -εος	[n.] sacred grove
ἀμφι-βαίνω	I go around; I guard
δενδρήεις, -εσσα, -εν	densely wooded
δυοκαίδεκα	[indecl.] twelve
Εὐάνθης, -εος	[m.] Euanthes
ἱ(ε)ρεύς, -ῆος	[m.] priest
Ἴσμαρος, -ου	[m.] the town of the Cicones
Μάρων, -ονος	[m.] Maron
οὕνεκα	because, seeing that
περι-έχομαι	I hold myself about, I protect
Φοῖβος, -ου	[m.] Phoebus ('the bright one'), name of Apollo

535. NOTES

62. ὅς : the antecedent is Ἀπόλλων .

62. ἀμφι-βεβήκει : the god had protected the city as its special guardian divinity before it was destroyed; or perhaps = an impf. (cp. Section 320, n. 3): he had made himself the city's protector and was such permanently while it existed.

536. COMMENT

59-61. With characteristic foresight and psychology, Odysseus sets out not only with a strong guard but with gifts— and just that sort of gift which is sure to be understood and welcomed. He will win over the stranger's friendship if possible, receiving aid and friendly gifts in return; but he can protect himself, too, if the natives are hostile. He feels ready for whatever may develop.

60. The wine is kept in a leather bag made of goatskin stitched together.

63-65. When he destroyed Ismarus, the Cicones' town (cp. Section 455), Odysseus had spared the priestly family at Apollo's shrine, out of reverence and in fear of the god's anger. How the good man's gifts of gratitude are now to work their blessing in Odysseus' favor will be seen as the tale unfolds.

537. THE TROJAN WAR (PART ONE)

Homer presupposes in the *Odyssey* (as does Vergil in the *Aeneid*) that his readers are already familiar with the main details in the traditional account of the Trojan War. You ought, then, to know at least the outlines of this, the most famous and widely referred to war in literature.

The story of the Trojan War, its causes and aftermath, was the subject of eight epic poems, two of which, the *Iliad* and the *Odyssey*, are extant. These poems belonged to what is called the Epic Cycle, a collection of early Greek epics. From summaries of their contents, compiled in antiquity, we are able to draw an outline of the legendary war at Troy.

At the marriage banquet of Peleus and Thetis, parents of Achilles, the goddess Strife (who had not been invited, because of her bad manners; she was always irritating people) throws onto the table from heaven a golden apple inscribed Καλλίστη. Since each of the goddesses present naturally thinks this was meant for herself, quarrels arise. The Trojan prince Paris is finally constituted judge, and on being promised by Aphrodite (Venus) that he would win Helen, most beautiful woman in the world, for wife, he awards her the prize.

But Helen is meanwhile married to Menelaus, king of Sparta in Greece. Paris nevertheless lays a plot, and gaining possession of Helen takes her to Troy. The Greek kings, shocked by the crime and this outrage to their honor, join forces under Agamemnon, king of Mycenae and brother of Menelaus. They had earlier sworn an oath, on Odysseus' urging, to support Helen's husband in defending her. In a mighty expedition of 100,000 men and 1186 ships (as described in Book 2 of the *Iliad*) they arrive, after many delays and strange incidents, at the coast of Troy and set up camp. Menelaus and Odysseus go to king Priam of Troy and demand Helen's return, with rich gifts as reparations. But the Trojans are led by Paris' insistence to refuse, and war is declared.

538. WRITE IN GREEK

1. Since we revered the holy man and saved his life, he gave us a great bag of honey-sweet wine, with which I was greatly pleased.

2. Whenever you (pl.) ask for it, you will receive a most splendid gift, which I was saving for you until you should arrive.

3. Some cruel (fellow), having seized the children's wagon and lifted it on high, hurled it afar into the river.

539. WORD STUDY

MELANCHOLY, MELANCHOLIC (χολή bile; a state of depression, gloom, constitutional low spirits, formerly ascribed in medical theory to an excess of 'black bile' getting into the bloodstream from the liver).

Lesson 80

540. MEMORIZE

ἄλοχος, -ου	[f.] wife
ἀμφίπολος, -ου	[f.] handmaid, female attendant
δμώς, δμωός	[m.] man-servant
ἑπτά	[indecl.] seven
εὐ-εργής, -ές	well made; fine
κρητήρ, κρητῆρος	[m.] mixing-bowl

541 TEXT

Maron's Gratitude

χρυσοῦ μέν μοι δῶκ' εὐεργέος ἑπτὰ τάλαντα,   66
δῶκε δέ μοι κρητῆρα πανάργυρον, αὐτὰρ ἔπειτα
οἶνον ἐν ἀμφιφορεῦσι δυώδεκα πᾶσιν ἀφύσσας,
ἡδὺν ἀκηράσιον, θεῖον ποτόν· οὐδέ τις αὐτὸν
ἠείδη δμώων οὐδ' ἀμφιπόλων ἐνὶ οἴκῳ,   70
ἀλλ' αὐτὸς ἄλοχός τε φίλη ταμίη τε μί' οἴη.

ἀκηράσιος, -ον	pure, unmixed
ἀμφι-φορεύς, -ος	[dat. pl. ἀμφιφορεῦσι] two-handled jar for wine; amphora
δυώδεκα	twelve
θεῖος, -η, -ον	divine, excellent
παν-άργυρος, -ον	all of silver
ποτόν, -οῦ	[n.] drink
τάλαντον, -ου	[n.] talent [a standard weight]
ταμίη, -ης	[f.] housekeeper

542. NOTES

68. ἐν ἀμφιφορεῦσι δυώδεκα πᾶσιν : "in twelve amphoras all-told"

70. ἠείδη : 3 sg. plpf. of οἶδα [= ᾔδη] cp. Section 491. δμώων, ἀμφιπόλων :
both genitives in this line are partitive, going with τις (cp. Section 18b).

71. The verb for these nominatives is to be carried over from the preceding line.

543. COMMENT

66-71. In his joy at being spared, the old priest gives Odysseus precious objects dear
to his heart. The bowl was likely a keepsake particularly admired for its artistic
ornamentation. The wine is obviously a very special treasure, because of its
remarkable flavor and fragrance— as we learn in the following lines.

Odysseus' humanity and respectful consideration, not expected from an enemy leader on a punitive expedition, are an indication of high character; it is fitting that they should be so well rewarded.

544. THE TROJAN WAR (PART TWO)

Unable to break through Troy's enormous god-built walls, the Greeks surround the city and keep it under blockade. There are occasional battles on the plain toward the sea, and many raiding expeditions on nearby towns for food and to prevent their assisting Troy. After ten years of such indecisive fighting, Agamemnon and the army wish to give up and return home, but Odysseus inspires them with courage to carry on. Achilles, greatest of Greek warriors, is insulted by Agamemnon and refuses to fight or allow his army to aid the others. An attempt to settle the war by a single combat between Menelaus and Paris fails, and violent battles go on for weeks.

Despite the brave efforts of many Greek heroes, and the momentary victory won by Odysseus and Diomedes in a night attack on one enemy camp, the Greeks are driven back to the sea by the noble Trojan leader Hector, who even sets fire to some of their ships.

Achilles, on the death of his dear friend Patroclus, finally reenters the war and in a fury of irresistible might drives the Trojans back within their walls, killing Hector and many others. When two new armies, of the Amazons and Ethiopians, come to aid Troy, Achilles slays their leaders and routs the host, but is himself slain by an arrow from Paris' bow. His armor is awarded to Odysseus, as bravest of the other Greeks, and, by his shrewdness in strategy, the greatest threat to Troy. This honor is again shown deserved when Odysseus, with Diomedes' aid, enters Troy in disguise and carries off from the temple a closely guarded sacred image of Athene, which had won the city divine protection. He is also in command of the troops within the great wooden horse by which Troy is finally tricked, entered, and destroyed. And it was he who thought up this clever stratagem for winning the war. Only a few Trojans escape with their lives, among them Aeneas, who finally sets up in Italy a new Troy later identified by the Romans as the origin of Rome.

There are, in Homer and the other poets, countless details filling out this general plot, and much vivid description and character portrayal. The story of Troy is one of the most fully and ingeniously developed of all legends. It forms the basis for a large proportion of the most famous writings of Greece, Rome, and the Middle Ages; and it enters extensively into the work of earlier English authors, including Chaucer, Spenser, and Shakespeare. Many modern poems and novels have also drawn on it in interesting ways.

545. WRITE IN GREEK

1. If he had been a wiser man, he would have put (θηκ-) the sweet but strong wine into that splendid black mixing-bowl which was lying beside him, and would have mixed seven measures of water with it.

2. In that great mountain we found a gigantic hollow cave, in which was concealed a most splendid treasure of gold.

546. WORD STUDY

HEPTAGON (γωνίη angle; a seven-sided geometrical figure); — CRATER (a 'bowl-shaped' cavity forming the mouth of a volcano); — TALENT (one's inborn 'amount of natural endowment'), TALENTED.

Lesson 81

547. MEMORIZE

ἀγήνωρ, ἀγήνορος	[adj.] manly, courageous
ἀπ-έχω	I hold back from, I refrain from
αὐτίκα	[adv.] at once
ἐμ-πίπλημι, ἐμ-πλήσω, ἔμ-πλησα	I fill (with)
ἐπ-έρχομαι	I come to, I come upon [+ dat., acc.]
θεσπέσιος, -η, -ον	heavenly, divine
χέω, χεύω, χεῦα	I pour; I heap up

548. TEXT

A Wine for the Gods

τὸν δ᾽ ὅτε πίνοιεν μελιηδέα οἶνον ἐρυθρόν,   72
ἓν δέπας ἐμπλήσας ὕδατος ἀνὰ εἴκοσι μέτρα
χεῦ᾽, ὀδμὴ δ᾽ ἡδεῖα ἀπὸ κρητῆρος ὀδώδει,
θεσπεσίη· τότ᾽ ἂν οὔ τοι ἀποσχέσθαι φίλον ἦεν.
τοῦ φέρον ἐμπλήσας ἀσκὸν μέγαν, ἐν δὲ καὶ ἦα
κωρύκῳ· αὐτίκα γάρ μοι ὀΐσατο θυμὸς ἀγήνωρ
ἄνδρ᾽ ἐπελεύσεσθαι μεγάλην ἐπιειμένον ἀλκήν,
ἄγριον, οὔτε δίκας εὖ εἰδότα οὔτε θέμιστας.   79

ἀλκή, -ῆς	[f.] prowess, strength
δέπας, -αος	[n.] cup, bowl
εἴκοσι	[indecl.] twenty
ἐπι-εῖμαι : pf. mid. of ἐπι-έννυμι	I clothe with [+ acc.]
ἐρυθρός, -ή, -όν	red
ἦα, -ων	[n. pl.] provisions
κώρυκος, -ου	[m.] bag, sack
ὀδμή, -ῆς	[f.] fragrance, scent
ὀδώδεα	plpf. with impf. sense of ὄζω: spread abroad [of an aroma]

549. NOTES

73. ἀνά here means "into, among" [= "over the extent of"]

72-73. ἕν...χεῦ᾽ : "Having filled one cup [of wine] he would pour it into twenty measures of water."

75. ἄν with a past indicative verb gives the clause a contrary to fact meaning.

76. τοῦ goes with ἀσκόν ; ἐν with κωρύκῳ.

77-79. ἄνδρ᾽ is the object of ἐπελεύσεσθαι, which is an inf. in indirect statement after ὀΐσατο.

550. COMMENT

72-75. From this description of the wine's merits it becomes evident why Maron kept it so well hidden and why Odysseus called it at line 69 "a drink fit for the gods."

73. Note that the ancient method of diluting was to pour the wine into water, not add water to the wine. The usual ratio was three parts of water to two of wine. Maron's concentrate therefore was especially potent.

76-79. Reflecting on the vast size of the sheep-pen as seen from the coast (lines 48-50), Odysseus suspected the cave's inhabitant might be a huge and burly fellow who likes his wine strong, and the easiest way to whose friendship would be a gift of food and a bag of wine—especially if this is of a quality he probably has never before known.

78. ἐπι-ειμένον : this is a common metaphor in Homer and other ancient authors. For instance, in the Old Testament, as *Ecclesiasticus* 17.2 "God clothed him with strength," *Job* 8.22 "thy enemies shall be clothed with confusion," and similar passages.

551. *ILIAD* AND *ODYSSEY*: ORAL TRADITION TO WRITTEN TEXT

In the thirteenth century BCE Greece was inhabited by speakers of an early form of Greek called "Mycenaean" after the home of Agamemnon in the *Iliad*. The people of this civilization (also called now "Achaean" after Homer's name for Greeks) could write. However, they used not the Greek alphabet you have learned but a syllabary. Moreover, they used writing to keep official records, not to preserve stories and poems, so far as we know, though such stories and poems certainly were passed on in an oral form.

Archaeology has uncovered a rich and refined way of life centered at palaces in Pylos, Argos, Mycenae, Tiryns, Thebes, Athens and elsewhere. For reasons about which we can only conjecture, Mycenaean civilization collapsed around 1200 BCE. The palaces, the nerve center of Mycenaean civilization, were destroyed and the sites largely abandoned. Thus, inhabitants were displaced, and the population declined steeply. Though a few areas continued to enjoy some prosperity thanks to unbroken trade relations with the Levant, most of Greece went into economic recession and can be described as backward, decentralized and disorganized, at least in comparison with the hierarchical civilization of the Mycenaeans. Burial practices changed, as did building and pottery styles. The period is called the Greek Dark Age. While we know that people continued to speak Greek throughout this period, they lost the art of writing it. Yet traditional tales were passed down orally, preserved by bards.

Archeological evidence suggests some renewal of prosperity by 1000 accompanied by more contact with peoples of the eastern Mediterranean— in particular, the Phoenicians, whose language was closely related to Hebrew. The Greeks borrowed the

Phoenician alphabet in the eighth century, adapting their Semitic script to the Greek language. Though it is not known exactly how this borrowing came about or for what purpose, it did make possible the eventual preservation, in a fixed form, of the oral epic tradition represented by the *Iliad* and the *Odyssey*. It is thought that these poems were written down sometime after 750 BCE. Many scholars believe that they were expanded, refined, and otherwise improved once in a written form.

552. WRITE IN GREEK

1. To refrain from shameful pleasures and endure trouble with a manly spirit is better than heaping up gold or becoming king of many kingdoms.

2. Whenever I would come (ἱκάνω) to this most holy temple, a heavenly peace seemed to fill (aor.) my heart.

3. Who would have thought that we would halt near the cave of a man neither revering right nor knowing truth?

553. WORD STUDY

OZONE (a blue gas with a pungent odor—it may be smelled in the air after a violent thunderstorm, being formed from oxygen by the passage of electricity through the atmosphere).

Lesson 82

554. MEMORIZE

ἄντρον, -ου	[n.]	cave
ἄρνες, ἀρνῶν	[no nom. sg.; acc.sg. ἄρνα] [m., f.]	lamb(s)
ἔνδον	[adv.]	within, inside
καρπάλιμος, -ον		swift, quick
πίων, πίονος	[adj.]	fat, rich
σηκός, -οῦ	[m.]	pen, fold
τυρός, -οῦ	[m.]	cheese

555. TEXT

Inside the Cave

καρπαλίμως δ' εἰς ἄντρον ἀφικόμεθ', οὐδέ μιν ἔνδον   80
εὕρομεν, ἀλλ' ἐνόμευε νομὸν κάτα πίονα μῆλα.
ἐλθόντες δ' εἰς ἄντρον ἐθηεύμεσθα ἕκαστα·
ταρσοὶ μὲν τυρῶν βρῖθον στείνοντο δὲ σηκοὶ
ἀρνῶν ἠδ' ἐρίφων· ναῖον δ' ὀρῷ ἄγγεα πάντα.

ἄγγος, ἄγγεος	[n.] vessel, pail
βρίθω, βρίσω, βρίσα	I am weighted down with a load of [+ gen.]
ἔριφος, -ου	[m.] kid
θηέομαι, θηήσομαι, θηησάμην	I gaze at (in wonder), I behold
ναίω	I am brimming with [+ dat.]
νομεύω	I tend (a flock)
νομός, -οῦ	pasture
ὀρός, -οῦ	[m.] whey [the clear yellow liquid that separates off from curdled milk]
στείνομαι	I am filled with a throng of [+ gen.]
ταρσός, -οῦ	wicker-basket

556. NOTES

81. κάτα here = "in" ["down the length of"]. When a preposition follows its object, its pitch-mark is moved back to the first syllable (cp. Section 408b on anastrophe).

557. COMMENT

80-84. The Greeks peer into the cave, whose vastness is even more impressive now that they see it close at hand. But no one seems to be within, or to answer their shouts of greeting. So they go inside and explore.

81. Odysseus learned that the Cyclops was afield with his flocks, not because he saw him there from the cave but by his entry later, which indicated where he had been.

83-84. It is evident to the visitors that the inhabitant of the cave is a herdsman or shepherd, and a very prosperous one at that, to judge from the abundance of food stored up and the large increase for his flocks. The young are kept inside for protection until they grow nimble and strong; the cheese is hung up on porous baskets to drip dry. The enormous size and quantity of everything holds the men in openmouthed wonder.

558. POETRY AND RHYTHM

You have probably already picked up some skill in following the verse-rhythm of Homer's lines. Here are some points to help you read the poem metrically with more understanding and enjoyment:

1. *Rhythm is a pattern cut in time.* It puts sounds into an orderly plan, molds them into an artistic design. It makes sounds follow one another in a flexible but regular sequence, so that recognizably the same pattern recurs at fixed intervals. Repetition yet variation; an intriguing blend of permanence and change; the combined pleasure of the return of what is familiar and the constant surprise of something new— these are the reasons why rhythmic sound possesses a natural interest and appeal for everybody, why all men love music.

2. *The poetic function of rhythm is threefold:* to add to the poem as a whole the charm and beauty of *music;* to interpret and emphasize the thought and deepen our emotional response to it by stirring up just the right *mood* for reacting more fully to the implications of what is being said; and to *elevate the language* above the level of ordinary speech or prose, for intensified artistic effect.

3. *Poetic technique.* A great rhythmic artist— and Homer is one of the world's supreme masters of this intricate art—will choose and arrange his words to gain all three of these effects in the highest degree, yet with complete ease and without in the least changing what he wants to *say.* The intangible charm of this rhythmic beauty, so perfectly fitted to the precise thought, is inevitably lost if the poem is put into other words or into another language. That is one reason why the *poetry* of a poem cannot be translated, but must be enjoyed in the original or not at all; and one reason why you are learning Greek is to be able to read Homer, the real Homer in all his original energy and life and melodic beauty.

4. *The type of rhythm* in a poem depends on three factors: (1) whether the recurring sound pattern is one of accent, tone, number of syllables in a line, time-length (**quantity**) of individual syllables, similar consonant-groups, or some other aspect of sound repeated in a regular cycle; (2) what is the formula for each such pattern or 'measure'; (3) how often this pattern is repeated, i.e., how many measures to a line.

The rhythmic scheme used by Homer (and many other ancient poets, e.g., Vergil) is the quantitative **dactylic hexameter**. Hence its pattern is determined by the **quantity** of the syllables, the length of time required to pronounce them—i.e., a pattern of long and short syllables, such as you already know; this pattern's formula is **long, short,**

short, or its equivalent, known as a **dactyl** because it has one long and two short sections like a finger; the pattern recurs six times each line, thus making it a six-measure verse or **hexameter** (cp. Section 179).

The simple rules for reading the Homeric hexameter rhythmically will be given in the next lesson.

559. WRITE IN GREEK

1. Let us then go quickly into the cave, to see the pens which have been built inside for the ram and the fat sheep.

2. We did not believe the man who told us that his daughter ate only cheese for nine days and still yearned for it.

3. O cruel woman, how did you have the heart to leave the children (dual) at the door of a stranger's house, where they would have perished if he had not received them kindly?

560. WORD STUDY

BUTTER (βού-τυρον 'cow-cheese', i.e., made from cow's milk, not goat's, which was more often used for drinking in ancient times than cow's milk); — THEATER (a 'place for gazing at' a dramatic performance), THEATRICAL; — THEORY (a 'beholding with the mind's eye' of some speculative or possible plan to be tested by experiment; hence, a proposed law in science or philosophy not yet accepted by everybody because not proved), THEORETICAL (hypothetical, probable but not certain, speculative as opposed to practical), THEORIZE: THEOREM (an accepted proposition in mathematics set up to be 'gazed at', thought over, and proved).

Lesson 83

561. MEMORIZE

αἴνυμαι	[pres. syst. only] I seize upon; I select
ἁλμυρός, -ή, -όν	salty, briny
ἦ	truly, indeed; also, an untranslatable interr. particle introducing a question
λίσσομαι, —, λισάμην	I entreat, I beg
ξείνιον, -ου	[n.] gift of hospitality, a present given by a host to a guest
πολύς, —, πολύ	much, many [Alternative m. and n. forms of πολλός, -ή, -όν]

562. TEXT

Hesitation

ἔνθ᾽ ἐμὲ μὲν πρώτισθ᾽ ἕταροι λίσσοντ᾽ ἐπέεσσι   85
τυρῶν αἰνυμένους ἰέναι πάλιν, αὐτὰρ ἔπειτα
καρπαλίμως ἐπὶ νῆα θοὴν ἐρίφους τε καὶ ἄρνας
σηκῶν ἐξελάσαντας ἐπιπλεῖν ἁλμυρὸν ὕδωρ·
ἀλλ᾽ ἐγὼ οὐ πιθόμην, ἦ τ᾽ ἂν πολὺ κέρδιον ἦεν,
ὄφρ᾽ αὐτόν τε ἴδοιμι, καὶ εἴ μοι ξείνια δοίη.   90
οὐδ᾽ ἄρ᾽ ἔμελλ᾽ ἑτάροισι φανεὶς ἐρατεινὸς ἔσεσθαι.

ἐξ-ελαύνω, ἐξ-ελάω, ἐξ-έλασ(σ)α	I drive out of [+ acc. and gen.]
ἐπι-πλέω	I sail over, upon
ἐρατεινός, -ή, -όν	delightful
ἔριφος, -ου	[m.] kid
πρώτιστα	[adv.] first of all, at the start

563. NOTES

85. -εσσι instead of -σι is sometimes used in the dat. pl.

86. τυρῶν is partitive. ἰέναι : pres. inf. of εἶμι ("I go"); the unstated subject of both infinitives ἰέναι and ἐπιπλεῖν, and of participles αἰνυμένους and ἐξελάσαντας, is ἡμέας.

90. The δοίη depends on ἴδοιμι carried over in thought. To review the form, see Sections 472 and 473.

564. COMMENT

85-90. Being soldiers hardened by long years of war and plundering of the enemy, Odysseus' men have no scruples about making the most of an opportunity and carrying off a few 'souvenirs.' Odysseus resists the tempting suggestion, in the hope that the stranger will freely offer some of his rich possessions as a token of friendly hospitality, according to universal custom and good manners in the Homeric world in regard to travelers. Besides, he is curious to see who lives in the vast cave.

89. Odysseus allows that it would have been better not to have awaited the stranger's return. It need not be interpreted to imply that they should have taken anything with them in leaving—though in Homeric ethics that would not have been considered a grave wrong under the circumstances.

90. Odysseus is characteristically eager to find out about things.

91. A somber foreshadowing of tragedy to come. But why the emphasis on companions? What will happen to their leader?

565. READING HOMER RHYTHMICALLY

1. **Quantity.** The rhythm of Greek and Latin verse is not built on a pattern of stressed and unstressed syllables (as in English poetry), but on one of long and short syllables—on their quantity or time-length when naturally pronounced. The rhythm of classical poetry, then, is built on the same principles as the rhythm of music.

    a. A syllable is **long**: (1) **by nature**, when it contains a long vowel or a diphthong: e.g., αὐτή, where both syllables are long (2) **by position**, when its vowel (even though naturally short) is followed by two or more consonants or by one of the double consonants ζ, ξ, ψ. E.g., ἔνδον (first syllable long), ἄνδρα (first syllable long), δὲ στείνοντο (first and third syllables long by position, the second by nature), ἄψ.

    b. A syllable is otherwise **short** — i.e., when it has a short vowel, alone or followed by only one simple consonant: e.g., δε, μιν

    Note: Sometimes the poet treats a mute followed by a liquid as a single consonant, so that the preceding vowel remains short (e.g., σχέτλιος, where ε is short); but ordinarily this combination makes the syllable long by position (e.g., ἔτλη, where ε is long).

    c. **Special:** a long vowel or diphthong is often treated as though short when it occurs in the last half of the foot and is followed by another vowel in the same or following word. This is really half-elision. For example, ἀλλ' ἐγὼ οὐ, where ω is short.

    A short vowel may be treated as long when it is in the first syllable of a foot, since it is there strengthened by the metrical stress. A short vowel may be treated as long for a different reason—because of a lost ϝ (digamma) whose influence remains and combines with a second consonant to make the vowel long by position in the regular way (e.g., ἐμὸν ἔπος, where the final syllable of ἐμὸν is long because of the digamma with which ἔπος once began [ϝεπος]).

    d.   **Synizesis.** Sometimes two adjacent vowels that would ordinarily be pronounced separately have to be forced into one syllable to fit the meter. This is done by pronouncing the first as y, combined with the second into one long syllable. This is called **synizesis** ('settling down together as one'). E.g., θεοι, δη ουτως

2.   **Pattern.** Each line has six measures or **feet**, corresponding to six bars in a phrase of music. The time-value of each foot is four beats. A short syllable gets one beat, a long syllable two.

Every foot begins with a long syllable; the second half of the foot may be either two short syllables or another long, in either case taking the same total time to pronounce: two beats.

    a.   The combination of a long syllable with two short (– ⌣⌣) is called a **dactyl**; two longs (– –) make a **spondee**.

    b.   Any foot except the last may be either a dactyl or a spondee; the last foot is generally a spondee, sometimes a half-dactyl with **anceps**, which is a space for long or short (×), but never a full dactyl. When the fifth foot is a spondee, the line is called a **spondaic line**, and the slow movement is quite noticeable.

    c.   The first syllable of every foot is **stressed**, i.e., receives the rhythmic accent, a swelling in volume. This is called the **ictus** (Latin for 'stroke').

    d.   Pattern of the **dactylic hexamete**r in general:

          – ⌣⌣ /– ⌣⌣ /– ⌣⌣ /– ⌣⌣ /– ⌣⌣ / – ×

    e.   Rhythmic technique: regularity is secured in this pattern by the fact that every line has twenty-four beats, broken up into six bars of four beats apiece and each beginning with a perceptible ictus; variety is obtained by changing the distribution and frequency of spondees in the basically dactylic scheme, by letting the pauses in thought and phrasing fall in different sections of the line, by altering the number of words in a verse, and by varying the frequency and position in the line where the end of a word coincides with the end of a foot. Homer uses practically every possible combination of all these factors, to give his hexameters their unrivaled variety, life, and interest.

    f.   Practical hints for reading the hexameter: (1) Remember that every line, and each new foot within the line, begins with a long, stressed syllable. (2) Don't hurry over long syllables, as though they were short, as we do in English poetry. (3) Get the rhythm into your head, like the melody of a song, by memorizing several lines according to exact meter and going over them frequently, until the rhythmic pattern is fixed firmly in your mind and flexible enough to fit any arrangement of long and short syllables as they come up. With a little attentive practice and repetition, all will quickly become natural and easy.

566. WRITE IN GREEK

1. My faithful comrade begged me to flee quickly back to the ships, but I wished to know if the monstrous shepherd would revere Zeus, the friend of strangers, and give us gifts of hospitality.

2. If we had selected some cheeses and sheep and had returned at once to the salty sea, truly many of my friends would not have perished in that savage cave.

3. Most men seem to be much worse than they are, and many of them who injure you (sg.) are trying to bring you some good. [Make "men" a partitive gen.]

567. WORD STUDY

LITANY (λιτ- for λισ-, a series of 'entreaties' addressed to God in prayer); — POLY- (prefix meaning 'many-' or 'much-') e.g., POLYPHONIC, POLYGAMY, POLYSYLLABLE, POLYMATH (a person possessed of 'many kinds of learning', POLYGON, etc.).

Lesson 84

568. REVIEW OF LESSONS 79-83

In the last five lessons you have read thirty-two more lines of the *Odyssey*, and have learned twenty-nine new words. Review and test your knowledge with this sample examination.

I. Vocabulary (25%)

    1.   black: f. dat. sg. =

    2.   εὐεργέων =

    3.   mixing-bowl: acc. sg. =

    4.   may they fill (aor.) =

    5.   ἄπ-εχες =

    6.   they entreated =

    7.   χεῦαι =

    8.   at once =

    9.   πολέεσσι =

    10.   fat: m. dat. pl. =

II. Text (50%)

    A. Translate accurately:

    1.   ὅν μοι δῶκε

    2.   πόρεν ἄγλαα δῶρα

    3.   οὐδέ τις αὐτὸν ᾔδη.

    4.   οὐδέ μιν ἔνδον εὕρομεν

    5.   ἄν κέρδιον ἦεν

    B. State the precise form, and the person referred to:

    1.   in line 72, πίνοιεν

    2.   in line 77, μοι

    3.   in line 64, ᾤκει

    4.   in line 90, δοίη

    C. Answer briefly:

    1.   Where and how did Odysseus get the wine?

    2.   What was remarkable about it?

    3.   Why did he decide to take some with him to the cave?

III. Grammar (25%)

A. Translate only the words in italics:

1. He met a man not *knowing* justice.

2. I thought I *would find* a monster.

3. No one *knew* (οἶδα) it.

4. To refrain *would not have been pleasant.*

5. I wondered if they *would give* me a present.

B. Scan lines 76-79 (i.e., write out the Greek, without breathings or pitch-marks, and indicate the *quantity of each syllable* and the foot-divisions).

Lesson 85

569. MEMORIZE

ἀπο-σεύω, —, ἀπο-σσύμην	[non-thematic 2 aor.] I rush away, I rush back (from)
ἔντοσθεν	[adv.] within, inside [prep. + gen] inside of
ἥμενος, -η, -ον	sitting, seated
εἷος [also ἧος or ἕως]	[conj.] while, until [+ ind. if purely factual; + purpose construction if anticipatory, like ὄφρα]
καίω, καύσω, κῆα	I kindle, I burn
νέμω, νεμέω, νεῖμα	I assign, I drive my flock; [in mid.] I possess, I feed on
ὄβριμος, -η, -ον	heavy, mighty
ὕλη, -ης	wood; forest

570. TEXT

A Terrifying Discovery

ἔνθα δὲ πῦρ κήαντες ἐθύσαμεν ἠδὲ καὶ αὐτοὶ   92
τυρῶν αἰνύμενοι φάγομεν, μένομέν τέ μιν ἔνδον
ἥμενοι, εἷος ἐπῆλθε νέμων. φέρε δ' ὄβριμον ἄχθος
ὕλης ἀζαλέης, ἵνα οἱ ποτιδόρπιον εἴη.
ἔντοσθεν δ' ἄντροιο βαλὼν ὀρυμαγδὸν ἔθηκεν·
ἡμεῖς δὲ δείσαντες ἀπεσσύμεθ' ἐς μυχὸν ἄντρου.   97

ἀζαλέος, -η, -ον	dried up, dry
ἄχθος, -εος	[n.] weight, load
θύω, θύσω, θῦσα	I offer sacrifice
μυχός, -οῦ	[m.] innermost part
ὀρυμαγδός, -οῦ	[m.] clatter, din
ποτιδόρπιος, -ον	useful for one's evening meal

571. NOTES

96. ἔθηκεν : to review the form, see Section 468.

97. ἐς : a common shortened form of εἰς

572. COMMENT

Curious to learn what sort of man lives in this cave and built the huge fold near its entrance, and hoping to gain from him friendly gifts as well as information about their route home, the Greeks decide to await his return, since it is now late afternoon and he must soon be coming back.

92. Thinking he will not begrudge his tired and hungry guests a bit of cheese from his vast supply, they prepare a lunch and eat it leisurely. But first they sacrifice a portion of it to the gods, as a sort of prayer to win divine favor; they build a small fire and cast into it some of the food, to be destroyed and thereby denied to themselves.

94-97. As evening falls, they hear a noisy commotion of bleating flocks outside. Then suddenly the great doorway is filled with an enormous form, indistinct in the twilight. And into the cave flies a huge bundle of logs, to fall with a terrifying crash onto the ground near where the men are sitting. In a flash they realize an appalling fact: the cave-dweller is not, as they had supposed, just a brawny native of the hills; he is a colossal giant of incredible size and strength. Speechless with horror they rush to the dark depths of the cave to elude notice and gather their wits for thinking out some means of escape.

95. The Cyclops will burn the wood for warmth and light while he has his meal, not for cooking, with which he doesn't bother.

573. ORAL COMPOSITION

In the late nineteen-twenties an American classicist named Milman Parry traveled to Yugoslavia to study Serbo-Croatian epic poetry, which was still a vital oral tradition at the time. Parry's scholarship described the training and practice of an oral poet, the performance and composition of the poetry, and the characteristics of the oral epic style.

Both the audiences and the poets were illiterate. The oral poet did not memorize or even rehearse a fixed script or text before his performance, but improvised as he sang. He was able to compose in this manner because he had mastered an extensive and traditional stock of stories, themes and formulaic phrases. His choice of a formula to express a given idea depended on the space available within the line of verse. As Parry put it in a famous definition of the formula: "an expression regularly used, under the same metrical conditions, to express an essential idea" (*The Making of Homeric Verse: the Collected Papers of Milman Parry.* ed. A. Parry, New York and Oxford 1987. p. 13). Thus, the oral poet did not need and did not seek alternative words for the same idea, except to fit different metrical conditions. Originality in that sense was not a goal or expectation, as it is for creative writers.

The various noun-epithet systems for people and things are the easiest examples of the formulaic method to grasp. You have noticed that there are several epithets for Odysseus. Odysseus can be inserted into different positions within a line and in different cases. In the nominative case, Homer can chose from πολύτλας δῖος Ὀδυσσεύς or just δῖος Ὀδυσσεύς, πολύμητις Ὀδυσσεύς, and πτολίπορθος Ὀδυσσεύς, to name but a few; each of these has a different metrical shape, allowing it to fit into a different part of the line. Aside from formulae in the nominative case, Odysseus can be named in other cases as well— for example, Ὀδυσσῆϊ μεγαλήτορι in the dative.

Besides noun-epithet phrases, appropriate formulae exist for every recurring concept or situation (called "themes"). The dawning of the sun in the morning, the sending of a message, the reception of a guest, the taking of a meal or bath, the gathering of an assembly are all themes with associated formulae that the poet used as he composed. He could also, by analogy, modify traditional formulae to fit new themes or ideas.

Parry's research established that for an oral poet such as Homer, the idea of an original or fixed text was unfamiliar. Every time an oral poet told a story, he was singing a somewhat different song. The tales of Odysseus' homecoming were certainly traditional, told many different times in different forms by different poets; Homer's version was undoubtedly many years in the making, and was told repeatedly by the poet in varied ways before he fashioned it into the epic we read today.

574. WRITE IN GREEK

1. We kept entreating the cruel and monstrous stranger to respect the gods and not to kill us with his mighty strength.

2. They rushed back into the cave and waited inside until they learned (πυθ-) whether he was savage or a friend to strangers.

3. Seizing the heavy door-stone from under the door, he hurled it upward into the sky with gigantic force.

575. WORD STUDY

CAUSTIC ('burning', e.g., an acid which corrodes or 'burns away' matter; or a remark full of 'burning' sarcasm), CAUTERIZE (to sear over by burning or exposing to a caustic acid); — ETHYL (the 'wood', i.e., substance, 'of ether'; a very inflammable and volatile chemical), ACETYLENE (a hot-burning gas containing the 'substance of acetic acid', a special carbon-radical molecule).

Lesson 86

577. MEMORIZE

ἀμέλγω	[pres. syst.] I milk
ἄρσην, -ενος [m., f.] ἄρσεν, ἄρσενος	[n.] male, masculine
βαθύς, -εῖα, -ύ	deep
ἐλαύνω, ἐλάω, ἔλασ(σ)α	I drive
ἐπι-τίθημι, ἐπι-θήσω, ἐπί-θηκα	I put on; I put in position
ὅσ(σ)ος, -η, -ον	as many as, as great as, as much as [see τόσ(σ)ος below]
τόσ(σ)ος, -η, -ον	so many, so great, so much [often correlative with ὅσ(σ)ος: so many…as…]

578. TEXT

Trapped!

αὐτὰρ ὅ γ᾽ εἰς εὐρὺ σπέος ἤλασε πίονα μῆλα,
πάντα μάλ᾽, ὅσσ᾽ ἤμελγε, τὰ δ᾽ ἄρσενα λεῖπε θύρηφιν,
ἀρνειούς τε τράγους τε, βαθείης ἔντοθεν αὐλῆς.   100
αὐτὰρ ἔπειτ᾽ ἐπέθηκε θυρεὸν μέγαν ὑψόσ᾽ ἀείρας,
ὄβριμον· οὐκ ἂν τόν γε δύω καὶ εἴκοσ᾽ ἄμαξαι
ἐσθλαὶ τετράκυκλοι ἀπ᾽ οὔδεος ὀχλίσσειαν·
τόσσην ἠλίβατον πέτρην ἐπέθηκε θύρησιν.

εἴκοσι	[indecl.] twenty
ἔντοθεν	[prep. + gen.] within, inside (of)
ἠλίβατος, -ον	towering, high
οὖδας, -εος	[n.] ground, floor
ὀχλίζω, —, ὄχλισσα	I raise, lift
τετράκυκλος, -ον	four-wheeled
τράγος, -ου	[m.] he-goat

579. NOTES

99. πάντα μαλ᾽ : a common idiom = "all" (intensified).

580. COMMENT

98-104. After throwing into the cave his great bundle of firewood, the giant separates out the males of the flock and drives the rest inside. Then he enters himself, closing up the cave's mouth with an enormous slab of rock.

101-104. The Cyclops easily lifts the huge stone and sets it in place —a mass so heavy that no human means could have budged it. The comparison to twenty-two wagons vividly evokes Polyphemus' size and strength compared to a man's. The size of the door-stone will be important to Odysseus' calculations for escape.

581. HOMER AND THE DIALECTS OF GREEK

Homer's Greek contains a mixture of dialects from different regions of the Greek world; for this reason, it is referred to as an "artificial" or "literary" dialect, since no real group spoke Homeric Greek. However, Homeric Greek's basis is Ionic, the dialect spoken on Euboea and on Chios and other islands of the eastern Aegean, as well as in Asia Minor. Attic Greek, the dialect of Athens and its environs, is a subdivision of Ionic, but Attic forms are rare in Homer. The dialect spoken on the northern islands such as Lesbos and on the northern mainland of Greece (Boeotia and Thessaly) was called Aeolic, whose forms appear often in Homer (e.g., infinitives ending in -εμεν). Finally, there are forms from the Arcado-Cyprian dialect, which is thought to have close links to the Mycenaean language of the second millennium. Examples include words with initial ππ-, such as πτόλεμος and πτόλις.

Some features and forms of the Homeric language are much older than others. This is explainable in terms of the oral traditional nature of the poems. Formulaic phrases often preserve the most ancient forms, suggesting that the poet inherited them from his long tradition. On the other hand, Homer himself may have introduced some of the later linguistic forms. In many cases, metrical convenience seems to explain the choice of a particular dialectical variation; Homer has available to him a whole range of metrical equivalents thanks to the dialectical richness he has inherited.

582. WRITE IN GREEK

1. If he had known we were within the cave, and had raised on high (ptc.) that mighty rock and thrown it at us, who of us would not then have perished by swift destruction? [for "at" use ἐπί + acc.]

2. They drove all our rams and fat sheep into seven great hollow wagons, and fled with them afar in a deep well-made ship to their own country.

3. Let us not flee like cowardly children, but let us stand here and fight for the sake of our lives (ψυχ-).

583. WORD STUDY

BATHOS (a laughable sudden 'drop to the depths', from the sublime to the ridiculous, in speaking or writing; startling anticlimax); — ELASTIC (spontaneously 'driving back' to a position from which the object has been forced—the real point in elasticity being the return to original position, not stretchability); — EPITHET (a descriptive modifier 'put on' to a person or thing, especially as a characteristic regularly associated with it; e.g., Richard 'Lion-hearted', 'Buffalo Bill' Cody); — CYCLE (a period in which things move around again to their starting-point, like a wheel), BICYCLE ('two-wheeled'), CYCLONE (violent revolving wind); — TRAGIC, TRAGEDY (probably from the song sung at the sacrifice of a goat [ᾠδή, contraction for ἀοιδή, song or ode]).

Lesson 87

584. MEMORIZE

αὖτε	[adv.] again; on the other hand
εἰσ-οράω, εἰσ-όψομαι, εἴσ-ιδον, etc.	I see, I look at
ἔμβρυον, -ου	[n.] a young one [of animals]
κατα-τίθημι, κατα-θήσω, κατά-θηκα	I put down
λευκός, -ή, -όν	bright, white
μοῖρα, -ης	[f.] due measure; portion; fate

585. TEXT

Discovered

ἑζόμενος δ' ἤμελγεν ὄϊς καὶ μηκάδας αἶγας,   105
πάντα κατὰ μοῖραν, καὶ ὑπ' ἔμβρυον ἧκεν ἑκάστῃ.
αὐτίκα δ' ἥμισυ μὲν θρέψας λευκοῖο γάλακτος
πλεκτοῖσ' ἐν ταλάροισιν ἀμησάμενος κατέθηκεν,
ἥμισυ δ' αὖτ' ἔστησεν ἐν ἄγγεσιν, ὄφρα οἱ εἴη
πίνειν αἰνυμένῳ καί οἱ ποτιδόρπιον εἴη.   110
αὐτὰρ ἐπεὶ δὴ σπεῦσε πονησάμενος τὰ ἃ ἔργα,
καὶ τότε πῦρ ἀνέκαιε καὶ εἴσιδεν, εἴρετο δ' ἡμέας·

ἄγγος, -εος	[n.] vessel, pail
ἀμάω, ἀμήσω, ἄμησα	I collect, I mass
ἀνα-καίω	I rekindle
γάλα, -ακτος	[n.] milk
μηκάς, -άδος	bleating
πλεκτός, -ή, -όν	woven, wicker
ποτιδόρπιος, -ον	used for one's evening meal
τάλαρος, -ου	[m.] basket

586. NOTES

106. πάντα κατὰ μοῖραν : a frequent idiom, = "everything just right." ἧκεν : aor. of ἵημι (Section 468)

107. θρέψας is aorist of τρέφω, which here has the special meaning "curdle".

109. ἔστησεν : aor. of ἵστημι (Section 526)

111. σπεῦσε : another instance of an aor. with plpf. force: "had hastened toiling" = "had quickly finished."

111. ἃ : recall the note on line 4.

112. ἡμέας : pronounce (and scan) as two syllables by *synizesis*.

587. COMMENT

105-110. Some of the milk (ἥμισυ μὲν) is to be made into cheese, while some (ἥμισυ δὲ) is for immediate consumption as a beverage with dinner (ποτιδόρπιον). The giant obtains what milk he needs for his own meal, then sets the mother animals to nourishing their young—the carefully guarded hope of his still richer possessions in the future.

107-108. He makes the cheese, no doubt, in the ordinary ancient way: he stirs juice from a wild fig-tree into the fresh milk, collects the curdled lumps resulting from this mixing, and presses them into reed baskets to drip and solidify.

111-112. All the while the Greeks have been watching him in the dim shadows from their refuge at the far end of the cave. But the giant, expecting no visitors and all intent on his work, has not acknowledged their silent presence. As the darkness increases, he relights the fire (the earlier one kindled by the Greeks for their sacrifice having died out). In the bright blaze which floods the whole cave with light, he suddenly discovers Odysseus and his men.

588. EXPLANATORY AND PURPOSE INFINITIVE

a.   The infinitive is often used in Greek to explain the sense of another word, to fill out its meaning. Some examples of this **explanatory** use of the infinitive:

> πρᾶγμα χαλεπόν ποιῆσαι
> *a thing difficult to do* (not necessarily difficult to imagine, plan, etc.)

> ἵνα ἔχω σῖτον φαγεῖν
> *that I may have bread to eat.* (not necessarily to share, serve, etc.)

b.   An **explanatory infinitive**, by answering the question "why?" may also express **purpose**, as in English. Often the future infinitive is preferred for this, but the present or aorist may also be used. This construction usually follows a verb meaning 'send, give, entrust, take, leave behind,' and the like.

> τοὺς ἔπεμψε πεύσεσθαι.   *He sent them to inquire.*

589. WRITE IN GREEK

1.   Having built a strong, deep pen for his rams and goats, everything just right, the mighty shepherd drove his fat white flocks inside.

2.   Have you (pl.) ever seen a larger or more splendid sheep than that one which they are looking at, lying, with her young one, so white and beautiful upon the black earth?

3.   Since the wisest of men, and not even the wisest of boys, does not know everything, we should no doubt obey (our) father and mother as wiser than we (gen.).

590. WORD STUDY

EMBRYO (an animal in its earliest stage of development; the human organism up to the third month after conception); — HYDRANGEA ('water-vessel': so named because the flower-cluster is like ancient water-jars); — GALAXY ('the Milky Way', a band of innumerable stars across the heavens; any cluster of millions of stars, e.g., an island-universe; hence a group of brilliant or famous people, e.g., 'a galaxy of famous authors attended the ceremony.').

Lesson **88**

591. MEMORIZE

ἀλάομαι, —, ἀλήθην, ἀλάλημαι	I wander [pf. has pres. force]
ἦτορ	[n., indecl.] heart
κέλευθος, -ου	[f., but frequently n. in pl.] way, path, course
οἷος, -η, -ον	(such) as, (of) what sort
πλέω, πλεύσομαι, πλεῦσα	I sail (over)
ὑγρός, -ή, -όν	fluid, watery
ὑπέρ or ὑπείρ	[prep. + gen. or acc.] over
φθόγγος, -ου	[m.] voice

592. TEXT

Inquiry

"ὦ ξεῖνοι, τίνες ἐστέ; πόθεν πλεῖθ' ὑγρὰ κέλευθα;
ἤ τι κατὰ πρῆξιν ἢ μαψιδίως ἀλάλησθε
οἷά τε ληϊστῆρες ὑπεὶρ ἅλα, τοί τ' ἀλόωνται   115
ψυχὰς παρθέμενοι, κακὸν ἀλλοδαποῖσι φέροντες;"
   ὣς ἔφαθ', ἡμῖν δ' αὖτε κατεκλάσθη φίλον ἦτορ,
δεισάντων φθόγγον τε βαρὺν αὐτόν τε πέλωρον.

ἀλλοδαπός, -ή, -όν	foreign, of another land
βαρύς, -εῖα, -ύ	heavy
κατα-κλάω, aor. pass. κατα-κλάσθην	I shatter
ληϊστήρ, -ῆρος	[m.] rover, pirate
μαψιδίως	[adv.] at random
παρα-τίθημι, aor. mid. ptc. παρ-θέμενος	I put aside, I risk
πέλωρον, -ου	[n.] monster
πρῆξις, -ιος	[f.] business

593. NOTES

115. οἷά τε : as adv. = "even as" or "like." ἀλόωνται : Homeric verbs in -άω sometimes become -όω by *assimilation*. When the α is short, the second vowel is often lengthened (here, ο to ω). See also Section 627.

117. φίλον here, as often elsewhere = "my (our, one's) own."

118. δεισάντων : the nearness of ἦτορ has drawn the ptc. away from agreement with ἡμῖν into a possessive genitive— which is, after all, the sense of ἡμῖν too.

594. COMMENT

113-116. Proper etiquette requires an extension of hospitality before the guests' identity is requested. The Cyclops, living aloof from others of his race and on an island far from human shores, is not used to visitors of any sort and is ignorant of the laws of hospitality. He is puzzled why these puny humans should have come to his cave, and how they found his island in the first place. They must be merchants driven off their course, or roving pirates in search of some rich victim.

117-118. At the sound of the giant's gruff, unfriendly voice thundering through the cave, and in the presence of his overwhelming build, the Greeks naturally are struck cold with fear, and their courage cracks.

118. We can hear in this line's heavy spondees and strongly emphasized long vowels a clear echo of the rolling thunder of that gigantic voice.

595. FORMS OF φημί

Memorize:

φημί, φήσω, φῆσα   I speak, I say, I tell, I claim

IMPF. ACTIVE AND MIDDLE (no difference in meaning; used according to metrical convenience in Homer):

	Sg.	*Pl.*	*Sg.*	*Pl.*
1st pers.	φῆν	φάμεν	φάμην	φάμεθα
2nd. pers.	φῆς(θα)	φάτε	φάο	φάσθε
3rd pers.	φῆ	φάσαν/φάν	φάτο	φάντο

596. WRITE IN GREEK

1. All strength fled from our limbs when with mighty voice he asked us why we were wandering in swift ships over the deep paths of the fluid sea.

2. Send (sg.) seven or more strong and brave men to seize those wild oxen and to make ready for us a great dinner there beside the river.

597. WORD STUDY

HYGROMETER (an instrument for measuring the wetness or humidity of the air); — DIPHTHONG ('double-sound', a sound produced by combining two vowels into a single syllable, or running them together as though but one); — BAROMETER (instrument for measuring the weight or pressure of the atmosphere), BARITONE ('the heavy tone', a voice between base and tenor); — HYPER- (a prefix meaning 'over, excessive', e.g., 'hyper-sensitive', 'hyperacidity'), HYPERBOLE (βολή a throwing, from βάλλω, 'an over-throwing' or over-statement, an exagerration), HYPERBOLA (a plane curve where the line is 'thrown over' upon itself in a broad arc of special pattern), HYPERBATON (βατός, -ή, -όν going, adj. from βαίνω, hence 'going over' from the normal word order to an unusual position for poetic effect, e.g., 'our foes among' for 'among our foes'); — EUPHEMISM ('speaking well', an agreeable or less offensive expression for something unpleasant, e.g., 'he passed away' instead of a blunt 'he died').

Lesson 89

598. MEMORIZE

Ἀγαμέμνων, Ἀγαμέμνονος   [m.] Agamemnon [king of Mycenae and commander in chief of Greeks at Troy]

Ἀχαιοί, -ῶν   Achaeans [a division of the Greeks; also, Greeks in general]

λαῖτμα, λαίτματος   [n.] gulf

οἴκαδε   [adv.] homeward

π(τ)όλις, πτόλιος   [f.] city

προσ-εῖπον   [2 aor.] I addressed, I spoke to [+ acc.]

599. TEXT

Identification

ἀλλὰ καὶ ὣς μιν ἔπεσσιν ἀμειβόμενος προσέειπον·
  "ἡμεῖς τοι Τροίηθεν ἀποπλαγχθέντες Ἀχαιοὶ   120
παντοίοισ' ἀνέμοισιν ὑπὲρ μέγα λαῖτμα θαλάσσης,
οἴκαδε ἱέμενοι, ἄλλην ὁδὸν ἄλλα κέλευθα
ἤλθομεν· οὕτω που Ζεὺς ἤθελε μητίσασθαι.
λαοὶ δ' Ἀτρεΐδεω Ἀγαμέμνονος εὐχόμεθ' εἶναι,
τοῦ δὴ νῦν γε μέγιστον ὑπουράνιον κλέος ἐστί·   125
τόσσην γὰρ διέπερσε πόλιν καὶ ἀπώλεσε λαοὺς
πολλούς.

ἀπο-πλάζω	I beat back; aor. pass. ἀπο-πλάγχθην I wander, I am driven from my course
Ἀτρεΐδης, -εω	son of Atreus [gen. ending special]
δια-πέρθω, δια-πέρσω, διά-περσα	I sack, I lay in ruins
ἵεμαι	I press on, I hasten eagerly
κλέος, κλέεος	[n.] renown; glory
μητίομαι, μητίσομαι, μητισάμην	I plan, I contrive
ὑπ-ουράνιος, -η, -ον	under heaven

600. NOTES

119. ἀλλὰ καὶ ὣς = "nevertheless". προσ-έειπον : when a verb that begins with a vowel takes the temporal augment, usually an original initial consonant has been lost. Here, that consonant is the digamma (= προσέϝειπον).

123. οὕτω = οὕτως

601. COMMENT

119. Despite his terror, Odysseus gains control over his emotions and answers the monster's questions.

120-126. With that tact and astute psychology for which he had won fame among Greeks and Trojans alike, Odysseus tries to win over the giant's good will. He shrewdly begins by referring to Troy, a magic name whose mention then, when news of the great war was uppermost in men's memories, would of itself arouse interest in most audiences. Quickly Odysseus explains that he has arrived here on the Cyclops' island by Zeus' will, driven off his homeward course, not by set purpose of meddling or attack. Then he returns to the basis on which he hopes for consideration: he and his men are subjects of far-famed Agamemnon, 'King of men' and mighty conqueror of Troy the impregnable, who is not someone to antagonize by harming his troops or friends. Odysseus expects his fame as a hero and his status as an associate of Agamemnon will further his claim on Polyphemus' hospitality.

602. COGNATE ACCUSATIVE

Intransitive verbs may govern the accusative of nouns whose meaning is closely related to that of the verb itself. This is called a **cognate** ('related') **accusative**, because both it and its verb have the same or kindred meaning. Cp. English "He died a glorious death," "We ran a race," where neither "death" nor "race" is a direct object of the verb. Similarly in Greek:

μακρὴν ὁδὸν ἤλθομεν. *We have come a long journey.*

σχέτλιον μαχέονται πόλεμον. *They are fighting a cruel war.*

603. WRITE IN GREEK

1. The Achaeans, followers of Agamemnon, fought most bravely around Troy, that they might bring back home(ward) the wife of the king's brother, who was said (λεγ-) to be the most beautiful of all women then living on the earth.

2. We addressed the monstrous shepherd with honey-sweet words, trying to win over his pitiless heart and save the lives of the Achaeans (dat.).

3. If you (pl.) should sail over the great gulf from one city to another, you would learn that Zeus protects his friends and sends good winds to all who revere his commands.

604. WORD STUDY

POLICE ('city guard'), POLITY (system of government in a city or nation), POLICY (administrative plan or program in governing; hence, any set principles of action in business or private conduct), POLITIC (diplomatic, discreet, in conducting oneself towards others), IMPOLITIC (indiscreet, injudicious, blundering), COSMOPOLITAN (considering the whole world as one's city, being at home everywhere; universal, international).

Lesson 90

605. REVIEW OF LESSONS 85-89

In Lessons 85-89, you have learned forty new words, read thirty-six more lines of the *Odyssey*, and studied the use of the explanatory and purpose infinitive and cognate accusative. Point your review by the aid of this quiz:

I. Vocabulary (45%)

1. we rushed away =
2. wood: acc. sg. =
3. ὑψόψε =
4. they will drive =
5. gulf: dat. pl. =
6. deep: f. acc. pl. =
7. λεύκοσι =
8. may they sail (aor.) =

9. homeward =
10. οἵησι =
11. he wandered (impf.) =
12. ὑπείρ =
13. let us address =
14. he was putting down =
15. κήαντες =

II. Text (40%)

1. εἷος ἐπ-ῆλθε νέμων =
2. In line 103, explain ὀχλίσσειαν.
3. δείσαντες ἀπ-εσσύμεθα =
4. When did the Cyclops first perceive the Greeks?
5. In line 113, explain πλεῖθ'.
6. ἄρσενα λεῖπε θύρηφιν =
7. What did the Cyclops do with the milk just collected?
8. In line 118, explain δεισάντων.

III. Grammar (25%)
Translate only the words in italics:

1. Twenty men *could not have lifted* it.
2. He seized the wine, to *drink* it.
3. *Our* hearts were broken with fear.
4. We went a *difficult way* around to the cave's back.
5. Happiness is easier *to desire* than to find.

Lesson 91

606. MEMORIZE

αἰδέομαι, αἰδέσ(σ)ομαι, αἰδεσσάμην	I venerate, I revere, I respect
ἱκέται, ἱκετάων	[m.] suppliants
ἱκνέομαι, ἵξομαι, ἱκόμην	I approach, I come [+ acc.]
κιχάνω, κιχήσομαι, κίχον	I come (by chance), I reach
νηλ(ε)ής, -ές	pitiless, ruthless
ὅπ(π)ῃ	[adv.] where, in what direction

607. TEXT

Odysseus' Appeal

> ἡμεῖς δ' αὖτε κιχανόμενοι τὰ σὰ γοῦνα
> ἱκόμεθ', εἴ τι πόροις ξεινήϊον ἠὲ καὶ ἄλλως
> δοίης δωτίνην, ἥ τε ξείνων θέμις ἐστίν.
> ἀλλ' αἰδεῖο, φέριστε, θεούς· ἱκέται δέ τοί εἰμεν.   130
> Ζεὺς δ' ἐπιτιμήτωρ ἱκετάων τε ξείνων τε,
> ξείνιος, ὃς ξείνοισιν ἅμ' αἰδοίοισιν ὀπηδεῖ."
> ὣς ἐφάμην, ὁ δέ μ' αὐτίκ' ἀμείβετο νηλέϊ θυμῷ·

αἰδοῖος, -η, -ον	honorable, worthy to be held in reverence
δωτίνη, -ης	[f.] gift, present
ἐπιτιμήτωρ, -ορος	[m.] patron, protector
ξεινήϊον, -ου = ξείνιον	[n.] gift given by a host to a guest
ξείνιος, -η, -ον	pertaining to guests or strangers [epithet of Zeus, "Guardian of guests"]
ὀπηδέω	I go along with, I accompany (as guardian)
φέριστος, -η, -ον	mightiest, noblest

608. NOTES

128. πόροις, δοίης depend on the idea of "to find out" implied in the preceding clause.

131. Ζεύς is the subject of an implied ἐστί.

609. COMMENT

127-132. It is customary in the Homeric world for those in a vulnerable position to seek protection from the powerful through supplication. The suppliant grasps the knees or falls down before the person he is supplicating; he invokes the value of reverence (αἰδώς), which requires forbearance and mercy towards the weak.

Odysseus, then, proclaims himself a suppliant by approaching the giant's knees in the name of the whole company. He implores the Cyclops to treat his guests with that kindness and that generosity in gifts of friendship which are expected from all in such circumstances. He is asking nothing special; only proper hospitality. To molest or ill-treat a suppliant would be the gravest moral wrong, a crime of the worst sort against the gods. Odysseus' appeal is to law and morality, enforced by the threat of otherwise incurring divine anger. For Zeus himself takes special care of men traveling at the mercy of others in a foreign land. He will personally avenge any harm or injustice inflicted on them.

610. WRITE IN GREEK

1. The truly wise venerate the gods always and entreat them as suppliants, that they may give them prosperity and a long and happy life.

2. Reaching a wide river which we had never seen, we asked the people living around the city if they would quickly give us a small ship and a pair of oars.

3. Not to seek and love truth is a shameful disease of the soul, which may we all avoid!

Lesson 92

611. MEMORIZE

αἰγίοχος, -η, -ον	aegis-bearing
ἆσσον	[adv.] near, close [often + gen. or dat.]
δύναμαι, δυνήσομαι, δυνησάμην	I can, I am able [+ inf.]
Κύκλωψ, Κύκλωπος	[m.] Cyclops
σχεδόν	[adv.] close by, near

612. TEXT

A Brutal Reply

"νήπιός εἰς, ὦ ξεῖν᾽, ἢ τηλόθεν εἰλήλουθας,
ὅς με θεοὺς κέλεαι ἢ δειδίμεν ἢ ἀλέασθαι.   135
οὐ γὰρ Κύκλωπες Διὸς αἰγιόχου ἀλέγουσιν
οὐδὲ θεῶν μακάρων, ἐπεὶ ἦ πολὺ φέρτεροί εἰμεν·
οὐδ᾽ ἂν ἐγὼ Διὸς ἔχθος ἀλευάμενος πεφιδοίμην
οὔτε σεῦ οὔθ᾽ ἑτάρων, εἰ μὴ θυμός με κελεύοι.
ἀλλά μοι εἴφ᾽, ὅπη ἔσχες ἰὼν εὐεργέα νῆα,   140
ἤ που ἐπ᾽ ἐσχατιῆς ἢ καὶ σχεδόν, ὄφρα δαείω."

ἀλέγω	I take heed of [+ gen.]
δάω, δαήσομαι, δάην	I know, I learn
ἐσχατιή, -ῆς	[f.] remotest part, edge [here = 'far shore']
ἔχθος, -εος	[n.] disfavor, enmity
τηλόθεν	[adv.] from afar
φείδομαι, πεφιδήσομαι, πεφιδόμην	I restrain myself from, I spare [+ gen.]
φέρτερος, -η, -ον	stronger, mightier

613. NOTES

134. εἰς : from εἰμί

135. δειδίμεν : pf. inf. of δείδω

140. εἴφ᾽ for εἰπέ. ἔσχες: i.e., "left". ἰὼν : see Section 468.

141. δαείω : alternate 3 aor. subj. 1 sg. of δάω [= δαήω].

614. COMMENT

134-139. Polyphemus addresses only Odysseus' plea to revere the gods, ignoring Odysseus' declaration of his fame and status, which obviously will win Odysseus no credit here. The Cyclops recognizes that Odysseus inhabits a different world when he says τηλόθεν εἰλήλουθας, but it is clear that, until Polyphemus speaks here, Odysseus still assumed, or at least hoped, that Agamemnon's μέγιστον ὑπουράνιον κλέος would have reached the land of the Cyclopes.

136. The aegis was a goatskin shield, symbol of the divine power of Zeus.

140-141. This imperious demand to know the whereabouts of Odysseus' ship and crew is a further indication of bad will. It is assumed he would put this information to evil purposes.

615. THE GODS IN HOMER

Homer's Odysseus has a human genealogy, but many of the prominent heroes in the Homeric poems have divine ancestry. Achilles' mother Thetis, the sea-nymph, is a goddess, and his paternal great-grandfather is Zeus. Ajax is a cousin of Achilles, with the same great-grandfather on his father's side. Agamemnon and Menelaus are also descended from Zeus through the paternal line. As we see in the passage we are reading from the *Odyssey*, the monster Polyphemus is a son of Poseidon. In other cases, the close bond between a god and a hero is due to a temperamental affinity; Athene loves Odysseus because he is clever, as she is.

Given the biological relationship between heroic mortals and gods, it is no surprise that the gods are stirred to action by human death or suffering. When Achilles is insulted by Agamemnon in the *Iliad*, his mother, then Zeus, then all the gods on Olympus become involved in the ensuing events. Athene is moved by the suffering of her favorite, Odysseus, to petition Zeus at the beginning of the *Odyssey*. In both of Homer's epics, the gods constitute an audience for the story unfolding below, but they intervene if their interests are threatened. Sometimes they actively take part, in disguise, and sometimes they inspire a beloved mortal with bravery or cunning, or sabotage his foe with delusion.

Athene plays the most active role of all the gods in the *Odyssey* as she monitors the interests of her Odysseus. She guides Telemachus on his journey to gather news of his missing father; she smoothes the way for Odysseus to be well-received by the Phaeacians; she warns him of the dangers awaiting him in Ithaca and fights at his side against the suitors; she personally resolves the final conflict with the suitors' kinsmen peacefully. In advancing the cause of Odysseus, Athene takes the side of justice and morality. Such an alignment is consistent with Zeus' pronouncement at the start of the poem, as he considers an instance of crime:

> "Alas, how mortals blame the gods!
> For they say evil things come from us. Rather they themselves
> By their own criminal wickedness have grief beyond what they are given."

I 32-34

The association between the gods and morality is also evident in the Cyclops episode, where Polyphemus' disregard of the gods (even if Poseidon is his father!) frees him to eat his guests (Section 612) and call it hospitality (Section 683). As Odysseus has put it earlier, a hospitable man is a god-fearing man (Section 508).

Later Greeks would reject Homer's gods because of their immorality and silliness or criticize Homer for portraying them so. Plato, for example, banned Homer's epics from his ideal educational curriculum. These critics had in mind the *Iliad*'s gods, who are indeed less single-minded about justice. Sometimes they are violent, sometimes childish and petty, and sometimes too carefree, even as they watch the suffering of mortals below. Although the gods know that many will die on the battlefield at Troy as a result of Achilles' quarrel with Agamemnon, they are shown feasting happily on Olympus as Hephaestus pours them drinks:

> Inextinguishable laughter rose up among the blessed gods
> As they watched Hephaestus puffing around the dining room.

I 599-600

616. WRITE IN GREEK

1. We could neither flee to our companions nor sail homeward, because the Cyclops had come down near the sea and standing close by, savage and pitiless, was throwing huge rocks towards our well-made ships. ["huge" = "largest"]

2. "Tell (sg.) me," he said, "how you justly expect others to respect you, who yourself do not wish with willing heart to revere aegis-bearing Zeus and the blessed gods."

3. Whenever we love those who love us, we do nothing great; but if (ever) we love those who hate us, then we are noble and splendid.

617. WORD STUDY

AEGIS or EGIS (protecting power, as 'under the aegis of a Government agency'); — DYNAMIC (powerful, forceful), DYNAMO (a machine for converting mechanical power of steam, waterfall, etc. into electrical energy), HETERODYNE (in radio, the method by which a receiving tube sets up oscillations of 'another force' similar to those coming from the transmitter), SUPERHETERODYNE; — CYCLOPEAN (colossal, gigantic, as 'cyclopean architecture' built from massive stones).

Lesson 93

618. MEMORIZE

αἰπύς, -εῖα, -ύ	steep; utter
μάρπτω, μάρψω, μάρψα	I seize
μηρός, -οῦ	[m.] thigh
πεῖραρ, πείρατος	[n.] end, boundary
Ποσειδάων, Ποσειδάωνος	[m.] Poseidon [brother of Zeus and god of the sea]

619. TEXT

Craft and Savagery

ὣς φάτο πειράζων, ἐμὲ δ' οὐ λάθεν εἰδότα πολλά,
ἀλλά μιν ἄψορρον προσέφην δολίοισ' ἐπέεσσι·
  "νέα μέν μοι κατέαξε Ποσειδάων ἐνοσίχθων,
πρὸς πέτρῃσι βαλὼν ὑμῆς ἐπὶ πείρασι γαίης,   145
ἄκρῃ προσπελάσας· ἄνεμος δ' ἐκ πόντου ἔνεικεν·
αὐτὰρ ἐγὼ σὺν τοῖσδε ὑπέκφυγον αἰπὺν ὄλεθρον."
  ὣς ἐφάμην, ὁ δέ μ' οὐδὲν ἀμείβετο νηλέϊ θυμῷ,
ἀλλ' ὅ γ' ἀναΐξας ἑτάροισ' ἐπὶ χεῖρας ἴαλλε,
σὺν δὲ δύω μάρψας ὥς τε σκύλακας ποτὶ γαίῃ   150
κόπτ'· ἐκ δ' ἐγκέφαλος χαμάδις ῥέε, δεῦε δὲ γαῖαν.

ἄκρη, -ης	[f.] highest point; headland
ἀν-αΐσσω, —, ἀν-άϊξα	I spring up
ἄψορρον	[adv.] back again; in reply
δεύω	I moisten, I dampen
δόλιος, -η, -ον	crafty
ἐγκέφαλος, -ου	[m.] brain
ἐνοσίχθων, -ονος	[m.] 'earth-shaker' [epithet of Poseidon]
ἐπι...ἰάλλω	I stretch out upon
κατ-άγνυμι, —, κατ-άξα	I break in pieces, I wreck
κόπτω, κόψω, κόψα	I smash, I beat
πειράζω	I try to get information
ποτί	[adv., prep.] down upon [=πρός]
προσ-πελάζω, —, προσ-πέλασα	I drive (something) into (something) [+ acc. and dat.]
πρόσ-φημι	I address
σκύλαξ, -ακος	[m.] puppy, whelp
ὑμός, -ή, -όν	your [pl.]
ὑπ-εκ-φεύγω, etc.	I flee out from under, I escape
χαμάδις	[adv.] to the ground

620. NOTES

142. εἰδότα : see οἶδα in Section 491.

144. νέα should be scanned as a monosyllable.

150. σύν : adv. = "together," "at the same moment."

621. COMMENT

142-147. Odysseus is too swift-witted to be trapped by the Cyclops' question into revealing anything that might jeopardize his companions back at the ship. Odysseus does not really answer the Cyclops' query at all. He does not say where he left his ship; he tells an imaginary story from which the monster, if he is willing to believe it, may think the ship destroyed and forget about it and its crew. This is, then, a dodge. It conceals the truth from an enemy by sidetracking his investigation.

144. Odysseus' lie about Poseidon has some dramatic irony in it: near the opening of the poem Zeus had explained to Athene that it was problematic for him to free Odysseus from Calypso's isle, since Odysseus had blinded Poseidon's son, Polyphemus, and Poseidon therefore held a grudge against him. Odysseus, however, is unaware of Polyphemus' parentage at this point.

148-151. The giant does not answer, but lunges forward and works sudden death on two of the companions nearest at hand.

622. HOMERIC DRESS

The Homeric poems contain the first references in literature to Greek clothing. Terms such as πέπλος (a woman's dress) and χίτων (a man's tunic), which will become standard elements in the vocabulary of Greek dress, appear here for the first time. While the poems cannot show us exactly what these garments looked like, they do give a sense of the importance of the textile arts in Greek culture.

Everyone knows that Penelope spent a lot of time weaving as she attempted to delay her marriage to one of her suitors. But weaving is a typical activity for the noble women of the Homeric poems. Helen, in both the *Iliad* and *Odyssey*, is pictured weaving. Andromache, the wife of Hector, weaves. King Alcinoos' wife, Queen Arete, weaves. So do the goddesses Circe, Calypso, and Athene— who was the patroness of weaving. Although slave women also are assigned weaving tasks, clearly the textile crafts have considerable prestige, and they are practiced with pride by the nobility. Queen Arete, for example, weaves a signature type of cloth (*Od.* 7.234). Social standing is reflected in the possession of abundant fine textiles, and clothing is used as an item of exchange in cementing alliances, in the form of guest-gifts, right along with talents of gold (e.g., *Od.* 8.390-441).

Unlike our garments today, clothing in ancient Greece was never tailored (cut, fitted, and sewn from several pieces). Garments were, rather, rectangular pieces of fabric; they were draped and often had multiple uses. The Homeric man's χίτων is a short garment, cinched with a belt. The cloak (χλαῖνα) he wears over it is of thick wool and can be used as a blanket as well. The cloak is fastened about the body with a brooch; Odysseus' golden brooch is engraved with a hound grasping a dappled fawn in its paws (19.226 ff.). More physically vigorous activities, such as boxing, wrestling, and warfare, are done in a ζῶμα, a sturdy loincloth.

The πέπλος or gown worn by Homeric women is long and is fastened across the shoulders by ornamental brooches and around the waist with a belt. These are colored and made of wool, and some are decorated with designs woven into the cloth itself. Women wear a veil, called a κρήδεμνον, with which they modestly cover their faces, or rip off as a gesture of mourning. A ζώνη or metal girdle cinches their waists.

623. WRITE IN GREEK

1. In order to avoid utter destruction, he told the monstrous shepherd that Poseidon had seized his ship and thrown it on the rocks at the boundaries of the land, afar.

2. According to the custom of men living at that time, whenever anyone prayed he always raised his hands towards heaven, to show that mortals receive all good things from the gods.

3. May he answer me nothing, but kill me at once, that I may not see the pains and death of more of my dear comrades.

624. WORD STUDY

ENCEPHALITIS (brain fever, inflammation of the brain).

Lesson 94

625. MEMORIZE

ἀνδρόμεος, -η, -ον	human [used only of flesh]
δόρπον, -ου	[n.] supper
κρέα, κρεῶν	[n. pl.] nom. sg. κρέας flesh, meat
ξίφος, ξίφεος	[n.] sword
ὁπλίζω, —, ὅπλισσα	I prepare
ὀστέον, -ου	[n.] bone

626. TEXT

A Ghastly Meal

τοὺς δὲ διὰ μελεϊστὶ ταμὼν ὁπλίσσατο δόρπον·   152
ἤσθιε δ' ὥς τε λέων ὀρεσίτροφος, οὐδ' ἀπέλειπεν,
ἔγκατά τε σάρκας τε καὶ ὀστέα μυελόεντα.
ἡμεῖς δὲ κλαίοντες ἀνεσχέθομεν Διὶ χεῖρας,
σχέτλια ἔργ' ὁρόωντες· ἀμηχανίη δ' ἔχε θυμόν.   156
αὐτὰρ ἐπεὶ Κύκλωψ μεγάλην ἐμπλήσατο νηδὺν
ἀνδρόμεα κρέ' ἔδων καὶ ἐπ' ἄκρητον γάλα πίνων,
κεῖτ' ἔντοσθ' ἄντροιο τανυσσάμενος διὰ μήλων.

ἄκρητος, -ον	undiluted
ἀμηχανίη, -ης	[f.] helplessness
ἀν-έχω	I hold up, I raise aloft
ἀπο-λείπω	I leave a remnant behind
γάλα, -ακτος	[n.] milk
ἔγκατα, -ων	[n. pl.] entrails
λέων, -οντος	[m.] lion
μελεϊστί	[adv.] limb by limb
μυελόεις, -εσσα, -εν	full of marrow
νηδύς, -ύος	[f.] belly
ὀρεσίτροφος, -η, -ον	mountain-bred
τάμνω, —, τάμον	I divide, I tear
τανύω, τανύω, τάνυσσα	I stretch out

627. NOTES

156. ὁρόωντες = ὁράοντες. Homeric verbs in -άω sometimes become -όω by *assimilation*. When the α is short, the second vowel is often lengthened (here, ο to ω). Cp. Section 593.

158. ἐπί is adverbial: "besides, on top of that" (="to wash down").

628. COMMENT

152-154. Polyphemus tears his victims into pieces to prepare them for his meal. In the *Iliad* the simile of the mountain-bred lion devouring freshly killed flocks is applied to the hero Menelaus dominating the battlefield. Note that at this point Odysseus identifies more with the vulnerable prey than with the predator.

155-156. The Greeks cry out in revulsion and dismay. Only in the gods, in Zeus, lover of justice and protector of guests, do they find any hope or strength; of themselves they are pitiably helpless. ἀμηχανίη appears only here in Homer; thus it is called a *hapax legomenon* ("once said"). Yet, knowing Odysseus as we do, we expect him to find a μῆχος ("device") for escape.

157-159. The Greeks watch Polyphemus drain off unmixed milk to complete his meal, then lie down stretched out among his flocks. ἄκρητον is elsewhere used only of wine, the drink Odysseus will in fact use as part of his μῆχος.

629. FOOD IN THE HOMERIC WORLD

It is interesting to know details about the way of life of these Homeric people with whom we are living in imagination throughout this course. Much can be learned about their food and drink by collecting the evidence from both poems.

The main staple of the diet is meat, roasted over an open fire or baked in bags of skin placed among the ashes; boiling is never mentioned. Beef, mutton, and pork are the common meats, with wild venison or boar or goat as occasional luxuries. Bread and cakes, made from wheat and barley, are the second major item, supplemented by soft cheese and occasionally by some vegetable, mainly beans or peas (not, of course, potatoes, corn, or tomatoes, which are New World crops). Onions are used as a relish; olive oil and salt, for flavoring.

Of fresh fruits there is mention of pears, pomegranates, apples, figs, olives, and grapes. Honey is very popular both in itself and as sweetening for other items. Fish is not much liked, but is eaten in the absence of other food.

The chief drink is wine, liberally diluted with water and often flavored with honey or spices. Wine is preferred aged, and is made in several varieties. Fresh spring-water, milk (mostly of goats), and whey are also fairly common for drinking, but on a secondary level to wine.

Usually there are two meals a day, a light one in the morning (ἄριστον) and the main meal (δεῖπνον) toward mid-day, but the time of the main meal varies. If the main meal is taken in the morning or at noon, a supper (δόρπον) ordinarily follows in the evening. Between meals and at intervals in the day's work a bit of wine is the customary refreshment.

630. WRITE IN GREEK

1. We wept when we saw the cruel Cyclops, sitting there in the cave among his sheep, seize with pitiless heart two faithful companions to eat.

2. Looking at him prepare a supper of human flesh and bones, I wished to draw my deadly sword from (παρά) my thigh and kill him.

3.   Tell me where you (sg.) found your companions, so many and brave. You are a happy king, O friend!

631. WORD STUDY

PANCREAS (a gland supplying the stomach juice for digesting fats and 'all flesh'), CREOSOTE ('flesh-saver', an oily liquid used as a wood preservative); — LEON, LEO — OSTEOPATH (a doctor who seeks to cure certain diseases by treatment of the bones, manipulation of the limbs, spine, and muscles).

Lesson 95

632. MEMORIZE

δῖος, -α, -ον	bright, glorious [f. usually keeps alpha through sg.]
ἐπι-μαίομαι, ἐπι-μάσσομαι, ἐπι-μασσάμην	I seek out; I feel, I touch
μεγαλήτωρ, μεγαλήτορος	[adj.] great-hearted, great, daring
ὅθι	[adv.] where
ὀξύς, -εῖα, -ύ	sharp, keen
στενάχω	[pres. syst. only] I groan, I lament

633. TEXT

The Wiser Second Thought

τὸν μὲν ἐγὼ βούλευσα κατὰ μεγαλήτορα θυμὸν   160
ἆσσον ἰών, ξίφος ὀξὺ ἐρυσσάμενος παρὰ μηροῦ,
οὐτάμεναι πρὸς στῆθος, ὅθι φρένες ἧπαρ ἔχουσι,
χείρ’ ἐπιμασσάμενος· ἕτερος δέ με θυμὸς ἔρυκεν.
αὐτοῦ γάρ κε καὶ ἄμμες ἀπωλόμεθ’ αἰπὺν ὄλεθρον·
οὐ γάρ κεν δυνάμεσθα θυράων ὑψηλάων   165
χερσὶν ἀπώσασθαι λίθον ὄβριμον, ὃν προσέθηκεν.
ὣς τότε μὲν στενάχοντες ἐμείναμεν Ἠῶ δῖαν.

ἀπ-ωθέω, ἀπ-ώσω, ἄπ-ωσα	I push from
ἐρύκω, ἐρύξω, ἔρυξα	I hold back, I restrain
ἧπαρ, -ατος	[n.] liver
οὐτάω	I stab, I pierce
προσ-τίθημι, etc.	I place in position
στῆθος, -εος	[n.] breast, chest

634. NOTES

162. φρένες here used in its literal sense: "midriff, diaphragm;" the usual meaning, "mind, spirit," is secondary, derived from the ancient opinion that the midriff, rather than the brain and heart, is the seat of intelligence and feeling.

162. ἔχουσι = "overlaps, enfolds"— an apt description of the way in which the diaphragm concavity encloses the upper surface of the liver.

163. χείρ’ is for χειρί, not χεῖρα.

164. καὶ ἄμμες : "we, too," in addition to the just-devoured comrades. αἰπὺν ὄλεθρον is cognate accusative (Section 602).

164-165. κε...ἀπωλόμεθ' and οὐ γὰρ κεν δυνάμεσθα· κε(ν) with the past ind. expresses potential in contrary to fact suppositions, i.e., "we would have perished..."

166. Ἠῶ : The acc. sg. Ἠόα is often thus contracted to Ἠῶ .

635. COMMENT

160-163. Odysseus' immediate plan typifies a warrior's way of thinking: he sees a chance of wounding the monster mortally. He will approach silently the slumbering figure, run his hand lightly over the massive frame until he locates a soft and vulnerable spot under the ribs, then plunge into the giant's vitals his keen-edged sword. One quick daring thrust, and they would be saved.

163-167. It occurs to Odysseus that in killing the Cyclops he and his companions would be entombed alive, because of the heavy door-stone. The *Odyssey* often makes this very point, that impulses must be checked or modified by calmer reason. Once again, Odysseus' clear thinking averts disaster.

636. FOLKTALES IN THE *ODYSSEY*

Folktales are traditional tales set in the indefinite past. They are vague about their geographic setting as well, and involve human or even animal characters who represent broad types; often they bear generic names or are unnamed.

The blinding of the giant Polyphemus is a widely known and popular folktale which the *Odyssey* incorporates into its epic narrative. Many versions of this tale of a trickster outwitting an ogre have been collected and studied by folklorists. Typically, a clever man, sometimes accompanied by companions, comes upon some sort of ogre in his isolated lair. Often the ogre is a giant and sometimes has only one eye. Because he is a cannibal, he decides to keep the man/men in his dwelling to round out his dinner. The trickster is able to blind the monster by means of a hot spit or boiling liquid. And being a trickster, he is good with disguises; he covers himself with a sheepskin, behaves like one of the sheep in the ogre's herd, and exits from the dwelling with the sheep. Often, after he has escaped, the trickster boasts to the ogre about his success.

The *Odyssey* omits one element that is found in many versions of this tale: the ogre possesses a talking ring that he throws to the escaped trickster. Once the trickster puts the ring on, it shouts, "Here I am!" over and over again, tipping off the blind monster to the trickster's whereabouts. Thus the trickster's escape requires that he cut off his finger, since the ring, once put on, cannot be removed. There are many possible reasons for this element to be omitted from the Homeric version, including the poem's emphasis on the technological backwardness of Cyclopean society (how would Polyphemus have gotten a hold of such a marvelous ring?); and the poem's preference for keeping its hero's body intact. Nevertheless, Polyphemus is able to do some harm to Odysseus through his curse at the end of the episode.

Odysseus' trick of calling himself "Nobody" is also similar to a ruse found in folktales from around the world. In these tales a man, when asked by a supernatural being for his name, identifies himself deceptively as 'Myself.' As the tale progresses, the man injures the supernatural being, who calls out for help from his neighbors. When they ask what is wrong, he shouts something like 'Myself has hurt me,' which response naturally leads his neighbors to assume that he has somehow caused his own problems.

Homer's *Odyssey* intertwines these two traditional folktales about a trickster outfoxing a more powerful being into the story of Odysseus' visit to the cave of Polyphemus. The tales provide lively and timeless affirmation of the poem's celebration of brains over brawn.

637. WRITE IN GREEK

1. If you (pl.) had been able to go close and feel the sharp rocks around the door with your hands, perhaps you would have found some way out of the cave and would not have remained there lamenting through the night. [For "go close and" use the ptc. alone.]

2. Whenever anyone asked the great-hearted king if he had a sword, he always drew it at once from beside his thigh and showed it to him, bright and keen.

3. Seeing the cruel deeds of the monstrous Cyclops, we wailed throughout the cave, and feared lest he might eat (φαγ-) us all.

638. WORD STUDY

OXYGEN (the 'acid-born, acid-making' element, present in acids and giving them their 'sharp' effect), OXYMORON (foolish; 'sharp-stupid', a figure of speech which joins two mutually opposed ideas for emphasis, e.g., 'a lawless law', 'O happy loss!'); — HEPATITIS (inflammation of the liver), HEPARIN (an anticoagulant drug derived from liver and lung tissue of animals); — STETHOSCOPE (an instrument for 'examining the chest' by listening to heartbeat and breathing).

Lesson 96

639. REVIEW OF LESSONS 91-95

In these lessons, you have memorized more vocabulary words and read forty-two more lines of the *Odyssey*. Review carefully; then try this sample test:

I. Vocabulary (30%)

    1.   may they reach : aor. =

    2.   νηλέας =

    3.   boundary : dat. pl. =

    4.   ὅπλισσον =

    5.   city : acc. pl. =

    6.   αἰπειῆσι =

    7.   we shall touch =

    8.   ἆσσον =

    9.   to respect : aor. inf. =

    10.   whenever we can : aor. subj. =

II. Syntax (30%): Translate only the words in italics:

    1.   I fear they will all perish a most cruel *death*.

    2.   We pushed the rock away with our *hands*.

    3.   If the storm had broken, *we would have reached* the island easily.

    4.   "Give me," he cried, "more of these puny men *to eat*."

    5.   *When he had filled* his huge belly, he slept.

III. Text (40%)

    1.   In line 130, explain αἰδεῖο.

    2.   Why did not Odysseus stab the giant as he slept?

    3.   In line 129, explain δοίης.

    4.   What motives did Odysseus use to appeal to the giant's mercy?

    5.   In line 162, explain οὐτάμεναι.

    6.   In line 164, explain ὄλεθρον.

    7.   In line 167, explain Ἠῶ.

    8.   How did Odysseus safeguard his men at the boat? Were his means justifiable?

Lesson 97

640. MEMORIZE

Ἀθήνη, -ης   [f.] Athene [a goddess, special patroness of Odysseus]

ἄψ   [adv.] back, back again

κλυτός, -όν   famous; excellent

τίνω or τίω,   I pay; [in mid.] I take vengeance upon, I punish
   [fut.] τείσω or τίσω,
   [aor.] τείσα or τῖσα

641. TEXT

New Cruelty and a New Plot

ἦμος δ᾽ ἠριγένεια φάνη ῥοδοδάκτυλος Ἠώς,
καὶ τότε πῦρ ἀνέκαιε καὶ ἤμελγε κλυτὰ μῆλα,
πάντα κατὰ μοῖραν, καὶ ὑπ᾽ ἔμβρυον ἧκεν ἑκάστῃ.   170
αὐτὰρ ἐπεὶ δὴ σπεῦσε πονησάμενος τὰ ἃ ἔργα,
σὺν δ᾽ ὅ γε δὴ αὖτε δύω μάρψας ὁπλίσσατο δεῖπνον.
δειπνήσας δ᾽ ἄντρου ἐξήλασε πίονα μῆλα,
ῥηϊδίως ἀφελὼν θυρεὸν μέγαν· αὐτὰρ ἔπειτα
ἂψ ἐπέθηχ᾽, ὡς εἴ τε φαρέτρῃ πῶμ᾽ ἐπιθείη.   175
πολλῇ δὲ ῥοίζῳ πρὸς ὄρος τρέπε πίονα μῆλα
Κύκλωψ· αὐτὰρ ἐγὼ λιπόμην κακὰ βυσσοδομεύων,
εἴ πως τεισαίμην, δοίη δέ μοι εὖχος Ἀθήνη.

ἀνα-καίω	I re-kindle
βυσσοδομεύω	I plan secretly
δειπνέω, δειπνήσω, δείπνησα	I take a meal
ἐξ-ελαύνω, εξ-ελάω, εξ-έλασ(σ)α	I drive out
εὖχος	[n.] prayed-for success; joyous triumph; thing one can boast about
πῶμα, -ατος	[n.] cover, lid
ῥοῖζος, -ου	[f.] whistling, calling
φαρέτρη, -ης	[f.] quiver (for arrows)

642. NOTES

172. σύν : adv. = "together, at once" (cp. line 149). δεῖπνον : here, the "morning meal."

175. τε : not translatable here, used in Homer in introducing similes; recall note on line 13. ὡς εἴ τε…: Polyphemus is so strong that he is able to replace the massive stone as effortlessly as, for example, an archer would replace the lid on his quiver.

177. λιπόμην : The aor. mid. of this verb often has passive sense.

178. εἴ πως : introduces an indirect question with the opt. ("I was wondering how I might…")

643. COMMENT

168-172. The repetition in partly identical, partly modified, form of several lines from earlier passages of the story serves as an artful memory hookup of the present action with what has gone before. We thus see the whole narrative more as a unit, and better perceive the place in it of what is now re-enacted. This is an example of formulaic composition.

172. By describing the dreadful death of two more Greeks in such a brief and unemotional way, Homer suggests that no other course of action was to be expected of him.

172. δεῖπνον : This term designates the principal meal of the day, ordinarily taken in the evening, but often at noon and sometimes, as here, before beginning the day's work.

173-175. Once more the ease with which the giant handles the huge rock slab brings home to us the immense strength at his command. The door-stone seems not to have reached to the very top of the cave's opening, but to have left some space for light and ventilation. That is how both the Cyclops and the Greeks knew when morning had arrived.

177-178. Foiled in their hopes of perhaps being able to escape when the giant opened the cave's mouth to let out his flocks, the Greeks are left behind as in a cage; they are choice morsels reserved for coming 'banquets.' It is a hopeless situation. But Odysseus, at least, does not give up, nor abandon hope. His sharp mind is busy with new schemes for vengeance and escape, and he trusts in the aid of the gods.

644. ACCUSATIVE OF SPECIFICATION

In Greek, an accusative is often used to explain or specify in what respect the idea contained in a verb, adjective, noun, or whole clause is true. This is called the accusative of specification or respect. Thus:

βάλε μιν χεῖρα.   He struck him *on the hand*.

γυνὴ καλὴ ὀφθαλμούς.   The woman is *fair-eyed*. (= fair in respect to eyes)

παῖς μὲν σῶμα, ἀρετὴν δὲ ἀνήρ.   He is a boy *in body*, but *as for valor* a man. (= a boy in respect to his body, a man in respect to valor)

645. WRITE IN GREEK

1. He left us there in the cave, planning how we might punish the Cyclops and go back again to our ships; but how could we lift that mighty door-stone out of the way?

2. The monstrous shepherd was cruel and savage, yet he well knew how to lead his excellent flocks over the mountains, to some place where they might find food. [For "knew how to" use οἶδα and inf.]

3.   Having drawn (aor.) my sharp sword easily from beside (my) thigh, I prepared
       destruction for the ruthless Cyclops, if somehow I might be able to kill him.

646. WORD STUDY

ATHENAEUM (a common name for a literary club, academy, reading-room, etc.,
Athene being in ancient myth the patroness of learning).

Lesson 98

647. MEMORIZE

ἐλαΐνεος, -η, -ον	(of) olive-wood
ἱστός, -οῦ	[m.] mast; loom [for weaving]
παρ-ίσταμαι, παρα-στήσομαι, παρά-στην	I stand by
χλωρός, -ή, -όν	greenish yellow, green

648. TEXT

Preparations for Attack

ἥδε δέ μοι κατὰ θυμὸν ἀρίστη φαίνετο βουλή·
Κύκλωπος γὰρ ἔκειτο μέγα ῥόπαλον παρὰ σηκῷ,   180
χλωρὸν ἐλαΐνεον· τὸ μὲν ἔκταμεν, ὄφρα φοροίη
αὐανθέν. τὸ μὲν ἄμμες εἴσκομεν εἰσορόωντες
ὅσσον θ᾽ ἱστὸν νηὸς ἐεικοσόροιο μελαίνης,
φορτίδος εὐρείης, ἥ τ᾽ ἐκπεράᾳ μέγα λαῖτμα·
τόσσον ἔην μῆκος, τόσσον πάχος εἰσοράασθαι.   185
τοῦ μὲν ὅσον τ᾽ ὄργυιαν ἐγὼν ἀπέκοψα παραστὰς
καὶ παρέθηχ᾽ ἑτάροισιν, ἀποξῦναι δ᾽ ἐκέλευσα·

ἀπο-κόπτω, ἀπο-κόψω, ἀπό-κοψα	I cut off
ἀπ-οξύνω, ἀπ-οξυνέω, ἀπ-όξυνα	I shape down, I taper
αὐαίνω, aor. pass. αὐάνθην	I dry out
ἐεικόσ-ορος, -ον	twenty-oared
εἴσκω	I judge to be
ἐκ-περάω, ἐκ-περήσω, ἐκ-πέρησα	I traverse, I sail across
ἐκ-τάμνω, —, ἔκ-ταμον	I cut out
ὄργυια, -ης	[f.] fathom (the length of the outstretched arms)
παρα-τίθημι, παρα-θήσω, παρά-θηκα	I set beside
πάχος, -εος	[n.] thickness, bulk
ῥόπαλον, -ου	[n.] club, staff
φορέω	I carry, I convey
φορτίς, -ίδος	[f.] merchant-ship

649. NOTES

181. The subject of the sentence has shifted from ῥόπαλον to Κύκλωψ. This change of subjects within a sentence is far more common in Greek than in Latin. φοροίη: contraction of φορεοίη, an alternate 3rd sing. pres. opt. act., equivalent to φορέοι.

182. εἰσορόωντες: = εἰσοράοντες. See the notes in Sections 593 and 627.

184. ἐκπεράᾳ: = ἐκπεράει; in verbs in -αω, α often prevails over an ε or η following it. λαῖτμα: i.e., the gulf of the sea

185. εἰσοράασθαι: = εἰσοράεσθαι

186. τοῦ μὲν ὅσον τ' ὄργυιαν ἐγὼν ἀπέκοψα : τοῦ ῥοπάλου τόσον ὅση ὄργυια γίγνεται ἀπέκοψα "I cut off so much (τόσον) of the club as (ὅση) a fathom is."

650. COMMENT

179-187. As he turns over in his mind several possible stratagems, Odysseus' eye is attracted by the huge stake of olive-wood leaning against the pen, obviously to dry out for use as a walking stick and club. This suggests to him the most workable plan of all, and he at once begins to set it in motion. Just what he intends to do neither his men nor we yet learn until 192ff.

182-185. Once again a simile makes the whole description much more vivid.

651. POLITICAL AND SOCIAL ORGANIZATION OF THE HOMERIC WORLD

Part 1: Political Organization

We have seen (Section 573) that the Homeric poems were the product of a long oral tradition stretching back to the Mycenaean period of the second millennium, when the inhabitants of Greece were governed from royal palaces; their society was centralized politically, socially, and economically; it was organized hierarchically and administered in a bureaucratic fashion (Section 551).

Yet the poems we have today present a world organized along different lines. The *Iliad* and *Odyssey* depict a local, small-scale society. Its basic political unit is the πόλις, the self-governing community anchored by a public gathering place called an ἀγορή, in which deliberation and decision-making take place. Two deliberative bodies are typical: a council (βουλή) of the leading men (βασιλῆες), and an assembly (also called ἀγορή) of the people (λαοί or δῆμος). Any important community issue is brought before these bodies; and while the people are not expected to speak out themselves, the βασιλῆες are concerned to win them over and create a consensus in order to legitimize communal actions. So, while the political system in the Homeric poems is obviously not democratic, popular opinion is respected and censure avoided. Such councils and assemblies are depicted in the *Odyssey's* Ithaca, but even the Greek army camped at Troy, far away from their various πόληες, governs itself through these institutions.

Archeological research has uncovered many such πόληες with central open spaces, and has dated them to the period after 1000 BCE, especially 850-700. The same era witnessed the beginning of colonization, the founding of new cities on the model of the parent city. Another product of this era was the Homeric poems, linking the political structure of the poems fairly closely with the late Dark Age.

652. WRITE IN GREEK

1. My comrades standing by thought that the tall green olive-wood tree was similar to the great mast of a deep, black ship, so great was it in length to look at.

2. "Lest another and more destructive war seize the suffering world, go yourselves," he said, "and teach men in every town and every land that they are all brothers to one another. Therefore they must love each other and not fight. There is no other way to peace."

3. Whenever any plan seems best to me in my knowing heart, my comrades always accept it, because they have faith in me.

653. WORD STUDY

CHLORINE (a greenish-yellow poisonous gas), CHLOROFORM (anaesthetic compound of chlorine and formic acid), HYDROCHLORIC (an acid formed of hydrogen and chlorine).

Lesson 99

654. MEMORIZE

ἀνώγω, ἀνώξω, ἄνωξα, ἄνωγα	[pf. has pres. sense; plpf. has impf. sense] I command, I urge
μοχλός, -οῦ	[m.] bar, stake
ὕπνος, -ου	[m.] sleep

655. TEXT

A Desperate Scheme

οἱ δ' ὁμαλὸν ποίησαν· ἐγώ δ' ἐθόωσα παραστὰς
ἄκρον, ἄφαρ δὲ λαβὼν ἐπυράκτεον ἐν πυρὶ κηλέῳ.
καὶ τὸ μὲν εὖ κατέθηκα κατακρύψας ὑπὸ κόπρῳ,   190
ἥ ῥα κατὰ σπείους κέχυτο μεγάλ' ἤλιθα πολλή·
αὐτὰρ τοὺς ἄλλους κλήρῳ πεπαλέσθαι ἄνωγον,
ὅς τις τολμήσειεν ἐμοὶ σὺν μοχλὸν ἀείρας
τρῖψαι ἐν ὀφθαλμῷ, ὅτε τὸν γλυκὺς ὕπνος ἱκάνοι.
οἱ δ' ἔλαχον, τοὺς ἄν κε καὶ ἤθελον αὐτὸς ἑλέσθαι,   195
τέσσαρες, αὐτὰρ ἐγὼ πέμπτος μετὰ τοῖσιν ἐλέγμην.

ἄφαρ	[adv.] quickly, briskly
ἤλιθα	[a strengthening adv.] very, in abundance
θοόω, θοώσω, θόωσα	I sharpen
κατα-κρύπτω. etc.	I hide away
κήλεος, -η, -ον	blazing
κλῆρος, -ου	[m.] lot
κόπρος, -ου	[f.] dung, filth
λαγχάνω, λήξομαι, λάχον	I draw the lot, I am assigned by lot
λέγω, λέξω, non-thematic 2 aor. mid. λέγμην	I choose, I collect, I count
ὁμαλός, -ή, -όν	smooth
πάλλω, —, πέπαλον	I shake, I cast; in mid: I draw lots
πέμπτος, -η, -ον	fifth
πυρακτέω	I harden (by fire), I temper
τέσσαρες, -α	four
τολμάω, τολμήσω, τόλμησα	I dare
τρίβω, τρίψω, τρίψα	I twist round, I grind, I rub

656. NOTES

191. σπείους : gen. sg. of σπεῖος, an alternate spelling of σπέος; see Section 514. κέχυτο: plpf. of χέω, with impf. force, = "lay scattered." Take μεγάλα adverbially ("high").

193. τολμήσειεν : depending on the idea 'to see' implicit in the preceding line.

195. τοὺς : the article used as a relative ("whom") with antecedent οἱ.

196. ἐλέγμην : translate this middle reflexively: "I chose myself" or "I counted myself"

657. COMMENT

188-194. When his men have smoothed down the entire log, Odysseus sharpens the tip and bakes it hard in the coals. Odysseus might have used his sword (ξίφος, 161) for this attack on the Cyclops, but he chooses to fashion instead this primitive weapon, a type used by early man. As he hides it away he explains his plan. He decides to determine who will share with him in this hazardous attempt by lot, the method commonly regarded in Greek culture as the fairest.

190-191. The years-old heaps of refuse covering the floor "all down the cave," from mouth to interior, are yet another indication of the Cyclops' uncivilized ways.

195-196. Odysseus is encouraged on finding the lot fall on just those men whose strength, dexterity, and proven courage make them most desirable. He sees here reason to trace the guiding hand of the gods.

658. POLITICAL AND SOCIAL ORGANIZATION OF THE HOMERIC WORLD

Part 2: Social Organization

The basic social unit in the Homeric poems is the household, or οἶκος. The household includes the head and his various dependents. A Homeric πόλις contains both modest and grand households, but typically the richest citizen (for Ithaca, that would be Odysseus) would head the most extensive. The οἶκοι of the paramount βασιλῆες include not just relatives and slaves, but also retainers, refugees from other πόληες, who are given status and protection in their new community in exchange for loyal service. The status of the preeminent βασιλεύς and his household can be challenged, as the situation in Ithaca during Odysseus' absence makes clear: the other leading men consider themselves to be nearly his equals and potentially his successors.

The lesser households do not receive attention in the Homeric poems, but they implicitly exist, since their heads sit in the assembly and follow the βασιλῆες to war as their λαοί. It appears that achievement in war could be an avenue to social advancement (see, for example, *Odyssey* 14. 199-234). Thus, class-boundaries are not insurmountable; and Odysseus' companions, though they are his social inferiors, are also his dear friends (φίλοι).

Besides the elite and non-elite land-owning farmers, the Homeric poems show us a class of professional artisans and specialists, such as bards, builders, seers, and doctors. Some craftsmen— potters, smiths, leatherworkers— have an ambiguous status in relation to households and communities. They probably worked for the οἶκοι. The hired worker, who did not have an ongoing tie to any οἶκος, stood at the bottom of the social ladder of all free men; slaves, in fact, who truly did "belong" to an οἶκος, were considered better off.

Long-distance commerce is the province of foreigners. Homer says little about local markets and exchange. However, the βασιλῆες regularly conduct raids in order to acquire goods and slaves. Moreover, the poems describe much gift exchange between the members of the elite; such exchange is a means of forging or cementing alliances.

A woman's role is confined to the household, where she supervises the slaves in their domestic work and does some herself: women are often shown weaving. Women in both of the Homeric poems are admonished to stay out of men's affairs (war, politics) and concentrate on their domestic tasks (see *Odyssey* 1. 356-59; *Iliad* 6. 490-93). A well-run household though, is critically important, as the story of Penelope's defense of Odysseus' household makes clear. Moreover, it is women who produce heirs.

Most scholars agree that, just as the political structure of the Homeric πόλις reflects late Dark Age reality, so also does the Homeric society. In the case of society, however, the evidence is not archeological but based on research on oral poetry. Traditional singers use traditional material (stories, diction), but elaborate on them so as to captivate and entertain the audience. Audiences are drawn to poems that are meaningful to them and with which they can identify. Oral songs typically depict dilemmas and conflicts familiar to the audience, though the characters and events may belong explicitly to some heroic past. In this sense, traditional poetry is highly adaptable and open to what is new. As Telemachus says:

> People surely applaud more the newest song to meet their ears.....
> *Odyssey* 1. 351-52

659. WRITE IN GREEK

1. I urged them to take the stake of green olive-wood and put it in the fire, that it might be made ready for the deed which we were about to do.

2. Who of my comrades would dare with me to raise the heavy stake and with it destroy that monstrous eye, when sleep should seize the cruel and pitiless shepherd?

3. He who is swift to obey but hesitates to command is indeed noble in soul and alone worthy to become king.

660. WORD STUDY

HYPNOTISM (artificially caused 'sleep' in which the mind becomes passive and easily directed by another), HYPNOTIST; HYPNOTIC (producing sleepiness or a state of hypnotism); — CLERIC (a religious official, churchman; so called from Deuteronomy 18.2: "The Lord Himself shall be their lot [i.e., inheritance, riches]"), CLERICAL (pertaining to clerics or the Church as a whole), CLERGY (by mispronunciation of 'clericy': Churchmen as a group), CLERK (shortened form of 'cleric': ancient name for a Churchman, later for any learned person or official in charge of records [e.g., City Clerk], now of anyone caring for business transactions); — DIATRIBE (a verbal attack or tirade, 'grinding through' a person's character or actions).

Lesson 100

661. MEMORIZE

αἷμα, αἵματος	[n.] blood
ὄνομα or οὔνομα, ὀνόματος	[n.] name
τρίς	[adv.] thrice, three times

662. TEXT

The Enemy Returns

ἑσπέριος δ᾽ ἦλθεν καλλίτριχα μῆλα νομεύων·   197
αὐτίκα δ᾽ εἰς εὐρὺ σπέος ἤλασε πίονα μῆλα,
πάντα μάλ᾽, οὐδέ τι λεῖπε βαθείης ἔντοθεν αὐλῆς,
ἤ τι ὀϊσάμενος, ἢ καὶ θεὸς ὣς ἐκέλευσεν.   200
αὐτὰρ ἔπειτ᾽ ἐπέθηκε θυρεὸν μέγαν ὑψόσ᾽ ἀείρας·
ἑζόμενος δ᾽ ἤμελγεν ὄϊς καὶ μηκάδας αἶγας,
πάντα κατὰ μοῖραν, καὶ ὑπ᾽ ἔμβρυον ἧκεν ἑκάστῃ.
αὐτὰρ ἐπεὶ δὴ σπεῦσε πονησάμενος τὰ ἃ ἔργα,
σὺν δ᾽ ὅ γε δὴ αὖτε δύω μάρψας ὁπλίσσατο δόρπον.

ἔντοθεν	[prep. + gen.] within, inside (of)
ἑσπέριος, -η, -ον	at evening
καλλίθριξ, καλλίτριχος	[adj.] with fair wool, fleecy [epithet of sheep and horses]
μηκάς, άδος	[adj.] bleating [epithet of goats]
νομεύω	I tend or drive (a flock)

663. NOTES

199. μάλα : recall note on line 99 in Section 579.

200. ἢ καὶ : καὶ here marks and emphasizes the distinction between alternatives.

201. ἐπέθηκε : Section 577

203. ἧκεν : see note on line 106 in Section 586

664. COMMENT

197-203. The Greeks watch the giant drive in his flocks and once more shut behind him that mighty barrier against all escape.

199-200. Odysseus speculates as to whether Polyphemus has some reason to drive in all the male animals, whereas before he had left them in the yard (Section 578). On the other hand, perhaps some god has so moved him. In any case, the variation in routine contributes to favorable circumstances for the ultimate fulfillment of Odysseus' plan.

665. THE GEOMETRIC STYLE

After the collapse of the rich and refined Mycenaean palace civilization (Section 551), life did go on, and practical products for daily living were still produced by the survivors. Yet these products were inferior technically and aesthetically to their Myceanean counterparts, and are called by scholars Submycenaean. In the eleventh century, pottery began to be produced at Athens using more advanced technology. Some improvement in design is evident, as well, as vases' shapes are accentuated and complemented by simple bands of paint, or with concentric semicircles. Occasionally, small figures of horses appear on these pots, but the prevalence of a geometric pattern is the reason that the style is called Protogeometric (1050 BCE initial date). The style evolved over time, phasing out the circular motifs for the rectilinear meander pattern that is still commonly identified with Greek decorative art. Vases became more fully covered with geometric designs, with animals being worked into the decorative bands of paint. Scholars distinguish this stage of design with a different label: Geometric, divided into subclasses Early (900 BCE), Middle (850 BCE), and Late (760 BCE), each with its own variations of the Geometric style.

Figural representation, which had disappeared during the Dark Age, increased in popularity and complexity in the second half of the ninth century; from the mid-eighth century—about the date assigned to Homer by scholars— jewelry with figure scenes engraved or in relief begin to appear in the archeological record, along with bronze figurines of men, animals and birds. Pottery was painted with multiple figure designs, showing funerary scenes and narrative scenes from mythology or epic. Chariot scenes and battle scenes were especially common. All figures on geometric pottery were painted so as to emphasize the geometrical forms underlying the bodily structure and to complement the surrounding geometric design. Geometric art has been likened to epic style: geometric design relies on stock motifs and ornamental formulas, and epic poems are constructed from stock formulas and traditional scenes. As we have noted, both art forms belong to the eighth century; perhaps, it is thought, their similarities reflect the aesthetics of their period.

As the eighth century came to a close, the Geometric style gave way to the Orientalizing style (700-625 BCE), named for its debt to contemporary Near Eastern styles. Geometric patterns were increasingly replaced by floral and animal motifs; the human figure was drawn with increasing naturalism and narrative scenes were designed with greater complexity.

666. WRITE IN GREEK

1. Perhaps some god ordered him to drive those excellent flocks this night into the high cave and not leave them where we had seen them near the sea.

2. He did not know, foolish one, what would happen to him when sweet sleep came and seized him in body and limbs. ["came and" = "coming should"]

3. Seeing his wild eyes and the blood on his hands, we thrice inquired of the stranger what was his name and country; but thrice he answered us nothing.

667. WORD STUDY

ANEMIA, ANEMIC ('bloodlessness', subnormal amount of red corpuscles or hemoglobin); — HEMO- (combining form meaning 'blood-' as in HEMOCYTE, HEMOPHILIA, HEMORRHAGE, HEMORRHOID);— ONOMATOPOEIA ('name-making', making the name imitate the sound of the thing designated, e.g., *splash, sizzle, murmur*); — SYNONYM ('with-name', a word with the same meaning as another, going with it as name for the same thing, e.g., begin and commence), ANONYMOUS ('nameless', of unknown authorship), METONYMY (a figure of speech in which a thing is 'named after' one of its parts or prominent attributes; e.g., "the ship was lost with all hands," i.e., all members of the crew; or "the crown" as meaning the royal government); — TRI- (prefix meaning 'thrice', 'three', as in TRISYLLABLE, TRICYCLE, TRIMETER, etc.), TRIAD (a group of three), TRILOGY (three literary works forming a unit and dealing with aspects of the same subject), TRIGONOMETRY (the mathematics of the triangle and its laws and measurement).

Lesson 101

668. MEMORIZE

αὖ   [adv.] again; but now

ἐλεέω, —, ἐλέησα   I pity, I have mercy on

προσ-αυδάω   I address

669. TEXT

A Wily Gift

καὶ τότ᾽ ἐγὼ Κύκλωπα προσηύδων ἄγχι παραστάς,   206
κισσύβιον μετὰ χερσὶν ἔχων μέλανος οἴνοιο·

"Κύκλωψ, τῆ, πίε οἶνον, ἐπεὶ φάγες ἀνδρόμεα κρέα,
ὄφρ᾽ εἰδῇς, οἷόν τι ποτὸν τόδε νηῦς ἐκεκεύθει
ἡμετέρη· σοὶ δ᾽ αὖ λοιβὴν φέρον, εἴ μ᾽ ἐλεήσας   210
οἴκαδε πέμψειας· σὺ δὲ μαίνεαι οὐκέτ᾽ ἀνεκτῶς.
σχέτλιε, πῶς κέν τίς σε καὶ ὕστερον ἄλλος ἵκοιτο
ἀνθρώπων πολέων; ἐπεὶ οὐ κατὰ μοῖραν ἔρεξας."

ἀνεκτῶς	[adv.] endurably
κισσύβιον, -ου	[n.] drinking bowl
λοιβή, -ῆς	[f.] libation
μαίνομαι	I rage, I act like a mad man
ποτόν, -οῦ	[n.] drink
τῆ	[impt.] here! come!
ὕστερον	[adv.] later

670. NOTES

208. κρέα : scan as monosyllable.

209. εἰδῇς : pf. subj. of οἶδα (Section 491). ἐκεκεύθει : plpf. of κεύθω (with impf. sense).

210. λοιβὴν : a λοιβή is an offering to a god. εἰ in context = "in the hope that…"

213. πολέων = πολλῶν: = "however many there be, anywhere in the world."

671. COMMENT

206-211. Maron's precious wine was brought along (60-79) as a friendly gift to the unknown inhabitant of the cave, though Odysseus did have a premonition that the wine might be useful against a bully (77-79). Now it becomes part of a deadly plot against the monster. Odysseus ironically flatters Polyphemus into accepting it by saying he brought it as a libation of gratitude (such as is offered to a god), if only he had treated them hospitably.

211-213. Odysseus sees Polyphemus as insane because he acts against his own self-interest: his inhospitality cuts him off from profitable interactions with men.

672. HERODOTUS, HISTORIAN WITH A SENSE OF HUMOR

The *History* of Herodotus is one of the world's best-loved books. Its delightful simplicity and directness of style, the genial humanism which pervades its thought, the buoyant eagerness and enthusiasm and sense of wonder with which events are told, together with the interesting nature of its varied contents and the author's wisdom and good-natured sense of humor combine to make Herodotus' book a most enjoyable sort of history. He is a master storyteller and has a sure eye for curious details and items of special human interest.

Herodotus, "The Father of History," lived about 480-425 BCE. Born at Halicarnassus, a prominent Greek city in Asia Minor, he traveled widely as a young man all over the Mediterranean world. Impressed by the recent defeat of the mighty, far-flung, monarchical Persian Empire by an alliance of Greek city-states through sheer bravery and love of freedom, he decided to tell the whole story as an inspiration for all time. In charmingly simple and graceful prose (very close to Homeric forms, and full of Homer's spirit), he wrote down a detailed account of the civilizations, customs, and interesting sights of Egypt, Lydia, Persia, Scythia, Babylon, Libya, Thrace and the story of their conquest and fusion into one vast Empire by the Persian kings. He then tells how all the resources of this powerful empire were twice massed against Greece and twice hurled back by the heroic valor and brilliant strategy of the small Greek forces in the famous battles of Marathon, Thermopylae, Salamis, and Plataea. It is a story known over the world.

Into this broad epic narrative, Herodotus has woven many colorful episodes, anecdotes, personal reflections, and entertaining stories, drawn from various informants and documents as well as local oral traditions. It is the earliest historical prose narrative we possess. The long narrative is given variety, interest, and a delightfully human tone by interspersed witty remarks, 'whoppers', fish-stories, and amusing descriptions.

673. WRITE IN GREEK

1. I stood near and with cunning addressed him as a god, bearing in my hands a splendid gift of the heavenly wine which that excellent man gave me at Apollo's temple.

2. This seemed to me the best plan: to conceal our ship beside the river and to approach the cave in the mountain while it was still dark night.

3. He was brave of (acc.) soul and mighty of strength, but kindly and friendly towards (those) doing worthy things.

674. WORD STUDY

ALMS (by mispronunciation of Old English *aelmesse*, derived from ἐλεημοσύνη 'pity-gift', alms), KYRIE ELEISON ('Lord, have mercy!', a prayer in the Mass, taken over from the Greek liturgy of the Eastern Church); — HYSTERON PROTERON (a figure of speech which puts 'the later thing first', inverting the logical order to emphasize the more important part of the thought, e.g., Vergil's 'Let us die and plunge into the midst of the fight!').

Lesson 102

675. REVIEW OF LESSONS 97-101

In these lessons, you have memorized seventeen more vocabulary words, have read forty-six lines of Homer, and have studied the use of the accusative of specification. Review all this carefully; then try this sample examination:

I. Vocabulary (20%)

    1.   they paid =

    2.   standing by (aor. masc. sg. dat.) =

    3.   ἀνώγεα =

    4.   mast: dat. pl. =

    5.   ἄψ =

II. Text (65%)

    1.   In line 211, explain πέμψειας.

    2.   In line 206, identify προσ-ηύδων.

    3.   Translate πίε οἶνον.

    4.   By the use of what simile does Homer show how easily the Cyclops handled the door-stone?

    5.   In line 185, explain εἰσ-οράασθαι.

    6.   Translate ἤλασε πίονα μῆλα.

    7.   How large was Polyphemus's new staff?

    8.   In line 185, explain μῆκος.

    9.   How many men were to thrust the pole into Polyphemus's eye? How were they chosen?

    10.   In line 175, identify and explain ἐπι-θείη.

    11.   Translate τὸν γλυκὺς ὕπνος ἵκανε.

    12.   What was unusual about Polyphemus's actions when he returned to the cave?

III. Syntax (15%) Translate the words in italics and identify the construction they exemplify:

    1.   The giant was a marvel *to look at*.

    2.   I was wondering if somehow *I might punish* him.

    3.   This savage monster was brutal *of voice* and terrifying *in strength*.

Lesson 103

676. MEMORIZE

αἰνῶς	[adv.] awfully, greatly
ἄρουρα, -ης	[f.] soil, earth
αὖτις	[adv.] back, again
τεός, -ή, -όν	your [sg.]

677. TEXT

Tricked!

ὣς ἐφάμην, ὁ δὲ δέκτο καὶ ἔκπιεν· ἥσατο δ᾽ αἰνῶς
ἡδὺ ποτὸν πίνων καί μ᾽ ᾔτεε δεύτερον αὖτις·   215

   "δός μοι ἔτι πρόφρων καί μοι τεὸν οὔνομα εἰπὲ
αὐτίκα νῦν, ἵνα τοι δῶ ξείνιον, ᾧ κε σὺ χαίρῃς.
καὶ γὰρ Κυκλώπεσσι φέρει ζείδωρος ἄρουρα
οἶνον ἐρισταφυλον, καί σφιν Διὸς ὄμβρος ἀέξει·
ἀλλὰ τόδ᾽ ἀμβροσίης καὶ νέκταρός ἐστιν ἀπορρώξ."   220

   ὣς ἔφατ᾽· αὐτάρ οἱ αὖτις ἐγὼ πόρον αἴθοπα οἶνον·
τρὶς μὲν ἔδωκα φέρων, τρὶς δ᾽ ἔκπιεν ἀφραδίῃσιν.

αἶθοψ, -οπος	glowing, sparkling
ἀμβροσίη, -ης	[f.] ambrosia [the food of the gods]
ἀπορρώξ, -ῶγος	[f.] sample, bit
ἀφραδίη, -ης	[f.] folly, recklessness
ἐκ-πίνω, etc.	I drink off
ἐρισταφυλος, -η, -ον	made from rich-clustering grapes [epithet of wine]
ζείδωρος, -ον	grain-giving, fruitful [epithet of the earth]
ποτόν, -οῦ	[n.] drink

678. NOTES

214. δέκτο : alternate 3 sg. impf. ind. of δέχομαι (= δέχετο)

216. δός : See Sections 472 and 473.

217. δῶ : 1 sg. 2 aor. subj. of δίδωμι, contracted form (Section 473).

217. ᾧ κε σὺ χαίρῃς.: relative clause of purpose: "in which you may…"

679. COMMENT

214-215. Polyphemus drinks the wine unmixed, just as he has the milk (158); Greeks would prefer to dilute their wine with water.

214-220. The giant's eagerness for more of Maron's wondrous wine, and his admission of its superiority over all he had before known or thought possible on earth, recalls the first account of the wine's merits, as a drink fit for the gods (lines 69-75).

216-217. In the Homeric world, a stranger's name was not asked at first meeting, but only later (perhaps days later), after proper hospitality had been proffered. However, in one respect Polyphemus is adhering to etiquette, for the giving of a ξείνιον should be preceded by an exchange of names.

221-222. Odysseus leads the Cyclops on to one draft after another of this potent drink (we recall it *should* be diluted twenty to one), with the idea of dulling his senses and slowing up his reactions, to make him an easier prey to the coming attack. The enemy's mighty strength is thus disorganized and confused by his 'puny' foe's keen-witted tactics. The sides are now more fairly matched, and the hope of victory grows brighter.

680. THE BIRTH OF TRAGEDY IN ATHENS

Aristotle in his *Poetics* states that tragedy originated in the choral hymns sung to the god Dionysus. This type of hymn, called the *dithyramb*, included verses for leaders (*exarchontes*), to which other singers would reply, while acting out in symbolic dance, sometimes with masks, the subject matter of the songs. Yet, there is no solid evidence to shed light on the early development of the genre from such origins at Athens until the plays of Aeschylus (525-456). Since Aeschylus dedicates a larger share of his dramas to the choral odes than do his successors, Sophocles and Euripides, it is generally agreed that tragedy before him must have gradually developed from a primarily choral performance into one which alternated choruses with lines spoken by actors. Aeschylus was apparently the first to present two actors, who impersonated the characters involved and engaged in dialogue among themselves and with the chorus. He thereby became the creator of tragedy in the full sense.

A bit later, Sophocles raised the dramatic art to perfection, introducing a third actor, improving the staging technique, and organizing the plot into a complete logical unity of actions springing naturally from the very characters of the persons involved. Euripides, his contemporary, was powerfully dramatic in his intensely vivid presentation of controversial topics. There were numerous other outstanding tragic poets, but these are the great three.

Although tragedy was performed elsewhere in Greece, it is from Athens and the surrounding district, Attica, that we have almost all our evidence about it. At some point in the sixth century, drama, including both tragedy and comedy, began to be performed in the state sponsored City Dionysia, a festival in honor of Dionysus. These yearly spring festivals also featured performances of dithyrambic odes, and sacrifices, libations, and processions. Three tragedians each produced three tragedies, and one of the three poets was awarded first prize by a panel of ten judges chosen for the occasion to represent the people of Athens.

Greek tragedy, which often takes its plots and characters from the Trojan War legend, has exerted obvious influence over later drama, inspiring modern rewritings of the myths popular in antiquity.

681. WRITE IN GREEK

1. Whenever we gave the Cyclops that strong dark wine, he took it eagerly and quickly drank it all.

2. Greatly pleased with my gift, he asked three times if I would give him the sweet wine again and tell him my name and from what place I had come.

3. Nature is always laboring for our sake; the soil, the sun, the rain produce many foods which we may eat, and many other beautiful things exist (πελ-) in which we may rejoice.

Lesson 104

682. MEMORIZE

μειλίχιος, -η, -ον	pleasing, winning
Οὖτις, Οὖτιος	Nobody
παχύς, -εῖα, -ύ	thick, stout
πρόσθε(ν)	[adv.] first, before, in front of

683. TEXT

Wile vs. Deceit

αὐτὰρ ἐπεὶ Κύκλωπα περὶ φρένας ἤλυθεν οἶνος,
καὶ τότε δή μιν ἔπεσσι προσηύδων μειλιχίοισι·

   "Κύκλωψ, εἰρωτᾷς μ᾽ ὄνομα κλυτόν; αὐτὰρ ἐγώ τοι   225
ἐξερέω· σὺ δέ μοι δὸς ξείνιον, ὥς περ ὑπέστης.
Οὖτις ἐμοί γ᾽ ὄνομα· Οὖτιν δέ με κικλήσκουσι
μήτηρ ἠδὲ πατὴρ ἠδ᾽ ἄλλοι πάντες ἑταῖροι."

   ὣς ἐφάμην, ὁ δέ μ᾽ αὐτίκ᾽ ἀμείβετο νηλέϊ θυμῷ·
"Οὖτιν ἐγὼ πύματον ἔδομαι μετὰ οἷσ᾽ ἑτάροισι,   230
τοὺς δ᾽ ἄλλους πρόσθεν· τὸ δέ τοι ξεινήϊον ἔσται."

εἰρωτάω	I ask [+ double acc.]
ἐξ-είρω, ἐξ-ερέω	I speak out, I tell
κικλήσκω	I call (by name)
ξεινήϊον, -ου	= ξείνιον, -ου
πύματος, -η, -ον	last
ὑφ-ίσταμαι, ὑπο-στήσομαι, ὑπό-στην	I promise

684. NOTES

223. περι...ἤλυθεν Κύκλωπα φρένας = "surrounded the Cyclops' senses;"
φρένας is an acc. of specification (Section 644).

226. δὸς : Section 473

230. μετὰ : "among" or "in the number of"

685. COMMENT

223-228. Odysseus makes very clever use of the Cyclops' inebriated state to improve his strategic position. His friendly, almost jovial tone, capitalizing on the giant's cheerful mood, lends persuasiveness to his words. His insertion of a renewed request for the promised gift before proceeding to tell his name comes at the right psychological moment, for the half-stupefied monster will be more ready to agree now, in order to get the desired information. And in giving the accusative also of his pretended name, Odysseus makes it sound more plausible, since it no longer appears to be merely the negative indefinite pronoun (whose accusative would be οὔ τινα) but a real name quite possible in Greek usage.

229-231. The protective deception works perfectly as planned. But here Polyphemus reveals his promise to be only a cynical jest. Though he is obviously violating the rules of hospitality when he eats his guests, yet his sarcasm enables him to designate his behavior as proper.

686. GREEK COMEDY

The word 'comedy' is from the Greek κωμῳδία, or 'κῶμος song.' A κῶμος is a procession of people carousing, singing and merry-making. Such a procession was part of the yearly Athenian festival called the City Dionysia. At some point, the κῶμος apparently took on a dramatic form, though there is inadequate evidence to explain how and when.

Greek comedy reached its artistic peak in Aristophanes (c. 448-380), whose plays combined brilliant stage effects (with choruses dressed up as clouds, birds, frogs, etc.) with clever situation and story, flashing wit, fierce satire of contemporary political or intellectual figures, fantasy, imaginative flights, puns, and ingenious parody. The comic hero in Aristophanes' plays typically feels oppressed by and dissatisfied with his (or her) situation at the start of the play; he concocts a fantastic scheme which aims at establishing, at least for himself, a peaceful and just utopia abundant in food, wine and sex. And the comic hero generally (with *Clouds* as an exception) succeeds: the comedies end on a festive note. But there is much serious and salutary criticism of personal and civic defects, too, and a vigorous intellectual point in his plays. It is comedy of a unique and very interesting sort.

Later comic writers, of whom Menander (342-292) is the most famous, abandoned satire and open criticism of public figures, for quieter themes concerned with the foibles, romances, and escapades of common people. There is much in common here with modern comedy, which has been deeply influenced by Greek technique and its Roman counterpart.

687. WRITE IN GREEK

1. Would you (sg.) have given your true name to the monstrous Cyclops, knowing his pitiless heart and what he did before to every mortal whom he could seize?

2. The stranger was stout and strong of body and winning in speech (pl.), but none of us knew if he were loyal or why he had come.

3. With winning words I kept requesting the pitiless stranger to pity us, but ruthless of heart he replied nothing.

688. WORD STUDY

PACHYDERM (δέρμα skin; a 'thick-skinned' animal, e.g., an elephant or hippopotamus), PACHYDERMOUS.

Lesson 105

688. MEMORIZE

ἅπτω, ἅψομαι, ἅψα	I fasten; [in mid.] I lay hold of; I catch fire
δαίμων, δαίμονος	[m., f.] a divinity, a superhuman power
ἦ	thus he spoke [3 sg. impf. of ἠμί]
ἐκ-σεύω, —, ἐκ-σσύμην	[non-thematic 2 aor.] I rush out of, I pour out of [intr.]
τάχα	[adv.] quickly, soon

689. TEXT

Final Preparations

ἦ, καὶ ἀνακλινθεὶς πέσεν ὕπτιος, αὐτὰρ ἔπειτα
κεῖτ' ἀποδοχμώσας παχὺν αὐχένα, κὰδ δέ μιν ὕπνος
ᾕρει πανδαμάτωρ· φάρυγος δ' ἐξέσσυτο οἶνος
ψωμοί τ' ἀνδρόμεοι· ὁ δ' ἐρεύγετο οἰνοβαρείων.   235
καὶ τότ' ἐγὼ τὸν μοχλὸν ὑπὸ σποδοῦ ἤλασα πολλῆς,
εἶος θερμαίνοιτο· ἔπεσσι δὲ πάντας ἑταίρους
θάρσυνον, μή τίς μοι ὑποδδείσας ἀναδύη.
ἀλλ' ὅτε δὴ τάχ' ὁ μοχλὸς ἐλάϊνος ἐν πυρὶ μέλλεν
ἅψασθαι, χλωρός περ ἐών, διεφαίνετο δ' αἰνῶς,   240
καὶ τότ' ἐγὼν ἄσσον φέρον ἐκ πυρός, ἀμφὶ δ' ἑταῖροι
ἵσταντ'· αὐτὰρ θάρσος ἐνέπνευσεν μέγα δαίμων.

ἀνα-δύω, —, ἀνά-δυν	I draw back, I flinch
ἀνα-κλίνω aor. pass. ἀνα-κλίνθην	I lean back
ἀπο-δοχμόω, —, ἀπο-δόχμωσα	I turn (something) aside, I cause (something) to droop
αὐχήν, -ένος	[m.] neck
δια-φαίνομαι	I appear through, I glow
ἐμ-πνέω, —, ἔμ-πνευσα	I breathe into
ἐρεύγομαι	I belch out, I disgorge, I vomit
θάρσος, -εος	[n.] courage, boldness
θαρσύνω, —, θάρσυνα	I encourage
θερμαίνω	I heat
οἰνοβαρείω	I am heavy with wine, I am drunk
παν-δαμάτωρ, -ορος	all-subduing [epithet of sleep]
σποδός, -οῦ	[f.] embers, hot ashes
ὑπο-δείδω, etc.	I grow fearful
ὕπτιος, -η, -ον	on the back, face up
φάρυξ, -υγος	[f.] throat
ψωμός, -οῦ	[m.] particle, scrap

690. NOTES

233. κὰδ = κατὰ (a common shortened form before δ).

236. τὸν μοχλὸν : τὸν here is demonstrative ("that [already mentioned] stake"); ὑπὸ : here refers not, as is usual with gen. to motion "from under", but "to a point under" the embers.

237. εἷος = ἧος

238. ὑποδδείσας = ὑποδείσας: the second δ stands for an original digamma (ὑποδϝείσας); ἀναδύη : opt. (see Section 306); μοι : ethical dat., conveying that their flinching would be to Odysseus' disadvantage (Section 18).

691. COMMENT

232-235. The poet gives a graphic description of Polyphemus' drunken stupor.

236-240. Odysseus has previously tempered the stake in the fire (189), but its tip is still green. Here he again heats it, inserting it under the embers until it glows and is on the verge of catching fire.

236-242. As he prepares the weapon of attack, Odysseus exhorts his companions to be brave; in addition, they are inspired with courage by some divine power. Both of these are elements in battle scenes in the *Iliad*, suggesting that the poet, or Odysseus himself, is evoking such scenes of heroic valor as he describes the assault on Polyphemus.

692. GREEK PHILOSOPHY

Ancient Greece gave birth to the discipline of philosophy as it has been practiced in the west. In the sixth and fifth centuries, thinkers now called pre-Socratics speculated about fundamental principles and substances that might explain the world as people experienced it. Their focus was often on the nature and origins of the material world, but they also attempted to explain the development of society.

The sophists (fifth century) are best remembered as the pioneers of the systematic study of persuasive argument. But they taught and lectured on a variety of topics, including political philosophy, mathematics, geography, and anthropology, as they traveled from city to city.

Plato (429-347 BCE) of Athens wrote dialogues remarkable for their style and dramatic vividness. In most of these, Socrates (469-399 BCE) is a participant, exposing the ignorance of his over-confident interlocutors. Socrates usually guides the conversation toward a definition of some moral excellence, such as justice or courage. Implicit in Plato's emphasis on definition is the existence of an ideal form of the object defined: an example of a courageous or just act does not suffice as a definition of courage. Plato in his middle and late dialogues brings out explicitly that knowledge is aimed not at particular instances but at abstract Forms, which are eternal and unchanging.

This Theory of Forms had implications for moral philosophy. Plato's theory argues for the objectivity of moral values such as justice and truth; in this, he goes against the general drift of sophistic thought, which, with its emphasis on argumentation, Plato regarded as morally relativistic.

Plato's Theory of Forms also had political ramifications. States cannot be well governed unless they are ruled in accordance with these objective, unchanging moral absolutes; in such a state, decisions are not reached through open debate or based on the majority preference; rather, those who are entrusted with governing need to be specially selected and trained to know the ideal Forms. Plato thus diverges not only from sophistic thought, according to which "Man is the measure of all things" (Protagoras), but from the principles of democracy, the political system of Plato's own Athens.

Plato's influence on his pupil Aristotle (384-322 BCE) is clear throughout Aristotle's wide-ranging writings. Yet Aristotle's interests obviously differed from Plato's. For example, Aristotle conducted groundbreaking biological research; it was unsurpassed in sophistication until the Renaissance, and was still admired by Charles Darwin in the nineteenth century. His contributions to fields within what we would now call philosophy included works in logic, ethics, metaphysics, and political philosophy. Although Aristotle wrote on so many subjects, his thinking was integrated and systematic, so that it is possible to venture a generalization about the direction of his arguments. Aristotle tends to claim a middle ground between Plato's absolutism and sophistic relativism. In ethics, for example, Aristotle both recognizes the reality of extenuating circumstances in reaching a moral decision, and yet holds that for any set of circumstances there is an objectively determinable right choice that will correspond to an absolute value. In political philosophy, he is critical of the authoritarian state proposed by Plato, yet rejects democracy as well. Aristotle believes that the state should ideally promote the happiness and welfare of its citizens, and that cooperative activity is necessary for the fullest extent of human happiness. Participation in government is the fundamental cooperative activity. However, since, in Aristotle's view, there are people without the capacity to contribute to political life (women, slaves, and manual laborers), not all people should be given citizenship.

Philosophy in the Hellenistic period (323-31 BCE) acquired a more practical orientation. The chief aim of the study of philosophy was happiness, often defined in negative terms as freedom from fear, pain, or anxiety. Even discussions in the fields of epistemology or logic were made to tie in to moral philosophy. Whereas Alexandria in Egypt developed into the cultural center of the Greek world, Athens remained the center for philosophical study. There, several distinct schools of philosophy formed and competed to attract students: the Stoics, Epicureans, Skeptics and Peripatetics (Aristotelians).

693. WRITE IN GREEK

1. We quickly seized the stout stake and put it in the fire until, about to catch fire, it should be able to destroy his big eye.

2. Some divinity surely supplied spirit to my companions, lest they fear his mighty strength and leave me alone to fight with so great a man.

3. Shall we then love and reverence our neighbor if he is wise, but not if he is foolish; if he is of this country, but not if he is of another; if he is white of body, but not if he is black? That would not be just.

694. WORD STUDY

DEMON (an evil superhuman power, a devil), PANDEMONIUM (disorderly uproar as though due to a 'gathering of all the demons'); — DIAPHANOUS ('showing through,' transparent).

Lesson **106**

695. MEMORIZE

ἀϋτμή, -ῆς	[f.] breath; vapor; blast
βλέφαρον, -ου	[n.] eyelid
δόρυ, δούρατος or δουρός	[n.] beam, plank; spear
ὀφρύς, ὀφρύος	[f.] eyebrow

696. TEXT

Assault!

οἱ μὲν μοχλὸν ἑλόντες ἐλάϊνον, ὀξὺν ἐπ' ἄκρῳ,
ὀφθαλμῷ ἐνέρεισαν· ἐγὼ δ' ἐφύπερθεν ἐρεισθεὶς
δίνεον, ὡς ὅτε τις τρυπᾷ δόρυ νήϊον ἀνὴρ   245
τρυπάνῳ, οἱ δέ τ' ἔνερθεν ὑποσσείουσιν ἱμάντι
ἁψάμενοι ἑκάτερθε, τὸ δὲ τρέχει ἐμμενὲς αἰεί·
ὣς τοῦ ἐν ὀφθαλμῷ πυριήκεα μοχλὸν ἑλόντες
δινέομεν, τὸν δ' αἷμα περίρρεε θερμὸν ἐόντα.
πάντα δέ οἱ βλέφαρ' ἀμφὶ καὶ ὀφρύας εὗσεν ἀϋτμὴ   250
γλήνης καιομένης· σφαραγεῦντο δέ οἱ πυρὶ ῥίζαι.

γλήνη, -ης	[f.] eyeball
δινέω	I twirl, I twist about
ἑκάτερθε	[adv.] on either side
ἐμμενές	[adv.] continuously
ἐν-ερείδω, —, ἐν-έρεισα	I press into, I thrust into
ἔνερθεν	[adv.] beneath, below
ἐρείδω, aor. pass. [with act. sense] ἐρείσθην	I press, I lean upon
εὕω, εὕσω, εὗσα	I singe
ἐφύπερθε(ν)	[adv.] from above
θερμός, -ή, -όν	warm, hot
ἱμάς, -άντος	[m.] leather strap, thong
νήϊος, -η, -ον	of, or for, a ship
περι-ρρέω	I flow about
πυρι-ήκης, -ες	fire-sharpened
ῥίζα, -ης	[f.] root
σφαραγέομαι	I crackle, I burst open
τρέχω, —, δράμον	I run
τρύπανον, -ου	[n.] drill
τρυπάω	I drill
ὑπο-σσείω	I make spin

697. NOTES

245. τρυπᾷ : 3rd sg. subj., contraction of τρυπάῃ.

249. τὸν...θερμὸν ἐόντα refers to the μοχλός. ἐόντα: see Section 190.

251. ῥίζαι : supply an understood γλήνης ("the roots of the eyeball").

698. COMMENT

243-249. Odysseus hands the glowing stake to his chosen helpers, then stands behind and above them. As soon as they drive the point into the eye of the Cyclops, who is supine, Odysseus throws himself on the upper end and with his hands twists it around, now one way now another. A simile compares the process to a ship-builder's use of a drill, though in that case it is the helpers who twirl the drill by pulling alternately from different sides on a thong wrapped around the drill-shaft.

249-251. Homer does not shrink from including all the gory details.

699. GREEK MEDICAL WRITING

Greek medicine included diverse and not always harmonious strains. Some of the surviving medical writings stress and demonstrate clinical observation and meticulous recording of symptoms as the only path towards effective medical practice. Others attempt to outline theories that would explain the functioning of the human body and its malfunctioning in disease but which owe little or nothing to clinical observation. Greek doctors were the trailblazers in surgery, anatomy, dentistry, dietetics, the descriptive study of the nervous and digestive systems, the structural analysis of the heart, brain, and other organs. They discovered many fundamental facts of physiology—e.g., that the body also breathes through the pores of the skin, that the physical seat of sensation is not the heart or diaphragm but the brain, that the pulsing of the arteries is caused by action of the heart.

The greatest figure in all this development was Hippocrates, "The Father of Medicine," who established a famous medical school at Cos about 425 BCE. The large corpus of medical essays bearing his name was in fact produced by numerous authors at different times, yet it constitutes the chief evidence for Greek evidence. The essays reflect a variety of viewpoints, and reveal the controversies dividing the medical field. Included are case histories, seen as the foundation for diagnostics and prognosis. Many of the treatises explain health and disease by analogy with physics and natural phenomena, such as balance and the four elements; the theory of the four humors (fluids) would dominate medical theory for many centuries. Some of the writings had a therapeutic focus, giving advice on diet, environment and life-style. Some therapies are drug based; and surgical approaches are also discussed in treatises on fractures, hemorrhoids, and wounds. Five hundred years later, Galen (129-216? CE) collected all ancient medical knowledge into a great twenty-two-volume encyclopedia, one of the most influential of ancient books.

It was the translation and wide distribution of the complete works of Hippocrates and Galen which inspired and guided much of the brilliant work of the founders of modern medicine from the fifteenth to the nineteenth century. New discoveries, the invention of the microscope and X-ray, recent diagnostic devices, and a staggering amount of collaborative research have advanced medical science far beyond Greek bounds and corrected many ancient errors. But it is on Greek foundations that all this vast structure still stands.

700. WRITE IN GREEK

1.   He said that the vapor of the burning eye quickly destroyed also all his eyelid and eyebrow.

2.   Blood seemed to hide the end (ἄκρον) of the olive-wood beam, and it flowed upon the ground, as when dark wine pours out of a bag.

3.   The cruel Cyclops himself then learned what all the best and wisest men always knew: one who does wrong must suffer. [Use χρὴ , with subject— "one who does wrong" —expressed by aor. ptc. alone.]

701. WORD STUDY

BLEPHARITIS (inflammation of the eyelids), BLEPHAROSPASM (spasmodic winking); — RHIZO- (a combining form meaning 'root'); — THERM (a unit of heat), THERMAL (having to do with heat), THERMOMETER, THERMOSTAT (instruments for measuring and regulating heat), THERMOS BOTTLE (trade name for a vacuum container to retain or exclude heat for liquids and foods).

Lesson 107

702. MEMORIZE

ἰάχω	[pres. syst. only] I shout; I hiss; I resound
ὧδε	[adv.] thus, so
οἰμώζω, οἰμώξομαι, οἴμωξα	I cry out in pain

703. TEXT

Gigantic Agony

ὡς δ' ὅτ' ἀνὴρ χαλκεὺς πέλεκυν μέγαν ἠὲ σκέπαρνον
εἰν ὕδατι ψυχρῷ βάπτῃ μεγάλα ἰάχοντα
φαρμάσσων· τὸ γὰρ αὖτε σιδήρου γε κράτος ἐστίν·
ὡς τοῦ σίζ' ὀφθαλμὸς ἐλαϊνέῳ περὶ μοχλῷ.   255
σμερδαλέον δὲ μέγ' ᾤμωξεν, περὶ δ' ἴαχε πέτρη,
ἡμεῖς δὲ δείσαντες ἀπεσσύμεθ'. αὐτὰρ ὁ μοχλὸν
ἐξέρυσ' ὀφθαλμοῖο πεφυρμένον αἵματι πολλῷ.

βάπτω	I dip, I plunge into (water)
ἐξ-ερύω, —, ἐξ-έρυσα	I pull out of
πέλεκυς, -εος	[m. acc. sg. -υν] axe-head
σίδηρος, -ου	[m.] iron
σίζω	I sizzle
σκέπαρνον, -ου	[n.] adze
σμερδαλέος, -η, -ον	dreadful, terrifying
φαρμάσσω	I temper, I harden
φύρω, —, φύρσα, —, πέφυρμαι	I mix with
χαλκεύς, -ῆος	[m.] smith, metal-worker
ψυχρός, -ή, -όν	cold

704. COMMENT

251-254. Again a simile likens these fantastic events to familiar things of daily life. Here it is the sharp hissing sound of hot metal suddenly plunged into water which helps Homer's audience hear more distinctly the hiss of the hot μοχλός as it sinks into Polyphemus' eye. Like the preceding simile of the shipbuilder using his drill, this reference to the smith at work constitutes a little picture in itself. This technology for tempering iron was introduced into Greece in the ninth century, which is later than the heroic era in which Odysseus' narrative is set; this is the sort of evidence that helps scholars to date the composition of the poem.

255-257. What an ear-shattering, thunderous scream the giant must have uttered in his pain! No wonder the Greeks fled for safety from the freed stake and his flailing hands.

705. WRITE IN GREEK

1. Whenever he cried out in pain, the whole cave resounded round about and we greatly feared destruction.

2. Seizing my spear, I hurled it with all my strength, but it missed the man, for some divinity was protecting him.

3. As bread and wine are food for the body, and we have need of them in order to live; so truth and justice are food of the soul, and we have need of them too in order to live a worthy life as human beings.

Lesson 108

In the last five lessons, you have memorized twenty-one new vocabulary words and read forty-five lines of Homer. Test your review with this sample examination.

I.   Vocabulary (35%)

    1.   name: dat. pl. =

    2.   ἅψαι =

    3.   before =

    4.   vapor: gen. pl. =

    5.   τάχα =

    6.   thick: n. pl. acc. =

    7.   ὀφρύων =

II. Text (65%)

    1.   Translate ἥσατο δ᾽ αἰνῶς

    2.   In 1. 215, identify ἤτεε.

    3.   In 1. 219, explain σφιν .

    4.   In 1. 222, explain ἀφραδίῃσιν.

    5.   In 1. 224, identify προσ-ηύδων.

    6.   Translate δός μοι ξείνιον .

    7.   In 1. 234, identify ᾕρει.

    8.   In 1. 238, explain ἀνα-δύη.

    9.   Translate μοχλὸς μέλλεν ἅψασθαι.

    10.   In 1. 256, explain σμερδαλέον.

    11.   With what simile does Homer describe the wounding of Cyclops' eye?

    12.   To what does he liken the sound of the burning eyeball?

Lesson 109

708. MEMORIZE

ἄλλοθεν	[adv.] from elsewhere
βοάω, βοήσω, βόησα	I shout, I roar
Πολύφημος, -ου	[m.] Polyphemus, a Cyclops [son of Poseidon]
ῥίπτω, ῥίψω, ῥῖψα	I hurl

709. TEXT

Clamor in the Night

τὸν μὲν ἔπειτ' ἔρριψεν ἀπὸ ἕο χερσὶν ἀλύων,
αὐτὰρ ὁ Κύκλωπας μεγάλ' ἤπυεν, οἵ ῥά μιν ἀμφὶς   260
ᾤκεον ἐν σπήεσσι δι' ἄκριας ἠνεμοέσσας.
οἱ δὲ βοῆς ἀΐοντες ἐφοίτων ἄλλοθεν ἄλλος,
ἱστάμενοι δ' εἴροντο περὶ σπέος, ὅττι ἑ κήδοι·

  "τίπτε τόσον, Πολύφημ', ἀρημένος ὧδ' ἐβόησας
νύκτα δι' ἀμβροσίην καὶ ἀΰπνους ἄμμε τίθησθα;   265
ἦ μή τίς σευ μῆλα βροτῶν ἀέκοντος ἐλαύνει;
ἦ μή τίς σ' αὐτὸν κτείνει δόλῳ ἠὲ βίηφι;"

ἀέκων, -οντος	[m. adj.] unwilling
ἀΐω	I hear the sound of [+ gen.]
ἄκρις, -ιος	[f.] hilltop, height
ἀλύω	I thrash about in pain
ἀμβρόσιος, -η, -ον	fragrant
ἀμφίς	same as ἀμφί
ἀρημένος, -η, -ον	distressed, harmed
ἄϋπνος, -ον	sleepless
βοή, -ῆς	[f.] shouting, cry
ἠνεμόεις, -εσσα, -εν	windy, windswept
ἠπύω	I call upon
κήδω	I trouble, I ail
τίπτε	[interr. adv.] what? why? [= τί ποτε]

710. NOTES

259. τὸν : that is, τὸν μοχλόν

259. χερσὶν should be taken with ἔρριψεν rather than with ἀλύων.

261. σπήεσσι : dat. pl. of σπέος

262. ἄλλοθεν ἄλλος : idiomatic for "from all directions" [lit. "one from one place, another from elsewhere"]

265. τίθησθα : 2 sg. pres. ind. of τίθημι.

266. ἦ μή = "surely no(t)…", Latin *num*.

711. COMMENT

259-261. The Cyclops flails about blindly. The other Cyclopes appear also to have been of an unsociable nature and to have lived for the most part alone, each in some cave in the cliff or hills throughout the island.

260-263. The Cyclopes are bewildered by this blood-chilling scream echoing through the night and run to investigate. Polyphemus ('Far-Famed': it is here that we first learn his name) must be suffering violence, an attack on his life or possessions. Yet who would dare assault so mighty and fierce a monster as he?

712. GREEK SCIENCE AND MATHEMATICS

The Greeks were pioneers in mathematics and the sciences. Their intellectual energy led them to seek out the causes of natural phenomena and the laws governing the external world. Though handicapped by lack of modern equipment, these scientists carried on experiments and complicated research investigations which laid the groundwork of several sciences and established many of the basic facts, principles, laws, and techniques which modern science builds on and incorporates.

Advanced mathematics did not originate with the Greeks, for Mesopotamians worked on problems in algebra and basic geometry. It is not certain whether this knowledge reached the Greek world; the Greeks themselves did not claim to have invented geometry, but to have learned it from the Egyptians. The Greeks, however, made fundamental advances in several branches of mathematics, including trigonometry (for use in astronomy) and conic sections; they developed geometry considerably, and devised the first algebraic notation.

In geography, they carried out daring explorations, early circumnavigated Africa, worked out with only slight error the shape, diameter, and circumference of the earth, and perfected cartography to a high level of accuracy and scientific technique. Geological phenomena were correctly explained as results of stresses, weathering, and the formative action of water, while Xenophanes (b. ?570 BCE) showed that shell-fossils were deposits from a prehistoric flood.

Physics and chemistry got their start from Greek experimentation and theory. Pythagoras (b. ?550 BCE) discovered basic laws of sound and musical harmonics; Aristotle developed this field and studied the nature of light and heat; Democritus (b. ?460 BCE) and Leucippus (5th century BCE) first proposed an atomic theory of the composition of matter, though not understanding the construction and laws of the invisible atoms themselves. Archimedes (287-211 BCE) was the great pioneer in mechanics, discovering the central laws of hydrostatics, building machines of war, and greatly improving the construction of cranes, pulleys, suction-screws for hoisting water, etc. The principles of the steam engine, waterpower, and jet propulsion were first demonstrated by Heron of Alexandria (1st century CE), but not then applied to practical uses.

Theophrastus' (371-287 BCE) book on plants is still an authority in its field. Aristotle's (384-322 BCE) work in biology and zoology was epoch-making in its thoroughness, accuracy, and acute methodology. Galen's (129-216 CE) experiments using vivisection contributed to the fields of anatomy and physiology; his work on the spinal chord made connections between vital functions and particular nerves. The extensive, interesting advances in astronomy and medicine made by Greek scientists are described in other lessons.

It is significant that there is no Greek equivalent for "scientist", though there were specific words for mathematicians, botanists, meteorologists, physiologists, and other specialists in the sciences. Science itself was called ἐπιστήμη by Aristotle. But the term used of the scientists described above was φιλόσοφος, a "lover of knowledge" or "learned man." φιλόσοφος also was applied to men with no interest in what we call science, such as the philosopher Socrates and the rhetorician and educator Isocrates. Commonly, however, the interests of a φιλόσοφος spanned the modern chasm separating science and the humanities, and science and the social sciences. Democritus, for example, besides outlining an atomic theory, also wrote on ethics, music, and anthropology.

713. WRITE IN GREEK

1. We saw monstrous Polyphemus, crying out in pain, take the cruel stake out of his eye and hurl it with mighty hand far away into the cave.

2. For many foolish men money is (their) soul and life.

3. "From what place have you come, strangers?" he shouted, "from Troy, or the land of the Achaeans, or elsewhere?"

Lesson **110**

714. MEMORIZE

ἀμύμων, ἀμύμονος	[adj.] blameless, excellent
βιάζω	I constrain, I use violence against
στείχω, —, στίχον	I go, I proceed

715. TEXT

The Ruse Succeeds

τοὺς δ᾽ αὖτ᾽ ἐξ ἄντρου προσέφη κρατερὸς Πολύφημος·
"ὦ φίλοι, Οὖτίς με κτείνει δόλῳ οὐδὲ βίηφιν."
   οἱ δ᾽ ἀπαμειβόμενοι ἔπεα πτερόεντ᾽ ἀγόρευον·   270
"εἰ μὲν δὴ μή τίς σε βιάζεται οἶον ἐόντα,
νοῦσόν γ᾽ οὔ πως ἔστι Διὸς μεγάλου ἀλέασθαι,
ἀλλὰ σύ γ᾽ εὔχεο πατρὶ Ποσειδάωνι ἄνακτι."
   ὣς ἄρ᾽ ἔφαν ἀπιόντες, ἐμὸν δ᾽ ἐγέλασσε φίλον κῆρ,
ὣς ὄνομ᾽ ἐξαπάτησεν ἐμὸν καὶ μῆτις ἀμύμων.   275

ἀγορεύω	I speak
ἀπ-αμείβομαι	I answer, I reply
ἀπ-ιών, -οῦσα, -όν	going away [ptc. from ἄπ-ειμι]
γελάω, γελάσομαι, γέλασσα	I laugh, I rejoice
ἐξ-απατάω, ἐξ-απατήσω, ἐξ-απάτησα	I trick, I beguile
μῆτις, -ιος	[f.] scheme, cunning

716. NOTES

272. ἔστι = it is possible (+ inf.). In this meaning, the pitch-mark is on the first syllable. Be alert to this clue.

274. ἔφαν : see Section 595.

717. COMMENT

268-275. A cleverly designed passage, about which the whole Cyclops episode turns. Polyphemus' words, shouted through the opening above the door-stone and across the great sheep fold outside, have been made ingeniously ambiguous. The distraught giant means to convey that this puny human Nobody is murdering him by craft; there is no force about it. He, Polyphemus, remains far mightier in strength; but the wily stranger has caught him off guard by a trick.

The Cyclopes, thinking Polyphemus means to reject all three implications of their question (266-7), and misunderstanding Οὖτις as a mere indefinite pronoun οὔ τις (as is shown by their μή τις in 271, an intended equivalent with altered negative to suit the changed sentence structure), consequently take οὐδὲ in the wrong sense too— as a simple "nor" following an introductory οὐ, instead of as "not" *contrasting* βίηφιν with δόλῳ. They think, then, that Polyphemus must have gone mad, and cried out because of some wild, insane imagining. They hurry off to their beds without more ado, not caring to mingle with a monster unsociable enough before and now violently crazy besides. There is, moreover, nothing they can do; madness is a disease from Zeus, and only a god can cure it. Let Poseidon himself come to his son's aid.

274-275. Odysseus' carefully thought-out plan has worked perfectly in all details and he is happy. The savage is punished, made unable to seize any more of the group for food, yet left alive and strong enough to lift away the great stone from the door, as he must decide to do sooner or later. In the μῆτις of line 275 is a further bit of wordplay, as we cannot miss its relation to Οὖτις and the thrice-repeated μή τις in the Cyclopes' words.

718. GREEK ASTRONOMY

In the clear, bright skies of Greece in ancient times the serene beauty of the stars, and their mystery, is more than usually impressive. Greek imagination was quick to discover in the sparkling panorama of the heavens meaning, life and pattern. Greek shepherds sitting through the night on the hills discovered in the maze of stars the seeming outlines of figures of men, animals, and things which form the constellations: the Great Bear, Andromeda, the Pleiades, and all the others. It was Greeks who wove around these figures in the sky those famous myths and stories whose poetic charm has lived on down the ages in literature and in the star-lore of the common people.

Similarly, the scientific and philosophical study of celestial phenomena made by Greek thinkers lies at the roots of modern astronomy. For strict scientific method and creative pioneering in reasoning out the nature and laws of the heavenly bodies, modern astronomers pay their great Greek predecessors the highest credit and respect. Lacking telescopes and other technical instruments, Greek astronomers still managed by sheer mathematics and accurate observation to discover most of the things knowable even now without special equipment.

As early as 585 BCE., Thales correctly predicted eclipses of the sun by working out the laws for such events on the basis of Babylonian records of earlier eclipses' dates. A century later, Anaxagoras gave the true scientific explanation of eclipses in terms of the position of the sun, moon, and earth in relation to each other. He also knew that it was rotary motion that separated the primeval mass of flaming matter into present star-systems. Aristotle and later observers proved the earth was a sphere by geometrical reasoning from the curved edge of the earth's shadow in a lunar eclipse and the shift in position of the fixed stars if seen from different latitudes.

Plato's pupil Heraclides (4th century BCE) correctly argued that the earth revolves on its axis and the planets move around the sun. Aristarchus of Samos (3rd century BCE) developed this concept into a complete heliocentric theory almost the same as that of Copernicus, who in fact got the idea and the start in his own investigations from reading about this theory in an old book. Plato's associate Eudoxus (390-340 BCE) tried to explain the baffling motions of the sun, moon, planets, and stars by a complicated geometrical pattern of concentric spherical orbits. Aristotle considered these spheres not as paths of motion but as fifty-six material globes turning around and through one another and carrying with them the heavenly bodies imbedded in their surface. (This theory was not displaced until Galileo and Kepler in the sixteenth century. It is the basis of many familiar ideas in literature, such as the "music of the spheres.")

About 225 BCE, Eratosthenes measured the earth's circumference with remarkably little margin of error. In the next century, Hipparchus, one of history's greatest scientific geniuses, immensely advanced astronomical knowledge in many fields. Besides numerous recondite achievements, he measured the distance of the sun and moon, computed the length of the solar year within five minutes of the modern estimate, determined the actual time-lapse of the moon's revolution around the earth (only one second off!), discovered the very subtle law of the 'precession of the equinoxes', and drew up a wonderfully accurate catalogue of the position of over a thousand fixed stars in relation to the ecliptic.

The last great ancient astronomer, Ptolemy, gathered up in his famous book the *Almagest* (c. 150 CE) all earlier Greek astronomical learning, adding much of his own. This was the standard textbook of astronomy for the next 1,400 years and has exerted much influence in literature and philosophy. Four centuries before Ptolemy, Aratus had summed up the whole contemporary astronomical theory in a learned didactic poem written in Homeric dialect, which Cicero later translated into Latin verse. Popular interest in astronomy was very widespread in the Greek world.

Even today, when an astronomer refers to a particular star he does so in Greek terms, by naming its constellation (in Latinized form) and that letter of the Greek alphabet by which it is designated and set apart from other stars in the same group. Vega, e.g., is α Lyrae; Pollux is β Geminorum, etc. Greek astronomy forms a permanent part of our own.

719. WRITE IN GREEK

1. A cruel fate would have constrained me to hide for nine days in that deadly cave with the pitiless Cyclops, if Zeus had not pitied me and saved me from utter destruction.

2. Seeing the admirable man, the brother of my dearest companion, proceeding alone down the road, I shouted and urged him to wait until I reached where he was.

3. Peace is the fruit not of force but of justice, and the world will never have it while men hate or wrong one another.

Lesson 111

720. MEMORIZE

ἐγγύθεν   [adv.] from close at hand, near

πετάννυμι, —, πέτασ(σ)α   I spread out

ὑφαίνω, ὑφανέω, ὕφηνα   I weave; I devise

721. TEXT

A Perilous Situation

Κύκλωψ δὲ στενάχων τε καὶ ὠδίνων ὀδύνῃσι,	276
χερσὶ ψηλαφόων, ἀπὸ μὲν λίθον εἷλε θυράων,	
αὐτὸς δ᾽ εἰνὶ θύρῃσι καθέζετο χεῖρε πετάσσας,	
εἴ τινά που μετ᾽ ὄεσσι λάβοι στείχοντα θύραζε·	
οὕτω γάρ πού μ᾽ ἤλπετ᾽ ἐνὶ φρεσὶ νήπιον εἶναι.	280
αὐτὰρ ἐγὼ βούλευον, ὅπως ὄχ᾽ ἄριστα γένοιτο,	
εἴ τιν᾽ ἑταίροισιν θανάτου λύσιν ἠδ᾽ ἐμοὶ αὐτῷ	
εὑροίμην· πάντας δὲ δόλους καὶ μῆτιν ὕφαινον,	
ὥς τε περὶ ψυχῆς· μέγα γὰρ κακὸν ἐγγύθεν ἦεν.	

καθ-έζομαι	I sit down
λύσις, -ιος	[f.] means of escape from, release from
μῆτις, -ιος	[f.] scheme, cunning
ὀδύνη, -ης	[f.] pain, torment
ὄχα	the very [intensifying adv.]
ψηλαφάω	I grope about
ὠδίνω	I am in agony, I writhe with anguish

722. NOTES

277. ψηλαφόων : = ψηλαφάων by *assimilation*; see Section 627, note on line 156.

278. εἰνί : lengthened alternative form for ἐν. Cp. εἰς for ἐς ; χεῖρε: see Section 459.

279. ὄεσσι : see Section 514; θύραζε : recall Section 422 a.

280. οὕτω goes with νήπιον.

284. ὥς τε περὶ ψυχῆς : "as is usual in matters of life and death"

723. COMMENT

276-280. The Cyclops, unable to see where the little men are, hopes to trap them going out the cave's mouth alongside his sheep. Odysseus tries to explain Polyphemus' tactic as the result of his underestimation of Odysseus' intelligence.

281-284. Odysseus, now that the door-stone has been removed, as foreseen, once more revolves in his mind all possible procedures until he is sure which is best. As always, he is guided by prudence and clear thinking, not hasty or reckless impulse. It is no accident that Homer characterized him in the very first line as πολύτροπος, "resourceful, of many turns of thought."

724. GREEK MILITARY TECHNOLOGY AND SCIENCE

In military tactics, Greek imaginative power and originality were much in evidence. New weapons, stratagems, defense measures, and improvements on the old. were constantly being thought up. A famous instance is the phalanx battle formation.

Epaminondas of Thebes, a brilliant general of the fourth century BCE, overcame far larger armies than his own by massing a solid column of spearmen fifty lines deep, with which he was able to break through and encircle the opposing forces. Philip of Macedon (382-336 BCE) took over this tactic and made it more flexible in maneuver. He arranged ten to sixteen lines of men in close formation, their long spears (up to twenty feet or more) resting on the shoulders of the men in front, so that five or six rows of spear points projected beyond the front rank, to form a terrifying and almost impenetrable barrier. Strict discipline and intensive drill enabled the whole mass to move as a unit. Its combined weight could ram it through almost any opposition. Supplies and replacements flowed easily from ranks deeper in, to maintain a solid fighting front.

It was largely by means of the phalanx that Alexander the Great (356-323 BCE) swept from victory to victory until in a few years he had military control of the whole eastern Mediterranean world and beyond into Mesopotamia and India. The principles of phalanx warfare were later embodied and improved on in the Roman legion, before which all other military formations generally fell apart in defeat.

725. WRITE IN GREEK

1. Lying in the dark cave, we saw him from close at hand lift the heavy stone from the door (pl.) and sit down where he hoped to seize us going past.
2. Those who die for the sake of (their) country will have great glory among mortals as most brave.
3. Whenever Polyphemus slept, he spread out his gigantic limbs among the sleeping flocks from one end of the cave to the other.

726. WORD STUDY

ANODYNE ('non-pain', a soothing medicine to relieve pain).

Lesson 112

727. MEMORIZE

ἀκέων, -ουσα   [adj., m. and f.] in silence, silent(ly)

ὕστατος, -η, -ον   last

728. TEXT

The Plan for Escape

ἥδε δέ μοι κατὰ θυμὸν ἀρίστη φαίνετο βουλή·	285
ἄρσενες ὄιιες ἦσαν ἐΰτρεφέες δασύμαλλοι,	
καλοί τε μεγάλοι τε, ἰοδνεφὲς εἶρος ἔχοντες·	
τοὺς ἀκέων συνέεργον ἐϋστρεφέεσσι λύγοισι,	
τῆσ᾽ ἔπι Κύκλωψ εὗδε πέλωρ, ἀθεμίστια εἰδώς,	
σύντρεις αἰνύμενος· ὁ μὲν ἐν μέσῳ ἄνδρα φέρεσκε,	290
τὼ δ᾽ ἑτέρω ἑκάτερθεν ἴτην σώοντες ἑταίρους.	

ἀθεμίστιος, -η, -ον	lawless
δασύμαλλος, -η, -ον	with thick fleece
εἶρος, -εος	[n.] wool
ἑκάτερθε(ν)	[adv.] on both sides
ἐΰ-στρεφής, -ές	well-twisted, well-plaited
ἐΰ-τρεφής, -ές	well-fed, fat
ἰοδνεφής, -ές	dark as violet
λύγος, -ου	[f.] willow-twig, withe
πέλωρ, -ωρος	[n.] monster
συν-έργω	I bind together
σύν-τρεις	three-together, three at a time

729. NOTES

285. ὄιιες : = ὄιες nom. pl. of ὄις. The initial οι- reflects metrical *thesis*, the lengthening of the first sylllable of each foot of the hexameter.

289. ἀθεμίστια εἰδώς : i.e., acknowledging no law. On εἰδώς see Section 491 and cp. line 53.

290. σύντρεις αἰνύμενος = "taking them three at a time"

291. τὼ δ᾽ ἑτέρω : nom. dual (Section 459); δέ is correlative to μέν in 290; ἴτην : impf. ind. act. 3 dual of εἶμι, I go. σώοντες : from the verb σώω, a variation of σώζω.

730. COMMENT

285-291. Odysseus, in thinking over various methods of escape, sees that it would be too risky to try to run out through the cave's mouth ahead of or after the flocks, and that if the men attempted to walk or crawl out among the animals they might be discovered by touch, or, more likely, crushed to death in the press of heavy beasts crowding through the door *en masse*. The safest plan, then, is this one of going out under the sheep, protected both from crushing and from discovery by the animals on either side.

286-287. We see now quite clearly how the Cyclops' unusual procedure of bringing in the rams too this night was indeed providential, in answer to the men's prayer for escape (see lines 199-200). The dark purple-black wool of the sheep would be considered especially valuable in ancient markets; it is, therefore, a sign of Polyphemus' wealth.

288-291. Odysseus straps the rams together into groups of three; each trio will carry one man, who will be lashed to the underbelly of the middle ram, though this is not made explicit until line 304, in Section 743. The length and fullness of the wool is crucial, as it will hide the thin withes from detection.

731. WRITE IN GREEK

1.   Though the last released, I arrived first at the ships and myself told what we had seen and how half of my companions had perished in that deadly cave.

2.   I saw my mother go silently to the door, to see if the children were still sleeping.

3.   Taking the olive-wood stake, we made (it) sharp, so that it might be for us like a spear with which we could fight.

732. WORD STUDY

IODINE (a dark violet-colored chemical antiseptic, the brownish tint of the drug store product being due to the addition of other components).

Lesson 113

734. MEMORIZE

γαστήρ, γαστέρος or γαστρός   [f.] belly

νῶτον, -ου   [n.] back

φώς, φωτός   [m.] man

735. TEXT

In Readiness

τρεῖς δὲ ἕκαστον φῶτ' ὄῖες φέρον· αὐτὰρ ἐγώ γε,
ἀρνειὸς γὰρ ἔην μήλων ὄχ' ἄριστος ἁπάντων,
τοῦ κατὰ νῶτα λαβών, λασίην ὑπὸ γαστέρ' ἐλυσθεὶς
κείμην· αὐτὰρ χερσὶν ἀώτου θεσπεσίοιο   295
νωλεμέως στρεφθεὶς ἐχόμην τετληότι θυμῷ.
ὣς τότε μὲν στενάχοντες ἐμείναμεν Ἠῶ δῖαν.

ἄωτος, -ου	[m.] wool
εἰλύω, aor. pass. ἐλύσθην	I curl up
λάσιος, -η, -ον	shaggy, woolly
νωλεμέως	[adv.] steadily, firmly
ὄχα	[adv.] by far
στρέφω, aor. pass. στρέφθην	I turn, I turn (face) upwards
τρεῖς, τρία	three

736. NOTES

293. ἀρνειὸς γὰρ ἔην…: understand this entire line parenthetically ("for there was a ram…")

294. τοῦ : refers to the ἀρνειὸς in the previous line; κατὰ…λαμβάνω· = "grasp."

296. ἐχόμην : middle ("I held myself on"); τετληότι : formed from τετληώς, -υῖα, -ός: pf. part. of τλάω, idiomatic for "steadfast, persevering."

737. COMMENT

292-296. After tying his men into place under the middle sheep of each group, Odysseus has to find some other means of escape himself. Since his friends cannot fasten him on in the same way, he decides to cling by his own hands beneath the largest of the sheep, the giant ram who is evidently king of the flock. He curls up (ἐλυσθεὶς) under its woolly belly. The wool is long enough to give a good hold and to cover over Odysseus' hands, concealing them from detection.

738. KOINE GREEK AND ITS LITERATURE

Alexander the Great's conquest of the Persian Empire in the fourth century BCE spread Greek culture and language throughout the Mediterranean world. His Macedonian Empire extended as far as the borders of India; its official language was based on the Attic dialect and is known now as Hellenistic Koine or simply Koine. The most significant and well known of texts written in Koine are the Greek translation of the Hebrew Torah (Pentateuch) called the Septuagint, and the New Testament.

One of the principal cities of the Hellenistic Greek world was Alexandria in Egypt, which with its Museum and Library was, in the third century BCE, developing into a cultural center. The Greek ruler of Egypt, Ptolemy II Philadelphus, requested for the Library a Greek translation of the Torah. Seventy-two learned Jewish scholars were sent from Jerusalem to put together what is now called the Septuagint ("seventy" in Latin). Over the next century or so, the rest of the Hebrew Bible and various Apocryphal books were also put into Greek. Although it was commissioned for inclusion in the Library, the Septuagint served the needs of Jews who had migrated to Egypt and other areas of the Greek world and were now speakers of Greek. Alexandria was one city with a large population of Hellenized Jews, and here as in other cities Jews now read and heard their sacred text in Greek. Jewish literature in Greek was also produced in other cities; several genres were represented, including history, epic, philosophy, and the novel, a popular literary form in the Hellenistic period.

Early Christians, who were predominantly Greek speaking, also used the Septuagint as their Bible; it was, therefore, the Bible for the writers of the New Testament. To this day, the Septuagint is the version of the Old Testament used in the Greek Orthodox Church.

The Holy Scripture of the early Christians was the Septuagint, which they interpreted allegorically. In addition, writings in Greek by Christians were being produced in profusion. The authority and authenticity of these writings were not universally accepted, however; theological controversies emerged early on. Some effort was made to establish a canonical set of texts that related the authentic and original story of Jesus, but none was supported by a consensus of churches.

It was a Greek theologian named Irenaeus who, after 180 CE, guided the selection of writings that were deemed to have been in use in the churches from the beginning. The four gospels of Matthew, Mark, Luke, and John were combined with the letters of the apostle Paul to constitute the New Testament, a Christian Bible to correspond to the pre-Christian Old Testament.

Other Christian writings in Koine include the works of the apologists, who wrote in defense of their faith against pagan attacks. Justin Martyr, who lived from 100-165 CE, was one such Christian apologist. He was certainly much influenced by classical Greek philosophy, including Plato; he argued that pagan philosophers presaged Christian truth. Clement of Alexandria (late second century), also well schooled in the classical tradition, continued to develop the link between Christian theology and Platonic philosophy. Origen (184-253), also of Alexandria and later of Judaea, likewise showed the influence of Plato. He was the most influential writer of the early Christian church, laying the foundations of early Christian theology.

739. WRITE IN GREEK

1. The Cyclops, having filled his monstrous belly with the strong wine, fell silently upon his back and slept, not knowing destruction was coming to him that very night.

2. A man's dearest possession, the wise man said, is not life but his immortal soul; for life passes, but the soul shall never die, neither can it be destroyed.

3. Whenever bright dawn, the early-born, appears over the lofty mountains, all the flocks rush out of the cave seeking food and water among the trees by the river.

740. WORD STUDY

GASTRIC (pertaining to the stomach, e.g., 'gastric juices' in digestion); — STROPHE (a group of lines to be sung by a dramatic chorus while 'turning' in dance from center of stage to one side; hence, in poetry, a group of lines, stanza).

Lesson 114

741. REVIEW OF LESSONS 109-113

In these lessons, you have memorized fifteen new vocabulary words and have read thirty-nine lines of the *Odyssey*. Make sure that you have really mastered the new vocabulary and are able to account for every form in the text of Homer. Then try this sample test:

I.   Vocabulary (45%)

    1.   στίχοιεν =

    2.   we shall devise =

    3.   ἀκεούσῃσι =

    4.   belly: acc. pl. =

    5.   φῶτας =

    6.   back: gen. pl. =

    7.   Polyphemus: dat. sg. =

    8.   πετάσσαι =

    9.   ἄλλοθεν =

    10. let us shout (aor.) =

    11. ἐβίαζε =

    12. to be about to hurl =

    13. ὧδε =

    14. from close at hand =

    15. ἀμύμοσι =

II.   Text (55%)

    1.   Translate ἐφοίτων, ἄλλοθεν ἄλλος.

    2.   In line 263, explain κήδοι.

    3.   In line 267, identify βίηφι.

    4.   Compare the sentiments expessed in lines 271-273 with the boasts of Polyphemus to Odysseus at their first meeting (lines 134-139). How do you explain the discrepancy?

    5.   In line 278, identify χεῖρε.

    6.   Translate οὕτω μ᾽ ἤλπετο νήπιον εἶναι

    7.   Scan line 278.

    8.   In line 281, explain γένοιτο.

    9.   In line 290, identify φέρεσκε.

    10. Why didn't the other Cyclopes assist Polyphemus?

    11. Describe the scheme by which Odysseus hoped to save his men and himself.

Lesson 115

742. MEMORIZE

θῆλυς, θήλεια, θῆλυ or θῆλυς, θῆλυ	female
πυκ(ι)νός, -ή, -όν	thick; close; shrewd
τείρω	[pres. syst. only] I wear out; I distress

743. TEXT

A Tense Moment

ἦμος δ' ἠριγένεια φάνη ῥοδοδάκτυλος Ἠώς,
καὶ τότ' ἔπειτα νομόνδ' ἐξέσσυτο ἄρσενα μῆλα,
θήλειαι δὲ μέμηκον ἀνήμελκτοι περὶ σηκούς·   300
οὔθατα γὰρ σφαραγεῦντο. ἄναξ δ' ὀδύνῃσι κακῇσι
τειρόμενος πάντων ὀΐων ἐπεμαίετο νῶτα
ὀρθῶν ἑσταότων· τὸ δὲ νήπιος οὐκ ἐνόησεν,
ὡς οἱ ὑπ' εἰροπόκων ὀΐων στέρνοισι δέδεντο.
ὕστατος ἀρνειὸς μήλων ἔστειχε θύραζε,   305
λάχνῳ στεινόμενος καὶ ἐμοὶ πυκινὰ φρονέοντι.

ἀνήμελκτος, -ον	unmilked
εἰροπόκος, -ον	woolly-fleeced
ἑσταώς, -υῖα, -ός	standing [nom. pf. ptc. act. of ἵστημι]
λάχνος, -ου	[m.] hair, wool
μηκάομαι	[irreg. plpf. with impf. endings and meaning: ἐμέμηκον] I bleat
ὀδύνη, -ης	[f.] pain, torment
νομός, -οῦ	[m.] pasture
οὔθαρ, -ατος	[n.] udder
στείνομαι	I am burdened, I am straitened
στέρνον, -ου	[n.] breast
σφαραγέομαι	I am full to bursting

744. NOTES

301. σφαραγεῦντο : the meaning here is different from 251.

304. ὡς = ὅτι ("that"); the accent is from the enclitic οἱ. δέδεντο is plpf. m.-p. of δέω.

745. COMMENT

298-301. At dawn, the Cyclops would normally (κατὰ μοῖραν) milk the females; now, with their master in pain and unable to milk them, they will experience discomfort, too.

302-304. The giant's hands pass searchingly over the backs of all the rams as they exit. The simple Cyclops does not perceive the trick; the upright, natural position of the rams averted all suspicion. Polyphemus' advantage in brute strength has been more than matched by Odysseus' strategic genius.

305-306. Odysseus' ordeal is not so quickly over. His peril is graver, in fact, because he is less well protected and his animal, in going out last, will draw the giant's undivided attention. The ram's slow pace, too, exposes Odysseus to greater danger.

746. GREEK'S FAMILY HISTORY

The Greek language is closely related to our own. In the family of languages, Greek and English are, as it were, cousins. They had a common origin in the distant past, and still retain under the surface many similar family traits.

The myriad languages of the world fall into several great groups, including Indo-European, Afro-Asiatic, Uralic, Sino-Tibetan, and Malayo-Polynesian, among others. Each of these language groups has numerous subdivisions. It is the Indo-European group to which both Greek and English belong.

Indo-European is the name given by historical linguists to a language or group of related dialects spoken by a people who lived about 6,000 years ago in a part of Europe or Asia, most likely around the Black Sea. Later, as this people migrated and dispersed to different and distant regions of India, Europe, and Asia Minor, the dialects changed, and developed eventually into distinct languages not understood outside their own localities. Related languages thus grew up, each distinct in many ways (pronunciation, inflection-endings, new words and meanings, etc.), yet all preserving the basic traits of their identical mother-tongue, Indo-European, in grammar and vocabulary.

These languages themselves developed as time went on, and many produced new groups of descended languages. Of the early sister-languages of Indo-European, Tocharian died out after its people moved to western China; primitive Albanian and Armenian survive without subfamilies; old Indo-Iranian developed into ancient Sanskrit, Pali, the Prakrit group, and eventually many of the modern languages of India; it also developed into Avestan and Old Persian, from which are descended, among others, Farsi and Kurdish; Balto-Slavic became in time Lithuanian, Latvian, Polish, Czech, Bulgarian, Russian, and other Slavic languages. Primitive Celtic developed into Gaelic, Welsh, Breton, Manx (on the Isle of Man, off England); old Germanic separated into many groups, from which came, among others, Old High German, Anglo-Saxon, and Scandinavian, with their modern descendants: German, English, Dutch, Flemish, Danish, Swedish, Norwegian, and Icelandic. Primitive Greek proved more stable, not breaking up into several languages, but only into partly differing dialects, the most important being Homeric (or Epic), Ionic, Aeolic, Doric, Attic, and Koine, which developed into Modern Greek. The early Italic speech, finally, divided into Oscan, Umbrian, and Latin, and from Medieval Latin arose Provencal, Italian, Spanish, French, Portuguese, and Romanian.

747. WRITE IN GREEK

1. The female sheep of the flock remained within, distressed, but all the males rushed out in a mass when they saw rosy-fingered Dawn had arrived. ["in a mass" = "closely, thickly"]

2. To know one another and to respect others' rights is the path for mortals into justice and peace.

3. Foolish in mind and cruel of heart, the mighty Cyclops hoped to seize and destroy us when we should try to flee out of the cave.

Lesson 116

748. MEMORIZE

δαμάζω, δαμάω, δάμασσα	I tame, I overpower
λυγρός, -ή, -όν	miserable, wretched
σταθμός, -οῦ	[m.] doorpost; farmyard

749. TEXT

Strange Behavior

τὸν δ᾽ ἐπιμασσάμενος προσέφη κρατερὸς Πολύφημος·
  "κριὲ πέπον, τί μοι ὧδε διὰ σπέος ἔσσυο μήλων
ὕστατος; οὔ τι πάρος γε λελειμμένος ἔρχεαι οἰῶν,
ἀλλὰ πολὺ πρῶτος νέμεαι τέρεν᾽ ἄνθεα ποίης   310
μακρὰ βιβάς, πρῶτος δὲ ῥοὰς ποταμῶν ἀφικάνεις,
πρῶτος δὲ σταθμόνδε λιλαίεαι ἀπονέεσθαι
ἑσπέριος, νῦν αὖτε πανύστατος. ἦ σύ γ᾽ ἄνακτος
ὀφθαλμὸν ποθέεις; τὸν ἀνὴρ κακὸς ἐξαλάωσε
σὺν λυγροῖσ᾽ ἑτάροισι, δαμασσάμενος φρένας οἴνῳ,   315
Οὖτις, ὃν οὔ πώ φημι πεφυγμένον ἔμμεν ὄλεθρον.

ἄνθος, -εος	[n.] flower, bud
ἀφ-ικάνω	I arrive at
ἀπο-νέομαι	I come back
βιβάς, -ᾶσα, -άν	striding along [nom. pres. ptc. act. sg. of βιβάω, parallel form of βαίνω]
ἐξ-αλαόω, ἐξ-αλασω, ἐξ-αλάωσα	I blind, I put (an eye) out
ἑσπέριος, -η, -ον	at evening
κριός, -οῦ	[m.] ram
παν-ύστατος, -η, -ον	last of all
πάρος	[adv.] before, formerly
πέπων, -ονος	[only in voc.] gentle, "softy"
ποίη, -ης	[f.] grass
ῥοή, -ῆς	[f.] stream, waters
σεύω, —, (σ)σύμην	[non-thematic aorist] I move forward
τέρην, -εινα, -εν	[m. and n. gen. τέρενος] tender

750. NOTES

308. μοι : weak dat. of reference, = "I say," "I pray."

309. λέλειμμένος is pf. m.-p. ptc. of λείπω, = lagging behind. οἰῶν (fused form of ὀΐων) is a gen. of separation (cp. Section 18).

311. μακρὰ is an adverb with βιβάς.

316. πέφυγμαι is pf. mid. of φεύγω. Here, the ptc. joined with pres. inf. functions the same as would the pf. inf. (πεφύχθαι) alone.

751. COMMENT

307-316. This speech is certainly the first (and only) instance of anything done or said by Polyphemus possessing pathos. The gentle tenderness of the Cyclops' words to the pet ram, his favorite among all his numerous flock, reveals an unexpected aspect of his character; yet that the monster's friend is an animal also underlines his social isolation.

310-313. A description of the proud bearing and spirited energy of the majestic leader of the flock. μακρὰ βιβάς is used formulaically of the proud strides of dominant warriors in the *Iliad*.

313-315. Polyphemus, puzzled by the ram's unusual conduct, tries to persuade himself that the noble beast is acting thus out of some sense of his master's loss, some sympathetic understanding of his pain.

316. The Cyclops claims that he will get revenge.

752. WORDS IN DISGUISE

As you saw in Section 746, there are many words in English that are identical in origin with those for the same thing in other Indo-European languages. You don't recognize the similarity because they have been camouflaged; their surface appearance in English is misleading and conceals their real nature. But it is easy to penetrate the disguise if you know the formula.

The changes in pronunciation which words undergo in the course of time and in the development of new languages out of old generally follow regular rules. One of the most important of these, and certainly the most famous, is Grimm's Law for mute-changes in the Germanic family of Indo-European. This phenomenon consists in original 'voiced' stops or mutes (*b, d, g*) becoming 'voiceless' (*p, t, k*, respectively). Conversely, *p, t, k* become *b, d, g*, by Verner's Law. However, when beginning a word or following an accented vowel, *p, t, k* become instead *f, th, h*, and when following *f, s,* or *h*, remain unchanged. Other factors may cause irregularities or a second change after the first, but the above rules work in most cases.

Not all words, of course, for a given thing in the various related languages have the same origin in a common Indo-European root, and some similarities are only apparent or accidental, not real. There are, besides, special laws for other consonants, and for vowels.

Here are some interesting examples of true 'cognate' words (in German, *v* is pronounced *f*):

GREEK	LATIN	POLISH	GERMAN	ENGLISH
πατήρ	pater		Vater	father
τρεῖς	três	trzy	drei*	three
βάκ-τρον	bac-ulum	bok		peg

ϝίδον	video	widziec		wit
πλή-ρης	ple-nus	pelny	voll	full
κολωνός	culmen, collis	(kalnas)**		holm, hill
νυκτ-ός	noct-is	noc	Nacht	ni(g)ht

*Second change, from th to d
**Lithuanian word

753. WRITE IN GREEK

1. Whenever the flocks proceeded from the cave to the river, or back again to the farmyard, this great ram always went first of all.

2. "Let us all pray together," he said, "to Zeus, that he may tame the Cyclops' pitiless heart and save us from utter destruction."

3. Two men sat beside the door-post of a wretched house, asking bread for themselves and their wives and children.

754. WORD STUDY

ADAMANT (a very hard mineral, 'untamable' by cutting instruments), ADAMANTINE (indestructible, impenetrable, all-resisting, like adamant); — ANTHO- (a prefix meaning 'flower'), ANTHOLOGY (a 'gathering of flowers' or select passages of literature, etc. from various sources); — HESPERUS (the evening star).

Lesson 117

755. MEMORIZE

μένος, μένεος   [n.] might; courage; wrath

τῶ   [adv., often used with conjunctive force] therefore; in that case

756. TEXT

Frustration and Success

  εἰ δὴ ὁμοφρονέοις ποτιφωνήεις τε γένοιο
εἰπεῖν, ὅππῃ κεῖνος ἐμὸν μένος ἠλασκάζει·
τῶ κέ οἱ ἐγκέφαλός γε διὰ σπέος ἄλλυδις ἄλλη
θεινομένου ῥαίοιτο πρὸς οὔδεϊ, κὰδ δέ τ᾽ ἐμὸν κῆρ   320
λωφήσειε κακῶν, τά μοι οὐτιδανὸς πόρεν Οὖτις."
  ὣς εἰπὼν τὸν κριὸν ἀπὸ ἕο πέμπε θύραζε.
ἐλθόντες δ᾽ ἠβαιὸν ἀπὸ σπείους τε καὶ αὐλῆς
πρῶτος ὑπ᾽ ἀρνειοῦ λυόμην, ὑπέλυσα δ᾽ ἑταίρους.

ἄλλυδις ἄλλη	[advs.] = in different directions, here and there [idiomatic]
ἐγκέφαλος. -ου	[m.] brain
ἠβαιός, -ή, -όν	little; [as adv.] = a little ways
ἠλασκάζω	I hide from [+ acc.]
θείνω	I strike down
κριός, -οῦ	[m.] ram
λωφάω, λωφήσω, λώφησα	I find relief from [+ gen]
ὁμο-φρονέω	I share understanding, I sympathize
οὔδας, -εος	[n.] floor, ground
οὐτιδανός, -ή, -όν	worthless
ποτι-φωνήεις, -εσσα, -εν	endowed with speech
ῥαίω, ῥαίσω, ῥαῖσα	I smash to pieces
ὑπο-λύω	loose from under, I unloose

757. NOTES

317. εἰ : recall Section 106.

318. εἰπεῖν : see Section 588.

320. θεινομένου agrees in sense with οἱ, which is a dat. of possession (cp. Section 504) and hence equivalent to a genitive.

320. κὰδ [= κατά] is used here as an adv., simply to intensify the general thought; translate "in full."

321. ἐλθόντες...λυόμην : the idea starts out as plural, then shifts in subject to singular, grammar giving way to vividness.

323. σπείους : alternative gen. sg. of σπέος

758. COMMENT

317-318. The futility of Polyphemus' wishful thinking is almost pathetic. It emphasizes how ineffective the blinded giant is in coping with this 'puny' enemy whom he still views with contempt. It stresses also the unbridgeable chasm between him and his beast, his only approximation to a friend.

319-321. The Cyclops would of course rely on violence in taking vengeance on his tiny but crafty attackers. Note the pun in his use of the adjective οὐτιδανὸς to describe Οὗτις.

322-324. The Cyclops sends his favorite ram out the door and, unwittingly, the Greeks as well. Their leader's cunning has snatched them from death's jaw.

759. MORE WORDS IN DISGUISE

Section 752 showed how the consonants of a word may change in passing from the IndoEuropean original into the various descended languages. It is interesting to know that an *n, m,* or *w* sound ordinarily does not change, and that an aspirated mute (*bh, gh, dh*) reacts differently from a simple *b, g,* or *d*– in English, losing the *h* sound instead of changing by Grimm's Law; in Greek and Latin, either shifting into another consonant or losing the *h*.

The following chart will reveal some perhaps unsuspected word-relationships.

INDO-EUR.	GREEK	LATIN	POLISH	GERMAN	ENGLISH
nome	ὄνομα	nomen		Name	name
(e)me	(ἐ)μέ	me	mnie	mi-ch	me
newos	νέ(ϝ)ος	novus	nowy	neu	new
v(o)ik	(ϝ)οῖκος	vicus	wies		War-wich
swadus	ἡδύς	suavis	slodki	süss	sweet
	[for σϝαδύς]	[for swadwis]			
bher-	φέρω	fero	bier-ac	ge-bären	bear
dh(w)or	θύρα	for-is	dwor	Tür	door
meg(h)	μέγας	mag[n]us	moc	Ich mag	I may

760. WRITE IN GREEK

1. We have been released, my men, from the Cyclops' deadly might! Therefore Zeus and Athene saved us, as we prayed.

2. When dawn appears, the sky is filled to overflowing with light. It is the beginning of another day, bringing to mortals both good things and bad.

3. Lying silently under the splendid rams, my companions awaited me, until having loosed myself I should approach and release them all.

Lesson 118

761. MEMORIZE

γοάω, γοήσομαι, γόησα   I weep (for) [+ acc.], I mourn

λίην   [adv.] exceedingly; καὶ λίην [adv.] truly

762. TEXT

Joyous Departure

καρπαλίμως δὲ τὰ μῆλα ταναύποδα, πίονα δημῷ,	325
πολλὰ περιτροπέοντες ἐλαύνομεν, ὄφρ' ἐπὶ νῆα	
ἱκόμεθ'· ἀσπάσιοι δὲ φίλοισ' ἑτάροισι φάνημεν,	
οἳ φύγομεν θάνατον· τοὺς δὲ στενάχοντο γοῶντες.	
ἀλλ' ἐγὼ οὐκ εἴων, ἀνὰ δ' ὀφρύσι νεῦον ἑκάστῳ,	
κλαίειν· ἀλλ' ἐκέλευσα θοῶς καλλίτριχα μῆλα	330
πόλλ' ἐν νηῒ βαλόντας ἐπιπλεῖν ἁλμυρὸν ὕδωρ.	
οἱ δ' αἶψ' εἴσβαινον καὶ ἐπὶ κληῖσι καθῖζον·	
ἑξῆς δ' ἑζόμενοι πολιὴν ἅλα τύπτον ἐρετμοῖς.	

ἀνα-νεύω	I shake my head "no", [literally "I nod up"]; I make a forbidding gesture
ἀσπάσιος, -η, -ον	welcome
δημός, -οῦ	[m.] fat
ἐπι-πλέω	I sail over
καλλίθριξ, -τριχος	fair-fleeced or -maned [epithet of sheep and horses]
περι-τροπέω	I turn about [trans.], I round up
ταναύπους, -ποδος	long-legged

763. NOTES

326. πολλά : used adverbially, = "time and again, often."

329. ἀνὰ δ' ὀφρύσι νεῦον ἑκάστῳ : explains ἀλλ' ἐγὼ οὐκ εἴων...κλαίειν

331. βαλόντας : the understood subject is the companions, and μῆλα the object.

764. COMMENT

325-327. The companions had lobbied Odysseus to steal the Cyclops' cheeses and flocks and sail away (85-90); Odysseus, curious about the stranger and hopeful of enrichment, had not been persuaded. Though he gives himself credit for his clever rescue of himself and his companions, it is also important to remember that he has admitted (89-91) that he erred in getting them into the danger in the first place. Now he does not hesitate to drive off the Cyclops' prize sheep. It is not easy, though, to keep the flock in hand, for they are constantly veering off by force of habit toward their usual grazing area among the hills some distance from the sea.

327-331. The men at the ships are happy to see their leader and his companions return, for their prolonged absence (a day and a half) on what was expected to be a mere visit of curiosity and information-gathering had raised anxiety over what had happened to them. How well founded their fears were they painfully discover on noting that six of the party are missing and, far more, on hearing the account of their horrible end. Odysseus, though fully sharing their grief, does not (as they) lose sight of the deadly peril for all if there is the least delay in setting out to sea. The giant may hear the sheep in this unaccustomed place, suspect that the men have somehow escaped and are driving off his flocks, and with a few great bounds be upon them in raging fury. As usual, Odysseus does not allow his emotions to cloud over his clear perception of what must be done.

765. WORD-WELDING IN GREEK

Like other languages, Greek has regular ways of building up new forms of words from basic parts by joining the root of the word with prefixes and suffixes of standardized meaning (cp. English true, tru-1y, tru-th, tru-th ful-ness, un-truth).

If you know what the regular force of these parts are, and recognize them in a word, it becomes easy to reason out the meaning of many words when you first meet them, without having to look them up in a dictionary. It gives you a more personal grasp on the principles of the language.

Here are a few hints on word-formation in Greek:

1. -αω, -εω, -ευω = to *be* or to *do* what is indicated by the root of the word (e.g., βο-άω, φιλ-έω, βουλ-εύω).

2. -οω = to *cause* to be (e.g., θο-όω I make sharp).

3. -αζω, -ιζω to *perform* the *action* (e.g., βι-άζω I use force, βαπτ-ίζω I perform a dipping).

4. -αιος, -ιος, -ος, -εις = *characterized* by, like (e.g., δίκ-αιος, πελώρ-ιος, ἱερ-ός, ἠνεμό-εις).

5. -κος, -ιτικος = *able to, connected with* (e.g., φυσι-κός, πολι-τικός, μαθημα-τικός).

6. -ιη, -η, -μη, -τις, -σις, -της (f.), -ος (n.) = *the general notion of a thing, its abstract noun,* (e.g., ἀληθε-ίη, δίκ-η, φή-μη, πίσ-τις, ποίη-σις, φιλό-της, κάλλ-ος, δημο-κρατ-ίη).

7. -της (m.), -τηρ, -ευς, -τωρ = *the doer, the person concerned* (e.g., ποιη-τής maker, σω-τῆρ savior, ἡγή-τωρ leader).

8. -μα = *the product, result* (e.g., ποίη-μα thing made, νόη-μα thought).

9. The principles already seen: alpha privative, special adverbial case endings -δε, -θεν, -φι(ν), prepositional compounds.

766. WRITE IN GREEK

1.   When I told my companions at the ship how our friends had perished by the pitiless Cyclops' hands, they mourned exceedingly, but also feared greatly for themselves.

2.   I, too, could become cruel in heart and wicked. May (it) never happen!

3.   Who would have supposed any mortal able to escape alive from that cave of death?

Lesson 119

767. MEMORIZE

γεγωνέω, γεγωνήσω,   [pf. with pres. meaning] I shout, I make myself heard
γεγώνησα, γέγωνα

ἔσθω   [pres. syst. only] I eat, I devour

768. TEXT

Parting Scorn

ἀλλ᾽ ὅτε τόσσον ἀπῆν, ὅσσον τε γέγωνε βοήσας,
καὶ τότ᾽ ἐγὼ Κύκλωπα προσηύδων κερτομίοισι·   335
"Κύκλωψ, οὐκ ἄρ᾽ ἔμελλες ἀνάλκιδος ἀνδρὸς ἑταίρους
ἔδμεναι ἐν σπῆϊ γλαφυρῷ κρατερῆφι βίηφι.
καὶ λίην σέ γ᾽ ἔμελλε κιχήσεσθαι κακὰ ἔργα,
σχέτλι᾽, ἐπεὶ ξείνους οὐχ ἅζεο σῷ ἐνὶ οἴκῳ
ἐσθέμεναι· τῶ σε Ζεὺς τείσατο καὶ θεοὶ ἄλλοι."   340

ἄναλκις -ιδος   cowardly, spiritless
κερτόμια, -ων   [n.] taunts, mockery [pl. only]

769. NOTES

334. τόσσον…ὅσσον : "as far…as;" ἀπ-ῆν : the unexpressed subject is either Κύκλωψ or νηῦς.

334. γέγωνε has for implied subject the indefinite τις. The aor. is generalizing, = pres.

336. οὐκ goes with ἀνάλκιδος: "It was no coward's companions…"

338. ἔργα is nom., subject of ἔμελλε.

339. οὐχ ἅζεο + inf. : "you did not scruple to…"

770. COMMENT

334-335. Once out of Polyphemus' reach, yet still within earshot, Odysseus exults over his victory and upbraids the Cyclops again for his inhospitality. Such κερτόμια are typically uttered by victorious warriors in the *Iliad* to their defeated foes, dead or alive.

336-340. Polyphemus had scorned the gods (134-139) when Odysseus supplicated him for hospitality in the name of Zeus (127-132). Odysseus' taunts take their shape from that exchange: Odysseus is the agent of Zeus ξείνιος, or Zeus as the overseer and protector of the stranger's claim to protection, which Polyphemus did not respect.

771. VOWEL SHIFT IN GREEK ROOTS

As you saw in Section 765, Greek, like other languages, often forms different related words from a common root. It sometimes happens that the vowel of this basic root undergoes change in the various offshoot words. This is called *Ablaut* or *Vowel Gradation*. It occurs in English too, as in the related words *sing, sang, sung, song.*

In Greek, vowel shift within the root consists in the lengthening, shortening, or entire omission of the vowel, or the substitution in its place of a weaker vowel. Here are some interesting examples: ἐλεύ-σομαι, εἰλή-λου-θα, ἔ-λυ-θεν, ἔ-λ-θον; λείπ-ω, λίπ-ον, λέ-λοιπ-α (pf.); φέρ-ω, φορ-έω, δί-φρ-ος (chariot, carrier), φαρ-έτρη (arrow-carrier, quiver); δῶ-ρον, δό-τε; τρέπ-ω, πολύ-τροπ-ος; φρήν, φρον-έω; φη-μί, ἔ-φα-το, φω-νή.

Awareness of this law of vowel change will help you realize the relationship of many words, and facilitate remembering their meanings. Be on the lookout for other examples among the words you read in Greek.

772. WRITE IN GREEK

1. As cruel Polyphemus discovered, whoever does evil deeds will himself sometime suffer; for there is justice in the world.

2. We tried to make ourselves heard from the river to our companions eating in the house, but we could not, for we were very far away.

3. Many things have I learned (aor.), but with none was I ever so pleased as with this account about the Cyclops and the Greeks, and how by craftiness and courage and the will of the gods they escaped alive from his cave.

Lesson 120

773. REVIEW OF LESSONS 115-119

In the last five lessons, you have memorized twelve new words and read forty-three more lines of Homer. Make sure that you have mastered everything; then check your knowledge with this test:

I.   Vocabulary (40%)

    1.   might: acc. sg. =

    2.   καὶ λίην =

    3.   in that case =

    4.   ἐγεγώνης =

    5.   they will weep =

    6.   θήλεϊ =

    7.   shrewd: m. dat. sg. =

    8.   δαμᾶ =

    9.   last: n. dat. pl. =

    10.   γοήσειε

II.   Text (60%)

    1.   Scan line 304.

    2.   In line 304, identify δέδεντο .

    3.   In line 299, explain νομόνδ'.

    4.   Translate δάμασσε φρένα οἴνῳ.

    5.   In line 319, explain οἱ.

    6.   Translate πρῶτος ὑπ' ἀρνειοῦ λυόμην.

    7.   In line 321, what part of speech is τά ?

    8.   In line 328, to what or whom does τοὺς refer?

    9.   In line 329, identify εἴων .

    10.   In line 339, what case is σχέτλ' and to whom does it refer?

    11.   What moral does Odysseus draw from this whole adventure?

    12.   Polyphemus' address to the ram is considered remarkable. What does it show of the character of the giant?

774. ADVENTURES CALLING!

As the ship sails away from the Cyclops' island, Polyphemus, infuriated by Odysseus' taunts, twice hurls an enormous rock, nearly sinking the ship with a mighty upsurge of waves. Odysseus boldly shouts back his true name, the giant replying with a prayer that his tormentors may be destroyed, or at least suffer prolonged woe on their homeward journey. The Cyclops episode thus ends on a note of dread foreboding, a fear that the gods may answer Polyphemus' prayer.

What lies before you is a story of many and varied new adventures, of thrilling events in far-off mysterious places, of joys and sorrows and gripping fears, of almost total disaster. There are interesting things awaiting you when you continue with Homer and the *Odyssey*!

Honor Work

Supplementary Text For Sight Reading
The Close of the Cyclops Story

Near Disaster

ὣς ἐφάμην, ὁ δ᾽ ἔπειτα χολώσατο κηρόθι μᾶλλον·   1
ἧκε δ᾽ ἀπορρήξας κορυφὴν ὄρεος μεγάλοιο,
κὰδ δ᾽ ἔβαλε προπάροιθε νεὸς κυανοπρῴροιο
ἐκλύσθη δὲ θάλασσα κατερχομένης ὑπὸ πέτρης·
τὴν δ᾽ ἂψ ἠπειρόνδε παλιρρόθιον φέρε κῦμα,   5
πλημυρὶς ἐκ πόντοιο, θέμωσε δὲ χέρσον ἱκέσθαι.
αὐτὰρ ἐγὼ χείρεσσι λαβὼν περιμήκεα κοντὸν
ὦσα παρέξ· ἑτάροισι δ᾽ ἐποτρύνας ἐκέλευσα
ἐμβαλέειν κώπῃσ᾽, ἵν᾽ ὑπὲκ κακότητα φύγοιμεν,
κρατὶ καταννεύων· οἱ δὲ προπεσόντες ἔρεσσον.   10

A Bold Revelation

ἀλλ᾽ ὅτε δὴ δὶς τόσσον ἅλα πρήσσοντες ἀπῆμεν,
καὶ τότε δὴ Κύκλωπα προσηύδων· ἀμφὶ δ᾽ ἑταῖροι
μειλιχίοισ᾽ ἐπέεσσιν ἐρήτυον ἄλλοθεν ἄλλος·

"σχέτλιε, τίπτ᾽ ἐθέλεις ἐρεθιζέμεν ἄγριον ἄνδρα;
ὃς καὶ νῦν πόντονδε βαλὼν βέλος ἤγαγε νῆα   15
αὖτις ἐς ἤπειρον, καὶ δὴ φάμεν αὐτόθ᾽ ὀλέσθαι.
εἰ δὲ φθεγξαμένου τευ ἢ αὐδήσαντος ἄκουσε,
σύν κεν ἄραξ᾽ ἡμέων κεφαλὰς καὶ νήϊα δοῦρα
μαρμάρῳ ὀκριόεντι βαλών· τόσσον γὰρ ἵησιν."
ὣς φάσαν, ἀλλ᾽ οὐ πεῖθον ἐμὸν μεγαλήτορα θυμόν,   20
ἀλλά μιν ἄψορρον προσέφην κεκοτηότι θυμῷ·

"Κύκλωψ, αἴ κέν τίς σε καταθνητῶν ἀνθρώπων
ὀφθαλμοῦ εἴρηται ἀεικελίην ἀλαωτύν,
φάσθαι Ὀδυσσῆα πτολιπόρθιον ἐξαλαῶσαι,
υἱὸν Λαέρτεω, Ἰθάκῃ ἔνι οἰκί᾽ ἔχοντα."   25

Vocabulary for lines 1- 25

ἀεικέλιος, -η, -ον	unseemly
ἀκούω, ἀκούσομαι, ἄκουσα	I hear the sound of [+ gen.]
ἀλαωτύς, -ύος	[f.] blinding
ἀπο-ρρήγνυμι, -ρρήξω, -ρρηξα	I break off

ἀράσσω, ἀράξω, ἄραξα	I smash, I crush
αὐδάω, αὐδήσω, αὔδησα	I speak
αὐτόθι	[adv.] then and there
ἄψορρον	[adv.] right back, again
βέλος, -εος	[n.] missile
ἐμ-βάλλω, etc.	I cast myself on
ἐξ-αλαόω,-αλαώσω, -αλάωσα	I blind
ἐπ-οτρύνω, -οτρυνέω, -ότρυνα	I urge on
ἐρεθίζω	I provoke, I anger
ἐρέσσω	I ply the oars, I row
ἐρητύω	I hold back, I seek to restrain [trans.]
ἤπειρος, -ου	[f.] land, shore
θεμόω, —, θέμωσα	I force [obj. is νῆα, understood from context]
ἵησι	3 sg. pres. ind. of ἵημι
Ἰθάκη, -ης	[f.] Ithaca
κακότης, -ητος	[f.] evil, danger, misery
κάρη, κρατός	[n.]
κατα-νεύω	I nod, I nod (assent)
κατα-θνητός, -ή, -όν	mortal [= θνητός, -ή, -όν]
κεκοτηώς, -υῖα, -ός	[pf. ptc. of κοτέω] angry
κεφαλή, -ῆς	[f.] head
κλύζω, aor. pass. κλύσθην	I surge up
κοντός, -οῦ	[m.] pole
κορυφή, -ῆς	[f.] peak, top
κυανόπρωρος, -ον	dark-prowed
κῦμα, -ατος	[n.] wave
κώπη, -ης	[f.] oar
Λαέρτης, -εω	[m.] [special gen.] Laertes [father of Odysseus]
μάλλον	[adv.] all the more
μάρμαρος, -ου	[m.] granite, quartz, marble
νήιος, -ον	for ships
Ὀδυσ(σ)εύς, -ῆος	[m.] Odysseus
οἰκίον, -ου	[n.] home, abode [only in pl.]
ὀκριόεις, -εσσα, -εν	jagged
παλιρρόθιος, -ον	backward-washing
παρέξ	[adv.] off, away
περιμηχής, -ές	long
πλημυρίς, -ίδος	[f.] flood-tide, swell
πρήσσω	I traverse, I go across
προπάροιθε(ν)	[adv., prep. + gen.] in front of, before
προ-πίπτω etc.	I fall to, I bend forward
πτολιπόρθιος, -ον	sacker of cities [epithet of Odysseus]
τίπτε = τί ποτε	[interrogative adv.] why?
ὑπ᾽ ἐκ…φεύγω	I flee from under, I escape
φάσθαι	inf. [here, = impt.] of φημί
φθέγγομαι, φθέγξομαι, φθεγξάμην	I make a noise
χέρσος, -ου	[f.] land
χολόομαι, κεχολώσομαι, χολωσάμην	I am enraged
ὠθέω, ὤσω, ὦσα	I push

A Prophecy Fulfilled

ὣς ἐφάμην, ὁ δέ μ’ οἰμώξας ἠμείβετο μύθῳ·
“ὢ πόποι, ἦ μάλα δή με παλαίφατα θέσφαθ’ ἱκάνει.
ἔσκε τις ἐνθάδε μάντις ἀνὴρ ἠΰς τε μέγας τε,
Τήλεμος Εὐρυμίδης, ὃς μαντοσύνῃ ἐκέκαστο
καὶ μαντευόμενος κατεγήρα Κυκλώπεσσιν·   30
ὅς μοι ἔφη τάδε πάντα τελευτήσεσθαι ὀπίσσω,
χειρῶν ἐξ Ὀδυσῆος ἁμαρτήσεσθαι ὀπωπῆς.
ἀλλ’ αἰεί τινα φῶτα μέγαν καὶ καλὸν ἐδέγμην
ἐνθάδ’ ἐλεύσεσθαι, μεγάλην ἐπιειμένον ἀλκήν·
νῦν δέ μ’ ἐὼν ὀλίγος τε καὶ οὐτιδανὸς καὶ ἄκικυς   35
ὀφθαλμοῦ ἀλάωσεν, ἐπεί μ’ ἐδαμάσσατο οἴνῳ.
ἀλλ’ ἄγε δεῦρ’, Ὀδυσεῦ, ἵνα τοι πὰρ ξείνια θείω,
πομπήν τ’ ὀτρύνω δόμεναι κλυτὸν ἐννοσίγαιον·
τοῦ γὰρ ἐγὼ πάϊς εἰμί, πατὴρ δ’ ἐμὸς εὔχεται εἶναι.
αὐτὸς δ’, αἴ κ’ ἐθέλῃσ’, ἰήσεται, οὐδέ τις ἄλλος   40
οὔτε θεῶν μακάρων οὔτε θνητῶν ἀνθρώπων.”
ὣς ἔφατ’, αὐτὰρ ἐγώ μιν ἀμειβόμενος προσέειπον·
αἲ γὰρ δὴ ψυχῆς τε καὶ αἰῶνός σε δυναίμην
εὖνιν ποιήσας πέμψαι δόμον Ἄϊδος εἴσω,
ὡς οὐκ ὀφθαλμόν γ’ ἰήσεται οὐδ’ ἐνοσίχθων.”   45

Polyphemus’ Prayer for Vengeance

ὣς ἐφάμην, ὁ δ’ ἔπειτα Ποσειδάωνι ἄνακτι
εὔχετο, χεῖρ’ ὀρέγων εἰς οὐρανὸν ἀστερόεντα·
   “κλῦθι, Ποσείδαον γαιήοχε κυανοχαῖτα·
εἰ ἐτεόν γε σός εἰμι, πατὴρ δ’ ἐμὸς εὔχεαι εἶναι,
δὸς μὴ Ὀδυσσῆα πτολιπόρθιον οἴκαδ’ ἱκέσθαι,   50
ἀλλ’ εἴ οἱ μοῖρ’ ἐστὶ φίλους τ’ ἰδέειν καὶ ἱκέσθαι
οἶκον ἐϋκτίμενον καὶ ἑὴν ἐς πατρίδα γαῖαν,
ὀψὲ κακῶς ἔλθοι, ὀλέσας ἄπο πάντας ἑταίρους,
νηὸς ἐπ’ ἀλλοτρίης, εὕροι δ’ ἐν πήματα οἴκῳ.”
   ὣς ἔφατ’ εὐχόμενος, τοῦ δ’ ἔκλυε κυανοχαίτης.   55
αὐτὰρ ὅ γ’ ἐξαῦτις πολὺ μείζονα λᾶαν ἀείρας
ἧκ’ ἐπιδινήσας, ἐπέρεισε δὲ ἶν’ ἀπέλεθρον·
κὰδ δ’ ἔβαλεν μετόπισθε νεὸς κυανοπρῴροιο
τυτθόν, ἐδεύησεν δ’ οἰήϊον ἄκρον ἱκέσθαι.
ἐκλύσθη δὲ θάλασσα κατερχομένης ὑπὸ πέτρης·   60
τὴν δὲ πρόσω φέρε κῦμα, θέμωσε δὲ χέρσον ἱκέσθαι.

Vocabulary for lines 26-61

ἄγε	[impt. of ἄγω; idiom] come!
Ἀΐδης, Ἀΐδος	[m.] Hades [god of underworld]
αἰών, -ῶνος	[m.] existence, being
ἄκικυς, —, ἄκικυ	feeble
ἀλαόω, ἀλοώσω, ἀλόωσα	I take away the sight of [+ gen.]
ἀλκή, -ῆς	[f.] strength
ἀλλότριος, -η, -ον	foreign, another's
ἀπέλεθρος, -ον	incalculable, stupendous
ἀστερόεις, -εσσα, -εν	starry
γαιήοχος, -ου	[m.] earth-holder [Epithet of Poseidon]
δεῦρο	[adv.] hither, here
δεύω, δευήσομαι, δεύησα	I just fail (to do something) [+ inf.]
δόμεναι	2 aor inf. of δίδωμι
δόμος, -ου	[m.] abode, house; realm
ἐδέγμην	1 sg. plpf. of δέχομαι (here= I [had] expected)
εἴσω	[+ acc.] into, to
ἐνθάδε	[adv.] here
ἐννοσίγαιος, -ου	[m.] earth-shaker [epithet of Poseidon]
ἐνοσίχθων, -ονος	[m.] earth-shaker [epithet of Poseidon]
ἐξαῦτις	[adv.] again, once more
ἐπ-ερείδω, -ερείσω, -έρεισα	I exert
ἐπι-δινέω, —, -δίνησα	I whirl around
ἐπι-ειμένος, -η, -ον	[pf. pass. ptc. of ἐπι-έννυμι + acc. of specification] arrayed in
ἔσκε	3 sg. iterative of εἰμί
ἐτεόν	[adv.] in truth, indeed
ἐϋκτίμενος, -η, -ον	well-built
εὖνις, -ιος	[adj., + gen.] deprived of
ἠΰς, —,ηΰ	goodly, admirable
θεμόω,—, θέμωσα	I cause [+ inf.]
θέσφατον, -ου	divine decree, oracle
ἰάομαι, ἰήσομαι, ἰησάμην	I heal
ἴς, ἰνός	[f.] strength, might
καίνυμαι,	pf. with pres. sense: κέκασμαι I excel
κατα-γηράω	I grow old
κλῦθι	[2 aor. impt. of κλύω] hear me!
κλύζω	aor. pass. κλύσθην I surge up
κλύω	I hear [+ gen.]
κυανόπρῳρος, -ον	dark-prowed
κυανοχαίτης	[voc. -τα] dark-haired [epithet of Poseidon]
κῦμα, -ατος	[n.] wave, billow
λᾶας, λᾶος, acc. λᾶαν	[m.] rock
μαντεύομαι	I act as a prophet
μάντις, -ιος	[m.] seer, prophet
μαντοσύνη, -ης	[f.] gift of prophecy
μετόπισθε	[prep. + gen.] behind
μῦθος, -ου	[m.] word, story, speech
οἰήϊον, -ου	[n.] steering-oar, rudder
ὀπίσσω	[adv.] afterwards, later
ὀπωπή, -ῆς	[f.] sight, vision
ὀρέγω	I stretch forth (a hand or hands)
ὀτρύνω	I urge on
οὐτιδανός, -ή, -όν	worthless, of no account
ὀψέ	[adv.] after long delay, late
παλαίφατος, -ον	spoken of old, ancient
παρ...θείω	alternate 1st pers. sg. 2 aor. subj. of παρα-τίθημι [cp. Section 472] I offer

πῆμα, -ατος	[n.] bane, woe
πομπή, -ῆς	[f.] conduct, escort, guidance
πρόσω	[adv.] forward
πτολίπορθος, -ον	sacker of cities [epithet only of Odysseus in the *Odyssey*]
τελευτάομαι, τελευτήσομαι	I come to pass
Τήλεμος Εὐρυμίδης	Telemus, son of Eurymis
τυτθός, -ή, -όν	little
χέρσος, -ου	[f.] land [here = the small island]
ὢ πόποι	Alas! Ah me!

The Fleet Reassembles and Sails Off

ἀλλ᾽ ὅτε δὴ τὴν νῆσον ἀφικόμεθ᾽, ἔνθα περ ἄλλαι
νῆες ἐΰσσελμοι μένον ἀθρόαι, ἀμφὶ δ᾽ ἑταῖροι
εἵατ᾽ ὀδυρόμενοι, ἡμέας ποτιδέγμενοι αἰεί,
νῆα μὲν ἔνθ᾽ ἐλθόντες ἐκέλσαμεν ἐν ψαμάθοισιν,   65
ἐκ δὲ καὶ αὐτοὶ βῆμεν ἐπὶ ῥηγμῖνι θαλάσσης.
μῆλα δὲ Κύκλωπος γλαφυρῆς ἐκ νηὸς ἑλόντες
δασσάμεθ᾽, ὡς μή τίς μοι ἀτεμβόμενος κίοι ἴσης.
ἀρνειὸν δ᾽ ἐμοὶ οἴῳ ἐϋκνήμιδες ἑταῖροι
μήλων δαιομένων δόσαν ἔξοχα· τὸν δ᾽ ἐπὶ θινὶ   70
Ζηνὶ κελαινεφέϊ Κρονίδῃ, ὃς πᾶσιν ἀνάσσει,
ῥέξας μηρί᾽ ἔκαιον· ὁ δ᾽ οὐκ ἐμπάζετο ἱρῶν,
ἀλλ᾽ ὅ γε μερμήριζεν, ὅπως ἀπολοίατο πᾶσαι
νῆες ἐΰσσελμοι καὶ ἐμοὶ ἐρίηρες ἑταῖροι.

ὣς τότε μὲν πρόπαν ἦμαρ ἐς ἠέλιον καταδύντα   75
ἥμεθα δαινύμενοι κρέα τ᾽ ἄσπετα καὶ μέθυ ἡδύ·
ἦμος δ᾽ ἠέλιος κατέδυ καὶ ἐπὶ κνέφας ἦλθε,
δὴ τότε κοιμήθημεν ἐπὶ ῥηγμῖνι θαλάσσης.
ἦμος δ᾽ ἠριγένεια φάνη ῥοδοδάκτυλος Ἠώς,
δὴ τότ᾽ ἐγὼν ἑτάροισιν ἐποτρύνας ἐκέλευσα   80
αὐτούς τ᾽ ἀμβαίνειν ἀνά τε πρυμνήσια λῦσαι.
οἱ δ᾽ αἶψ᾽ εἴσβαινον καὶ ἐπὶ κληῖσι καθῖζον,
ἑξῆς δ᾽ ἑζόμενοι πολιὴν ἅλα τύπτον ἐρετμοῖς.

ἔνθεν δὲ προτέρω πλέομεν ἀκαχήμενοι ἦτορ,
ἄσμενοι ἐκ θανάτοιο, φίλους ὀλέσαντες ἑταίρους.   85

Vocabulary for lines 62-85

ἀθρόος, -η, -ον	in a group, together
ἀκαχήμενος, -η, -ον	[pf. ptc. of ἀχέω] aching, weighed down
ἀμβαίνω	[= ἀνα-βαίνω] I embark
ἀνάσσω	I lord over, I am king over [+ dat.]
ἀπ-ολοίατο	recall Section 385 h
ἄσμενος, -η, -ον	glad (to be) [aor. ptc. of ἥδομαι]
ἄσπετος, -ον	abundant, copious
ἀτέμβω	I unjustly deprive of [+ gen.]

δαίνυμαι	I banquet, I feast
δαίω	I divide into shares
δατέομαι, δάσομαι, δασ(σ)άμην	I divide, I appoint shares
εἵατο	3 pl. impf. [= ἥατο] of ἧμαι
ἐμπάζομαι	I take heed of [+ gen.]
ἔξοχα	[adv.] pre-eminently, most
ἐπ-οτρύνω, -οτρυνέω, -ότρυνα	I urge on
ἐϋκνήμις, -ιδος	equipped with sturdy leg-guards [epithet of Achaeans and of the companions]
ἐΰσσελμος, -ον	equipped with sturdy rowing-benches [epithet of ships]
ἧμαι	I sit, I remain (doing something)
θίς, θινός	beach, shore
ἱρῶν	= ἱερῶν
ἶσος, -η, -ον	equal [μοίρης is to be understood]
κατα-δύω, -δύσω, -δυν	I go down, I set
κελαινεφής, -ές	god of the black cloud [epithet or name of Zeus]
κέλλω, —, κέλσα	I beach, I land
κίω	I go
κνέφας, -αος	[n.] darkness
κοιμάομαι, κοιμήσομαι, κοιμήθην	I sleep, I lie down to rest
Κρονίδης, dat. -ίδη	[m.] son of Kronos [Zeus]
κυανοχαίτης	dark-haired [epithet of Poseidon]
μέθυ	[indecl. n.] wine
μερμηρίζω	I ponder, I contrive
μηρίον, -ου	[n.] thigh, ham
νῆσος, -ου	[f.] island
ὀδύρομαι	I am sorrowful, I am sad
ποτι-δέγμενος, -η, -ον	[aor. ptc. of ποτι-δέχομαι] awaiting apprehensively
πρό-πας, -πασα, -παν	entire, whole
προτέρω	[adv.] onward
πρυμνήσιον, -ου	[n.] mooring cables [holding the ship to something firm on shore]
ῥέζω	here in technical religious sense, "I offer up, I sacrifice"
ῥηγμίς, -ῖνος	[f.] surf, breakers
ψάμαθος, -ου	[f.] sand

Appendix A

Summary of Grammar

DECLENSION ENDINGS

	1st DECL.		2nd DECL.		3rd DECL.	
	βι-	γαι-	θε-	δωρ-	ἀνακτ-	ἐπε-
N	-η	-α	-ος	-ον	----	----
G	-ης	-ης	-ου/οιο	-ου/οιο	-ος	-ος
D	-ῃ	-ῃ	-ῳ	-ῳ	-ι	-ι
A	-ην	-αν	-ον	-ον	-α/-ν	----
N	-αι	-αι	-οι	-α	-ες	-α
G	-αων	-αων	-ων	-ων	-ων	-ων
D	-ῃσ(ι)	-ῃσ(ι)	-οισ(ι)	-οισ(ι)	-(εσ)σι	-(εσ)σι
A	-ας	-ας	-ους	-α	-ας	-α
GEND.	all f.		m.; a few f.	all n.	m., f., n. (cp. Lesson 27)	

ADJECTIVE AND PARTICIPLE TYPES

1. 1st and 2nd decl.   -ος, -η, -ον
2. 1st and 3rd decl.   -ων, -ουσα, -ον (m./n. gen. -οντ-ος)   -υς, -εια, -υ (m./n. gen. -ε-ος)
   -ας, -ασα, -αν (m./n. gen. -αντ-ος)   -ως, -υια, -ος (m./n. οτ-ος)
   -εις, -εσσα/-εισα, -εν (m./n. gen. -εντ-ος)
3. 3rd decl. only   -ης, -ες (gen. -ε-ος)   -ων, -ον (gen. -ον-ος)
4. Single termination (e.g., μάκαρ)

COMPARISON OF ADJECTIVES

1. Adj. in -ος w. last syllable of stem long: add to stem   -οτερος, -οτατος
2. Adj. in -ος w. last syllable of stem short: add to stem   -ωτερος, -ωτατος
3. Adj. in -ων: add to stem   -εστερος, -εστατος
4. Adj. in -ης, some in -υς: add to stem   -τερος, -τατος

IRREGULAR COMPARISON

ἀγαθός	ἀρείων	ἄριστος
καλός	καλλίων	κάλλιστος
μέγας	μείζων	μέγιστος
πολλός	πλείων	πλεῖστος
φίλος	φίλτερος	φίλτατος
ταχύς	θάσσων	τάχιστος

VOCATIVE

Same as nom. except:
1. 2nd decl. m. sg. -ε (φίλε)
2. 3rd decl. -ευς, -ις drop -ς (ζεῦ, πόλι)
3. 3rd decl. long vowel of nom. shortens if it also does in gen. (πάτερ)
4. Special: θεός, γύναι

SPECIAL CASE ENDINGS

1. -δε added to acc. = *place to which* (οἰκόνδε); -δε blends with ς into -ζε (θυράζε)
2. -θεν added to gen minus ς or υ = *place from which* (οὐρανόθεν)
3. -φι(ν) added to gen. minus ς or υ = *by, at, from, with, on, in* (βίηφι, θύρηφι)
4. DUAL: 2nd decl. -ω, 3rd decl. -ε (χεῖρε ἐμῶ)

VERB ENDINGS: ACTIVE AND AORIST PASSIVE

	PRES. SYSTEM λυ-	FUT. SYSTEM λυσ-	1 AOR. SYSTEM λυσ-	2 AOR. SYSTEM ιδ-	3 AOR. SYSTEM βη-	PF. ACT. SYSTEM λελυκ-	AOR. PASS. SYSTEM λυθ-
IND.	-ω	-ω				-α	
	-εις	-εις				-ας	
	-ει	-ει				-ε(ν)	
	-ομεν	-ομεν				-αμεν	
	-ετε	-ετε				-ατε	
	-ουσι(ν)	-ουσι(ν)				-ασι(ν)	
	(impf.)					(plpf.)	
	-ον		-α	-ον	-ν	-εα, -η	-ην
	-ες		-ας	-ες	-ς	-ης	-ης
	-ε(ν)		-ε(ν)	-ε(ν)	--	-ει	-η
	-ομεν		-αμεν	-ομεν	-μεν	-εμεν	-ημεν
	-ετε		-ατε	-ετε	-τε	-ετε	-ητε
	-ον		-αν	-ον	-σαν	-εσαν	-ησαν
SUBJ.	-ω		-ω	-ω	-ω	-ω	-ω
	-ῃς		-ῃς	-ῃς	-ῃς	-ῃς	-ῃς
	-ῃ		-ῃ	-ῃ	-ῃ	-ῃ	-ῃ
	-ωμεν		-ωμεν	-ωμεν	-ωμεν	-ωμεν	-ωμεν
	-ητε		-ητε	-ητε	-ητε	-ητε	-ητε
	-ωσι(ν)		-ωσι(ν)	-ωσι(ν)	-ωσι(ν)	-ωσι(ν)	-ωσι(ν)
OPT.	-οιμι		-αιμι	-οιμι	-αιην*	-οιμι	-ειην
	-οις		-ειας	-οις	-αιης	-οις	-ειης
	-οι		-ειε(ν)	-οι	-αιη	-οι	-ειη
	-οιμεν		-αιμεν	-οιμεν	-αιμεν	-οιμεν	-ειμεν
	-οιτε		-αιτε	-οιτε	-αιτε	-οιτε	-ειτε
	-οιεν		-ειαν	-οιεν	-αιεν	-οιεν	-ειεν
IMPT.	-ε		-ον	-ε	-θι	-ε	-ηθι
	-ετε		-ατε	-ετε	-τε	-ετε	-ητε
INF.	-ειν	-ειν	-αι	-(ε)ειν	-ναι	-εναι	-ηναι
	-(ε)μεν	-(ε)μεν		-(ε)μεν		-εμεν(αι)	-ημεναι
	-(ε)μεναι	-(ε)μεναι		-(ε)μεναι			
PTC.					β-　　γν-*	-ως	-εις
	-ων	-ων	-ας	-ων	-ας　-ους	-υια	-εισα
	-ουσα	-ουσα	-ασα	-ουσα	-ασα　-ουσα	-ος	-εν
	-ον	-ον	-αν	-ον	-αν　-ον		

*Incorporating the stem vowel (See Lesson 43)

Note: the Subj. 3 sg. ending is sometimes -ῃσι, the 2 sg. sometimes -ῃσθα.

VERB ENDINGS: MIDDLE AND PASSIVE

PRES. SYSTEM λυ-	FUT. SYSTEM λυσ-	1 AOR. SYSTEM λυσ-	2 AOR. SYSTEM ιδ-	PF. M-P SYSTEM λελυ-
IND.				
-ομαι	-ομαι			-μαι
-εαι	-εαι			-σαι
-εται	-εται			-ται
-ομεθα	-ομεθα			-μεθα
-εσθε	-εσθε			-σθε
-ονται	-ονται			-αται/νται
(impf.)				(plpf.)
-ομην		-αμην	-ομην	-μην
-εο		-αο	-εο	-σο
-ετο		-ατο	-ετο	-το
-ομεθα		-αμεθα	-ομεθα	-μεθα
-εσθε		-ασθε	-εσθε	-σθε
-οντο		-αντο	-οντο	-ατο/ντο
SUBJ.				
-ωμαι		-ωμαι	-ωμαι	
-ηαι		-ηαι	-ηαι	
-ηται		-ηται	-ηται	
-ωμεθα		-ωμεθα	-ωμεθα	
-ησθε		-ησθε	-ησθε	
-ωνται		-ωνται	-ωνται	
OPT.				
-οιμην		-αιμην	-οιμην	
-οιο		-αιο	-οιο	
-οιτο		-αιτο	-οιτο	
-οιμεθα		-αιμεθα	-οιμεθα	
-οισθε		-αισθε	-οισθε	
-οιατο /οιντο		-αιατο /-αιντο	-οιατο /-οιντο	
IMPT.				
-εο/ -ευ		-αι	-εο/ευ	-σο
-εσθε		-ασθε	-εσθε	-σθε
INF.				
-εσθαι	-εσθαι	-ασθαι	-εσθαι	-σθαι
PTC.				
-ομενος	-ομενος	-αμενος	-ομενος	-μενος
-η	-η	-η	-η	-η
-ον	-ον	-ον	-ον	-ον

Notes:

1. In the 1 pl., -μεσθα may be used for -μεθα.
2. The Subj. 2 sg. -ηαι may contract to -ῃ.

SPECIAL VERB FORMS

εἰμί *I am*		οἶδα *I know*	
IND. PRES.		[PF. ENDINGS]	
εἰμί	εἰμέν	οἶδα	ἴδμεν
ἐσσί/εἶς	ἐστέ	οἶσθα	ἴστε
ἐστί(ν)	εἰσί(ν)	οἶδε	ἴσασι
IND. IMPF.		[PLPF. ENDINGS]	
ἦα	ἦμεν	ἤδεα	ἴδμεν
ἦσθα	ἦτε	ἤδης	ἴστε
ἦεν/ἦν/ἔην	ἦσαν/ἔσαν	ἤδη	ἴσαν
IND. FUT.			
ἔσ(σομαι	ἐσ(σ)ομεθα	εἰδήσω, etc.	
ἔσ(σ)εαι	ἔσ(σ)εσθε		
ἔσ(σ)εται/ἔσται	ἔσ(σ)ονται		
SUBJ. PRES.		[PF. ENDINGS]	
ὦ	ὦμεν	[εἰδῶ	εἴδομεν
ᾖς	ἦτε	εἰδῇς	εἴδετε
ᾖ	ὦσι(ν)	εἰδῇ	εἰδῶσι]
OPT. PRES.			
εἴην	εἶμεν	[εἰδείην	εἰδεῖμεν
εἴης	εἶτε	εἰδείης	εἰδεῖτε
εἴη	εἶεν	εἰδείη	εἰδεῖεν]
IMPT. PRES.			
[ἴσθι	ἔστε]	ἴσθι	ἴστε
INF. PRES.			
εἶναι/ ἔμμεν(αι)		ἴδμεν(αι)	
INF. FUT.			
ἔσεσθαι		[εἰδησέμεν]	
PTC. PRES.			
ἐών, ἐοῦσα, ἐόν		εἰδώς, -υῖα, -ός	
PTC. FUT.			
ἐσόμενος, -η, -ον			

-μι VERBS: FORMS USED IN THIS TEXT (for more complete paradigms, see Lesson 65.)

	ἵημι I send forth	δίδωμι I give		τίθημι I put	
IND. PRES.				--	--
				[τίθησθα]	--
				--	--
IND. IMPF.	ἵειν/ ἵην	--		--	--
	ἵεις	--		--	--
	ἵει	--		τίθει	--
2 AOR. IND.		--	--	--	--
		--	--	--	--
		--	[δόσαν]	--	θέσαν
SUBJ. 2 AOR.		[δῶ]	--		
		--	--		
		δώῃ	--		
OPT. 2 AOR.		δοίην	δοῖμεν	θείην	θεῖμεν
		δοίης	δοῖτε	θείης	θεῖτε
		δοίη	δοῖεν	θείη	θεῖεν
IMPT. 2 AOR.		δός	δότε		
PTC. 2 AOR. MID.				[θέμενος, -η, -ον]	

φημί I speak				
IND. IMPF. ACT.			**MID.**	
φῆν	φάμεν		φάμην	φάμεθα
φῆς(θα)	φάτε		φάο	φάσθε
φῆ	φάσαν/φάν		φάτο	φάντο

A Reading Course in Homeric Greek

PRONOUNS

I.	Relative	ὅς (ὁ), ἥ, ὅ (τό)	*who, which, that*
	Intensive	αὐτός, -ή, -ό	*who, which, that*
	Demonstrative	(ἐ)κεῖνος, -η, -ο	*that (one)*
		ὁ, ἡ, τό	*that (one), the*
		ὅδε, ἥδε, τόδε	*this (one)*

For complete paradigms, see Lessons 14 and 15.

Paradigm of ὁ, ἡ, τό   *that (one), the*

ὁ	ἡ	τό
τοῦ, τοῖο	τῆς	τοῦ, τοῖο
τῷ	τῇ	τῷ
τόν	τήν	τό
οἱ (τοί)	αἱ (ταί)	τά
τῶν	τάων	τῶν
τοῖσι, τοῖς	τῇσι, τῇς	τοῖσι, τοῖς
τούς	τάς	τά

Use: 1. Demonstrative when modifying a noun.
2. Relative when following a definite antecedent.
3. Third person personal pronoun when standing in place of a noun already mentioned.

II.	Interrogative	τίς, τί	*who? which? what?*
	Indefinite	τις, τι	*some(one), some(thing), any, a certain*

Paradigms

τίς	τί	τις	τι
τεῦ	τεῦ	τευ	τευ
τῷ, τέῳ	τῷ, τέῳ	τῳ, τεῳ	τῳ, τεῳ
τίνα	τί	τινα	τι
τίνες	τίνα	τινες	τινα
τέων	τέων	τεων	τεων
τέοισι	τέοισι	τεοισι	τεοισι
τίνας	τίνα	τινες	τινα

Notes:

1. For the use of the indefinite and interrogative pronouns and adjectives, see Lesson 31.

2. For the declension of the indefinite relative and the indirect interrogative pronouns/adjectives, see Lesson 31.

III. Personal

Paradigms

1st person *I*		2nd person *you*		3rd person *he, she, it*	
ἐγώ(ν)	ἡμεῖς/ἄμμες	σύ	ὑμεῖς	--	--
μευ /ἐμεῖο	ἡμέων	σεῦ/σεῖο	ὑμέων	ἕο	σφεων
ἐμοί, μοι	ἡμῖν/ἄμμιν	σοί/τοι	ὑμῖν	οἱ	σφί(ν)/σφισι
ἐμέ/με	ἡμέας/ἄμμε	σέ	ὑμέας	μιν/ἑ	σφεας

For use of the personal pronouns and more complete paradigms, see Lessons 32, 33, and 34.

PREPOSITIONS

	+ Genitive	+ Dative	+ Accusative
ἄγχι	near ἄγχι Τροίης		
ἅμα		at same time ἅμα νυκτί together with ἅμα ἑταίροις	
ἀμφί		on both sides ἀμφὶ οἴκῳ around ἀμφὶ νηῷ concerning ἀμφὶ δώροις	on both sides ἀμφὶ οἴκον around ἀμφὶ νηόν concerning ἀμφὶ δῶρα
ἀνά	on(to) ἀνὰ νεῶν	on [at rest] ἀνὰ νηί	on(to) ἀνὰ νῆα over ἀνὰ γαῖαν
ἀπάνευθε	away from ἀπάνευθε οἴκου apart from ἀπάνευθε πόνου far from ἀπάνευθε φίλων		
ἀπό	away from ἀπὸ πέτρης from ἀπὸ ψυχῆς		
διά	through διὰ πυρός		through διὰ πῦρ among [motion] διὰ ἑταίρους on account of διὰ χρυσόν
ἐγγύς	near ἐγγὺς θαλάσσης		
εἵνεκα	on account of εἵνεκα πολέμου for the sake of εἵνεκα σεῦ		
εἰς			into εἰς γαῖαν to εἰς θάλασσαν
ἐκ, ἐξ	out of ἐκ πέτρης from ἐξ ἀρχῆς		
ἐν		in ἐν ψυχῇ on ἐν πέτρῃσι among ἐν φίλοις	
ἐπί	upon ἐπὶ πέτρης	on ἐπὶ πέτρῃ at, beside ἐπὶ θαλάσσῃ	to(wards) ἐπὶ πέτρας after [in search] ἐπὶ δόξαν
κατά	down from κατὰ πέτρης		down (along) κατὰ ποταμόν according to κατὰ δίκην throughout κατὰ γαῖαν
μετά		among μετὰ δενδρέοισι with μετὰ ἀγάπῃ	into the midst μετὰ ξείνους after μετὰ πόλεμον
παρά	from παρὰ φίλων	at, beside παρὰ ποταμῷ	to παρὰ θάλασσαν along(side) παρὰ ποταμόν
περί	about περὶ βουλῆς excelling περὶ πάντων	about περὶ σώματι for περὶ δώροις	about περὶ σῶμα for περὶ δῶρα
πρός	from πρὸς ἄνακτος	on πρὸς γαίῃ at πρὸς θαλάσσῃ	to(ward) πρὸς θάλασσαν
σύν		with σὺν σοφοῖσι	
ὑπέρ	over ὑπὲρ θύρης		over ὑπὲρ πόντον
ὑπό	from under ὑπὸ πέτρης by [agent] ὑπὸ ψυχῆς	under [at rest] ὑπὸ πέτρῃ	under [motion to] ὑπὸ πέτρην

Position of preposition:

1. Ordinarily, before its object or object's modifier (πρός με, σὺν πολλοῖς ἑταίροις)
2. For poetic purposes, after its object, or between modifier and object (χειρὸς ἄπο, πολλοῖς σὺν ἑταίροις)
3. In compound words, directly joined (προσφέρω)
4. As adverb (ἀμφὶ ῥα πάντες ἔστησαν).

VARIA

NU MOVABLE

ν may be added before a vowel, at end at end of a sentence, occasionally before a consonant, to the final -σι of the 3rd pl. or dat. pl. and to the final -ε of the 3rd. sg.; also in a few other words ending in -σι or -ε.

ELISION

For easier pronunciation, a short final vowel (except υ), and sometimes a final -αι or -οι may drop out before an initial vowel or diphthong and in compounds (ἀπ' ἀρχῆς, πάρ-ην).

Elision does not occur in the dat. pl. of the 3rd decl., or in περί, πρό, ὅτι, τι, or in words which take ν movable.

When elision brings π, τ, or κ before a rough breathing, they change to φ, θ, χ (ἀφ-αιρέω).

DISTINCTION OF οὐ and μή

οὐ negates statements of concrete fact, μή statements of possibility, condition, general, wish, suppositions.

ADVERBS

Formation

1. By adding -ως to neuter stem (καλ-ῶς, ταχέ-ως)
2. Simple n. acc., sg. or pl. (πρῶτον)
3. Special (νῦν, τότε etc.)
4. Prepositions used adverbially

Comparison

1. n. acc. sg. of the comp. adj. (θᾶσσον)
2. n. acc. pl. of the supl. adj. (τάχιστα)

DEPONENT VERBS

Have mid. or pass. endings only, but w. active force (μάχομαι)

The mid. of deponent and of many act. verbs often is intransitive (τρέπομαι I turn).

-μι VERBS

Irregular only in pres. and 2 aor. systems, where they lack the thematic vowel and have some special endings.

Subj. mid. retains the usual long thematic vowel, which absorbs the final α or ε of the stem and contracts with final ο to ω.

AUGMENT IN PAST INDICATIVE

1. Stems beginning w. consonant(s) prefix ἐ (e.g., aor. λύσα becomes ἔλυσα). Initial ρ often doubles (ἔρρεε).
2. Stems beginning w. a short vowel or a diphthong that is not the reduplication lengthen the initial vowel (e.g., οἴκεον becomes ᾤκεον). Initial ε lengthens to η usually; but ε lengthens to ει in the following verbs: ἔχω, ἐάω, ἕπομαι, ἕλκω, ἕρπω, ἑρπύζω, ἕλον.
3. Stems beginning w. a long vowel (e.g., ἠσάμην) or a vowel-reduplication (e.g., ἔγνωσμαι) take no augment.

CONSONANT CHANGES

In dat. pl. :

$$κ, γ, χ + σ = ξ$$

$$π, β, φ + σ = ψ$$

τ, δ, θ, ν drop before σ (When both ντ drop, the preceding ε lengthens to ει, ο lengthens to ου.)

In pf. mid. of consonant stems, principal part ending in

μ + σ = ψ	γ + σ = ξ	σ + σ = σ
μ + τ = πτ	γ + τ = κτ	σ + τ = στ
μ + σθ = φθ	γ + σθ = χθ	σ + σθ = σθ
μ + ντ = φατ	γ + ντ = χατ	σ + ντ = θατ

VOWEL CONTRACTIONS

1. αε becomes α. αει becomes ᾳ
2. αο, αω, αου become ω
3. εε, εει become ει
4. εο, εου become ευ/ου
5. οε, οο become ου.

REDUPLICATION IN PF. STEM

1. Stems beginning w. single consonant prefix initial consonant and ε (e.g., λυ- becomes λέλυκ-).
2. Stems beginning w. two consonants simply prefix ε (e.g., στέλλ- becomes ἔσταλκ-).
3. Stems beginning w. short vowel or w. diphthong lengthen initial vowel (e.g., ἁμαρτάν- becomes ἡμάρτηκ-; αἱρέ- becomes ᾕρηκ-).
4. Stems beginning w. mute plus liquid (π, β, φ, κ, γ, χ, τ, δ, θ plus λ, μ, ν or ρ) prefix the mute with ε (e.g., γράφ- becomes γέ-γραφ-).
   a. but initial γν follows rule 2, above.
   b. Initial φ, χ, θ become π, κ, τ in reduplicating (e.g., φιλε- becomes πε-φίληκ-).
5. Some reduplications are irregular.

SYNTAX OF THE NOUN

1. NOMINATIVE: case of subject of a finite verb.
2. GENITIVE: possession, partitive (whole), contents, material, separation; w. certain verbs, adjectives, prepositions.
3. DATIVE: indirect object, reference, possession; instrumental (means, manner); locative (where, when); w. certain verbs, adjectives, prepositions.
4. ACCUSATIVE: case of object of action, motion, thought (direct object, place to which, subject of infinitive in indirect discourse, w. certain prepositions). Special uses: a) cognate, governed by intransitive verb of related meaning, e.g., μακρὴν ὁδὸν ἤλθομεν. *We came a long journey.* b) specification, specifying in what respect the idea contained in an accompanying word is true, e.g., νόον ἐσθλός *Noble in mind.*
5. VOCATIVE: case of direct address.

SYNTAX OF THE VERB BY MOODS

1. INDICATIVE (tenses indicate time, as well as aspect of action):

   a. Statements of fact: past, present, future time; simple, continuous, completed aspect. Negative οὐ.

      ἔρχεται. *He comes. (He is coming.)*
      ἔρχετο. *He was coming.*
      ἦλθεν. *He came.*
      ἑώραται. *He has been seen.*
      οὐ λέξω. *I shall not say.*

   b. Past and present contrary-to-fact: impf. or aor. ind. in both clauses, ἄν or κε(ν) in conclusion (apodosis). Negative μή in if- clause (protasis), οὐ in conclusion (apodosis).

      εἰ μὴ τόδε πίνεν, οὐκ ἂν θάνεν.
      If he had not drunk this, he would not have died.

2. SUBJUNCTIVE (tenses indicate aspect, not time):

   a. Hortatory: requested or proposed actions referring to the speaker himself; in first person, sg. or pl. Negative μή.

      μή τῇδε μένωμεν, ἑταῖροι, ἀλλὰ φύγωμεν.
      Let us not remain here, comrades, but let us flee.

   b. Present purpose: to express intended action, after primary main verb; introduced by ἵνα, ὡς, ὅπως, ὄφρα. Negative ἵνα μή, sometimes μή alone.

      πεύθομαι ἵνα γιγώνσκωμεν.
      I inquire in order that we may know.

      πεύθομαι ὄφρα μὴ νήπιος ὦ.
      I inquire in order that I may not be foolish.

   c. Vivid future (future general) construction: to express a probable future supposition; often with ἄν or κε(ν). Negative μή.

      εἰ (κεν) ἔλθῃ, δέξομαί μιν πρόφρων.
      If he comes, I shall receive him eagerly.

   d. Present general: to indicate repeated occurrence in the present; may take ἄν or κε(ν). Negative μή.

      ὅτε (ἄν) βούληται, ἐπὶ θάλασσαν ἔρχεται.
      Whenever he wishes, he goes to the sea.

      N.B. The main verb is regularly pres. ind., negative οὐ.

3. OPTATIVE (tenses indicate aspect, not time):

   a. Wishes: to express possible and impossible wishes (often equivalent to a polite imperative); may be introduced by εἰ, εἴθε, εἰ γάρ ("if only," "would that"), especially if an impossible wish.

      πολλά γε μανθάνοιμι.
      At least, may I learn many things!

      εἴθε μὴ χαλεπὸν εἴη.
      If only it were not difficult!

   b. Past purpose: to express intended action after secondary main verb; introduced by ἵνα, ὡς, ὅπως, ὄφρα. Negative ἵνα μή, sometimes μή alone.

      θάνε αὐτὸς ὄφρα σώζοι ἡμέας.
      He himself died in order to save us.

      θάνε αὐτὸς ἵνα μὴ ἀπολοίμεθα.
      He himself died in order that we might not perish.

c. Future contrary to fact (should-would) construction: to indicate a less likely future supposition and its assumed consequence; both clauses may take ἄν or κε(ν). Negative of supposition (protasis) is μή, of conclusion (apodosis) is οὐ.

N.B. The apodosis may sometimes be more definite, using an impt. or hortatory subj.

d. Potential: to express an opinion as to what might, could, or would happen if certain unstated circumstances should prevail; usually takes ἄν or κε(ν). Negative οὐ. (This construction is equal to the apodosis of a should-would construction.)

> μὴ βῆτε· κτείνειε γάρ κεν ὑμέας πάντας.
> *Do not go, for he might kill all of you!*

e. Expectation: a potential optative with special force, indicating what one desires or expects to happen under assumed circumstances, and equivalent to English "can, will" rather than "could, would, might." Same rule as potential optative.

> εὕρωμέν τινα ὃς ἂν ἡμῖν ὁδὸν φαίνοι.
> *Let's find someone who can show us the way.*

f. Past general: to indicate repeated occurrence in the past. Negative μή.

> ὅτε βούλοιτο, ἐπὶ θάλασσαν ἔρχετο.
> *Whenever he wished, he came to the sea.*

N.B. The main verb is ordinarily impf. ind., rarely aor.; negative οὐ.

g. Indirect questions: the verb within a question depending on a secondary main verb of asking, knowing, etc., ordinarily shifts from the ind. (or subj.) of the direct question into the corresponding tense of the opt., though it may stay unchanged. Negative as in direct question form.

> ἔρετο τίς ἡμέας πέμψειεν (πέμψεν).
> *She asked who sent us.*

4. IMPERATIVE (tenses indicate aspect, not time):

a. Commands: to express what one desires or orders another to do. Negative μή.

> μὴ εὕδετε· μανθάνειν γε πειράετε.
> *Don't sleep; at least try to learn!*

5. INFINITIVE (tenses indicate aspect, except in indirect discourse, where time is indicated):

a. Complementary: after certain verbs (wishing, planning, attempting, etc.) to complete the sense. Negative μή.

> σοφοὶ μανθάνειν πειράουσιν.
> *The wise attempt to learn.*

b. Explanatory: to explain the sense of another word and fill out its meaning. Negative μή.

> χαλεπὸν μὲν ἔρδειν, αἰσχρὸν δὲ μὴ ἔρξαι.
> *To act is indeed difficult, but not to act is shameful.*

c. Purpose: to explain why an action is done; usually follows a verb meaning "send." Negative μή.

> πέμψε σφέας ὕδωρ ζητέειν.
> *She sent them to seek water.*

d. As noun: subject or object of another verb. Negative μή.

> φαγέμεναι καὶ ἀνάγκη ἐστὶ καὶ ἡδονή.
> *Eating (to eat) is both a necessity and a pleasure.*

e. As imperative: to express command. Negative μή.

> τὰ γιγνῶσκεις, λέγειν.
> *Say what you know!*

f. Indirect discourse: to express an action depending on a main verb of saying, thinking, perceiving, etc. Subject is in accusative case; tenses are in relation to the main verb (pres. inf. for action contemporaneous with main verb; aor. inf. for action prior to main verb; future for action subsequent to main verb). Negative οὐ.

> ἔφη πατέρα ἑὸν χρήματα ποτε σχέθειν πολλά, νῦν δὲ οὐκ ἔχειν οὐδὲ αἶψα σχήσειν.
>
> *He said that his father once had many possessions, but that he did not now have nor would quickly have many.*

6. PARTICIPLE (tenses indicate time):

a. Circumstantial: to indicate cause, condition, manner, or circumstances attending the action of the main verb. Negative οὐ if fact, otherwise μή.

> εὕδων ἐπὶ γαῖαν πέσε καὶ ἀπόλετο.
> *While sleeping, he fell to the ground and was killed.*

b. Adjectival: modifying a noun or pronoun. Negative οὐ.

> τὸν μὲν φεύγοντα ὁράω, ἄνακτα δὲ διώκοντα.
> *I see that man fleeing, but I seeing the king in pursuit (pursuing).*

SYNTAX OF THE VERB BY CONSTRUCTIONS

1. CIRCUMSTANTIAL: ptc. indicates the circumstances under which the main action takes place. Negative οὐ if fact, otherwise μή.

> μαχεόμενος θάνεν.
> *While fighting, he died.*

2. COMMANDS: expressed by impt., inf., opt. when less forceful. Negative μή.

> τὰ γιγνῶσκεις, λέγε (λέγεις, λέγοις).
> *Say what you know!*

3. CONTRARY-TO-FACT IN PAST: impf. or aor. ind. in both clauses, ἄν or κε(ν) in conclusion (apodosis). Negative μή in if- clause (protasis), οὐ in conclusion (apodosis).

> εἰ μὴ τόδε πίνεν, οὐκ ἂν θάνεν.
> *If he had not drunk this, he would not have died.*

4. EXPECTATION: indicating what one desires or expects to happen under assumed circumstances, and equivalent to English "can, will" rather than "could, would, might." Optative, usually with ἄν or κε(ν). Negative οὐ.

> εὕρωμέν τινα ὃς ἂν ἡμῖν ὁδὸν φαίνοι.
> *Let's find someone who can show us the way.*

5. EXPLANATORY: inf. explaining sense of another word. Negative μή. Also, by ἐπεί or ὅτι with ind. Negative οὐ.

> χαλεπὸν νοῆσαι.
> *It is difficult to perceive (To perceive is difficult.)*

> ὅτι σε φιλῶ, ἤλυθον.
> *Because I love you, I came.*

6. FACT: ind. and proper tense to indicate both time and aspect of action. Negative οὐ.

   ἔρχεται.
   He comes. (He is coming.)

   ἔρχετο.
   He was coming.

   ἦλθεν.
   He came.

   οὐ λέξω.
   I shall not say.

7. FUTURE SUPPOSITIONS

   a. Vivid future (future general) construction: to express a probable future supposition; subj., often with ἄν or κε(ν). Main verb in fut. ind. or impt. Negative of subj. and impt. is μή, of ind. οὐ.

      εἴ κεν ἔλθῃ. δέξομαί μιν.
      If he comes, I shall receive him.

      εἰ δὲ μὴ χρυσὸν ἔχῃ, πόρε οἱ σύ.
      If, however, he has no gold, give him (some gold).

   b. Future contrary to fact (should-would) construction: to indicate a less likely future supposition and its assumed consequence; optative in both supposition (protasis) and conclusion (apodosis), and both clauses may take ἄν or κε(ν). Negative of protasis is μή, of apodosis is οὐ.

      εἰ μὴ ἔλθοις, οὐκ ἄν ἐθέλοιμι ἔρχεσθαι αὐτός.
      If you should not go, I would not wish to go myself.

8. GENERAL (repeated occurrence)

   a. Present: subj., may take ἄν or κε(ν). Negative μή. Main verb is regularly pres. ind., negative οὐ.

      ὅτε ἄν βούληται, ἐπὶ θάλασσαν ἔρχεται.
      Whenever she wishes, she goes to the sea.

   b. Past: opt. Negative μή. Main verb is ordinarily impf. ind. rarely aor.; negative οὐ.

      ὅτε βούλοιτο, ἐπὶ θάλασσαν ἔρχετο.
      Whenever she wished, she went (would go) to the sea.

9. HORTATORY: subj., first person (sg. or pl.) only. Negative μή.

   μὴ τῇδε μένωμεν, ἑταῖροι, ἀλλὰ φύγωμεν.
   Let us not remain here, comrades, but let us flee.

10. INDIRECT DISCOURSE: after a main verb of saying, thinking, perceiving, etc. Verb is inf., with subject in acc. case; tenses are in relation to the main verb (pres. inf. for action contemporaneous with main verb; aor. inf. for action prior to main verb; future for action subsequent to main verb). Negative οὐ.

    ἔφη σφέας δέξασθαι τάδε δῶρα ἀπὸ ἄνακτος.
    He said that they had received these gifts from the king.

A Reading Course in Homeric Greek

11. INDIRECT QUESTIONS: after primary tense main verb of asking, wondering, etc., the verb within the subordinate clause (the question itself) remains unchanged in mood.; however, the verb within a question depending on a secondary main verb ordinarily shifts from the ind. (or subj.) of the direct question into the corresponding tense of the opt., though it may stay unchanged. Negative as in direct question form.

εἴρεται τίς ἡμέας πέμψεν.
He asks who sent us.

ἔρετο τίς ἡμέας πέμψειεν (πέμψεν).
He asked who sent us.

12. POTENTIAL: to express an opinion as to what might, could, or would happen if certain unstated circumstances should prevail; usually takes ἄν or κε(ν). Negative οὐ. (This construction is equal to the apodosis of a should-would construction.)

μὴ βῆτε· κτείνειε γάρ κεν ὑμέας πάντας.
Don't go, for he might kill you all!

13. PURPOSE (introduced by ἵνα, ὡς, ὅπως, ὄφρα. Negative ἵνα μή, sometimes μή alone)

a. Present purpose: to express intended action, after primary main verb; verb in subj., introduced by ἵνα, ὡς, ὅπως, ὄφρα. Negative ἵνα μή, sometimes μή alone.

πεύθομαι ἵνα γιγνώσκωμεν.
I inquire in order that we may know.

πεύθομαι ὄφρα μὴ νήπιος ὦ.
I inquire in order that I may not be foolish.

b. Past purpose: to express intended action after secondary main verb; verb in opt., introduced by ἵνα, ὡς, ὅπως, ὄφρα. Negative ἵνα μή, sometimes μή alone.

θάνε αὐτὸς ὄφρα σώζοι ἡμέας.
He himself died in order to save us.

θάνε αὐτὸς ἵνα μὴ ἀπολοίμεθα.
He himself died in order that we might not perish.

14. SHOULD-WOULD: see above, 7b.

15. WISHES, both possible and impossible of fulfillment: opt.; may be introduced by εἰ, εἴθε, εἰ: γάρ ("if only," "would that"), especially if an impossible wish.

πολλά γε μανθάνοιμι.
At least, may I learn many things!

εἴθε μὴ χαλεπὸν εἴη.
If only it were not difficult!

Appendix B

Appendix B (Vocabulary by Lesson)

19. (Lesson 6)

ἀπό	[prep. + gen.] away from, from
γὰρ	[conj.; never first word] for
ἐκ	(ἐξ before vowels) [prep. + gen.] out of
ἐν	[prep. + dat.] in, on, among
ἐπί	[prep. + gen.] upon [prep. +dat.] on, at, beside [prep. + acc.] to, towards; after [in search or attack]
καί	[conj.] and; even, also
σύν	[prep. + dat.] with
ὑπό	[prep. + gen.] from under; under the influence of, = by [personal or impersonal agent] [prep. + dat.] under [at rest] [prep. + acc.] under [motion to]

25. (Lesson 7)

ἀληθείη, -ης	[f.] truth
ἀρετή, -ῆς	[f.] manliness, virtue
βίη, -ης	[f.] force
δίκη, -ης	[f.] justice; custom
εἰρήνη, -ης	[f.] peace
καλή, -ῆς	[f. adj.] beautiful, noble
πέτρη, -ης	[f.] rock
ψυχή, -ῆς	[f.] soul; life

31. (Lesson 8)

ἀλλά	[conj.] but
γαῖα. -ης	[f.] earth, land
δόξα, -ης	[f.] opinion; glory
ἡδεῖα, -ης	[f. adj.] sweet, pleasant
θάλασσα, -ης	[f.] sea
μὲν…δὲ	[correlative particles marking contrast] indeed…but; on the one hand…on the other; δέ [alone] but, however; and
οὐ	[οὐκ before smooth breathing, οὐχ before rough breathing] not, no
οὔτε	and not, nor [following a negative clause]
οὔτε…οὔτε	neither…nor

36. (Lesson 9)

ἀγαθή, -ῆς	[f. adj.] good, brave
αἰεί	[adv.] ever, always, forever
ἀνάγκη, -ης	[f.] necessity, need
ἀρχή, -ῆς	[f.] beginning

δή	[adv.] clearly, indeed
νῦν	[adv.] now, at the present time
οὔτως	[adv.] thus, in this way, so
φωνή, -ῆς	[f.] voice, sound

42. (Lesson 10)

αἶψα	[adv.] quickly, suddenly
εἰ	[conj.] if
εἰς	[prep. + acc.] into, to
κατά	[prep. + gen.] down from [prep. + acc.] down (along); throughout; according to
λέγω	I say, I tell; I call
πότε	ever, (at) some time, once
πρός	[prep. + gen.] from [prep. + dat.] on, at [prep. + acc.] to, towards
φίλη, -ης	[f. adj.] dear (to), friendly (to) [+ dat.]

47. (Lesson 11)

ἄνθρωπος, -ου	[m.] man, human being
θεός, -οῦ	[m., f.] god, goddess
ἰητρός, -οῦ	[m.] physician
λόγος, -ου	[m.] word; account
μοῦνος, -η, -ον	alone, only
νήπιος, -η, -ον	simple; foolish
σοφός, -ή, -όν	wise
ὑψηλός, -ή, -όν	high
φίλος, -ου	[m. adj. as noun] friend

54. (Lesson 12)

βίος, -ου	[m.] life
δένδρεον, -ου	[n.] tree
δίκαιος, -η, -ον	just, honorable
εἵνεκα	[prep. +. gen.] on account of, for the sake of
θάνατος, -ου	[m.] death
κακός, -ή, -όν	cowardly, bad, evil
ὁμοῖος, -η, -ον	like to, similar to
π(τ)όλεμος, -ου	[m.] war
χρυσός, -οῦ	[m.] gold

62. (Lesson 13)

δῶρον, -ου	[n.] gift
ἔργον, -ου	[n.] work, deed
ἐσθλός, -ή, -όν	noble, excellent
θυμός, -οῦ	[m.] heart, spirit
ξεῖνος, -ου	[m.] guest, stranger

ὀλίγος, -η, -ον	small, few
σχέτλιος, -η, -ον	cruel, pitiless; reckless
τέ	[postpositive conj.] and τέ...τέ both...and; τέ...καί both...and

71. (Lesson 14)

ἐγγύς	[adv.; prep. + gen.] near
ἕτερος, -η, -ον	(the) other
ἡμέτερος, -η, -ον	our
καρπός, -οῦ	[m.] fruit
ὀφθαλμός, -οῦ	[m.] eye
πολλός, -ή, -όν	much; many
πόνος, -ου	[m.] toil, trouble
ποταμός, -οῦ	[m.] river

79. (Lesson 15)

βροτός, -ή, -όν	mortal, human
ἑός, -ή, -όν	own; his, her
θησαυρός, -οῦ	[m.] treasure
θνητός, -ή, -όν	mortal
κρατερός, -ή, -όν	strong
νόος, -ου	[m.] mind
νοῦσος, -ου	[f.] disease
πονηρός, -ή, -όν	worthless, base, wicked
χαλεπός, -ή, -όν	difficult

85. (Lesson 16)

αἰσχρός, -ή, -όν	shameful
γιγνώσκω	I know
λίθος, -ου	[m.] stone
λύω	I loose, I release
ὄλβος, -ου	[m.] happiness, prosperity
ὁράω	I see, I look at
ῥηίδιος, -η, -ον	easy
χρόνος, -ου	[m.] time

92. (Lesson 17)

ἄγω	I lead
εὕδω	I sleep
θνήσκω	I die
μανθάνω	I learn
μή	not; μηδέ and not, nor, not even
φέρω	I bear, I bring
φιλέω	I love
ὡς	[adv. and conj.] as, that, how

99. (Lesson 18)

ἐννέπω	I say, I tell
ἐπεί	[conj.] when; since
ἔχω	I have, I hold
ἵνα	[adv.] where; [conj.] that, in order that, to
κεύθω	I hide
ὅπως	[conj.] that, in order that, to
ὅτι	[conj.] that; because
ὄφρα	[conj.] that, in order that, to

παρ-έχω	I supply
ῥέζω	I do

107. (Lesson 19)

ἀδικέω	I (do) wrong, I injure
διώκω	I pursue
ἐσθίω	I eat
ἱκάνω	[pres. syst. only] I come
κελεύω	I command [+ acc., dat., inf.]
ποιέω	I make, I produce, I do
φοιτάω	I roam (back and forth)

115. (Lesson 20)

ἐθέλω	I wish
ζώω	I live
ἠδέ	[conj.] and
νοέω	I think, I perceive
νομίζω	I consider, I think, I believe
παρά	[prep. + gen.] from; [prep. + dat.] at, beside; [prep. + acc.]to, along
φεύγω	I flee, I escape

124. (Lesson 21)

ἀθάνατος, -η, -ον	immortal, eternal
ἁμαρτάνω	I fail of, I miss, I err [often + gen.]
διδάσκω	I teach
δίς	[adv.] twice, a second time
δοκέω	I seem, I appear
ὄμβρος, -ου	[m.] rain, storm
οὐδέ	and not, nor, not even
παντοῖος, -η, -ον	of all sorts
πάρ-ειμι	I am present
πίπτω	I fall
που	[indef. adv.] perhaps, suppose,of course, no doubt
ποῦ	[interr. adv., always with circumflex] where?
σπεύδω	I hasten
τρέφω	I nourish, I feed, I rear
φρονέω	I consider, I have understanding

133. (Lesson 22)

ἀέξω	I increase; [in mid.]: I increase (myself), I grow
αἰτέω	I ask, I request
ἥδομαι	I am pleased with [+ dat.]
λαμβάνω	I take, get
μάχομαι (μαχέομαι)	I fight (against)
μετά	[prep. + dat.] among, with [prep. + acc.] into the midst, after
οὖν	therefore, then [not of time!]
πλησίος, -η, -ον	near; neighbor
τρέπω	I turn

141. (Lesson 23)

ἀν-έχομαι	I hold up under, I endure
γίγνομαι	I am born, I become, I am, I happen
ἑταῖρος, -ου	[m.] companion, comrade
ἠέλιος, -ου	[m.] sun
μισέω	I hate
ὀρθός, -ή, -όν	straight, true
πίνω	I drink
ὦ	O! [in direct address]

149. (Lesson 24)

ἄπ-ειμι	I am away
αὐτάρ	but, yet
δυνατός, -ή, -όν	able, possible [+εἰμί and inf.] able (to)
μέλλω	I am about, I am going, I intend, I am destined (to) [+ inf.]
ὄφρα	(in order) that, to
πέλω	I come to be, I am
or deponent form: πέλομαι	
πέμπω	I send
σός, -ή, -όν	your [sg.]
τοί	surely, you see [postpositive]

157. (Lesson 25)

ἀμείβομαι	I (ex)change; I reply
γε	[enclitic particle] at least, in fact
δείδω	I fear [+ inf. or μή and purpose construction]
εἴρομαι	I ask
ἱερός, -ή, -όν	holy, sacred
νηός, -οῦ	[m.] temple
πεύθομαι	I learn (by inquiry), I inquire (from), I hear of [+ acc. of thing heard, + gen. of person heard]
πρῶτος, -η, -ον	first
σώζω	I save

165. (Lesson 26)

ἀπ-ολλύω	I kill, I destroy; I lose; [in pf. and mid.] I perish, I am lost
ἐμός, -ή, -όν	my, mine
ἔρχομαι	I come, I go
ζωή, -ῆς	[f.] life
κασιγνητός, -οῦ	[m.] brother
οὐρανός, -οῦ	[m.] heaven, sky
παρ-έρχομαι	I go past, I pass
πῶς	[interr. adv.] how?
πως	[enclitic adv.] somehow, in anyway
σῖτος, -ου	[m.] bread, food

175. (Lesson 27)

ἄναξ, ἄνακτος	[m.] king, lord
ἀνήρ, ἀνέρος or ἀνδρός	[m.] dat. pl. ἄνδρεσσι or ἄνδρασι man, male
γέρων, γέροντος	[m.] old man
ἕκαστος, -η, -ον	each
ἤ	or, than; ἤ...ἤ either...or, whether...or
μέτρον, -ου	[n.] measure
παῖς, παιδός	[m., f.] child, boy, girl
πατήρ, πατέρος or πατρός	[m.] father
περ	[enclitic particle] surely, by far [adds force]; [+ ptc.] though
πόλις, πόλιος or πόληος	[f.] city
φύσις, φύσιος	[f.] nature
φαίνω	I show, I reveal; in mid: φαίνομαι, φανέομαι. aor. pass. w. act. force: φάνην I show myself, I appear

182. (Lesson 28)

διά	[prep. + gen.] through [prep. + acc.] through; among, on account of
ἔπος, ἔπεος	[n.] word
κῆρ, κῆρος	[n.] heart
μῆκος, μήκεος	[n.] length
πρᾶγμα, πράγματος	[n.] deed; [in pl.] trouble, deeds
πῦρ, πυρός	[n.] fire
σῶμα, σώματος	[n.] body, corpse
τῇ	where [rel. adv.]; there
τῇδε	[adv.] here
φάος, φάεος	[n.] light
χρῆμα, χρήματος	[n.] possession, property; [in pl.] wealth

191. (Lesson 29)

αἱρέω	I seize; [in mid.] I pick for myself, I choose
ἀληθής, -ές	true
ἡδονή, -ῆς	[f.] pleasure
ἡδύς, ἡδεῖα, ἡδύ	sweet, pleasant
κρίνω	I pick out; I separate; I judge
μάκαρ, -αρος	happy, blessed
πρόφρων, -ον	willing, eager, ready
πτερόεις, -εσσα, -εν	winged
χρηστός, -ή, -όν	worthy, good

200. (Lesson 30)

ἀκούω	I hear
ἅπας, ἅπασα, ἅπαν	[m./ n. gen. ἅπαντος] all, the whole
εἷς, μία, ἕν	[m./n. gen. ἑνός] one
ἥμισυς, -(εια), -υ	half

μηδείς, μηδεμία, μηδέν	no one, none
οὐδείς, οὐδεμία, οὐδέν	no one, none
πατρίς, πατρίδος	[f.] fatherland, country; [as f. adj.] of one's fathers, ancestral
πᾶς, πᾶσα, πᾶν	[m./ n. gen. παντός] all, every, the whole
πειράω	I make trial of [+ gen.]; I attempt, I try [+ gen., or + inf.]

215. (Lesson 31)

ἄνεμος, -ου	[m.] wind
ἄρα, ῥα	[postpositive] therefore, then [not of time!]
ἔρδω	I do
ἔτι	[adv.] yet, still; οὐκ ἔτι no longer
νέκταρ, νέκταρος	[n.] nectar [the special drink of the gods]
πείθω	I persuade, I win over; [in mid.] I am persuaded by, I am obedient to, I obey [+ dat.]

222. (Lesson 32)

ἄλλος, -η, -ο	other, another, else
βούλομαι	I desire, I prefer
γλυκύς, -εῖα, -ύ	sweet, delightful
ἔνθεν	[adv.] from there; then [of time]
μίσγω	I mix (something, in acc.) with (something, in dat.), I mingle with
Μοῦσα, -ης	[f.] Muse, a goddess of poetry and art
ὕδωρ, ὕδατος	[n.] water
φρήν, φρενός	[f.] mind, spirit

229. (Lesson 33)

δέχομαι	I receive, I accept
εὑρίσκω	I find, I discover
εὐρύς, -εῖα, -ύ	wide, broad
λαός, -οῦ	[m.] people [a nation]; followers
ὁδός, -οῦ	[f.] way, road; journey
οἶνος, -ου	[m.] wine
πόθεν	[adv.] from what source? whence?

238. (Lesson 34)

γόνυ, γούνατος	[n.] knee
εἰσ-έρχομαι	I enter
ἐντολή, -ῆς	[f.] command, order
ζητέω	I seek, I search after
πύλη, -ης	[f.] gate, entrance
υἱός, -οῦ or υἱέος	[m.] son

248. (Lesson 35)

Ἀπόλλων, Ἀπόλλωνος	[m.] Apollo [the god]
δύω or δύο	[indecl.] two

ἐπήν	contraction of ἐπεὶ ἄν
ἤν	contraction of εἰ ἄν
μάλα	[adv.] very, quite, greatly
ὅτε	{adv. conj.} when, whenever
τεύχω	I build; I make ready. [pf. pass. often = I am]

256. (Lesson 36)

βουλεύω	I plan, I consider whether to or how to
βουλή, -ῆς	[f.] plan, advice, will
γαμέω	I marry
θέμις, θέμιστος	[f.] a right, custom; θέμις ἐστί it is right, lawful [+ acc. and inf.]
λανθάνω	I elude, I escape someone's notice, I deceive; [in mid.] I am forgetful of
πω	[+ neg.] [adv.] never yet, in no way, not at all

263. (Lesson 37)

βασιλείη, -ης	[f.] kingdom
ἐάω	I leave (alone); permit, allow (to do or be something) [+ inf.]
πάσχω	I suffer, I experience
πονέομαι	I labor, I toil at, I am busy about
χάρις, χάριτος	[f.] acc.sg. χάριν beauty, charm, grace

271. (Lesson 38)

ἀείρω	I lift up, I take up, I raise
ἦμαρ, ἤματος	[n.] day
μῆλον, -ου	[n.] sheep; flock
πιστεύω	I believe (in), I have faith in [+ dat.]
χαίρω	[aor. pass. w. act. force] I rejoice (in)
χρή	it is necessary

278. (Lesson 39)

ἄκρος, -η, -ον	top(most), outermost, extreme; [as n. noun] edge, tip
ἄλληλοι, -ων	[pl. only] one another, each other
ἅμα	[adv., or prep. + dat.] at the same time, together, with
ἔπειτα	[adv.] then, thereupon
κόσμος, -ου	[m.] world
μακρός, -ή, -όν	long, large [in space or time]

286. (Lesson 40)

αὐλή, -ῆς	[f.] courtyard, farmyard, fold
ἔλπω or ἔλπομαι	[pres. syst. only] I expect, I hope, I suppose [+ inf.]
εὔχομαι	I claim to be, I boast, I exult; I pray (to) [+ inf.]
ποιμήν, ποιμένος	[m.] shepherd

293. (Lesson 41)

ἀπάνευθε	[adv., and prep. + gen.] away (from), apart (from), afar
εἶπον	[2 aor. syst. only] I said, I told
περί	[adv.] round about; especially [prep. + gen.] about; excelling [prep. + dat. or acc.] about; for
πόρον	[2 aor. syst. only] I gave, I offered
τελέω	I fulfill, I accomplish, I complete

300. (Lesson 42)

βαίνω	I go
δύω	I enter
ῥέω	[present syst.] I flow
στῆν	[3 aor. syst. of ἵστημι I stand] I stood [intr.]
τλάω	I endure (something) patiently, I have the heart, I dare (to do something) [+ inf.]

307. (Lesson 43)

ἄλγος, ἄλγεος	[n.] pain, distress, woe
λείπω	I leave
ὀΐω or ὀΐομαι	I think, I suppose, I imagine
ποθέω	I long (to do something), I yearn (to do something) [+ inf.], I miss (a person or thing)

314. (Lesson 44)

βάλλω	I throw, I strike
εὖ	[adv.] well
μένω	I remain, I stay; I await
σάρξ, σαρκός	[f.] flesh

323. (Lesson 45)

ἀγάπη, -ης	[f.] love, charity
γυνή, γυναικός	[f.] woman, wife
δόλος, -ου	cunning, craftiness; trickery; bait for catching fish
ἔοικα	I seem, I am like to; it is fitting

331. (Lesson 46)

μέσ(σ)ος, -η, -ον	middle (of), midst (of) [followed by noun in same case]
οἶκος, -ου	[m.] house, home
πάλιν	[adv.] back (again); again
σφέτερος, -η, -ον	their(s)

340. (Lesson 47)

κεῖμαι	[pf. mid. syst.] I have been placed, I lie (down)
κρύπτω	I conceal
τότε	[adv.] then

347. (Lesson 48)

ἀμφί	[adv.; prep. + dat. or acc.] on both sides, around, concerning
κτείνω	I kill
μήτηρ, μητέρος or μητρός	[f.] mother
πατήρ, πατέρος or πατρός	[m.] father

356. (Lesson 49)

ἄφρων, -ον	senseless
δεύτερος, -η, -ον	second
Ζεύς, Διός or Ζηνός	Zeus [father and chief of the gods]

364. (Lesson 50)

δέκατος, -η, -ον	tenth
μέγας, μεγάλη, μέγα	great, large, big
νύξ, νυκτός	[f.] night
οἰκέω	I dwell, I inhabit

371. (Lesson 51)

ἅζομαι	[pres. syst. only] I respect, I revere; I hesitate to or shrink from [+ inf.]
μέλος, μέλεος	[n.] member (of the body), limb
χείρ, χε(ι)ρός	[f.] hand

379. (Lesson 52)

ἀνα-βαίνω	I go up, I ascend
κέρδιον	[comp. adv.] more beneficial, better
λιλαίομαι	[pres. syst. only] I long (to do something) [+ inf.]

387. (Lesson 53)

ἀλέομαι	I avoid, I shrink before
θύρη, -ης	[f.] door
κράτος, κράτεος	[n.] strength, power
νηῦς, νηός or νεός, dat. pl. νηυσί	[f.] ship
οὖλος, -η, -ον	whole, entire

436. (Lesson 61)

Τροίη, -ης	[f.] Troy, Ilion

441. (Lesson 62)

ἄστυ, ἄστεος	[n.] town
(ἐ)ρύομαι	I save, I rescue, I protect
νόστος, -ου	[m.] return (home)
πόντος, -ου	[m.] sea, the deep
ὥς, ὧς	[adv.] thus, so [always with pitch-mark]

448. (Lesson 63)

ἀφ-αιρέομαι	I take away
βοῦς, βοός	[m., f.] [dat. pl. also βουσί] ox, cow
θυγάτηρ, θυγατέρος or θυγατρός	[f.] daughter
νόστιμος, -η, -ον	of one's homecoming
ὄλλυμι	I kill, I destroy, I lose; in pf. and mid. I perish, I am lost
Ὑπερίων, Ὑπερίονος	[m.] Hyperion

455. (Lesson 64)

ἀτάρ	[adversative particle or conj.] but
ἔδω	[pres. syst. only] I eat
εἶδαρ, εἴδατος	[n.] food
ἐννῆμαρ	[adv.] for nine days
ἐπι-βαίνω	[+ gen.] I land upon, I go upon
Λωτοφάγοι, -ων	[m.] Lotus-eaters [a legendary people]
ὀλοός, -ή, -όν	destructive, deadly

462. (Lesson 65)

ἀφύσσω	I draw; I heap up
δεῖπνον, -ου	[n.] dinner, meal
ἔνθα	[adv.] there, then
θοός, -ή, -όν	swift

468. (Lesson 67)

δίδωμι	I give
ἵημι	I send forth, I cast; I place
ἰών, ἰοῦσα, ἰόν	going [pres. act. ptc. of εἶμι go]
ὀπάζω	I send with (someone); I present
πατέομαι	I partake of [+ gen.]
προ-ίημι	I send forth, I hurl
τίθημι	I put, I place, I cause
χθών, χθονός	[f.] earth

476. (Lesson 68)

λωτός, -οῦ	[m.] lotus
μήδομαι	I contrive, I plan
ὄλεθρος, -ου	[m.] destruction

482. (Lesson 69)

αὐτοῦ	[adv.] in the same place, there
μελιηδής, -ές	honey-sweet
νέομαι	[pres. syst. only] I return

487. (Lesson 70)

γλαφυρός, -ή, -όν	hollow
δέω	I tie, I fasten
ἐρίηρος, -ον	[pl. 3 decl. ἐρίηρες, etc.] faithful, loyal
ἐρύω	I drag, I draw
κέλομαι	I order

κλαίω	I weep, I wail
ὠκύς, -εῖα, -ύ	swift, nimble

493. (Lesson 71)

ἅλς, ἁλός	[f.] sea
ἕζομαι	I sit down; [in aor.] I cause to be seated
ἑξῆς	[adv.] in order, in rows
ἐρετμόν, -οῦ	[n.] oar
καθ-ίζω	I seat myself; I cause to be seated
κληΐς, κληῖδος	[f.] oar-lock; bolt
πολιός, (-ή), -όν	grayish, white
τύπτω	I strike, I beat

500. (Lesson 73)

ἦμος	[conj.] when
ἠριγένεια, -ης	the early-born (one)
Ἠώς, Ἠόος	[f.] Eos [the personified goddess of the dawn]
μίμνω	[pres. syst. only] I remain, I await
ῥοδοδάκτυλος, -ον	rosy-fingered

507. (Lesson 74)

ἄγριος, (-η), -ον	wild, savage
ἀνά or ἄμ	[adv.] up; back [prep. + gen.] on (to) [prep. + dat.] on [at rest] [prep. + acc.] on (to), over

514. (Lesson 75)

ἄγχι	[adv., and prep. + gen.] near, close by
αἴξ, αἰγός	[m., f.] goat
ἀφ-ικνέομαι	I come to, I arrive [+ acc.]
ὄϊς, ὄϊος	[dat. pl. always ὄεσσι, acc. pl. always ὄϊς] [m., f.] sheep
σπέος, σπέος or σπῆος	[n.] cave
χῶρος, -ου	[m.] place, region

520. (Lesson 76)

ἀπόπροσθεν	[adv.] far away, aloof
ἰδέ	[conj.] and [= ἠδέ]
οἶος, -η, -ον	alone
πελώριος, -η, -ον	gigantic, monstrous

526. (Lesson 77)

ἀρνειός, -οῦ	[m.] ram [full-grown]
θυρεός, -οῦ	[m.] door-stone
ἵστημι	I put; I halt [trans.]
ἵσταμαι	I stand, I halt [intr.]
ὄρος, ὄρεος	[n.] mountain

533. (Lesson 79)

ἀγλαός, -ή, -όν	splendid
ἄμαξα, -ης	[f.] wagon

ἀσκός, -οῦ	[m.] bag
μέλας, μέλαινα, μέλαν	[m. and n. gen. μέλανος] dark, black
ὑψόσε	[adv.] on high, upwards

540. (Lesson 80)

ἄλοχος, -ου	[f.] wife
ἀμφίπολος, -ου	[f.] handmaid, female attendant
δμώς, δμωός	[m.] man-servant
ἑπτά	[indecl.] seven
εὐ-εργής, -ές	well made; fine
κρητήρ, κρητῆρος	[m.] mixing-bowl

547. (Lesson 81)

ἀγήνωρ, ἀγήνορος	[adv.] manly, courageous
ἀπ-έχω	I hold back from, I refrain from
αὐτίκα	[adv.] at once
ἐμ-πίπλημι	I pour; I heap up I fill (with)
ἐπ-έρχομαι	I come to, I come upon [+ dat., acc.]
θεσπέσιος, -η, -ον	heavenly, divine
χέω	I pour; I heap up [+ acc., gen.]

554. (Lesson 82)

ἄντρον, -ου	[n.] cave
ἄρνες, ἀρνῶν	[no nom. sg.; acc.sg. ἄρνα] [m., f.] lamb(s)
ἔνδον	[adv.] within, inside
καρπάλιμος, -ον	swift, quick
πίων, πίονος	fat, rich
σηκός, -οῦ	[m.] pen, fold
τυρός, -οῦ	[m.] cheese

561. (Lesson 83)

αἴνυμαι	[pres. syst. only]I seize upon; I select
ἁλμυρός, -ή, -όν	salty, briny
ἦ	truly, indeed; also [an untranslatable interr. particle introducing a question]
λίσσομαι	I entreat, I beg
ξείνιον, -ου	[n.] gift of hospitality, a present given by a host to a guest
πολύς, —, πολύ	much, many [alternative m. and n. forms of πολλός, -ή, -όν]

569. (Lesson 85)

ἀπο-σεύω	[non-thematic 2 aor.] I rush away, I rush back (from)
ἔντοσθεν	[adv.] within, inside [prep. + gen] inside of
ἥμενος, -η, -ον	sitting, seated
εἷος [also ἧος or ἕως]	[conj.] while, until
καίω	I kindle, I burn
νέμω	I assign, I drive my flock; [in mid.] I possess, I feed on

ὄβριμος, -η, -ον	heavy, mighty
ὕλη, -ης	wood; forest

577. (Lesson 86)

ἀμέλγω	[pres. syst.] I milk
ἄρσεν, ἄρσενος	[n.] male
βαθύς, -εῖα, -ύ	deep
ἐλαύνω	I drive
ἐπι-τίθημι	I put on; I put in position
ὅσ(σ)ος, -η, ον	as many as, as great as
τόσ(σ)ος, -η, ον	so many, so great

584. (Lesson 87)

αὖτε	again; on the other hand
εἰσ-οράω	I see, I look at
ἔμβρυον, -ου	[n.] a young one [of animals]
κατα-τίθημι	I put down
λευκός, -ή, -όν	bright, white
μοῖρα, -ης	[f.] due measure; portion; fate

591. (Lesson 88)

ἀλάομαι	I wander [pf. has pres. force]
ἦτορ	[n., indecl.] heart
κέλευθος, -ου	[f., but frequently n. in pl.] way, path, course
οἷος, -η, -ον	such as, what sort (of)
πλέω	I sail (over)
ὑγρός, -ή, -όν	fluid, watery
ὑπέρ or ὑπείρ	[prep. + gen. or acc.] over
φθόγγος, -ου	[m.] voice

598. (Lesson 89)

Ἀγαμέμνων, Ἀγαμέμνονος	[m.] Agamemnon [king of Mycenae and commander in chief of Greeks at Troy]
Ἀχαιοί, -ῶν	Achaeans, a division of the Greeks; also, Greeks in general
λαῖτμα, λαίτματος	[n.] gulf
οἴκαδε	[adv.] homeward
προσ-εῖπον	I address, I speak to [+ acc.]
π(τ)όλις, π(τ)ολιος	[f.] city

606. (Lesson 91)

αἰδέομαι	I venerate, I revere, I respect
ἱκέται, ἱκετάων	[m.] suppliants
ἱκνέομαι	I approach, I come [+ acc.]
κιχάνω	I come (by chance), I reach
νηλ(ε)ής, -ές	pitiless, ruthless
ὅπ(π)η	[adv.] where, in what direction

611. (Lesson 92)

αἰγίοχος, -η, -ον	aegis-bearing [epithet of Zeus]
ἆσσον	[adv.] near, close [often + gen. or dat.]
δύναμαι	I can, I am able [+ inf.]

| Κύκλωψ, Κύκλωπος | [m.] Cyclops |
| σχεδόν | [adv.] close by, near |

618. (Lesson 93)

αἰπύς, -εῖα, -ύ	steep; utter
μάρπτω	I seize
μηρός, -οῦ	[m.] thigh
πεῖραρ, πείρατος	[n.] end, boundary
Ποσειδάων, Ποσειδάωνος	[m.] Poseidon [brother of Zeus and god of the sea]

625. (Lesson 94)

ἀνδρόμεος, -η, -ον	human [used only of flesh]
δόρπον, -ου	[n.] supper
κρέα, κρεῶν	[n. pl.] nom. sg. κρέας flesh, meat
ξίφος, ξίφεος	[n.] sword
ὁπλίζω	I prepare
ὀστέον, -ου	[n.] bone

632. (Lesson 95)

δῖος, -α, -ον	bright, glorious [f. usually keeps alpha through sg.]
ἐπι-μαίομαι	I seek out; I feel, I touch
μεγαλήτωρ, μεγαλήτορος	[adj.] great-hearted, great, daring
ὅθι	[adv.] where
ὀξύς, -εῖα, -ύ	sharp, keen
στενάχω	[pres. syst. only] I groan, I lament

640. (Lesson 97)

Ἀθήνη, -ης	[f.] Athene [a goddess, special patroness of Odysseus]
ἄψ	[adv.] back, back again
κλυτός, -όν	famous; excellent
τίνω or τίω	I pay; [in mid.] I take vengeance upon, I punish

647. (Lesson 98)

ἐλαΐνεος, -η, -ον	(of) olive-wood
ἱστός, -οῦ	[m.] mast; loom [for weaving]
παρ-ίσταμαι	I stand by
χλωρός, -ή, -όν	greenish yellow, green

654. (Lesson 99)

ἀνώγω	[pf. has pres. sense; plpf. has impf. sense] I command, I urge
μοχλός, -οῦ	[m.] bar, stake
ὕπνος, -ου	[m.] sleep

661. (Lesson 100)

αἷμα, αἵματος	[n.] blood
ὄνομα or οὔνομα, ὀνόματος	[n.] name
τρίς	[adv.] thrice, three times

668. (Lesson 101)

αὖ	[adv.] again; but now
ἐλεέω	I pity, I have mercy on
προσ-αυδάω	I address

676. (Lesson 103)

αἰνῶς	[adv.] awfully, greatly
ἄρουρα, -ης	[f.] soil, earth
αὖτις	[adv.] back, again
τεός, -ή, -όν	your [sg.]

682. (Lesson 104)

μειλίχιος, -η, -ον	pleasing, winning
Οὖτις, Οὔτιος	Nobody
παχύς, -εῖα, -ύ	thick, stout
πρόσθε(ν)	[adv.] first, before, in front (of)

688. (Lesson 105)

ἅπτω	I fasten; [in mid.] I lay hold of; I catch fire
δαίμων, δαίμονος	[m., f.] a divinity, a superhuman power
ἐκ-σεύω	[non-thematic 2 aor.] I rush out of, I pour out of [intr.]
ἦ	thus he spoke [3 sg. impf. of ἠμί]
τάχα	[adv.] quickly, soon

695. (Lesson 106)

ἀϋτμή, -ῆς	[f.] breath; vapor; blast
βλέφαρον, -ου	[n.] eyelid
δόρυ, δούρατος or δουρός	[n.] beam, plank; spear
ὀφρύς, ὀφρύος	[f.] eyebrow

702. (Lesson 107)

ἰάχω	[pres. syst. only] I shout; I hiss; I resound
οἰμώζω	I cry out in pain
ὧδε	[adv.] thus, so

708. (Lesson 109)

ἄλλοθεν	[adv.] from elsewhere
βοάω	I shout, I roar
Πολύφημος, -ου	[m.] Polyphemus [a Cyclops, son of Poseidon]
ῥίπτω	I hurl

714. (Lesson 110)

ἀμύμων, ἀμύμονος	[adj.] blameless, excellent
βιάζω	I constrain, I use violence against
στείχω	I go, I proceed

720. (Lesson 111)

ἐγγύθεν	[adv.] from close at hand, near
πετάννυμι	I spread out
ὑφαίνω	I weave; I devise

727. (Lesson 112)

ἀκέων, -ουσα	[adj., m. and f.] in silence, silent(ly)
ὕστατος, -η, -ον	last

734. (Lesson 113)

γαστήρ, γαστέρος or γαστρός	[f.] belly
νῶτον, -ου	[n.] back
φώς, φωτός	[m.] man

742. (Lesson 115)

θῆλυς, -εια , -υ	[adj.] female
πυκ(ι)νός, -ή, -όν	thick; close; shrewd
τείρω	[pres. syst. only] I wear out; I distress

748. (Lesson 116)

δαμάζω	I tame, I overpower
λυγρός, -ή, -όν	miserable, wretched
σταθμός, -οῦ	[m.] doorpost; farmyard

755. (Lesson 117)

μένος, μένεος	[n.] might; courage; wrath
τῷ	[adv., often used with conjunctive force] therefore; in that case

761. (Lesson 118)

γοάω	I weep (for) [+ acc.], I mourn
λίην	[adv.] exceedingly; καὶ λίην [adv.] truly

767. (Lesson 119)

γεγωνέω	[pf. with pres. meaning] I shout, I make myself heard
ἔσθω	[pres. syst. only] I eat, I devour

Appendix C

Rules for Writing Pitch-Marks (Accents)

1. The **acute** (´) may stand on the last, the second-last, or the third-last syllable, but not on the third-last syllable if the last syllable is long.

2. The **circumflex** (˜) never stands on the third-last syllable, or on any short syllable; it may not stand on the second-last syllable if the last syllable is long.

3. The **grave** (`) may stand only on the last syllable.

4. Placement. The accent marks are placed over the vowel of the accented syllable (e.g., καλὸν δῶρον) . The accent mark is written over the second vowel of a diphthong (e.g., νοῦσος, Οὖτις). Accents are placed in front of an initial vowel when upper case (e.g., Ὅμηρος). Breathing marks are written before the acute and grave (e.g., οἵ), but under the circumflex (e.g., εἶς).

5. Grave accent. The acute on a final syllable becomes a grave if followed by another word of the same sentence without intervening punctuation (e.g., πρὸς ποταμὸν μέγαν, not πρός ποταμόν μέγαν).

6. Enclitics and Proclitics. Rule 5 does not apply (1) if the word is interrogative (τίς ποταμός;) or (2) if the word is followed by an **enclitic**: the personal pronouns μεῦ, μοί, μέ, σεῦ, σοί, σέ, ἔο, οἵ, ἕ, σφίσι, the indefinite pronoun τις, τι in all its cases, the indefinite adverbs πού, πή, ποθί, ποθέν, ποτέ, πώ, πώς, the particles γε, τέ, τοί, πέρ, κέ(ν), and all forms of the present indicative of εἰμί (*I am*) and φημί (*I say*) except the monosyllabic second person singular (εἶς, φής).

   Enclitics tend to throw their pitch marks back onto the preceding word (e.g., ἄνθρωπός τις) but not if it is a dissyllabic enclitic following a word with the acute on the next-to-last syllable (e.g., λόγων τινῶν).

   Ten monosyllabic words, called **proclitics**, have no accent. These include: the forms of the article that begin with a vowel (ὁ, ἡ, οἱ, αἱ); the prepositions εἰς/ἐς, ἐκ/ἐξ, ἐν; the conjunction εἰ (*if*), ὡς (*as, that*); the negative adverb οὐ/οὐκ/οὐχ. However, there are conditions under which proclitics acquire an accent mark: when they precede an enclitic (e.g., ἔν σφισι *among them*); when ἐξ, ἐν, εἰς are placed after their objects (e.g., κακῶν ἔξ *out of evils*); when ὡς is placed after its noun (e.g., ἀνὴρ ὥς *as a man*).

7. Final -οι and -αι are regarded as short (ἄνθρωποι, Μοῦσαι), except in the optative of verbs (e.g., κεύθοι, not κεῦθοι).

8. The third-last syllable can have the acute only.

9. The second-last syllable, if marked and long, has the circumflex if the last syllable is short (e.g., νῆσος).

10. If the final syllable is long, the acute cannot stand on the third-last syllable, nor the circumflex on the second-last. Therefore the acute that is on the third-last

syllable in some forms of a word (e.g., ἄνθρωπος, αἰδέομαι) shifts to the second-last when the final syllable becomes long (ἀνθρώπου, αἰδεόμην); a circumflex likewise will change to an acute if the last syllable of its word becomes long (δῶρον, δώρου).

11. If the final syllable is short, the pitch-mark on the final syllable itself is always an acute (e.g., σοφός); on the second-last, it is acute if that syllable is short, but a circumflex if the second-last syllable is long (e.g., νόμος, δῶρον); on the third-last syllable it is always an acute (e.g., ἔρχετο).

12. In most verb forms, the pitch-mark is **recessive**: it is placed as many syllables from the end of the word as the above rules allow. Nouns and adjectives (as well as a few verb forms) have **persistent** accents: their accents remain where they are placed in the nominative case, unless forced to move or change nature by the rules above.

13. There are names for the last three syllables of a Greek word:
the last syllable: **ultima**
the next to the last syllable: **penult**
the one before the next to the last syllable: **antepenult**

14. There are specific names for words of each accent pattern:
acute on the ultima: **oxytone**
acute on the penult: **paroxytone**
acute on the antepenult: **proparoxytone**
circumflex on the ultima: **perispomenon**
circumflex on the penult: **properispomenon**

Appendix D

REVIEW EXERCISES

LESSON 10

I. Change the following imperfect tense forms of the verb εἰμί to the present tense, keeping the same person and number.

   E.g., ἦα   Answer: <u>εἰμί</u>

   1. ἔην
   2. ἦμεν
   3. ἦσθα
   4. ἦν
   5. ἦσαν
   6. ἦτε
   7. ἔσαν
   8. ἦεν
   9. ἦα

II. The following sentences all have singular subjects and verbs. Change each subject to the plural, and then also change the verb and any modifying adjective to agree with the subject. Do not change the verb tense.

   E.g., ἦεν καλὴ θάλασσα.   Answer: <u>ἦσαν καλαὶ θάλασσαι.</u>

   1. φωνή ἐστι καλή.
   2. πέτρη ἐπὶ γαίης ἦν.
   3. καλὴ ἦα.
   4. φίλη ἐσσί.
   5. δίκη ἐστίν.

ANSWERS

I. 1. ἐστί(ν)   2. εἰμέν   3. ἐσσί (εἶς)   4. ἐστί(ν)   5. εἰσί(ν)
   6. ἐστέ   7. εἰσί(ν)   8. ἐστί(ν)   9. εἰμί

II. 1. φωναί εἰσι καλαί.   2. πέτραι ἐπὶ γαίης ἦσαν.   3. καλαὶ ἦμεν.
   4. φίλαι ἐστέ.   5. δίκαι εἰσίν.

LESSON 11

I. Say whether each of the following dictionary entries is for an adjective or noun. If it is for a noun, identify which declension.

1. καρπός, -ου
2. κρατερός, -ή, -όν
3. μοῖρα, -ης
4. μοῦνος, -η, -ον
5. πύλη, -ης

II. Decline following noun-adjective pairs.

1. ἰητρὸς σοφός
2. ἄνθρωπος νήπιος
3. ἀνάγκη ὑψηλή
4. δόξα μούνη

ANSWERS

I. 1. noun, 2nd decl.   2. adjective   3. noun, 1st decl.   4. adjective
5. noun, 1st decl.

II.

1. | ἰητρὸς σοφός | ἰητροὶ σοφοί |
    | ἰητροῦ σοφοῦ | ἰητρῶν σοφῶν |
    | ἰητρῷ σοφῷ | ἰητροῖσι σοφοῖσι |
    | ἰητρὸν σοφόν | ἰητροὺς σοφούς |

2. | ἄνθρωπος νήπιος | ἄνθρωποι νήπιοι |
    | ἀνθρώπου νηπίου | ἀνθρώπων νηπίων |
    | ἀνθρώπῳ νηπίῳ | ἀνθρώποισι νηπίοισι |
    | ἄνθρωπον νήπιον | ἀνθρώπους νηπίους |

3. | ἀνάγκη ὑψηλή | ἀνάγκαι ὑψηλαί |
    | ἀνάγκης ὑψηλῆς | ἀναγκάων ὑψηλάων |
    | ἀνάγκῃ ὑψηλῇ | ἀνάγκῃσι ὑψήλῃσι |
    | ἀνάγκην ὑψηλήν | ἀνάγκας ὑψηλάς |

4. | δόξα μούνη | δόξαι μοῦναι |
    | δόξης μούνης | δοξάων μουνάων |
    | δόξῃ μούνῃ | δόξῃσι μούνῃσι |
    | δόξαν μούνην | δόξας μούνας |

LESSON 12

I. Modify each of the following nouns with the correct form of the adjective καλός, -ή, -όν. Remember that, to agree, an adjective must be put into the same case, gender and number as its noun, but that the endings will not necessarily look alike.

1. βίου
2. ἔργα
3. εἰρήνη
4. θεούς
5. θανάτων

6. θάλασσαν
7. πόλεμοι
8. δενδρέοις
9. γαῖα
10. λόγῳ

II. Translate the above noun-adjective phrases.

ANSWERS

I. 1. καλοῦ 2. καλά 3. καλῇ 4. καλούς 5. καλῶν 6. καλήν 7. καλοί 8. καλοῖς 9. καλή 10. καλῷ

II. 1. of a noble life 2. noble deeds (as subject or object) 3. by/for/to a noble peace 4. noble gods (as object) 5. of noble deaths 6. beautiful sea (as object) 7. noble wars 8. by/to/for beautiful trees 9. beautiful earth 10. by/to/for a noble word

LESSON 13

I. Indicate whether each of the following adjective and noun phrases show agreement. When they do not, supply the correct form of the adjective:

1. δῶρα καλή
2. δῶρον καλόν
3. δώροις καλοῖσι
4. δώρων καλῷ
5. γαῖα καλά
6. γαίη καλῇ
7. γαῖαν καλήν
8. ξεῖνον καλόν
9. ξεῖνους καλάς
10. ξείνου καλοῦ
11. βίαι καλή

ANSWERS

1. No: δῶρα καλά 2. Yes 3. Yes 4. No: δώρων καλῶν 5. No: γαῖα καλή 6. Yes 7. Yes 8. Yes 9. No: ξεῖνους καλούς 10. Yes 11. No: βίαι καλαί

CHAPTER 14

I.   Translate the following phrases into Greek:

1.   those fruits (nom.)
2.   of that fruit
3.   those fruits (acc.)
4.   by means of the same fruit
5.   they themselves (nom. f.)
6.   they themselves (acc. m.)
7.   of those (things) (n.)
8.   of those (men)
9.   to the woman herself
10. for the man himself

II. Translate each of the following pronouns according to the case and number, indicating gender:

1.   (ἐ)κείνας
2.   (ἐ)κεῖνα
3.   (ἐ)κείνῳ
4.   (ἐ)κεῖνον
5.   (ἐ)κεῖνο
6.   αὐτάων
7.   αὐτοί
8.   αὐτῇσ(ι)
9.   αὐτά

ANSWERS

I.   1. (ἐ)κεῖνοι καρποί   2. (ἐ)κείνου καρποῦ   3. (ἐ)κείνους καρπούς
4. αὐτῷ καρπῷ   5. αὐταί   6. αὐτούς   7. (ἐ)κείνων   8. (ἐ)κείνων
9. αὐτῇ   10. αὐτῷ

II. 1. those (acc. f.)   2. those (nom./acc. n.)   3. by/for/to that (m./n.)
4. that (acc. m.)   5. that (nom./acc. n.)   6. of them themselves (f.)
7. they themselves (nom. m.)   8. by/for/to them themselves (f.)
9. they themselves (nom./ acc. n.)

CHAPTER 15

I. Give the Greek for each of the following phrases, using the correct forms of the weak demonstrative ὁ, ἡ, τό and of the demonstrative ὅδε, ἥδε, τόδε.

1.   by means of this treasure
2.   those treasures (nom.)
3.   the treasures (acc.)
4.   of that treasure
5.   of these treasures
6.   for that disease (note the gender of 'disease')
7.   these diseases (nom.)
8.   this disease (acc.)
9.   of those diseases
10. the diseases (nom.)

II. Identify each of the demonstratives in the sentences in Section 80 as a pronoun or adjective.

ANSWERS

I.   1. θησαυρῷ τῷδε   2. οἱ θησαυροί   3. τοὺς θησαυρούς
4. τοῦ θησαυροῦ   5. τῶνδε θησαυρῶν   6. τῇ νούσῳ   7. αἵδε νοῦσοι
8. τήνδε νοῦσον   9. τάων νούσων   10. αἱ νοῦσοι

II.   1. τοῖσι pronoun   2. κεῖνοι pronoun; τῶν pronoun   3. τοῖο pronoun
4. τῶνδε adjective   5. ὅδε adjective   6. τῆς adjective   7. αἵδε pronoun;
τάων pronoun   8. no demonstrative in this sentence   9. τῆς pronoun
10. ἥδε pronoun

CHAPTER 16

I.   Based on the information in Section 83, classify each of the following as a voice, mood, or tense.

1. indicative

2. aorist

3. passive

4. middle

5. optative

6. imperfect

7. imperative

8. subjunctive

9. pluperfect

10. active

11. present

II. Based on the chart in Section 84, indicate the aspect (completed, progressive, or simple) of each of the following English verb phrases:

1. I had eaten

2. We shall be eating

3. They will have eaten

4. I ate

5. We shall eat

6. They were eating

7. He has eaten

8. She is eating

9. They eat

ANSWERS

I.   1. mood   2. tense   3. voice   4. voice   5. mood   6. tense   7. mood
8. mood   9. tense   10. voice   11. tense

II.   1. completed   2. progressive   3. completed   4. simple   5. simple
6. progressive   7. completed   8. progressive   9. simple

LESSON 17

I. In each of the following sentences, identify the subject (S) and, where there is one, direct object (O) of the verb. Translate the sentences.

1. ἀνθρώπους νῦν ἄγω.
2. ἐοὶ φίλοι λίθους φέρουσιν.
3. μάνθανον ἀληθείην.
4. πολλὰ μάνθανεν.
5. εὕδεις.
6. θνήσκει.
7. γιγνώσκω ολίγα.
8. ἀγαθαὶ ἀγαθοὺς φιλέετε.
9. ὅδε κεῖνον λύεν.
10. τούσδε κεῖνος λύεν.
11. φίλος ἀγαθός ἐστιν.
12. νούσος σχετλίη.
13. ἐκεῖνον ποταμὸν ὁράεις;
14. αἰσχρὰ οὐ γιγνώσκομεν.
15. οἱ φίλοι δῶρα καλὰ φέρον.

II. Identify each of the following as either statements of fact or contrary-to-fact. Translate.

1. φέρε λίθους πολλούς.
2. εἰ μὴ φέρε λίθους πολλούς, οὐκ ἂν θνήσκεν.
3. εἰ φέρε δῶρα, οὐκ ἂν θνήσκεν.
4. φέρε δὴ λίθους.
5. οὐ φέρε δῶρα.
6. θνήσκεν.
7. βίος σχέτλιος.
8. εἰ μὴ βίος σχέτλιος ἦεν, οὐκ ἂν θνήσκεν.

ANSWERS

I. 1. **S** I **O** ἀνθρώπους (I am now leading men.) 2. **S** ἐοὶ φίλοι **O** λίθους (His/her friends carry/ are carrying stones.) 3. **S** I/they **O** ἀληθείην (I/they were learning truth.) 4. **S** he/she/it **O** πολλὰ (He/she/it was/were learning many things.) 5. **S** You (sg.) **O** none (intransitive verb) (You (sg.) are sleeping.) 6. **S** he/she/it **O** none (intransitive verb) (He/she/it is dying.) 7. **S** I **O** ολίγα (I know few things.) 8. **S** you (pl.) **O** ἀγαθοὺς (You brave women love brave men.) 9. **S** ὅδε **O** κεῖνον (This man was releasing that man.) 10. **S** κεῖνος **O** τούσδε (That man was releasing these men.) 11. **S** φίλος / he **O** none (intransitive or linking verb) (A/the friend is good. He is a good friend.) 12. **S** νούσος **O** none (intransitive or linking verb) (A/the disease is cruel.) 13. **S** you **O** ἐκεῖνον ποταμὸν (Do you see that yonder river?) 14. **S** we **O** αἰσχρὰ (We do not know shameful things.) 15. **S** οἱ φίλοι **O** δῶρα (Those/the friends were bringing fine gifts.)

II. 1. Fact (He was carrying many stones.) 2. Contrary-to-fact (If he were not carrying many stones, he would not be dying.) 3. Contrary-to-fact (If he were carrying gifts, he would not be dying.) 4. Fact (He was in fact carrying stones.) 5. Fact (He was not carrying gifts.) 6. Fact (He was dying.) 7. Fact (Life is cruel.) 8. Contrary-to-fact (If life were not cruel, he would not be dying.)

LESSON 18

I. Complete the Greek versions of the English sentences below. You will need to put the
    nouns and adjectives in parentheses into the correct cases.

1. They have many treasures.
   (πολλοὶ θησαυροὶ) ἔχουσιν.

2. Were you hiding the treasure?
   κεύθες (θησαυρός);

3. We are doing this in order that we may supply good things to our friends.
   (τόδε) ῥέζομεν ἵνα παρ-έχωμεν ἀγαθὰ (ἡμέτεροι φίλοι).

4. Noble men always love noble things.
   ἐσθλοὶ (ἐσθλὰ) αἰεὶ φιλέουσιν.

5. Let me not lead a life of toil.
   (βίος) πόνου μὴ ἄγω.

6. Let us learn the truth.
   μανθάνωμεν (ἀληθείη).

7. That person is our guest.
   ἐκεῖνος ἄνθρωπός ἐστιν (ξεῖνος ἡμέτερος).

8. She is speaking the truth in order that you may not love that worthless man.
   (ἀληθείη) ἐννέπει ὄφρα (ὁ πονηρὸς) μὴ φιλέῃς.

9. They know many people.
   γιγνώσκουσι (πολλοί ἄνθρωποι).

10. He was always sleeping, but he loved his friends.
    αἰεὶ μὲν εὕδεν, (ἑοὶ φίλοι) δὲ φίλεεν.

II. Change the verbs (in parentheses) in the following purpose clauses into the
    subjunctive mood, retaining the same person and number. Translate each sentence.

1. αἰσχρὰ κεύθει ἵνα (ὁράεις) μοῦνα ἐσθλά.

2. αἰσχρὰ κεύθει ὄφρα (ἔχει) θησαυρόν.

3. αἰσχρὰ κεύθει ὅπως μὴ (γιγνώσκετε) αἰσχρά.

4. αἰσχρὰ κεύθει ἵνα μὴ (εἰσι) αἰσχροί.

5. αἰσχρὰ κεύθει ὡς (μανθάνομεν).

ANSWERS

I. 1. πολλοὺς θησαυροὺς   2. θησαυρόν   3. τόδε/φίλοισιν ἡμετέροισιν
4. ἐσθλά   5. βίον   6. ἀληθείην   7. ξεῖνος ἡμέτερος   8. ἀληθείην/τὸν
πονηρὸν   9. πολλοὺς ἀνθρώπους   10. ἑοὺς φίλους

II. 1. ὁράῃς He is hiding shameful things in order that you may see only noble
things.   2. ἔχῃ He is hiding shameful things in order that he may have treasure.
3. γιγνώσκητε He is hiding shameful things in order that you may not know
shameful things.   4. ὦσι He is hiding shameful things in order that they may not be
shameful (men).   5. μανθάνωμεν He is hiding shameful things in order that we
may learn.

LESSON 19

I. Hortatory and wish. For each of the following indicative statements, give a subjunctive (hortatory) or optative (wish) version, as indicated. Translate both versions.

1. ἄγετε. wish:
2. οὐκ ἀδικέομεν. hortatory:
3. τούσδε διώκω. hortatory:
4. οὐ ποιέεις κακά. wish:
5. βίον κακὸν οὐκ ἄγω. hortatory:
6. βίον κακὸν οὐκ ἄγω. wish:
7. οὐκ αἰεὶ φοιτάουσιν. wish:
8. νῦν ἐσθίομεν. hortatory:
9. νῦν εὕδει. wish:
10. νῦν θνήσκω. wish:
11. καλαί εἰμεν. hortatory:

II. Change each of the following from a primary sequence purpose clause to a secondary sequence purpose clause, changing the mood of the purpose clause verb accordingly. Translate the new sentences.

1. In order that they may not do worthless things, they are learning many things.
   ἵνα μὴ ῥέζωσι πονηρά, πολλὰ μανθάνουσιν.

2. We injure their eyes, that they may not see.
   ἀδικέομεν τῶν ὀφθαλμούς, ὅπως μὴ ὁράωσιν.

3. I supply fruit, in order that you all may eat.
   παρ-έχω καρπόν, ἵνα ἐσθίητε.

4. He pursues happiness in order to lead a just life.
   ὄλβον διώκει ὄφρα ἄγῃ βίον δίκαιον.

5. You never do cruel deeds, in order that you may have prosperity.
   σχέτλια ἔργα οὔ ποτε ποιέεις, ἵνα ἔχῃς ὄλβον.

ANSWERS

I.   1. You all lead. ἄγοιτε. May you all lead!   2. We are not doing wrong. μὴ ἀδικέωμεν. Let us not do wrong!   3. I am pursuing these men. τούσδε διώκω. Let me pursue these men!   4. You do not do bad things. μὴ ποιέοις κακά. May you not do bad things!   5. I do not lead an evil life. βίον κακὸν μὴ ἄγω. Let me not live an evil life!   6. I do not lead an evil life. βίον κακὸν μὴ ἄγοιμι. May I not lead an evil life!   7. They do not wander forever. μὴ αἰεὶ φοιτάοιεν. May they not wander forever!   8. Now we are eating. νῦν ἐσθίωμεν. Now let us eat!   9. Now he is sleeping. νῦν εὕδοι. Now may he sleep!   10. Now I am dying. νῦν θνήσκοιμι. Now may I die!   11. We are beautiful. καλαί ὦμεν. Let us be beautiful!

II.   1. ἵνα μὴ ῥέζοιεν πονηρά, πολλὰ μάνθανον. In order that they might not do worthless things, they were learning many things.   2. ἀδικέομεν τῶν ὀφθαλμούς, ὅπως μὴ ὁράοιεν. We were injuring their eyes, that they might not see.   3. πάρ-εχον καρπόν, ἵνα ἐσθίοιτε. I was supplying fruit, in order that you all might eat.   4. ὄλβον δίωκε ὄφρα ἄγοι βίον δίκαιον. He was pursuing happiness in order to lead a just life.   5. σχέτλια ἔργα οὔ ποτε ποίεες, ἵνα ἔχοις ὄλβον. You never did cruel deeds, in order that you might have prosperity.

A Reading Course in Homeric Greek

LESSON 20

I. Change the following direct statements to indirect statements, using the introducing verb given in parentheses. Translate.

    1.   (νόμιζον) οἱ νήπιοι πονηρὰ δίωκον.

    2.   (νομίζομεν) ἐκεῖνός ἐστιν ἀγαθός.

    3.   (λέγει) ὁ φίλος ἐθέλει πόνον φεύγειν.

    4.   (λέγω) δένδρεά ἐστι ὑψηλά.

    5.   (λέγε) φίλε ἑὸς φίλος δίκην.

    6.   (νομίζεις) οἱ δίκαιοι οὔ ποτε φοιτάουσιν.

    7.   (λέγει) οὐ θνήσκει ὅδε ἄνθρωπος ἀλλὰ εὕδει.

    8.   (λέγουσι) ποταμὸς λίθους εἰς θάλασσαν φέρει.

    9.   (λέγουσι) οἱ ἱκάνουσιν.

    10.   (νομίζετε) σοφοὶ γίγωνσκον πολλά.

II. Convert the following indicative statements to commands. Translate both versions.

    1.   κείνην οὐ φιλέεις.   4.   φωνὴν οὔ ποτε ποιέετε.

    2.   ἄγεις βίον δίκαιον.   5.   ἱκάνεις.

    3.   οὐ φέρετε θησαυρούς.

III. Identify the way in which each infinitive is used, i.e., as a noun, as the verb in indirect statement, or as a complement to a verb of wishing. Translate.

    1.   φεύγειν πονηρόν ἐστιν.   4.   χαλεπὸν φιλέεμεν.

    2.   οὐκ ἐθέλει φεύγειν.   5.   αἰεὶ ἐσθιέμεναι ἐθέλω.

    3.   λέγες τοὺς εἶναι πονηρούς.

ANSWERS

I. *(some but not all alternative forms of the present infinitive are given in parentheses)*
1. νόμιζον τοὺς νηπίους πονηρὰ διώκειν (διώκεμεν/διωκέμεναι). I/They used to believe those foolish men were pursuing base things. 2. νομίζομεν ἐκεῖνον εἶναι (ἔμμεν/ἔμμεναι) ἀγαθόν. We consider(ed) that man to be brave. (We thought that man was brave.) 3. λέγει τὸν φίλον ἐθέλειν (ἐθέλεμεν/ἐθελέμεναι) πόνον φεύγειν. He says that friend wishes to flee from toil. 4. λέγω δένδρεα εἶναι (ἔμμεν/ἔμμεναι) ὑψηλά. I say the trees are tall. 5. λέγε φιλέειν (φίλεμεν/ φιλέμεναι) ἑὸν φίλον δίκην. He kept on saying that his friend loved justice. 6. νομίζεις τοὺς δικαίους οὔ ποτε φοιτάειν (φοιτάεμεν/φοιταέμεναι). You believe just people never wander. 7. λέγει οὐ θνήσκειν (θνήσκεμεν/ θνησκέμεναι) τόνδε ἄνθρωπον ἀλλὰ εὕδειν (εὕδεμεν/εὐδέμεναι). He says this man is not dying but is sleeping. 8. λέγουσι ποταμὸν λίθους εἰς θάλασσαν φέρειν (φέρεμεν/φερέμεναι). They say the river carries stones to the sea. 9. λέγουσι τοὺς ἱκάνειν (ἱκάνεμεν/ἱκανέμεναι). They say those men are coming. 10. νομίζετε σοφοὺς γιγώνσκειν (γιγνώσκεμεν/γιγνωσκέμεναι) πολλά. You all think the wise knew many things.

II. 1. You do not love that woman. κείνην μὴ φίλεε. Do not love that woman!
2. You lead a just life. ἄγε βίον δίκαιον. Lead a just life!   3. You all are not
carrying treasures. μὴ φέρετε θησαυρούς. Do not carry treasures!   4. You all never
make a sound. φωνὴν μή ποτε ποιέετε. Never make a sound!   5. You are
coming. ἵκανε. Come!

III. 1. Noun. To flee is base.   2. Complementary. He/She does not wish to flee.
3. Indirect statement. You were saying that those (men) were base.   4. Noun. To
love is difficult.   5. Complementary. I always wish to eat.

LESSON 22

I. Translate each of the following verb forms. (All are in the indicative mood.)

1. ἀέξεαι	10. λαμβάνεο	19. φρονέετο
2. ἀέξετο	11. λαμβάνεις	20. φρονέει
3. ἀέξομεν	12. τρέποντο	21. φρόνεε
4. αἰτέεις	13. τρέπονται	22. φρονέεο
5. αἰτεόμην	14. τρέπουσι	23. φρονέεαι
6. αἰτεόμεθα	15. τρέφω	24. ἥδοντο
7. λαμβάνεται	16. τρέφομαι	25. ἥδετο
8. λάμβανον	17. τρέφεσθε	
9. λαμβάνουσι	18. τρέφετε	

ANSWERS

I.   1. you (sg.) grow/are growing   2. he/she/it was growing   3. we increase/are
increasing (something), we were increasing (something)   4. you (sg.) ask/ are asking
5. I was asking for myself (mid.), I was being asked (pass.)   6. we ask/ are asking for
ourselves, we were asking for ourselves (mid.), we are/ were being asked (pass.)
7. he/she/it takes/ is taking for himself/herself/itself (mid.), he/she/it is (being) taken
(pass.)   8. I/they were taking   9. they take/are taking   10. you (sg.) were taking for
yourself (mid.), you were being taken (pass.)   11. you (sg.) take/are taking   12. they
were turning themselves (mid.), they were being turned (pass.)   13. they are turning
themselves (mid.), they are (being) turned (pass.)   14. they turn /are turning
(something)   15. I nourish/ am nourishing   16. I nourish / am nourishing myself
(mid.), I am nourished (pass.)   17. you (pl.) nourish/ are/ were nourishing yourselves
(mid.), you are/ were being nourished (pass.)   18. you (pl.) nourish/ are
nourishing   19. He/she/it was considering for himself/herself/itself (mid.), he/she/it
was being considered   20. he/she/it considers/ is considering   21. he/she/it was
considering   22. you (sg.) were considering for yourself (mid.), you were being
considered (pass.)   23. you (sg.) consider/ are considering for yourself (mid.), you are
considered (pass.)   24. they were pleased with   25. he/she/it was pleased with

A Reading Course in Homeric Greek

LESSON 23

I. Where an indicative middle-passive verb is given in brackets in the following Greek clauses of purpose, supply the corresponding form of the subjunctive or optative according to the rules of syntax. Retain the same person, number, voice and tense. A translation is supplied.

1. οἱ φίλοι φέρουσι καλὰ δῶρα, ὡς μὴ [μισέονται] ὑπὸ θεῶν.
   The friends are bringing fine gifts, lest they be hated by the gods.

2. οἱ φίλοι φέρον καλὰ δῶρα, ἵνα μὴ [μισέονται] ὑπὸ θεῶν.
   The friends were bringing fine gifts, lest they be hated by the gods.

3. οἱ φίλοι φέρουσι πολλὰ δῶρα, ὄφρα ὄλβῳ [ἡδόμεθα].
   The friends are bringing many gifts, that we may enjoy prosperity.

4. οἱ φίλοι φέρον πολλὰ δῶρα, ὄφρα ὄλβῳ [ἡδόμεθα].
   The friends were bringing many gifts, in order that we might enjoy prosperity.

5. ἐκεῖνοι πλησίοι φέρουσι παντοῖα δῶρα, ἵνα [γίγνεσθε] ἑταῖροι.
   Those neighbors are bringing all sorts of gifts, in order that you may become comrades.

6. ἐκεῖνοι πλησίοι φέρον παντοῖα δῶρα, ὅπως [γίγνεσθε] ἑταῖροι.
   Those neighbors were bringing all sorts of gifts, in order that you might become comrades.

7. δίκαιοι φέρουσι δῶρα, ὡς φίλοι [λύονται].
   Righteous men are bringing gifts, in order that their friends may be released.

8. δίκαιοι φέρον δῶρα, ὡς φίλοι [λύονται].
   Righteous men were bringing gifts, in order that their friends might be released.

II. Convert the following indicative statements into hortatory subjunctive constructions. Translate.

1. οὐκ αἰτεόμεθα χρυσόν.
   We don't request gold for ourselves.

2. διδασκόμεθα ὑπό τε σοφῶν καὶ δικαίων.
   We are taught by both wise and just men.

3. οὐ γιγνώσκομαι ὡς σχετλίη.
   I am not known as cruel.

III. Convert the following indicative statements into wishes, using the optative mood. Translate.

1. οὔ ποτε ἥδομαι θησαυρῷ.
   I never take pleasure in treasure.

2. δίκη τοῖσι φίλη γίγνεται.
   Justice is becoming dear to them.

3. οἱ ἑταῖροι οὐκ αἰεὶ ἐν ἐκείνῃ γαίῃ μάχονται.
   The comrades are not still fighting in that land yonder.

4. ἀνέχεσθε πόνον θυμῷ ἀγαθῷ.
   You (pl.) endure toil with a brave spirit.

5. φίλεαι ὑπὸ πολλῶν δικαίων.
    You are loved by many righteous people.

ANSWERS

I. 1. μισέωνται 2. μισεοίατο 3. ἡδώμεθα 4. ἡδοίμεθα 5. γίγνησθε
6. γίγνοισθε 7. λύωνται 8. λυοίατο

II. 1. μὴ αἰτεώμεθα χρυσόν. Let us not request gold for ourselves!
2. διδασκώμεθα ὑπό τε σοφῶν καὶ δικαίων. Let us be taught by both wise and
just men! 3. μὴ γιγνώσκωμαι ὡς σχετλίη. Let me not be known as cruel!

III. 1. μή ποτε ἡδοίμην θησαυρῷ. May I never take pleasure in treasure!
2. δίκη τοῖσι φίλη γίγνοιτο. May justice become dear to them! 3. οἱ ἑταῖροι
μὴ αἰεὶ ἐν ἐκείνῃ γαίῃ μαχοίατο. I hope the comrades are not still fighting in
that land yonder! 4. ἀνέχοισθε πόνον θυμῷ ἀγαθῷ. May you (pl.) endure toil
with a brave spirit! (or, as polite imperative) Please endure toil with a brave spirit!
5. φιλέοιο ὑπὸ πολλῶν δικαίων. May you be loved by many just people!

LESSON 24

I. Supply the infinitive of the verb in parentheses in the correct voice (active, middle or
passive) to complement each of the following finite verbs:

1. He wishes to be sent.
    ἐθέλει (πέμπω).

2. Are you about to die?
    μέλλεις (θνήσκω);

3. They were able to drink.
    δυνατοὶ ἦσαν (πίνω).

4. I wish to be asked.
    ἐθέλω (αἰτέω).

5. Those things are going to be taken.
    κεῖνα μελλεῖ (λαμβάνω).

6. We wish not to fight.
    ἐθέλομεν μὴ (μάχομαι).

7. She wishes to become wise.
    ἐθέλει (γίγνομαι) σοφή.

8. He wishes to be carried.
    ἐθέλει (φέρω).

9. Are you able to do that deed?
    δυνατοί ἐσσι (ποιέω) ἔργον ἐκεῖνο;

10. I myself wish to endure.
    αὐτὸς ἐθέλω (ἀν-έχομαι).

11. They were going to take the treasure for themselves.
    μέλλον (λαμβάνω) θησαυρόν.

12. He was able to request fine things for himself.
    δυνατὸς ἦεν (αἰτέω) καλά.

II. Change the following imperative mood verbs into infinitives with the force of an imperative. Keep the same voice, and translate.

1. πέμπετε
2. πέμπεσθε
3. ἀν-έχευ
4. μὴ λύεο
5. μὴ λύε

6. ἥδεσθε
7. ἥδευ
8. μὴ μίσεε
9. ἀέξεσθε
10. μὴ ἁμαρτάνετε

ANSWERS

I. 1. πέμπεσθαι 2. θνῄσκειν 3. πίνειν 4. αἰτέεσθαι 5. λαμβάνεσθαι
6. μάχεσθαι 7. γίγνεσθαι 8. φέρεσθαι 9. ποιέειν 10. ἀν-έχεσθαι
11. λαμβάνεσθαι 12. αἰτέεσθαι

II. 1. πέμπειν Send! 2. πέμπεσθαι Send for yourself! Be sent!
3. ἀν-έχεσθαι Endure! 4. μὴ λύεσθαι Do not loose for yourself! Do not be
loosed! 5. μὴ λύειν Do not loose! 6. ἥδεσθαι Be pleased! 7. ἥδεσθαι
Be pleased! 8. μὴ μισέειν Do not hate! 9. ἀέξεσθαι Grow!
10. μὴ ἁμαρτάνειν Do not miss!

LESSON 26

I. Change the present tense verbs in the following sentences to the future tense, retaining the original person, number and voice. For your convenience, the second principal part of the verb to be changed is given in parentheses. Translate each sentence.

1. οἱ φίλοι δῶρα πέμπουσιν. (πέμψω)
2. οἱ φίλοι εἰς θάλασσαν ἔρχονται. (ἐλεύσομαι)
3. οἱ νήπιοι πίπτουσιν; (πέσομαι)
4. κασιγνητοὶ ἐμοὶ ἔχουσιν ὄλβον. (ἕξω)
5. κασιγνητοὶ ἐμοὶ ἐθέλουσιν ἔχειν ὄλβον. (ἐθελήσω)
6. κασιγνητὸς ἐμὸς πολλοὺς σώζει. (σώσω)
7. κασιγνητὸς ἐμὸς αἶψα ἀμείβεται. (ἀμείψομαι)
8. ἀληθείην πευθόμεθα. (πεύσομαι)
9. οὐχ ἥδονται ὄμβρῳ. (ἥσομαι)
10. δένδρεα τρέφει ὄμβρος. (θρέψω)
11. γίγνεσθε ἀθάνατοι; (γενήσομαι)
12. τόδε πρῶτος γιγνώσκεις. (γνώσομαι)

II. Insert the correct form of the relative pronoun into the relative clauses of the following Greek sentences. The underlined words in the English translations correspond to the pronouns that you will supply.

1. ὁ ἄνθρωπος _____ ἔρχεται κασιγνητὸς ἐμός ἐστιν.
The person <u>who</u> is going is my brother.

2. ὁ ἄνθρωπος _____ ὄψεαι κασιγνητὸς ἐμός ἐστιν.
   The person <u>whom</u> you will see is my brother.

3. ὁ ἄνθρωπος _____ σῖτον λάμβανες κασιγνητὸς ἐμός ἐστιν.
   The person <u>whose</u> food you were taking is my brother.

4. ὁ ἄνθρωπος σὺν _____ ἐλεύσεαι κασιγνητὸς ἐμός ἐστιν.
   The person with <u>whom</u> you will go is my brother.

5. οἱ ἄνθρωποι _____ μίσεεν ἐμὸς κασιγνητὸς ἱκάνεμεν ἐθέλουσιν.
   The people <u>whom</u> my brother hated wish to come.

6. οἱ ἄνθρωποι _____ μαχόμεθα ἀπ-ολέσονται.
   The people <u>with whom</u> we are fighting will perish.

7. οἱ ἄνθρωποι _____ καλοὶ γίγνοντο οὔ ποτε ἀδικέουσιν.
   The people <u>who</u> are noble never do wrong.

8. ὁράετε τὸν νηὸν ἐν_____ ἐμὸς κασιγνητὸς ἀπ-ολλύετο;
   Do you see the temple in <u>which</u> my brother perished?

9. ὁράετε τὸν νηὸν _____ ἐμὸς κασιγνητὸς σῶζεν;
   Do you see the temple <u>that</u> my brother was saving?

10. ὁράετε τὸν νηὸν _____ ἱερὸς πέλει;
    Do you see the temple <u>that</u> is holy?

11. ὁράετε τὸν νηὸν ἀπὸ _____ ἐμὸς κασιγνητὸς φεύγεν;
    Do you see the temple out <u>of which</u> my brother fled?

12. ἔργα _____ δίκαιος ποιέει θεοὶ φιλέουσιν.
    The gods love the deeds <u>that</u> a just man does.

13. ἔργα _____ δίκαιά ἐστι θεοὶ φιλέουσιν.
    The gods love the deeds <u>that</u> are just.

14. ἐθέλω ἔχειν δῶρα _____ ἥδεαι.
    I wish to have the gifts <u>with which</u> you are pleased.

15. τὰ δῶρα, _____ δοκέει εἶναι καλαί, ἐπὶ πέτρησί ἐστιν.
    The gifts, <u>which</u> seem to be noble, are beside the rocks.

ANSWERS

I.   1. πέμψουσιν. The friends will send gifts.   2. ἐλεύσονται. The friends will go to the sea.   3. πέσονται. Will the fools fall?   4. ἕξουσιν. My brothers will have happiness.   5. ἐθελήσουσιν. My brothers will wish to have happiness.
6. σώσει. My brother will save many.   7. ἀμείψεται. My brother will respond quickly.   8. πευσόμεθα. We shall find out the truth.   9. ἥσονται. They will not be pleased with rain.   10. θρέψει. The rain will nourish the trees.
11. γενήσεσθε. Will you (pl.) become immortal?   12. γνώσεαι. You will know this first.

II.   1. ὅς   2. ὃν   3. οὗ   4. ᾧ   5. οὕς   6. οἷσι   7. οἳ   8. ᾧ   9. ὃν
10. ὅς   11. οὗ   12. ἃ   13. ἃ   14. οἷσι   15. ἃ

LESSON 27

I. Below are the dictionary entries, including the genitive, of some masculine and feminine third declension nouns. Find the stem for each.

1. παῖς, παιδός [m., f.] child, boy, girl
2. φύσις, φύσιος [f.] nature
3. ἀνήρ, ἀνέρος or ἀνδρός [m.] man
4. Ποσειδάων, Ποσειδάωνος [m.] Poseidon
5. ποιμήν, ποιμένος [m.] shepherd
6. σάρξ, σαρκός [f.] flesh
7. χθών, χθονός [f.] earth
8. φώς, φωτός [m.] man
9. κρητήρ, κρητῆρος [m.] mixing-bowl
10. γαστήρ, γαστέρος or γαστρός [f.] belly
11. πόλις, πόλιος or πόληος [f.] city

II. Give the dative singular for each of the nouns above.

ANSWERS

I. 1. παιδ- 2. φύσι- 3. ἀνέρ- or ἀνδρ- 4. Ποσειδάων- 5. ποιμέν-
6. σαρκ- 7. χθον- 8. φωτ- 9. κρητῆρ- 10. γαστέρ- or γαστρ-
11. πόλι- or πόλη-

II. 1. παιδί 2. φύσιι 3. ἀνέρι or ἀνδρί 4. Ποσειδάωνι 5. ποιμένι
6. σαρκί 7. χθονί 8. φωτί 9. κρητῆρι 10. γαστέρι or γαστρί
11. πόλιι or πόληι

LESSON 28

I. Given the nominative and genitive of the following nouns, which ones are third declension neuter and which are second declension masculine?

1. μῆκος, μήκεος length
2. ἄνεμος, ἀνέμου wind
3. θυρεός, θυρεοῦ door-stone
4. σπέος, σπῆος cave
5. σηκός, σηκοῦ pen for animals
6. υἱός, υἱέος son
7. υἱός, υἱοῦ son
8. τυρός, τυροῦ cheese

II. Modify the following third declension nouns with the correct form of the adjective καλός, -ή, -όν. (The dictionary entries for the masculine and feminine nouns in this exercise are given in the Review Exercise I for Lesson 27.)

1. ἔπεα
2. ἐπέεσσι
3. ἔπεσι
4. πυρός
5. πυρῶν
6. πῦρ
7. σώματι
8. σωμάτεσσι
9. σώμασι
10. χθονός
11. χθόνα
12. χθονῶν
13. φώς
14. φῶτες
15. φῶτας
16. φάος
17. φάεος
18. φάει
19. φάεα
20. φαέων

ANSWERS

I. 1. 3rd, n.   2. 2nd, m.   3. 2nd, m.   4. 3rd, n.   5. 2nd., m.   6. 3rd, m. (an exception to the rule given in Section 181)   7. 2nd, m. (this noun is declined in both declensions)   8. 2nd, m.

II. 1. ἔπεα καλά   2. ἐπέεσσι καλοῖσι   3. ἔπεσι καλοῖσι   4. πυρός καλοῦ   5. πυρῶν καλῶν   6. πῦρ καλόν   7. σώματι καλῷ   8. σωμάτεσσι καλοῖσι   9. σώμασι καλοῖσι   10. χθονός καλῆς   11. χθόνα καλήν   12. χθονῶν καλάων   13. φώς καλός   14. φῶτες καλοί   15. φῶτας καλούς   16. φάος καλόν   17. φάεος καλοῦ   18. φάει καλῷ   19. φάεα καλά   20. φαέων καλῶν

LESSON 29

I. Below are some dictionary entries for adjectives. Identify each adjective by type as set forth in this lesson, i.e., Type A, Type B, Type C.

1. πυκινός, -ή, -όν   thick; shrewd
2. μέλας, μέλαινα, μέλαν   dark
3. μελιηδής, μελιηδές   honey-sweet
4. ὄβριμος, -η, -ον   heavy, mighty
5. νηλεής, νηλεές   ruthless
6. ὀξύς, ὀξεῖα, ὀξύ   sharp
7. μακρός, -ή, -όν   long
8. εὐεργής, εὐεργές   well-made
9. γλυκύς, γλυκεῖα, γλυκύ   sweet
10. ἀρείων, ἄρειον   better
11. ἀνθεμόεις, ἀνθεμόεσσα, ἀνθεμόεν   flowery
12. καρπάλιμος, -ον   swift

II. Use the examples given for Type B and Type C adjectives to predict the genitive singular for each of the following adjectives:

1. μελιηδής
2. ὀξύς
3. εὐεργές
4. ἀρείων
5. ἀνθεμόεις

ANSWERS

I. 1. Type A   2. Type B   3. Type C   4. Type A   5. Type C   6. Type B
7. Type A   8. Type C   9. Type B   10. Type C   11. Type B   12. Type A (see Note 2 under Type A)

II.   1. μελιηδέος   2. ὀξέος   3. εὐεργέος   4. ἀρείονος   5. ἀνθεμόεντος

LESSON 30

I. Give the correct form of the present or future participle of the verb in parentheses to agree with each noun. Keep the participle in the voice and tense in which the verb in parentheses is shown. Translate each phrase. For example,

πατέρων (φιλέομαι)

Answer: πατέρων φιλεομένων of the fathers being loved/ of the fathers loving for themselves (mid.)

1. σώματι (θνήσκω)
2. πέτραι (πίπτω)
3. ἀνδρῶν (πίνω)
4. ἄναξ (λύσω)
5. πατρίδα (εἰμί)

6. ἡδονή (φιλέομαι)
7. πόλιος (λύσομαι)
8. πράγμασι (γίγνομαι)
9. φίλῳ (μάχομαι)
10. πῦρ (εἰμί)

II. Each of the following sentences contains a subordinate clause of a type (causal, temporal, purpose, conditional, relative) that could also be expressed by a participial clause, as outlined in this chapter. Change each of the subordinate clauses, which have been italicized in the English translation, into participial clauses. Attempt to translate (though sometimes a strictly literal English translation of the participial clause does not work). For example,

ἐπεὶ ἐμὸν κασιγνητὸν φίλεν, τὸν σώζεν.
Since she loved my brother, she saved him.

Answer: φιλέουσα ἐμὸν κασιγνητόν, τὸν σώζεν.
Loving my brother, she saved him.

1. ἐπεὶ ἐκεῖνος *νῦν* θνήσκει, μὴ τὸν ἀδικεώμεν.
   Since that man is now dying, let's not injure him. (causal)

2. οἵδε φέρον γέρουσι δῶρα, ὅτι ἔθελον γίγνεσθαι φίλοι.
   These men were carrying gifts to the old men, *because they wished to become friends.* (causal)

3. ὄφρα παῖδες εὗδον, τοὺς φέρομεν.
   While the children slept, we carried them (the children). (temporal)

4. δῶρα φέρομεν γέροντι ὃς δίδασκε παῖδας.
   We were bringing gifts to the old man *who was teaching the children.* (relative)

5. ἔρχεται ἵνα κεύθη θησαυρόν.
   He is coming *in order that he may hide the treasure.* (purpose)

6. τὸν πατέρα τοῦ ἀνδρὸς ὃς παρ-έχει καρπὸν ὁράεις;
   Do you see the father of the man *who supplies fruit?* (relative)

7. εἰ μὴ ἐκείνη ἐμὸν κασιγνητὸν ἀδίκεον, τὴν ἂν φίλεον.
   If that woman were not harming my brother, I would love her. (conditional)

8. ἡδόμεθα ἐκείνοισι δώροισι ἐπεὶ καλά ἐστιν.
   We are pleased with those gifts *because they are lovely.* (causal)

ANSWERS

I.   1. σώματι θνήσκοντι to/for/by a body dying/ dying body   2. πέτραι πίπτουσαι falling rocks   3. ἀνδρῶν πινόντων of men drinking/ drinking men   4. ἄναξ λύσων a lord being about to loose   5. πατρίδα ἐοῦσαν being a fatherland/ a fatherland being   6. ἡδόνη φιλεομένη pleasure being loved   7. πόλιος λυσομένης of a city being about to be loosed/ of a city being about to loose for itself   8. πράγμασι γιγνόμενοισι to/for/by troubles happening   9. φίλῳ μαχομένῳ to/for a friend fighting/ fighting friend   10. πῦρ ἐόν being a fire/ a fire being

II.   1. ἐκεῖνον ἄνδρα θνήσκοντα μὴ ἀδικεώμεν. Let us not harm that dying man (since he is dying).   2. οἵδε φέρον γέρουσι δῶρα ἐθέλοντες γίγνεσθαι φίλοι. These men, wishing to become friends, were carrying gifts to the old man.   3. παῖδας εὕδοντας φέρομεν. We carried the sleeping children.   4. δῶρα φέρομεν γέροντι διδάσκοντι παῖδας. We were bringing gifts to the old man teaching the children.   5. ἔρχεται κεύσων θησαυρόν. He is coming intending to hide the treasure.   6. τὸν πατέρα τοῦ ἀνδρὸς παρ-έχοντος καρπὸν ὁράεις; Do you see the father of the man supplying fruit?   7. ἐκείνην ἐμὸν κασιγνητὸν μὴ ἀδικέουσαν ἂν φίλεον. I would love that woman (if she were) not harming my brother.   8. ἡδόμεθα ἐκείνοισι δώροισι ἐόντεσσι καλοῖσιν. We take pleasure in those gifts, being beautiful (the gifts, that is).

LESSON 31

I. Fill in the blanks with the correct form of the interrogative pronoun/adjective τίς, τί.

1. Who (sg.) will send this? ____ τόδε πέμψει;
2. Who (pl.) will send this? ____ τόδε πέμψουσιν;
3. Whom (sg.) are you sending? ____ πέμπεις;
4. Whom (pl.) are you sending? ____ πέμπεις;
5. To whom (sing.) shall we send gifts? εἰς ____ δῶρα πέμψομεν;
6. In what do I take pleasure? (By what am I pleased?) ____ ἥδομαι;
7. With whom (sg.) are you all coming? σὺν ____ ἔρχεσθε;
8. With what friend are you coming? σὺν ____ φίλῳ ἔρχεαι;
9. By means of what words does that man persuade him? ____ λόγοισι τὸν ἐκεῖνος πείθει;
10. What man does he obey? ____ ἀνέρι πείθεται;
11. In what virtues do they take pleasure? ____ ἀρετῇσι ἥδονται;
12. What children do not love sweet fruit? ____ παῖδες καρπὸν ἡδὺν οὐ φιλέουσιν;
13. What word do you hear? ____ ἔπος ἀκούεις;
14. What sound do you all hear? ____ φωνὴν ἀκούετε;
15. From what city are they coming? ἀπὸ ____ πόλιος ἔρχονται;

II. Put the following phrases into Greek, using the indefinite pronoun/adjective.

1. someone
2. for certain wisemen
3. some words
4. of some gold
5. something
6. for some child
7. certain winds (acc.)
8. some truth
9. of some nectar
10. certain treasures

III. Change each direct question below into indirect questions introduced by αἰτέει and αἴτεε (he/she asks, he/she asked) and using the indirect interrogative pronoun and the optative in secondary sequence where possible.

1. τί μάχονται; (Why are they fighting?)
2. τίνες μάχονται; (Who (pl.) is fighting?)
3. τί ἔρδει; (What is she doing?)
4. τίς τόδε ἔρδει; (Who does this?)
5. τίς νέκταρ πίνει; (Who drinks nectar?)
6. τίνα φιλέεις; (Whom do you love?)

ANSWERS

I.   1. τίς   2. τίνες   3. τίνα   4. τίνας   5. τίνα   6. τέῳ   7. τέῳ
8. τέῳ   9. τέοισι   10. τῷ   11. τέοισι   12. τίνες   13. τί   14. τίνα
15. τεῦ

II.   1. τις   2. σοφοῖσι τεοῖσι   3. λόγοι τινές   4. χρυσοῦ τευ   5. τι
6. παιδί τεῳ   7. ἀνέμους τινάς   8. ἀληθείη τις   9. νέκταρός τευ
10. θησαυροί τινες

III.   1. αἰτέει τί μάχονται. αἴτεε τί μαχοίατο.   2. αἰτέει οἵ τινες
μάχονται. αἴτεε οἵ τινες μαχοίατο.   3. αἰτέει ὅ τι ἔρδει. αἴτεε ὅ τι
ἔρδοι.   4. αἰτέει ὅς τις τόδε ἔρδει. αἴτεε ὅς τις τόδε ἔρδοι   5. αἰτέει ὅς τις
νέκταρ πίνει. αἴτεε ὅς τις νέκταρ πίνοι.   6. αἰτέει ὅν τινα φιλέεις. αἴτεε ὅν
τινα φιλέοις.

LESSON 32

I.   Complete the Greek sentences with the correct form of the Greek first personal
pronoun.

1.   The voice of the Muse is sweet <u>to me</u>.   φωνὴ Μούσης ἐστί _____ ἡδεῖα.

2.   The words of wise men always persuade <u>me</u>.   λόγοι σοφῶν αἰεί _____
πείθουσιν.

3.   <u>We</u> always obey the words of wise men.   _____ λόγοις σοφῶν αἰεὶ
πειθόμεθα.

4.   The treasure is <u>ours</u>.   θησαυρός ἐστι _____.

5.   <u>My</u> gold was hidden among the rocks.   χρυσός _____ κεύθετο ἐν τῇσι
πέτρῃσι.

6.   Speak sweet words <u>to me</u>!   ἔννεπέ _____ ἔπεα γλυκέα.

7.   He asked who saved <u>us</u>.   αἴτεε ὅς τις _____ σώζοι.

8.   They heard <u>us</u> speaking.   ἄκουον _____ λεγόντων.

9.   Why are you making trial of <u>me</u>?   τί _____ πειράεις;

10. They are bringing <u>me</u> into the city in order that they might make trial of <u>me</u>.
     φέρουσί _____ εἰς πόλιν ἵνα πειράωσί _____.

ANSWERS

I.   1. μοι   2. με.   3. ἡμεῖς   4. ἡμῖν. (dat. of possession)   5. μευ   6. μοι
7. ἡμέας   8. ἡμέων (ἀκούω + gen.)   9. μευ (πειράω + gen.)   10. με, μευ

LESSON 33

I. Change the verb form in the following sentences to agree with the nominative personal pronoun. Translate.

1. ἐγὼ νηπίῳ ἐκείνῳ οὐ πείσομαι.   *I shall not obey that fool.*

    σὺ νηπίῳ ἐκείνῳ οὐ _____.

    ἡμεῖς νηπίῳ ἐκείνῳ οὐ _____.

    ὑμεῖς νηπίῳ ἐκείνῳ οὐ _____.

2. ἡμεῖς οἶνον οὔ ποτε πίνομεν.   *We never drink wine.*

    ὑμεῖς οἶνον οὔ ποτε _____.

    ἐγὼ οἶνον οὔ ποτε _____.

    σὺ οἶνον οὔ ποτε _____.

3. σὺ βούλεαι διδάσκεσθαι.   *You wish to be taught.*

    ὑμεῖς _____ διδάσκεσθαι.

    ἡμεῖς _____ διδάσκεσθαι.

    ἐγὼ _____ διδάσκεσθαι.

ANSWERS

I.   1. πείσεαι *You* will not obey that fool. πεισόμεθα *We* shall not obey that fool. πείσεσθε *You* (pl.) will not obey that fool.   2. πίνετε *You* (pl.) never drink wine. πίνω *I* never drink wine. πίνεις *You* never drink wine.
3. βούλεσθε *You* (pl.) wish to be taught. βουλόμεθα *We* wish to be taught. βούλομαι *I* wish to be taught.

LESSON 34

I. Replace the underlined words with the correct form of the third personal pronoun. Translate.

1. ἱκάνω δῶρα εἰς σέ φέρων, ὡς <u>ἐκείνας φίλας</u> λύσῃς.
2. λαοὶ <u>τόδε ἔργον</u> ἔρξουσιν.
3. λέγω <u>τοῖσι ἄνδρεσσι</u> ἀληθείην.
4. φιλέωμεν πάντες <u>κασιγνητούς</u>.
5. αἴτεες ὅς τις ζητέοι <u>τὸν υἱόν</u>.
6. μήποτε <u>παῖδα</u> ἀδικέωμεν.
7. τί μισέετε <u>τοῦ ἀνδρὸς</u> υἷους;
8. οὐ γίγνωσκον ἥντινα ὁδὸν <u>ἐκείνῳ</u> φαίνοιεν.
9. <u>ἄλλοισι ἀνθρώποισι</u> βούλοντο μίσγειν.
10. ὁ πόλεμος ἦεν <u>τῷ</u> χαλεπός.

ANSWERS

I. 1. σφεας I come bearing gifts for you, in order that you may free those friends/ them.   2. μιν/ἑ The people will do this work/ it.   3. σφιν/σφισι I speak the truth to the men/ them.   4. σφεας Let us all love our brothers/ them.   5. ἑ/ μιν You were asking who was seeking the son/ him.   6. ἑ /μιν Let us never injure a child/ him!   7. ἑο Why do you (pl.) hate the sons of that man/ him?   8. οἱ I did not know what road they were showing to that man/ him.   9. σφι/ σφισι They wished to mingle with other men/ them.   10. οἱ The war was difficult for someone/ him.

LESSON 35

I. Change each underlined verb to the aorist tense, keeping the same person, number, and mood. The aorist stem is given in parentheses. Translate.

1. ἐκεῖνον ἀγαθὸν <u>ἀδικέουσι</u> οἱ πονηροί. (ἀδίκησ-)
2. <u>αἴτεες</u> τίνα φιλέοι. (αἴτησ-)
3. <u>ἀκούετέ</u> ἑο λέγοντος; (ἄκουσ-)
4. <u>δείδω</u> τοὺς ἀγαθοὺς ἀπολλύειν. (δεῖσ-)
5. <u>δίωκέ</u> σφεας ἀπὸ θαλάσσης εἰς πόλιν. (δίωξ-)
6. ἔχειν πολλοὺς φίλους <u>ἐθέλωμεν</u>. (ἐθέλησ-)
7. ὑμέας διώκομεν ὄφρα <u>σπεύδητε</u>. (σπεῦσ-)

II. Translate, identifying each type of condition as either a Future More Vivid (FMV) or Present General (PG).

1. εἴ κεν ἔρξῃ πολλὰ ἔργα κακά, ἀπολέσω μιν.
2. ὅτε ἔρξωσι πολλὰ ἔργα κακά, ἀπολλύω σφεας.
3. οἵ τινες ἔρξωσι πολλὰ ἔργα κακά, θανέονται.
4. ἢν αἰεὶ εὕδῃς, οὔ ποτε μαθήσεαι.

5. ἢν αἰεὶ εὕδητε, οὐδὲν μανθάνετε.

6. ἐπὴν παῖδες εὕδήσωσιν, οὐδὲν μανθάνουσιν.

7. εἴ κέν τις πίνῃ πολλὸν οἶνον, πίπτει.

8. ὅς τις πίνῃ πολλὸν οἶνον, πέσεται.

9. ὃς πίνῃ πολλὸν οἶνον, πίπτει.

10. ὅτε πῦρ πόλιας ἀπόλεσῃ, πολλοὶ θνήσκουσιν.

III. Identify from these dictionary entries which type of aorist each of the following verbs has. (Review Section 244)

1. δοκέω, δοκήσω, δόκησα

2. ἔρχομαι, ἐλεύσομαι, ἔλθον

3. ἐσθίω, ἔδομαι, φάγον

4. εὑρίσκω, εὑρήσω, εὗρον

5. λύω, λύσω, λύσα

6. γιγνώσκω, γνώσομαι, γνῶν

7. ζώω, ζώσω, ζῶσα

ANSWERS

I.   1. ἀδίκησαν The vile men injured that brave man.   2. αἴτησας You asked whom he loved.   3. ἀκούσατε Did you hear him speaking?   4. δεῖσα I feared to kill the brave men.   5. δίωξέ He pursued them from the sea to the city. 6. ἐθλήσωμεν Let us wish to have many friends!   7. σπεύσητε. We are pursuing you (pl.) in order that you may hurry (make haste).

II.   1. If he does many bad deeds, I shall kill him. FMV   2. When they do many bad deeds, I kill them. PG   3. Whoever does (pl. subject) many bad deeds will die. FMV   4. If you are always sleeping, you will never learn. FMV   5. If you (pl.) are always sleeping, you learn nothing.   6. When children are sleeping, they are learning nothing. PG   7. If some one drinks much wine, he falls. PG   8. Whoever drinks a lot of wine will fall. FMV   9. (A man) who drinks a lot of wine falls.   10. When fire destroys cities, many die. PG

III.   1. 1st   2. 2nd   3. 2nd   4. 2nd   5. 1st   6. 3rd   7. 1st

LESSON 36

I. Change the participles in the following sentences into the aorist tense. (The aorist stem is given in parentheses.) Then translate the new sentences.

1. πείθοντες ἡμέας ἑ λῦσαι, ἐπὶ νηὸν ἔρχοντο. (πεῖσ-)
    (While) persuading us to free him, they were going to the temple.

2. ἐσθίεις καρπὸν ἀπολλύων περ τοὺς χρηστούς; (ἀπόλεσ-)
    Are you eating fruit although (you are) killing those worthy men?

3. θεὸν τὴν πόλιν σώσοντα γίγνωσκον. (σῶσ-)
    They knew that the god was about to save the city. (They knew the god being about to save the city.)

4. ὁ θεὸς τὴν πόλιν σώζων πέμπει ὄμβρον. (σῶσ-)
    The god, (while) saving the city, sends a storm.

5. βουλεύων περ δίδαξαι ἡμέας, οὐ πολλὸν γιγνώσκει. (βούλευσ-)
    Although planning to teach us, he does not know much.

II. Change the underlined verbs into the aorist tense. (The aorist stem is given in parentheses.) Translate.

1. <u>βουλεύοι ἔρδεμεν</u> καλά. (βούλευσ-, ἔρξ-)

2. χρηστὰς υἱοί μευ <u>γαμέοιεν</u>. (γάμησ-)

3. μούνα ἀγαθὰ <u>νοέοιμι</u>. (νόησ-)

4. ἐθελήσαμεν γίγνεσθαι θεοὶ ἵνα <u>ῥέζοιμεν</u> πάντα ἃ βουλόμεθα. (ῥέξ-)

5. οἶνον ἔνεικας ὄφρα μηδείς σε <u>μισέοι</u>. (μίσησ-)

ANSWERS

I. 1. πείσαντες (After) Having persuaded us to free him, they were going to the temple.   2. ἀπολέσας Are you eating fruit although having killed those worthy men? (although you have killed these worthy men)   3. σώσαντα They knew that the god saved the city. (the god having saved the city)   4. σώσας The god, (after) having saved the city, sends a storm.   5. βουλεύσας Although having planned to teach us, he does not know much.

II. 1. βουλεύσειεν ἔρξαι May he plan to do noble things!   2. γαμήσειαν May my sons marry worthy women!   3. νοήσαιμι May I think/perceive only good things!   4. ῥέξαιμεν We wished to become gods in order that we might do everything that we wanted.   5. μισήσειεν You brought wine in order that no one might hate you.

LESSON 37

I. Convert each of the following imperfects to aorists (stem in parentheses), and then translate. Remember to keep the verb in the same voice, but remember that in the aorist system the passive endings are different from the middle endings.

1. πονεόμην (πονησ-) I was toiling

2. τεύχοντο (τευξ-) they were building for themselves/they were being built

3. ζητέεο (ζητησ-) you were seeking for yourself/you were being sought

4. πέμπετο (πεμψ-) he/she was sending for him/herself/he/she was being sent

5. (ἐγώ) βούλευον (βουλευσ-) I was considering

6. γαμέομεν (γαμησ- or γῆμ-) we were marrying

7. αἰτέεσθε (αἰτησ-) you were asking for yourselves/you were being asked

8. μίσγεο (μιξ-) you were mixing for yourself/you were being mixed

9. ἥδετο (ἡσ-) he/she was enjoying

10. ἔρδετο (ἐρξ-) he/she/it was doing for him/her/itself/it was being done

11. ῥέζοντο (ῥεξ-) they were doing for themselves/they were being done

12. ποιέοντο (ποιησ-) they were making for themselves/they were being made

13. πείθεσθε (πεισ-) you (pl.) were obeying

14. φαίνετο (φην-) he/she was showing for him/herself/he/she was being shown

15. φιλεόμην (φιλησ-) I was loving for myself/I was being loved

ANSWERS

I.   1. πονησάμην I toiled   2. τεύξαντο they built for themselves
3. ζητήσαο you sought for yourself   4. πέμψατο he/she sent for him/herself
5. βούλευσα I planned   6. γαμήσαμεν/γήμαμεν we married
7. αἰτήσασθε you asked for yourselves   8. μίξαο you mixed for yourself
9. ἥσατο he/she enjoyed   10. ἔρξατο he/she did for him/herself
11. ῥέξαντο they did for themselves   12. ποιήσαντο they made for
themselves   13. πείσασθε you (pl.) obeyed   14. φήνατο he/she/it showed for
itself/seemed   15. φιλησάμην I loved for myself

LESSON 38

I. Translate each of the following sentences. Then identify or describe the construction it represents (e.g., Future More Vivid, Purpose Clause in Primary Sequence, etc.).

1. εἰ κε πράγματα χρηστὰ πονήσησθε, ὄλβῳ ἥσεσθε.
2. ὅτε πράγματα χρηστὰ πονήσησθε, ὄλβῳ ἥδεσθε.
3. πράγματα χρηστὰ πονήσαντο ἵνα ὄλβῳ ἡσαίατο.
4. πράγματα χρηστὰ πονησώμεθα ὄφρα ὄλβῳ ἡσώμεθα.
5. ἢν πράγματα χρηστὰ πονησάμην, ὄλβῳ ἂν ἡσάμην.
6. ὅς τις πράγματα χρηστὰ πονήσηται, ὄλβῳ ἥσεται.
7. οἵ τινες πράγματα χρηστὰ πονήσωνται, ὄλβῳ ἥσονται
8. μή ποτε πράγματα πονηρὰ πόνησαι.
9. ὄλβῳ ἥσασθε.
10. ὄλβῳ ἥσαιο.
11. πράγματα χρηστὰ πονήσαισθε.
12. πράγματα χρηστὰ πονησώμαι.
13. πράγματα χρηστὰ πονησάμενοι, ὄλβῳ ἥσαντο.
14. πράγματα χρηστὰ πονεόμενοι, ὄλβῳ ἥσαντο.
15. πράγματα χρηστὰ πονησάμενος, ὄλβῳ ἥδεται.
16. πράγματα χρηστὰ πονησαμένη, ὄλβῳ ἥσομαι.
17. ὄλβῳ ἡδομένη, πράγματα χρηστὰ πόνησαο.
18. ὄλβῳ ἡδόμεναι, πράγματα χρηστὰ πονέοντο.
19. ἐπεὶ ὄλβῳ ἂν ἥσηαι, πράγματα χρηστὰ πονέεαι.
20. εἰ κεν ὄλβῳ ἥσηται, πονήσεται πράγματα χρηστά.

ANSWERS

I. 1. If you (pl.) work at worthy deeds, you will enjoy prosperity. Future More Vivid 2. When you (pl.) work at worthy deeds, you enjoy prosperity. Present General 3. They worked at worthy deeds in order that they might enjoy prosperity. Secondary Sequence Purpose Clause 4. Let's work at worthy deeds in order that we may enjoy prosperity! Primary Sequence Purpose Clause 5. If I had worked at worthy deeds, I would have enjoyed prosperity. Past Contrary to Fact 6. Whoever works at worthy deeds will enjoy prosperity. Future More Vivid 7. Whoever (pl.) works at worthy deeds will enjoy prosperity. Future More Vivid 8. Never work at vile deeds! (Sg. Imperative) 9. Enjoy prosperity! (Pl. Imperative) or You (pl.) enjoyed prosperity. 10. May you (sg.) enjoy prosperity! Wish 11. May you (pl.) work at worthy deeds! Wish 12. Let me work at worthy deeds! Hortatory 13. Having worked at worthy deeds, they enjoyed prosperity. Participial clause, time prior to main verb 14. (While) Working at worthy deeds, they enjoyed prosperity. Participial clause, time simultaneous with main verb 15. (After) Having worked at worthy deeds, he is enjoying prosperity. Participial clause, time prior to main verb 16. (After) Having worked at worthy deeds, I shall enjoy prosperity. Participial clause, time prior to main verb 17. (While) Enjoying prosperity, you worked at worthy deeds. Participial clause, time simultaneous with main verb 18. (While) Enjoying prosperity, they were working at noble deeds. Participial clause, time simultaneous with main verb 19. When you enjoy prosperity, you are working at worthy deeds. Present General 20. If he enjoys prosperity, he will work at worthy deeds. Future More Vivid

LESSON 40

I. Identify and translate each of the following conditions, and then change them to Future Less Vivid conditions, and translate.

1. εἰ ὑμέας ἴδον ἐκεῖνοι, φῆναν ἂν ὑμῖν τὴν ὁδόν.
2. εἰ δίκαιοι εὔξωνται ἀγαθοί εἶναι, ἀληθείην λέγουσιν.
3. εἰ ποιμὴν ἔλθεν εἰς ἄκρον γαίης, μῆλα ἕο εὗρεν ἄν.
4. εἰ κόσμος ἀπ-ολλύηται, ἡμεῖς πάντες θανεόμεθα.
5. εἰ φιλέωμεν ἀλλήλους, εἰρήνην σχήσομεν.

II. Change the following wishes into potential optative sentences. Translate both types of sentences.

1. ποιμήν τε ζητήσειε καὶ εὕροι μῆλα ἕο.
2. μῆλα μὴ ποιμένα λάθοι.
3. πολλοὶ ποιμένες διώξειαν τὰ μῆλα ἃ οὐ δυνατοί εἰμεν εὑρεῖν.
4. μῆλα ἔλθοι εἰς αὐλήν.
5. ποιμὴν ἴδοι μῆλα ἕο.

ANSWERS

I. 1. Past Contrary to Fact. If those men had seen you (pl.), they would have shown the way to you. FLV: εἰ ὑμέας ἴδοιεν (ἂν) ἐκεῖνοι, φήνειε (ἂν) ὑμῖν ὁδόν. If those men should see you, they would show the way to you.
2. Present General. If righteous men claim to be brave, they are speaking the truth. FLV: εἰ δίκαιοι εὐξαίατο (ἂν) ἀγαθοί εἶναι, ἀληθείην λέγοιεν (ἂν). If righteous men should claim to be brave, they would be speaking the truth.
3. Past Contrary to Fact. If the shepherd had come to the edge of the land, he would have found his sheep. FLV: εἰ ποίμην ἔλθοι εἰς ἄκρον γαίης, μῆλα ἕο εὕροι (ἂν).   4. Future More Vivid. If the world perishes, we shall all die. FLV: εἰ κόσμος ἀπ-ολλύοιτο, ἡμεῖς πάντες θάνοιμεν/θνήσκοιμεν (ἂν). If the world were to perish, we would all die/ be dying.   5. Future More Vivid. If we love one another, we shall have peace. FLV: εἰ φιλέοιμεν ἀλλήλους, εἰρήνην σχέθοιμεν (ἂν). If we were to love one another, we would have peace.

II. 1. May the shepherd both seek and find his sheep! ποιμήν τε ζητήσειε καὶ εὕροι ἂν μῆλα ἕο. The shepeherd could/ might/would both seek and find his sheep.   2. May the sheep not escape the shepherd's notice! μῆλα οὐ ποιμένα ἂν λάθοι. The sheep could/might/would not escape the shepherd's notice.
3. May many shepherds pursue the sheep that we are not able to find! πολλοὶ ποιμένες διώξειαν ἂν τὰ μῆλα ἃ οὐ δυνατοί εἰμεν εὑρεῖν. Many shepherds might/could/ would pursue the sheep that we are not able to find.   4. May the sheep come to the fold! μῆλα ἔλθοι ἂν εἰς αὐλήν. The sheep might/ could/ would come to the fold.   5. May the shepherd see his sheep! ποιμὴν ἴδοι ἂν μῆλα ἕο. The shepherd might/ could/ would see his sheep.

LESSON 41

I. Form the 3rd person singular imperfect and aorist indicative of each verb below. (The first three principal parts are given.)

1. αἱρέω, αἱρήσω, ἕλον
2. ἀμείβομαι, ἀμείψομαι, ἀμειψάμην
3. ἁμαρτάνω, ἁμαρτήσομαι, ἅμαρτον
4. γίγνομαι, γενήσομαι, γενόμην
5. δέχομαι, δέξομαι, δεξάμην
6. ἐννέπω, ἐνίψω, ἔνισπον
7. ἔρχομαι, ἐλεύσομαι, ἔλ(υ)θον
8. ἐσθίω, ἔδομαι, φάγον
9. εὑρίσκω, εὑρήσω, εὗρον
10. εὔχομαι, εὔξομαι, εὐξάμην
11. ἔχω, ἕξω or σχήσω, σχόν or σχέθον
12. κεύθω, κεύσω, κύθον
13. κρίνω, κρινέω, κρῖνα
14. λαμβάνω, λήψομαι, λάβον
15. λανθάνω, λήσω, λάθον
16. μανθάνω, μαθήσομαι, μάθον
17. ὁράω, ὄψομαι, ἴδον
18. πάσχω, πείσομαι, πάθον
19. πείθω, πείσω, πεῖσα or πέπιθον
20. πεύθομαι, πεύσομαι, πυθόμην
21. πίνω, πίομαι, πίον
22. πίπτω, πέσομαι, πέσον

ANSWERS

I. 1. αἵρεε/ ἕλε 2. ἀμείβετο/ ἀμείψατο 3. ἁμάρτανε/ ἅμαρτε
4. γίγνετο/ γένετο 5. δέχετο/ δέξατο 6. ἔννεπε/ ἔνισπε 7. ἔρχετο/ ἔλ(υ)θε 8. ἔσθιε/ φάγε 9. εὕρισκε/ εὗρε 10. εὔχετο/ εὔξατο 11. ἔχε/ σχέ, σχέθε 12. κεῦθε/ κύθε 13. κρίνε/ κρῖνε 14. λάμβανε/ λάβε
15. λάνθανε/ λάθε 16. μάνθανε/ μάθε 17. ὅραε/ ἴδε 18. πάσχε/ πάθε
19. πεῖθε/ πεῖσε, πέπιθε 20. πεύθετο/ πύθετο 21. πίνε/ πίε
22. πίπτε/ πέσε

LESSON 42

I. Conjugate the third aorist verb στῆν (I stood) in all the moods, just as has been done with βῆν.

II. Change each of the following underlined imperfect tense verbs to the aorist indicative, maintaining the same person and number. Translate.

1. <u>βαῖνον</u> κεῖνοι παῖδες ἀπὸ πόλιος πρὸς ποταμόν.
2. <u>βαῖνε</u> κεῖνος παῖς ἀπὸ πόλιος πρὸς ποταμόν.
3. διὰ ἤματος παντὸς εὑδήσας, σὺ <u>βαῖνες</u> εἰς πόλιν.
4. <u>γιγνώσκετε</u> τὸν γέροντα ἑὸν βίον τελέσαντα;
5. <u>γίγνωσκες</u> τὸν γέροντα ἑὸν βίον τελέσαντα;
6. σοφοὶ ἐόντες <u>γιγνώσκομεν</u> ἀληθείην.
7. <u>τλάον</u> δὴ ἐγὼ μαχήσασθαι εἵνεκα πατρίδος.
8. <u>τλάομεν</u> δὴ ἡμεῖς μαχήσασθαι εἵνεκα πατρίδος.
9. πάντες <u>δύον</u> νηόν ὄφρα πόροιεν ἀθάνατοις δῶρα.
10. πᾶς <u>δύε</u> νηόν ὄφρα πόροι ἀθάνατοις δῶρα.

ANSWERS

I.

	Indicative		Subjunctive	
	Sg.	*Pl.*	*Sg.*	*Pl.*
1st pers.	στῆν	στῆμεν	στήω	στήωμεν
2nd pers.	στῆς	στῆτε	στήῃς	στήητε
3rd pers.	στῆ	στῆσαν	στήῃ	στήωσι

	Optative	
	Sg.	*Pl.*
1st pers.	σταίην	σταῖμεν
2nd pers.	σταίης	σταῖτε
3rd sing.	σταίη	σταῖεν

	Imperative	
	Sg.	*Pl.*
2nd pers.	στῆθι	στῆτε

Infinitive   στῆναι

Participle (m. f. n. nom.)   στάς, στᾶσα, στάν

II. 1. βῆσαν Those children went from the city to the river. 2. βῆ That child went from the city to the river. 3. βῆς Having slept for the whole day, you went to the city. 4. γνῶτε Did you (pl.) know that the old man completed his life (died)? 5. γνῶς Did you (sg.) know that the old man completed his life (died)? 6. γνῶμεν Being wise (since we were wise), we knew the truth. 7. τλῆν I indeed dared to fight for the sake of my fatherland. 8. τλῆμεν We indeed dared to fight for the sake of our fatherland. 9. δῦσαν/δῦν Everybody entered the temple in order that they might give gifts to the immortals. 10. δῦ Each man entered the temple in order that he might give gifts to the immortals.

A Reading Course in Homeric Greek

LESSON 43

I. Change the underlined verbs to the aorist, maintaining the same person, number, voice and mood (unless a change in mood is required by rules of syntax). Then translate.

1. εἰ <u>γιγνώσκοις</u>, <u>ἐννέποις</u> ἄν.
2. εἰ <u>γιγνώσκῃς</u> ἀληθείην, χρή σε <u>ἐννέπειν</u>.
3. ὅτε <u>δύῃ</u> ὁ ξεῖνος εἰς ποταμόν, εὑρήσει ὕδωρ πολλόν.
4. ὅτε <u>δύοι</u> ὁ ξεῖνος εἰς ποταμόν, εὕροι ἄν ὕδωρ πολλόν.
5. <u>βαίνοντές</u> περ εἰς πόλεμον, οὐκ ἔλπουσι πείσεσθαι (from πάσχω).
6. εἰ <u>βαίνοιμεν</u>, <u>εὑρίσκοιμεν</u> ἄν σῖτον.
7. <u>γίγνωσκε</u> σὲ αὐτόν.
8. <u>βαίνετε</u> νῦν καὶ <u>σώζετέ</u> με.
9. <u>βαίνοιεν</u> ἄν.
10. <u>μανθάνω</u> πολλὰ ἵνα <u>γιγνώσκω</u> (subjunctive) ἀληθείην.
11. <u>τλάες</u> πόνους πολλοὺς ἵνα <u>γαμήσειας</u> κείνην;
12. οἱ νήπιοι <u>πίπτον</u> καὶ <u>δύον</u> εἰς ποταμόν.

ANSWERS

I. 1. εἰ <u>γνοίης</u>, <u>ἐνίσποις</u> ἄν. If you should know, then you would say.
2. εἰ <u>γνώῃς</u> ἀληθείην, χρή σε <u>ἐνισπεῖν</u>. If you know the truth, it is necessary for you to say. 3. ὅτε <u>δύῃ</u> ὁ ξεῖνος εἰς ποταμόν, εὑρήσει ὕδωρ πολλόν. When the stranger enters the river, he will find much water. 4. εἰ <u>δυίη/δύῃ</u> ὁ ξεῖνος εἰς ποταμόν, εὕροι ἄν ὕδωρ πολλόν. If the stranger should enter the river, he would find much water. 5. <u>βάντες</u> περ εἰς πόλεμον, οὐκ ἔλπουσι πείσεσθαι. Although having gone to war, they are not expecting to suffer.
6. εἰ <u>βαῖμεν</u>, <u>εὕροιμεν</u> ἄν σῖτον. If we should go, we would find food.
7. <u>γνῶθι</u> σὲ αὐτόν. Know yourself. 8. <u>βῆτε</u> νῦν καὶ <u>σώσατε</u> με. Come (pl.) now and save me! 9. <u>βαῖεν</u> ἄν. They could go. 10. <u>μάθον</u> πολλὰ ἵνα <u>γνοίην</u> ἀληθείην. I studied many things in order that I might know the truth.
11. <u>τλῆς</u> πόνους πολλοὺς ἵνα <u>γαμήσειας</u> κείνην; You endured many toils in order that you might marry that woman? 12. οἱ νήπιοι <u>πέσον</u> καὶ <u>δῦσαν/δῦν</u> εἰς ποταμόν. The fools fell and sank into the river.

LESSON 45

I. After referring to the following principal parts, form the perfect and pluperfect third person singular and plural.

1. αἱρέω, αἱρήσω, ἕλον, ᾕρηκα
2. ἁμαρτάνω, ἁμαρτήσομαι, ἅμαρτον, ἡμάρτηκα
3. γίγνομαι, γενήσομαι, γενόμην, γέγαα
4. ἔρχομαι, ἐλεύσομαι, ἔλ(υ)θον, εἰλήλουθα
5. ἐσθίω, ἔδομαι, φάγον, ἐδήδοκα
6. εὑρίσκω, εὑρήσω, εὗρον, εὕρηκα
7. ἔχω, ἕξω or σχήσω, σχόν or σχέθον, ὄχωκα
8. κεύθω, κεύσω, κύθον, κέκευθα
9. κρίνω, κρινέω, κρῖνα, κέκρικα
10. λαμβάνω, λήψομαι, λάβον, εἴληφα
11. λανθάνω, λήσω, λάθον, λέληθα
12. μανθάνω, μαθήσομαι, μάθον, μεμάθηκα
13. ὁράω, ὄψομαι, ἴδον, ἑώρακα
14. πάσχω, πείσομαι, πάθον, πέπονθα
15. πείθω, πείσω, πεῖσα or πέπιθον, πέπεικα
16. πέμπω, πέμψω, πέμψα, πέπομφα
17. πίπτω, πέσομαι, πέσον, πέπτωκα

II. Translate the third person plural perfect and pluperfects from I.

ANSWERS

I.   1. ᾕρηκε/ ᾑρήκει ᾑρήκασι/ ᾑρήκεσαν   2. ἡμάρτηκε/ ἡμαρτήκει ἡμαρτήκασι/ ἡμαρτήκεσαν   3. γέγαε/ γεγάει γεγάασι/ γεγάεσαν   4. εἰλήλουθε/ εἰληλούθει εἰληλούθασι/ εἰληλούθεσαν   5. ἐδήδοκε/ ἐδηδόκει ἐδηδόκασι/ ἐδηδόκεσαν   6. εὕρηκε/ εὑρήκει εὑρήκασι/ εὑρήκεσαν   7. ὄχωκε/ὀχώκει ὀχώκασι/ὀχώκεσαν   8. κέκευθε/ κεκεύθει κεκεύθασι/ κεκεύθεσαν   9. κέκρικε/ κεκρίκει κεκρίκασι/ κεκρίκεσαν   10. εἴληφε/ εἰλήφει εἰλήφασι/ εἰλήφεσαν   11. λέληθε/ λελήθει λελήθασι/ λελήθεσαν   12. μεμάθηκε/ μεμάθηκει μεμαθήκασι/ μεμαθήκεσαν   13. ἑώρακε/ ἑωράκει ἑωράκασι/ ἑωράκεσαν   14. πέπονθε/ πεπόνθει πεπόνθασι/ πεπόνθεσαν   15. πέπεικε/ πεπείκει πεπείκασι/ πεπείκεσαν   16. πέπομφε/ πεπόμφει πεπόμφασι/ πεπόμφεσαν   17. πέπτωκε/ πεπτώκει πεπτώκασι/ πεπτώκεσαν

II.   1. they have seized/ they had seized   2. they have erred/ they had erred   3. they have been born/ they had been born   4. they have come/ they had come   5. they have eaten/ they had eaten   6. they have found/ they had found   7. they have had/ they had had   8. they have hidden/ they had hidden (both transitive)   9. they have picked out/ they had picked out   10. they have taken/ they had taken   11. they have escaped notice/ they had escaped notice   12. they have learned/ they had learned   13. they have seen/ they had seen   14. they have suffered / they had suffered   15. they have persuaded/ they had persuaded   16. they have sent / they had sent   17. they have fallen / they had fallen

LESSON 46

I. ἀπ-όλωλα is the perfect of the verb ἀπ-ολλύω, *I destroy, I kill.* However, the perfect has the meaning *I am lost, I perish.* (Likewise, the second aorist middle ἀπ-ολόμην means *I was lost, I perished.*) Conjugate the perfect ἀπ-όλωλα.

        a) indicative perfect and pluperfect

        b) subjunctive

        c) optative

        d) imperative

        e) infinitive

        f) participle (give the nom. sg. forms)

ANSWERS

I.

a)

indicative perfect	pluperfect
ἀπ-όλωλα	ἀπ-ολώλεα/η
ἀπ-όλωλας	ἀπ-ολώλεας
ἀπ-όλωλε	ἀπ-ολώλει
ἀπ-ολώλαμεν	ἀπ-ολώλεμεν
ἀπ-ολώλατε	ἀπ-ολώλετε
ἀπ-ολώλασι	ἀπ-ολώλεσαν

b)

subjunctive	optative
ἀπ-ολώλω	ἀπ-ολώλοιμι
ἀπ-ολώλῃς	ἀπ-ολώλοις
ἀπ-ολώλῃ	ἀπ-ολώλοι
ἀπ-ολώλωμεν	ἀπ-ολώλοιμεν
ἀπ-ολώλητε	ἀπ-ολώλοιτε
ἀπ-ολώλωσι	ἀπ-ολώλοιεν

e)

imperative	
ἀπ-όλωλε	ἀπ-ολώλετε

f)

infinitive

ἀπ-ολωλέναι/ ἀπ-ολωλέμεν(αι)

g)

participle

ἀπ-ολωλώς ἀπ-ολωλυῖα ἀπ-ολωλός

LESSON 47

I. Using the consonant changes chart in Section 339 for reference, conjugate the perfect and pluperfect middle-passive forms of a) λείπω, b) τεύχω, c) πεύθομαι. Their fifth principal parts are, respectively: λέλειμμαι, τέτυγμαι, and πέπυσμαι.

ANSWERS

I.

a)
λέλειμμαι	λελείμμεθα
λέλειψαι	λέλειφθε
λέλειπται	λελείφαται

λελείμμην	λελείμμεθα
λέλειψο	λέλειφθε
λέλειπτο	λελείφατο

b)
τέτυγμαι	τετύγμεθα
τέτυξαι	τέτυχθε
τέτυκται	τετύχαται *

τετύγμην	τετύγμεθα
τέτυξο	τέτυχθε
τέτυκτο	τετύχατο **

c)
πέπυσμαι	πεπύσμεθα
πέπυσαι	πέπυσθε
πέπυσται	πεπύθαται

πεπύσμην	πεπύσμεθα
πέπυσο	πέπυσθε
πέπυστο	πεπύθατο

* frequently spelled τετεύχαται
** frequently spelled τετεύχατο

LESSON 48

I. For each of the following forms of the perfect active participle, give the corresponding form in the middle-passive. Use the chart below to check your answer.

1. λελυκότι
2. λελυκυῖαι
3. λελυκότων
4. λελυκώς
5. λελυκυιάων
6. λελυκός
7. λελυκόσι
8. λελυκότα
9. λελυκότεσσι
10. λελυκυίαν

PF. ACT. PART.

	M	F	N
Sg.			
N	λελυκώς	λελυκυῖα	λελυκός
G	λελυκότος	λελυκυίης	λελυκότος
D	λελυκότι	λελυκυίη	λελυκότι
A	λελυκότα	λελυκυίαν	λελυκός
Pl.			
N	λελυκότες	λελυκυῖαι	λελυκότα
G	λελυκότων	λελυκυιάων	λελυκότων
D	λελυκότεσσι (λελυκόσι)	λελυκυίησ(ι)	λελυκότεσσι (λελυκόσι)
A	λελυκότας	λελυκυίας	λελυκότα

PF. M.-P. PART.

	M	F	N
Sg.			
N	λελυμένος	λελυμένη	λελυμένον
G	λελυμένου	λελυμένης	λελυμένου
D	λελυμένῳ	λελυμένη	λελυμένῳ
A	λελυμένον	λελυμένην	λελυμένον
Pl.			
N	λελυμένοι	λελυμέναι	λελυμένα
G	λελυμένων	λελυμένων	λελυμένων
D	λελυμένοισι	λελυμένῃσι	λελυμένοισι
A	λελυμένους	λελυμένας	λελυμένα

LESSON 49

I. Form the comparative (nominative, masculine, singular) and the superlative of each of the following adjectives. For help with the irregular forms, consult Section 354.

1. σοφός, -ή, -όν wise
2. ἱερός, -ή, -όν holy
3. νηλής, -ές pitiless
4. γλυκύς, -εῖα, -ύ sweet
5. πονηρός, -ή, -όν vile
6. πρόφρων, -ον willing
7. χλωρός, -ή, -όν green
8. εὐεργής, -ές well-made
9. ταχύς, -εῖα, -ύ swift (irreg.)
10. πολλός, -ή, -όν many (irreg.)
11. ἀγαθός, -ή, -όν good (irreg.)
12. φίλος, -η, -ον dear (irreg.)
13. καλός, -ή, -όν beautiful (irreg.)
14. μέγας, μεγάλη, μέγα (irreg.)
15. αἰσχρός, -ή, -όν shameful

II. Translate the following noun adjective phrases

1. ἀμείνων μήτηρ
2. ἀμείνονος μητρός
3. ἀμεινόνεσσι μητέρεσσι
4. ἀρίστην μητέρα
5. Ζεὺς ἱερώτατος
6. Διὸς ἱερωτάτου
7. Ζηνὸς ἱερωτάτου
8. Δία πατέρα ἱερώτατον
9. οἶκος εὐεργέστερος
10. οἴκων εὐεργεστάτων
11. ἔργον γλύκιον
12. ἔργα γλύκιονα
13. ἔργῳ γλυκίστῳ

ANSWERS

I. 1. σοφώτερος / σοφώτατος 2. ἱερώτερος / ἱερώτατος
3. νηλέστερος, νηλέστατος 4. γλυκίων / γλύκιστος 5. πονηρότερος / πονηρότατος 6. προφρονέστερος / προφρονέστατος 7. χλωρότερος / χλωρότατος 8. εὐεργέστερος / εὐεργέστατος 9. θάσσων / τάχιστος 10. πλείων / πλεῖστος 11. ἀρείων, ἀμείνων / ἄριστος
12. φίλτερος / φίλτατος 13. καλλίων / κάλλιστος 14. μείζων / μέγιστος 15. αἰσχίων / αἴσχιστος

II. 1. better mother 2. of (a) better mother 3. to/for better mothers
4. best mother (acc.) 5. holiest Zeus 6. of holiest Zeus 7. of holiest Zeus
8. holiest father Zeus (acc.) 9. better-made house 10. of best-made houses
11. sweeter deed 12. sweeter deeds 13. to/for (a) sweetest deed

LESSON 50

I.   Form the positive degree of the adverbs from each of the following adjectives by adding -ως to the neuter stem. Translate the adverb.

1.   μακρός, -ή, -όν long, large (in space or time)
2.   αἰσχρός, -ή, -όν shameful
3.   βαθύς, -εῖα, -ύ deep
4.   δίκαιος, -η, -ον just
5.   ἐσθλός, -ή, -όν noble
6.   ἱερός, -ή, -όν holy
7.   γλυκύς, -εῖα, -ύ sweet
8.   κακός, -ή. -όν bad
9.   κρατερός, -ή, -όν strong
10. ὀρθός, -ή, -όν straight, correct
11. ἀληθής, -ές true
12. βαρύς, -εῖα, -ύ heavy
13. χαλεπός, -ή, -όν difficult
14. ἄφρων, -ον senseless
15. μέγας, μεγάλη, μέγα big, great

II. Translate the following comparatives and superlatives as adverbs.

1.   φίλτερον, φίλτατα
2.   ἀληθέστερον, ἀληθέστατα
3.   κάλλιον, κάλλιστα
4.   μακρώτερον, μακρώτατα
5.   ἄμεινον, ἄριστα
6.   αἴσχιον, αἴσχιστα
7.   ἥδιον, ἥδιστα
8.   δικαιότερον, δικαιότατα
9.   ἱερώτερον, ἱερώτατα
10. πλεῖον, πλεῖστα

ANSWERS

I.   1. μακρῶς at great length, slowly   2. αἰσχρῶς shamefully   3. βαθέως deeply   4. δικαίως justly 5. ἐσθλῶς nobly 6. ἱερῶς holily 7. γλυκέως sweetly 8. κακῶς badly   9. κρατερῶς strongly   10. ὀρθῶς correctly 11. ἀληθέως truly   12. βαρέως heavily   13. χαλεπῶς with difficulty 14. ἀφρόνως senselessly   15. μεγάλως greatly

II.   1. more dearly, most dearly   2. more truly, most truly   3. more beautifully, most beautifully   4. at greater length/ more slowly, at greatest length/ most slowly 5. better, best   6. more shamefully, most shamefully   7. more sweetly, most sweetly 8. more justly, most justly   9. more holily, most holily   10. more, most

LESSON 51

I. Change each of the following imperfect passive indicatives to aorist passive indicatives, keeping the same person and number. Translate both the imperfect and aorist forms.

1. λύοντο
2. λύεο
3. λύεσθε
4. ὁραόμην
5. ὁραόμεθα
6. ὁράετο
7. γιγνωσκόμεθα
8. γιγνώσκεσθε
9. γιγνώσκετο
10. χαίρεο *
11. χαιρόμην *
12. φαίνοντο
13. φαίνετο
14. φαινόμεθα
15. φαινόμην

ANSWERS

I.

1. λύθησαν   they were being loosed/ They were loosed
2. λύθης   you (sg.) were being loosed/ you were loosed
3. λύθητε   you (pl.) were being loosed/ you were loosed
4. ὄφθην   I was being seen/ I was seen
5. ὄφθημεν   we were being seen/ we were seen
6. ὄφθη   he/she was being seen/ he/she was seen
7. γνώσθημεν   we were being known/ we were known
8. γνώσθητε   you all were being known/ you all were known
9. γνώσθη   he/she was being known/ he/she was known
10. χάρης   you (sg.) were rejoicing/ you rejoiced
11. χάρην   I was rejoicing/ I rejoiced
12. φάνησαν   they were appearing/ they appeared
13. φάνη   he/she was appearing/ he/she appeared
14. φάνημεν   were were appearing/ we appeared
15. φάνην   I was appearing/ I appeared

* The verb χαίρω has the same meaning in the active, middle and passive voices.

LESSON 52

I. Change each of the following from a primary sequence purpose clause to a secondary sequence purpose clause. Change the main verb into either the imperfect or aorist indicative (retaining the same mood, voice, person and number); change the verb in the subordinate clause from the subjunctive to the optative mood (retaining the same tense, voice, person and number). Translate.

1. πονεόμεθα πολλὸν ὄφρα ὦμεν ἄρισται.
2. πονέομαι πολλὸν ὄφρα ὦ ἀρίστη.
3. πονέεται πολλὸν ὄφρα ᾖ ἀρίστη.
4. πονέονται πολλὸν ὄφρα ὦσι ἄρισται.
5. πονέεαι πολλὸν ὄφρα ᾖς ἀρίστη.
6. πονέεσθε πολλὸν ὄφρα ἦτε ἄρισται.
7. ἀνα-βήσομαι ταχέως ἵνα μὴ ὀφθῶ.
8. ἀνα-βήσονται ταχέως ἵνα μὴ ὀφθῶσι.
9. ἀνα-βήσεαι ταχέως ἵνα μὴ ὀφθῇς.
10. ἀνα-βήσεται ταχέως ἵνα μὴ ὀφθῇ.
11. ἀνα-βήσεσθε ταχέως ἵνα μὴ ὀφθῆτε.
12. ἀνα-βησόμεθα ταχέως ἵνα μὴ ὀφθῶμεν.

ANSWERS

1. πονεόμεθα / πονησάμεθα πολλὸν ὄφρα εἶμεν ἄρισται.
   We were toiling/We toiled much in order that we might be best.

2. πονεόμην / πονησάμην πολλὸν ὄφρα εἴην ἀρίστη.
   I was toiling/ I toiled much in order that I might be best.

3. πονέετο / πονήσατο πολλὸν ὄφρα εἴη ἀρίστη.
   She was toiling/ She toiled much in order that she might be best.

4. πονέοντο / πονήσαντο πολλὸν ὄφρα εἶεν ἄρισται.
   They were toiling/ They toiled much in order that they might be best.

5. πονέεο / πονήσαο πολλὸν ὄφρα εἴης ἀρίστη.
   You (sg.) were toiling/ You toiled much in order that you (sg.) might be best.

6. πονέεσθε / πονήσασθε πολλὸν ὄφρα εἶτε ἄρισται.
   You (pl.) were toiling/ You toiled much in order that you (pl.) might be best.

7. ἀνά-βαινον/ ἀνά-βην ταχέως ἵνα μὴ ὀφθείην.
   I was going up/ I went up swiftly in order that I might not be seen.

8. ἀνά-βαινον/ ἀνά-βησαν ταχέως ἵνα μὴ ὀφθεῖεν.
   They were going up/ They went up swiftly in order that they might not be seen.

9. ἀνά-βαινες/ ἀνά-βης ταχέως ἵνα μὴ ὀφθείης.
   You (sg.) were going up/ You went up swiftly in order that you (sg.) might not be seen.

10. ἀνά-βαινε/ ἀνά-βη ταχέως ἵνα μὴ ὀφθείη.
    He was going up/ He went up swiftly in order that he might not be seen.

11. ἀνα-βαίνετε/ ἀνά-βητε ταχέως ἵνα μὴ ὀφθεῖτε.
    You (pl.) were going up/ You went up swiftly in order that you (pl.) might not be seen.

12. ἀνα-βαίνομεν/ ἀνά-βημεν ταχέως ἵνα μὴ ὀφθεῖμεν.
    We were going up/ We went up swiftly in order that we might not be seen.

LESSON 54

I. The verb forms in the left and right columns below are almost identical except for the presence of the augment and in some cases the accent mark. First (a) translate the augmented forms in the left column. Then (b) identify the forms in the right hand column, *assuming that they are not indicative.*

1.	ἔλυε	λύε
2.	ἐλύετε	λύετε
3.	ἔλυσας	λύσας
4.	ἔλυσαν	λῦσαν
5.	ἐλελύκετε	λελύκετε
6.	ἐλελύκεμεν	λελυκέμεν
7.	ἐλύεο	λύεο
8.	ἐλύσασθε	λύσασθε
9.	ἐλέλυσο	λέλυσο
10.	ἐλέλυσθε	λέλυσθε
11.	ἔλειπε	λεῖπε
12.	ἐλείπετε	λείπετε
13.	ἔλειπον	λεῖπον
14.	ἐλείπεο	λείπεο
15.	ἐλείπεσθε	λείπεσθε
16.	ἔλιπε	λίπε
17.	ἐλίπετε	λίπετε
18.	ἐλίπεο	λίπεο
19.	ἐλίπεσθε	λίπεσθε
20.	ἔλιπον	λιπόν

ANSWERS

1. a. He was loosing
    b. Loose! (pres. impt. act. 2 sg.)

2. a. You (pl.) were loosing
    b. Loose! (pres. impt. act. 2 pl.)

3. a. You (sg.) loosed
    b. having loosed (aor. ptc. act. nom. m. sg.)

4. a. They loosed
    b. having loosed (aor. ptc. act. nom./acc. n. sg.)

5. a. You (pl.) had loosed
    b. Loose once and for all! (pl.) (pf. impt. act. 2 pl.)

6. a. We had loosed
    b. to have just loosed (pf. inf. act.)

7. a. You (sg.) were loosing for yourself / you were being loosed
    b. Loose for yourself!   Be loosed! (pres. impt. m.-p. 2 sg.)

8. a. You (pl.) loosed for yourselves/ you were loosed
    b. Loose for yourselves! Be loosed! (aor. impt. m.-p. 2 pl.)

9. a. You (sg.) had loosed for yourself / you had been loosed
    b. Loose for yourself once and for all! Be loosed once and for all!
       (pf. impt. m.-p. 2 sg.)

10. a. You (pl.) had loosed for yourselves / you had been loosed
    b. Loose for yourselves once and for all! Be loosed once and for all!
       (pf. impt. m.-p. 2 pl.)

11. a. He was leaving.
    b. Leave! (pres. impt. act. 2 sg.)

12. a. You (pl.) were leaving.
    b. Leave! (pres. impt. act. 2 pl.)

13. a. I was/ They were leaving.
    b. leaving (pres. ptc. nom./acc. n. sg.)

14. a. You (sg.) were leaving for yourself / you were being left
    b. Leave for yourself! Be left for yourself! (pres. impt. m.-p. 2 sg.)

15. a. You (pl.) were leaving for yourselves / you were being left.
    b. Leave for yourselves! Be left for yourselves! (pres. impt. m.-p. 2 pl.)

16. a. He left.
    b. Leave! (aor. impt. act. 2 sg.)

17. a. You (pl.) left.
    b. Leave! (aor. impt. act. 2 pl.)

18. a. You (sg.) left for yourself.
    b. Leave for yourself! (aor. impt. mid. 2 sg.)

19. a. You (pl.) left for yourselves.
    b. Leave for yourselves! (aor. impt. mid. 2 pl.)

20. a. I/ They left.
    b. having left (aor. ptc. act. nom./acc/ n. sg.)

Greek-English Vocabulary

Containing all words in the "Memorize" sections; the number in parentheses after entry indicates the lesson in which the word is first introduced.

( ) enclose words not necessarily needed in translating; [ ] contain explanatory information

A

ἀγαθός, -ή, -όν good, brave (11)

Ἀγαμέμνων, Ἀγαμέμνονος [m.] Agamemnon [king of Mycenae and commander in chief of Greeks at Troy] (89)

ἀγάπη, -ης [f.] love, charity (45)

ἀγήνωρ, ἀγήνορος [adj.] manly, courageous (81)

ἀγλαός, -ή, -όν splendid (79)

ἄγριος, (-η), -ον wild, savage (74)

ἄγχι [adv., or prep. + gen.] near, close by (75)

ἄγω, ἄξω, ἄγαγον I lead (17)

ἀδικέω, ἀδικήσω, ἀδίκησα I (do) wrong, I injure (19)

ἀείρω, —, ἄειρα I lift up, I take up, I raise (38)

ἀέξω, ἀεξήσω, ἀέξησα I increase [trans.]; [intr. in mid.] I increase (myself), I grow (22)

ἄζομαι [pres. syst. only] I respect, I revere; I hesitate to or shrink from [+ inf.] (51)

ἀθάνατος, -η, -ον immortal, eternal (21)

Ἀθήνη, -ης [f.] Athene [a goddess, special patroness of Odysseus] (97)

αἰγίοχος, -η, -ον aegis-bearing [epithet of Zeus] (92)

αἰδέομαι, αἰδέσ(σ)ομαι, αἰδεσσάμην I venerate, I revere, I respect (91)

αἰεί [adv.] ever, always, forever (9)

αἷμα, αἵματος [n.] blood (100)

αἴνυμαι [pres. syst. only] I seize upon; I select (83)

αἰνῶς [adv.] awfully, greatly (103)

αἴξ, αἰγός [m., f.] goat (75)

αἰπύς, -εῖα, -ύ steep; utter (93)

αἱρέω, αἱρήσω, ἕλον I seize; [in mid.] I pick for myself, I choose (29)

αἰσχρός, -ή, -όν shameful (16)

αἰτέω, αἰτήσω, αἴτησα I ask, I request (22)

αἶψα [adv.] quickly, suddenly (10)

ἀκέων, -ουσα [adj., m. and f.] in silence, silent(ly) (112)

ἀκούω, ἀκούσομαι, ἄκουσα I hear (30)

ἄκρος, -η, -ον top(most), outermost, extreme; [as n. noun] edge, tip (39)

ἀλάομαι, —, ἀλήθην, ἀλάλημαι I wander [pf. has pres. force] (88)

ἄλγος, ἄλγεος [n.] pain, distress, woe (43)

ἀλέομαι, — , ἀλεάμην or ἀλευάμην I avoid, I shrink before (53)

ἀληθείη, -ης [f.] truth (7)

ἀληθής, ές true (29)

ἀλλά [conj.] but (8)

ἀλλήλοι, -ων [pl. only] one another, each other (39)

ἄλλοθεν [adv.] from elsewhere (109)

ἄλλος, -η, -ο other, another, else (32)

ἀλμυρός, -ή, -όν salty, briny (83)

ἄλοχος, -ου [f.] wife (80)

ἅλς, ἁλός [f.] sea (71)

ἅμα [adv., or prep. + dat.] at the same time, together with (39)

ἅμαξα, -ης [f.] wagon (79)

ἁμαρτάνω, ἁμαρτήσομαι, ἅμαρτον I fail of, I miss, I err [often + gen.] (21)

ἀμείβομαι, ἀμείψομαι, ἀμειψάμην I (ex)change; I reply (25)

ἀμέλγω [pres. syst.] I milk (86)

ἄμμε [acc. pl. pron.] us

ἄμμες [nom. pl. pron.] we

ἄμμιν [dat. pl. pron.] to/for us

ἀμύμων, ἀμύμονος [adj.] blameless, excellent (110)

ἀμφί [adv.; prep. + dat. or acc.] on both sides, around, concerning (48)

ἀμφίπολος, -ου [f.] handmaid, female attendant (80)

ἀνά or ἄμ [adv.] up; back; [prep. + gen.] on (to); [prep. + dat.] on [at rest]; [prep. + acc.] on (to), over (74)

ἀνα-βαίνω, ἀνα-βήσομαι, ἀνά-βην I go up, I ascend (52)

ἀνάγκη, -ης [f.] necessity, need (9)

ἄναξ, ἄνακτος [m.] king, lord (27)

ἀνδρόμεος, -η, -ον human [used only of flesh] (94)

ἄνεμος, -ου [m.] wind (31)

ἀν-έχομαι, ἀν-έξομαι or ἀνα-σχήσομαι, ἀνά-σχον or -σχεθον I hold up under, I endure (23)

ἄνθρωπος, -ου [m.] man, human being (11)

ἀνήρ, ἀνέρος ορ ἀνδρός [m.] dat. pl. ἄνδρεσσι or ἀνδράσι man, male (27)

ἄντρον, -ου [n.] cave (82)

ἀνώγω, ἀνώξω, ἄνωξα, ἄνωγα [pf. has pres. sense; plpf. has impf. sense] I command, I urge (99)

ἀπάνευθε [adv., or prep. + gen.] away (from), apart (from), afar (41)

ἅπας, ἅπασα, ἅπαν [m./ n. gen. ἅπαντος] all, the whole (30)

ἄπ-ειμι I am away (24)

ἀπ-έχω I hold back from, I refrain from (81)

ἀπό [prep. + gen.] away from, from (6)

ἀπ-ολλύω, ἀπ-ολέσω, ἀπ-όλεσ(σ)α, ἀπ-όλωλα, [2 aor. mid.] ἀπ-ολόμην I kill, I destroy; I lose; [in pf. and mid.] I perish, I am lost (26)

Ἀπόλλων, Ἀπόλλωνος [m.] Apollo [god of prophecy] (35)

ἀπόπροσθεν [adv.] far away, aloof (76)

ἀπο-σεύω, —, ἀπο-σσύμην [non-thematic 2 aor.] I rush away, I rush back (from) (85)

ἅπτω, ἅψομαι, ἅψα I fasten; [in mid.] I lay hold of; I catch fire (105)

ἄρα or ῥα [postpositive] therefore, then [not of time!] (31)

ἀρείων, ἄρειον [comp. of ἀγαθός, -ή, -όν] better (49)

ἀρετή, -ῆς [f.] manliness, virtue (7)

ἄριστος, -η, -ον [supl. of ἀγαθός, -ή, -όν] best (49)

ἀρνειός, -οῦ [m.] ram [full-grown] (77)

ἄρνες, ἀρνῶν [no nom. sg.; acc.sg. ἄρνα] [m., f.] lamb(s) (82) ἄρουρα, -ης [f.] soil, earth (103)

ἄρσην, -ενος [m., f.] ἄρσεν, ἄρσενος [n.] male, masculine (86)

ἀρχή, -ῆς [f.] beginning (9)

ἀσκός, -οῦ [m.] bag (79)

ἆσσον [adv.] near, close [often + gen. or dat.] (92)

ἄστυ, ἄστεος [n.] town (62)

ἀτάρ [adversative particle or conj.] but, however, but yet (64)

αὖ [adv.] again; but now (101)

αὐλή, -ῆς [f.] courtyard, farmyard, fold (40)

αὐτάρ [conj.] but, yet (24)

αὖτε again; on the other hand (87)

αὐτίκα [adv.] at once (81)

αὖτις [adv.] back, again (103)

ἀϋτμή, -ῆς [f.] breath; vapor; blast (106)

αὐτός, -ή, -ό self, same, very; himself, herself, itself; him, her, it [not in nom. in last sense] (14)

αὐτοῦ [adv.] in the same place, there (69)

ἀφ-αιρέομαι, ἀφ-αιρήσομαι, ἀφ-ελόμην I take away (63)

ἀφ-ικνέομαι, ἀφ-ίξομαι, ἀφ-ικόμην I come to, I arrive [+ acc.] (75)

ἄφρων, -ον senseless (49)

ἀφύσσω, ἀφύξω, ἄφυσ(σ)α I draw; I heap up (65)

Ἀχαιοί, -ῶν Achaeans [a division of the Greeks; also, Greeks in general] (89)

ἄψ [adv.] back, back again (97)

B

βαθύς, -εῖα, -ύ deep (86)

βαίνω, βήσομαι, βῆν, βέβηκα I go (42)

βάλλω, βαλέω, βάλον I throw, I strike (44)

βασιλείη, -ης [f.] kingdom (37)

βιάζω I constrain, I use violence against (110)

βίη, -ης [f.] force (7)

βίος, -ου [m.] life (12)

βλέφαρον, -ου [n.] eyelid (106)

βοάω, βοήσω, βόησα I shout, I roar (109)

βουλεύω, βουλεύσω, βούλευσα I plan, I consider whether to or how to [+ inf., or ὅπως + purpose construction] (35)

βουλή, -ῆς [f.] plan, advice, will (35)

βούλομαι, βουλήσομαι, βουλόμην I desire, I prefer (32)

βοῦς, βοός [m., f.] [dat. pl. also βουσί] ox, cow (63)

βροτός, -ή, -όν mortal, human (15)

Γ

γαῖα, -ης [f.] earth, land (8)

γαμέω, γαμέω, γάμησα or γῆμα I marry (35)

γὰρ [conj.; never first word] for (6)

γε [enclitic particle] at least, in fact (25)

γέγαα pf. of γίγνομαι

γεγωνέω, γεγωνήσω, γεγώνησα, γέγωνα [pf. with pres. meaning] I shout, I make myself heard (119)

γέρων, γέροντος [m.] old man (27)

γίγνομαι, γενήσομαι, γενόμην, γέγαα I am born, I become, I am, I happen (23)

γιγνώσκω, γνώσομαι, γνῶν, ἔγνωκα, ἔγνωσμαι, γνώσθην I know (16)

γλαφυρός, -ή, -όν hollow (70)

γλυκύς, -εῖα, -ύ sweet, delightful (32)

γοάω, γοήσομαι, γόησα I weep (for) [+ acc.], I mourn (118)

γόνυ, γούνατος or γουνός [n.] knee (34)

γυνή, γυναικός [f.] woman, wife (45)

Δ

δαίμων, δαίμονος [m., f.] a divinity, a superhuman power (105)

δαμάζω, δαμάω, δάμασσα I tame, I overpower (116)

δέ [alone] but, however; and (8)

δείδω, δείσομαι, δεῖσα, δείδια I fear [+ inf., or μή + purpose construction; pf. has pres. sense] (25)

δεῖπνον, -ου [n.] main meal, meal (65)

δέκατος, -η, -ον tenth (50)

δένδρεον, -ου [n.] tree (12)

δεύτερος, -η, -ον second (49)

δέχομαι, δέξομαι, δεξάμην I receive, I accept (33)

δέω, δήσω, δῆσα I tie, I fasten (70)

δή [adv.] clearly, indeed (9)

διά [prep. + gen.] through [prep. + acc.] through; among, on account of (28)

διδάσκω, διδάξω, δίδαξα I teach (21)

δίδωμι, δώσω, δῶκα I give [see Appendix A for irreg. forms] (67 and 68)

δίκαιος, -η, -ον just, honorable (12)

δίκη, -ης [f.] justice; custom (7)

δῖος, -α, -ον bright, glorious [f. usually keeps alpha through sg.] (95)

δίς [adv.] twice, a second time (21)

διώκω, διώξω, δίωξα I pursue (19)

δμώς, δμωός [m.] man-servant (80)

δοκέω, δοκήσω, δόκησα I seem, I appear (21)

δόλος, -ου [m.] cunning, craftiness; trickery; bait for catching fish (45)

δόξα, -ης [f.] opinion; glory (8)

δόρπον, -ου [n.] supper (94)

δόρυ, δούρατος or δουρός [n.] beam, plank; spear (106)

δῦν 3 aor. of δύω I go down, I sink (42)

δύναμαι, δυνήσομαι, δυνησάμην I can, I am able [+ inf.] (92)

δυνατός, -ή, -όν a) [adj.] able, possible; b) [vb.] [+ εἰμί and inf.] able (to do something) (24)

δύω, δύσω, δῦν I enter (42)

δύω or δύο [indecl.] two (35)

δῶρον, -ου [n.] gift (13)

E

ἑ him, her [acc. sg. of 3 pers. pron.]

ἐάω, ἐάσω, ἔασα I leave (alone); permit, allow (to do or be something) [+ inf.] (37)

ἐγγύθεν [adv.] from close at hand, near (111)

ἐγγύς [adv.; prep. + gen.] near (14)

ἔγνωκα, ἔγνωσμαι pf. of γιγνώσκω

ἐγώ(ν) I

ἔδομαι fut. of ἐσθίω

ἔδω [pres. syst. only] I eat (64)

ἕζομαι, —, ἔσα I sit down; [in aor.] I cause to be seated (71)

ἐθέλω, ἐθελήσω, ἐθέλησα I wish (20)

εἰ [conj.] if (10); εἰ γάρ if only [+ opt. in impossible wish] (19); εἰ μή unless

εἶδαρ, εἴδατος [n.] food (64)

εἴθε if only, would that (19)

εἰμί I am (see Appendix A for forms)

εἵνεκα [prep. +. gen.] on account of, for the sake of (12)

εἷος [also ἧος or ἕως] [conj.] while, until [+ ind. if purely factual; + purpose construction if anticipatory, like ὄφρα] (85)

εἶπον [2 aor. syst. only] I said, I told (41)

εἰρήνη, -ης [f.] peace (7)

εἴρομαι, εἰρήσομαι, ἐρόμην I ask (25)

εἰς [prep. + acc.] into, to (10)

εἷς, μία, ἕν [m./n. gen. ἑνός] one (30)

εἰσ-έρχομαι, εἰσ-ελεύσομαι, εἰσ-ἔλθον I enter (34)

εἰσ-οράω, εἰσ-όψομαι, εἴσ-ιδον, etc. I see, I look at (87)

ἐκ (ἐξ before vowels) [prep. + gen.] out of (6)

ἕκαστος, -η, -ον each (27)

(ἐ)κεῖνος, -η, -ο that (one) (14)

ἐκ-σεύω, —, ἐκ-σσύμην [non-thematic 2 aor.] I rush out of, I pour out of [intr.] (105)

ἔκτοθεν [adv.] outside (86)

ἐλαΐνεος, -η, -ον (of) olive-wood (98)

ἐλαύνω, ἐλάω, ἔλασ(σ)α I drive (86)

ἐλεέω, —, ἐλέησα I pity, I have mercy on (101)

ἕλον 2 aor. of αἱρέω

ἔλπω or ἔλπομαι [pres. syst. only] I expect, I hope, I suppose [+ inf.] (40)

ἔλ(υ)θον 2 aor. of ἔρχομαι

ἔμβρυον, -ου [n.] a young one [of animals] (87)

ἐμός, -ή, -όν my, mine (26)

ἐμ-πίπλημι, ἐμ-πλήσω, ἔμ-πλησα I pour; I heap up I fill (with) (81)

ἐν [prep. + dat.] in, on, among (6)

ἔνδον [adv.] within, inside (82)

ἔνεικα aor. of φέρω

ἔνθα [adv.] there, then (65)

ἔνθεν [adv.] from there; then [of time] (32)

ἐννέπω, ἐνίψω, ἔνισπον I say, I tell (18)

ἐννῆμαρ [adv.] for nine days (64)

ἔντοθεν [adv.] inside; [prep. + gen.] inside of (86)

ἐντολή, -ῆς [f.] command, order (34)

ἔντοσθεν [adv.] within, inside; [prep. + gen] inside of (85)

ἐξ = ἐκ before vowels

ἑξῆς [adv.] in order, in rows (71)

ἑο of him/her [gen. sg. of 3 pers. pron.]

ἔοικα [pf. with pres. force; ἐῴκεα plpf. with impf. force] I seem, I am like to; [in 3 sg. impersonal construction, which may take acc. and inf.] it is fitting (45)

ἑός, -ή, -όν own; his, her (15)

ἐπεί [conj.] when; since (18)

ἔπειτα [adv.] then, thereupon (39)

ἐπ-έρχομαι I come to, I come upon [+ dat., acc.] (81)

ἐπήν contraction of ἐπεὶ ἄν (35)

ἐπί [prep. + gen.] upon; [prep. + dat.] on, at, beside; [prep. + acc.] to, towards; after [in search or attack] (6)

ἐπι-βαίνω, ἐπι-βήσομαι, ἐπί-βην, ἐπι-βέβηκα I land upon, I go upon [+ gen.] (64)

ἐπι-μαίομαι, ἐπι-μάσσομαι, ἐπι-μασσάμην I seek out; I feel, I touch (95)

ἐπι-τίθημι, ἐπι-θήσω, ἐπί-θηκα I put on; I put in position (86)

ἔπος, ἔπεος [n.] word (28)

ἑπτά [indecl.] seven (80)

ἔργον, -ου [n.] work, deed (13)

ἔρδω, ἔρξω, ἔρξα I do (31)

ἐρετμόν, -οῦ [n.] oar (71)

ἐρίηρος, -ον [pl. 3 decl. ἐρίηρες, etc.] faithful, loyal (70)

(ἐ)ρύομαι, (ἐ)ρύσσομαι, (ἐρ)ρυσάμην I save, I rescue, I protect (62)

ἐρύω, —, ἔρυσ(σ)α I drag, I draw (70)

ἔρχομαι, ἐλεύσομαι, ἔλ(υ)θον, εἰλήλουθα I come, I go (26)

ἐσθίω, ἔδομαι, φάγον I eat (19)

ἐσθλός, -ή, -όν noble, excellent (13)

ἔσθω [pres. syst. only] I eat, I devour (119)

ἑταῖρος, -ου [m.] companion, comrade (23)

ἕτερος, -η, -ον (the) other (14)

ἔτι [adv.] yet, still; οὐκ ἔτι no longer (31)

εὖ [adv.] well (44)

εὕδω, εὑδήσω, εὕδησα I sleep (17)

εὐ-εργής, -ές well made; fine (80)

εὑρίσκω, εὑρήσω, εὗρον I find, I discover (33)

εὐρύς, -εῖα, -ύ wide, broad (33)

εὔχομαι, εὔξομαι, εὐξάμην I claim to be, I boast, I exult; I pray (to) [+ inf.] (40)

ἔφη he/she said [irreg. from φημί]

ἔχω, ἕξω or σχήσω, σχόν or σχέθον I have, I hold (18)

ἕως [also ος or εἷος] [conj.] while, until [+ ind. if purely factual; + purpose construction if anticipatory, like ὄφρα] (85)

Z

Ζεύς, Διός or Ζηνός Zeus [father and chief of the gods] (49)

ζητέω, ζητήσω, ζήτησα I seek, I search after (34)

ζωή, -ῆς [f.] life (26)

ζώω, ζώσω, ζῶσα I live (20)

H

ἤ or, than; ἤ...ἤ either...or; ἤ...ἤ whether...or (27)

ἦ truly, indeed; also, an untranslatable interrogative particle introducing a question (83)

ἦ thus he spoke [3 sg. impf. of ἠμί] (105)

ἠδέ [conj.] and (20)

ἥδομαι, ἥσομαι, ἡσάμην I am pleased with [+ dat.] (22)

ἡδονή, -ῆς [f.] pleasure (29)

ἡδύς, ἡδεῖα, ἡδύ sweet, pleasant (8 and 29)

ἠέ = ἤ

ἦε = ἤ or ἦ

ἠέλιος, -ου [m.] sun (23)

ἦμαρ, ἤματος [n.] day (38)

ἡμεῖς we [nom. pl. personal pron.]

ἥμενος, -η, -ον sitting, seated (85)

ἡμέτερος, -η, -ον our (14)

ἠμί I speak [only in 3 sg. impf.] (105)

ἥμισυς, (-εια), -υ half (30)

ἦμος [conj.] when (73)

ἤν contraction of εἰ ἄν (35)

ἧος [also εἷος or ἕως] [conj.] while, until [+ ind. if purely factual; + purpose construction if anticipatory, like ὄφρα] (85)

ἠριγένεια, -ης the early-born (one) (73)

ἦτορ [n., indecl.] heart (88)

Ἠώς, Ἠόος [f.] Eos [the personified goddess of the dawn] (73)

Θ

θάλασσα, -ης [f.] sea (8)

θάνατος, -ου [m.] death (12)

θάσσων, θᾶσσον [comp. of ταχύς, -εῖα, -ύ] swifter (49)

417

θέμις, θέμιστος [f.] a right, custom; θέμις ἐστί it is right, lawful [+ acc. and inf.] (36)

θεός, -οῦ [m., f.] god, goddess (11)

θεσπέσιος, -η, -ον heavenly, divine (81)

θῆλυς, θήλεια, θῆλυ or θῆλυς, θῆλυ female (115)

θησαυρός, -οῦ [m.] treasure (15)

θνήσκω, θανέομαι, θάνον I die (17)

θνητός, -ή, -όν mortal (15)

θοός, -ή, -όν swift (65)

θρέψω, θρέψα fut. and aor. of τρέφω

θυγάτηρ, θυγατέρος or θυγατρός [f.] daughter (63)

θυμός, -οῦ [m.] heart, spirit (13)

θυρεός, -οῦ [m.] door-stone (77)

θύρη, -ης [f.] door (53)

Ι

ἰάχω [pres. syst. only] I shout; I hiss; I resound (107)

ἰδέ [conj.] and [= ἠδέ] (76)

ἱερός, -ή, -όν holy, sacred (25)

ἵημι, ἥσω, ἧκα I send forth, I cast; I place (67)

ἰητρός, -οῦ [m.] physician (11)

ἱκάνω [pres. syst. only] I come (19)

ἱκέται, ἱκετάων [m.] suppliants (91)

ἱκνέομαι, ἵξομαι, ἱκόμην I approach, I come [+ acc.] (91)

ἵνα [adv.] where; [conj.] that, in order that, to (18)

ἵστημι, στήσω, στῆσα I put; I halt [trans.] (77)

ἵσταμαι, στήσομαι, στῆν I stand, I halt [intr.; mid. of ἵστημι] (77)

ἱστός, -οῦ [m.] mast; loom [for weaving] (98)

ἰών, ἰοῦσα, ἰόν going [pres. act ptc. of εἶμι go] (67)

Κ

κάδ = κάτα before δ

καθ-ίζω, —, κάθισα I seat myself; I cause to be seated (71)

καί [conj.] and; even, also (6)

καίω, καύσω, κῆα I kindle, I burn (85)

κακός, -ή, -όν cowardly, bad, evil (12)

καλέω, καλέω, κάλεσ(σ)α I call, I summon, I invite

κάλλιστος, -η, -ον supl. of καλός, -ή, -όν

καλλίων, -ον comp. of καλός, -ή, -όν

καλός, -ή, -όν beautiful, noble (7)

καρπάλιμος, -ον swift, quick (82)

καρπός, -οῦ [m.] fruit (14)

κασιγνητός, -οῦ [m.] brother (26)

κατά [prep. + gen.] down from; [prep. + acc.] down (along); throughout; according to (10)

κατα-τίθημι, etc. I put down (87)

κεῖμαι [pf. mid. syst.] I have been placed, I lie (down) (47)

κεῖνος, -η, -ο that (one) (14)

κέλευθος, -ου [f., but frequently n. in pl.] way, path, course (88)

κελεύω, κελεύσω, κέλευσα I command [+ acc., dat., inf.] (19)

κέλομαι, κελήσομαι, κεκλόμην I order (70)

κε(ν) particle giving a theoretical, general, expected, or contrary to fact coloring to clause. (17)

κέρδιον [comp. adv.] more beneficial, better (52)

κεύθω, κεύσω, κύθον I hide [trans.] (18)

κῆρ, κῆρος [n.] heart (28)

κιχάνω, κιχήσομαι, κίχον I come (by chance), I reach (91)

κλαίω, κλαύσω, κλαῦσα I weep, I wail (70)

κληΐς, κληῖδος [f.] oar-lock; bolt (71)

κλυτός, -όν famous; excellent (97)

κόσμος, -ου [m.] world (39)

κούρη, -ης [f.] daughter

κρατερός, -ή, -όν strong (15)

κράτος, κράτεος [n.] strength, power (53)

κρέα, κρεῶν [n. pl.] [nom. sg. κρέας] flesh, meat (94)

κρητήρ, κρητῆρος [m.] mixing-bowl (80)

κρίνω, κρινέω, κρῖνα I pick out; I separate; I judge (29)

κρύπτω, κρύψω, κρύψα I conceal (47)

κτείνω, κτενέω, κτεῖνα or κτάνον I kill (48)

Κύκλωψ, Κύκλωπος [m.] Cyclops (92)

Λ

λαῖτμα, λάιτματος [n.] gulf (89)

λαμβάνω, λήψομαι, λάβον I take, get (22)

λανθάνω, λήσω, λάθον I elude, I escape someone's notice, I deceive; [in mid.] I am forgetful of [+ gen.] (36)

λαός, -οῦ [m.] people [a nation]; followers (33)

λέγω, λέξω, λέξα I say, I tell; I call (10)

λείπω, λείψω, λίπον I leave (43)

λευκός, -ή, -όν bright, white (87)

λίην [adv.] exceedingly; καὶ λίην [adv.] truly (118)

λίθος, -ου [m.] stone (16)

λιλαίομαι [pres. syst. only] I long (to do something) [+ inf.] (52)

λίσσομαι, —, λισάμην I entreat, I beg (83)

λόγος, -ου [m.] word; account (11)

λυγρός, -ή, -όν miserable, wretched (116)

λύω, λύσω, λῦσα, λέλυκα, λέλυμαι, λύθην I loose, I release (16)

λωτός, -οῦ [m.] lotus (68)

Λωτοφάγοι, -ων [m.] Lotus-eaters [a legendary people] (64)

Μ

μάκαρ, -αρος [adj.] happy, blessed (29)

μακρός, -ή, -όν long, large (in space or time) (39)

μάλα [adv.] very, quite, greatly (35)

μανθάνω, μαθήσομαι, μάθον I learn (17)

μάρπτω, μάρψω, μάρψα I seize (93)

μάχομαι (μαχέομαι), μαχήσομαι, μαχεσ(σ)άμην I fight (against) [+ dat.] (22)

μεγαλήτωρ, -ορος [adj.] great-hearted, great, daring (95)

μέγας, μεγάλη, μέγα [m. acc. sg. μέγαν, n. acc. sg. μέγα, rest of m. and n. is 2nd declension, on stem μεγαλ-] great, large, big (50)

μείζων, μεῖζον [comp. of μέγας, μεγάλη, μέγα] bigger (49)

μειλίχιος, -η, -ον pleasing, winning (104)

μέλας, μέλαινα, μέλαν [m. and n. gen. μέλανος] dark, black (79)

μελιηδής, -ές honey-sweet (69)

μέλλω, μελλήσω, μέλλησα I am about, I am going, I intend, I am destined (to do something) [+ inf.] (24)

μέλος, μέλεος [n.] member (of the body), limb (51)

μὲν...δὲ [correlative particles marking contrast] indeed...but; on the one hand...on the other (8)

μένος, μένεος [n.] might; courage; wrath (117)

μένω, μενέω, μεῖνα I remain, I stay; I await (44)

μέσ(σ)ος, -η, -ον middle (of), midst (of) [modifying noun in same case] (46)

μετά [prep. + dat.] among, with; [prep. + acc.] into the midst, after (22) μέτρον, -ου [n.] measure (27)

μή not; μηδέ and not, nor, not even (17)

μηδείς, μηδεμία, μηδέν no one, none (30)

μήδομαι, μήσομαι, μησάμην I contrive, I plan (68)

μῆκος, μήκεος [n.] length (28)

μῆλον, -ου [n.] sheep; flock (38)

μηρός, -οῦ [m.] thigh (93)

μήτηρ, μητέρος or μητρός [f.] mother (48)

μίμνω [pres. syst. only] I remain, I await (73)

μιν him/her [acc. sg. of pers. pron.]

μίσγω, μίξω, μίξα I mix (something, in acc.) with (something, in dat.), I mingle with (32)

μισέω, μισήσω, μίσησα I hate (23)

μοῖρα, -ης [f.] due measure; portion; fate (87)

μοῦνος, -η, -ον alone, only (11)

Μοῦσα, -ης [f.] Muse [a goddess of poetry and art] (32)

μοχλός, -οῦ [m.] bar, stake (99)

N

νέκταρ, νέκταρος [n.] nectar [the special drink of the gods] (31)

νέμω, νεμέω, νεῖμα I assign, I drive my flock; [in mid.] I possess, I feed on (85)

νέομαι [pres. syst. only] I return (69)

νηλ(ε)ής, -ές pitiless, ruthless (91)

νηός, -οῦ [m.] temple (25)

νήπιος, -η, -ον simple; foolish (11)

νηῦς, νηός or νεός, dat. pl. also νηυσί [f.] ship (53)

νοέω, νοήσω, νόησα I think, I perceive (20)

νομίζω, νομιῶ, νόμισα consider, think, believe (20)

νόος, -ου [m.] mind (15)

νόστιμος, -η, -ον of one's homecoming (63)

νόστος, -ου [m.] return (home) (62)

νοῦσος, -ου [f.] disease (15)

νῦν [adv.] now, at the present time (9)

νύξ, νυκτός [f.] night (50)

νῶτον, -ου [n.] back (113)

Ξ

ξείνιον, -ου [n.] gift of hospitality, a present given by a host to a guest (83)

ξεῖνος, -ου [m.] guest, stranger (13)

ξίφος, ξίφεος [n.] sword (94)

Ο

ὁ, ἡ, τό that, the [modifying noun or substantive]; who, which, that [w. def. antecedent]; he, she, it [as pron. standing alone] (15)

ὄβριμος, -η, -ον heavy, mighty (85)

ὅδε, ἥδε, τόδε [demonstrative pron./adj.] this (one) (15)

ὁδός, -οῦ [f.] way, road; journey (33)

ὅθι [adv.] where (95)

οἶδα, εἰδήσω [irreg.; see Appendix A for forms] I know

οἴκαδε [adv.] homeward (89)

οἰκέω, οἰκήσω, οἴκησα I dwell, I inhabit (50)

οἶκος, -ου [m.] house, home (46)

οἰμώζω, οἰμώξομαι, οἴμωξα I cry out in pain (107)

οἶνος, -ου [m.] wine (33)

οἶος, -η, -ον alone (76)

οἷος, -η, -ον (such) as, (of) what sort (88)

ὄϊς, ὄϊος [dat. pl. also ὄεσσι, acc. pl. always ὄϊς] [m., f.] sheep (75)

οἴσω fut. of φέρω

ὀΐω or ὀΐομαι, ὀΐσομαι, ὀϊσάμην I think, I suppose, I imagine (43)

ὄλβος, -ου [m.] happiness, prosperity (16)

ὄλεθρος, -ου [m.] destruction (68)

ὀλίγος, -η, -ον small, few (13)

ὄλλυμι, ὀλέσω, ὄλεσ(σ)α, ὄλωλα 2 aor. mid. ὀλόμην I kill, I destroy, I lose; [in pf. and mid.] I perish, I am lost (63)

ὀλοός, -ή, -όν destructive, deadly (64)

ὄμβρος, -ου [m.] rain, storm (21)

ὁμοῖος, -η, -ον like to, similar to (12)

ὄνομα or οὔνομα, ὀνόματος [n.] name (100)

ὀξύς, -εῖα, -ύ sharp, keen (95)

ὀπάζω, ὀπάσσω, ὄπασ(σ)α I send (someone) as a companion; I present (67)

ὁπλίζω, —, ὥπλισσα I prepare (94)

ὅπ(π)η [adv.] where, in what direction (91)

ὅπως [conj.] that, in order that, to (18)

ὁράω, ὄψομαι, ἴδον, ἑώρακα, ἑώραμαι, ὤφθην I see, I look at (16)

ὀρθός, -ή, -όν straight, true (23)

ὄρος, ὄρεος [n.] mountain (77)

ὅς, ἥ, ὅ [rel. pron.] who, which, that (26); ὅς τις, ἥ τις, ὅ τι/ ὅττι [indef. rel. pron.] whoever, whatever (31)

ὅσ(σ)ος, -η, -ον as many as, as great as, as much as [see τόσ(σ)ος] (86)

ὀστέον, -ου [n.] bone (94)

ὅτε [adv. conj.] when, whenever (35)

ὅτι [conj.] that; because (18)

οὐ [οὐκ before smooth breathing, οὐχ before rough breathing] not, no (8)

οὐδέ and not, nor, not even (21)

οὐδείς, οὐδεμία, οὐδέν no one, none (30)

οὐκέτι [adv.] no longer

οὖλος, -η, -ον whole, entire (53)

οὖν [adv.] therefore, then [not of time!] (22)

οὐρανός, -οῦ [m.] heaven, sky (26)

οὔτε and not, nor [following a neg. clause] (8)

οὔτε…οὔτε neither…nor (8)

Οὖτις, Οὔτιος Nobody (104)

οὕτως [adv.] thus, in this way, so (9)

ὀφθαλμός, -οῦ [m.] eye (14)

ὄφρα [conj.] that, in order that, to [+ subj. or opt. in purpose construction] (18); while, until [+ ind. if purely factual, + purpose construction if anticipatory] (24)

ὀφρύς, ὀφρύος [f.] eyebrow (106)

Π

παῖς, παιδός [m., f.] child, boy, girl (27)

πάλιν [adv.] back (again); again (46)

παντοῖος, -η, -ον of all sorts (21)

παρά [prep. + gen.] from; [prep. + dat.] at, beside; [prep. + acc.] to, along (20)

πάρ-ειμι I am present (21)

παρ-έρχομαι I go past, I pass (26)

παρ-έχω, παρ-έξω or παρα-σχήσω, παρά-σχον I supply (18)

παρ-ίσταμαι, παρα-στήσομαι, παρά- στην I stand by (98)

πᾶς, πᾶσα, πᾶν [m./ n. gen. παντός] all, every, the whole (30)

πάσχω, πείσομαι, πάθον I suffer, I experience (37)

πατέομαι, —, πασ(σ)άμην I partake of [+ gen.] (67)

πατήρ, πατέρος or πατρός [m.] father (27, 48)

πατρίς, πατρίδος [f.] fatherland, country; [as f. adj.] of one's fathers, ancestral (27)

παχύς, -εῖα, ύ thick, stout (104)

πείθω, πείσω, πεῖσα or πέπιθον, 2 aor. mid. πιθόμην I persuade, I win over; [in mid.] I am persuaded by, I am obedient to, I obey [+ dat.] (31)

πεῖραρ, πείρατος [n.] end, boundary (93)

πειράω, πειρήσω, πείρησα I make trial of [+ gen.]; I attempt, I try [+ gen., or + inf.] (30)

πέλω, —, πέλον or deponent form πέλομαι, —, πλόμην I come to be, I am (24)

πελώριος, -η, -ον gigantic, monstrous (76)

πέμπω, πέμψω, πέμψα I send (24)

περ [enclitic particle] surely, by far [adds force]; [+ ptc.] though (27)

περί [adv.] round about; especially; [prep. + gen.] about; excelling (over); [prep. + dat. or acc.] about; for (41)

πετάννυμι, —, πέτασ(σ)α I spread out (111)

πέτρη, -ης [f.] rock (7)

πεύθομαι, πεύσομαι, πυθόμην I learn (by inquiry), I inquire (from), I hear of [+ acc. of thing heard, + gen. of person heard] (25)

πίνω, πίομαι, πίον I drink (23)

πίπτω, πέσομαι, πέσον I fall (21)

πιστεύω, πιστεύσω, πίστευσα I believe (in), I have faith in [+ dat.] (38)

πίων, πίονος fat, rich (82)

πλεῖστος, -η, -ον [supl. of πολλός, -ή, -όν] most (49)

πλείων, πλεῖον [comp. of πολλός, -ή, -όν] more (49)

πλέω, πλεύσομαι, πλεῦσα I sail (over) (88)

πλησίος, -η, -ον near; neighbor(ing) (22)

πόθεν [interr. adv.] from what source? whence?

ποθέω, ποθήσω, πόθεσα I long (to do something), I yearn (to do something) [+ inf.], I miss (a person or thing) (43)

ποιέω, ποιήσω, ποίησα I make, I produce, I do (19)

ποιμήν, ποιμένος [m.] shepherd (40)

πόλεμος, -ου [m.] war (see π(τ)όλεμος)

πολιός, (-ή), -όν grayish, white (71)

πόλις, πόλιος or πόληος [f.] city (27)

πολλός, -ή, -όν much; many (14)

πολύς, —, πολύ much, many [alternative m. and n. forms of πολλός, -ή, -όν] (83)

Πολύφημος, -ου [m.] Polyphemus [a Cyclops, son of Poseidon and the nymph Thoösa] (109)

πονέομαι, πονήσομαι, πονησάμην I labor, I toil at, I am busy about (37)

πονηρός, -ή, -όν worthless, base, wicked (15)

πόνος, -ου [m.] toil, trouble (14)

πόντος, -ου [m.] sea, the deep (62)

πόρον [2 aor. syst. only] I gave, I offered (41)

Ποσειδάων, -ωνος [m.] Poseidon [brother of Zeus and god of the sea] (93)

ποταμός, -οῦ [m.] river (14)

ποτέ [enclitic adv.] ever, (at) some time, once (10)

που [indefinite adv.] perhaps, I suppose, of course, no doubt (21)

ποῦ [interr. adv., always with circumflex] where? (21)

πρᾶγμα, πράγματος [n.] deed; [in pl.] trouble, deeds (28)

προ-ίημι, προ-ήσω, προ-ῆκα I send forth, I hurl (67)

πρός [prep. + gen.] from; [prep. + dat.] on, at; [prep. + acc.] to, towards (10)

προσ-αυδάω I address (101)

προσ-εῖπον I address, I speak to [+ acc.] (89)

πρόσθε(ν) [adv.] first, before, in front of (104)

πρόφρων, -ον willing, eager, ready (29)

πρῶτος, -η, -ον first (25)

πτερόεις, -εσσα, -εν winged (29)

π(τ)όλεμος, -ου [m.] war (12)

π(τ)όλις, π(τ)όλιος [f.] city (89)

πυκ(ι)νός, -ή, -όν thick; close; shrewd (115)

πύλη, -ης [f.] gate, entrance (34)

πῦρ, πυρός [n.] fire (28)

πω [+ neg.] [adv.] never yet, in no way, not at all (36)

πῶς [interr. adv.] how? (26)

πως [enclitic adv.] somehow, in anyway (26)

Ρ

ῥα [See under ἄρα]

ῥέζω, ῥέξω, ῥέξα I do (18)

ῥέω [pres. syst.] I flow (42)

ῥηίδιος, -η -ον easy (16)

ῥίπτω, ῥίψω, ῥῖψα I hurl (109)

ῥοδοδάκτυλος, -ον rosy-fingered [epithet of Eos, goddess of the dawn] (73)

ῥύομαι, ῥύσομαι, ῥυσάμην [See under (ε)ρύομαι]

Σ

σάρξ, σαρκός [f.] flesh (44)

σηκός, -οῦ [m.] pen, fold (82)

σῖτος, -ου [m.] bread, food (26)

σός, -ή, -όν your [sg.] (24)

σοφός, -ή, -όν wise (11)

σπέος, σπέος or σπῆος [n.] cave (75)

σπεύδω, σπεύσω, σπεῦσα I hasten (21)

σταθμός, -οῦ [m.] doorpost; farmyard (116)

στείχω, —, στίχον I go, I proceed (110)

στενάχω [pres. syst. only] I groan, I lament (95)

στῆν [3 aor. syst. of ἵστημι I stand] I stood [intr.] (42)

σύ you [nom. sg. pers. pron.]

σύν [prep. + dat.] with (6)

σφέτερος, -η, -ον their(s) (46)

σφι(ν), σφισι(ν) to/ for them [dat. pl. pers. pron.]

σχεδόν [adv.] close by, near (92)

σχέθον 2 aor. of ἔχω

σχέτλιος, -η, -ον cruel, pitiless; reckless (13)

σχήσω fut. of ἔχω

σώζω, σώσω, σῶσα I save (25)

σῶμα, σώματος [n.] body, corpse (28)

Τ

τάχα [adv.] quickly, soon (105)

ταχύς, -εῖα, -ύ swift (49)

τέ [postpositive conj.] and τέ...τέ both...and; τέ...καί both...and (13)

τείρω [pres. syst. only] I wear out; I distress (115)

τελέω, τελέω, τέλεσα I fulfill, I accomplish, I complete (41)

τεοισι dat. pl. of τις, τι

τεός, -ή, -όν your [sg.] (103)

τεύχω, τεύξω, τεῦξα, pf. mid. τέτυγμαι I build; I make ready. [pf. pass. often = I am] (35)

τεων gen. pl. of τις, τι

τῇ where [rel. adv.]; there (28)

τῇδε [adv.] here (28)

τίθημι, θήσω, θῆκα I put, I cause, I make (67)

τίνω or τίω, [fut.] τείσω or τίσω, [aor.] τείσα or τῖσα I pay; [in mid.] I take vengeance upon, I punish (97)

τίς, τί who? which? what? [interrog. pron.]; τί [interrog. adv.] why? (31)

τις, τι some(one), some(thing), one, a certain, any(one) [indef. pron.]; τι [adv.] somehow, in some respect (31)

τλάω, τλήσομαι, τλῆν I endure (something) patiently, I have the heart, I dare (to do something) [+ inf.] (42)

τοί surely, you see [postpositive] (24)

τόσ(σ)ος, -η, -ον so many, so great, so much [often correlative with ὅσ(σ)ος: so many…as…] (86)

τότε [adv.] then (47)

τρέπω, τρέψω, τρέψα I turn [trans.]; [in mid.] I turn (myself) [intr.] (22)

τρέφω, θρέψω, θρέψα I nourish, I feed, I rear (21)

τρίς [adv.] thrice, three times (100)

Τροίη, -ης [f.] Troy, Ilion (61)

τύπτω, τύψω, τύψα I strike, I beat (71)

τυρός, -οῦ [m.] cheese (82)

τῶ [adv., often used with conjunctive force] therefore; in that case (117)

Υ

ὑγρός, -ή, -όν fluid, watery (88)

ὕδωρ, ὕδατος [n.] water (32)

υἱός, -οῦ or υἱέος [m.] son (34)

ὕλη, -ης wood; forest (85)

ὑμεῖς you all [nom. pl. of personal pron.]

ὑπέρ or ὑπείρ [prep. + gen. or acc.] over (88)

Ὑπερίων, Ὑπερίονος [m.] Hyperion (63)

ὕπνος, -ου [m.] sleep (99)

ὑπό [prep. + gen.] from under; under the influence of, = by [personal or impersonal agent]; [prep. + dat.] under [at rest]; [prep. + acc.] under [motion to] (6)

ὕστατος, -η, -ον last (112)

ὑφαίνω, ὑφανέω, ὕφηνα I weave; I devise (111)

ὑψηλός, -ή, -όν high (11)

ὑψόσε [adv.] on high, upwards (79)

Φ

φάγον 2 aor. of ἐσθίω

φαίνω, φανέω, φῆνα I show, I reveal; [in mid.] φαίνομαι, φανέομαι. aor. pass. w. act. force φάνην I show myself, I appear (27)

φάος, φάεος [n.] light (28)

φέρω, οἴσω, ἔνεικα I bear, I bring (17)

φεύγω, φεύξομαι, φύγον I flee, I escape (20)

φημί, φήσω, φῆσα I say, I claim [see Appendix A for irreg. forms]

φθόγγος, -ου [m.] voice (88)

φιλέω, φιλήσω, φίλησα I love (17)

φίλος, -η, -ον dear (to), friendly (to) [+ dat.] (10)

φίλος, -ου [m. adj. as noun] friend (11)

φοιτάω, φοιτήσω, φοίτησα I roam (back and forth) (19)

φρήν, φρενός [f.] mind, spirit (32)

φρονέω, φρονήσω, φρόνησα I consider, I have understanding (21)

φύσις, φύσιος [f.] nature (27)

φωνή, -ῆς [f.] voice, sound (9)

φώς, φωτός [m.] man (113)

Χ

χαίρω, χαιρήσω, χάρην [aor. pass. with active force] I rejoice (in) (38)

χαλεπός, -ή, -όν difficult (15)

χάρις, χάριτος [f.] acc. sg. χάριν beauty, charm, grace (37)

χείρ, χε(ι)ρός [f.] hand (51)

χέω, χεύω, χεῦα I pour; I heap up [+ acc., gen.] (81)

χθών, χθονός [f.] earth (67)

χλωρός, -ή, -όν greenish yellow, green (98)

χρή [+ inf. w. acc. sub.] it is necessary (38)

χρῆμα, χρήματος [n.] possession, property; [in pl.] wealth (28)

χρηστός, -ή, -όν worthy, good; useful, serviceable (29)

Χριστός, -οῦ [m.] Christ ["the anointed one"]

χρόνος, -ου [m.] time (16)

χρυσός, -οῦ [m.] gold (12)

χῶρος, -ου [m.] place, region (75)

Ψ

ψυχή, -ῆς [f.] soul; life (7)

Ω

ὦ O! [in direct address] (23)

ὧδε [adv.] thus, so (107)

ὠκύς, -εῖα, -ύ swift, nimble (70)

ὡς [adv. or conj.] as, that, how (17)

ὥς, ὣς [adv.] thus, so [always with pitch-mark] (62)

English-Greek Vocabulary

( ) enclose words not always used in translation; [ ] contain explanatory information.

For more detail (i.e., principal parts of verbs, case usage after prepositions, etc.), consult the fuller entry in the Greek-English Vocabulary.

A

able δυνατός, -ή, -όν I am able δύναμαι, δυνήσομαι, δυνησάμην

about a) περί [prep. + gen., dat., acc.]; b) [vb.] I am about μέλλω, μελλήσω, μέλλησα

above (all) περί [prep. + gen.]

accept δέχομαι, δέξομαι, δεξάμην

accomplish τελέω, τελέω, τέλεσα

according to κατά [prep. + acc.]

account λόγος, -ου [m.]; on account of διά [prep. + acc.], είνεκα [prep. + gen.]

Achaeans Ἀχαιοί, -ῶν [m.]

address προσ-αυδάω, προσ-εῖπον [+ acc.]

admirable ἀμύμων, ἀμύμονος

advice βουλή, -ῆς [f.]

aegis-bearing αἰγίοχος, -η, -ον

afar ἀπάνευθε [adv.]

after (in search or attack) ἐπί [+ acc.]; (in time or position) μετά [+ acc.]

again αὖ, αὖτε, αὖτις, πάλιν

Agamemnon Ἀγαμέμνων, Ἀγαμέμνονος [m.]

all πᾶς, πᾶσα, πᾶν [m./ n. gen. παντός]; ἅπας, ἅπασα, ἅπαν [m./ n. gen. ἅπαντος]

allow ἐάω, ἐάσω, ἔασα [+ inf.]

alone μοῦνος, -η, -ον; οἶος, -η, -ον

along παρά [prep. + acc.]

aloof ἀπόπροθεν [adv.]

also καί

although περ [+ ptc.]

always αἰεί [adv.]

am a) εἰμί [see appendix for forms] b) πέλω, —, π(έ)λον or mid. πέλομαι, —, πλόμην c) γίγνομαι, γενήσομαι, γενόμην. γέγαα

among ἐν [prep. + dat.]; μετά [prep. + dat.]; διά [prep. + acc.]

ancestral πατρίς, πατρίδος [as f. adj.]

and καί, ἠδέ, δέ; δέ, τε [never first word]; and not οὐδέ, μηδέ, οὔτε

another ἄλλος, -η, -ο

any(one) τις, τι

apart (from) [adv., or prep. + gen.] ἀπάνευθε

Apollo Ἀπόλλων, Ἀπόλλωνος [m.]

appear φαίνομαι, φανέομαι, φάνην; appear [seem] δοκέω, δοκήσω, δόκησα

approach ἱκνέομαι, ἵξομαι, ἱκόμην [+ acc.]

around ἀμφί [adv.; prep. + dat. or acc.]; ἀμφίς [adv.]

arrive ἀφ-ικνέομαι, ἀφ-ίξομαι, ἀφ-ικόμην [+ acc.]

as ὡς; as many, as great, as much ὅσ(σ)ος, -η, -ον [often correlative with τόσ(σ)ος, -η, -ον· so many (etc.)…as]

ascend ἀνα-βαίνω, etc.

ask αἰτέω, αἰτήσω, αἴτησα; εἴρομαι, εἰρήσομαι, ἐρόμην

assign νέμω, νεμέω, νεῖμα

at ἐπί, παρά, πρός [preps. + dat.]; at least γε [enclitic particle]; at once αὐτίκα

Athene Ἀθήνη, -ης [f.]

attempt πειράω, πειρήσω, πείρησα [+ inf.]

attendant ἀμφίπολος, -ου [f.]

avoid ἀλέομαι, — , ἀλεάμην or ἀλευάμην; ἀλεείνω

await μένω, μενέω, μεῖνα; μίμνω [pres. syst. only]

away (from) ἀπό [prep. + gen.]; ἀπάνευθε [adv., or prep. + gen.]; I am away ἄπ-ειμι

awfully αἰνῶς [adv.]

B

back a) [adv.] αὖτις, ἄψ, πάλιν, ἀνά or ἄμ; back again ἄψ, πάλιν b) [noun] νῶτον, -ου [n.]

bad κακός, -ή, -όν

bag ἀσκός, -οῦ [m.]

bait (for catching fish) δόλος, -ου [m.]

bar μοχλός, -οῦ [m.]

base πονηρός, -ή, -όν

be [see "am"]

beam δόρυ, δούρατος or δουρός [n.]

bear φέρω, οἴσω, ἔνεικα

beat τύπτω, τύψω, τύψα

beautiful καλός, -ή, -όν [comp. καλλίων, -ον; supl. κάλλιστος, -η, -ον]

beauty χάρις, χάριτος [acc. sg. χάριν] [f.]

because ὅτι [conj.]

become γίγνομαι, γενήσομαι, γενόμην. γέγαα

before πρόσθε(ν) [adv.]

beg λίσσομαι, —, λισάμην

beginning ἀρχή, -ῆς [f.]

believe (in) πιστεύω, πιστεύσω, πίστευσα [+ dat.]

belly γαστήρ, γαστέρος or γαστρός [f.]

beneficial, more κέρδιον [comp. adv.]

beside ἐπί, παρά [preps. + dat.]

best ἄριστος, -η, -ον [supl. of ἀγαθός, -ή, -όν] best

better κέρδιον [comp. adv.]; ἀρείων, ἄρειον [comp. of ἀγαθός, -ή, -όν]

big μέγας, μεγάλη, μέγα [m. acc. sg. μέγαν, n. acc. sg. μέγα, rest of m. and n. is 2nd decl., on stem μεγαλ- ; comp. μείζων, -ον; supl. μέγιστος, -η, -ον]

black μέλας, μέλαινα, μέλαν [m. and n. gen. μέλανος]

blameless ἀμύμων, ἀμύμονος

blast ἀϋτμή, -ῆς [f.]

blessed μάκαρ [gen. μάκαρος]

blood αἷμα, αἵματος [n.]

boast εὔχομαι, εὔξομαι, εὐξάμην [+ inf.]

body σῶμα, σώματος [n.]

bolt κληίς, κληῖδος [f.]

bone ὀστέον, -ου [n.]

born, I am γίγνομαι, γενήσομαι, γενόμην, γέγαα

both...and τε...τε, τε...καί; on both sides ἀμφί [adv.; prep. + dat. or acc.]

boundary πεῖραρ, πείρατος [n.]

boundless ἀπείρων, -ον

boy παῖς, παιδός [m.]

brandish τινάσσω, τινάξω, τίναξα

brave ἀγαθός, -ή, -όν [comp. ἀρείων, -ον; supl. ἄριστος, -η, -ον]

bread σῖτος, -ου [m.]

breath ἀϋτμή, -ῆς [f.]

bright δῖος, -α, -ον [f. usually keeps alpha through sg.]; λευκός, -ή, -όν

bring φέρω, οἴσω, ἔνεικα; bring to a halt ἵστημι, στήσω, στῆσα [trans.]; bring oneself to a halt ἵσταμαι, στήσομαι, στῆν [intr.]

briny ἁλμυρός, -ή, -όν

broad εὐρύς, -εῖα, -ύ

brother κασιγνητός, -οῦ [m.]

build τεύχω, τεύξω, τεῦξα, pf. mid. τέτυγμαι

burn καίω, καύσω, κῆα [trans.]

busy about, I am πονέομαι, πονήσομαι, πονησάμην

but ἀλλά, αὐτάρ, ἀτάρ; δέ [never first word; following a phrase or clause introduced by μέν]; but now αὖ

by [cause or agent] ὑπό [+ gen.]

C

call λέγω, λέξω, λέξα; καλέω, καλέω, κάλεσ(σ)α; call (by name) ὀνομάζω, ὀνομάσω, ὀνόμασα

can δύναμαι, δυνήσομαι, δυνησάμην [+ inf.]

carry φέρω, οἴσω, ἔνεικα

cast προ-ίημι, προ-ήσω, προ-ῆκα

catch fire ἅπτομαι, ἅψομαι, ἁψάμην

cause τίθημι, θήσω, θῆκα; I cause to be seated ἕσα [aor. of ἕζομαι] or καθ-ίζω, —, κάθ-ισα

cave ἄντρον, -ου [n.]; σπέος, σπέος or σπῆος [n.]

certain, a [indef. adj. and pron.] τις, τι [for forms, see Section 212]

change ἀμείβομαι, ἀμείψομαι, ἀμειψάμην

charity ἀγάπη, -ης [f.]

charm χάρις, -χάριτος [acc. sg. χάριν]

cheese τυρός, -οῦ [m.]

child παῖς, παιδός [m., f.]

choose αἱρέομαι, αἱρήσομαι, ἑλόμην [mid. of ἁρέω]

Christ Χριστός, -οῦ

city π(τ)όλις, π(τ)όλιος [f.]

claim (to be) εὔχομαι, εὔξομαι, εὐξάμην

clearly δή [adv.]

close a) [adj. = compact] πυκ(ι)νός, -ή, -όν; b) [adv.] ἆσσον; close by ἄγχι [adv., or prep. + gen.], σχεδόν [adv.]

come a) ἔρχομαι, ἐλεύσομαι, ἔλ(υ)θον, εἰλήλουθα; b) ἱκνέομαι, ἵξομαι, ἱκόμην [+ acc.]; c) ἱκάνω [pres. syst. only] d) I come (by chance) κιχάνω, κιχήσομαι, κίχον; e) I come to ἐπ-έρχομαι, etc. [+ dat. or acc.]; ἀφ-ικνέομαι, etc. [+ acc.]; f) I come to be πέλω, —, πέλον or deponent form: πέλομαι, —, πλόμην; γίγνομαι, γενήσομαι, γενόμην, γέγαα; g) I come upon ἐπ-έρχομαι [+ dat. or acc.]

command a) [vb.] ἀνώγω, ἀνώξω, ἄνωξα, ἄνωγα [pf. has pres. sense; plpf. has impf. sense]; κελεύω, κελεύσω, κέλευσα [+ acc., dat., inf.]; b) [noun] ἐντολή, -ῆς [f.]

companion ἑταῖρος, -ου; ἕταρος, -ου [m.]

complete τελέω, τελέω, τέλεσα

comrade ἑταῖρος, -ου; ἕταρος, -ου [m.]

conceal κρύπτω, κρύψω, κρύψα

concerning ἀμφί [adv.; prep. + dat. or acc.]

consider φρονέω, φρονήσω, φρόνησα; νομίζω, νομιῶ, νόμισα; consider whether or how to βουλεύω, βουλεύσω, βούλευσα [+ inf., or ὅπως + purpose construction]

constrain βιάζω [pres. syst. only]

contrive μήδομαι, μήσομαι, μησάμην

corpse σῶμα, σώματος [n.]

could [= potential fut. supposition expressed by vb. in opt. + κε(ν) or ἄν]

country a) homeland πατρίς, πατρίδος [f.]; b) rural area, as opposed to city ἀγρός, -οῦ [m.]

courage μένος, μένεος [n.]

courageous ἀγήνωρ [gen. ἀγήνορος]

course a) [noun] κέλευθος, -ου [f., but frequently n. in pl.]; b) [indef. adv.] of course που

courtyard αὐλή, -ῆς [f.]

cow βοῦς, βοός [m., f.] [dat. pl. also βουσί]

cowardly κακός, -ή, -όν

craftiness δόλος, -ου [m.]

cruel σχέτλιος, -η, -ον

cry out in pain οἰμώζω, οἰμώξομαι, οἴμωξα

cunning δόλος, -ου [m.]

custom δίκη, -ης [f.]; θέμις, θέμιστος [f.]

Cyclops Κύκλωψ, Κύκλωπος [m.]

D

dare τλάω, τλήσομαι, τλῆν [+ inf.]

daring [adj.] μεγαλήτωρ [gen. μεγαλήτορος]

dark μέλας, μέλαινα, μέλαν [m. and n. gen. μέλανος]

daughter θυγάτηρ, θυγατέρος or θυγατρός [f.]; κούρη, -ης [f.]

Dawn [= goddess] Ἠώς, Ἠόος [f.]

day ἦμαρ, ἤματος [n.]; for nine days ἐννῆμαρ [adv.]

dead body σῶμα, σώματος [n.]

deadly ὀλοός, -ή, -όν

dear (to) φίλος, -η, -ον [comp. φίλτερος, -η, -ον; supl. φίλτατος, -η, -ον]

death θάνατος, -ου [m.]

deceive λανθάνω, λήσω, λάθον

deed ἔργον, -ου [n.]; πρᾶγμα, πράγματος [n.]

deep a) [adj.] βαθύς, -εῖα, -ύ; b) [noun = sea] πόντος, -ου [m.]

delightful γλυκύς, -εῖα, -ύ

desire βούλομαι, βουλήσομαι, βουλόμην

destroy ὀλλύω, ὀλέσω, ὄλεσ(σ)α; ἀπ-ολλύω, etc. [= destroy utterly]

destruction ὄλεθρος, -ου [m.]

destructive ὀλοός, -ή, -όν

devise ὑφαίνω, ὑφανέω, ὕφηνα

devour ἔσθω [pres. syst. only]

die θνήσκω, θανέομαι, θάνον

difficult χαλεπός, -ή, -όν

dinner δεῖπνον, -ου [n.]

discover εὑρίσκω, εὑρήσω, εὗρον

disease νοῦσος, -ου [f.]

distress a) [noun] ἄλγος, ἄλγεος [n.]; b) [vb.] τείρω [pres. syst. only]

divine θεσπέσιος, -η, -ον

divinity δαίμων, δαίμονος [m., f.]

do ῥέζω, ῥέξω, ῥέξα; ἔρδω, ἔρξω, ἔρξα; ποιέω, ποιήσω, ποίησα; I do wrong ἀδικέω, ἀδικήσω, ἀδίκησα door θύρη, -ης [f.]

door-post σταθμός, -οῦ [m.]

door-stone θυρεός, -οῦ [m.]

doubt, no doubt που [indef. adv.]

down (from) κατά [prep. + gen.]; down (along) κατά [prep. + acc.]; down (to) κατά [prep. + acc.]

drag ἐρύω, —, ἔρυσ(σ)α; ἕλκω

draw ἐρύω, —, ἔρυσ(σ)α; I draw (water or wine) ἀφύσσω, ἀφύξω, ἄφυσ(σ)α

drink πίνω, πίομαι, πίον

drive ἐλαύνω, ἐλάω, ἔλασ(σ)α; I drive a flock νέμω, νεμέω, νεῖμα

due measure μοῖρα, -ης [f.]

dwell οἰκέω, οἰκήσω, οἴκησα

E

each ἕκαστος, -η, -ον; other ἀλλήλοι, -ων [pl. only]

eager(ly) πρόφρων, -ον

early-born (one) ἠριγένεια, -ης [f.]

earth [= world, globe] γαῖα. -ης [f.]; [= ground] χθών, χθονός [f.]; [= soil, arable land] ἄρουρα, -ης [f.]

easy ῥηΐδιος, -η -ον

eat ἐσθίω, ἔδομαι, φάγον; ἔδω [pres. syst. only]; ἔσθω [pres. syst. only]

edge ἄκρον, -ου [n.]

either...or ἤ...ἤ; [after neg.] οὐδέ...οὐδέ

else ἄλλος, -η, -ο

elude λανθάνω, λήσω, λάθον

end πεῖραρ, πείρατος [n.]

endure ἀν-έχομαι, ἀν-έξομαι or ἀνα-σχήσομαι, ἀνά-σχον or -σχεθον; I endure patiently τλάω, τλήσομαι, τλῆν

enter εἰσ-έρχομαι, εἰσ-ελεύσομαι, εἰσ-έλθον; δύω, δύσομαι, δυσάμην or δῦν

entire οὖλος, -η, -ον

entrance πύλη, -ης [f.]

entreat λίσσομαι, —, λισάμην

err ἁμαρτάνω, ἁμαρτήσομαι, ἅμαρτον

escape φεύγω, φεύξομαι, φύγον; I escape the notice of (someone) λανθάνω, λήσω, λάθον

especially περί [adv.]

eternal ἀθάνατος, -η, -ον

even καί; not even οὐδέ, μηδέ

ever [= forever] αἰεί [adv.]; [= at some time] ποτέ [enclitic adv.]

every πᾶς, πᾶσα, πᾶν [m./ n. gen. παντός]

evil κακός, -ή, -όν

exceedingly λίην [adv.]; περί [adv.]

excellent ἐσθλός, -ή, -όν; κλυτός, -ον; ἀμύμων, ἀμύμονος

excelling (over) περί [prep. + gen.]

(ex)change ἀμείβομαι, ἀμείψομαι, ἀμειψάμην

expect ἔλπω or ἔλπομαι [+ inf.] [pres. syst. only]

experience πάσχω, πείσομαι, πάθον

extreme ἄκρος, -η, -ον

exult εὔχομαι, εὔξομαι, εὐξάμην

eye ὀφθαλμός, οῦ [m.]

eyebrow ὀφρύς, ὀφρύος [f.]

eyelid βλέφαρον, -ου [n.]

F

fail of ἁμαρτάνω, ἁμαρτήσομαι, ἅμαρτον [often + gen.]

faith in, I have πιστεύω, πιστεύσω, πίστευσα [+ dat.]

faithful ἐρίηρος, -ον [pl. 3 decl.: ἐρίηρες, etc.]

fall πίπτω, πέσομαι, πέσον

famous κλυτός, -ον

far away ἀπόπροσθεν [adv.]

farmyard αὐλή, -ῆς [f.]; σταθμός, -οῦ [m.]

fast ταχύς, -εῖα, -ύ [comp. θάσσων, θᾶσσον; supl. τάχιστος, -η, -ον]

fasten ἅπτω, ἅψομαι, ἅψα; δέω, δήσω, δῆσα

fat πίων, πίονος

fate μοῖρα, -ης [f.]

father πατήρ, πατέρος or πατρός [m.]

fatherland πατρίς, πατρίδος [f.]

fear δείδω, δείσομαι, δεῖσα, δείδια [+ inf. or μή + purpose construction; pf. has pres. sense]

feed [trans.] τρέφω, θρέψω, θρέψα; feed (upon) [intr., = graze] νέμομαι, νεμέομαι, νειμάμην

feel ἐπι-μαίομαι, ἐπι-μάσσομαι, ἐπι-μασσάμην

fellow ἄνθρωπος, -ου [m.]

female θῆλυς, θήλεια, θῆλυ [or adj. of two endings θῆλυς, θῆλυ]

few ὀλίγος, -η, -ον

fight (against) μάχομαι (μαχέομαι), μαχήσομαι, μαχεσ(σ)άμην [+ dat.]

fill (with) ἐμ-πίπλημι, ἐμ-πλήσω, ἔμ-πλησα; I fill to overflowing ναίω

find εὑρίσκω, εὑρήσω, εὗρον

fine εὐ-εργής, -ές

fire πῦρ, πυρός [n.]

first a) [adj.] πρῶτος, -η, -ον; b) [adv.] at first πρῶτον

fitting, it is ἔοικα [in 3 sg. impers. construction, which may take acc. and inf.]

flee φεύγω, φεύξομαι, φύγον

flesh σάρξ, σαρκός [f.]; κρέα, κρεῶν [n. pl.] nom. sg. κρέας

flock μῆλον, -ου [n.]

flow ῥέω [pres. syst.]

fluid ὑγρός, -ή, -όν

fold [= pen for animals] αὐλή, -ῆς [f.]; σηκός, -οῦ [m.]

followers λαός, -οῦ [m.]

food σῖτος, -ου [m.]; εἶδαρ, εἴδατος [n.]

foolish νήπιος, -η, -ον

for [conj., never first word in clause] γάρ; for περί [prep. + dat. or acc.]; for the sake of εἵνεκα [prep. +. gen.]

force βίη, -ης [f.]

forest ὕλη, -ης

forever αἰεί [adv.]

forgetful of, I am λανθάνομαι, λήσομαι, λαθόμην [+ gen.]

friend φίλος, -ου [adj. as noun]

friendly (to) φίλος, -η, -ον [+ dat.]

from ἀπό, ἐκ, παρά, πρός [preps. + gen.]; down from κατά [prep. + gen.]; from close at hand ἐγγύθεν [adv.]; from elsewhere ἄλλοθεν [adv.]; from there ἔνθεν [adv.]; from under ὑπό [+ gen.]; from what place or source? [interr. adv.] πόθεν

fruit καρπός, -οῦ [m.]

fulfill τελέω, τελέω, τέλεσα

G

gate πύλη, -ης [f.]

gave πόρον [2 aor. syst. only]

get λαμβάνω, λήψομαι, λάβον

gift δῶρον, -ου [n.]; gift of hospitality, guest-gift ξείνιον, -ου [n.]

gigantic πελώριος, -η, -ον

girl παῖς, παιδός [f.]

give δίδωμι, δώσω, δῶκα [see appendix for irreg. forms]; ὀπάζω, ὀπάσσω, ὄπασ(σ)α; πόρον [2 aor. syst. only]

glorious δῖος, -α, -ον [f. usually keeps alpha through sg.]

glory δόξα, -ης [f.]

go βαίνω, βήσομαι, βῆν, βέβηκα; ἔρχομαι, ἐλεύσομαι, ἔλ(υ)θον, εἰλήλουθα; στείχω, —, στίχον; I go up ἀνα-βαίνω, etc; I go upon ἐπι-βαίνω, etc. [+ gen.]; I go past παρ-έρχομαι, etc.

goat αἴξ, αἰγός [m., f.]

god θεός, -οῦ [m., f.]

going ἰών, ἰοῦσα, ἰόν [pres. act. ptc. of εἶμι go]

gold χρυσός, -οῦ [m.]

good ἀγαθός, -ή, -όν [comp. ἀρείων, -ον; supl. ἄριστος, -η, -ον]; χρηστός, -ή, -όν; good-for-nothing λυγρός, -ή, -όν

grace χάρις, χάριτος [f.] acc. sg. χάριν

grayish πολιός, (-ή), -όν

great μέγας, μεγάλη, μέγα [m. acc. sg. μέγαν, n. acc. sg. μέγα, rest of m. and n. is 2nd decl., on stem μεγαλ- ; comp. μείζων, -ον; supl. μέγιστος, -η, -ον]; as great as ὅσ(σ)ος, -η, -ον [see as]; so great as τόσ(σ)ος, -η, -ον [see so]

great-hearted μεγαλήτωρ [gen. μεγαλήτορος] [adj.]

greatly μάλα [adv.]

Greeks Ἀχαιοί, -ῶν [m.]

green, greenish-yellow χλωρός, -ή, -όν

greyish πολιός, (-ή), -όν

groan στενάχω [pres. syst. only]

grow a) [trans.] ἀέξω, ἀεξήσω, ἀέξησα b) [intr.] ἀέξομαι, ἀεξήσομαι, ἀεξησάμην

guest ξεῖνος, -ου [m.]

gulf λαῖτμα, λάιτματος [n.]

H

half ἥμισυς, -(εια), -υ

halt a) [trans.] ἵστημι, στήσω, στῆσα b) [intr.] ἵσταμαι, στήσομαι, στῆν

hand χείρ, χε(ι)ρός [f.]

handmaid ἀμφίπολος, -ου [f.]

happen γίγνομαι, γενήσομαι, γενόμην, γέγαα; happen upon τυγχάνω, τεύξομαι, τύχον

happiness ὄλβος, -ου [m.]

happy μάκαρ [gen. μάκαρος]

hasten σπεύδω, σπεύσω, σπεῦσα

hate μισέω, μισήσω, μίσησα

have ἔχω, ἕξω or σχήσω, σχόν or σχέθον; have mercy on ἐλεέω, —, ἐλέησα; have the heart (to) τλάω, τλήσομαι, τλῆν

he a) ὁ; ὅδε; αὐτός b) him [pron. in gen., dat., acc.] see Lesson 34

heap up χέω, χεύω, χεῦα; ἀφύσσω, ἀφύξω, ἄφυσ(σ)α

hear ἀκούω, ἀκούσομαι, ἄκουσα; I hear of πεύθομαι, πεύσομαι, πυθόμην

heart θυμός, -οῦ [m.]; κῆρ, κῆρος [n.]; ἦτορ [n., indecl.]; I have the heart (to) τλάω, τλήσομαι, τλῆν

heaven οὐρανός, -οῦ [m.]

heavenly θεσπέσιος, -η, -ον

heavy ὄβριμος, -η, -ον

her a) [pron., see she]; b) [adj.] ἑός, -ή, -όν

here τῆδε [adv.]

hereafter ὄπισθεν, ὀπίσ(σ)ω [adv.]

herself [see himself, herself, itself]

hesitate to ἅζομαι [pres. syst. only] [+ inf.]

hide [trans.] κεύθω, κεύσω, κύθον; κρύπτω, κρύψω, κρύψα

high ὑψηλός, -ή, -όν

him [see he]

himself, herself, itself αὐτός, -ή, -ό

his ἑός, -ή, -όν

hiss ἰάχω [pres. syst. only]

hold ἔχω, ἕξω or σχήσω, σχόν or σχέθον; hold back from ἀπ-έχω; hold up under ἀν-έχομαι, etc.

hollow γλαφυρός, -ή, -όν

holy ἱερός, -ή, -όν

home οἶκος, -ου [m.]

homecoming a) [noun] νόστος, -ου [m.] b) [adj., = of one's homecoming] νόστιμος, -η, -ον

homeward οἴκαδε [adv.]

honey-sweet μελιηδής, -ές

honorable δίκαιος, -η, -ον

hope ἔλπω or ἔλπομαι [+ inf.] [pres. syst. only]

house οἶκος, -ου [m.]

how ὡς [adv.]; how? πῶς [interr. adv.]

however δέ [never first word]

human βροτός, -ή, -όν; [used only of flesh] ἀνδρόμεος, -η, -ον; human being ἄνθρωπος, -ου [m.]

hurl ῥίπτω, ῥίψω, ῥῖψα; ἵημι, ἥσω, ἧκα; προ-ίημι, προ-ήσω, προ-ῆκα

Hyperion Ὑπερίων, Ὑπερίονος [m.]

I

I ἐγώ(ν) [for forms, see Appendix A]

if εἰ; if only [=impossible wish] εἰ, εἰ γάρ, εἴθε [+ opt.]

Ilion Τροίη, -ης [f.]

imagine ὀίω or ὀίομαι, ὀίσομαι, ὀισάμην

immortal ἀθάνατος, -η, -ον

in ἐν [prep. + dat.]; in any way πως [enclitic adv.]; in fact γε [enclitic particle]; in front of πρόσθε(ν) [adv.]; in order ἑξῆς [adv.]; in order that ἵνα, ὡς, ὅπως, ὄφρα [conj.]; in silence ἀκέων, -ουσα, —; in that case [=therefore] τῷ [conj.]; in the same place αὐτοῦ [adv.]

increase a) [trans.] ἀέξω, ἀεξήσω, ἀέξησα; b) [intr. = I increase (myself), I grow] ἀέξομαι, ἀεξήσομαι, ἀεξησάμην

indeed ἦ; δή [adv.]; [in contrasts followed by δέ] μέν

inhabit οἰκέω, οἰκήσω, οἴκησα

injure ἀδικέω, ἀδικήσω, ἀδίκησα

inquire (from) πεύθομαι, πεύσομαι, πυθόμην

inside (of) a) [adv.] ἔνδον, ἔντοσθεν; b) [prep. + gen.] inside of ἔντοσθεν

intend (to do something) μέλλω, μελλήσω, μέλλησα [+ inf.]

into εἰς [prep. + acc.]; into the midst μετά [prep. + acc.]

it [if gender is unclear] τό; τόδε; αὐτό

itself αὐτό [gen. αὐτοῦ]

J

journey ὁδός, -οῦ [f.]

judge κρίνω, κρινέω, κρῖνα

just δίκαιος, -η, -ον

justice δίκη, -ης [f.]

K

keen ὀξύς, -εῖα, -ύ

kill κτείνω, κτενέω, κτεῖνα or κτάνον; ἀπ-ολλύω, etc.

kindle καίω, καύσω, κῆα

kindly πρόφρων, -ον

king ἄναξ, ἄνακτος [m.]

kingdom βασιλείη, -ης [f.]

knee γόνυ, γούνατος or γουνός [n.]

know γίγνώσκω, γνώσομαι, γνῶν, ἔγνωκα, ἔγνωσμαι, γνώσθην; οἶδα, εἰδήσω [irreg.; see Appendix A for forms]

L

labor at πονέομαι, πονήσομαι, πονησάμην

lamb(s) ἄρνες, ἀρνῶν [no nom. sg.; acc.sg. ἄρνα] [m., f.]

lament στενάχω [pres. syst. only]

land a) [noun] γαῖα. -ης [f.]; b) [vb.] ἐπι-βαίνω, ἐπι-βήσομαι, ἐπί-βην, ἐπι-βέβηκα [+ gen.]

large a) μέγας, μεγάλη, μέγα [m. acc. sg. μέγαν, n. acc. sg. μέγα, rest of m. and n. is 2nd decl., on stem μεγαλ- ; comp. μείζων, -ον; supl. μέγιστος, -η, -ον]; b) μακρός, -ή, -όν

last ὕστατος, -η, -ον

lawful, it is θέμις ἐστί [+ acc. and inf.]

lay hold of ἅπτομαι, ἅψομαι, ἁψάμην

lead ἄγω, ἄξω, ἄγαγον

learn μανθάνω, μαθήσομαι, μάθον; I learn by inquiry πεύθομαι, πεύσομαι, πυθόμην

least, at γε [enclitic particle]

leave λείπω, λείψω, λίπον; leave (alone) ἐάω, ἐάσω, ἔασα [+ inf.]

length μῆκος, μήκεος [n.]

lest μή, ἵνα μή [+ subj. or opt. in purpose construction]

let a) let me, let us [expressed by vb. in 1st pers. hortatory subj.] b) let him, her, it [expressed by vb. in 3rd pers. opt.] c) let alone [= allow, permit] ἐάω, ἐάσω, ἔασα [+ inf.]

lie (down) κεῖμαι [pf. mid. syst. only]

life ζωή, -ῆς [f.]; βίος, -ου [m.]; ψυχή, -ῆς [f.]

lift up ἀείρω, —, ἄειρα

light φάος, φάεος [n.]

like (to) a) [adj. + dat.] ὁμοῖος, -η, -ον; b) [vb.] I am like to ἔοικα [pf. with pres. force; ἐῴκεα plpf. with impf. force]

limb μέλος, μέλεος [n.]

live ζώω, ζώσω, ζῶσα

lofty ὑψηλός, -ή, -όν

long a) [adj.] μακρός, -ή, -όν b) [vb.] I long (after) ποθέω, ποθήσω, πόθεσα; I long (to do something) ποθέω, ποθήσω, πόθεσα [+ inf.], λιλαίομαι [+ inf.] [pres. syst. only]

look (at) ὁράω, ὄψομαι, ἴδον, ἑώρακα, ἑώραμαι, ὄφθην; εἰσ-οράω, εἰσ-όψομαι, εἶσ-ιδον

loom [for weaving] ἱστός, -οῦ [m.]

loose λύω, λύσω, λύσα, λέλυκα, λέλυμαι, λύθην

lord ἄναξ, ἄνακτος [m.]

lose ἀπ-ολλύω, ἀπ-ολέσω, ἀπ-όλεσ(σ)α

lost, am ὀλλύομαι, ὀλέσομαι, ὀλόμην, ὄλωλα; ἀπ-ολλύομαι, etc.

lotus λωτός, -οῦ [m.]

Lotus-eaters Λωτοφάγοι, -ων [m.]

love a) [noun] ἀγάπη, -ης [f.]; b) [vb.] φιλέω, φιλήσω, φίλησα

loyal ἐρίηρος, -ον [pl. 3 decl.: ἐρίηρες, etc.]

M

make ποιέω, ποιήσω, ποίησα; I myself heard γεγωνέω, γεγωνήσω, γεγώνησα, γέγωνα [pf. with pres. meaning]; I make trial of πειράω, πειρήσω, πείρησα [+ gen.]

male ἄρσην, -ενος [m., f.] ἄρσεν, ἄρσενος [n.]

man [=human being] ἄνθρωπος, -ου [m.]; [= male] ἀνήρ, ἀνέρος or ἀνδρός [m.] dat. pl. ἄνδρεσσι or ἄνδρασι ; [= person] φώς, φωτός [m.]

manliness ἀρετή, -ῆς [f.]

manly ἀγήνωρ, ἀγήνορος [adj.]

man-servant δμώς, δμωός [m.]

many πολλός, -ή, -όν; [m./n. also 3rd decl. πολύς, -ύ; comp. πλείων, -ον; supl. πλεῖστος, -η, -ον]; as many as ὅσ(σ)ος, -η, -ον [see as]; so many as τόσ(σ)ος, -η, -ον [see so]

marry γαμέω, γαμέω, γάμησα or γῆμα

mast ἱστός, -οῦ [m.]

meal δεῖπνον, -ου [n.]

measure μέτρον, -ου [n.]; due measure μοῖρα, -ης [f.]

meat κρέα, κρεῶν [n. pl.] nom. sg. κρέας

member (of the body) μέλος, μέλεος [n.]

middle (of) μέσ(σ)ος, -η, -ον [modifying noun in same case]

midst (of) μέσ(σ)ος, -η, -ον [modifying noun in same case]

might μένος, μένεος [n.]

mighty ὄβριμος, -η, -ον

milk ἀμέλγω [pres. syst. only]

mind νόος, -ου [m.]; φρήν, φρενός [f.]

mine ἐμεῖο; μευ; ἐμός, -ή, -όν

mingle (with) μίσγω, μίξω, μίξα [+ dat.]

miserable λυγρός, -ή, -όν

miss ἁμαρτάνω, ἁμαρτήσομαι, ἅμαρτον [often + gen.]; miss (an absent person or thing) ποθέω, ποθήσω, πόθεσα [+ acc.]

mix (something with something) μίσγω, μίξω, μίξα

mixing-bowl κρητήρ, κρητῆρος [m.]

money χρήματα, χρημάτων [pl. of χρῆμα]

monstrous πελώριος, -η, -ον

more [see many]

mortal θνητός, -ή, -όν; βροτός, -ή, -όν

most [see many]

mother μήτηρ, μητέρος or μητρός [f.]

mountain ὄρος, ὄρεος [n.]

mourn γοάω, γοήσομαι, γόησα

much a) [adj.] πολλός, -ή, -όν; [m./n. also 3rd decl. πολύς, -ύ; comp. πλείων, -ον; supl. πλεῖστος, -η, -ον]; as much as ὅσ(σ)ος, -η, -ον [see as]; so much as τόσ(σ)ος, -η, -ον [see so]; b) [adv.] πολύ

Muse Μοῦσα, -ης [f.]

my ἐμός, -ή, -όν

myself a) 1st personal pron. + αὐτός in same case; b) often expressed by mid. voice of vb.

N

name ὄνομα or οὔνομα, ὀνόματος [n.]

nature φύσις, φύσιος [f.]

near a) [adv.] ἐγγύς, ἄγχι, ἆσσον, ἐγγύθεν, σχεδόν b) [preps. + gen.] ἐγγύς, ἄγχι, ἆσσον c) [prep. + dat.] ἆσσον d) [adj.] πλησίος, -η, -ον

necessary, it is χρή [+ inf. w. acc. sub.]

necessity ἀνάγκη, -ης [f.]

neck αὐχήν, αὐχένος [m.]

nectar νέκταρ, νέκταρος [n.]

need ἀνάγκη, -ης [f.]

neighbor(ing) πλησίος, -η, -ον

neither...nor οὔτε...οὔτε

never (yet) πω [+ neg.] [adv.]

night νύξ, νυκτός [f.]

nimble ὠκύς, -εῖα, -ύ

nine days, for ἐννῆμαρ [adv.]

no, nor οὐ [οὐκ before smooth breathing; οὐχ before rough breathing]; μή [οὐ generally is the neg. of concrete fact, μή of possibility, condition, command, general, dependence, etc.]; no doubt που; no longer οὐκ ἔτι or οὐκέτι [adv.]; in no way πω [+ neg.]; no one οὐδείς, οὐδεμία, οὐδέν; μηδείς, μηδεμία, μηδέν

noble ἐσθλός, -ή, -όν; καλός, -ή, -όν [comp. καλλίων, -ον; supl. κάλλιστος, -η, -ον]

nobody οὐδείς, οὐδεμία, οὐδέν; μηδείς, μηδεμία, μηδέν; Nobody Οὖτις, Οὔτιος

none οὐδείς, οὐδεμία, οὐδέν; μηδείς, μηδεμία, μηδέν

nor a) οὐδέ; μηδέ b) [following a neg. clause] οὔτε; c) neither...nor οὔτε...οὔτε

not [see *no*]; not at all πω [+ neg.]; not even οὐδέ; μηδέ; nothing οὐδέν

nourish τρέφω, θρέψω, θρέψα

now [= at the present time] νῦν; [not of time; = therefore] δή

O

O! [in direct address] ὦ

oar ἐρετμόν, -οῦ [n.]

oar-lock κληΐς, κληῖδος [f.]

obey, am obedient to πείθομαι, πείσομαι, πιθόμην [+ dat.]

of a) expressed by gen. case b) [adv.] of course που

offered πόρον [2 aor. syst. only]

old man γέρων, γέροντος [m.]

olive-wood, of ἐλαΐνεος, -η, -ον

on ἐπί; ἐν; πρός [preps. + dat.]; ἀνά or ἄμ [prep. + gen., dat., acc.]; on account of διά [prep. + acc.], εἵνεκα [prep. + gen.]; on high [adv.] ὑψόσε; on the one hand μέν; on the other hand δέ; αὖτε

once [= some time] ποτέ [enclitic adv.]; at once αὐτίκα

one εἷς, μία, ἕν [m./n. gen. ἑνός]

one another ἄλληλοι, -ων [pl. only]

only μοῦνος, -η, -ον

opinion δόξα, -ης [f.]

or ἤ; ἠέ

order a) [noun] ἐντολή, -ῆς [f.]; b) [vb.] κέλομαι, κελήσομαι, κεκλόμην; c) [conj. = in order that] ἵνα, ὅπως, ὡς, ὄφρα [neg. μή]; d) [adv.] ἑξῆς

other ἄλλος, -η, -ο ; (the) other(s) ἕτερος, -η, -ον

ought χρή [+ inf. w. acc. sub.]

our ἡμέτερος, -η, -ον

out of ἐκ (ἐξ before vowels) [prep. + gen.]

outermost ἄκρος, -η, -ον

over ἀνά or ἄμ [prep. + acc.]; ὑπέρ or ὑπείρ [prep. + gen. or acc.]

overpower δαμάζω, δαμάω, δάμασσα

own (his/her own) ἑός, -ή, -όν

ox βοῦς, βοός [m., f.] [dat. pl. also βουσί]

P

pain ἄλγος, ἄλγεος [n.]

pair of [expressed by the dual]

partake (of) πατέομαι, —, πασ(σ)άμην [+ gen.]

pass (by) παρ-έρχομαι, etc.

path κέλευθος, -ου [f., but frequently n. in pl.]

pay τίνω or τίω, [fut.] τείσω or τίσω, [aor.] τείσα or τῖσα

peace εἰρήνη, -ης [f.]

pen σηκός, -οῦ [m.]

people λαός, -οῦ [m.]

perceive νοέω, νοήσω, νόησα

perhaps που [indef. adv.]

perish ὀλλύομαι, ὀλέσομαι, ὀλόμην, ὄλωλα; ἀπ-ολλύομαι, etc.

persuade πείθω, πείσω, πεῖσα or πέπιθον

physician ἰητρός, -οῦ [m.]

pick for myself αἱρέομαι, αἱρήσομαι, ἑλόμην [mid. of αἱρέω]; pick out κρίνω, κρινέω, κρῖνα

pitiless σχέτλιος, -η, -ον; νηλ(ε)ής, -ές

pity ἐλεέω, —, ἐλέησα

place a) [noun] χῶρος, -ου [m.]; b) [vb.] ἵημι, ἥσω, ἧκα; I have been placed κεῖμαι [pf. mid. syst. only]

plan a) [noun] βουλή, -ῆς [f.]; b) [vb.] plan how to βουλεύω, βουλεύσω, βούλευσα [+ inf., or ὅπως + purpose construction]; μήδομαι, μήσομαι, μησάμην

plank δόρυ, δούρατος or δουρός [n.]

pleasant ἡδύς, ἡδεῖα, ἡδύ

please [expressed by verb in opt.]

pleased with, I am ἥδομαι, ἥσομαι, ἡσάμην [+ dat.]

pleasing μειλίχιος, -η, -ον

pleasure ἡδονή, -ῆς [f.]

pole μοχλός, -οῦ [m.]

Polyphemus Πολύφημος, -ου [m.]

portion μοῖρα, -ης [f.]

Poseidon Ποσειδάων, -ωνος [m.]

possess νέμομαι, νεμέομαι, νειμάμην

possession χρῆμα, χρήματος [n.]

possible δυνατός, -ή, -όν

pour [trans.] χέω, χεύω, χεῦα; I pour out of [intr.] ἐκ-σεύω, —, ἐκ-σσύμην [non-thematic 2 aor.]

power κράτος, κράτεος [n.]; a superhuman power or divinity δαίμων, δαίμονος [m.]

pray (to) εὔχομαι, εὔξομαι, εὐξάμην [+ dat. and inf.]

prefer βούλομαι, βουλήσομαι, βουλόμην

prepare τεύχω, τεύξω, τεῦξα, —, τέτυγμαι; ὁπλίζω, —, ὅπλισσα

present a) [adv., = now] at present νῦν b) [vb.] ὀπάζω, ὀπάσσω, ὄπασ(σ)α; I am present πάρ-ειμι [see εἰμί in Appendix A for forms]

proceed στείχω, —, στίχον

produce ποιέω, ποιήσω, ποίησα

property χρῆμα, χρήματος [n.]

prosperity ὄλβος, -ου [m.]

protect (ἐ)ρύομαι, (ἐ)ρύσσομαι, (ἐρ)ρυσάμην

punish τίνομαι, τίσομαι, τισάμην

pursue διώκω, διώξω, δίωξα

put ἵστημι, στήσω, στῆσα; τίθημι, θήσω, θῆκα; put down κατα-τίθημι, etc.; put in position, put on ἐπι-τίθημι, etc.

Q

quick καρπάλιμος, -ον

quickly αἶψα; τάχα; καρπαλίμως [adv.]

quite μάλα [adv., modifying adj. or adv.]

R

raft σχεδίη, -ης [f.]

rage μενεαίνω, —, μενέηνα

rain ὄμβρος, -ου [m.]

raise ἀείρω, —, ἄειρα

ram ἀρνειός, -οῦ [m.]

reach (by chance) κιχάνω, κιχήσομαι, κίχον

ready a) [adj.] πρόφρων, -ον b) [vb.] I make ready τεύχω, τεύξω, τεῦξα, pf. mid.: τέτυγμαι

rear τρέφω, θρέψω, θρέψα

reason λόγος, -ου [m.]

receive δέχομαι, δέξομαι, δεξάμην

reckless σχέτλιος, -η, -ον

refrain from ἀπ-έχω

region χῶρος, -ου [m.]

rejoice (in) χαίρω, χαιρήσω, χάρην [aor. pass. with active force]

release λύω, λύσω, λύσα, λέλυκα, λέλυμαι, λύθην

remain μένω, μενέω, μεῖνα; μίμνω [pres. syst. only]

reply ἀμείβομαι, ἀμείψομαι, ἀμειψάμην

request αἰτέω, αἰτήσω, αἴτησα

rescue (ἐ)ρύομαι, (ἐ)ρύσσομαι, (ἐρ)ρυσάμην

resound ἰάχω [pres. syst. only]

respect αἰδέομαι, αἰδέσ(σ)ομαι, αἰδεσσάμην; ἅζομαι [pres. syst. only]

return a) [vb.] νέομαι [pres. syst. only] b) [noun = return home] νόστος, -ου [m.]

reveal φαίνω, φανέω, φῆνα

revere ἅζομαι [pres. syst. only]; αἰδέομαι, αἰδέσ(σ)ομαι, αἰδεσσάμην

reverence αἰδέομαι, αἰδέσ(σ)ομαι, αἰδεσσάμην

rich πίων, πίονος

right ὀρθός, -ή, -όν; a right θέμις, θέμιστος [f.]; it is right θέμις ἐστί [+ acc. and inf.]

rivalry ἔρις, ἔριδος [f.]

river ποταμός, οῦ [m.]

road ὁδός, -οῦ [f.]; κέλευθος, -ου [f, but frequently n. in pl.]

roam (back and forth) φοιτάω, φοιτήσω, φοίτησα

roar βοάω, βοήσω, βόησα

rock πέτρη, -ης [f.]

rosy-fingered ῥοδοδάκτυλος, -ον

round about περί [adv.]

rush away, rush back (from) ἀπο-σεύω, —, ἀπο-σσύμην [non-thematic 2 aor.]; rush out of ἐκ-σεύω, —, ἐκ-σσύμην

ruthless νηλ(ε)ής, -ές

S

sacred ἱερός, -ή, -όν

said [3 sg.] ἔφη [irreg. from φημί]; I said εἶπον [2 aor. syst. only]

sail (over) πλέω, πλεύσομαι, πλεῦσα

sake: for the sake of εἵνεκα [prep. +. gen.]

salty ἁλμυρός, -ή, -όν

same a) [adj.] αὐτός, -ή, -ό; b) [adv., or prep. + dat.] at the same time ἅμα

savage ἄγριος, (-η), -ον

save σώζω, σώσω, σῶσα; (ἐ)ρύομαι, (ἐ)ρύσσομαι, (ἐρ)ρυσάμην

say λέγω, λέξω, λέξα; ἐννέπω, ἐνίψω, ἔνισπον; εἶπον [2 aor. syst. only]; φημί, φήσω, φῆσα [see Section 595 for impf. forms]

sea θάλασσα, -ης [f.]; [=the deep] πόντος, -ου [m.]; ἅλς, ἁλός [f.]

search after ζητέω, ζητήσω, ζήτησα

seat myself καθ-ίζω, —, κάθισα

seated ἥμενος, -η, -ον

second δεύτερος, -η, -ον; a second time δίς [adv.]

see ὁράω, ὄψομαι, ἴδον, ἑώρακα, ἑώραμαι, ὄφθην ; [= watch, look at] εἰσ-οράω, etc.

seek ζητέω, ζητήσω, ζήτησα; seek out ἐπι-μαίομαι, ἐπι-μάσσομαι, ἐπι-μασσάμην

seem δοκέω, δοκήσω, δόκησα; ἔοικα [pf. with pres. force; ἐῴκεα plpf. with impf. force]

seize αἱρέω, αἱρήσω, ἕλον ; seize upon αἴνυμαι [pres. syst. only]

seize μάρπτω, μάρψω, μάρψα

select αἱρέομαι, αἱρήσομαι, ἑλόμην [mid. of αἱρέω]; αἴνυμαι [pres. syst. only]

self αὐτός, -ή, -ό

send πέμπω, πέμψω, πέμψα; ἵημι, ἥσω, ἧκα; I send forth ἵημι, ἥσω, ἧκα; I send (someone) as a companion ὀπάζω, ὀπάσσω, ὄπασ(σ)α [+ acc. and dat.]

senseless ἄφρων, -ον

separate κρίνω, κρινέω, κρῖνα

servant [man] δμώς, δμωός [m.]; [woman] δμωή, -ῆς [f.]

seven ἑπτά [indecl.]

shameful αἰσχρός, -ή, -όν

sharp ὀξύς, -εῖα, -ύ

she a) ἡ; ἥδε; αὐτή; b) her [pron. in gen., dat., acc.] see Lesson 34

sheep μῆλον, -ου [n.]; ὄϊς, ὄϊος [dat. pl. also ὄεσσι, acc. pl. always ὄϊς] [m., f.]

shepherd ποιμήν, ποιμένος [m.]

ship νηῦς, νηός or νεός, dat. pl. also νηυσί [f.]

shout βοάω, βοήσω, βόησα; ἰάχω [pres. syst. only]; γεγωνέω, γεγωνήσω, γεγώνησα, γέγωνα [pf. with pres. meaning]

show φαίνω, φανέω, φῆνα; I show myself φαίνομαι, φανέομαι, φάνην

shrewd πυκ(ι)νός, -ή, -όν

shrink before ἀλέομαι, — , ἀλεάμην or ἀλευάμην

sickness νοῦσος, -ου [f.]

silent(ly) ἀκέων, -ουσα

similar to ὁμοῖος, —, -ον [+ dat.]

simple νήπιος, -η, -ον

since ἐπεί [conj.]

sit down ἕζομαι, —, ἕσα

sitting ἥμενος, -η, -ον

sky οὐρανός, -οῦ [m.]

sleep a) [vb.] εὕδω, εὑδήσω, εὕδησα; b) [noun] ὕπνος, -ου [m.]

small ὀλίγος, -η, -ον

so οὕτως, ὧδε, ὥς, ὡς [adv.]; so many, so great, so much τόσ(σ)ος, -η, -ον [often correlative with ὅσ(σ)ος, -η, -ον: so many (etc.)...as]

soft μαλακός, -ή, -όν

soil ἄρουρα, -ης [f.]

some(one), some(thing) τις, τι

somehow πως [enclitic adv.]; τι [enclitic adv.]

sometime(s) ποτέ [enclitic adv.]

son υἱός, -οῦ or υἱέος [dat. pl. υἱάσι] [m.]

soon τάχα [adv.]

sort a) [adj.= of what sort] οἷος, -η, -ον; b) [adj. = of all sorts] παντοῖος, -η, -ον

A Reading Course in Homeric Greek

soul ψυχή, -ῆς [f.]

sound φωνή, -ῆς [f.]

speak φημί, φήσω, φῆσα [see Section 595 for impf. forms]; speak to προσ-εῖπον [or προσ-έειπον] [+ acc.]

spear δόρυ, δούρατος or δουρός [n.]

speech λόγος, -ου [m.]

spirit [= heart, soul, life] θυμός, -οῦ [m.]; [= mind] φρήν, φρενός [f.]

splendid ἀγλαός, -ή, -ον

spoke ἦ [= thus he spoke]

spread out πετάννυμι, —, πέτασ(σ)α

stake μοχλός, -οῦ [m.]

stand [intr.] ἵσταμαι, στήσομαι, στῆν; I stand by παρ-ίσταμαι, etc.

stay μένω, μενέω, μεῖνα; μίμνω [pres. syst. only]

steep αἰπύς, -εῖα, -ύ

still ἔτι [adv.]

stone λίθος, -ου [m.]

stood [intr.] στῆν [3 aor. syst. of ἵστημι I stand]

storm ὄμβρος, -ου [m.]

stout παχύς, -εῖα, ύ

straight ὀρθός, -ή, -όν

stranger ξεῖνος, -ου [m.]

strength κράτος, κράτεος [n.]

strike βάλλω, βαλέω, βάλον; τύπτω, τύψω, τύψα

strong κρατερός, -ή, -όν

such a) [adv., modifying adj. or adv.] οὕτως b) [adj. = (such) as] οἷος, -η, -ον

suddenly αἶψα

suffer πάσχω, πείσομαι, πάθον

sun ἥλιος, -ου [m.]

superhuman power [a divinity] δαίμων, δαίμονος [m., f.]

supper δόρπον, -ου [n.]

suppliants ἱκέται, ἱκετάων [m.]

supply παρ-έχω, etc.

suppose a) [vb.] ὀΐω or ὀΐομαι, ὀΐσομαι, ὀϊσάμην; ἔλπω or ἔλπομαι [pres. syst. only]; b) που [indef. adv.]

surely περ, τοι [enclitic particles]

sweet ἡδύς, ἡδεῖα, ἡδύ ; γλυκύς, γλυκεῖα, γλυκύ; γλυκερός, -ή, -όν

swift ταχύς, -εῖα, -ύ [comp. θάσσων, θᾶσσον; supl. τάχιστος, -η, -ον]; ὠκύς, -εῖα, -ύ; θοός, -ή, -όν; καρπάλιμος, -ον

sword ξίφος, ξίφεος [n.]

T

take λαμβάνω, λήψομαι, λάβον; take away ἀφ-αιρέομαι, ἀφ-αιρήσομαι, ἀφ-ελόμην; take hold of αἴνυμαι [pres. syst. only]; take up ἀείρω, —, ἄειρα; I take vengeance upon τίνομαι, τίσομαι, τισάμην

tame δαμάζω, δαμάω, δάμασσα

teach διδάσκω, διδάξω, δίδαξα

tell λέγω, λέξω, λέξα; ἐννέπω, ἐνίψω, ἔνισπον; εἶπον [2 aor. syst.]; φημί, φήσω, φῆσα [see Section 595 for impf. forms]

temple νηός, -οῦ [m.]

tenth δέκατος, -η, -ον

than ἤ [or use comp. gen.]

that a) demonstr. adj./pron. ὁ , ἡ, τό; (ἐ)κεῖνος, -η, -ο; b) [conj. = in order that] ἵνα, ὅπως, ὡς, ὄφρα [neg. μή]; c) [conj. after vb. of saying, thinking, etc. in indirect statement] ὅτι

their(s) σφέτερος, -η, -ον

them see *they*

themselves αὐτοί, -αί, -ά

then [of time] ἔνθα, ἔνθεν, τότε, ἔπειτα [adv.]; [not of time, = therefore] οὖν, ἄρα or ῥα [postpositive]

there [adv.] αὐτοῦ, τῇ, ἔνθα

therefore οὖν, ἄρα or ῥα [postpositive], τῷ

thereupon ἔπειτα [adv.]

they a) [nom.] οἱ, αἱ; οἵδε, αἵδε; αὐτοί, -αί; (ἐ)κεῖνοι, -αι; b) them [gen., dat., acc.]; see Lesson 34

thick παχύς, -εῖα, -ύ; πυκ(ι)νός, -ή, -όν

thigh μηρός, -οῦ [m.]

think ὀΐω or ὀΐομαι, ὀΐσομαι, ὀϊσάμην; νοέω, νοήσω, νόησα; νομίζω, νομιῶ, νόμισα

this (one) [demonstrative pron. and adj.] ὅδε, ἥδε, τόδε

though περ [+ ptc.]

three times τρίς [adv.]

thrice τρίς [adv.]

through διά [prep. + gen., acc.]

throughout κατά [prep. + acc.]

throw βάλλω, βαλέω, βάλον

thus οὕτως; ὧδε, ὥς, ὡς [adv.]; thus he spoke ἦ

tie δέω, δήσω, δῆσα

time a) [noun] χρόνος, -ου [m.]; b) [adv.] at the present time νῦν; at the same time ἅμα; at some time, at any time ποτέ

tip ἄκρον, -ου [n.]

to a) [prep. + acc.] ἐπί [= upon, e.g., "It fell *to* earth."], εἰς [= into, toward]; πρός [= up to], παρά [= up alongside]; b) [conj. = in order that] ἵνα, ὡς, ὅπως, ὄφρα, or expressed by fut. ptc. or fut. inf.

together with ἅμα [adv., or prep. + dat.]

toil a) [noun] πόνος, -ου [m.] b) [vb.] I toil at πονέομαι, πονήσομαι, πονησάμην

told εἶπον [2 aor. syst. only]

topmost ἄκρος, -η, -ον

touch ἐπι-μαίομαι, ἐπι-μάσσομαι, ἐπι-μασσάμην

towards ἐπί, πρός [preps. + acc.]

town ἄστυ, ἄστεος [n.]

treasure θησαυρός, οῦ [m.]

tree δένδρεον, -ου [n.]

trial, make trial of πειράω, πειρήσω, πείρησα [+ gen.]

trickery δόλος, -ου [m.]

trouble πόνος, -ου [m.]; πράγματα, πραγμάτων [pl. of πρᾶγμα, πράγματος]

Troy Τροίη, -ης [f.]

true ὀρθός, -ή, -όν ; ἀληθής, ές

truly ἦ ; καὶ λίην [adv.]

trusty ἐρίηρος, -ον [pl. 3 decl.: ἐρίηρες, etc.]

truth ἀληθείη, -ης [f.]

try πειράω, πειρήσω, πείρησα [+ gen. or + inf.]

turn τρέπω, τρέψω, τρέψα [trans.]; τρέπομαι, τρέψομαι, τρεψάμην [intr.]

twice δίς

two δύω or δύο [indecl.]

U

under a) [= at rest under] ὑπό [prep. + dat.]; b) [= motion up under] ὑπό [prep. + acc.]; c) [= from under, under the influence of, by] ὑπό [prep. + gen.]

understanding, I have φρονέω, φρονήσω, φρόνησα

unless εἰ μή

until εἷος [also ἧος or ἕως] or ὄφρα [+ ind. if purely factual; + purpose construction if anticipatory] up ἀνά or ἄμ [adv.]

upon ἐπί [prep. + gen.]

upwards ὑψόσε [adv.]

urge ἀνώγω, ἀνώξω, ἄνωξα, ἄνωγα [pf. has pres. sense; plpf. has impf. sense]

us [see pron. forms in appendix]

use violence against βιάζω [pres. syst. only]

useful χρηστός, -ή, -όν

utter αἰπύς, -εῖα, -ύ

V

vapor ἀϋτμή, -ῆς [f.]

venerate αἰδέομαι, αἰδέσ(σ)ομαι, αἰδεσσάμην

vengeance, I take vengeance upon τίνομαι, τίσομαι, τισάμην

very μάλα [adv., modifying adj. or adv.]

violence βίη, -ης [f.]; I use violence against βιάζω [pres. syst. only]

virtue ἀρετή, -ῆς [f.]

voice φωνή, -ῆς [f.]; φθόγγος, -ου [m.]

W

wagon ἄμαξα, -ης [f.]

wail κλαίω, κλαύσω, κλαῦσα

wait μίμνω [pres. syst. only]

wander ἀλάομαι, —, ἀλήθην, ἀλάλημαι [pf. has pres. force]

war π(τ)όλεμος, -ου [m.]

water ὕδωρ, ὕδατος [n.]

watery ὑγρός, -ή, -όν

wave κῦμα, κύματος [n.]

way a) [noun] κέλευθος, -ου [f., but frequently n. in pl.]; ὁδός, -οῦ [f.] b) [adv., = in this way] οὕτως

we [see pron. forms in Appendix A]

wealth χρήματα, χρημάτων [pl. of χρῆμα]

wear out [tr.] τείρω [pres. syst. only]

weave ὑφαίνω, ὑφανέω, ὕφηνα

weep for γοάω, γοήσομαι, γόησα [+ acc.]; κλαίω, κλαύσω, κλαῦσα [+ acc.]

well εὖ [adv.]

well made εὐ-εργής, -ές

what a) see *who* b) [adv.] in what direction [= whither] ὅπ(π)η c) [adj.] (of) what sort οἷος, -η, -ον

whatever ὅ τι/ ὅττι [indef. rel. pron.] [see Section 214]

whence? πόθεν [interr. adv.]

when(ever) ἐπεί, ὅτε, ἦμος [conj.]

where a) [not interr.] ὅθι, ἵνα [adv.]; τῇ [rel. adv.]; b) [interr. adv.] where? ποῦ [always w. circumflex]; from where? πόθεν

whether [in indirect question] εἰ ; whether...or ἤ...ἤ

which [see *who*]

while εἷος [also ἧος or ἕως] or ὄφρα [+ ind. if purely factual; + purpose construction if anticipatory]

white λευκός, -ή, -όν; πολιός, (-ή), -όν

who, which, what a) interr. pron./ adj.] τίς, τί b) [rel. pron.] ὅς, ἥ, ὅ c) [rel. pron. w. def. antecedent] ὁ, ἡ, τό

whoever, whatever ὅς τις, ἥ τις, ὅ τι/ ὅττι [indef. rel. pron.] [see Section 214]

whole ἅπας, ἅπασα, ἅπαν [m./n. gen.ἅπαντός]; πᾶς, πᾶσα, πᾶν [m./ n. gen. παντός]; οὖλος, -η, -ον

why? τί [interr. adv.]

wicked πονηρός, -ή, -όν

wide εὐρύς, -εῖα, -ύ

wife γυνή, γυναικός [f.]; ἄλοχος, -ου [f.]

wild ἄγριος, (-η), -ον

will βουλή, -ῆς [f.]

willing heart, with πρόφρων, -ον

win over πείθω, πείσω, πεῖσα or πέπιθον

wind ἄνεμος, -ου [m.]

wine οἶνος, -ου [m.]

winged πτερόεις, -εσσα, -εν

winning μειλίχιος, -η, -ον

wise σοφός, -ή, -όν

wish ἐθέλω, ἐθελήσω, ἐθέλησα

with μετά [prep. + dat.]; σύν [prep. + dat.]

within ἔνδον [adv.]; ἔντοσθεν [adv.]

woe ἄλγος, ἄλγεος [n.]

woman γυνή, γυναικός [f.]

wood ὕλη, -ης

word λόγος, -ου [m.]; ἔπος, ἔπεος [n.]

work ἔργον, -ου [n.]

world κόσμος, -ου [m.]

worthless πονηρός, -ή, -όν

worthy χρηστός, -ή, -όν

would that [=impossible wish] εἰ, εἰ γάρ, εἴθε [+ opt.]

wrath μένος, μένεος [n.]

wretched λυγρός, -ή, -όν

Y

yearn (after) ποθέω, ποθήσω, πόθεσα

yet ἔτι [=of time]; αὐτάρ [=nevertheless]; δέ [after μέν, in contrasts]

you [sg and pl.: see pron. forms in Appendix A and Lesson 33]

you see [enclitic adv.] τοί

young one [of animals] ἔμβρυον, -ου [n.]

your [sg.] σός, -ή, -όν; τεός, -ή, -όν; σεῖο, σευ; [pl.] ὑμέτερος, -η, -ον; ὑμέων

yourself [sg., or pl.] 2 personal pron. + same case of αὐτός, -ή, -όν

Z

Zeus Ζεύς, Διός or Ζηνός [m.]

Index of Grammatical Terms

(by Section numbers)